Twentieth-Century Caribbean and Black African Writers

First Series

Dictionary of Literary Biography® • Volume One Hundred Seventeen

Twentieth-Century Caribbean and Black African Writers

First Series

Edited by
Bernth Lindfors and Reinhard Sander

A Bruccoli Clark Layman Book
Gale Research Inc.
Detroit, London

Printed in the United States of America

Published simultaneously in the United Kingdom
by Gale Research International Limited
(An affiliated company of Gale Research Inc.)

The paper used in this publication meets the minimum requirements
of American National Standard for Information Sciences—Permanence
Paper for Printed Library Materials, ANSI Z39.48-1984.

Library of Congress Catalog Card Number 92-8972
ISBN 0-8103-7594-X

10 9 8 7 6 5 4 3 2

Contents

Plan of the Series

The advisory board, the editors, and the publisher of the *Dictionary of Literary Biography* are joined in endorsing Mark Twain's declaration. The literature of a nation provides an inexhaustible resource of permanent worth. We intend to make literature and its creators better understood and more accessible to students and the reading public, while satisfying the standards of teachers and scholars.

To meet these requirements, *literary biography* has been construed in terms of the author's achievement. The most important thing about a writer is his writing. Accordingly, the entries in *DLB* are career biographies, tracing the development of the author's canon and the evolution of his reputation.

The purpose of *DLB* is not only to provide reliable information in a convenient format but also to place the figures in the larger perspective of literary history and to offer appraisals of their accomplishments by qualified scholars.

The publication plan for *DLB* resulted from two years of preparation. The project was proposed to Bruccoli Clark by Frederick C. Ruffner, president of the Gale Research Company, in November 1975. After specimen entries were prepared and typeset, an advisory board was formed to refine the entry format and develop the series rationale. In meetings held during 1976, the publisher, series editors, and advisory board approved the scheme for a comprehensive biographical dictionary of persons who contributed to North American literature. Editorial work on the first volume began in January 1977, and it was published in 1978. In order to make *DLB* more than a reference tool and to compile volumes

that individually have claim to status as literary history, it was decided to organize volumes by topic, period, or genre. Each of these freestanding volumes provides a biographical-bibliographical guide and overview for a particular area of literature. We are convinced that this organization—as opposed to a single alphabet method—constitutes a valuable innovation in the presentation of reference material. The volume plan necessarily requires many decisions for the placement and treatment of authors who might properly be included in two or three volumes. In some instances a major figure will be included in separate volumes, but with different entries emphasizing the aspect of his career appropriate to each volume. Ernest Hemingway, for example, is represented in *American Writers in Paris, 1920-1939* by an entry focusing on his expatriate apprenticeship; he is also in *American Novelists, 1910-1945* with an entry surveying his entire career. Each volume includes a cumulative index of the subject authors and articles. Comprehensive indexes to the entire series are planned.

With volume ten in 1982 it was decided to enlarge the scope of *DLB*. By the end of 1986 twenty-one volumes treating British literature had been published, and volumes for Commonwealth and Modern European literature were in progress. The series has been further augmented by the *DLB Yearbooks* (since 1981) which update published entries and add new entries to keep the *DLB* current with contemporary activity. There have also been *DLB Documentary Series* volumes which provide biographical and critical source materials for figures whose work is judged to have particular interest for students. One of these companion volumes is entirely devoted to Tennessee Williams.

We define literature as the *intellectual commerce of a nation:* not merely as belles lettres but as that ample and complex process by which ideas are generated, shaped, and transmitted. *DLB* entries are not limited to "creative writers" but extend to other figures who in their time and in their way influenced the mind of a people. Thus the series encompasses historians, journalists, publishers, and screenwriters. By this means

---

*From an unpublished section of Mark Twain's autobiography, copyright© by the Mark Twain Company

readers of *DLB* may be aided to perceive literature not as cult scripture in the keeping of intellectual high priests but firmly positioned at the center of a nation's life.

DLB includes the major writers appropriate to each volume and those standing in the ranks immediately behind them. Scholarly and critical counsel has been sought in deciding which minor figures to include and how full their entries should be. Wherever possible, useful references are made to figures who do not warrant separate entries.

Each *DLB* volume has a volume editor responsible for planning the volume, selecting the figures for inclusion, and assigning the entries. Volume editors are also responsible for preparing, where appropriate, appendices surveying the major periodicals and literary and intellectual movements for their volumes, as well as lists of further readings. Work on the series as a whole is coordinated at the Bruccoli Clark Layman editorial center in Columbia, South Carolina, where the editorial staff is responsible for accuracy of the published volumes.

One feature that distinguishes *DLB* is the illustration policy—its concern with the iconography of literature. Just as an author is influenced by his surroundings, so is the reader's understanding of the author enhanced by a knowledge of his environment. Therefore *DLB* volumes include not only drawings, paintings, and photographs of authors, often depicting them at various stages in their careers, but also illustrations of their families and places where they lived. Title pages are regularly reproduced in facsimile along with dust jackets for modern authors. The dust jackets are a special feature of *DLB* because they often document better than anything else the way in which an author's work was perceived in its own time. Specimens of the writers' manuscripts are included when feasible.

Samuel Johnson rightly decreed that "The chief glory of every people arises from its authors." The purpose of the *Dictionary of Literary Biography* is to compile literary history in the surest way available to us—by accurate and comprehensive treatment of the lives and work of those who contributed to it.

The *DLB* Advisory Board

Foreword

Since the mid 1980s scholarly interest in postcolonial (including Caribbean and African) writing has grown considerably in most literature departments at colleges and universities in the United States and elsewhere. In recent years many high-school students have been exposed to works such as *Things Fall Apart* (1958) by Nigerian writer Chinua Achebe, which appear on new multicultural reading lists. In 1986 another Nigerian writer, Wole Soyinka, was the first African to receive the Nobel Prize for literature. Therefore it seems timely for the *DLB* to publish two volumes of biobibliographical critical essays on some of the major anglophone writers from Africa and the Caribbean. These volumes are meant as research and reference tools for teachers, students, and general readers; it is hoped that they will also contribute to the realization—to quote the Caribbean writer George Lamming—"that the English language does not belong to the Englishman. It belongs to a lot of people who do a lot of things with it; it is really a tree that has now grown innumerable branches, and you cannot any longer be alarmed by the size or quality of the branch."

When Christopher Columbus and other mariners embarked on their voyages half a millennium ago, they set in motion a process that led to Europe's military, economic, and cultural domination of much of the rest of the world. Spain and Portugal, soon challenged by Great Britain and other European powers, carved out colonial possessions for settlement or exploitation around the globe. The colonizers' treatment of the indigenous peoples they encountered ranged from genocide—as committed in parts of the Americas—to various forms of direct and indirect rule, as practiced throughout Africa. The process also led to vast movements of people within the colonized countries and between continents. The enslavement and transportation of millions of Africans across the Atlantic during the early phase of colonialism set the stage for subsequent developments in the Caribbean—where people of African descent were to outnumber all others—that closely paralleled those on the African continent. This connection is evident in the chronology of the decolonization process that began after World War I and in the cross-fertilization of ideas concerning the anticolonial struggle. African and Caribbean nationalists developed similar political and cultural strategies for achieving independence.

Europeans differed widely in their attitudes toward the peoples and cultures they colonized, but their policies invariably facilitated the imposition and dissemination of European languages. European immigration to North and South America and Australia, and the establishment of smaller European enclaves in parts of Africa and Asia, accelerated the process of linguistic unification and domination.

The internationalization of English during the period of colonialism has had interesting literary consequences, for it has led to the creation of new literatures in English all over the world. These literatures emerged first in areas of European settlement such as the United States, Canada, and Australia, where English was the native language of many immigrants. But it also has occurred more recently in parts of South Asia, East Asia, and Africa, where English gained a foothold mainly as a second language spoken by an educated elite. In the British Caribbean, English-based creole languages eclipsed African languages such as Igbo, Yoruba, Kikongo, and Wolof and were used by all sections of the society, including postemancipation Asian indentured laborers and the offspring of the original colonizers. However, the plantation system and various debilitating socioeconomic factors delayed the spread of English as a written language—and thus the creation of a written literature.

Literatures written in English by non-European speakers of the language developed contemporaneously with the ongoing movements for independence during the twentieth century and generally supported them. Since World War II, when Europe increasingly lost its direct grip on its colonial territories, these literatures have grown prodigiously, especially in the Caribbean, India, Nigeria, South Africa, Kenya, and

Zimbabwe, to name only the liveliest areas. Not all of this vigorous, new anglophone writing comes from former British colonies. One also finds it, for example, in Puerto Rico and the Philippines, where English was introduced by the United States.

The sixty-five writers included in the two series of *Twentieth-Century Caribbean and Black African Writers* are drawn from fourteen nations in Africa and the Caribbean, with the greatest number coming from Nigeria (16), South Africa (11), Jamaica (8), Trinidad and Tobago (6), Guyana (5), Ghana (5), and Kenya (4). There are many reasons for the numerical imbalance in Africa, the foremost being the availability of Western education in the countries concerned. Nigeria, Africa's most heavily populated nation, may have more university graduates than the rest of anglophone Africa combined. South Africa, Ghana, and Kenya also have a relatively high percentage of people with a Western education, compared with neighboring states. In some nations—particularly Nigeria and South Africa—local publishers of books, journals, and popular magazines have provided indigenous outlets for new writing. Of special importance have been *Drum*, *Black Orpheus*, *Okike*, and *Nigeria Magazine*. There have also been active writers' groups, such as the Mbari Clubs in Nigeria, that have sponsored literary competitions, staged plays, organized cultural festivals and book fairs, encouraged the production of children's literature, and sought to protect the financial interests of authors. Such activities have helped to launch and sustain strong anglophone literary movements in areas of the world where English is a language learned at school.

In the British Caribbean, where a distinct variety of English is spoken by the educated sections of the society, some of the same social and institutional forces have been at work. Education was not available to the majority of the population until the last quarter of the nineteenth century, but by the middle of the twentieth century the Caribbean possessed some of the best secondary schools in the British Empire. Furthermore, the foundations had been laid for the establishment of the University of the West Indies, whose campuses in Jamaica, Barbados, and Trinidad boast several published writers among their former students and current faculties. The Caribbean has produced a large number of writers, many of whom—like tens of thousands of their countrymen—have left the Caribbean to seek their fortunes elsewhere, especially in Great Brit-

ain, Canada, and the United States. However, the indigenous publishing industries that have begun to flourish in the Caribbean and Africa are much in evidence in this volume, as more than half the authors represented here published their first book in their native area, eight of them in Africa (primarily Nigeria) and eight in the Caribbean. The other fourteen authors saw their first book published in Great Britain or the United States, but several of those also later published in their home countries or regions. It is, however, two British firms, Heinemann and Longman, that continue to dominate the publishing of African and Caribbean writing through their paperback series aimed at secondary-school and college students.

Nearly all the African writers in this *DLB* volume are bilingual, and some are fluent in three or more languages as well as in a local pidgin. Recently some have switched from writing in English to publishing first in African languages and then translating their texts into English. Caribbean authors express themselves mainly in English. However, their published work often also draws on the patois or creole languages of the particular island on which they grew up. In Africa and the Caribbean, ready access to other languages and dialects has led to adventurous stylistic innovations, as authors seek to capture the complex verbal texture of the pluralistic environment they and their characters inhabit. By bending and twisting the English language, they are able to evoke the complexity of African and West Indian social realities. They are forcing an old language to tell new truths.

While many African and Caribbean writers of the 1950s and 1960s tended to explore the colonial past and the colonial experience in their writings, more recent writers have turned to probing various facets of postcolonial life. In carrying out this task, African writers in particular have frequently attracted the censure of their governments and have been imprisoned or forced into exile. Those able to continue writing in such circumstances have developed fresh perspectives on the vulnerability of their societies to economic and political pressures exerted by the outside world, which has resulted in writings that examine the black experience in the context of global power struggles. Close linkages of thought and feeling unite politically committed African, Caribbean, and African-American authors. Their novels, plays, and poems increasingly transcend parochial, domestic concerns and address wider international issues that have an impact on the entire black world. Since African and Caribbean writers are citizens of societies that share a common set of postcolonial problems, they often seek answers to the same vexing sociopolitical questions. They are drawn together by history and geography as well as by race.

One of the authors in this volume, Olaudah Equiano, who is discussed in the appendix, wrote in the eighteenth century. All the rest—in this and the second volume—are men and women who began to have their work published in the twentieth century, though three (H. G. de Lisser, Claude McKay, and Jean Rhys) were born in the late nineteenth century. The selection was based entirely on influence and reputation: those writers most written about, most widely studied in schools and universities, and most frequently read for pleasure were the ones chosen for inclusion. While we considered it appropriate to in-

clude a Caribbean writer of European descent (Rhys), white South African writers were excluded because they belong to a different literary tradition, one shaped by a peculiar set of social, cultural, and historical experiences not shared by other African writers or by writers from the Caribbean.

In the interest of providing a balanced mix of talents from Africa and the Caribbean in each volume, we have included the writers from Gambia, Ghana, Guyana, St. Lucia, and Dominica in the first series, and those from Kenya, Uganda, Sudan, Somalia, Barbados, and Trinidad and Tobago in the second series. The many authors from Nigeria, South Africa, and Jamaica have been divided between the two volumes.

—Bernth Lindfors and Reinhard Sander

Acknowledgments

This book was produced by Bruccoli Clark Layman, Inc. Karen L. Rood is senior editor for the *Dictionary of Literary Biography* series. Jack Turner was the in-house editor.

Production coordinator is James W. Hipp. Projects manager is Charles D. Brower. Photography editors are Edward Scott and Timothy C. Lundy. Layout and graphics supervisor is Penney L. Haughton. Copyediting supervisor is Bill Adams. Typesetting supervisor is Kathleen M. Flanagan. Systems manager is George F. Dodge. The production staff includes Rowena Betts, Teresa Chaney, Patricia Coate, Janet Connor, Rebecca Crawford, Gail Crouch, Henry Cuningham, Margaret McGinty Cureton, Bonita Dingle, Mary Scott Dye, Denise Edwards, Sarah A. Estes, Robert Fowler, Avril E. Gregory, Ellen McCracken, Kathy Lawler Merlette, John Myrick, Pamela D. Norton, Jean W. Ross, Thomasina Singleton, Maxine K. Smalls, Jennifer C. J. Turley, and Betsy L. Weinberg.

Walter W. Ross and Dennis Lynch did library research. They were assisted by the following librarians at the Thomas Cooper Library of the University of South Carolina: Jens Holley and the interlibrary-loan staff; reference librarians Gwen Baxter, Daniel Boice, Faye Chadwell, Jo Cottingham, Cathy Eckman, Rhonda Felder, Gary Geer, Jackie Kinder, Laurie Preston, Jean Rhyne, Carol Tobin, Virginia Weathers, and Connie Widney; circulation-department head Thomas Marcil; and acquisitions-searching supervisor David Haggard.

The volume editors would like to thank Rhonda Cobham, Margaret Groesbeck, Nuhad Jamal, and Michael Kasper—all of Amherst College—for their substantial help with this project.

Twentieth-Century Caribbean and Black African Writers
First Series

Dictionary of Literary Biography

Peter Abrahams
(19 March 1919 -   )

Michael Wade
Hebrew University of Jerusalem

BOOKS: *Here, Friend* (Durban, circa 1940);
A Blackman Speaks of Freedom! (Durban: Universal, 1941);
Dark Testament (London: Allen & Unwin, 1942);
Song of the City (London: Crisp, 1945);
Mine Boy (London: Crisp, 1946; New York: Knopf, 1955);
The Path of Thunder (New York: Harper, 1948; London: Faber & Faber, 1952);
Wild Conquest (New York: Harper, 1950; London: Faber & Faber, 1951);
Return to Goli (London: Faber & Faber, 1953);
Tell Freedom (London: Faber & Faber, 1954; New York: Knopf, 1954);
A Wreath for Udomo (London: Faber & Faber, 1956; New York: Knopf, 1956);
Jamaica: Island Mosaic (London: Her Majesty's Stationery Office/Corona, 1957);
A Night of Their Own (London: Faber & Faber, 1965; New York: Knopf, 1965);
This Island Now (London: Faber & Faber, 1966; New York: Knopf, 1967; revised and enlarged, London: Faber & Faber, 1985);
The View from Coyaba (London & Boston: Faber & Faber, 1985).

Peter Abrahams was the first black South African author to choose the path of exile; he was the first to establish an international literary reputation; he was the first to publish a substantial body of novels in English; and his fiction and nonfiction commanded attention and respect throughout the English-speaking world in the 1940s and 1950s, especially among those interested in the historical and political development of Africa in general and South Africa in particular. Another reason for his importance was his profound influence on the next generation of African writers, partly because he exemplified for them the existence of the black person as writer and partly as a result of the themes he chose and the way he wrote about them. Among the founders of modern African fiction in English who have declared Abrahams a key influence on their work are Cyprian Ekwensi of Nigeria and Ngugi wa Thiong'o of Kenya.

Abrahams was born on 19 March 1919 in the Johannesburg slum suburb of Vrededorp; he is the son of a "Cape Coloured" (South African) mother, Angelina DuPlessis Abrahams, and—according to his autobiography *Tell Freedom* (1954)—an Ethiopian nobleman, James Henry Abrahams, who had traveled to South Africa to find work in the gold mines of the Witwatersrand. Because of family poverty the young Abrahams began his schooling late, at the age of eleven, but in his mid teens he studied at two elite secondary schools for blacks, Diocesan Training College at Grace Dieu, near Pietersburg, and St. Peter's Rosettenville, in Johannesburg, where Es'kia (Ezekiel) Mphahlele was his contemporary and where Oliver Tambo, a president of the African National Congress, had also received a secondary education. Before going to high school, Abrahams had found work at the Bantu Men's Social Centre, a Johannesburg institute set up by American Board missionaries in the 1920s, and it was there in the mid 1930s that an encounter crucial to the development of African literature took place. As Abrahams describes it in *Tell Freedom,*

Peter Abrahams (photograph copyright by Bailey's African Photo Archives)

while he was waiting to be interviewed for a job, he heard a phonograph record of Paul Robeson singing "Old Man River." From there Abrahams went to the Centre's library, where he found W. E. B. Du Bois's *The Souls of Black Folk* (1903) and an anthology called *The New Negro* (1925), in whose pages he encountered poems by Countee Cullen, Langston Hughes, Claude McKay, and others.

It seems fashionable to deprecate the role of the American Board missionaries in South Africa in the early decades of the twentieth century on the grounds that they aimed at creating and reinforcing a more or less docile African middle class that, because of its stake in the status quo, would accept a gradualist means of political change. In this light it may seem odd that Abrahams's crucial literary influences, encountered at the board-inspired Bantu Men's Social Centre, all come from a radical-activist position within the black movement in the United States.

While he was attending Diocesan, Abrahams's earliest successful poems were published in the white-owned *Bantu World*, a newspaper catering to black readers. Some of these poems

are collected in two small booklets, *Here, Friend* (circa 1940) and *A Blackman Speaks of Freedom!* (1941), which Abrahams published before leaving South Africa. When he was at St. Peter's, according to Mphahlele, Abrahams often talked about Marcus Garvey and expressed Pan-Africanist ideas. At St. Peter's he also made friends with a young white couple who initiated him into Marxism, and for the next few years, until he left South Africa, he wrote short stories, sketches, and poems and engaged in political activity, working in trade unions in Johannesburg with the Trotskyite Max Gordon and then moving to Cape Town, where he was for a while the protégé of the Gool family, aristocrats of the colored community, who were also leaders of a Trotskyite faction. After working in a school in circumstances of exceptional physical deprivation on the Cape Flats and becoming (by his own account) disenchanted with the sectarian struggles of the Left in the Cape, the young Abrahams moved across country to Durban, where he came under orthodox Stalinist-Communist influence, and, after attracting the attention of the authorities, he went into exile by signing on as a crew member of a

Dust jacket for Abrahams's 1942 book, a collection of short stories and sketches that reflect his left-wing political views

freighter bound for England. He arrived there in 1941, worked for a left-wing book distributor, and was for a time on the staff of the Communist party organ, the *Daily Worker*.

In 1942 Abrahams married Dorothy Pennington; the marriage was dissolved in 1948. On 1 June of that year, he married Daphne Elizabeth Miller, and they have three children: Anne, Aron, and Naomi.

Abrahams's youthful short stories and sketches, collected under the title *Dark Testament* (1942), express with uncontrolled emotion the feelings of loneliness and despair of the young writer and intellectual in the context of political struggle. Given his color and the rarity of left-wing writers of fiction in South Africa in the late 1930s, it is not surprising that Abrahams felt isolated. But another conflict was also palpable: between Abrahams's simultaneous attraction to and distrust of strong ideological frameworks. This tension was to become a distinguishing mark of his literary career.

In this first phase of his career Abrahams was deeply involved with the specifics of urban life, which was, of course, a reflection of his own youthful experience and of one of the major preoccupations of liberal and left-wing theoreticians and ideologues. The growing black industrial proletariat and the parallel dispossession of many rural whites, who also became migrant workers in industry (if they could find work), in the depression years of the 1930s led to an intensification of racial conflict and polarization in South Africa. The thrust of liberal thinking in the late 1930s and early 1940s was in the direction of pragmatic crisis containment rather than resolution, and this stance was accompanied by eloquent expressions of concern for the collapse of traditional agrarian African social systems. Abrahams, writing his first full-length novels in exile, remarkably and explicitly dismissed this dimension of liberal thought as irrelevant.

His first novel, *Song of the City* (1945), exhibits literary qualities that are almost as fumbling and incompetent as its young hero's first attempts at coping with urban life. The action takes place about the time of the outbreak of World War II, and the plot deals with the political crisis in the white community over whether to enter the war on the side of the Allies or to remain neutral. The protagonist, Dick, never emerges from stereotyping, and some of the less important characters are more interesting; but Abrahams characteristically provides a full, schematic view of the South African political spectrum—from cautious white and black liberals, whose scenario for segregation anticipates ideological apartheid, though their motives are more sincere; rightward to the pro-Nazi extremes of Afrikaners; and left to include a socialist trade-union activist. Dick works as domestic servant in the house of a white liberal professor and inevitably runs afoul of the laws controlling the lives of blacks in urban areas. For him the question is: "How does one learn not to fear?" This basic concern points to Abrahams's instinctive predilection for the unvarnished truth over the ideologized version—a strong point in his writing that is sometimes compromised by deficiencies in his rhetoric. Dick learns to phrase the question while waiting in custody together with a politically sophisticated young black man, who shows no fear of the white policeman. Though Abrahams grants his hero a return to the pastoral, when he convalesces from a physical illness in his home village, Abrahams then returns him to the city. For Abrahams the urbanization of blacks is inevitable, and history begins from there, though at this stage he was not yet ready to spell out a doctrine of economic necessity. Concerning whites, the book is at its most convincing in the description of the love between the Englishwoman Myra and the Afrikaner member of Parliament who is her husband. Myra opts for separation and a return to England when her husband, Van der Merwe, the minister for native affairs, votes to keep South Africa out of World War II. The disintegration of their marriage is allegorical, though with all his satiric dismissal of bourgeois liberalism and its impotent segregationist panaceas, Abrahams did not foresee the success of Afrikaner nationalism in winning overall white support for its apartheid grand design.

Abrahams's second novel, *Mine Boy* (1946), is the highest achievement of the first phase of his career as writer. With it he staked his claim to a permanent place in South Africa's literary history on three solid and impressive grounds. First, he presents objective urban reality from a black point of view; second, for the first time in a South African novel, a convincing account of the state of mind of urban blacks is presented; and third, he is the first South African novelist to pose a possible solution to the continuing crisis of black experience in the industrial city. He succeeds through a powerful, detailed challenge to a hitherto unquestioned set of conventions in white South African fiction. These conventions were generated by the comprehensive myth system projected and inhabited by white South Africans as an area of psychic refuge and expressed as fully in their literature as in their everyday behavior. Since large-scale black urbanization has always threatened the psychic stability of the whites, while being at the same time essential to their material comfort and self-esteem, their mythic defenses have had to work overtime in this area. Thus, depiction of urban black life in literature was determined by rock-hard conventions in the works of Olive Schreiner, W. C. Scully, William Plomer, Sarah Gertrude Millin, and others, though the most influential treatment of these conventions was yet to appear, in Alan Paton's *Cry, the Beloved Country* (1948).

The conventional matrix dictates that blacks flood to the towns because they practice primitive farming methods and are incapable of learning better ones; this migration is causally connected to the "breakdown of the tribal system." Once in the towns the blacks are feckless, lazy, irre-

Dust jacket for Abrahams's 1946 novel, a graphic account of poverty and oppression in South Africa

sponsible, and unable to improve their miserable material conditions; this situation is largely because of their innate disabilities. They are drawn to criminal activities. All this trouble is perhaps the fault of the whites to a very limited degree, but there is really no "solution." The best way to deal with this self-generated problem is probably to encourage as many blacks as possible to return to the countryside and try to learn better farming techniques. The worst possible approaches to the problem are to advocate making education more widely available to blacks, or to allow missionaries to influence them. Black politicians are invariably both corrupt and cowardly as well as being inordinately self-seeking when they are not actually criminal. Such is the literary-historical setting of *Mine Boy*, which was the first Marxist bildungsroman in South African literature. The migrant laborer Xuma, the protagonist, is totally displaced from his rural origin, which is, in fact, never described (a telling silence, and quite against the stream of the white writers' insistence on portraying the black rural "tribal" ambience, or, for that matter, the next generation of African writers' fascination with rural roots as an aspect of precolonial experience). Xuma makes himself from scratch in the city, from raw materials composed of physical strength, moral integrity, and a capacity to endure suffering. This is the second specific challenge to the conventions of the genre, the first being the dismissal of the traditional rural background. Xuma rises almost immediately to the position of "boss boy," or gang leader, for a white, left-wing-thinking foreman nicknamed the "red one," and Xuma engages in lucid dialogue with him over whether the workers' first loyalty is to ethnic group or class. Xuma develops his ideas in this respect so that, when the crisis of the novel arrives, he is able to synthesize his own views, based on his experiences in the city, with those conveyed by the foreman and to face the responsibilities that leadership entails for a politicized urban black man (in this case, imprisonment and persecution).

That, says Abrahams, is the meaning of urbanization and the direction of the future: not the ignominious retreat of the blacks, wounded physically and morally, from urban to rural slum, there to spin out their hungry days in the decayed framework of some vanishing "tribal system," but the emergence of the black proletariat to political consciousness; the struggle against the mine owners, the police, and the state that backs them; and the move toward a classless society in which race will be irrelevant. Abrahams's characters reinforce his challenge to stereotypes. Xuma's first love, the schoolteacher Eliza, whom he meets on his first night in the city, at the shebeen managed by the imposing Leah, is a character torn by her longing for a decent material existence. The neurosis bred by her reasonable aspirations and the impossibility of fulfilling the smallest part of them makes her incapable of happiness or sustaining a relationship—incapable of loving or accepting love. Eliza's position is an allegory of the present, just as Xuma's points to the future. Multiply her condition by the number of blacks trapped in it, Abrahams is saying, and a fundamental element in the pathology of the oppressed becomes clear.

Part of Abrahams's success in challenging the conventions of the novel of urbanization is based on his avoidance of stereotyping: this is true in the case of Eliza; of Maisie, the proletarian woman with whom Xuma eventually falls in love; of Daddy, the ruined alcoholic who was once a leader of the struggle; and, of course, of Leah, the wise, attractive, and powerful shebeen keeper (the first of a long series of strong mother figures to appear in Abrahams's fiction), who is eventually crushed by the law. But Abrahams's highest achievement in this novel is his description of Xuma's working life. As in the presentation of the secondary characters, the technical keynote is the easy and convincing movement between the subjective and the objective, creating a sense of truth for the reader. Abrahams dwells first on the psychic confusion of the men in transition, the migrant workers squeezed dry in the economic forces represented by the gold mine. He then moves from a subjective impression of the workers' responses to the objective conditions of physical labor. The details of the physical actuality of the work are effective in themselves, and such a description is a rarity in South African literature. Abrahams's success in tightly controlled description should also be seen in the general context of the proletarian novel, in which such passages are also rare. But the achievement does not end here: he evokes the myth of Sisyphus, thus tying the objective and subjective into a unified experience of mine labor. The result is a graphic description of the capitalist process of production, in which the producer is cut off from the product of his labor and as a result suffers the psychic agonies of alienation. Abrahams locates the black, urban proletariat in South Africa firmly in the universal context of class exploitation. He shows in the novel that, for him, the inevitable progression was from exploitation to class struggle. At the end of the novel Xuma is reborn, politicized, and prepared for leadership, sacrifice, and suffering in the name of a revolutionary transformation to come.

In the first stage of his writing career Abrahams's concern was, by dramatizing contemporary reality, to counter the white myth structure and endow South Africa with an alternative, revolutionary teleology. This stage culminated with *The Path of Thunder* (1948), which challenges another particularly potent area of mythic defenses—those opposing love between individuals of different colors. With the startling exception of William Plomer in *Turbott Wolfe* (1926), white African writers have been unanimously horrified (and compulsively fascinated and attracted) by the subject. Their main characters suffer the most elementally inevitable and harrowing fates, which is a necessary climactic discharge for the tension and anxiety involved for both white writers and their audience. The problem inherent in the subject matter is the unavoidability of granting the black partner in a transpigmentary sexual relation a degree of individuality (which the white myth structure is self-designed to prevent at all costs; novels of urbanization do so by a comprehensive reliance on stereotype). One result is often a singularly vindictive rage directed by the writer at his black character.

In *The Path of Thunder* the central character, Lanny Swartz, has roots in the rural colored proletariat but is no longer of it. He is a young intellectual, a newly graduated schoolteacher who, out of an obstinate sense of mission, returns from the relative liberal ease of Cape Town student life, after turning down a prestigious high-school teaching post in the city, to the karoo village of Stilleveld, where he was born, there to serve the impoverished community that had sent him to the university.

Abrahams draws an important distinction between the poverty of coloreds in urban and rural settings: in Cape Town coloreds were poor but psychologically free; in the rural areas they were completely broken. He depicts the feudal relationship between the coloreds and the white landowners in rural areas of the Cape, and he suggests that the complete dependence and powerlessness of coloreds in relation to whites is reflected in an exploitative pattern of sexual relations. Lanny learns that he is half brother to the violently racist lord of the local manor, Gert Villier; he also falls in love with Gert's ward, Sarie, and the feeling is reciprocated. Lanny makes friends with two intellectuals: Isaac, the son of the local Jewish storekeeper; and Mako, a young black teacher who runs the black school. Abrahams uses their friendship to air political issues, some of which must have been painful for the author himself—they surface also in *Return to Goli* (1953), the autobiographical account of his return to South Africa. These issues concern the role of the colored group in the struggle for racial equality. Abrahams's critique of the colored elite is directed against their political conservatism, their subservience to whites, and their pathetic expectation of reward for this subservience.

In *The Path of Thunder* Abrahams develops an emphasis on the centrality of the individual—a theme by no means new in his writing but hitherto contained within the conceptual framework of Marxist political activism. Thus the discursive interludes in this novel all tend to support the love story, and the conclusive resolution

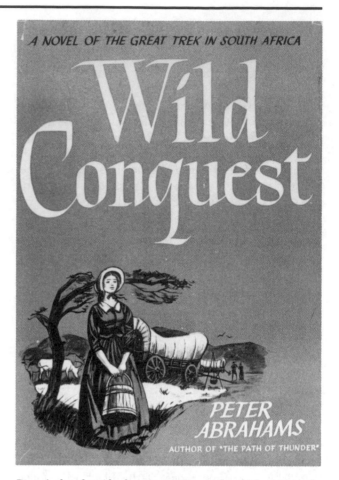

Dust jacket for Abrahams's 1950 novel, which depicts the Dutch migration north from the Cape in 1834 and a parallel movement of rebellious Zulus

of the conflicts within the South African polity is presented in terms of the ability of individuals to transcend the limitations inherent in their situations through their relations with others. This novel is the first unambiguous evidence of a pronounced ideological shift, which has driven some critics of Abrahams's work to a pitch of irrationality characteristic of the highly politicized arena of contemporary South African studies, exemplified by the way critics who are concerned to attack what they call "liberalism" for failing to bring about change in South Africa simply ignore or dismiss the implications of the ending of this novel. Lanny and Sarie, their planned escape across the border of South Africa blocked, take up arms and shoot it out with the white racists who have trapped them. Outnumbered and cut off from flight, they are killed, but not before three of their attackers perish. For the first time in black South African writing a black man in a contemporary setting takes the white man's symbol of technological and political supremacy and turns it on the whites themselves. Lanny Swartz and Sarie Villier demonstrate that there is more than one path of thunder. The figure of Lanny firing his rifle at his white attackers is the first icon of the South African revolution.

Despite the shift toward liberalism, Abrahams does not abandon the analysis of poverty and oppression he uses in the first two novels of his triptych on contemporary South Africa. Oppression's feudal roots in the rural setting are clearly presented, and the economic basis for institutionalized racism is both explicit and implicit in the text. Abrahams has added a dimension, though, in which he describes the actions of individuals determined to be free of their historic constraints. In the end it is Lanny who quotes Percy Bysshe Shelley on individual freedom and not the avowed black nationalist, Mako, who takes up arms against the racist state. Of course, South African miscegenation novels by whites often posit tragedy, though usually without nobility, and often consisting of degeneration into poverty and bitterness. Abrahams's challenge to this convention precludes easy options: his central figures, though they plan to escape South Africa, fail to do so, and they die heroically, fighting for their freedom.

Abrahams's next novel, *Wild Conquest* (1950), again takes an established theme in the white novel and challenges its conventions. The Great Trek, the migration of many Cape Dutch families northward beginning in 1834, shortly after the British abolished slavery at the Cape, intensified already existing conflicts over land possession between blacks and whites and led to the eventual spread of white political hegemony throughout South Africa south of the Limpopo, except for three small territorial pockets whose black rulers sought protection from the British crown against the land-hungry and technologically better-equipped forerunners of Afrikaner nationalism. The trek generated a vast literature, a fair proportion of it in English, mostly doctrinal, romantic statements about the heroism of the white trekkers, their taming of the wilderness, and their victories over savages who are usually depicted as cunning and bloodthirsty, with the occasional exception—almost always a faithful family retainer who saves the life of a female trekker at the cost of his own.

Wild Conquest initiated the middle phase of Abrahams's fiction, a phase marked by the emergence of a typically liberal mixture of passion and skepticism, and a thorough rejection of formu-

Dust jacket for Abrahams's autobiography (1954), inspired by his visit to South Africa on assignment for the Observer *of London*

lated ideology as a guide or framework. As a result his challenge to the conventions of white Great Trek literature seems halfhearted, and in the end the novel is a failure both as historical treatment and demythologizing agent. It differs from the white norm in presenting another mass migration—that of the Matabele, a rebellious Zulu group—as having equal historic importance to that of the trekkers. The dramatization of black life is heavily indebted to Sol T. Plaatje's historic romance *Mhudi*, written about 1919, published in 1930, and largely forgotten when Abrahams consulted it. Abrahams presents his black characters in stereotyped form, often coming close to adopting white conventions on matters such as the influence of witchcraft in black society, the brutality of the Matabele armies, and the failure to produce any but the most superficial account of the causes of black migration. In *Wild Conquest* his teleology is deeply pessimistic, with the potential standard-bearers of liberal values, both black and white, dying on the battlefield in the fateful encounter between Boer and Matabele. Abrahams's problem in *Wild Conquest* is that while he recognizes the existence of two opposed cultures in the historic arena, he fails to find an appropriate idiom for the blacks. Though he proposes a joint rhetoric of liberalism for the enlightened characters of both camps, the effect is stilted and wooden. The only discourse that is rhetorically effective in the novel is that of the racist whites—a tragic indication, perhaps, of the degree to which Abrahams, growing up colored in a Johannesburg slum, internalized the vocabulary of the racism directed against him.

Abrahams's liberal voice gains confidence and resonance in the next two books of his middle period, however—the autobiographical works *Return to Goli* and *Tell Freedom*. These two books state clearly and vigorously Abrahams's ideological position in the middle of his creative life. In the opening pages of *Return to Goli* (which describes a visit to South Africa sponsored by the liberal London Sunday paper, the *Observer*) Abrahams describes his disillusion with communism and his break, in the 1940s, with its institutionalized British version. He then expresses in anecdotal form how living in Britain helped him free himself from the victim pathology of racism, and he goes on to quote Shelley and E. M. Forster in support of his new personal creed of liberalism. In this approach he is not much different from the host of writers and other artists who supported communism in the 1930s and 1940s as the best means to fight fascism and recanted because of disillusionment with Stalinist tyranny. Though there are specific elements distinguishing Abrahams's case—his South African origin, his blackness, the fact that he was a victim of racism—the most interesting aspect of his intellectual progression is its closeness to the norm.

Return to Goli and *Tell Freedom* possess a stylistic vigor and directness that his novels lack. In these two works Abrahams succeeds in letting events and people speak for themselves. The result is that the ideological texture is felt by the reader as a living web of ideas rather than the heavy hand that tends to deaden the narrative in his novels. The nonfiction books are also characterized by a considerable sense of humor, sadly absent from his fiction. Like *Mine Boy*, *Tell Freedom* and *Return to Goli* occupy positions of major importance in the development of South African literature.

The next three novels of Abrahams's middle, liberal phase are expressions of tragic disillu-

sionment. *A Wreath for Udomo* (1956) deals prophetically with the problems of a newly independent black state in Africa. Ghana (still the Gold Coast in 1956) was to attain its independence from Britain the following year and was the first African territory in the Commonwealth to do so; Abrahams had lodged with Francis Kwame Nkrumah in London in the 1940s and had been party to the organization of the Pan-Africanist Congress in Manchester in 1946. In *A Wreath for Udomo* Abrahams anticipates the crushing implications of neocolonialism for newly independent states. He also predicts the downfall of the modernizing leadership that took power with the advent of independence. His central character, Michael Udomo, leads his country to independence only to fall victim to forces of ultranationalism combined with obscurantism. What Abrahams sees as the intolerably restrictive forces of traditional tribal life triumph over the virtues of Western liberal individualism, expressed in Udomo's modernizing zeal. In *Udomo* Abrahams is obsessed by betrayal. The plot moves from immediate postwar London—including the cold and bleak Hampstead area where foreign students and political exiles congregate—to the steaming African state of Panafrica (modeled on Ghana), with a brief excursion to the shore of the southern Mediterranean. Udomo is a powerful, charismatic, single-minded man who betrays his English mistress by getting her flatmate pregnant. The price of getting the foreign expertise needed to accelerate Panafrica's modernization is the betrayal of his friend and comrade in arms, Mhendi, who seeks to lead a revolution against white rule in his country, the neighboring Pluralia. In the end Udomo himself is betrayed by two close associates, the doctor Adebhoy and the sinister market woman Selina, who control the political party Udomo founded. They accuse him of selling out to the white man and thereby betraying his own people.

Abrahams links their accusation with a concept of backwardness, superstition, and obscurantism wrapped up in the word *tribalism*, as stereotyped in Manichaean ugliness during the Matabele bone-throwing episode in *Wild Conquest*. Udomo is ritually murdered by his house guards, who revert to savagery at the prompting of native drums that beat out the refrain "Udomo traitor Udomo die." This assassination is orchestrated by the tribalists in his party. But Abrahams also has his hero succumb to the hypnotic beat of the drums: Udomo's will is paralyzed, and he cannot resist his assassins.

At the point of death, Udomo feels additional agony over his betrayal of Lois, the English mistress, who symbolizes the whole structure of liberal values. His betrayal of her is worse, for him, than his selling his comrade Mhendi into the hands of the whites. In *Udomo* Abrahams presents a picture of African reality that is profoundly pessimistic—but it is judged in only one light, that of Western liberalism.

In the mid 1950s the British Colonial Office commissioned Abrahams, who had established his reputation as a travel writer, to write a popular history of Jamaica, which was published in 1957, and Abrahams and his family moved to Jamaica, where they remained. His two novels of the 1960s push the liberal pessimism of *A Wreath for Udomo* still further.

A Night of Their Own (1965) returns to South Africa after the well-known Rivonia trial and describes a love affair between a black artist (of liberal convictions, who has lived in London), smuggled into South Africa with funds for the underground resistance, and an Indian woman, a political activist whose task is to conceal him from the secret police until he can be spirited abroad. *This Island Now* (1966) relates how an Udomo-like figure becomes ruler of a Caribbean state and tries to modernize it against a whole spectrum of vested interests, ranging (again) from the Western imperialist powers, through the local rich mercantile caste, to the backward and intensely conservative peasantry. He is forced to violate most of the liberal shibboleths and ends up isolated, a lonely autocrat in danger of assassination. In neither book is much action described: each has its liberal hero, and both heroes are weighed down by the moral problem of assessing the motives and likely consequences of political action. There is little progression of thought in these novels, despite Abrahams's deep and genuine commitment to the black struggle in South Africa and his obvious knowledgeability and affection for the Caribbean. Abrahams seems to have been confronted—and stopped in his tracks—by the hard fact that the liberal individualism that served him well as a moral framework in the arena of ideological conflict, demarcated by East and West, had no answer to the situations that mattered most to him. The problem of where to turn next was to preoccupy him for nineteen years, before he published another novel.

At the end of *This Island Now* Andy Simpson, the island's presidential secretary, once devoted to the mission of transferring political and economic power from the expatriate elite to the humble black people of the island, waits with a high-velocity rifle for President Albert Josiah to drive past him on a lonely road in the hills. Simpson, young, black, brilliant, and appointed because of his support for Josiah's goals, has suffered a cumulative means-and-ends crisis, characteristic of liberals who involve themselves in action toward massive social and political change. However, again characteristic of liberal sensibility, when faced with the problem of action, he fails to pull the trigger.

In 1985 Abrahams produced a slightly revised version of *This Island Now*, with an additional half chapter that enforces the extraordinary pessimism of the ending, and he also surprised the African literary world in the same year with a new novel, *The View from Coyaba*. The scope is far greater than in any of Abrahams's previous, rather overfocused plots, and the content is astonishing in that it marks a return to ideology combined with an entirely new synthesis.

The novel traces the story of a family created by two runaway slaves in the late 1820s and ends in Uganda after the tyranny of Idi Amin. In a complex, multilayered design Abrahams revives issues and ideological positions that had all but disappeared from his writing in its most recent phase, reassesses them in the light of history, and integrates them into the pattern of his design. *The View from Coyaba* is a novel of reconciliation, creating an existential harmony between conflicting elements of Abrahams's early and later life and thought. The central character, Jacob Brown, is the grandchild of the original couple of runaway slaves, who had successfully created a cooperative settlement in the Jamaican hills based on a biblical Christianity and centered on an impressive church structure, which the white-run Anglican establishment would later burn down. He is sent to a university in Georgia in the early years of the twentieth century, where he sits at the feet of W. E. B. Du Bois and falls in love with another student—the daughter of an Alabama sharecropper—who will marry him only if he commits himself for life to the black struggle in the Deep South. They eventually part, and Jacob, after completing his studies and being ordained, goes to Liberia as a missionary for a black independent church. There he is appointed bishop, and later he marries and is sent to Uganda, where he builds a flourishing mission based on cooperative and self-help ideas. This early period is presented as a lacuna, and the

Peter Abrahams
was born in 1919 in Johannesburg, South Africa, where he remained until he was twenty. He attended the Church of England Mission schools and colleges there. Except for two years at sea as a stoker during the war, he has earned his living solely by writing. The London *Observer* sent him to South Africa and Kenya in 1952 to do a series of articles, which attracted considerable attention and were also run in the European edition of the *Herald Tribune*. In 1955 the British Government sent him to Jamaica to gather material for an official report on the British West Indies, and he has been living in Jamaica with his wife and three children since then. He was the editor of the *West Indian Economist*; the controller of the *West Indian News*, a daily radio-news network of the West Indian Federation; and a news commentator on Jamaican radio and television broadcasts. During this period he also wrote pieces for *Holiday* magazine. Early in 1964 he gave up most of his other activities to make more time for writing fiction. Among Mr. Abrahams's previous books are the novels *A Wreath for Udomo* (1956) and *Path of Thunder* (1948), and the autobiography of his early years in Africa, *Tell Freedom* (1954).

Dust jacket for the American edition of Abrahams's 1965 novel, about a love affair between two political activists, a black man and an Indian woman, in South Africa

reader meets the present-day Brown for the first time after his departure from Liberia, at his wife's funeral in Uganda following many years of work there. But Brown is estranged from his son, David, a doctor who has rejected Christianity for radical Pan-Africanism and socialism and is involved in preparations for the Algerian uprising against French colonial rule. David returns to Uganda a day late for his mother's funeral (piloting a small aircraft solo from Algeria: the icon of the black man mastering technology, confidently at the controls of the machine, is a significant one for Abrahams, though its force may escape the general reader). The second half of the novel describes the father and son's reconciliation to ideological and filial fulfillment, through the time of the decolonization of black Africa, the persecution of the church by the Amin tyranny, a retreat to ancestral roots in Jamaica, and a planned return, as Jacob Brown nears the end of his life, to the place of ultimate origins, Africa. By the end of the novel the reconciliation between father and son in *The View from Coyaba* is so perfect that David Brown (now married to a Ugandan woman) decides to become a medical missionary.

Throughout his writing life Abrahams has struggled with the implications of black disadvantage, political, economic, and social, wherever it has occurred. The explanations offered by different ideological systems have afforded partial satisfaction at times, and he records in *Tell Freedom* his sense of clarity and relief when in late adolescence he first encountered a Marxist economic analysis of the racial tyranny he suffered in South Africa. Later, when he divested his thinking of Marxist scaffolding, he was forced back into despair, which sometimes broke disturbingly through the surface of his rhetoric. (Perhaps the best example is a sentence describing the artist Mabi during one of the crises in the plot of *A Wreath for Udomo*: "And all the guilt of Africa was in his voice.") Abrahams's passion is apparent when he first addresses the problem in *The View from Coyaba*, by having a runaway slave condemn the white master's practice of employing slaves to whip other slaves. Abrahams, perhaps for the first time in his career, succeeds in creating an effective metaphor for the variety of shapes and forms of black disadvantage and dispossession. There will always be those who are prepared to

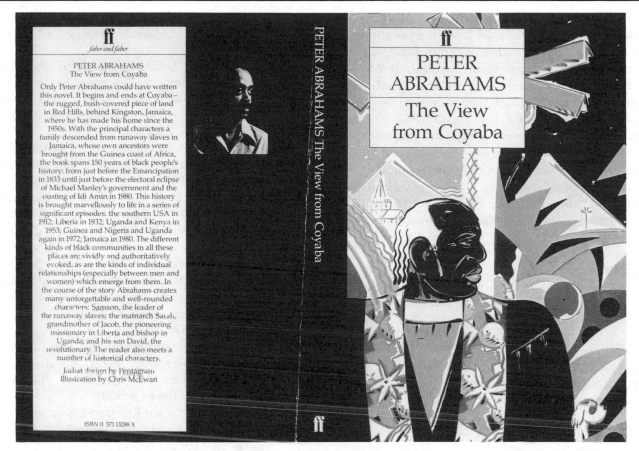

Dust jacket for Abrahams's 1985 book, a family novel with a far broader scope than any of his earlier works of fiction

sell their identity to the real exploiters in exchange for power. The black slave who whips his fellow stands for members of black elites who sell their countries into economic and political thralldom or carry out the policies of their neocolonial masters. The effects on the black soul, Abrahams suggests, are severely demoralizing.

The conflict between father and son in *The View from Coyaba* is finally resolved at the ancestral home in Jamaica, where David and Jacob debate the appropriate response of blacks to white racism and oppression and finally decide to follow "the greatest revolutionary who ever lived . . . the Christ who taught love and kindness and compassion." This is the existential answer the mature Abrahams, near the end of his career as novelist, offers to the questions he has examined so relentlessly and with such integrity in his fiction since that career began. David and his wife, Emma, widow of the black bishop martyred by Amin, will return to Africa to build a new militant church, dedicated to fighting (with firearms if need be) for a new synthesis, beginning with a black withdrawal from the embraces of both West and East.

Thus the book closes the circle of reconciliation between father and son, as David accepts the distilled wisdom of Jacob's life as Christian pastor and missionary. It also sets the seal on David's own Christian commitment and the remarkable change that this seems to signal in Abrahams's own beliefs. David's final act in the book is to take his wife's African maiden name as his surname, so the dual commitment is altogether specific: "Doctor David Batari of Uganda."

The issue of what was later called black consciousness begins early in Abrahams's work and is debated thoroughly in *Mine Boy*, his first major novel. There it is considered sympathetically but rejected in favor of a universalist Marxist ethic. From then until 1966, up to and including the publication of the first version of *This Island Now*, as his political thought changed and developed, it remained vigorously universalist in orientation. The changes in *The View from Coyaba* may be more apparent than real: by yoking his "withdrawal" into a version of black consciousness with the universalist ethic of Christianity, Abrahams keeps the flag of consistency flying. The contradictions must be embraced: the black world has failed so far to exploit the historic opportunity of decolonization and emerge from white domination, but the struggle must continue. It will succeed, but it must be based on Christian universalism; otherwise it faces the danger of becoming just another racism. Abrahams's final statement in *The View from Coyaba* is thus not very different from the ardent utopianism of his earliest writing or even the liberal skepticism of his middle period: humankind may have to become free one segment at a time, but there is no freedom without recognition and acceptance of human unity.

Bibliography:

Kolawole Ogungbesan, "Peter Abrahams: A Selected Bibliography," *World Literature Written in English*, 13 (November 1974): 184-190.

References:

Ursula A. Barnett, *A Vision of Order: A Study of Black South African Literature in English (1914-1980)* (London: Sinclair Browne / Amherst: University of Massachusetts Press, 1983);

V. A. February, *Mind Your Colour: The "Coloured" Stereotype in South African Literature* (London & Boston: Kegan Paul, 1981);

Shatto Arthur Gakwandi, *The Novel and Contemporary Experience in Africa* (London: Heinemann / New York: Africana, 1977);

Albert Gérard, "Peter Abrahams et la littérature sud-africaine," *Revue Nouvelle*, 45 (1967): 651-654;

Gérard, "Le roman néo-africaine: Peter Abrahams," *Revue Nouvelle*, 38 (1963): 374-381;

Cynthia Hamilton, "Work and Culture: The Evolution of Consciousness in Urban Industrial Society in the Fiction of William Attaway and Peter Abrahams," *Black American Literature Forum*, 21 (Spring-Summer 1987): 147-163;

Michael Harris, "South Africa Past and Future in Peter Abrahams' *Wild Conquest*," *World Literature Written in English*, 28 (Spring 1988): 1-11;

Christopher Heywood, "The Novels of Peter Abrahams," in *Perspectives on African Literature*, edited by Heywood (London: Heinemann / New York: Africana, 1971), pp. 157-172;

Vladimir Klima, *South African Prose Writing in English* (Prague: Oriental Institute in Academia, 1969);

Kimberly A. Koza, "Telling of Freedom: The Novels of Peter Abrahams," in *Essays on Contemporary Post-Colonial Fiction*, edited by Hedwig Bock and Albert Wertheim (Munich: Hueber, 1986), pp. 101-113;

Charles R. Larson, *The Emergence of African Fiction* (Bloomington & London: Indiana University Press, 1972);

Bernth Lindfors, "Exile and Aesthetic Distance: Geographical Influences on Political Commitment in the Works of Peter Abrahams," *International Fiction Review*, 13 (1986): 76-81;

Chukwudi T. Maduka, "Colonialism, Nation-Building and the Revolutionary Intellectual in Peter Abrahams' *A Wreath for Udomo*," *Journal of Southern African Affairs*, 2, no. 2 (1977): 245-257;

Maduka, "Limitation and Possibility: The Intellectual as Hero-Type in Peter Abrahams' *A Wreath for Udomo*," *Zagadnienia Rodzajow Literackich*, 24 (1981): 51-60;

Hena Maes-Jelinek, "Race Relationships and Identity in Peter Abrahams' 'Pluralia,'" *English Studies*, 50 (1969): 106-112;

Serge Menager, "Peter Abrahams, Icare Metis," *Commonwealth Essays and Studies*, 12 (Spring 1990): 91-100;

Ezekiel Mphahlele, *The African Image* (London: Faber & Faber, 1974);

Kolawole Ogungbesan, *The Writing of Peter Abrahams* (London: Hodder & Stoughton / New York: Holmes & Meier, 1979);

James Olney, *Tell Me Africa: An Approach to African Literature* (Princeton, N.J.: Princeton University Press, 1973);

Robert Philipson, "Images of Colonized Childhood: Abrahams, Wright and Laye," in *Literature of Africa and the African Continuum*, edited by Jonathan A. Peters, Mildred P. Mortimer, and Russell V. Linnemann (Washington, D.C.: Three Continents Press & the African Literature Association, 1989), pp. 75-81;

Paul A. Scanlon, "Dream and Reality in Abrahams's *A Wreath for Udomo*," *Obsidian*, 6, nos. 1-2 (1980): 25-32;

Michael Wade, *Peter Abrahams* (London & Ibadan: Evans, 1972);

Sylvia Wynter, "The Instant Novel Now," *New World Quarterly*, 3, no. 3 (1967): 78-81.

Chinua Achebe
(16 November 1930 -   )

G. D. Killam
University of Guelph

BOOKS: *Things Fall Apart* (London: Heinemann, 1958; New York: McDowell, Obolensky, 1959);

No Longer at Ease (London: Heinemann, 1960; New York: Obolensky, 1961);

The Sacrificial Egg, and Other Short Stories (Onitsha, Nigeria: Etudo, 1962);

Arrow of God (London: Heinemann, 1964; New York: Day, 1967; revised, London: Heinemann, 1974);

Chike and the River (Cambridge: Cambridge University Press, 1966);

A Man of the People (London: Heinemann, 1966; New York: Day, 1966);

Beware, Soul Brother, and Other Poems (Enugu, Nigeria: Nwankwo-Ifejika, 1971; revised and enlarged edition, London: Heinemann, 1972; Enugu, Nigeria: Nwamife, 1972; republished as *Christmas in Biafra and Other Poems* (Garden City, N.Y.: Anchor/Doubleday, 1973);

Girls at War and Other Stories (London: Heinemann, 1972; Garden City, N.Y.: Doubleday, 1973);

How the Leopard Got His Claws, by Achebe and John Iroaganachi (Enugu, Nigeria: Nwamife, 1972; New York: Third Press, 1973);

Morning Yet on Creation Day: Essays (London: Heinemann, 1975; enlarged edition, Garden City, N.Y.: Anchor/Doubleday, 1975);

The Drum: A Children's Story (Enugu, Nigeria: Fourth Dimension, 1977);

The Flute: A Children's Story (Enugu, Nigeria: Fourth Dimension, 1979);

The Trouble with Nigeria (Enugu, Nigeria: Fourth Dimension, 1983; London & Exeter, N.H.: Heinemann, 1984);

The World of the Ogbanje (Enugu, Nigeria: Fourth Dimension, 1986);

Anthills of the Savannah (London: Heinemann, 1987; New York: Anchor/Doubleday, 1988);

Hopes and Impediments: Selected Essays, 1965-1987 (London: Heinemann, 1988; New York: Doubleday, 1989);

The University and the Leadership Factor in Nigerian Politics (Enugu, Nigeria: Abic, 1988);

A Tribute to James Baldwin (Amherst: University of Massachusetts Press, 1989).

Collection: *The African Trilogy: Things Fall Apart; No Longer at Ease; Arrow of God* (London: Picador, 1988).

OTHER: *The Insider: Stories of War and Peace from Nigeria*, edited by Achebe and others (Enugu, Nigeria: Nwankwo-Ifejika, 1971);

Don't Let Him Die: An Anthology of Memorial Poems for Christopher Okigbo (1932-1967), edited by Achebe and Dubem Okafor (Enugu, Nigeria: Fourth Dimension, 1978);

Aka Weta: Egwu aguluagu Egwu edeluede, edited by Achebe and Obiora Udechukwu (Nsukka, Nigeria: Okike, 1982);

African Short Stories, edited by Achebe and C. L. Innes (London & Portsmouth, N.H.: Heinemann, 1985).

SELECTED PERIODICAL PUBLICATIONS—UNCOLLECTED: "The Role of the Writer in the New Nation," *Nigeria Magazine*, 81 (June 1964);

"The Novelist as Teacher," *New Statesman*, 69 (29 January 1965);

"The English Language and the African Writer," *Insight* (October-December 1966);

"Named for Victoria, Queen of England," *New Letters*, 40 (October 1973): 15-22.

Chinua Achebe is arguably the most discussed African writer of his generation. His first novel, *Things Fall Apart* (1958), has become a classic. It has been read and discussed by readers throughout the anglophone world and has been translated into some forty languages. Sales are estimated to be in excess of three million copies. His other novels—*No Longer at Ease* (1960), *Arrow of God* (1964), *A Man of the People* (1966), and *Anthills of the Savannah* (1987)—are equally re-

Chinua Achebe circa 1962 (photograph by George Hallett)

spected. A substantial body of scholarship and criticism has grown up around each of these books.

Achebe was born on 16 November 1930 in the village of Ogidi in eastern Nigeria. His mother was Janet Iloegbunam Achebe. His father, Isaiah Okafor Achebe, was a catechist for the Church Missionary Society, and the young Achebe's primary education was in the society's school in Ogidi. He was eight when he began to learn English and fourteen when he went, as one of the few boys selected, to the Government College at Umuahia, one of the best schools in West Africa. He enrolled in 1948 at University College, Ibadan, as a member of the first class to attend this new school. He intended to study medicine but soon switched to English literary studies and followed a syllabus that almost exactly resembled the University of London honors degree program, Ibadan's college being then a constituent college of the University of London. He contributed stories, essays, and sketches to the *University Herald*. (The stories were published in 1972 in *Girls at War and Other Stories*.) After graduating in 1953 he firmly decided to be a writer.

Achebe is a master of the craft of fiction; he has extended the capability of English beyond the limits it had achieved to the point when he published his first novel. His control of language is absolute, and his wide range of usage is appropriate to the multiplicity of his interests.

Things Fall Apart first received attention, however, because of the social purposes he assigned to it and to himself as writer. The novel was published two years before Nigerian independence was gained in 1960. The timing was superb: while Africans—Nigerians in this case—looked forward with excitement and optimism to the political freedom they would attain after more than a half century of colonial rule, Achebe understood the necessity of showing his countrymen the strength of their own cultures to assist in the task of nation building, a strength greatly diminished by the imposition of an alien culture: "as far as I am concerned the fundamental theme . . . is that African people did not hear of culture for the first time from Europeans; that their societies were not mindless but frequently had a philosophy of great depth and value and beauty, that

Achebe in the 1950s

tion of Africans by Europeans, the more so because Cary was working hard at getting the presentation right and not writing fiction that deliberately, often cynically, exploited the stereotypes of Africans and African society that informed the hundreds of novels written by Englishmen about Africa during the imperial-colonial period. It was precisely because Cary was a liberal-minded and sympathetic writer, as well as a colonial administrator, that Achebe felt the record had to be set straight.

Achebe's purpose, then, is to write about his own people and for his own people. His five novels to date form a continuum of time over some one hundred years of Igbo civilization. Europeans have not yet penetrated Umuofia, the setting of the first novel, when this period begins. When it ends, colonial rule has been established, significant change has taken place, and the character of the community—its values and freedoms—have been substantially and irrevocably altered. *Arrow of God*, his third novel, has much the same setting as *Things Fall Apart* with the difference that colonial rule has been consolidated and the lives of the villagers are completely circumscribed by it. The action of *No Longer at Ease* (his second novel) takes place in the period immediately before independence from British colonial rule in Nigeria; *A Man of the People* and *Anthills of the Savannah* are located in unspecified African countries (strongly resembling Nigeria) in the immediate postindependence period. The novels therefore form an imaginative history of a segment of a major group of people in what eventually became Nigeria, as seen from the perspective of a Christian Igboman.

Achebe has said in various places that the fact of his Christian upbringing was important in his evolution as a writer. The Christian rituals, which shaped his upbringing, he later detected in the Igbo religion itself, and it is this recognition that has shaped his art and might be said to be a controlling metaphor of it. He writes, in the introduction to *African Short Stories* (1985): "The Igbo world is an arena for the interplay of forces. It is a dynamic world of movement and flux.... In some cultures an individual may worship one of the gods or goddesses in the pantheon and pay scant attention to the rest. In Igbo religion such selectiveness would be unthinkable. All the people must placate all the gods all the time! For there is a cautionary proverb which states that even when a person has satisfied Udo completely he may be killed by Ogwugwu! The degree of peril

they had poetry and, above all, they had dignity. It is this dignity that African people all but lost during the colonial period, and it is this that they must now regain" ("The Role of the Writer in the New Nation," *Nigeria Magazine*, June 1964).

Interested in stories and storytelling since his youth, Achebe had his interest in becoming a writer confirmed when he encountered Joyce Cary's novel *Mister Johnson* (1939): "one of the things that probably finally decided me was a novel set in Nigeria ... called *Mister Johnson*, which is quite famous, and I feel that ... in spite of [Cary's] ability, in spite of his sympathy and understanding, he could not get under the skin of his African. They just did not communicate. And I felt if a good writer could make this mess perhaps we ought to try our hand" (*African Writers Talking*, 1972). For Achebe, the character Mister Johnson represents the worst kind of presenta-

propounded by this proverb is only dimly apprehended until one realises that Ogwugwu is Udo's loving consort."

Given Achebe's purposes as an artist—the duty to the art and the social purposes he has said he means it to serve—one can say that his is a distinctly Igbo sensibility. His art reflects in all its variety the endless permutations of the essential duality of Igbo life. The connection between this worldview and artistic irony is, of course, apparent. Achebe's art is essentially an art of irony, from the simple to the profound. What makes Achebe's irony different from that of writers from purely literary cultures is that, while their uses of irony are cultivated, his is instinctive, generating as it does from the substance of his culture and being inseparable from it.

There was a five-year gap between the publication of his stories in the university paper and the release of *Things Fall Apart*. In that interval Achebe taught for a year and then embarked on a twelve-year career as a producer for the Nigerian Broadcasting Corporation. In 1957 he went to London to attend the British Broadcasting Corporation Staff School. One of his teachers there was the British novelist and literary critic Gilbert Phelps. Phelps recognized the quality of *Things Fall Apart* and recommended it for publication. Achebe has remarked that he never had to endure the experience of the struggling artist.

There are other related reasons why there was a gap between the stories of student days and the publication of *Things Fall Apart*. There was the purely practical reason of finding time to write in the midst of a full professional life. He was appointed director of the Voice of Nigeria (external broadcasting) by the Nigerian Broadcasting Corporation in 1961. That same year, on 10 September, he married Christie Chinwe Okoli and became involved in domesticity. But some reasons were more profound. Having determined that one of his purposes was essentially a political one—to set straight the record propounded about Nigerian life by Europeans—he had to find out in more detail than he knew at the time what the native philosophy was and what the basis was for its depth and value and beauty. More than that, and most difficult and elusive in accounting for, he had to discover the appropriate form and language for his fictional evocations.

As Achebe admits (in "Named for Victoria, Queen of England," *New Letters*, October 1973), he largely "picked up" the history of his society: "this was the life that interested me, partly the

life I lived and the life that was lived around me, supported by what I heard in conversation—I was very keen on listening to old people—and what I learned from my father, so it was sort of picked up here and there. There was no research in the library. . . ." But Achebe was aware of and read the writing of colonial administrators and missionaries, especially the quasi-anthropological treatises of G. T. Basden, who was a close friend of Achebe's father. (Basden performed the wedding ceremony for Achebe's parents and was honored by Achebe's village, Ogidi, with a carved tusk.) Like Cary's, presumably Basden's heart was in the right place, and it was precisely because he was sincere and earnest that his woefully wrongheaded interpretations of Igbo customs could not go unchallenged. He was ineluctably one of those who, through his writing, contributed to what Achebe called the "almost complete disaster for the black races . . . the warped mental attitudes of both black and white . . . the traumatic experience" that was the legacy of Africa's long encounter with Europe. Achebe read Basden's and others' accounts and absorbed them.

As he says in "The Novelist as Teacher" (*New Statesman*, 29 January 1965), he conceives his role as partly that of "teacher"—"perhaps what I write is applied art as distinct from pure. But who cares?" However, he is not a "preacher": "I'm very fully aware and fully conscious of the dangers of idealization. . . . I bend over backwards to paint in all the unsavoury, all the unfavourable aspects of that culture. Because what I think I am is a kind of witness and I think I would not be doing justice to my cause if I could be faulted on the matter of truth."

Things Fall Apart is "an act of atonement with my past, the ritual return and homage of a prodigal son." Conceived first as a story that would deal with the lives of three men in a family over three generations—Okonkwo, Nwoye (who later takes the Christian name Isaac), and Obi Okonkwo—the novel was originally divided into three parts with two of the parts eventually expanded to tell the full story of only two lives, those of Okonkwo (in *Things Fall Apart*) and Obi Okonkwo (in *No Longer at Ease*). Nwoye's complete story has never been told (though interesting speculative articles on what that life might have comprised have been published by critics and scholars). *Things Fall Apart* primarily tells the story of Okonkwo and his life and career in the village of Umuofia. His father is Unoka, a wastrel, known in "all the clan for the weakness of his ma-

Cover for the first volume in Heinemann's African Writers Series, a 1962 edition of Achebe's first novel

chete and his hoe" (who nonetheless embodies qualities admirable in themselves if not admired and supported in the clan). Okonkwo is determined through hard work to achieve the highest titles in his clan. He embodies the qualities most valued by his people (if in an exaggerated form)— energy, a strong sense of purpose, and a sense of communal cooperativeness that at the same time is marked by a strong sense of individuality.

When readers meet him, Okonkwo's fame is already established: "Okonkwo was well-known throughout the nine villages and even beyond. His fame rested on solid personal achievements." As a young man he had thrown Amalinze, the Cat, "the great wrestler who for seven years was unbeaten from Umuofia to Mbaino." Okonkwo thus brought "honor to his village." Since that time his fame has grown like a "bush fire in the harmattan": he has achieved wealth and wives and children and is a member of the highest council of the clan. Okonkwo's rise to a position of

wealth and authority is in part accounted for by the strength of his will, his back, and his arms. Burdened with an improvident father and—due to one very bad year—an early failure as a farmer, Okonkwo does not yield to despair: "it always surprised him that he did not sink under the load of despair. He knew he had been a fierce fighter, but that year had been enough to break the heart of a lion." Recognizing his capacity for survival, he believes that " 'since I survived that year . . . I shall survive anything.' He put it down to his inflexible will." Okonkwo's whole life is "dominated by fear, the fear of failure and weakness . . . and so Okonkwo's whole life was ruled by one passion—to hate everything that his father Unoka had loved."

In metaphysical terms, however, in accordance with the beliefs of the clan, Okonkwo's success is attributed to his *chi*. In the concept of the *chi*, Achebe secures the philosophical basis of the novel and reveals the essential duality of Igbo be-

lief. Okonkwo's success is attributed to a benevolent *chi*. The Ghanaian writer and critic Kofi Awoonor says that "the 'chi' is a personal god or man's deital expression, the ultimate mission brought by man from the creator's house, a deity that makes each man's unique personality or being." Relating this to Achebe's achievement, Awoonor writes: "Achebe's thematic construction and dramatisation of the conflict in *Things Fall Apart* utilises the 'chi' concept. The structure of the novel is firmly based in the principles that are derived from this piece of Igbo ontological evidence. Okonkwo's life and actions seem to be prescribed by those immutable laws inherent in the 'chi' concept. It is the one significant principle that determines the rhythm and tragic grandeur of the novel. Okonkwo's rise and fall are seen in the significant way in which he challenges his 'chi' to battle."

Okonkwo's story is set against the background of daily life in Umuofia, an agrarian society governed by rules of religion and politics, always discussed, debated, and amended as circumstances dictate. It is a democratic society in which titles are taken (or given) on merit and can be taken away if the proscriptions for holding them are violated. The tension in the society and, at the same time, its stability arise out of the balance struck between individuality—which in Okonkwo's case displays itself in a single-minded pursuit of acquiring wealth and thus respect and influence—and communality. Individual enterprise is valued and rewarded. But a strong religious principle keeps this individualism in check. Achebe has written that "Igbo society has always been materialistic. This may sound strange because Igbo life had at the same time a strong spiritual dimension—controlled by other gods, ancestors, personal spirits or 'chi' and magic" ("The Role of the Writer in a New Nation").

The *chi* is the dominating ambiguous force in the life of an individual, but his life is also circumscribed by gods, ancestors, and magic. All these forces contain the community in *Things Fall Apart*, which displays community members in dynamic relationships with the seasons: subject to periods of intense labor in the planting and harvest seasons, followed by periods of leisure; and subject to the vagaries of the climate, leavened by song, dance, and music.

This is the society readers see in the first (and longest) part of the novel, a homogeneous society not without its inner tensions and problems, both personal and communal, but which operates based on codes of religious and political belief supported by custom. The first section of *Things Fall Apart* is set in Umuofia before the coming of Europeans, and it is here that Achebe best demonstrates his concern that "the past needs to be recreated not only for the enlightenment of our detractors but even more for our own education. Because . . . the past with all its imperfections, never lacked dignity. . . . This is where the writer's integrity comes in. Will he be strong enough to overcome the temptation to select only those facts which flatter him?"

Part 1 comprises thirteen chapters and presents the Umuofian agricultural year; the games and festivals at its climax; the affairs of prominent citizens and their relations, both as individuals and as families within the clan; and the arrival in the clan of Ikemefuna, the boy who becomes like a son to Okonkwo and, more importantly in terms of the novel's purposes, almost a brother to Okonkwo's son, Nwoye. Following

Achebe in Lagos in 1964, when he was the director of the Voice of Nigeria

these affairs and events, part 1 focuses on Okonkwo's crisis (brought on by his accidentally shooting a man), culminating in his seven-year banishment to the village of his mother.

Part 2 is situated in Mbanta, and readers learn of the arrival of the white man and of the religion and colonial government gradually introduced into the area. The economy of Achebe's prose and his restraint in telling his story belie the complexity of the issues. Because the coming of the foreigners is gradual, the processes by which these new values are established are insidious. At first the Christian church attracts only the "worthless" members of village society. But gradually men of prominence in the clan join the ranks of converts, and this, together with the establishment of a political-judicial system administered by Europeans (and supported by African police) and the introduction of a cash-based trading economy, causes things to change irreversibly.

Okonkwo witnesses, without being able to ra-

tionalize them, the inevitable processes of historical change. The new religion has sufficient appeal to undermine traditional religion. At the same time, through the incentives of the new value placed on palm oil and palm kernels, the acquisitive nature of the society is enhanced. The traditional balance is upset.

Part 3 of the novel, proceeding from Okonkwo's return to Umuofia, brings the novel swiftly to a close. The climax is reached after a sacred python—the embodiment of a sacred spirit—is killed by a Christian: reprisal is taken by the villagers, who burn the Christian church. The district officer calls Okonkwo and other elders to his office on the pretext that he wishes to discuss the animosities between the two factions, but he behaves treacherously by putting them in jail and in irons. Following this, for Okonkwo, there is nothing left to do but fight. He kills a government messenger, and when Okonkwo sees that he stands alone, he hangs himself. This abominated form of death ironically earns for him what he had sought all his life to avoid: a dishonorable burial like the one given his father.

The final paragraphs of the novel reveal irony of a different kind. The dangling body of Okonkwo is merely an "undignified detail" to the district officer, who plans to write a book called *The Pacification of the Primitive Tribes of the Lower Niger*. In this book Okonkwo's story will make "interesting reading," even if only an almost incidental detail.

The meaning of Achebe's novel is sustained by the consummate control he has over his materials, as these are presented in a manner appropriate to all of the moods and modes of the story. Achebe has said in many places that the words must sound right in his ear before he sets them down. His statement about the kind of English appropriate to the writer's task is well known: "The price a world language must be prepared to pay is submission to many different kinds of use. The African writer should aim to use English in a way that brings out his message best without altering the language to the extent that its value as a medium for international exchange will be lost. He should aim at fashioning out an English which is at once universal and able to carry his peculiar experience" ("The English Language and the African Writer," *Insight*, October-December 1966).

Things Fall Apart is an account of colonial history from the point of view of the colonized rather than the colonizer: the perspective is African ontology instead of Eurocentric historiography. The novel explores the philosophical principles of an African community, which is autonomous at the outset. But Achebe's discussion, direct and inferred, does not have the depth of his third novel, *Arrow of God*.

Achebe's second novel, *No Longer at Ease*, is set in modern Nigeria in the days immediately before independence from British colonial rule. The novel reveals the changes to Nigerian society that result from foreign intervention—the extent to which things have fallen apart. The nature of these changes is revealed through the experiences, actions, and beliefs of Obi Okonkwo, the grandson of Okonkwo. *No Longer at Ease* records Obi's professional, social, and moral declines as they arise from and run parallel to a confusion of values in modern Nigerian society. Obi is a highly individualized character who nevertheless seems typical of young Nigerians of his generation. Obi's is the tragic story of a modern man:

Dust jacket for Achebe's 1964 novel, which examines conflicts between villagers and the British Colonial Service in early-twentieth-century Nigeria

his values are shaped by his links with his Igbo culture as revealed by his mother: but they are contorted by his formal, alien education overseas—he has a B.A. with honors in English from London University. The novel also tells of the tragedy of a modern state, for through Obi's experiences Achebe provides a record of the nature of "modernity"—in terms of its social, political, and economic implications—derived through colonial rule as Nigerians have accommodated themselves to it, and of the price Nigerians have paid for this kind of modernity.

Obi is not an admirable character: his distanced, literary, and supercilious responses to events in the traditional society of his village and at his "European" job in the capital city are smug and callow. His tragic flaw is that he has no moral reserves with which to deal with the calamities he brings down on his own head. Yet his experiences testify to the oppressive weight of doubt, guilt, and regret that the colonial experience has occasioned in Nigeria.

Achebe returns to the past in *Arrow of God.* He evokes a world much like that of Okonkwo's but more dynamic, in comprehensive detail, a world redolent of the complexities of daily domestic, social, political, and religious living but further complicated by the religious and political prescriptions the colonial force has introduced into Igbo society, rules that are now institutionalized. The dynamics of the lives of the people of Umuaro are rendered in detail for the purpose of displaying the tragedy of Ezeulu, the chief priest of Ulu and the spiritual and political leader of his people. When readers meet him, Ezeulu's power is supreme. But secure as his power and influence are, he is compelled to defend it against Nwaka, a wealthy chief and principal supporter of Ezidemili, chief priest of the god Idemili, a once powerful deity Ulu has displaced.

The novel is a meditation on the nature and uses of power, and on the responsibility of the person who wields it. Ezeulu becomes engaged in a struggle for power with both the people of his village and the officers of the British Colonial Service. Always sensitive to the source of his power (the people), Ezeulu is forced to try to reconcile the contending impulses in his nature: to serve the needs of his people and to indulge his desire for greater personal power through pushing his authority to its limits. Out of the contending impulses his tragedy arises.

The novel focuses on a moment when an attempt at resolution of the dilemma is forced on him. For political reasons Ezeulu is put in jail at British administrative headquarters. (He has offended the district officer by refusing his offer of a warrant chieftaincy.) During Ezeulu's period of imprisonment two new moons pass; two sacred yams—by which ceremony the calendar year passes and the planting season is determined— remain uneaten while he determines to thwart both the British administration and, more important, his own clansmen. On his return to the village after being released by the British, and despite the warm welcome accorded him, Ezeulu determines to eat the two yams in sequence, thus delaying the harvest. New yams rot in the ground, and the clan is faced with a famine. Ultimately the clan—and his god, Ulu—abandon Ezeulu. The Christian mission offers succor to members of the clan, some of whom bring thanksgiving offerings to the mission. Ezeulu wrestles with his conscience, seeking to respond to the absolute need of his people to harvest their annual food supply and yet determined to honor his god by observing and defending custom with reference to the eating of the ceremonial yams. He makes the wrong choice, and tragedy results. Achebe displays the processes, both social and psychological, that bring down the priest-leader and his god.

A religious ambience pervades the society, and Achebe, according to Awoonor, through his dramatization of Ezeulu's function in the community is able "to centralize the theological arguments that emerge in an African religious situation which outsiders may think is devoid of intellectual debate." Achebe has said, "we make the gods we worship," and Ezeulu has persistent cause to meditate on the nature of his power: "Whenever Ezeulu considered the immensity of his power over the year and the crops and, therefore, over the people he wondered if it was real. . . . He was merely a watchman."

Ezeulu's consideration of his powers soon becomes more than speculation. With the presence of white society and with Ezeulu's recognition that it is an influence that will alter and reshape his society, he is determined to understand this influence and turn it to his own profit (and that of the villagers). Ezeulu knows that the clan is no longer in full control of its own affairs, that political power has been taken from it, and that personal animosities are not at issue. Nevertheless, his motives are not entirely disinterested. For while he seeks to understand and accommodate the power of the new, imposed regime—the better to understand and convert it to the use of the clan—he also seeks to exploit new knowledge for personal use.

Ezeulu thus incurs the suspicion of some and jealousy of others within the clan and the anger of the British political officers, who impute to him the wrong motives for supporting certain of their political actions. What he fails to take fully into account is the way in which the governing colonial power has compromised his authority.

The irony is that the renewed rivalry between the two priests, which threatens to divide the clan, is rendered obsolete by the consequences of Ezeulu's decision to castigate the clan by refusing to announce the harvest; by the defection of large numbers of villagers to the Christian fold—where dispensation to survive is provided; by the death of his son Obika, who, although ill with fever, runs a funeral race on behalf of a dead clansman, determined if possible

Achebe in 1972, when he received a D.Litt. degree from Dartmouth College

to retrieve something of his father's reputation; and ultimately by Ezeulu's madness: "At any other time Ezeulu would have been more than equal to his grief. He would have been equal to any grief not compounded with humiliation. . . . Perhaps it was the constant, futile throbbing of these thoughts which finally left a crack in Ezeulu's mind. . . . But this . . . allowed Ezeulu, in his last days, to live in the haughty splendour of a demented high priest and spared him the knowledge of the final outcome."

Ezeulu's tragedy results from his own rationalization of his responsibility, the nature of his power, and his decision on a course of action. He is the author of his own destiny; no external force is ultimately responsible. But the British authority has been an agent in his destiny. Ezeulu fails because he acts in a way that will bring about his community's destruction through starvation. Personal motives become entangled with pub-

lic, political, and religious motives, and through Ezeulu's destruction the Igbo aphorism that "no man however great can win a judgment against the clan" is proven. In other words, he fails to integrate the present circumstances with his recognition of his priestly role. In the end the collective will, determined to ensure survival of the villagers, prevails. Survival is more important than ritual.

The consequences of the loss of predictable political power at the village level can bring personal tragedy; at the national level the consequences are, of course, more widespread and longer lasting. It is to this latter reality that Achebe turns in his fourth novel, *A Man of the People*. The novel is set in the postcolonial period in an independent African country. The governance of the country is, nominally, in the hands of the people, and it is the quality of the leadership and the response of the people to that leadership that concern Achebe. There is no collective will in the people; there is no responsible leadership.

Moreover, a collective voice manifest at the village level, through which collective agreement is articulated, as seen in *Things Fall Apart* and *Arrow of God*, does not exist: "You see, the oral tradition of Igboland worked because the community was small in size, and the man who got up to speak was not judged entirely by what he was saying then: he was judged by what was known of him ten years ago. . . . But you can't have that kind of safeguard today in the context of an 80 million nation. You simply do not know the man who is talking to you and therefore you must devise more sophisticated ways of assessing him" (*Chinua Achebe in Conversation with C. L. Innes*, June 1981).

A Man of the People is about Chief Nanga and his colleagues, senior ministers of government, and their rivals in other political parties who have produced what Achebe describes in the novel as a "fat-dripping, gummy, eat-and-let-eat regime . . . which inspired the common saying that a man could only be sure of what he had put away safely in his gut or, in language more suited to the times: 'you chop, me self I chop, palaver finish. . . .' "

Whereas the Achebe novels set in the past display a society in which a balance between collective religious observance and individual monetary pursuits is achieved, contemporary society is revealed in *A Man of the People* as devoid of religious concerns. Only a vestige remains of the religious beliefs that kept the acquisitiveness of the society in balance. Therefore, in *A Man of the People*, there is an atmosphere of unrestrained acquisitiveness in the midst of political corruption: there is no national voice but only a confusion of competing village voices, an atmosphere where it is every man for himself in acquiring as large a piece of the national financial cake as possible and by whatever means are the most effective. Odili, who tells the story, is, when readers meet him, a cynical and politically disaffected university graduate who once had placed his faith in university-trained, public-minded leaders who would ensure through their education and actions that a unified nation, economically viable and politically stable, would be developed in the postcolonial period. But political opportunists, Nanga prominent among them, have caused high-minded, disinterested, well-educated leaders to be discredited in the name of Africanization, thus making sure that they, the people of the people, as it were, can extend their personal fortunes at the expense of the taxed public purse.

The novel is a retrospective narration told in the first person by Odili, and the purposes of the story are revealed in the relations between Odili and Nanga, their various political activities, and the confrontations between them, which culminate in a national economic crisis and scandal, a rigged election, and finally military intervention. A principal and related purpose is the examination of public and private motives that inform political action.

The strength of the argument of the book is summed up in Odili's statement that mere anarchy has replaced the laws of the village and that such confusion is made worse by the tension in the relationship between Odili and Nanga. Nanga is an engaging and credible character: this is what makes his apostasy so terrifying.

The novel is open-ended. An impasse in the political system has been reached, but military intervention is plainly not a solution to the problems of public governance. However, this is where the novel ends. Nigeria—and other African countries as well (thus the applicability of the circumstances Achebe dramatizes in *A Man of the People* to African states, or to any other countries in like circumstances)—has gone through hard political times and a series of military coups. There is still the ultimate hope of a return to civilian government.

A Man of the People continues Achebe's contemplation of the changes wrought in Nigerian life during the twentieth century. Against a background of changing and evolving social and political realities, Achebe reveals his concern with individual humanity and with the responses of his heroes to the social problems in which they become enmeshed. His interest is in the failures and the tragic destinies of his heroes, for out of their responses to their failures (and out of awareness of the causes) new possibilities arise.

A prophetic novel, *A Man of the People* was published in January 1966 and coincided almost exactly with the first military coup d'état in Nigeria. Facts emulated art. The worsening political situation in Nigeria led to persecution of Igbo people, at first those living outside of Igboland, most notably in northern Nigeria, where a series of massacres took place. Achebe resigned from his job with the Nigerian Broadcasting Corporation after these acts of genocide and returned to his homeland. The Eastern Region declared itself an independent state, called Biafra, in 1967 shortly after

*Dust jacket for the volume that collects Achebe's short fiction
from the early 1950s to 1972*

the devastating civil war in Nigeria or with explorations of theological positions in Igbo culture.

The opening poem, "1966," offers a contrast between the indifference to the possibility of civil war in Nigeria in 1966 and the increasing imminence of the war itself. Similarly, "Christmas in Biafra" contrasts the Christmas setting—the manger, the palms, the plaster-cast scene of the divine birth in Bethlehem, the serene holy family, and the "Child Jesus plump wise-looking and rose-cheeked"—with a Biafran woman and her dying child who lay "flat like a dead lizard / on her shoulder his arms and legs / cauterized by famine . . . a miracle / of its own kind."

Achebe has said of the Igbo insistence of the duality of things that "Wherever Something stands, there also Something Else will stand." This is consistent with Achebe's attitude that historical cultural preferences will always inform contemporary considerations—indeed, as his political writings show plainly, it is important that they do so. Nothing is static. What is important is that dualities and cultural premises must be examined carefully so as to determine what among them will prove serviceable to a contemporary generation of Nigerians. Out of such considerations, examinations, and choices come the materials for building an adequate society and providing a vital leadership.

Achebe, in light of his concern for the personal plight of those who have suffered terribly through the war, passes on the responsibility to those who survive and to whom will fall the responsibility—if they have the vision and the courage—to "inaugurate / a season of atonement and rescue / from fingers calloused by heavy deeds / the tender rites of reconciliation" ("Remembrance Day").

Thirteen of Achebe's short stories, collected as *Girls at War and Other Stories*, were published in 1972. He writes in the preface to the volume that "it was with something of a shock that I realised my earliest short stories were published as long ago as twenty years in the Ibadan student magazine, *The University Herald*," and that just over a "dozen pieces in twenty years must be accounted a pretty lean harvest by any reckoning." The stories display the conflict between traditional and modern values, and, intimately related to this, the nature of religious belief apposite to the present. Some stories focus on the social contexts of contemporary Nigerian life in circumstances that transcend the values agreed upon and upheld at the local or village level; others deal with aspects

a thirty-month civil war began. Throughout the war Achebe traveled widely on Biafran affairs, to Europe and North America. There was neither time nor inclination to write long fiction during this period. Rather, Achebe produced most of the poems in the volume *Beware, Soul Brother, and Other Poems* (1971; later revised, enlarged, and republished in the United States as *Christmas in Biafra and Other Poems*, 1973).

In a note to the poem "Misunderstanding," Achebe writes: "The Igbo people have a firm belief in the duality of things. . . . Igbo proverbs bring out this duality of existence very well. Take any proverb which puts forward a point of view or a 'truth' and you can always find another that contradicts it or at least puts a limitation on the absoluteness of its validity." In most of the poems in the slim volume, Achebe exploits this cultural axiom as an elaborated, controlling, sustaining poetic device, whether the poems deal with considerations of the social and humane implications of of the Nigeria-Biafra War. In his stories as in his novels Achebe's vision is multifaceted, scrupulously honest, and layered with irony. The harvest of stories is small, but it is not lean. The stories display his full range as a writer—from the humor of "Uncle Ben's Choice," through the various levels of irony in "The Madman," "The Voter," "Akueke," and "Dead Man's Path," to scathing assaults on the final follies of men in the political sphere.

In 1975 Achebe published a volume of fifteen essays, *Morning Yet on Creation Day*, written between 1962 and 1973, on various literary and political subjects. The collection is divided into two parts. Part 1 has eight essays dealing specifically with the role of the African writer in his society: Achebe discusses the central position of art in African society—"artists lived and moved and had their being in society, and created their art for the good of that society"—and addresses the question of the language the artist should employ, the role of critic, and the kind of critical standards that should be developed to evaluate the new literatures from Africa. In part these essays are a rebuttal of some of the critical standards developed and applied by expatriate critics of African literature. These essays are not so much concerned with the abstractions of literary criticism, though this is part of their importance. Their major thrust is with the function of the writer and critic in a dynamic relationship—"in assuming responsibility for our problems and our situation in the world. . . ." The essays in the second part are more personal in nature, although there is also a public application to the conclusions drawn. Of special interest is the essay " 'Chi' in Igbo Cosmology" for the light it throws on the *chi* in Achebe's first and third novels.

The 1975 collection has been superseded by *Hopes and Impediments* (1988), which retains some of the essays of the earlier volume and adds essays and addresses produced in the intervening years. Of special note are "The Truth of Fiction" and "What Has Literature Got to Do with It?" (the latter being Achebe's address on receiving the Nigerian National Merit Award).

In the midst of a busy literary life Achebe has been recognized at home and abroad with honorary degrees and visiting academic appointments, and he has been involved in other literary activities within Nigeria and abroad. He has continued to comment on the political life of Nigeria. The question of the kind of leadership that would best serve the country is at the center

Achebe lecturing at the University of Massachusetts—Amherst, 1974 (photograph by Bernth Lindfors)

of his concern. In 1983, in the face of an impending federal election, he published *The Trouble with Nigeria*. The opening pages of the book declare its thesis: "The trouble with Nigeria is simply and squarely a failure of leadership. There is nothing basically wrong with the Nigerian character. There is nothing wrong with the Nigerian land or climate or water or air or anything else. The Nigerian problem is the unwillingness or inability of its leaders to rise to the responsibility, to the challenge of personal example which are the hallmarks of true leadership."

He describes the country as "One of the most disorderly, insensitive, inefficient places under the sun," and as "dirty, callous, noisy, ostentatious, dishonest and vulgar." But he says that his statements proceed from love, that they are not negative but are predicated on the belief that change is possible in Nigeria. The political system of democracy left by the British did not work, and Nigerian leaders have been too complacent about finding a political system that will. The questions that must be addressed and the problems that must be solved if such a system is to be found are suggested in the various chapter headings of the book—"Tribalism," "False Images of Ourselves," "Patriotism," "Social Injustice and the Cult of Mediocrity," "Indiscipline," "Corruption," and "The Igbo Problem." The final chapter, "The Example of Aminu Kano," comments on the qualities of the ideal leader for Nigeria in Achebe's view. Aminu Kano was, in Achebe's words, a man "I admired [for] his commitment to the welfare and redemption of the oppressed. He was a saint and a revolutionary at the same time." Kano died before the election, and Achebe was asked to stand as a presidential candidate. Instead he became the deputy national president, an honorary title. Before the election was held, the military intervened, and it has been suggested that Achebe's words in part prompted this action.

Achebe continues to be involved in the quest to determine a just system of governance for Nigerians and to ally his thoughts to the place of literature in serving society's needs. In 1986 Achebe was awarded the Nigerian National Merit Award for the second time. In his acceptance speech he acknowledged that "the comprehensive goal of a developing nation like Nigeria is, of course, development or its somewhat better variant, modernization" and that literature is central in the quest for achieving this goal: "Literature, whether handed down by word of mouth or in print, gives us a second handle on reality; enabling us to encounter in the safe manageable dimensions of make-believe the very same threats to integrity that may assail the psyche in real life; and at the same time providing through the self-discovery which it imparts, a veritable weapon for coping with these threats whether they are found within our problematic and incoherent selves or in the world around us."

Gustave Flaubert, in one of his letters to Ivan Turgenev, said that there was nothing new for the writer to say, but there had to be new ways of saying the old things. Such is not the case with Achebe: the old things said about Africa over a long period of history, predicated on denigrative racial assumptions, were not worth saying again; indeed, they had to be refuted. Achebe has new things to say, and he has found a new way of saying them. He sets the record of history straight: no one can think about Africa in terms applied before his first novel was written.

He restores his people's faith in themselves and provides a context by which they can "articulate their values and define their goals in relation to the cold, alien world around them."

Achebe confirmed his place as the leading African novelist with the publication of *Anthills of the Savannah* in 1987. The novel is set in the fictional West African country of Kangan, which resembles Nigeria, and it takes up the inquiry initiated by *A Man of the People*. *Anthills of the Savannah* ends with yet another military coup: history goes on repeating itself, a measure of how far the country is from solving its political problems. Achebe examines the consequences of military, as opposed to civilian, rule. By all accounts military leadership is not much better than the Nanga-ism of the regime it replaced. In fact it is worse: political chaos has been replaced by a dictatorship; cynical self-interest has been replaced by megalomania. *Anthills of the Savannah* elaborates and adumbrates many of the problems Achebe identified in *The Trouble with Nigeria*.

Kangan is ruled by a military governor and a cabinet of civilian ministers, a regime that can take no credit for its accomplishments, as one of the characters muses:

> The prime failing of this government also began to take on a clearer meaning for him. It can't be the massive corruption though its scale and pervasiveness are truly intolerable; it isn't the subservience to foreign manipulation, degrading as it is; it isn't even this second-class, hand-me-down capitalism, ludicrous and doomed; nor is it the damnable shooting of striking railway-workers and demonstrating students and the banning thereafter of independent unions and cooperatives. It is the failure of our rulers to establish vital inner links with the poor and dispossessed of this country, with the bruised heart that throbs painfully at the core of the nation's being.

Anthills of the Savannah, with a multiplicity of viewpoints, is contemporary in setting yet includes the relevance of historical tradition. It tells the tragic story of Sam, His Excellency and would-be President for Life; Ikem Osodi, poet and editor of the *National Gazette*; and Chris Oriko, minister of information in the cabinet. They have been friends for twenty-five years, and Ikem and Chris have been instrumental in helping Sam to power. Achebe characterizes Sam's career in a brief burst: "From school to Sandhurst; then first African Second Lieutenant in the Army; ADC to the Governor; Royal Equerry during the Queen's

Chinua and Chinwe Achebe at their silver wedding anniversary celebration in September 1986, with three of their four children: Nwando, Chidi, and Ike (Mike's Photos, Nsukka, Nigeria)

visit; Colonel at the time of the coup; General and His Excellency, then Head of State, after."

Noting that Sam, through his Sandhurst training, has cultivated the style of an English gentleman, Ikem says that Sam could do worse: "I believe that a budding dictator might choose models far worse than the English gentleman of leisure. . . . The English have for all practical purposes, ceased to menace the world. . . . The real danger is from that fat, adolescent and delinquent millionaire, America, and from all those virulent, misshapen freaks like Amin and Bokassa sired on Africa by Europe. Particularly those ones."

Sam begins well enough, even though surrounded by "court jesters" and "mesmerised toadies." But after he attends a meeting at the OAU and apparently meets Haile Selassie (not named

in the novel but aptly characterized) and the fictional-though-archetypal President-for-life Ngongo, Sam's dreams of ultimate and enduring political power begin to take shape: he "sees for the first time the possibilities for his drama in the role of an African Head of State and withdraws to prepare his own face and perfect his arts." Sam heeds the advice of Ngongo that "your greatest risk is your boyhood friends, those who grew up with you in your village. Keep them at arm's length and you will live long." Boyhood friends become grown-up victims. Ikem is accused of participating in a plot to overthrow the regime and of planning "regicide" when he makes a snide comment on Sam's plan to have his head minted on Kangan coinage. He is arrested and murdered by the state police. Chris uses his connections with the international press to tell the

Dust jacket for the American edition of the novel in which Achebe argues for reforming society "around what it is, its core of reality; not around an intellectual abstraction"

truth about Ikem's death. He is forced into hiding and, while seeking safety in the northern territory of the country, is shot and killed by a soldier, ironically on the day when Sam's overthrow is broadcast to the nation.

For Achebe the trouble with Kangan is its leadership. *The Trouble with Nigeria* seems a gloss on the novel. Admitting that external factors have a bearing on the problems of the nation, he has Ikem say: "to blame all these things on imperialism and international capitalism as our modish radicals want us to do is, in my view, sheer cant and humbug." Nor is the leadership problem to be solved by a "democratic dictatorship of the proletariat," because no two groups have been more derelict than workers and students in their commitment to public and civil causes. Ikem castigates both groups roundly in chapter 12 of the novel, the core of Achebe's analysis. Achebe's solution is a humanist one: "We can only hope to rearrange some details in the periphery of human personality. Any disturbance of its core is an irre-

sponsible invitation to disaster. . . . It has to be the same with society. You reform it around what it is, its core of reality; not around an intellectual abstraction."

The writer's role is central in effecting this solution. *Anthills of the Savannah* is a novel about the concept of narrative. There are persistent references to the role of "story" and the "storyteller" in the book: "the story owns and directs us . . . the story is everlasting"; "storytellers are a threat. They threaten all the champions of control, they frighten usurpers of the right-to-freedom of the human spirit—in state, in church or mosque, in party congresses, in the university or wherever"; "every artist contains multitudes and expresses the ultimate enmity between art and orthodoxy"; "Writers don't give prescriptions—they give headaches." There is, moreover, a metafictional element in the novel, made plain by the fact that three of the principal characters—Ikem, Chris, and Beatrice—are writers: Beatrice tells the story of the closing days of

Sam's regime, of the integrity and sacrifice of Ikem and Chris, and of the horror of the regime that replaces Sam's. A reflexive reference to *Things Fall Apart* is included. Beatrice senses her identity with "Chielo in the novel, the priestess and prophetess of the Hills and Caves," an avatar of the ambiguous purposes of the deity. She knows, as well, the legend of Idemili and the role of Mother Idoto in advocating it. Idemili was sent to wrap "around Power's rude waist a loincloth of peace and modesty." When that power is abused by Sam, Beatrice assumes the role of avenging goddess and, seducing him, reminds him of his responsibility.

In *Anthills of the Savannah* Achebe aims at giving the story back to the people, at reclaiming the art of storytelling in a society in which oral wisdom is in danger of dying out because of the increasing development of the modern technocratic society and where the communal and public act of storytelling is yielding to the private form of the printed word. *Anthills of the Savannah* reveals that the two distinct forms can meet and assist in closing the gap between the educated and the uneducated, so that the story is capable of fulfilling its traditional role.

Chinua Achebe dominates the African novel and has a central place in contemporary literature because he has reflectively and unobtrusively modified the traditions of fiction, deriving forms distinctively his own for the purpose of envisaging and conveying experiences that are deeply convincing. Profundity, discriminating insight, mental and moral fastidiousness, elegance, and lucidity—these are the hallmarks of Achebe's art.

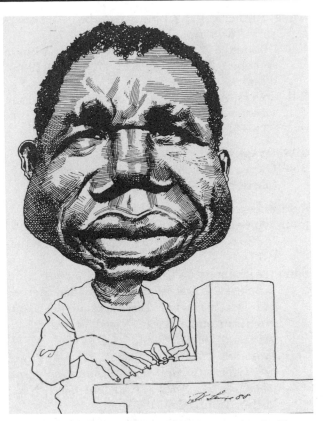

Chinua Achebe (drawing by David Levine; reprinted with permission from the New York Review of Books; *copyright 1988 Nyrev, Inc.)*

Interviews:

"Chinua Achebe on Biafra," *Transition*, 36 (July 1968): 31-37;

Dennis Duerden and Cosmo Pieterse, eds., *African Writers Talking: A Collection of Radio Interviews* (London: Heinemann / New York: Africana, 1972), pp. 3-17;

Bernth Lindfors, Ian Munro, Richard Priebe, and Reinhard Sander, eds., *Palaver: Interviews with Five African Writers in Texas* (Austin: African and Afro-American Research Institute, University of Texas, 1972), pp. 8-12;

Ernest Emenyonu and Pat Emenyonu, "Achebe: Accountable to Our Society," *Africa Report*, 17 (May 1972): 21, 23, 25-27;

Karen L. Morell, ed., *In Person: Achebe, Awoonor, and Soyinka at the University of Washington* (Se-

attle: African Studies Program, Institute for Comparative and Foreign Area Studies, University of Washington, 1975), pp. 19-58;

Phanuel Akubueze Egejuru, *Towards African Literary Independence: A Dialogue with Contemporary African Writers* (Westport, Conn.: Greenwood Press, 1980);

Chinweizu, "An Interview with Chinua Achebe (Nsukka, 20 January 1981)," *Okike*, 20 (February 1981): 19-32;

Kalu Ogbaa, "An Interview with Chinua Achebe," *Research in African Literatures*, 12 (Spring 1981): 1-13;

Jonathan Cott, "Chinua Achebe: At the Crossroads," *Parabola*, 6 (May 1981): 30-39;

Chinua Achebe in Conversation with C. L. Innes, [recording], British Council Literature Recordings, CW02, June 1981;

Anthony Appiah, John Ryle, and D. A. N. Jones, "An Interview with Chinua Achebe," *Times Literary Supplement*, 26 February 1982, p. 209;

J. O. J. Nwachukwu-Agbada, "An Interview with Chinua Achebe," *Massachusetts Review*, 28, no. 2 (1987): 273-285;

Anna Rutherford, "Chinua Achebe: An Interview," *Kunapipi*, 9, no. 2 (1987): 1-7;

Kay Bonetti, "An Interview with Chinua Achebe," *Missouri Review*, 12, no. 1 (1989): 62-83;

Bill Moyers, *A World of Ideas*, edited by Betty Sue Flowers (New York: Doubleday, 1989), pp. 333-344.

Bibliography:

Bole Okpu, *Chinua Achebe: A Bibliography* (Lagos: Libriservice, 1984).

References:

John Agetua, ed., *Critics on Chinua Achebe, 1970-76* (Benin City, Nigeria: Agetua, 1977);

Edna Aizenberg, "Cortazar's *Hopscotch* and Achebe's *No Longer at Ease*: Divided Heroes and Deconstructive Discourse in the Latin American and African Novel," *Okike*, 25-26 (February 1984): 10-26;

Kofi Awoonor, *The Breast of the Earth: A Survey of the History, Culture and Literature of Africa South of the Sahara* (Garden City, N.Y.: Anchor/Doubleday, 1975);

E. A. Babalola, "A Reconsideration of Achebe's *No Longer at Ease*," *Phylon*, 47 (1986): 139-147;

F. Odun Balogun, *Tradition and Modernity in the African Short Story* (New York: Greenwood, 1991);

Hugh R. Brown, "Igbo Words for the Non-Igbo: Achebe's Artistry in *Arrow of God*," *Research in African Literatures*, 12 (1981): 69-85;

Lloyd W. Brown, "Cultural Norms and Modes of Perception in Achebe's Fiction," *Research in African Literatures*, 3 (1972): 21-35;

David Carroll, *Chinua Achebe* (New York: Twayne, 1970);

Rosemary Colmer, " 'The Start of Weeping is Always Hard': The Ironic Structure of *No Longer at Ease*," *Literary Half-Yearly*, 21, no. 1 (1980): 121-135;

David Cook, *African Literature: A Critical View* (London: Longman, 1977);

Denise Coussy, *L'Oeuvre de Chinua Achebe* (Paris: Presence Africaine, 1985);

Coussy, *Le Roman nigérian* (Paris: Silex, 1988);

M. J. C. Echeruo, "Chinua Achebe," in *A Celebration of Black and African Writing*, edited by Bruce King and Kolawole Ogungbesan (Ibadan & Zaria, Nigeria: Ahmadu Bello University Press & Oxford University Press, 1975), pp. 150-163;

R. N. Egudu, "Achebe and the Igbo Narrative Tradition," *Research in African Literatures*, 12 (1981): 43-54;

Holger G. Ehling, ed., *Critical Approaches to "Anthills of the Savannah"* (Amsterdam & Atlanta: Rodopi, 1991);

Ernest Emenyonu, "Early Fiction in Igbo," *Research in African Literatures*, 4 (1973): 7-20;

Emenyonu, *The Rise of the Igbo Novel* (Ibadan: Oxford University Press, 1978);

Robert Fraser, "A Note on Okonkwo's Suicide," *Kunapipi*, 1, no. 1 (1979): 108-113;

Shatto Arthur Gakwandi, *The Novel and Contemporary Experience in Africa* (London: Heinemann / New York: Africana, 1977);

Simon Gikandi, *Reading Achebe* (London: Currey, 1991);

Gikandi, *Reading the African Novel* (London: Currey, 1987);

Judith Gleason, *This Africa: Novels by West Africans in English and French* (Evanston, Ill.: Northwestern University Press, 1965);

Ian Glenn, "Heroic Failure in the Novels of Achebe," *English in Africa*, 12, no. 1 (1985): 11-27;

K. L. Goodwin, "A Rhetoric of Contraries in Chinua Achebe's Poetry," *Literary Half-Yearly*, 21, no. 1 (1980): 40-49;

Gareth Griffiths, *A Double Exile: African and West Indian Writing Between Two Cultures* (London: Boyars, 1978);

Griffiths, "Language and Action in the Novels of Chinua Achebe," *African Literature Today*, 5 (1971): 88-105;

C. L. Innes, *Chinua Achebe* (Cambridge: Cambridge University Press, 1990);

Abiola Irele, "The Tragic Conflict in Achebe's Novels," *Black Orpheus*, 17 (1965): 24-32;

Abdul R. JanMohamed, *Manichean Aesthetics: The Politics of Literature in Colonial Africa* (Amherst: University of Massachusetts Press, 1983);

G. D. Killam, "Chinua Achebe's Novels," *Sewanee Review*, 79 (1971): 514-541;

Killam, *The Novels of Chinua Achebe* (London: Heinemann, 1969); revised as *The Writings of Chinua Achebe* (London: Heinemann, 1977);

Charles R. Larson, *The Emergence of African Fiction* (Bloomington: Indiana University Press, 1971);

Bernth Lindfors, *Early Nigerian Literature* (New York: Africana, 1982);

Achebe speaking at the British Studies Faculty Seminar, University of Texas at Austin (photograph by Nancy Guiles, Multimedia Center, University of Texas at Austin)

Lindfors, *Folklore in Nigerian Literature* (New York: Africana, 1973);

Lindfors, ed., *Approaches to Teaching "Things Fall Apart"* (New York: Modern Language Association, 1991);

Thomas Melone, *Chinua Achebe et la tragédie de l'histoire* (Paris: Presence Africaine, 1973);

Gerald Moore, *Twelve African Writers* (Bloomington: Indiana University Press, 1980);

Ngugi wa Thiong'o, *Homecoming: Essays on African and Caribbean Literature, Culture and Politics* (London: Heinemann, 1972);

Benedict Chiaka Njoku, *The Four Novels of Chinua Achebe: A Critical Study* (New York: Lang, 1984);

Charles R. Nnolim, "A Source for *Arrow of God*," *Research in African Literatures*, 8 (1977): 1-26;

D. Ibe Nwoga, "The Igbo World of Achebe's *Arrow of God*," *Research in African Literatures*, 12 (1981): 14-42;

Emmanuel Obiechina, *Culture, Tradition and Society in the West African Novel* (Cambridge: Cambridge University Press, 1975);

Kalu Ogbaa, *Folkways in Chinua Achebe's Novels* (Oguta, Nigeria: Zim, 1990); republished as *Gods, Oracles, and Divination: Folkways in Chinua Achebe's Novels* (Trenton, N.J.: Africa World, 1992);

Umelo Ojinmah, *Chinua Achebe: New Perspectives* (Ibadan: Spectrum, 1991);

Emmanuel M. Okoye, *The Traditional Religion and Its Encounter with Christianity in Achebe's Novels* (New York: Lang, 1987);

James Olney, *Tell Me, Africa: An Approach to African Literature* (Princeton, N.J.: Princeton University Press, 1973);

Oyekan Owomoyela, *African Literatures: An Introduction* (Waltham, Mass.: Crossroads, 1979);

Jonathan Peters, *A Dance of the Masks: Senghor, Achebe, Soyinka* (Washington, D.C.: Three Continents, 1978);

Richard K. Priebe, *Myth, Realism and the West African Writer* (Trenton, N.J.: Africa World, 1988);

Arthur Ravenscroft, *Chinua Achebe* (Harlow, U.K.: Longmans, Green, 1969);

Adrian Roscoe, *Mother Is Gold: A Study of West African Literature* (Cambridge: Cambridge University Press, 1971);

Wole Soyinka, *Myth, Literature and the African World* (Cambridge: Cambridge University Press, 1978);

Danièle Stewart, *Le Roman africain anglophone depuis 1965: D'Achebe à Soyinka* (Paris: L'Harmattan, 1988);

Oladele Taiwo, *Culture and the Nigerian Novel* (London: Macmillan, 1976);

Marjorie Winters, "Morning Yet on Judgment Day: The Critics of Chinua Achebe," *Journal of the Literary Society of Nigeria*, 1 (1981): 26-31;

Winters, "An Objective Approach to Achebe's Style," *Research in African Literatures*, 12 (1981): 55-68;

Robert M. Wren, *Achebe's World: The Historical and Cultural Context of the Novels of Chinua Achebe* (Washington, D.C.: Three Continents, 1980).

Ama Ata Aidoo

(23 March 1942 -)

Naana Banyiwa Horne
University of Wisconsin—Madison

BOOKS: *The Dilemma of a Ghost* (London & Accra: Longmans, 1965; New York: Collier, 1971);

Anowa (Harlow, U.K.: Longmans, 1970; Washington, D.C.: Three Continents, 1980);

No Sweetness Here (Harlow, U.K.: Longman, 1970; Garden City, N.Y.: Doubleday, 1971);

Our Sister Killjoy; or, Reflections from a Black-Eyed Squint (London: Longman, 1977; New York: NOK, 1979);

Someone Talking to Sometime (Harare, Zimbabwe: College Press, 1985);

The Eagle and the Chickens and Other Stories (Enugu, Nigeria: Tana, 1986);

Birds and Other Poems (Harare, Zimbabwe: College Press, 1987);

Changes: A Love Story (London: Women's Press, 1991).

PLAY PRODUCTION: *The Dilemma of a Ghost*, Legon, Ghana, Students' Theatre, 12 March 1964.

OTHER: "The African Poet, His Critics and His Future," *Legonite* (1964): 57-59;

Ayi Kwei Armah, *The Beautyful Ones Are Not Yet Born*, introduction by Aidoo (New York: Collier/Macmillan, 1969), pp. i-iv;

"No Saviours," in *African Writers on African Writing*, edited by G. D. Killam (New York: Africana, 1973), pp. 14-18;

"Unwelcome Pals and Decorative Slaves—or Glimpses of Women as Writers and Characters in Contemporary African Literature," in *Medium and Message: Proceedings of the International Conference on African Literature and the English Language*, edited by Ernest Emenyonu (Calabar, Nigeria: University of Calabar, 1981), I: 17-37;

"To Be an African Woman Writer—an Overview and a Detail," in *Criticism and Ideology: Second African Writers' Conference, Stockholm 1986*, edited by Kirsten Holst Petersen (Uppsala: Scandinavian Institute of African Studies, 1988), pp. 155-172.

Ama Ata Aidoo (photograph by Adam Gadsby)

Ama Ata Aidoo's identity as an African woman is a propelling force governing her artistic vision, and she is one of the few African writers who persist in exploring the colonial history of the continent, especially its legacy of slavery – hence the prominence of African-Americans in her works. One of the principal characters in the play *The Dilemma of a Ghost* (first performed in 1964; published in 1965) is African-American; so is a character in the short story "Other Versions" (in *No Sweetness Here*, 1970). The theme of slavery is highlighted in both her plays. In *The Dilemma of a Ghost* Eulalie's slave origin becomes an issue of contention to Ato's family. In *Anowa* (1970) the female protagonist awakens negative sentiments with her questions regarding slavery: "Did the men of the land sell other men of the land, and women and children to pale men from beyond the horizon who looked like you or me peeled, like lobsters boiled or roasted? . . . What happened to those who were taken away? Do people hear from them?"

Though Western educated, Aidoo derives her artistic integrity from her strong African ties. She was born on 23 March 1942 in the Fanti town of Abeadzi Kyiakor, near Dominase, in the central region of Ghana. One of the children of

Nana Yaw Fama, a chief of Abeadzi Kyiakor, and his wife, Maame Abba Abasema, she was raised in the royal household, an environment that proved instrumental in raising her consciousness of traditional lore and ritual, appropriateness in the use of language, and human drama in general. She went to Wesley Girls' High School in Cape Coast and from 1961 to 1964 attended the University of Ghana, Legon, an institution with a school of drama and a writers' workshop. Little wonder then that her first literary accomplishments were two plays and a collection of short stories that she conceived of as oral performances written mainly to be heard. *The Dilemma of a Ghost* was completed in 1964, the year of her graduation with a B.A. in English (honors program), and the play was presented the same year for three nights on 12, 13, and 14 March by the Students' Theatre, Legon. It has since been produced elsewhere in Ghana, Nigeria, the United States, and other parts of the world.

The play is in the tradition of culture conflict; it highlights the alienation crippling the educated class in Africa. A young Ghanaian man, Ato Yawson, educated in America, returns home with Eulalie Rush, his African-American wife, whom he has married without forewarning his family. This action generates the main conflict in the play. Western individual values are posited against African communal ones. The volatility of the situation is compounded by the immaturity, ignorance, and exasperating arrogance of Eulalie and by Ato's inability to reconcile the opposing forces in his world, or to offer his wife the needed guidance for adjustment to a culture that is alien to her. In the end the strength, wisdom, resilience, and sheer humaneness of Ato's mother save the situation, asserting the integrative nature of traditional African norms and values over the disruptive Western ones that threaten the familial sense of harmony and stability.

In this play Aidoo directs her attention to those thematic and structural concerns she comes to articulate even more strongly in her subsequent works. In various publications she expresses her views on theater as a social microcosm. Contemporary African drama, she contends, should maintain integrity by evolving out of contemporary African experience and situations, and it should aim at integrating African oral-narrative forms and Western literary forms. *The Dilemma of a Ghost* is Aidoo's first attempt to support these propositions in her own works, and it iterates her concerns as a woman writer. The play questions social conventions as they relate to the roles and identities of women, in addition to underscoring the dislocation caused within individuals, families, and even whole societies, particularly the gulf created among black peoples in Africa and the New World, as a result of Africa's colonial history. She weaves oral-narrative techniques—the folktale, the gossip of women, the play of children—into literary conventions to advance her structure and themes.

Since its publication, *The Dilemma of a Ghost* has attracted considerable attention, the various responses exposing the strengths and weaknesses of a first play. The weaknesses are mostly structural, growing out of Aidoo's innovative efforts to blend African oral and Western literary elements, and, for a short play, *Dilemma* has too many acts. These shortcomings notwithstanding, Aidoo often succeeds in integrating her themes, language, and characterization. According to the critic Dapo Adelugba, "Her success in creating levels of language, in matching literary grace with veracity of characterization, in suiting . . . the action to the word, the word to the action, is commendable in such a young dramatist" (*African Literature Today*, 1976).

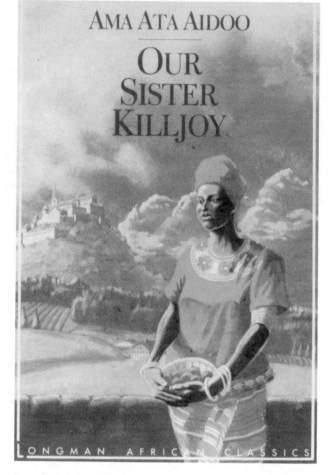

Dust jacket for Aidoo's experimental first novel, which combines prose, poetry, and epistolary fiction

Anowa displays an even sharper awareness of history and culture, and it articulates more strongly certain questions pertaining to the role and identity of women. It is set during a significant period in the colonial history of the Gold Coast, and the ethical implications of colonialism and slavery heighten the dramatic action, revealing conflicting attitudes toward issues such as wealth and slavery. The play focuses on Anowa's growing awareness of herself as a woman and the forces that militate against the female's struggle to attain her full potential. *Anowa* unveils Aidoo's strong feminist penchant and shows her talent for creating articulate, assertive, but sensitive female characters. The play centers on a beautiful and talented young woman who rejects all the suitors approved of by her parents and marries Kofi Ako, the man of her choice. Later he turns against her and tries to drive her away. Refusing to be divorced without reason, Anowa takes up her own defense, repudiates the insinuations of barrenness that are automatically leveled against women in childless marriages, and puts the blame on him. Totally deflated by this threat to his manhood, Kofi kills himself, and Anowa also commits suicide, overwhelmed by the futility of finding meaning in life.

Anowa, structured around a familiar folktale, attests to Aidoo's maturing dramatic skills, demonstrating a more skillful integration of thematic and structural features and folkloristic and literary conventions; the critical responses acknowledge these improvements. In the folktale, a girl marries a disguised monster; Aidoo transforms the monster into human incompatibility, which results in conflicting attitudes between Anowa and Kofi on all major issues—work ethics, wealth, children, and marital relations—and aborts the couple's dreams of marital bliss, eventually destroying them. In the folktale the girl is rescued; in Aidoo's realistic drama, there is no rescue. The tragedy is absolute. And as the critic Eldred Jones points out, *Anowa* "takes on the dimensions of myth without losing its social relevance. . . ."

Aidoo's two plays introduced her to the literary world as a dramatist; however, it is as a short-story writer that her dramatic skills and control of her artistic medium are best exhibited. She displays a firm manipulation of dialogue, dramatic action, characterization, and themes, transforming each story into a microcosm of the inner world of women and of society. The stories are characterized by minimal narration and the prevalence of dialogue, often combined with interior monologue. Characters and themes are unfolded primarily through what the characters say, for Aidoo seems to let them speak for themselves, thus stamping each story with the distinctive personality of the protagonist. The collection *No Sweetness Here* includes Aidoo's most successful efforts at integrating African oral techniques and Western literary conventions. She has remarked, "I pride myself on the fact that my stories are written to be heard, primarily."

Her feminist concerns are most apparent in *No Sweetness Here*: eleven stories written over a four-to-five-year period. This gallery of female portraits offers perceptive images of womanhood, exposing sexism and degradation, and celebrating the physical and intellectual capabilities of women. In this panorama Aidoo covers a wide range of issues: budding girlhood and the identity crisis emanating from growing up female in a sexist environment ("The Late Bud"); moderniza-

tion and its impact on both rural and urban women ("Everything Counts," "For Whom Things Did Not Change," "In the Cutting of a Drink," "Certain Winds from the South," "Two Sisters," "Something to Talk About on the Way to the Funeral"); and transcendence over degradation, followed by the assertion of humanist values ("The Message," "No Sweetness Here," "A Gift from Somewhere," "Other Versions"). Aidoo's interests are comprehensive and essentially tragic, with all the stories echoing the same theme: the absence of any quintessential sweetness in life. Her sympathy infuses the stories with pathos, and as Daniele Stewart observes, "raises them to a universal level seldom achieved in contemporary literature."

After Aidoo published three works in five years, establishing a reputation as a distinguished author, several years elapsed before the publication of her next work, *Our Sister Killjoy*, in 1977. Though the problems of publishing contributed to this long silence, Aidoo admits that "part of the reason is just one's inability to put all the different strands in one's life together, sufficiently to sit down and write." Starting in 1970 she was a lecturer in English at the University of Cape Coast, Ghana, and, among other engagements, served as consulting professor to the Washington bureau of the Phelps-Stokes Fund's Ethnic Studies Program (1974-1975). Aidoo's literary silence was undoubtedly aggravated by the political climate in Ghana at the time: a long, orchestrated display of military brutality and blatant corruption, climaxing in indiscriminate incarceration, especially of Ghana's intelligentsia and students. The full extent of Aidoo's artistic vision is revealed in her ability to cast the political repression and corruption of her immediate surroundings into a global mold.

Our Sister Killjoy, subtitled *Reflections from a Black-Eyed Squint*, is an innovative novel blending prose, poetry, and the epistolary form. Its caustic tone and aggressive mood mirror the critical, committed stance of its well-meaning but enraged and politically conscious writer. It comprises a prologue and three parts. "In a Bad Dream," the prologue, sets the general tone and mood for the novel. "The Plums" recounts the protagonist Sissie's impressions of Germany, particularly her encounters with Marija, a young German housewife. "From Our Sister Killjoy," based on Sissie's encounters in England, probes the psychological bondage, an aftermath of colonialism, that keeps African students lingering abroad despite the al-

Ama Ata Aidoo (photograph by Satoru Tsuchiya)

most subhuman conditions of their existence there. The last part, "A Love Letter," exploits the epistolary form to address spiritual and material problems bedeviling the world. This last part tempers the strident tone that characterizes the rest of the work.

The novel condemns oppression. Aidoo's scope is global and extensive, spanning exploitation and degradation in all their forms. The condition of women is cast within the general context of human history, which Aidoo analyzes as the search by self-proclaimed superior groups for methods of freeing themselves of burdens and placing them on others. Womanhood becomes a metaphor depicting the condition of oppressed and exploited humankind in general. This novel has drawn provocative responses. While there is consensus regarding Aidoo's impact as a social critic, uneasiness about the pointedness of her attacks against the Western world has been expressed by some. The overall strength of the novel, however, is captured in Chikwenye O. Ogunyemi's comparison of Aidoo's style to both James Baldwin's *The Fire Next Time* (1963) and Jean Toomer's *Cane* (1923).

In 1985 the College Press of Zimbabwe published the first collection of Aidoo's poetry, *Someone Talking to Sometime*, which contains some of her older poems that have appeared in anthologies and other poetry collections and some new

ones. The two parts of the collection—"Of Love and Commitment" and "Someone Talking to Sometime"—total forty-four poems. Opening the collection is an invocation to her ancestors in Fanti; it is followed by a poem, "Crisis."

Someone Talking to Sometime reiterates various themes articulated in Aidoo's other works. In characteristic Aidoo fashion, criticism is blended with affirmation, and tragedy and pain are toned down with wit and humor. Political corruption is humorously depicted in "From the Only Speech that Was Not Delivered at the Rally": the insanity and collapse of order in contemporary Africa are suggested by the image of being overtaken "by / winter at the height of an / equatorial noon." Highly condemnatory poems, such as "Nation Building" and "A Salute to African Universities" and those in the "Routine Drug" sequence, are balanced by more affirmative poems—"Of Love and Commitment," "Lorisnrudi," and "For Kinna II." Aidoo employs a conversational style to lend humor to the essentially tragic nature of existence and to invest the poems with the enduring quality of the blues.

Ama Ata Aidoo has established herself as a versatile and impressive writer for adults, and she has also written stories and poetry for children (*The Eagle and the Chickens and Other Stories* [1986] and *Birds and Other Poems* [1987]). Her most recent work, *Changes: A Love Story* (1991), is a novel that presents a critical look at options in love and marriage for contemporary African women. Through the female character Esi, who is an educated ambitious, career-oriented Ghanaian, Aidoo explores such issues as marital rape and career choices, and their impact on love and marital relationships, highlighting the role of compromise. She scrutinizes through fiction the age-old institutions of monogamy and polygamy.

Aidoo has also pursued a career teaching, giving readings and lectures, and conducting seminars at universities in West and East Africa and the United States, and she has held high political office as a minister of education in Ghana. She has traveled extensively in Africa, the United States, and Eastern and Western Europe. Currently living in Harare, Zimbabwe, Aidoo is a full-time writer and the mother of one daughter, Kinna Likimani.

Interviews:

Maxine Lautre McGregor, "Ama Ata Aidoo," in *African Writers Talking*, edited by Cosmo Pieterse and Dennis Duerden (New York: Africana, 1972), pp. 19-27;

Theo Vincent, ed., *Seventeen Black and African Writers on Literature and Life* (Lagos: Centre for Black and African Arts and Civilization, 1981), pp. 1-8;

Oliver Nyika, "Ama Ata Aidoo: Mother of Africa," *Mahogany* (October-November 1983): 46-47;

Patricia Made, "An Artist Unfolds Her Struggles and Hopes," *Moto*, 28 (1984): 23-24;

George Alagiah, "The Loneliness of the African Writer," *South* (October 1985): 191;

Jane Bryce, "Ama Ata Aidoo: A Further Departure," *New African*, 218 (November 1985): 46.

References:

Dapo Adelugba, "Language and Drama: Ama Ata Aidoo," *African Literature Today*, 8 (1976): 72-84;

Adelugba, "*No Sweetness Here*: Literature as Social Criticism," *Ba Shiru*, 6, no. 1 (1974): 15-24;

J. Amankulor, "Ama Ata Aidoo: *The Dilemma of a Ghost*," *Okike Educational Supplement*, 3 (1982): 137-150;

Brenda Berrian, "The Afro-American-West African Marriage Question: Its Literary and Historical Contexts," *African Literature Today*, 15 (1987): 152-159;

Lloyd Brown, "Ama Ata Aidoo: The Art of the Short Story and Sexual Roles in Africa," *World Literature Written in English*, 13 (November 1974): 172-183;

Brown, *Women Writers in Black Africa* (Westport, Conn.: Greenwood Press, 1981), pp. 84-121;

Charlotte Bruner, "Child Africa as Depicted by Bessie Head and Ama Ata Aidoo," *Studies in the Humanities*, 7, no. 2 (1979): 5-12;

Karen Chapman, Introduction to Aidoo's *The Dilemma of a Ghost* (New York: Collier, 1971), pp. 7-25; reprinted in *Sturdy Black Bridges: Visions of Black Women in Literature*, edited by Roseann Bell, Bettye Parker, and Beverly Guy Sheftall (Garden City, N.Y.: Doubleday, 1979), pp. 25-38;

Maryse Condé, "Three Female Writers in Modern Africa: Flora Nwapa, Ama Ata Aidoo and Grace Ogot," *Presence Africaine*, 82 (1972): 132-143;

Denise Coussy, "Is Life Sweet? The Short Stories of Ama Ata Aidoo," in *Short Fiction in the New Literatures in English*, edited by Jacqueline Bardolph (Nice: Faculté des Lettres & Sciences Humaines de Nice, 1989), pp. 285-290;

Arlene Elder, "Ama Ata Aidoo and the Oral Tradition: A Paradox of Form and Substance," *African Literature Today*, 15 (1987): 109-118;

Mildred Hill-Lubin, "The Relationship of African Americans and Africans: A Recurring Theme in the Works of Ama Ata Aidoo," *Presence Africaine*, 124 (1982): 190-201;

Hill-Lubin, "The Storyteller and the Audience in the Works of Ama Ata Aidoo," *Neohelicon*, 16, no. 2 (1989): 221-245;

Eldred Jones, "Ama Ata Aidoo: *Anowa*," *African Literature Today*, 8 (1976): 142-144;

Marion Kilson, "Women and African Literature," *Journal of African Studies*, 4 (Summer 1977): 161-166;

G. C. M. Mutiso, "Women in African Literature," *East African Journal*, 8, no. 3 (1971): 4-14;

John Nagenda, "Generations of Conflict: Ama Ata Aidoo, J. C. de Graft and R. Sharif Easmon," in *Protest and Conflict in African Literature*, edited by Cosmo Pieterse and Donald Munro (New York: Africana, 1970), pp. 101-108;

Chimalum Nwankwo, "The Feminist Impulse and Social Realism in Ama Ata Aidoo's *No Sweetness Here* and *Our Sister Killjoy*," in *Ngambika: Studies of Women in African Literature*, edited by Carole Boyce Davies and Anne Adams Graves (Trenton, N.J.: African World, 1986), pp. 151-159;

Chikwenye O. Ogunyemi, "Womanism: The Dynamics of the Contemporary Black Female Novel in English," *Signs*, 11 (Autumn 1985): 63-80;

Chinyere G. Okafor, "Ama Ata Aidoo: *Anowa*," *Okike Educational Supplement*, 4 (1985): 137-146;

Kofi Owusu, "Canons Under Siege: Blackness, Femaleness and Ama Ata Aidoo's *Our Sister Killjoy*," *Callaloo*, 13 (Spring 1990): 341-363;

Cosmo Pieterse, "Dramatic Riches," *Journal of Commonwealth Literature*, 2 (December 1966): 168-171;

Geoffrey Ridden, "Language and Social Status in Ama Ata Aidoo," *Style*, 8 (Fall 1974): 452-461;

Daniele Stewart, "Ghanaian Writing in Prose: A Critical Survey," *Presence Africaine*, 91 (1974): 73-105;

Susanne Thies-Torkornoo, "Die Rolle der Frau in der afrikanischen Gesellschaft: Eine Betrachtung von Ama Ata Aidoos *Anowa* and Efua T. Sutherlands *Foriwa*," *Matatu*, 1, no. 1 (1987): 53-67.

T. M. Aluko
(14 June 1918 -   )

Patrick Scott
University of South Carolina

BOOKS: *One Man, One Wife* (Lagos: Nigerian Printing and Publishing Company, 1959; revised edition, London & Ibadan: Heinemann, 1967);

One Man, One Matchet (London: Heinemann, 1964);

Kinsman and Foreman (London: Heinemann, 1966);

Chief the Honourable Minister (London: Heinemann / New York: Humanities Press, 1970);

His Worshipful Majesty (London: Heinemann, 1973);

Wrong Ones in the Dock (London & Exeter, N.H.: Heinemann, 1982);

A State of Our Own (London: Macmillan, 1986).

OTHER: "The New Engineer," in *African New Writing: Short Stories by African Authors*, edited by T. Cullen Young (London & Redhill, U.K.: Lutterworth, 1947), pp. 33-36;

"The Upgrading of Privy Methods of Sewage Disposal by the Biodisc Process," Ph.D. dissertation, University of Newcastle upon Tyne, 1976.

SELECTED PERIODICAL PUBLICATIONS—UNCOLLECTED:

FICTION

"Strange Captain of the North," *West African Review* (April 1948): 393-395;

"No Welcome for the Ghost," *West African Review* (January 1949): 43-47;

"Art of Dentistry," *West African Review* (October 1949): 1141-1143;

"Silence in Court!," *West African Review* (October 1953): 1097-1099.

NONFICTION

"Case for Fiction," *West African Review* (November 1949): 1237-1239;

"Polygamy and the Surplus Women," *West African Review* (March 1950): 259-260;

"Outlook for Better Housing in Nigeria," *Occasional Papers on Nigerian Affairs* (London), 2 (October 1955): 42-53.

Timothy Mofolorunso Aluko

T. M. Aluko is one of the most productive, though most undervalued, of modern Nigerian novelists, and his seven novels offer a distinctive insight into Nigerian society during the middle decades of the twentieth century. As early as the 1940s he received recognition for his short stories, but since then for much of his writing career critics have been almost uniformly hostile toward his satiric portraits of villagers, administrators, politicians, and clergymen. He has never been a full-time writer. His primary occupation has been civil engineering—in the civil service, as a university professor, and in consultancy work—and his books reflect the realism and perhaps the inevitable elitism of his special vantage point; they certainly reflect a practical man's impatience with more theoretical commentators. His distanced irony and his political skepticism distinguish him from the cultural committedness general in writers of the immediate prein-

dependence and postindependence periods, and such qualities seem to preclude any widespread acclaim for his writings from African critics. Though his last two novels have raised renewed political criticism, his major novels from the 1960s have in recent years received increased critical attention, especially for their skillful control of style and tone, and thus it is now more possible to understand Aluko's development sympathetically and to reassess the critical realism of his commentary on Nigerian politics and society.

Timothy Mofolorunso Aluko was born on 14 June 1918, the son of a polygamous though church-connected family, at Ilesha, near Ife, in what was then the protectorate area within the Southern Provinces of Nigeria. He received his early education at a local church primary school and his secondary schooling at Government College, Ibadan, founded on British "public school" lines to train a modern Nigerian leadership class.

In 1939 he moved to Yaba Higher College, near Lagos, then the most advanced educational institution in Nigeria, and, after graduation in 1942, he held posts as a junior engineer in the Public Works Departments of Lagos and Ilorin.

In the 1940s, a decade before most other modern Nigerian writers had done so, Aluko first came to notice as a fiction writer, through short-story contests sponsored by the British Council. From the contests came readings on Nigerian radio and his first publication, "The New Engineer," a comic piece about a lazy road gang, in the British-edited anthology *African New Writing* (1947). After Aluko went to Britain in 1946 to study engineering and town planning at King's College, London, he contributed regularly to the Liverpool-based *West African Review*, and many of the recurring topics of his novels appear in these early stories and essays, including satire on the local law courts ("Silence in Court!"); on public letter writers and the uprooted culture of urban Lagos ("No Welcome for the Ghost"); and on the forced Britishness of government officials ("Art of Dentistry" and the cricket story "Strange Captain of the North"). His important 1949 essay "Case for Fiction" argues strongly for "stories and novels written by African writers with an essentially African background and atmosphere, and for an essentially African reading public." Aluko was prescient in recognizing the underlying practical questions that faced African writers, about limited publishing outlets and the choice between European and vernacular language; he called for more African literary magazines and, for reasons of national unification, leaned toward English as the preferred medium, though he understood the theoretical difficulty of "rendering African thought in English."

In 1950 Aluko returned to Nigeria, soon to become a senior public works engineer, with tours in Oyo, Oshogbo, and Ikoyi, and in 1956 he became town engineer for the growing city of Lagos. His first book, *One Man, One Wife* (1959), dedicated "to the African writer of tomorrow" and "the great cause of African literature," was a historic landmark, the first modern Nigerian novel to be published by a Nigerian firm (though it was printed in Britain). It is set in the small village of Isolo, apparently in the 1930s, and the multiple plots all revolve around the clash, sharpened by a smallpox epidemic, between traditional Yoruba religion and the new religion of mission Christianity. The novel introduces a wonderful cast of village characters—the pastor, the old

chief, and village elders; the staunch churchman Bible Jeremiah; and most notably the semieducated teacher and catechist, the rogue Royasin, who is chased from the village for adultery but flourishes in a nearby town as a public letter writer, "Friend of the Illiterate and Advocate of the Oppressed."

Unlike most Nigerian novels of the independence period, *One Man, One Wife* seems strangely uncommitted regarding the tradition-modernization conflict. It is only in occasional incidents, like the storytelling under the Odan tree in the second chapter, that Aluko shows any identification with traditional village culture. The village Christians and the worshippers of Shango and Shonponna are all shown as superstitious and manipulative, and traditional greeting forms as well as Christian hymns are presented as falsifying experience. In his preface Aluko makes the rather disingenuous disclaimer that "any seeming sarcasm on any . . . administration or religious movement" is "purely accidental," but his satire was nonetheless condemned by reviewers such as Ulli Beier (*Black Orpheus*, November 1959) as "objectionable," "sensationalist," and "imperialist."

Aluko modified the book a little for its 1967 edition, but there remain unresolved conflicts within it, because the novel's symbolism pulls against its satire. Much of the symbolism is heavily, even heavy-handedly, protraditionalist, as for instance in the very self-conscious symbolic contrast between the village church as a bud still growing toward flowers and fruit, and the counterimage of the much older and more deeply rooted Odan tree "inhabited by the god of the village"; and in the contrast between the literal water that Shango brings to the village stream and the metaphorical water of life offered by the church. This protradition imagery, however, seems unconvincing by comparison with the comedy. There also remain unresolved problems in the book's ending, where a new Christian prophet preaches a minimally syncretist religion under the Odan tree, and the runaway girl is saved by marriage to a local policeman. The first reviews seem unduly harsh, and subsequent critics have pointed out the traditional Yoruba roots of Aluko's broad satiric method in the novel and his sharp ear for imitating the variety of English style among the different characters (the piety of the vicar, the exuberant unfairness of Royasin's newspaper article). The damaging difference between this first novel and Aluko's mature fiction is its limited focus on an increasingly old-

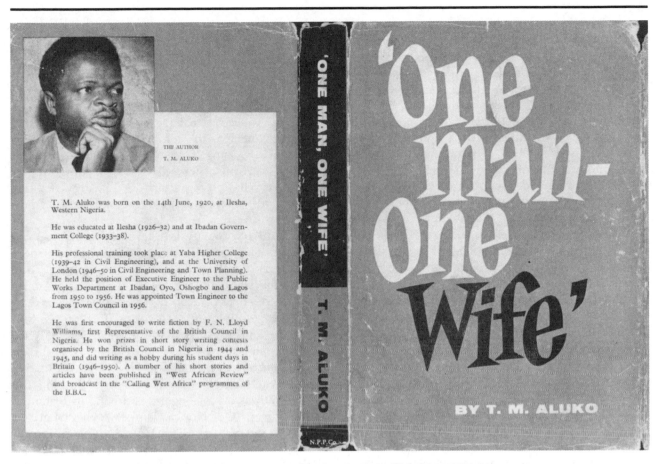

THE AUTHOR
T. M. ALUKO

T. M. Aluko was born on the 14th June, 1920, at Ilesha, Western Nigeria.

He was educated at Ilesha (1926–32) and at Ibadan Government College (1933–38).

His professional training took place at Yaba Higher College (1939–42 in Civil Engineering), and at the University of London (1946–50 in Civil Engineering and Town Planning). He held the position of Executive Engineer to the Public Works Department at Ibadan, Oyo, Oshogbo and Lagos from 1950 to 1956. He was appointed Town Engineer to the Lagos Town Council in 1956.

He was first encouraged to write fiction by F. N. Lloyd Williams, first Representative of the British Council in Nigeria. He won prizes in short story writing contests organised by the British Council in Nigeria in 1944 and 1945, and did writing as a hobby during his student days in Britain (1946–1950). A number of his short stories and articles have been published in "West African Review" and broadcast in the "Calling West Africa" programmes of the B.B.C.

Dust jacket for the first modern Nigerian novel to be published by a Nigerian company

fashioned village life, a life that evoked conventional respect among those encouraging African fiction in the 1950s, but a life-style to which Aluko no longer really belonged.

His next three novels, his major works, all gain by moving the focus from village life to the problems and preoccupations of Aluko's own educated but apolitical African elite. In this changed focus he found his distinctive voice and theme. Following Nigerian independence in 1960, Aluko was appointed permanent secretary in the Western Ministry of Works and Transport, the highest administrative engineering post in his region. His second novel, *One Man, One Matchet* (1964), follows the career of a new Nigerian district officer as he attempts to implement central government tax and agricultural policy in the face of traditionalist obstruction. It is set in the early 1950s, and the protagonist, Udo Akpan, has to deal not only with an outbreak of cocoa disease but also with a self-serving political agitator, Benja-Benja, who turns the local Oba (the traditional ruler) and elders against Akpan. The about-face of government policy over the cocoa disease—from erad-

icating diseased plants to fostering new, disease-resistant varieties—raises obvious parallels to changes in colonial government attitudes toward nationalist politicians; the parallel becomes explicit in Akpan's closing lesson from Benja-Benja's dishonesty, that "whatever brand of democracy we import into this country we must make sure that we sift out the seed of the disease that will otherwise choke to death" the new freedom. Aluko clearly suggests that the independence process has favored corrupt politicians rather than the selfless, apolitical administrative elite such as Akpan, who have to deal with actual policy implementation.

The strength of the novel lies not only in the comic exuberance with which it portrays Benja-Benja's exploitation of his supporters' greed and local pride but also in the much more subtle irony with which it explores the constraints under which Akpan works in colonial administrative procedures and language. Moreover, the novel is not wholly one-sided. Akpan's problems are partly of his own making as well as of Benja-Benja's. Indeed, Marxist critic James Booth has paid tribute to the complex realism in Aluko's analysis of Akpan's relation to the Ipaja villagers; Booth argues that Aluko's elite perspective reveals the political contradictions of the modernizing process and so makes them available for reinterpretation. Even at the end of the book, as Aluko moves from fiction to direct political debate, Akpan concludes with a question rather than an answer: "How can we make the whole thing operate with efficiency? How?"

Aluko retained his focus on the new Nigerian district-level administrators in his next novel, *Kinsman and Foreman* (1966). The protagonist, Titus Oti, has been posted as the first Nigerian district engineer to his hometown, where he discovers that his father's cousin Simeon, the public works foreman, has been taking bribes and fiddling with his expenses. A useful comparison is with Chinua Achebe's novel *No Longer at Ease* (1960), which also depicts a Nigerian civil servant facing traditional kinship obligations; Aluko's hero is much stronger and more effective than Achebe's. Titus is squarely against peculation and deceit, but, like Achebe's Obi, his dilemmas are those of conflicting social pressures rather than simply of moral choices—not only the head of his family, but his widowed mother, his parish clergyman, and his former school friend Chris the lawyer, all want him to condone and protect his kinsman's crimes. Titus suffers a nightmare crisis of psychological identity when he goes on a tour of his district and stops at a rest house where years ago a colonial officer had been killed. He comes to believe he himself is literally under attack, and though his breakdown is brief, it reinforces another of the powerful recurrent images in the book, that of a furiously driven, badly maintained, and wildly out-of-control mammy-wagon (truck), rather hopefully named *Safe Journey*, which Titus as district engineer is meant to inspect for roadworthiness but whose dangers he can do little about. The engineer's breakdown and the truck's disrepair are crucial images for Aluko's attitude in the mid 1960s toward Nigerian politics. His administrator Titus can plan, with great difficulty, the building of roads and bridges, but he has little control over the modern Nigeria that will use them.

Indeed, the novel leaves a very negative picture of the future. In this book, unlike Aluko's first, the local prophetic sect, the *alasoteles*, can offer only psychic escape, not cultural synthesis, with their apocalyptic promise of a sudden end to this conflict-ridden world. The modern central government is shown as weak and unrealistic in controlling crime, when Simeon is twice cleared of his embezzlement, once in court and again before an internal commission of inquiry. And the attitude of Westerners to modern Africa is satirized when some Chicago benefactors decide, after reading an American magazine article, to endow the village church as the center for a new black theology. Titus himself, like Udo in the previous novel, can only stick with his job, and hope to find psychic integration in facing realities, though the lawyers and contractors seem to flourish unchecked.

Aluko's fourth novel, *Chief the Honourable Minister* (1970), reflects Aluko's move into more senior and politicized civil-service postings, and the politicization of the service itself, but it also reflects the breakup of his civil-service world in Nigeria's double military coups of 1966. Following the coups, Aluko had retired from the civil service and started a second career as a university lecturer, briefly at the University of Ibadan and then at the University of Lagos; in 1968 and 1969 he was out of Nigeria, studying in Britain at the University of Newcastle upon Tyne, where he received an M.S. in public health engineering. Unlike any other of Aluko's books, *Chief the Honourable Minister* is set not in the provinces but in central government, in the capital of a fictional new African nation, "Afromarcoland," and its focus is the gradual breakdown of civilian rule and the inevitable coming of a military coup, as had happened in Nigeria in 1966.

Aluko's book clearly invites comparison with Achebe's book on the same theme, *A Man of the People* (1966), yet the differences between the two works are as significant as the similarities. Achebe's hero is an intellectual outside the government, and Achebe's politician is a villain, a blatantly opportunistic rogue; by contrast, Aluko's central character, Alade Moses, is both intellectual and politician at once, a former schoolmaster who has been brought into the government after independence and who has switched from his original profession—teaching engineering—to become minister of works (switched, that is, from theory and hope to the pressing practicalities of "nation-building"). Moses is drawn by his supporters and colleagues not only into political trade-offs, bid rigging, and election fraud, but also into a disturbing rapprochement with traditional culture, into secret blood oaths scientifically administered with a hypodermic syringe, and a chieftaincy initiation that is purely for political propaganda. Unlike Achebe, who uses a first-person narrative to allow readers inside the experience of his politically alienated protagonist, Aluko uses the more objective third-person voice, to chart, almost clinically, the way weakness, rather than wickedness, leads to Alade Moses's fall from power. There are satiric cameos, too, of the way both expatriate and African civil servants get caught up in collusion with their new political masters.

The problem once again with Aluko's tragicomic view of politics is in its perspective on the future, or sense of an ending; the main narrative of the novel rests on an ironic distance from the political rhetoric of the characters, implying at best a troubled outcome, while his final chapter, where the new military ruler announces his coup on national radio, seems to have a straightforward seriousness and firmness of political program. This disjunction of modes is clearly of historical significance, in assessing the initial attitude of African elites to the military coups of the 1960s, as well as of literary significance, in indicating Aluko's final reluctance to relinquish his early idealistic hopes for a totally ironic detachment.

The book marks the end of a major phase in Aluko's writing career, for his three subsequent novels turn away from mainstream questions of political development to focus instead on smaller-scale case studies in Nigerian affairs. In the early 1970s Aluko served as a civilian state commissioner of finance, but the novels appear to evade any direct comment on politics at that level or of that period. Indeed, according to his 1973 interview with Kole Omotoso, younger Nigerians fiercely criticized his "timidity" and "refusal to take moral stands." His later books, too, avoid even the conditional and troubled sense of hope that Aluko had maintained in his three novels from the 1960s. Yet these later books may also, in light of the indirect and symbolic approach to political commentary used in *One Man, One Matchet* and *Kinsman and Foreman*, be read as commentary on the contemporary state of the Nigerian nation.

In *His Worshipful Majesty* (1973), Aluko steps back dramatically in time to the early 1950s and returns his focus to the local level, but with some interesting differences from the early novels. The book deals with the introduction in 1952 of the Western Region's new Local Government Act, which was intended to set up modern democratic local councils alongside the traditional structure of chiefs and elders, formerly protected under the colonial policy of indirect rule. Local government reform was a small-scale version of the larger general problem of the relocation of power as traditional societies modernized, and the novel skillfully dramatizes the inevitable clashes of two incompatible political patterns. Some critics have argued that in this book Aluko shows a new sensitivity to the values of traditional Yoruba culture, and certainly his picture of the new council chairman, the Lagos lawyer Morrison, satirizes the outsider's ignorance of local tradition and shows him having to learn about it. The book dwells, too, at much greater length than earlier ones had done, on the ceremonial grandeur, as well as the stubborn resistance to change, of the traditional ruler, the Alaiye. But this change of attitude toward traditional culture is partly one of point of view, rather than of basic value.

Aluko tells the story through the eyes of Kale Roberts, who combines the posts of secretary to the Alaiye and to the new local council, a man with a deep investment in both worlds, comic in his self-interested efforts not to drop between the old and new; Kale's account seems like self-justification rather than objective narrative. Indeed, some of the novel's satire seems to argue that modern, educated Nigerians can never recover the traditional culture they have lost: Morrison's newfound interest in local tradition seems merely diplomatic, and his ultimate fate (madness and then death, after being administered a traditional cure) is hardly encouraging. The very length and number of the Alaiye's speeches make it difficult for the reader to stand securely outside the traditionalist point of view, but the plot of the novel shows the Alaiye's resistance to change as stubborn and selfish rather than heroic. Insofar as Morrison is a symbol of modern government, a government that seemed by the 1970s to have broken down and gone mad, the novel would seem to argue for firmer and more committed modernization and against renewed deference to cultural tradition. In this small, good-humored, often comic case study of local reform, Aluko is concerned with exploring the human complexity of social change, but he never questions its inevitability or necessity.

For the remainder of the 1970s Aluko returned to his teaching post at Lagos, and his sixth novel, *Wrong Ones in the Dock* (1982), is set in that city. He earned a Ph.D. from the University of Newcastle upon Tyne in 1976, for research on biodisc methods of urban sewage disposal, and he retired as an associate professor in

Aluko in 1986 (photograph by Bernth Lindfors)

to influential lawyers and the police, so that, through his eyes, the reader, unlike the suspects, fully understands the excruciatingly slow and unpredictable legal process through which the case must go. The suspects and their family are much less educated than the narrator, and the crime was committed in a crowded, lower-class, urban housing development, where the population is constantly shifting and witnesses are both hard to find and reluctant to come forward. The police and the lawyers have no understanding of the urban culture in which such domestic violence occurs, nor much interest in the human suffering their legal process causes. Both the prisons and the courts are shown to be corrupt and inefficient.

In the climax of the novel several suspects die from suffocation in an unair-conditioned British-style police van, as they are shuttled back and forth from court to prison; Jonathan and Paul survive and are eventually released, but Jonathan's health and life have been ruined. The police-van incident forms a fitting symbol for the novel's attitude to the Nigerian legal system, but it also stands as a symbol for the larger frustration and despair Aluko projects about Nigerian government and society. Only in the rather powerless human decency of the narrator himself do any real positives emerge from the novel.

Aluko's *A State of Our Own* (1986) focuses on the multiplication of state governments within the Nigerian federal structure, but it places the responsibility for governmental inefficiency less on inherited colonial structures than on the individuals who want to change those structures for ultimately selfish purposes. The book describes the plans, and lobbying campaign, of a group of ambitious faculty members at the University of Sogal ("Unisog") to set up a new state in their home region; not coincidentally this will also create not only a new set of openings for cabinet ministers, civil servants, and state assemblymen but also a new university, where they can all be full professors. The book details their caucuses, their fundraising techniques, and their employment of an extravagant American-style lobbying firm, as well as their growing mutual distrust as they come to realize the full implications and costs of getting their proposed state approved in a federal system. Their own students at Unisog riot in protest against the new state, and the commission of inquiry into the protests allows Aluko to put forward, through the student leaders, a remarkable indictment of the shortsightedness, greed, and am-

Lagos in 1979. The novel is a thriller about the Lagos law courts and the injustices caused by an antiquated British-style legal system that is breaking down under the sheer pressures of African urban life. The dedication, "To Jacob, whose needless suffering inspired the writing of this novel," suggests that the initial impulse for the book was simply journalistic and reformist, to tell the story of a wrongful arrest for murder; it takes the unlucky suspects, Jonathan and Paul, twenty months of suffering and anguish before their friends can prove their innocence and regain their freedom.

The narrator of the novel is an educated Nigerian much like Aluko himself, with social ties

bition of the novel's main characters. The first-person narrator, Moses Erinosho, a low-level university administrator who had hoped to become registrar of the new university, is increasingly persuaded by arguments against the new state.

The novel's message seems to be that only the breakdown of political order can make the educated elite face up to political and economic realities. It is, again, an almost wholly negative message. At the end, symbolically, Moses leaves his office where the new state had been planned: "enough was enough," and his resolution is firm ("I was through with the movement and for what the movement stood"). But he has "nowhere in particular in mind" to go, and he wanders "purposelessly" toward the library before turning down toward the shore. The problems of ambition and factionalism within the university parallel those in state-level politics; indeed, through the selfishness and self-importance of the Unisog faculty, Aluko can miniaturize, and so make absurd, the initially more stirring and plausible self-importance of politicians. As an indictment of elite selfishness, the novel is detailed and absorbing, but it will inevitably be criticized for the bleak political prospect it offers.

Aluko's achievements can now be seen in much clearer perspective. Though his first six books all received the accolade of inclusion in the Heinemann African Writers Series, they have remained rather marginal to the canon of modern African literature. Several of them received scathing criticism from the original reviewers, initially for what was labeled their "abusive" attitude to traditional Yoruba culture, and latterly for a blinkered, "civil service" view of Nigerian life, where Aluko's inside knowledge of the Public Works Department leads to a style like "limp xeroxes of contracts and tenders" (*Times Literary Supplement*, 16 October 1970). In the early 1970s, too, young writers questioned Aluko's ties with the Nigerian governmental establishment and projected their distrust onto the novels, as mentioned in the Omotoso interview: "he has held office till now," wrote one, "more like an instrument than a dynamic person . . . one searches his novels in vain for the high moral seriousness . . . of committed artists." Even critics sympathetic to his kind of satire, such as Bernth Lindfors, have sometimes seen him as merely a "facile and witty writer . . . a gadfly without a sting" (*African Literature Today*, 1971), though such criticisms could hardly be brought against his dark later novels.

But alongside these criticisms there has also been continuing appreciation, both for his social satire and for his developing skill in handling tone and style. Oladele Taiwo, for instance, praises Aluko's realism as establishing "a relevant link between tradition and modern experience," and both Taiwo and Ayo Banjo have documented Aluko's "technical sophistication" in handling Nigerian English across "a much wider range of linguistic activities than one finds in many another Nigerian novelist" (Taiwo, *Culture and the Nigerian Novel*, 1976). From his work as a whole, moreover, there emerge recurring images, of lonely protagonists and nightmarelike breakdowns, of rooted and transplanted trees, of health and disease and contagion, of water and streams and rains, that suggest behind the surface satire a deeper and more poetic imaginative vision.

As time recedes from the immediate topics of Aluko's political satire, and his novels become less contemporary, critics and readers may perhaps appreciate more fully the less time-bound qualities of this tragicomic vision and reevaluate Aluko's place in Nigerian literature. In the meantime, however, his most recent books remain unabashed in their dark polemic satire on contemporary issues; political questions seem likely therefore to remain central, as debate continues about Aluko's brand of critical realism and the insights it can offer into the contradictions of contemporary Nigeria.

Interviews:

Kole Omotoso, "Interview with T. M. Aluko," *Afriscope*, 3 (June 1973): 51-52;

Lee Nichols, "T. M. Aluko of Nigeria" [recording and booklet], *Conversations with African Writers* (Washington, D.C.: Voice of America, 1978).

References:

A. O. Aboderin, "Conflict as a Binding Force in Five Novels of T. M. Aluko," *Journal of Teacher Education*, 2, no. 2 (1986): 124-138;

'Ladipo Adamolekun, "T. M. Aluko," *Afriscope*, 5 (February 1975): 57-59;

F. O. Balogun, "The Criticism of T. M. Aluko: The Need for Re-examination," *Lagos Review of English Studies*, 8 (1986): 159-166;

Ayo Banjo, "Language in Aluko: The Use of Colloquialisms, Nigerianisms," *Ba Shiru*, 5 (1971): 59-69;

Sibusiso M. E. Bengu, *Chasing Gods Not Our Own* (Pietermaritzburg, S.A.: Shuter & Shooter, 1976);

James Booth, "Democracy and the Elite: T. M. Aluko," in his *Writers and Politics in Nigeria* (New York: Africana, 1981), pp. 82-92;

Donald Carter, "Sympathy and Art: Novels and Short Stories," *African Literature Today*, 5 (1971): 137-142;

Harold R. Collins, "The Novel in Nigeria," in *Writers the Other Side of the Horizon*, edited by Priscilla Taylor (Champaign, Ill.: N.C.T.E., 1964), pp. 51-58;

Oscar R. Dathorne, *The Black Mind* (Minneapolis: University of Minnesota Press, 1974);

Arthur Drayton, "The Return to the Past in the Nigerian Novel," *Ibadan*, 10 (1960): 27-30;

S. A. Dzeagu, "T. M. Aluko as a Social Critic," *Legon Journal of the Humanities* (Legon, Ghana), 2 (1976): 28-41;

Viney Kirpal, "The Structure of the Modern Nigerian Novel and the National Consciousness," *Modern Fiction Studies*, 34 (Spring 1988): 45-54;

Margaret Laurence, *Long Drums and Cannon* (London: Macmillan, 1968; New York: Praeger, 1969), pp. 169-177;

Bernth Lindfors, "Characteristics of Yoruba and Igbo Prose Styles in English," in his *Folklore in Nigerian Literature* (New York: Africana, 1973), pp. 153-175;

Lindfors, "T. M. Aluko: Nigerian Satirist," *African Literature Today*, 5 (1971): 41-53;

Ngugi wa Thiong'o [as James Ngugi], "Satire in Nigeria: Chinua Achebe, T. M. Aluko, and Wole Soyinka," in *Protest and Conflict in African Literature*, edited by Cosmo Pieterse and Donald Munro (New York: Africana, 1969), pp. 56-69; reprinted as "Wole Soyinka, T. M. Aluko, and the Satiric Voice," in his *Homecoming* (London: Heinemann, 1972; New York & Westport, Conn.: Lawrence Hill, 1973), pp. 55-66;

Francis E. Ngwaba, "From the Artifice to Art: The Development of T. M. Aluko's Technique," *Literary Half-Yearly*, 23 (January 1982): 115-127;

Ngwaba, "T. M. Aluko and the Theme of the Crisis of Acculturation," *Nsukka Studies in African Literature*, 2, no. 1 (1979): 3-11;

Emmanuel N. Obiechina, *Culture, Tradition and Society in the West African Novel* (Cambridge: Cambridge University Press, 1975);

Tejumola Olaniyan, "Timothy Aluko," *Guardian* (Lagos), 31 August 1985, p. 13;

Oluwaniyi Osundare, "Speech Narrative in Aluko: An Evaluative Stylistic Investigation," *Journal of the Nigerian English Studies Association*, 8, no. 1 (1976): 33-39;

Eustace Taiwo Palmer, "Development and Change in the Novels of T. M. Aluko," in his *Growth of the African Novel* (London: Heinemann, 1979), pp. 102-123;

Patrick Scott, "The Cultural Significance of T. M. Aluko's Novels," in *When the Drumbeat Changes*, edited by Carolyn Parker (Washington, D.C.: Three Continents, 1981), pp. 215-239;

Scott, "The Older Generation: T. M. Aluko and Gabriel Okara," in *European-Language Writing in Sub-Saharan Africa*, 2 volumes, edited by Albert Gérard (Budapest: Akadémiai Kiadó, 1986), II: 689-697;

Beatrice Stegeman, "The Courtroom Clash in T. M. Aluko's *Kinsman and Foreman*," *Critique*, 17, no. 2 (1975): 26-35;

Stegeman, "The Divorce Dilemma: The New Woman in Contemporary African Novels," *Critique*, 15, no. 3 (1974): 81-93;

Oladele Taiwo, "T. M. Aluko: The Novelist and his Imagination," in his *Culture and the Nigerian Novel* (London: Macmillan / New York: St. Martin's Press, 1976), pp. 149-180;

Kashim Ibrahim Tala, "T. M. Aluko's *One Man, One Wife*: A Re-evaluation," *New Horizons*, 1, no. 2 (1981): 45-57;

Robert M. Wren, "Anticipation of Civil Conflict in Nigeria: Aluko and Achebe," *Studies in Black Literature*, 2 (1970): 21-32.

Elechi Amadi
(12 May 1934 -   )

Emmanuel Obiechina
University of Nigeria at Nsukka

BOOKS: *The Concubine* (London: Heinemann, 1966);

The Great Ponds (London: Heinemann, 1969; New York: Day, 1973);

Sunset in Biafra (London: Heinemann, 1973);

Isiburu: A Play (London: Heinemann, 1973);

Peppersoup and The Road to Ibadan (Ibadan: Onibonoje, 1977);

The Slave (London: Heinemann, 1978);

Dancer of Johannesburg (Ibadan: Onibonoje, 1978);

Ethics in Nigerian Culture (Ibadan: Heinemann, 1982);

Estrangement (London & Portsmouth, N.H.: Heinemann, 1986).

SELECTED PERIODICAL PUBLICATION—
UNCOLLECTED: "The Novel in Nigeria," *Afriscope*, 4, no. 11 (1974): 40-41, 43, 45; reprinted in *Oduma*, 2, no. 1 (1974): 33, 35-37.

Elechi Amadi circa 1966

Few African novelists writing in English have portrayed rural life in Africa with as much authenticating care and detail as has Elechi Amadi in his novels. He is one of the foremost chroniclers of the African village in creative literature. In his novels African villagers come alive in the immense variety of their individual and group activities, which are deeply informed by a shared sense of religion, ethics, social etiquette, and culture. His novels tend to project the image of an idyllic and stable world. But this world does not remain stable for long: it is sometimes undermined by the intervention of fate and the supernatural forces that determine the destinies of men and women in the traditional society; and in some cases by the people themselves, who, through stupidity or excessive passion, knock down the walls of the stability of their world. In Amadi's novels the idyllic is never too distant from the tragic.

Amadi himself was a child of an African village. Born to Daniel W. and Enwere Weke Amadi on 12 May 1934 in Aluu, in the rainforest belt of southeastern Nigeria, near Port Harcourt, he had his early upbringing in that region. Later he ventured outward to receive his secondary education at Umuahia Government College and his university education at University College, Ibadan (earning a B.S. in physics and mathematics in 1959). Then he taught science and mathematics in Merchant of Light from 1960 to 1963, before joining the army, but the village remained embedded in his consciousness and was readily drawn upon when he turned his mind to fiction. His first three novels are each set in the cluster of villages around where he was raised, while his fourth novel is set principally in Port Harcourt, the largest urban center in Rivers State. The success of Amadi's novels is attributable to the surefootedness with which he describes the setting and the cultural environment. He describes village life and experience, sports and games, and rituals and social practices with a degree of verisimilitude possible only for an insider.

Amadi's best contribution to the novel in Africa, however, remains his having perfected a style of narration and dialogue that captures the rhythms of traditional speech. It is a style of great flexibility and lends itself admirably to the dramatization of action, the expression of emotion, and the exposition of ideas.

Many commentators on his novels have noted this achievement of his art, his having evolved a simple but profound narrative style akin to the style of the classical storytellers. Indeed, Henry Tube, the reviewer of *The Great Ponds* (1969) for the *Spectator* (10 September 1969), had in mind Amadi's narrative style as well as the world of his novel when he wrote, "If there is something of Homer and Virgil in the physical descriptions of battles and parleys . . . there is still more in the powerful sense of what it is like to be ruled by supernatural forces." And in 1981 Alastair Niven described *The Concubine* (1966) as "a novel of classic simplicity."

A mild and intensely private man not given to self-dramatization, Amadi has nonetheless a very clear view of what he set out to achieve in his fictional works. In one of his few statements on the role of the novelist in Africa (as quoted by Theophilus Vincent in 1974), he asserts that "an African writer who really wants to interpret the African scene has to write in three dimensions at once. There is the private life, the social life and what you may call the supernatural." Each of his rural novels illustrates the validity of this statement.

The Concubine is regarded as a successful first novel and has been acclaimed for combining formal excellence with depth of meaning. Critics agree that it is a well-controlled narrative with a proper balance between character and situation and between action and background. The title character is Ihuoma, a beautiful young woman of inimitable charm, the crown jewel of feminine propriety and the pride of the village of Omokachi. Unknown to her, she has been betrothed to the Sea King, a malevolent spirit who is content to allow her to become a concubine but not the wife of any mortal man. Any man who falls in love with her and seriously contemplates marrying her is soon struck down and exterminated by the ever-vigilant Sea King. Such is the fate of

Emenike the noble villager, Madume the land-grabber, and Ekwueme the lovesick young man. In the middle of all the upheaval is the tragic heroine, totally oblivious to this immense potential for destruction.

On the most superficial level, the story would seem to belong to the genre of pure folklore, with the heroine in the archetypal role of the fatal female who brings disaster to her lovers. But the strength of *The Concubine* rests on the fact that it is not folklore but realistic-style fiction, in spite of its strong penetration by the supernatural.

Amadi's success in this novel can be attributed to two main accomplishments. First, he has drawn a convincing picture of the traditional society in which he situates the action. In this society, human beings are in close contact with the world of gods, spirits, and ancestors. The close interplay of the natural and the supernatural, of the physical and the metaphysical, and of the secular and the spiritual provides a strong backdrop to the drama played out by the characters. Second, the characters themselves are clearly drawn, and their actions are given dramatic effect through Amadi's superbly controlled dialogue. His skillful portrayal of the characters and their society and his matter-of-fact handling of the supernatural combine to produce a convincing illusion of reality and to make *The Concubine* a significant novel.

Between the publications of his first and second novels, Amadi resigned from the army, taught at Ikerre/Etche Grammar School for a year (1966-1967), then rejoined the army. He served with the Federal Commandos during the Nigerian civil war.

The Great Ponds, his second book, is about a feud between two fishing villages near the Niger delta for the possession of a communal fishing pond. The pond of Wagaba is really of no greater consequence than other ponds, but its symbolic value has risen by the degree of prestige invested by each community in the effort to possess it exclusively. In the tradition of heroic contests, the possession of the pond becomes a challenge and a channel through which the warriors on each side celebrate their bravery, martial sagacity, and magical prowess. On either side there is a champion whose destiny is coterminous with that of his community: Olumba of Chiolu, and Wago the leopard-killer of Aliakoro.

Amadi's understanding of traditional life is again revealed by his detailed description of the arts of war and peace, including his recourse to

Dust jacket for Amadi's first novel, in which he combines supernatural legends with a realistic style

the supernatural to break the impasse when war begins to prove too costly for the contestants. The resolution of the controversy is subtle and unexpected, including the structural use of the influenza epidemic of 1918. Amadi is a master of plot construction, for, even though the end of the tale is unexpected, there is nothing forced or overtly contrived about it. He succeeds in trimming the action away from fantasy and exaggerated gestures and toward empiricism.

Beginning in 1973 and continuing until his retirement in 1983, Amadi worked in the Rivers State Public Service as a permanent secretary. This secure job gave him the stability to hone his writing skills further.

The Slave (1978) is even more restrained than *The Great Ponds*, because Amadi has imposed on it the necessary demands of conventional realism. Even though a degree of heightening is essential to sustain interest in a work of fiction, Amadi deliberately reins in his enthusiasm and plays down the sense of wonder to keep the action within a proper range of credibility; the magical is kept down in the novel.

The Slave tells the story of Olumati, a young son of a dying family, whose parents have been victimized by their village and stampeded into seeking refuge in the service of a god in a neighboring village, thus embracing slavery as a means of securing their lives. As a grown young man, Olumati attempts to reclaim his patrimony by restoring his family to social respectability, but the forces that oppressed his family reassert themselves and combine with his own deeply embedded complexes to nullify his effort. In a mood of extreme despondency he escapes into voluntary slavery as his parents had done before him. *The Slave* is a very pessimistic tale, and it is Amadi's best effort so far at exploring the inner life of a character. Whatever social obstacles lie in the way of Olumati's efforts to restore his family's place and reputation are not as formidable as the state of deep unease and insufficiency within himself. In the end his failure becomes inevitable because he has suffered psychological damage from which he cannot recover. Not even the help of his friends and some of the people of the village could restore him, because his problem is both within and without. The internal sickness is more

51

difficult to cure than the external. For him, the test of his acceptability would have been to marry Enaa, the village elder's daughter whom Olumati has come to regard as a justifiable prize for his economic success. When she is betrothed to his friend who is an artist, Olumati regards the action as a sign of his rejection by the community, and he goes away to embrace his destiny as a slave in the shrine house.

Like *The Concubine* and *The Great Ponds, The Slave* is also set in precolonial eastern Nigeria and is written in the same evocative style. But it is somewhat misleading to present the three novels as a trilogy, as some critics and publishers have tried to do. There is no organic relationship or unifying theme among the novels; neither do the characters link up in any way.

In his fourth and latest novel, *Estrangement* (1986), Amadi shifts the focus of his fiction from precolonial times to the postcolonial period, and specifically to the period of the Nigerian civil war, also called the Biafran War (1967-1970). The novel deals with how the war affects Alekiri, a young, devoted housewife from Port Harcourt, a Biafran city that has fallen to the Federal soldiers: her marriage collapses, and she is driven into the arms of Maj. Sule Dansuku, a Federal field commander. The novel gives a glimpse of the dilemmas and tragedies that faced individuals in one of the monumental disasters of modern history. Every one of the major characters bears the scar of the war—Alekiri, Major Dansuku, and Ibekwe, Alekiri's alienated husband—but the end of the war also finds them gathering together the pieces of their shattered lives. However, the old stabilities have gone forever for some of the people.

Amadi explores his themes and his characters' predicaments with integrity and compassion and gives a touching picture of the community's effort to help its members to heal the wounds of the war. He shows that the trauma of this terrible upheaval did not completely destroy the traditional community's vitality, even though the community is not as strong as those in Amadi's novels set in precolonial times.

Amadi experienced the Biafran War firsthand. He was detained in Biafra during the war, before he escaped to join the Federal side. Two years before the war, he had retired from the Nigerian Army with the rank of captain in the Educational Corps. Rejoining the army after leaving Biafra, he became a major. His experiences during the civil war are described in his third book, *Sun-*

Cover for the novel that prompted Henry Tube of the Specta-tor *to compare Amadi's powers of description to those of Homer and Virgil*

set in Biafra (1973), a memoir that, as Niven said in 1981, "is written in a compelling narrative form as though it were a novel."

In addition to novels and memoirs, Amadi has written four plays directed mainly at secondary-school audiences. These are *Isiburu* (1973), a ritualistic play about a famous wrestler who, in spite of the odds, becomes the chosen favorite of the gods; *Peppersoup and The Road to Ibadan* (1977), a combined publication, the first play a comedy on interracial marriage and the other a civil-war story that seems to anticipate *Estrangement*; and *Dancer of Johannesburg* (1978), a spy story with an unexpected ending that features an African High Command and the defeat of apartheid.

Amadi has also written a nonfiction book on morality and culture in Nigeria, *Ethics in Nigerian Culture* (1982). It is a work of good scholarship and could become a useful companion to Amadi's novels, because it discusses many of the cultural institutions and values from which the novels take their moral and sociological bearings. The book reveals that, in addition to being an excellent storyteller, Amadi is also a thoughtful and well-read philosopher.

From 1984 to 1987 he was writer in residence at Rivers State College of Education. In 1987 he rejoined the civil service when he was appointed commissioner for education in the Rivers State Cabinet. Since 1989 he has served as commissioner for lands and surveys. His job makes heavy demands on his time, but he remains a devoted family man. (In December 1957 he married Dorah Nwonne Ohale, a midwife. They have several children, all of whom either graduated from or are attending college.) And Amadi continues to write. He has shown that he is a talented novelist with broad visions and wide sympathies that encompass modern as well as traditional settings. He has the potential of becoming a great novelist.

References:

S. O. Aje, "Music and Dance as Metaphors of Language in Elechi Amadi's *The Concubine*," *Neohelicon*, 16, no. 2 (1989): 187-199;

Naana Banyiwa-Horne, "African Womanhood: The Contrasting Perspectives of Flora Nwapa's *Efuru* and Elechi Amadi's *The Concubine*," in *Ngambika: Studies of Women in African Literature*, edited by Carole Boyce Davies and Anne Adams Graves (Trenton, N.J.: Africa World, 1986), pp. 119-129;

K. M. Chandar, "Elechi Amadi's *The Concubine*," *Literary Half-Yearly*, 21, no. 2 (1980): 123-133;

Ebele Eko, "African Aesthetics in Elechi Amadi's *The Slave*," *Literary Criterion*, 23, nos. 1-2 (1988): 143-153;

Eko, *Elechi Amadi: The Man and His Work* (Lagos: Kraft, 1991);

Ernest M. Emenyonu, "The Horrors of War: *Sunset in Biafra*," in *African Literature for Secondary Schools*, edited by Emenyonu and Benaiah E. C. Oguzie (Ibadan: University Press, 1985), pp. 163-172;

Geoffrey I. Finch, "Tragic Design in the Novels of Elechi Amadi," *Critique*, 17, no. 2 (1975): 5-16;

Simon Gikandi, "Myth, Language and Culture in Chinua Achebe's *Arrow of God* and Elechi Amadi's *The Concubine*," in his *Reading the African Novel* (London: Currey / Nairobi & Portsmouth, N.H.: Heinemann, 1987), pp. 149-170;

Barry Ivker, "Elechi Amadi: An African Writer Between Two Worlds," *Phylon*, 33 (1972): 290-293;

Alfred Kiema, "The Fantastic Narrative in Elechi Amadi's Works: Narrating and Narrator," *Commonwealth Essays and Studies*, 12, no. 2 (1990): 86-90;

Prema Nandakumar, "Another Image of African Womanhood: An Appreciation of Elechi Amadi's *The Concubine*," *Africa Quarterly*, 13 (1973): 38-44;

Rodney Nesbit, *Notes on Elechi Amadi's "The Concubine"* (Nairobi: Heinemann, 1975);

Alastair Niven, "The Achievement of Elechi Amadi, *The Concubine*," in *Common Wealth*, edited by Anna Rutherford (Aarhus, Denmark: Akademisk Boghandel, 1972);

Niven, *Elechi Amadi's "The Concubine": A Critical View* (London: Collings, 1981);

Chimalum Nwankwo, "The Metaphysical as Tangible Presence: Elechi Amadi," in *Subjects Worthy of Fame: Essays on Commonwealth Literature in Honour of H. H. Anniah Gowda*, edited by A. L. McLeod (New Delhi: Sterling, 1989), pp. 88-96;

George Nyamdi, *The West African Village Novel, with Particular Reference to Elechi Amadi's The Concubine* (Berne: Lang, 1982);

Wole Ogundele, "Chance and Deterministic Irony in the Novels of Elechi Amadi," *World Literature Written in English*, 28 (Spring 1988): 189-203;

Benaiah E. C. Oguzie, "Predestination? Elechi Amadi's *Concubine*," in *African Literature for Secondary Schools*, pp. 25-38;

Niyi Osundare, "As Grasshoppers to Wanton Boys: The Role of the Gods in the Novels of Elechi Amadi," *African Literature Today*, 11 (1980): 97-109;

Ndiawar Saar, "*The Concubine*: Roman sur la societé Africaine traditionelle," *Université de Dakar Annales*, 8 (1978): 139-152;

John Updike, "Books: Shades of Black," *New Yorker*, 49 (21 January 1974): 84-94;

Theophilus Vincent, ed., *The Novel and Reality in Africa and America* (Lagos: U.S. Information Service, 1974), pp. 13-14.

Ayi Kwei Armah

(28 October 1939 -   )

Derek Wright
Northern Territory University, Darwin, Australia

BOOKS: *The Beautyful Ones Are Not Yet Born* (Boston: Houghton Mifflin, 1968; London: Heinemann, 1969);

Fragments (Boston: Houghton Mifflin, 1970; London: Heinemann, 1974; Nairobi: East African Publishing House, 1974);

Why Are We So Blest? (New York: Doubleday, 1972; London: Heinemann, 1974; Nairobi: East African Publishing House, 1974);

Two Thousand Seasons (Nairobi: East African Publishing House, 1973; London: Heinemann, 1979; Chicago: Third World, 1979);

The Healers (Nairobi: East African Publishing House, 1978; London: Heinemann, 1979).

OTHER: "Aftermath," in *Messages: Poems from Ghana*, edited by Kofi Awoonor and G. Adali Mortty (London: Heinemann, 1970), pp. 89-91.

SELECTED PERIODICAL PUBLICATIONS—
UNCOLLECTED:

FICTION

"The Ball," *Harvard Advocate*, 98, no. 2 (1964): 35-40;

"The Night Club Girl," *Drum* (January 1964): 35-39; reprinted as "The Offal Kind," *Harper's Magazine*, 238 (January 1969): 79-84;

"Contact," *New African*, 4 (December 1965): 244-248;

"Asemka," *Okyeame*, 3 (December 1966): 28-32;

"Yaw Manu's Charm," *Atlantic* (May 1968): 89-95;

"An African Fable," *Présence Africaine*, 68 (1968): 192-196;

"Halfway to Nirvana," *West Africa* (24 September 1984): 1947-1948;

"Doctor Kamikaze," *Mother Jones*, 14 (October 1989): 34-38, 46; reprinted as "The Development Agent," *CODESRIA Bulletin*, 4 (1990): 11-14.

POETRY

"Speed," *West Africa* (13-19 February 1989): 227.

Ayi Kwei Armah (photograph by Vasco Nerses)

NONFICTION

"La mort passe sous les blancs," *L'Afrique Littéraire et Artistique*, 3 (February 1960): 21-28;

"Letter from Ghana" (anonymous), *New York Review of Books* (12 October 1967): 34-39;

"Pour les ibos, le régime de la haine silencieuse," *Jeune Afrique*, 355 (29 October 1967): 18-20;

"African Socialism: Utopian or Scientific?," *Présence Africaine*, 64 (1967): 6-30;

"A Mystification: African Independence Revalued," *Pan-African Journal*, 2 (Spring 1969): 141-151;

"Fanon: The Awakener," *Negro Digest*, 18 (October 1969): 4-9, 29-43;

"Sundiata, An Epic of Old Mali," *Black World*, 23 (May 1974): 51-52, 93-96;

"Chaka," *Black World*, 24 (February 1975): 51-52, 84-90; reprinted as "The Definitive Chaka," *Transition*, 50 (1976): 10-15;

"Larsony [*sic*], or Fiction as Criticism of Fiction," *Asemka*, 4 (September 1976): 1-14; reprinted in *New Classic*, 4 (November 1977): 33-45;

"Masks and Marx: The Marxist Ethos vis-à-vis African Revolutionary Theory and Praxis," *Présence Africaine*, 131 (1984): 35-65;

"Islam and 'Ceddo,'" *West Africa* (8 October 1984): 2031;

"The View from PEN International," *West Africa* (26 November 1984): 2384-2385;

"The Oxygen of Translation," *West Africa* (11 February 1985): 262-263;

"The Lazy School of Literary Criticism," *West Africa* (25 February 1985): 355-356;

"The Caliban Complex," *West Africa* (18 and 25 March 1985): 521-522; 570-571;

"The Festival Syndrome," *West Africa* (15 April 1985): 726-727;

"Our Language Problem," *West Africa* (29 April 1985): 831-832;

"The Teaching of Creative Writing," *West Africa* (20 May 1985): 994-995;

"One Writer's Education," *West Africa* (26 August 1985): 1752-1753;

"Flood and Famine, Drought and Glut," *West Africa* (30 September 1985): 2011-2012;

"Africa and the Francophone Dream," *West Africa* (28 April 1986): 884-885;

"Dakar Hieroglyphs," *West Africa* (19 May 1986): 1043-1044;

"Writers as Professionals," *West Africa* (11 August 1986): 1680;

"The Third World Hoax," *West Africa* (25 August 1986): 1781-1782;

"A Stream of Senegalese History," *West Africa* (9 March 1987): 471-473.

Ayi Kwei Armah is perhaps the most versatile, innovative, and provocative of the younger generation of postwar African novelists, and like all authors who express extreme views in their books, he has become a controversial figure—in both African and Western critical circles—but the controversy has centered exclusively on the works and not on the man, about whom extremely little is known. Armah is a very private person. He gives no interviews, attends no confer-ences or writers' workshops, releases no press statements, and does not seek to promote or publi-cize his work outside of Africa in any way. Only twice, when provoked beyond endurance by the American critic Charles Larson's misreading of his novels and later, in a mellower mood, when correcting an African critic's errors about his edu-cation, has Armah broken his rule of silence about himself and his work, and it is to these two essays that Western critics owe nearly all of their biographical information about him.

Born at the start of World War II to Fante-speaking parents in Sekondi-Takoradi, a seaport of the then-British colony of the Gold Coast, Armah apparently was too young to take in the full import of his country's postwar social unrest—the strikes, unemployment, and the shooting by British authorities of demonstrating ex-ser-vicemen recently back from the colonial war. But the first twenty years of his life coincided with the growth of Ghana, through a mixture of politi-cal negotiation and violent struggle, into Africa's first independent state, and the violence of this period and the nationalist hopes of the indepen-dence movement clearly left their marks on him. These events are convincingly documented in the sixth chapter of his first novel, *The Beautyful Ones Are Not Yet Born* (1968), where the reminiscences of the two characters provide a collective autobiog-raphy of the new nation.

Armah left Ghana in 1959 on an American scholarship to Groton School in Groton, Massa-chusetts, and then on to Harvard—shortly before his twentieth birthday, two years after Ghanaian independence, and before President Kwame Nkrumah had turned Ghana into a one-party state and shut down all political opposition. No doubt Armah carried with him to America, then caught in the throes of civil-rights agitation, the youthful idealism of Nkrumah socialism. The be-trayal of that idealism in the 1960s and the subse-quent disillusionment were to color all of Armah's early writings. His short stories and po-lemical essays on African socialism, on indepen-dence, and on the ideas of Frantz Fanon, works Armah wrote in the decade of post-in-dependence disenchantment, contain in embry-onic form the themes of his novels: Africa's contin-uing oppression under the "mystification" of inde-pendence and its entrapment in a cycle of neocolonial dependency in both the political and economic spheres; the failure of human reciproc-ity in the lives of modern urban Africans under the pressure of a manipulative and exploitative system of relationships; and the resistance to genuine revolutionary growth and regeneration in the politics of the postcolonial world. Notable among these early pieces are the essay "A Mystification: African Independence Revalued" (Spring 1969), which charts the unchanging economic-flow pattern from African province to Western metropole in the neocolonial economy; and the story "Yaw Manu's Charm" (May 1968), a remarkable and disturbing study of the far-reaching effects of neocolonial psychology, even at the lowest levels of aspiration, in the lives of westernized clerks. The American-set story "Contact" (December 1965) is a subtle exploration of the ways in which the racial stereotypes of colonial history still penetrate the private corners of interpersonal and sexual relationships, and, along with the novel *Why Are We So Blest?* (1972), it clearly draws upon Armah's experience of America in those years of racial confrontation that marked a shift from integrationist to black-separatist politics. An early poem, "Aftermath" (1970), which telescopes themes of personal, artistic, and racial betrayal, reveals an early fondness for the syncretic image, a marked feature of his mature work.

Armah has financed his fiction writing by a mixture of teaching, scriptwriting, translating, and editing, and his work, along with his desire to write from an African base and find a genuinely African focus for his novels, has taken him to several African countries. He has worked as a translator for *Revolution Africaine* in Algiers (1963), and, in his native Ghana, as a scriptwriter for Ghana Television and as an English teacher at Navrongo School (1966). In late 1970—after a productive six-year period that saw the publication of his first novel, the completion of a second, and commencement upon a third—he moved to Tanzania and then taught African literature and creative writing at the College of National Education at Chang'ombe from 1972 to 1976, when he left to teach the same subjects at the National University of Lesotho. Armah also spent periods in Paris as an editor of *Jeune Afrique* (1967-1968), and in the United States as an assistant professor at the University of Massachusetts (1970) and as an associate professor at the University of Wisconsin (1979). He has since returned to Africa and settled in Dakar, Senegal.

Armah's early departure and lengthy absences from his native Ghana, together with his setting of his early novels in an unashamedly modern, urban, and westernized Africa, have helped to create the impression that his writing reveals little knowledge of or interest in traditional African culture. The fact that he has always eschewed the notion of exile and has spent his longest periods of residence not in America and Europe but in other parts of Africa seems to have done little to correct this misapprehension. Armah's combination of an African background with an American education has made the question of the literary sources of his fiction a vexed one. During the 1970s the notion that the vision and techniques of his first three novels were foreign derived or at least foreign inspired became a commonplace in the criticism of African fiction, and Western commentators who detected echoes of French writing—including that of Jean-Paul Sartre, Samuel Beckett, Alain Robbe-Grillet, and Celine—were legion. In the case of Armah's third novel, *Why Are We So Blest?*, black American literature and polemic might have been added to the list of influences.

More seriously, the divergence of Armah's visionary, symbolic fictional modes from the realist mainstream of African fiction has provoked charges from African critics, notably Chinua Achebe, that his characterization and style are "un-African" and have more in common with expatriate fiction about Africa written by Europeans than with African writing. In fact the modern malaise of the alienated "been-to" hero in Armah's second and third novels is not simply a foreign literary imposition, either of existential angst or absurdist ennui, which upholds an un-African view of the universe. Armah is a historically minded writer who trained as a social scientist, and the Western-induced paralysis diagnosed by his heroes in their own conditions goes much further and deeper than mere literary influence. This paralysis is transparently the product of an exploitative politico-economic process through which the West not only exports its psychological maladies to its former colonies but maintains a stultifying interference in and control of African affairs: this prevailing existence in Africa is upheld indirectly by means of political influence, educational programs, and economic strangleholds that force Africa to remain a subordinate partner in what is still an essentially colonial, cash-crop economy.

Armah delves deeper than the personal disenchantment of his protagonists, to historical determinants and, most especially, to the colonial continuities identified by Fanon in his analysis of postcolonial society. Armah's small body of fiction, like Fanon's political theory, reveals a deepening suspicion of all conceptual systems derived from Europe, and this connection is extended, finally, to their concomitant literary styles and techniques. In the exclusively literary zone of influence, there are no doubt vestiges of the French *nouveau roman* in the descriptive tableaux of *The Beautyful Ones Are Not Yet Born*, indicating francophone leanings that are unusual in an anglophone African author. But these westernized stylistic excesses are pressed into the service of ritualistic and peculiarly African concepts, particularly in the matter of the spatial conceptualization of time: the first novel's hallucinated epic descriptions of journeys up a staircase or along a coast, suppressing event in favor of sheer phenomena, give occasion to a descriptive treatment of time, as object and state rather than motion and process, which owes more to African than to European thought. Neither do the hero's anonymity and impersonality in the first novel have anything to do with an everyman typicality or a generic significance as "working man," after the pattern of Western allegory. The protagonist, called simply "the man," is not representative but atypical of his society and his class of railway clerks and, in a world of westernized go-getters with Anglo-African names, his unassuming honesty and ordinariness are singled out as different and given special and peculiar expression in anonymity. Remote from class identity, this anonymity has to do essentially with his society's refusal of an identity to one estranged from its values and its sheer incapacity for recognizing value beyond its own narrowly materialistic definitions. Significantly the unnamed man and the Teacher represent the novel's only coherent subjectivities, while the named characters are shallow stereotypes used for purposes of satiric representation.

Bound up with the focus in the early novels on the dilemmas of the isolated and estranged individual is Armah's neglect or negative evaluation of the African extended-family system; his attitude has come under fire from Achebe and other African critics. In Armah's treatment of the family, he appears to offend all the traditional pieties. Children are generally cause for mourning rather than joy. For the unnamed man of the first novel they mean both the cesarean scar that deadens desire and the increased pressure to acquire material commodities, and his wife's initial pregnancy is seen to have trapped him in the deadness of familial materialism. On returning from American studies, in Armah's second novel, *Fragments* (1970), Baako, the only son of the Onipa family, is regarded by them as a human conveyor belt for Western cargo, and the outdoor ceremony for his newborn nephew is simply a pretext for making money out of the child: the ceremony is brought forward to coincide with payday, with the result that the child is exposed too soon and, by a cruel irony, dies before his birth has been properly celebrated. Everywhere in these novels children have more to do with death than with birth (the new Ghana is even seen as a death-child, born out of war and anarchy), but this attitude is chiefly because the erstwhile communalizing energy of the African family system has, in its transposition to a modern urban context, become locked into the service of a viciously selfish and deadly materialism. Far from upholding or condoning the westernizing corruption of traditional family values, Armah exposes and excoriates the perverted individualism that so completely undermines them that they are no longer the expression of a genuinely communal ethic.

Once the linchpin of the traditional community, the extended family structure originally acted as a bulwark against social discontent by ensuring some share of prosperity for all, but, in the different circumstances of the centralized nation-state, the system no longer functions in this way. Only a few families have power and influence, concentrating more wealth into fewer hands, and, instead of serving the community, the system undermines it by turning against it the hedonistic interests of a few powerful careerists. As Baako perceives in *Fragments*, the return of material cargo by the westernized "been-to" serves only the false microcommunities of selected "loved ones" at the expense of the larger community, and when the provider falls from political favor, new families enjoy the prospect of prosperity. The family has come to reflect the modern state insofar as it has ceased to be a solidarity of reciprocal interests and has become a means for manipulation.

In *The Beautyful Ones Are Not Yet Born*, Armah uses the grand, crystallizing, syncretic image of a white fish's cannibalized body to draw together in a logical chain the power-elite scrambling after white power from the corpse of colonialism, the communal body fed off of by a few privileged families, and the family members themselves feeding parasitically upon the single providing member. When the Nkrumah regime is toppled in the novel, the corrupt minister Koomson bribes his way to safety, quoting to the boatman

Dust jacket for the British edition (1969) of Armah's first novel, which depicts political corruption and the breakdown of traditional values in the newly independent nation of Ghana

the traditional proverb, "When the bull grazes, the egret also eats." But current ethics have twisted the saying out of its proper meaning by providing huge short-term gratification for the "bull," a few pickings for the smaller animals in his vicinity, and nothing for the rest. The politician, like the short-changing conductor on the symbolic social bus in the first chapter, offers to those who have found him out only a fraternity of fraud, a false community of corruption. Inverting the traditional pattern, the bull feeds from the egret, the big fish from the little ones. Personal greed is furthered by a system originally designed to check such excesses, and the paradoxical result is that anyone with a surviving spirit of community, like Baako and the anonymous man, is cut off from the body that his beliefs were intended to serve. By a similar irony modern Africa's rejection of Baako's traditional priestlike

approach to his artistic vocation, as a self-effacing communal servant, drives him reluctantly inward into the position of the Western artistic recluse, thus alienating him further from his audience.

Parallel perversions have befallen traditional ritual practices, which are kept solely for convenience, expedience, and profit. In *Fragments* libation is a pretext for an uncle's bibulous indulgence; the sacrifice of a ram to mark the birth of a child is performed with an irreverence appropriate to a drunken feast; and the greedy acceleration of the outdoor ritual speeds Baako's nephew and namesake in and out of the world before the baby has completed his first week of life. Armah's picture of the modern family in urban Africa is scathing, but it is also full of poignant ironies and is touched by a deep sadness about disappearing and debased traditions.

Early critical allegations that there are few "Africanisms" in Armah's first two novels and that the books do not draw upon Ghanaian settings, speech, or history have not held up under the pressures of close investigation. But, beyond these pedestrian issues, these books are so imbued with surviving ritual forms, ceremonial motifs, local mythologies, and residual ancestral beliefs that traditional West African culture is always powerfully, if vestigially, present, both in its superior ethical imperatives and its inherent deficiencies. The cyclic pattern and pollution concepts of an indigenous purification rite form a hauntingly ironic backcloth to the protagonist's involvement with and rescue of Koomson in *The Beautyful Ones Are Not Yet Born*, and in *Fragments* Armah again underpins the narrative with a ritualistic subtext that, in this case, draws upon arcane areas of Akan custom and theology to rehabilitate a dead order of value as a living presence in the novel. In both these works the exploration of debased ritual practices establishes a complex and problematic continuity between a corrupt modern present and a corruptible traditional past.

Armah's contemporary urban Africa is a complicated amalgam of vanishing but unvanquished pasts and bleakly futureless presents. In this fictional realm, traditionally honored ancestors are starved of libations by drunken modern priests, and the few remaining gods are being driven out by self-worshiping materialism. Racked by a self-distrust that reflects a national failure of confidence in the constructive potential of indigenous culture, the contemporary cognates of traditional chanters and sculptors have gone overseas in search of foreign approval. Even local folk myths, such as the Mammy Water legend in *Fragments*, have been tampered with and turned into insidious neocolonial propaganda by television technocrats angling for foreign foundations. Yet, in spite of this degenerative process, and as if in willful resistance to it, the past in the early novels contrives to be dormant rather than dead: its complex interplay with the modern world in which it has a residual presence is expressed through Armah's imaginative possession of ancient West African coastal mythologies and ritual forms and the traditional religious beliefs that inform them. The author's figurative treatment of the intricacies of ritual process gives his work an unexpected and seldom-noticed common ground with work from which his own art has been thought far removed, such as the tradition-oriented plays of the early Wole Soyinka, and with the writing of authors who

have adopted a hostile critical stance toward him, such as Kofi Awoonor. Those African commentators—notably Solomon O. Iyasere and D. S. Izevbaye—who adhere to more broadly hospitable, catholic concepts of traditionalism have drawn attention to the first novel's indebtedness both to African fable and to the graphic personifications of the oral tradition, and to the second novel's striking simulation of the oracular and editing devices of griotarary narrative. Thus the "Africanness" of Armah's imagination is not a shallow property that can be easily substantiated or refuted but a subtle, elusive, and many-sided quality that reveals itself to a correspondingly subtle and probing critical approach, and the author may have done himself something of a disservice by his later statements, quoted in Gwendolyn Brooks's 1972 autobiography, about the first novel lacking "an absolutely African focus."

The Beautyful Ones Are Not Yet Born burst upon the international literary scene in 1968 and quickly became a classic of African fiction. Armah's talent seemed to have been sprung upon his readers fully formed, matured, and without any apprenticeship, but this impression probably owed something to the fact that the novel had been a long time in the making. It was written between 1964 and 1967, a period of composition sufficiently protracted to permit the incorporation of events surrounding the anti-Nkrumah coup of February 1966. There is in Armah's first novel a kind of inverse proportion between its formidable stylistic complexities and the simplicity of its plot, which divides, symmetrically, into three cyclic parts of roughly equal length. During the first part the anonymous hero goes through the cycle of a single day. He battles to retain his integrity against an onslaught of temptation, which takes the form of bribes proffered or accepted by traders and bus conductors, the graft of venal fellow clerks at the railway office where he works, and the corrupt invitations of an influential family relation, Koomson. The latter tries to persuade the man to act as the nominal owner and partner in the fraudulent purchase of a luxurious boat that Koomson's facade of socialist politics prevents him from undertaking in his own name. Later in the novel the hero, under pressure from both his wife, Oyo, and his mother-in-law to enter into the corrupt boat deal, finally relents. The first part of the novel dwindles to a halt with the man's arrival, in the evening, at the house of his friend, "the Teacher." Then, in part 2, the narrative movement is suspended, and the day cycle gives way to recollections of the violent birth of the independence movement and the cycle of growth and decline of the Nkrumah regime, which is only a few weeks away from its downfall. The nine years of the first independence government are figuratively contracted to the life span of a man-child who completes his whole life cycle and dies, prematurely aged, at the end of his seventh year.

The final part of the novel stretches over an indefinite period of weeks, ending with the February coup and the lurid episode of Koomson's escape. During the man's rescue of Koomson, by way of a latrine hole and the back lanes and sewers that lead to the sea and the escape boat, the malodorous minister is described in terms of the filth and excrement that pile the streets and latrines throughout the novel, and the whole highly stylized finale appears to owe something to the purification rite of the carrier in West African coastal communities, in which the detritus of the dying year, its ills and misfortunes, are ceremonially carried out to sea in the form of a miniature wooden boat. The protagonist's fanatic bathing rituals, before and after each contact with the Koomsons, have emphasized his need for constant purification from the Koomsons' pollutive presence, as if to strengthen his purity in preparation for an act of social decontamination. The symbolism of the surreal climax invests Koomson with the twin identity of the nation's collected excrement—about to be evacuated through the national latrine hole and carried off by the communal latrine man—and, closely linked with this, the collected ills of the moribund Nkrumah regime, which must be ritually expelled at the completion of its life cycle and carried to sea so that a new historical era can be born.

Armah's implied view of postcolonial history as the hoarded accumulation of evils, in a cycle of consumption, waste, and disposal, calls for the imagery of consumer waste and excreta to be pushed to its extremity. Thus the power-elite's intemperate devouring of the country's resources without performing any productive work in return becomes the cause of a spectacular physiological imbalance, instanced in the growling entrails and thundering flatulence of the fugitive Koomson, and it leads, by an interior poetic logic, to mountains of feces and dirt in the environment. There is also a socioeconomic rationale, since the privileged consumer-elite who produces the waste also embezzles the municipal funds allocated for its disposal. But this is not all. The nov-

el's two twilight creatures, the office sweeper and the latrine man, both of whom are proleptic of the hero's cleansing role, find more dirt in the Ghanaian environment than can ever be cleaned away, enough to provide the sweeper with three daily cleaning jobs. Orgies of description are lavished upon refuse heaped around litter boxes, impetuously piled excrement in latrines, the viscous organic rot of a staircase banister, and the decaying junk on the shoreline, "so old it has become more than mere rubbish. . . . It has fused with the earth underneath."

The implication seems to be that all the filth of Africa's history is still in existence, and the failure to jettison the old has contaminated the new. Amankwa, the timber trader who tries to bribe the protagonist, is a walking antiquity who speaks with "the voice of ages" through "generations" of "piled up teeth." Neocolonialism in independent Africa has reincarnated colonial and precolonial evils that were never properly expelled, and the daunting task facing the unnamed man in his mock-ritual role at this late stage of African history is the purgation of this vast accumulated filth, as a new start for Africa's future demands nothing less than a complete break with the past, a thorough sweeping away of ancient corrupt heritages. In an environment polluted by the unpurged rot of history, things are born infected and prematurely aged by what came before: hence the man-child, the aged new leaders, the putrid polish on floor and stair, and the ancient smell of the new banknote. The accelerated overuse, wearing out, and emptying of resources, bequeathing a growing detritus and diminishing means to the next generation, is the novel's paradigm for African history.

But the ritualized fantasy of a panoramic cleansing of history, like the Teacher's thwarted millenarian faith in messianic saviors bringing "future goodness," falls victim to the irony of events. The only practical possibility envisaged is a break with the immediate past of the Nkrumah regime, but the inveteracy of corrupt practices prevents the nation from availing itself even of this limited opportunity. Koomson's excretory "rebirth" through the latrine hole (he is symbolically naked and pushed headfirst by the man as midwife for the new age) is the purest parody, a mock ritual of passage too deliberately droll in tone and surreal in style for the ritual disguise of escape as expulsion to be anything but ironic. Koomson gets away to the Ivory Coast, where, readers may assume, his corrupt way of life starts

over again, and it is significant that, in the totalitarian ethos of this novel, the era of bribery is itself
banished by a bribe (Koomson, with the man's
help, bribes his way onto the escape boat). Corruption, eternally self-renewing, is expelled by more
of the same: the last purgative act of the old
order triggers the first guilt of the new one.
Koomson's last words to the man—"We shall
meet again"—suggest that his evils, like the de-
bris heaped by the returning tide, will not be
washed very far away. The forced celebrations at
the coup are tainted by fear and suspicion, and
the new regime is only a few hours old when the
bribes begin again. The bribing of the policeman
by the driver of the shiny new bus on the last
page brings the novel full circle by repeating the
corrupt practices of the conductor on the old rotting bus on the first page. As the protagonist
reaches the shore after his purifying immersion
in the sea, he awakens to the reality that there
can be "no saviors," "no answers," and no permanent expulsion of ills of the kind ritually simulated by his own act. The knowledge brings only
a solitary release, a limited personal renewal that
is not transferred to the community at large. Nothing has altered much. The beautiful ones have
not been born, and the man wearily returns to
the cycle of things that do not change: "Oyo, the
eyes of the children after six o'clock, the office
and every day. . . . "

The conclusion of the novel is, with a few
qualifications, a despairing one, and the overall
view of political developments in independent Africa is pessimistically one-sided. Trimmed to fit
Fanonian theories about unproductive bourgeois
administrations in postcolonial countries, Armah's political cartoon of Nkrumah's Ghana records the speed, waste, abortive plans, and false
public utilities but leaves out the industry and the
constructive achievements. What rescues the novel from the banality of the political themes, the
bareness of the plot, and the suspicious simplicity
of the cyclic view of history is the sheer penetration of Armah's imagination and the vitality of
his style. The power of *The Beautyful Ones Are Not
Yet Born* lies in the performance of language and,
most especially, in dazzlingly inventive, graphic hyperbole, influenced at least in part by African
oral tradition. With a kind of grim exhilaration,
Armah's indefatigable scatology flatulates breath,
constipates voices, and turns fraud and corrupt
ambition into urinary and excretory activities
until the metaphoric attributions have wholly invaded, possessed, and become their objects. Orga-

nizing and orchestrating them is an intricate and
formidably symmetrical network of correspondences between the human ingestion-evacuation
cycle, the body politic, and the Ghanaian environment. Along this metaphoric labyrinth the
courses of political regimes rise and fall, shrink satirically to the dimensions of the physiological cir-
cuit, and swell to the ritualized calendrical evacua-
tion of the nation at the climax of the novel.
There is poetic intensity and symbolic composition—particularly in the man's seashore epiph-
anies and the Teacher's recollections of the *wee*
(marijuana) smokers—which were new to African
fiction, and a metaphoric richness that, with the
possible exception of Soyinka's fictions, has not
been surpassed.

This richness is not diminished in Armah's
semi-autobiographical novel *Fragments*, which
tells the story of a "been-to" who is hounded into
madness by his family because what he brings
back from his stay in America is not the instant return of material possessions and prestige that
they expect of him but a moral idealism that interferes with the selfish materialism they have taken
over from Western culture. Baako is not the conventional "been-to," caught between Africa and
the West or even between a modern and a traditional Africa: divided instead between the West
and a vulgarly westernized Africa, he reviles the
place he returns to only insofar as it imitates the
one he has fled. The only help Baako receives in
his purgatorial passage through the increasingly
foreign world of his native Ghana comes from
the companionship, both spiritual and sexual, of
the Puerto Rican psychiatrist Juana and from the
traditional wisdom of his blind grandmother,
Naana. The latter's ancient order of values is reflected in the Akan chapter titles that divide the
novel into the thirteen lunar months of the traditional Akan year, and though she can neither
make sense of the modern world nor resign herself to the mindless reception of its confusing material impressions, it is Naana's encircling monologue and epilogue that enclose in a timeless
frame the historical fragmentation recorded in
the linear narratives of Baako and Juana. Naana
reflects on this disintegration: "The larger meaning which lent sense to every small thing and
every momentary happening years and years ago
has shattered into a thousand and thirty useless
pieces. Things have passed which I have never
seen whole, only broken and twisted against themselves."

In the new, urbanized Africa depicted in

Photograph by Douglas Harris

29, was educated at Achimota, Ghana, then at Groton and Harvard. After three years at home he left Ghana late in 1967 to work for the magazine *Jeune Afrique* in Paris. He is currently at Columbia University, participating in the Graduate Writing Program there on a grant from the Farfield Foundation.

Besides his novels he has published short fiction in *Harper's* and the *Atlantic*.

Dust jacket for the semi-autobiographical novel in which Armah describes a Ghanaian's disillusionment with his westernized native country after his return from a stay in the United States

the novel, an Africa besotted by commodity and status, the uncritical eye is dazzled and overwhelmed by the aggressive, superficial beauty of external things: empty titles and ceremonials, pompous-sounding sinecures, and the gaudy trinkets of Western technology in airports and hotels. The general failure to penetrate the luminously impressive outward show to reach the inner paucity—thus mistaking the visible appearance of things for the things themselves—causes form to fragment from meaning, and perception to separate from understanding. In particular, attention is diverted from the inherent power and value resident within traditional ritual properties to their material exteriors, turning the furniture of festivals into a succession of spiritless objects and, as in the fantastic airport reception of the returning "big man" Brempong, making ceremonial forms evasions rather than expressions of reality—hence the novel's strangely disembodied descriptive style, the obsessive lingering on hard shiny surfaces, the awe of language in the presence of material objects. The notion of partial perception, the inability to see beyond surfaces and being uninformed by any guiding moral or intel-

lectual vision, is reinforced by a rhetoric that does not merely shrink characters like the Brempongs to the size of their objects of worship but physically fragments them into partial people, into collections of disjointed limbs that appear to operate independently of any thinking or organizing consciousness and do not add up to complete human beings. As Armah's first novel graphically endows characters with excremental characteristics that take on a quasi-literal status, the second one effectively disintegrates them, rendering them as fragmented and as incomplete as their perception of the world.

Although *Fragments* is about fragmentation, it is the most intricately structured and least fragmented of Armah's novels. Each of the novel's partial and often mutually uncomprehending viewpoints contributes some important mythological fragment to what is really a single diffused consciousness. Meanwhile the thirteen narrative fragments are bound by a sometimes heavy-handed and over-suggestive network of foreshadowings and echoes, turning large stretches of the novel into a tone poem whose limping narrative and dialogue are borne along on a tide of recurring leitmotivs. The specter of a dog murdered in a mock-sacrificial manner in Juana's opening narrative prowls the pages of the succeeding chapters and appears again during the hounding of Baako by his relatives in a ritualized chase across the city. The motif of penetrating walls between worlds links Baako's "expanded consciousness" with that of visionaries and madmen observed in both the Parisian and Ghanaian sections of his narrative; and the conscious decision of Juana, her husband, and the other expatriates to accept the necessity of fragmented perception and a limited wholeness is epitomized in Naana's blindness as a refuge from insanity, "which would surely have come with seeing so much that was not to be understood." The leading metaphor of the returning ghost recurs in the form of the resurrected cargo-spirit, the reincarnated ancestor, the repatriated "been-to," and the visionary lover of Mammy Water, back from the sea: the figures advance concurrently across the novel's seamless myth fabric, each going to come again and amplifying the pattern of an outward passage, an actual or figurative death and rebirth into an altered state, and a beneficial return, bearing what may be doubtful blessings. In the rich and multilayered tapestry of this poetic novel, sentences such as the following, from Naana's dream— "But Baako walked among them neither touched nor seen, like a ghost in an overturned world in which all human flesh was white"—conflate allusions to cargo-ghosts, the ancestral dead turned white in the spirit world, the lonely African in American exile, and the missionary "been-to," unwelcome because of his idealism and walking unheeded, both invisible and untouchable, among westernized Ghanaians.

Most important, the pivotal episode of the death by careless exposure of Baako's week-old nephew has a protracted imminence in the novel. Foretold by Naana, feared by Baako, and alluded to by a plethora of omens and danger signals in the chapter "Awo" (Birth), it becomes a key metaphor for the premature truncation of life that pervades the book. The failure of the Onipa family to keep its offspring alive because of its greed for riches has logical socioeconomic extensions in the aborted public utilities of schools and roads quickly abandoned by self-aggrandizing governments, the shutdown distilleries and disused industrial rail tracks, and the architectural miscarriage of Efua's (Baako's mother's) dream house, which is the sequel to the five actual miscarriages her daughter has. Omnipresent in the novel is the de-

struction or desertion of whatever fails to provide instant fulfillment, by those who cannot themselves produce or possess: a syphilitic dog-slayer; a crew of Ghanavision technicians wrecking a last disputed television set; and an impecunious "nexologist" who, like a cargo-cult devotee, destroys what little he has left to get more. This sterility is exacerbated by a "cargo-mentality," a colonial-derived dependency complex that causes contemporary Ghanaians to continue to attribute to the white world godlike powers of invention and innovation that they are unwilling to develop themselves. The persecution of Baako follows the pattern of the dog slaying by the sexually disabled and the quasi-infanticide of the outdoor rite, insofar as it is an attempt to exorcise a general impotence. Mistaking his artistic self-communings for madness, his acquisitive family declares him a bad investment and packs him off to the lunatic asylum. The overriding implication, as Robert Fraser has observed in *The Novels of Ayi Kwei Armah* (1980), is that this community is jealously resentful of any creative energy or quickness and, even if it does not go so far as to kill what it cannot create, at least it tries to make those who possess creative gifts responsible for its own frustrating sterility, and perversely demands that they, too, be made like its own barren self. The family's crippling neurosis enables the sick ones to stay well by making the well ones sick: it passes its own madness onto its son, who expresses its illness for it.

There are signs in *Fragments* of a darkening of Armah's vision. The more openly aggressive and destructive pressures to conform in the second novel call for something stronger than the protagonist's passive endurance in the first. The intolerances of Ghana demand offerings for the altars of their respective materialism and purblind racism, and since their sins against humanity are deadlier and less forgivable than the corruption of the first book, a heavier price than mere relief actions must be paid for their purgation. The man in *The Beautyful Ones Are Not Yet Born* seems to offer some kind of purification; Baako and Modin (in *Why Are We So Blest?*) are, more immediately, sacrificial victims. They are also scapegoats whose suffering should, in theory, release the community from the burden of false hope and shame that it has heaped upon their heads and, through the pain of loss and remorse at their disintegration or death, restore to that community the traditional wisdoms that were missing. But the sacrificial pattern focuses the somber insight that it is only the trauma of death, whether from maternal neglect (as in the case of Baako's nephew) or bureaucratic incompetence (exemplified by the death of Skido), that has the power to shock contemporary Ghanaians back into a sense of real value and human dignity. Only the crises of birth and death bring out what is still good in them, and only in the sudden experiences of fraternity that these inspire, and the brief and bitter wisdom gotten from error, can Baako find any faith in his people.

There is in *Fragments* a reluctance to believe in total loss and waste, given its purest and most positive expression by Naana: "Each thing that goes away returns and nothing in the end is lost." Nevertheless, it remains uncertain whether any painful redemption, either of family or community, has emerged from Baako's sacrifice. Near the end of the book, Baako's mother takes him to the ruined foundations of her unbuilt mansion and, formally lifting her curse on her son, confessionally loads onto him the burden of her disappointed hopes and thwarted cravings. But the purity of Efua's "soul-cleaning" is suspect because her relief at being lightened of the weight of her dreams is still mixed with grudging regrets that they could not be fulfilled, and the result is that Baako is left with a load of guilt that is the crucial factor in his drift toward madness. Upon his slow recovery in the asylum, Baako is finally rescued from the clutches of his vampiric family, but his rescuer, Juana, is the first to admit that psychiatry's periodic patching up of broken souls has no permanent value since it will always have to be repeated, and her concern is, moreover, with one man's personal salvation—or, more precisely, salvage—and not with some wider social regeneration.

The ambivalence of *Fragments* is perhaps most poignant in the presentation of Naana's beliefs and the traditional order of value in which they are rooted. In Armah's first novel, ancient African customs, such as the giving of *kola*, appear to be still moribundly alive and potent with their own corruption, like the still viscous, aged filth in the latrine tunnel. In his second book, however, they seem rather to have died and been cynically resurrected in altered forms that have no kinship with their original spirit. Folk myths pass to propagandizing poetasters, outdooring rituals to private profiteers, and praise songs to toadying television producers who disguise sycophantic opportunism as traditional respect for elders. In a faithless age the surviving religious emotions of awe

and wonder have been exchanged for modern technology's glittering profane paradise of material objects and the bringers of its gifts. Thus are the unseen ancestors of Naana's dream visibly vulgarized into flesh by Sissie Brempong: "Oh, they have made you a white man. The big man has come again.... The air where he has been is pure, not like ours." Efua beholds her newly returned son as a semisupernatural being, inquiring after his car "in a near whisper filled with wonder and gladness."

Yet, the sudden death of the past notwithstanding, its order of value insinuates itself in the novel through its surviving representative and spokeswoman Naana, whose ancient ghostly traditions appear to some extent to revenge themselves upon their modern violators. Naana is the novel's "ritual consciousness." She foresees and reviews events, and she issues reminders of the lost ritual values that attach to customs: for example, the original communal significance of the outdooring rite, now perverted into an exhibition of private wealth and prestige; and the traditional importance of libation in maintaining the cyclic continuity and interdependence of the living, the ancestors, and the unborn. In Akan belief the destinies of the newly born are closely bound up with devotion to the ancestors who watch over them and with care of the elders who are closest to the ghost world from which new lives are sent. The neglect of one end of this circular continuum interferes with developments at the other, and it is significant that Araba's five miscarriages coincide with the five years of Baako's exile, during which Naana's power as an elder within the family suffers a drastic decline.

Araba's childlessness is a traditional form of poetic justice: those who prematurely forget the elders are allowed no progeny so that they themselves will be quickly forgotten at their deaths. Naana's traditional wisdom is allied to commonsense values, which tell her that "a child too soon exposed is bound to die," but, above and beyond this practical wisdom, the birth and outdooring of the child are surrounded by a ritualistic subtext that uses mythological allusion to evoke the gathering forces of an offended moral order and an atmosphere of mounting danger. The money-making ceremony takes place in the week of traditional harvest festivities, giving pay cycles priority over seasonal ones, and becomes a somber earth festival, a grimly inverted fertility rite presided over by Efua, who kills the grandchildren arriving with the harvest: in the death scene it is Efua, repeatedly linked with the things of earth, who switches on the fan and turns the air current directly against the cradle. The poetic logic implies that the outraged earth, in order to punish those who abuse its fertility at a time when it is ritually renewed, demands the sacrifice of the child itself: a pattern repeated one year later at the drowning of the lorry driver Skido, when a ferry holdup prevents him from bringing the harvest to market.

Events appear orchestrated in such a way as to color them with Naana's moral and teleological perspective and give life to a dormant and suppressed Akan ethos. Her fears that the scanted and omitted libations at Baako's departure and the outdooring will provoke ancestors and elders alike into withdrawing their protection from the young travelers are similarly borne out by events: Baako is driven to a mental breakdown; and the child, as foreseen, dies as the dire consequence of the premature ceremony. The traditional responsibilities urged by Naana upon Baako as maternal uncle are also vindicated to the extent that Baako, in his distant concern for the child's welfare, proves to be a fitter father than Kwesi, who allows his wife to blackmail him into endangering their son's life.

At the same time, however, the reader is made painfully aware that this traditional order of value is a dead order, artificially resuscitated by an allusive subtext to breathe some moral energy into a spiritual wilderness, and that, in the final analysis, it has its unity and power only in the minds of Armah and Naana. Its superior but obsolete ethical imperatives form a backcloth of nonfunctioning values that consistently declare their absence from and failing relevance to a world in which they can have no continuing currency or claim. The centrality that the Akan ethic assumes in the novel's composite psyche is inversely proportionate to its influence on behavior: no one listens to Naana, and at the outdooring the family looks to Baako not for avuncular moral guidance but for the prestige his educated presence lends to the proceedings. In the last chapter, which brings the year full circle, Naana dies, and, in her own mind at least, is reborn into the world of the ancestors. Her death, along with the deterioration of her family and nation, is subsumed into a cycle of renewal and restoration charted by the unceasing progress of the spirit: "The great friend throws all things apart and brings all things together again." But from the more material viewpoint of the age, the histori-

cal process has already subverted this circular passage. Naana's name, the singular of *nananom* (ancestors), figuratively renders her as the last fragment of a community of elders and ancestors, and in the epilogue she effectively sings her own funeral dirge, knowing that no one in the family will sing it for her. Presented as the sole survivor of a lost past whose beliefs die with her, she implicitly brings to an end the age of cyclic belief, and her release into the spirit community betokens the continuing captivity of the living. Moreover, the infiltration of Naana's Akan eschatology by salvationist notions of terminality from Christian religion suggests that she has not escaped complicity with the demise of traditional African beliefs. Meanwhile, Baako's slow emergence from his entombment in the asylum holds out faint prospects of new beginnings.

Finally Armah's occult structuring of the novel by prefigurative devices, coincidence, and underlying ritual patterns offers only a fragile aesthetic unity in token resistance to material fragmentation: Naana's random "momentary happenings" are reassembled into the only kind of ordered wholeness or "larger meaning"— an artistic one that is available. Her monologues offer not a practical corrective to an errant contemporary Africa but an abstract and merely imaginative, otherworldly alternative, and her spiritual meditations, like Baako's artistic ones, are taken as signs of madness in a materialistic age. For Baako, who is not ready to trade a physical for a spiritual existence, the cyclic passages and transactions between the seen and unseen worlds in her faith have no value beyond the metaphorical. The strong intimations that Naana's traditional view of the universe is better than what has replaced it, or what it has been corrupted into, are balanced by the realistic admission that there is no longer any way to draw upon the old to improve or temper the new. *Fragments* does not fatuously urge a return to values rooted in a way of life that has vanished: Naana's is a lost and failed order that cannot be restored. The timeless perspective of the Akan worldview that frames and contains the novel's interior linearities and deteriorative historical processes is also undermined and exploded by them. The problematic positioning of her circumscriptive narrative at the outer ring of the novel, denoting at once an absolute overview and her peripheral remoteness—her distance from the center of things—leaves uncertain the final value that is to be attached to Naana's vision.

Though flawed by some facile social and political satire, *Fragments* is a complex and problematic work and is the most densely textured and richly poetic of Armah's novels. His next novel, in contrast, displays a rarefied thinness of texture unparalleled in his writing. *Why Are We So Blest?* takes little trouble over the sensuous evocation of fictional locales, merely pegging notebook speculations to settings that are no more than their names, and its overworked symbolic shorthand of predator and factor archetypes, and white deserts and bleached Africans, though powerful and startling, is disappointingly telegraphic after the labyrinthine metaphoric structures of the first two books. Set largely in the North African city of Laccreyville (a thin disguise for post-revolutionary Algiers), the novel traces, through their respective diary entries, the encounters and relations of three characters: Solo, a failed revolutionary and artist from one of the unliberated Portuguese colonies; Modin, a Harvard-educated Ghanaian student in search of African revolution but still clinging to liberal beliefs in interracial harmony; and Aimée, a thrill-seeking, bogusly revolutionary white American girl with whom Modin has become fatally infatuated and who, when he is murdered by marauding O.A.S. terrorists in the desert at the climax of the novel, reveals herself to be a vicious psychopath.

The bleakly cynical, disillusioned portrait of African revolutionaries, which grew out of Armah's stay in Algiers in 1963, provides some continuity with the political skepticism of the first two novels. The Laccreyville sections of *Why Are We So Blest?* constitute Armah's requiem for the Algerian revolution and epitaph to Fanon's hopes for his adopted country. Armah's "Afrasia" is a war-ruined nation of crippled freedom fighters, partisans, and orphaned beggars, ruled from former colonial mansions by privileged managerial cadres who combine a colonial "white hunter" mentality with the traditional chauvinism and machismo of Islam. Punning on the meaning of "essence," Solo explains grimly to an old *mutilé de guerre* (victim of war) in the hospital that the militants now excluded from government serve as the sacrificial fuel for the revolution, carrying its opportunistic executives and diplomats to power on their backs: they are cynically duped pawns whose Sisyphean struggle installs a new French-supported hierarchy in a "colony only freshly disguised as a nation." In this haven for sham revolutionaries, the Portuguese-colonized "Congherians" receive little inspiration from their Afrasian

hosts. Ensconced in luxurious first-floor offices behind facades of ground-floor austerity and constantly currying favor with the white international press, the Congherian exiles find their will to action sapped and their power emasculated in the midst of a revolution very much in decline. A little more decadence and they could sit for Armah's satiric essay portrait (in "African Socialism") of "fiery revolutionaries who have never ventured within smelling distance of a revolution, freedom fighters whose suits are made in Paris and whose most hair-raising campaigns are fought and won in the scented beds of posh hotels." In the mythological scheme of the novel, these men are parodied Prometheans, at heart secret Olympians who hanker after the trappings of the West, and their entrails are hardened to withstand not the punitive tortures of colonial oppressors but their own hypocrisies. Jorge Manuel, for example, defers and then rejects Modin's application to join the movement, because Modin's situation is identical with Manuel's: he is a Western-educated intellectual with an American lover. After being kept hanging around for months, the demoralized Modin is finally persuaded to attempt an individual, backdoor entry to Congheria and is goaded by Aimée into the foolhardy Saharan crossing that leads to his death.

Armah's reflexive ironies question the value that any legend taken from the mythological store of the oppressor can have as a blueprint for revolution or model for progress in Africa. Nevertheless, although Modin steals no knowledge worthy of the name from the American Olympus and dies a useless, unenlightening death, the pervasive imagery of fire, entrails, livers, and predators invests him with Promethean pretensions. The idealistic "been-to," like the Greek demigod, tries to shed privilege and crosses over to the side of oppressed humanity to place his gift of education at their disposal. The endeavor leaves him stranded between, on the one hand, the whites who do not accept him and their black stooges whose privileges he has betrayed; and, on the other, the oppressed whose interests he is estranged from and opposed to because of his new knowledge. Even before he speculates about Promethean descents and becomes the tortured prey of the American "eagle" Aimée, Modin is seen as the Western-trained African intellectual who is doomed to punitive elevation on a lonely, lofty educational peak far above his people. Since knowledge is the property of the alien, the thirst for knowledge alienates. For the intellectual to stay at

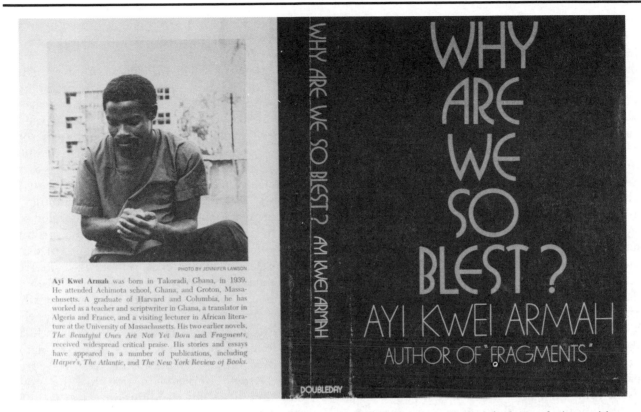

PHOTO BY JENNIFER LAWSON

Ayi Kwei Armah was born in Takoradi, Ghana, in 1939. He attended Achimota school, Ghana, and Groton, Massachusetts. A graduate of Harvard and Columbia, he has worked as a teacher and scriptwriter in Ghana, a translator in Algeria and France, and a visiting lecturer in African literature at the University of Massachusetts. His two earlier novels, *The Beautyful Ones Are Not Yet Born* and *Fragments*, received widespread critical praise. His stories and essays have appeared in a number of publications, including *Harper's*, *The Atlantic*, and *The New York Review of Books*.

Dust jacket for the novel that grew out of Armah's disillusionment with the African revolutionaries he met during a visit to Algiers in 1963

home is to join the "peripheral" masses who are afflicted by "manipulation, mystification, planned ignorance," while the alternative is to gravitate guiltily toward manipulatory Western "centres" where there is "high information" and "overall clarity" but also isolation and betrayal.

"The things he wrote of were in general not events; they were more like concatenations of ideas," Solo summarizes Modin's journal, and he is himself admonished by a Congherian exile: "You interest yourself in abstractions. There are concrete problems." Reading at times more like a treatise than a novel, *Why Are We So Blest?* stands accused of the same charges. The lonely pondering mind of its Lusophone narrator (Solo) broods over the notebooks of its anglophone one (Modin), rearranging their contents after Modin's death and subjecting them to a theoretical analysis that shows more interest in patterns and processes than in people: the "exchanges" between the two men are not the dramatic interaction of living people but the posthumous dialogue of ghosts. Exposition, hitherto essentially confined to the discursive sixth chapter of Armah's first novel and Baako's abstract screenplays and cargo theories in the second, now swamps the narra-

tive, and its central thesis is that, in the self-inclusive words of Manuel, "an African in love with a European is a pure slave ... with the heart of a slave, with the spirit of a slave." Interracial sexual relationships are doomed to reenact racially predetermined roles and thus to serve as a microcosm of Africa's historical encounter with the West.

The lethal aspects of Western imperialism are seen to penetrate beyond the political and economic arenas into the most private corners of human relationships, making the colonial model of exploitation and servitude the key to each, and black expectations of white friendship, under the impression that certain basic human values transcend racial divisions, are judged to be universally suicidal. A powerful device in the novel and also, finally, a source of its weakness, is the politico-sexual allegory that passes each of its sexual relationships through a kind of political "blender," in which personal and political fates—the private disposition of black to white and Africa's deadly molestation by the West—are telescoped so as to become virtually the same thing. Thus, the acquisition of white mistresses is blamed for Manuel's introduction of a class hierarchy and Western luxury into his government-in-exile and for the failure of Solo's political aspirations and his current defeatism. The colonial-sexual paradigm postulates quasi-organic, causative connections that make the proximity of the white woman spell the automatic debilitation and decline of the black man, and the sexual attraction of black to white is uniformly characterized as a "sickness" or "disease." The result is the often bizarre metaphoric transposition of the West's devouring of Africa's material resources into a corresponding draining of black sexual energy by white women and of Europe's economic rape of the continent into America's psychosexual consumption. By day the obedient "factor" and puppet trained by his neocolonial academic masters to further America's African interests, Modin is by night the exotic rarity needed to titillate the jaded sexual appetites of their wives and daughters.

The characterization of the white women in the novel suffers accordingly. They are given virtually no traits other than a frigidity meant to represent white America's arid sensibility or, alternatively, depraved sexual hungers, which symbolize the West's plundering of the manpower and material wealth of a subsequently impotent Africa. Aimée herself is an almost entirely schematic personality; her need to sexualize the public life to compensate for the frigidity of her private one makes her a ready tool in the politico-sexual allegory. Aimée's rapacious sexuality is principally a political metaphor, significant for its exploitative and antirevolutionary nature. In Africa she sleeps her way through the ruling bourgeois elites and imaginatively identifies with murdered white colons in bullet-holed bedrooms, and in America her sexual fantasies transform the Harvard scholar Modin into Mwangi, a colonial steward-boy, and help her conjure up orgasms while listening to the statistics of massacred African freedom fighters in history lectures. Aimée, the dominant archetype of colonial predation, transforms oral sexual practices into a murderous cannibalism, and at the surreal climax, when Modin is simultaneously fellated by Aimée and castrated by French terrorists who then rape her, her carnivorous carnality burgeons into a full sexual vampirism. The improbable finale takes the novel on a flight into metaphor and is perhaps best read on an abstract level: for example, the terrorists' use of Aimée to arouse Modin and so excite her, in turn, for their own use, suggests the white world's temptation of the African with privi-leges he desires but is not allowed to enjoy, while perversely siphoning off Africa's energies for its own profit.

The habitual identification of white seduction with political infiltration, fusing political tenor and sexual vehicle, promotes resistance to white sexual charms almost into an article of the new revolutionary faith and produces some unreal oppositions and misleading parallels: Modin's positing of American stud service as the natural alternative to renewed contact with his people's deprivation; and Solo's twinning of Aimée's psychopathy with Sylvia's weak-willed submission to Portuguese racism on the grounds that both are white girls. As an allegory of black-white relations presented in remorselessly destructive sexual terms, *Why Are We So Blest?* overlooks exceptions and discrepancies. Redeeming white virtues are outside its racial polemic, as the white depravity manifested in slavery and genocide are outside the scope of the crass, self-congratulatory *New York Times* Thanksgiving editorial from which Armah derived his title for the novel. James Booth has described this novel as a racist fiction about racist fictions. Certainly white racism as presented in the novel assumes almost metaphysical proportions, as if the result of some mysterious, inherent diabolism or inheritable genetic disorder, which places whites beyond ordinary human understanding. Moreover, the symbolism does appear to decry those white-promulgated sexual myths that degrade black self-images, while it assents to those that flatter such images—notorious myths of white deficiency and black prowess, and of fantasy-ridden "clitoral" white sex and perfectly reciprocal "vaginal" black sex.

The extreme vision of Armah's third novel is partly accounted for by its origins. Although the book has its setting and genesis in his first American visit and education at Harvard, from 1959 to 1963, it was completed after his second visit, from 1968 to 1970, and its militantly separatist racial polemics and uncompromising sexual attitudes represent a stage of black revolutionary thought a decade on from the period of its setting. These are best seen against a backcloth of late 1960s black radicalism—notably Black Power—which saw American race oppression as a species of internal colonization, and American integration schemes as variations on colonial assimilation programs, and which dissociated itself from the whole edifice of white civilization, including white revolution. In the novel, the "African" and "Negro" experiences have, in their common uprooting and alienation, become almost interchangeable, and the dramatic evidence for Africa's victim status in Modin's paradigm is drawn almost entirely from his American experiences. The book's racial typology of sexual jealousy and revenge, rape and castration (not to mention a Negro called Lynch), owes more to black America than to colonial Africa, and black American polemics supply the scenario for the sexual psychology, in which white male impotence and the subsequent nymphomania of wives combine to project upon the figure of the black man a mythical sexual vigor. The resulting sexual paranoia about blacks in the white mind awakens deeply secret sadomasochistic longings and fears and the desire to see them enacted: thus Mrs. Jefferson's orgasmic moans guide her sexually dormant husband to the spot where she lies with Modin, so that he may, in prurient self-torture, briefly relish his wife's forbidden pleasures before assaulting their supplier.

Armah transposes this essentially American model to a colonial context. The mentally overdeveloped Western nations in receipt of African sexual aid appear to need, in order to revive their exhausted sensibilities, fantasy reenactments of the original colonial violence that deadened them. In their sexual recolonization of Africans, Mrs. Jefferson and Aimée orchestrate their respective orgasms to the phallic stab of a knife blade and the explosion from a gun barrel aimed at the head of a steward-boy seducer: during the real-life enactment of the Mwangi fantasy by the O.A.S thugs, Aimée reaches the peak of her sexual excitement at the moment of Modin's lethal castration. In the novel's sexual allegorization of 1960s American politics—in which revolutionary energy, black and male, is sapped by the powers of reaction, white and female—Modin's various lovers represent the stereotypes of a traditional paternalism (Mrs. Jefferson), a hypocritical civil-rights integrationism (Sandra), and a sensation-seeking, slogan-mouthing Marxism (Aimée), which attach themselves like leeches to the causes of black minorities. On the other side of the racial divide, the tender and expert black lover Naita, who warns Modin off white women, links black separatism to sexual harmony as integration has been linked to sexual discord and exploitation.

In Armah's third novel urgent polemical pressures, many of them coming from outside Africa, have rigidified his vision and left the enemy perhaps too easily identifiable: it is "the West" and, beyond that, the whole white race, fired by a pathological lust for destruction and materially powerful enough to replenish its spiritual void by draining the superior vitality of its victims. In the first two novels the white world is not wholly diabolical, and the enemy is, rather, the Ghanaians who, mindlessly or cynically, adopt its worst elements and collaborate with the alien values that are destroying their culture. The three-story universe of the third book crudely polarizes this more densely textured world into "blest" and "damned"; Sacred Mountain and Plain; and American Olympus and Third World Tartarus awaiting Promethean deliverance. Among these levels wander the half-blest, half-cursed *évolués* who have been spirited away from their native cultures by Western education. Armah has not entirely lost sight of the Koomsons and Brempongs who enslave their people from within, but in his third novel even the betrayers are recast as victims. The Jorge Manuels are themselves manipulated and, albeit willingly, programmed into positions of privilege and prosperity by Western educational schemes that isolate them from the people whose revolutions they profess to lead.

Why Are We So Blest? is an ideographic construct with bold outlines and low specificity. Its facile, uninvestigative symbolism opposes to a stereotypical idea of the West an equally stereotyped, stage-set Africa, shorn of its multiple complexities and contradictions; and the higher visibility and sparser texture are especially noticeable in the areas of ritual and mythology. One of the secret strengths of the early novels is the subtextual pattern of ritual process, which runs beneath and often counter to the narrative. The purification motif in *The Beautyful Ones Are Not Yet Born* invests the coup with the potential of a turning point in Ghanaian history, and in *Fragments* the Onipas have the theoretical option of embracing the artistic gifts that Baako, like the singer in the Mammy Water myth, brings back from across the sea, although in practice the collective and familial wills prove too weak to make use of the opportunities. These ritual options in the fictive subconscious are absences that have the power of presences; negatives that function, albeit with guarded promise, as positives. But in the third novel their quiet potencies have been dissolved, and the ritualistic dimensions of the narrative are emptied of their suggestiveness: the unapparent is too apparent; the subconscious is self-conscious. This texture is due chiefly to a change in the mode of rituality, from an implicit and largely metaphoric presence, charged with the independent significances and determinisms of the African tradition, to the grotesquely artificial, sinister foreign arrangement of the American educational process, which trains the African neophyte in mindless obedience to the dogma of Western superiority: "alien communal rituals designed to break me and my kind," comments Modin, "a ritual celebrating of a tradition called great because it is European, Western, white." The rule of these "rites of secrecy" is that the initiate will duly decry his race whenever prompted and confirm that his exceptional intelligence is proof of the general rule of African stupidity.

In Armah's cross-cultural conspiracy cartoon, American educational aid programs constitute a series of pseudo-Promethean reverse crossings, which in fact co-opt into power a minority from the underprivileged to help keep the many out: the cause of black revolution is thus kept perpetually self-defeating by maintaining a subversive input of Western-educated intellectuals into the leadership. America expends a few philanthropic flames to dampen the revolutionary blaze and the small loan of fire is returned with interest to stoke the Olympian furnace. Meanwhile, the blind and uphill Sisyphean struggle of the real revolutionaries—who become the slain or mutilated militants—is doomed because its repeated failure is ordained within the Olympian system. This "elitist ritual for selecting slave traders" enjoys, in the political and sexual arenas of the novel, a preordination that makes white values and neuroses the black man's fate and makes the African's life a creation of whites. "Our disease is ordained," Solo concludes. In a world where educational exchanges have caused white-imitative aspirations to permeate even antiwhite revolution, it is no surprise to find the novel's sole traditional African image—a mask of Ananse—in the custody of an Afro-American academic integrant. Neither is it odd that the complementarity that marks much African ritual process should be viciously appropriated in defense of universal inequalities by the obtuse American student who reads out the titular editorial. The Western-controlled, fabricated form of rituality is given its most theatrical expression in the cult murder of Modin at the mock-sacrificial climax: the French terrorists swoop in, fatelike, from the desert to crucify and castrate Modin on the back of an O.A.S. jeep, while Aimée, as malevolent American priestess, erotically prepares the passive victim and then catches his blood.

In this novel, ritual symbolism no longer controls the protagonists and narrative consciousnesses; it no longer undermines the action but is itself undermined. By bringing myths and archetypes to the full glare of consciousness, this new ambience of self-regarding, self-advertising pseudoritual denies the rituals their latent power and severs them from the African origins that have hitherto been their source in Armah's work. Modin remarks that there are "other myths of enlightened reverse crossings, apart from the Promethean one, and indeed his own West African coast has a few (those of Ogun and Mammy Water, for example), but for the first time in Armah's fiction these "other myths"— the African ones—are completely silent. The internationalized voices give the impression that, on a Europeanized earth where Africa is a mere prop to Western supremacy, African myths are either extinct or have lost their authenticity, and there are no remaining intellectual or spiritual properties that are not white originated. What is interesting and hopeful about *Why Are We So Blest?*, however, is the transmission of these anxieties to the search for appropriate artistic form. Solo argues that when the black race has to borrow the stylistic devices and narrative techniques of its exploiters and destroyers to bewail its own destruction, then writing itself becomes an act of betrayal and destruction. He is aware that his rearrangement of Modin's fragments, never anything more than a spurious aesthetic refuge from chaos, reflects in its dislocated time schemes and multiple consciousnesses only the splintered life of the Europeanized *évolué* and, more seriously, imitates the "discrete beauty" of a despised European modernism. Solo's seduction by Western aestheticism parallels the political and sexual infatuations of Manuel and Modin: he is the artistic middleman, or factor, whose art bears the Olympian seal of approval and is designed essentially for Olympian consumption. He makes interesting art out of defeated revolution, aesthetic success from political failure; his task is to turn thwarted rebellion and its punishment into high tragedy for the purification of an Olympian conscience that craves exorcising insights into its own iniquity.

Why Are We So Blest? is a milestone along Armah's own chosen route out of the circle of the expatriate African "blest" and out of the dilemma of the factor-writer who is invited to enrich himself by writing about black oppression for a primarily white audience, and whose literary capitalization on distress effectively disarms revolutionary energy by its sublimation of suffering. Along with the hint of a radical shift of focus goes a growing distrust of ritual process, either as a fatalistic and diversionary substitute for real change or as a force that enshrines the cult of the special, outstanding individual and upholds a subjectivism that Armah has been keen to avoid in his later work. His dissatisfaction with inherited artistic forms, already discernible in his treatment of artist figures in *Fragments*, has in his third novel come to include his own narrative mode in that novel. The aesthetic form reflexively declares its achievement to be worthless, signaling Armah's arrival at a terminus and the imminence of some radical formal innovation: "There is no creative art outside the destruction of the destroyers," Solo declares. "In my people's world revolution would be the only art, revolutionaries the only creators."

For those readers who have registered these warning signals, the next book is not the total shock to the sensibility that appears to have been its intended effect upon Western audiences. Nevertheless, after Armah's first three works, the fourth one, written during his six-year stay in Tanzania, comes as an alarming corrective. *Two Thousand Seasons* (1973) localizes the historical experience of the whole African people to the troubled migrations of the Akan nation from its Sudanic origins, through slavery, exile, Arab and European imperialism, guerrilla resistance, and decolonization to its settlement in modern Ghana and future task of reconstruction. As such, the novel is only in part recorded history, and the narrative does not draw on specific local tribal memories but on the hypothetical race consciousness of a fictitious pan-African brotherhood whose names are taken from all parts of the continent. In this book Armah surprisingly bursts the bounds of historical realism, period setting, and naturalistic narrative, as he moves into the terrain of myth, legend, and racial memory. The group experience is paramount, so characterization is minimal and presents collective states and feelings rather than the fine delineation of individuals. The reader is addressed by a pluralized narrative voice, an anonymous and timeless "We," which represents the whole social body throughout its wanderings across history.

Two Thousand Seasons does not purport to be a "novel" in any sense of the word. Few novels create deliberately unmemorable characters who are merely functions of a collective will, or ramble episodically over vast spans of time in pursuit of racial destinies. Even fewer novels start from the premise that certain racial groups and their imperial underlings have engrossed most of the human vices and are helplessly predictable in the evil of their own natures. Abandoning critical investigation for partisan invective, Armah makes no claim to criticize subtly his colonial "destroyers" and "predators" and their African quislings, but he simply hurls abuse at them, more after the fashion of the Ewe *halo* than that of Western satire. It seems rather that he has evolved a strange and arresting new literary form by some daring experimentation with the devices of an indigenous African tradition that has an ancient pedigree: the tradition of the *griot*, storyteller, or oral historian, for which the nearest equivalents in European narrative would be those epics, sagas, and chronicles that also trace the migrations of whole peoples and celebrate the founding of nations and empires. The *griot* speaks with the voice of the whole community, and his legends, folktales, and proverbs are stored in the communal memory. Armah's griotary narrator self-effacingly assumes a common identity both with the specific audience his tale is designed to educate and with the characters of the tale itself; thus the "reciprocity" he preaches is enacted among storyteller, tale, and listeners.

The alienated individuals of the early Armah novels are implicitly reproved and outgrown, as instanced in the exemplary harsh treatment of "the selfish, cut off spirit" Dovi and Abena's selfless sacrifice, which submerges the individual self into the group mentality: "There is no self to save apart from all of us." Furthermore, by an interesting historical sleight-of-hand, Armah is able to grapple with the problems of artistic form confronted by Solo in the previous novel. In *Two Thousand Seasons* he artificially resolves the dilemma of the contemporary African artist by setting his tale in an indeterminate past when the artist was not yet alienated from his society but still immersed in a collective and egalitarian ethos, and then by using the *griot* voice vicariously to advocate communal commitment and popular revolution in a period of fragmentation and elitist privilege. This deliberate polemical strategy carries an urgent ideological message. Armah's newly Africanized narrative mode is, of necessity, a pseudo-oral, simulated exercise in which the traditional communal intimacy of artist and audience is a mere fiction of the plural voice. Lacking a traditional audience, the book is aimed rather at those anglicized Africans who have ventured furthest from what Armah postulates as Africa's true self. His didactic purpose is to cure an errant Africa of its diseased distrust in its own indigenous forms and values, not to reproduce an exact copy of those forms, and there is thus no inconsistency between the form of the book and its initial African publication.

In practice, however, the greatest strengths of the oral tale seldom survive its transposition to written form, and it may be questioned whether, in execution, any real justice is done to Armah's oral models by his peculiar mixture of oracular and idiomatic styles, his portentously inverted vatic utterances, his lusterless demagogic jargon of a precolonial African "Way," and the rhetorical redundancies that result from oral modes of editing (by recantation rather than omission). The presentation of the ideology of the Way is marked by a banality, a vagueness of definition, and a disregard for concrete particulars, which are, in fact, quite alien to the oral tradition. Paradoxically, the dazzling inventiveness and exuberant hyperbole of the *griot* are more in evidence in the scatology of the supposedly Western-oriented first novel than in the affected "griotature" of *Two Thousand Seasons*, where the literary compromise with oral form, far from being enriched by it, results in a restricted and impoverished verbal code.

Two Thousand Seasons succeeds, however, as a kind of therapeutic exorcism, both for its author and for its African readership. The book works from the assumption that the remembrances of oral narrative are no more unreliable than recorded history, especially when the written record is a European one colored by colonial prejudices; the novel argues that a starkly monochromatic portrait of white devilry and black victimization is at least compatible with Africa's narrow experience of the white man as slaver and colonizer—as material and spiritual destroyer. The dogma of the Way follows from the premise that one ethnocentric history, serving indigenous ideological needs, is as good as or better than another that serves alien needs. *Two Thousand Seasons* thus stands, self-consciously, in the same relation to the work of black ethnologists and historians such as Cheikh Anta Diop and Chancellor Williams as Rider Haggard and Joseph Conrad do to the Eurocentric ethnology of Western scholarship. Armah's rhetoric in the prologue, of fragmentation and dismemberment, reminds the reader that it is the fragmented part of Africa's history—the colonial period that cut the continent off from its past—that, until recently, has alone constituted "African History" in Western study.

As Armah's writing heads beyond the tensions and ambivalences of realist fiction into the unifying simplicities of mythology, the growing tendency to blame all Africa's woes on the West stiffens, in *Two Thousand Seasons*, into an explicit racism, which portrays whites as pathologically evil. The systematic direction of hatred at Arab and European "whites" is intended to exorcise the sensations of helplessness induced by colonialism and to clear the air of negative feelings so that the work of construction may begin: it is a healing catharsis that prepares the mind for the creation of radical alternatives to the societies left by the imperialists. These alternatives necessarily involve a large element of hypothesis and wish-fulfillment since they are ideal projections yet to be realized, not experienced life forms to be restored—for example, the ideal of an egalitarian, nonethnic African fraternity, which flies in the face of tribal, social, and national divisions.

Armah does not so much record history as correct and reinvent it: the successful slave rebellion in the second half of the book is history as it might and should have been and as it might yet be if the conditions of the Way are adhered to. This revisionism makes for rousing racial propaganda, but for somewhat unengaging fiction. The principal aim is the remythologizing of history, or what Soyinka has called "the visionary reconstruction of the past for the purposes of a social direction." Armah's ethical manifestos belong to a higher, speculative order of reality and provide a frame of reference from which the prevailing destruction in the existing reality can be condemned and surmounted. As *griot*-like activist, he joins in the struggle between creation and destruction depicted in his tale, paradoxically valorizing new models for progress by inventing a mythical ancestry for them in the form of the doctrine of the Way.

The historical myths of *Two Thousand Seasons* are fleshed out in Armah's next novel, *The Healers* (1978). In this work the prism through which he chooses to refract Africa's destruction, wrought by both external depredations and internal divisions, is the specific historical episode of the fall of the Ashanti empire. The abstract oppositions of *Two Thousand Seasons*—of "Destruction" and "Unconnectedness" to "Creation" and "Reciprocity"—give way to the more substantial one of "Manipulation," as demonstrated by the shal-

Dust jacket for the British edition (1979) of Armah's historical novel based on the dissolution of the Ashanti Empire and its aftermath

low colonial stooge and court intriguer Ababio, and "Inspiration," as practiced by Damfo's outlawed and persecuted healing enclaves. The mission of the latter is to serve as the Ashanti and, ultimately, the African historical conscience and to minister to the wounded Ashanti spirit, torn from its true course by the incursions of colonialism. More concretely than *Two Thousand Seasons*, the novel turns from the pain of the past to a more hopeful future, from the black diaspora to eventual reunification. At its conclusion the historical wheel is brought, perhaps too neatly, to a full circle by the enforced regathering of the black peoples of the world in the white captivity that first sundered them. Anna Nkroma's wishful speculations at the closing dance inject a note of optimistic resolution, albeit forced and unwarranted by events: "Here we healers have been wondering about ways to bring our people together again. And the whites want ways to drive us further apart. Does it not amuse you, that in their wish to drive us apart the whites are actually bringing us work for the future?" Its ending notwith-

standing, *The Healers* is a better-executed novel than *Two Thousand Seasons*. Its wealth of circumstantial detail manages to supply something of the feel of lived history; the solemn racial vituperation of *Two Thousand Seasons* has at least mellowed to sardonic scorn (as in the portraits of John Glover and Garnet Wolseley); and the values and behavioral patterns entailed by a communal ethos are more precisely realized.

The historical novels are an important turning point in Armah's career. His penitential submergence of his earlier isolated artists and visionaries in a communal vision is clearly an attempt to give his art a more democratic basis and seems, on the surface, to be a step toward a more overt espousal of "authentic" African values. The rejection of despair and the rousing call for a halt to the further fragmentation of African society by the doubtful blessings of Western culture are positive gestures in a new direction. If his first novel approximates the "assimilation phase" of Fanon's tripartite scheme for the decolonized writer, insofar as it is partly influenced by the literary techniques of the colonial power, and Armah's next two novels fit into the second phase of disturbance and painful liberation, in which the uprooted writer tries unsuccessfully to recross the immense distance between himself and the African community, then these last two novels clearly subscribe to the militant posture of Fanon's "fighting phase," in which the writer devises a future-oriented revolutionary literature to address and awaken his own people. His novels are also flamboyantly original achievements, the works of a tireless experimenter who never does the same thing twice and who has a genius for finding new mediums for old messages.

The most striking shift of emphasis in these two books lies in their historical outlook, which constitutes a largely negative departure rather than a positive development from early practice. In the complex, shifting vision of *Fragments* and *The Beautyful Ones Are Not Yet Born*, the past is by turns an ideal yardstick, a lost alternative, and a vulnerable mine of temptation, already potent with its own corruption. In the histories, however, vanished cultures have been regimented into the simplistic dogma of a pristine, indigenously African "Way," a harmonious mode of being anterior even to the evils of precolonial society from which colonialism and neocolonialism germinated, and signposted by the mystical healing seers Isanusi and Damfo. This fabricated, ideological "Africanness" is very different from that which resides in the subtextual undercurrents of the first two novels; the fictive richness that arises from the imaginative engagement between myth, ritual, and historical realism is clearly lost in the historical novels when there is a substitution of ideological for historical imagination, and of type for complex consciousness. Since they deliberately mix realism and fantasy in a fictional mode that has its eye as much on the future as on the past, it would be inappropriate to fault Armah's histories for being "unhistorical." But the remoteness of their settings results in those weaknesses that are often the lot of historical fantasy: unreal dialogue, a thinness of characterization, and a general failure to create a convincing, authentic world. Naana's gnomic utterances, in *Fragments*, give her a numinous quality that makes her a stranger to the modern world she finds herself in, but she remains a creature of a solidly historical past, with its own finely delineated customs, rituals, and faiths; her reality is never in doubt.

Isanusi and Damfo are, in comparison, ethereal otherworldly creatures, beings of another order too distant for identification, and their codes of behavior are no more than imaginative hypotheses. The repetition of Isanusi's sacred trinity of neologisms—"Reciprocity," "Connectedness," and "Creation"—is accompanied by so little explication of what they practically involve that they tend to become lifeless verbal tags, self-enclosed abstractions, which leave the Way an essentially unknown quantity. Defined mainly in negatives, as everything that "Destruction" is not, the Way at times seems to be no more than a convenience category for lost virtues, and its rather drab and joyless communalism emerges as something more non-European, and anti-European, than specifically and recognizably African. In fact, certain features, such as the total rejection of family and kin urged upon Dovi and Araba Jesiwa in the name of a higher ideal and the overriding of territorial instincts by abstract ideological loyalties, would appear to be highly unAfrican. Forgotten and not yet rediscovered, the Way, to which the enlightened few act as spiritual guardians, never becomes the code of the community. The latter, in reality, is always heedless of or opposed to the Way, and in its advancement toward the status-seeking materialism of Armah's modern Ghana, the community isolates integrity and intelligence with such ease that the communal narrative view and the validity of a responsible communal ethic are constantly undermined.

Armah's search for a more overtly African focus in his later works is, by virtue of his choice of different genres, necessarily marked by a corresponding loss of subtlety and complexity in both characterization and symbolism. It may yet prove to be the case that this African focus is really most profound and authentic where it is least insistent—when immanent in a fabric of ritual and mythological allusion, as in the early novels— and, conversely, least authentic where it is explicitly formulated and unambiguously schematized into ideology, as in his two historical books. The histories have had a mixed reception. Some Western critics, notably Gerald Moore and Bernth Lindfors, have expressed reservations about them, and there seems to be a consensus in the West that they show signs of waning inspiration and declining artistic achievement. Robert Fraser, on the other hand, has argued strenuously that their apparent radical line of departure is really a curve in an arc of continuous development and achievement from the early novels, and he has fewer reservations about the method and manner by which the beautiful ones are finally "born" in Armah's fiction. Meanwhile, his two historical novels have been widely hailed by African critics as evolving a major new style for African literature.

References:

Chinua Achebe, "Africa and Her Writers," in his *Morning Yet on Creation Day* (London: Heinemann, 1975), pp. 19-29;

Chidi Amuta, "Ayi Kwei Armah and the Mythopoesis of Mental Decolonisation," *Ufahamu*, 10 (Spring 1981): 44-56;

Amuta, "Ayi Kwei Armah, History and 'The Way': The Importance of *Two Thousand Seasons*," *Komparatistische Hefte*, 3 (1981): 79-86;

Amuta, "The Contemporary African Artist in Armah's Novels," *World Literature Written in English*, 21 (Autumn 1982): 467-476;

Sunday Anozie, "Le Nouveau roman africain," *Conch*, 2, no. 1 (1970): 29-32;

Kofi Anyidoho, "Historical Realism and the Visionary Ideal: Ayi Kwei Armah's *Two Thousand Seasons*," *Ufahamu*, 11, no. 2 (1981-1982): 108-130;

Anyidoho, "Literature and African Identity: The Example of Ayi Kwei Armah," *Bayreuth African Studies Series*, 6 (1986): 23-42;

Kofi Awoonor, "Africa's Literature Beyond Politics," *Worldview*, 15, no. 3 (1972): 21-25;

Rand Bishop, "The Beautyful Ones Are Not Yet Born: Armah's Five Novels," *World Literature Written in English*, 21 (Autumn 1982): 531-537;

Y. S. Boafo, "The Nature of Healing in Ayi Kwei Armah's *The Healers*," *Komparatistische Hefte*, 13 (1986): 95-104;

James Booth, "*Why Are We So Blest?* and the Limits of Metaphor," *Journal of Commonwealth Literature*, 15 (August 1980): 50-64;

Gwendolyn Brooks, "African Fragment," in her *Report from Part One* (Detroit: Broadside, 1972), pp. 87-130;

Abena Busia, "Parasites and Prophets: The Use of Women in Ayi Kwei Armah's Novels," in *Ngambika: Studies of Women in African Literature*, edited by Carole Boyce Davies and Anne Adams Graves (Trenton, N.J.: Africa World, 1986), pp. 89-114;

Sarah Chetin, "Armah's Women," *Kunapipi*, 6, no. 3 (1984): 47-57;

John Coates, "The Mythic Undercurrent in *The Beautyful Ones Are Not Yet Born*," *World Litera-*

ture Written in English, 28 (Autumn 1988): 155-170;

Harold Collins, "The Ironic Imagery of Armah's *The Beautyful Ones Are Not Yet Born*: The Putrescent Vision," *World Literature Written in English*, 20 (1971): 37-50;

Rosemary Colmer, "The Human and the Divine: *Fragments* and *Why Are We So Blest?*," *Kunapipi*, 2, no. 2 (1980): 77-90;

Margaret Folarin, "An Additional Comment on Ayi Kwei Armah's *The Beautyful Ones Are Not Yet Born*," *African Literature Today*, 5 (1971): 116-129;

Robert Fraser, "The American Background in *Why Are We So Blest?*" *African Literature Today*, 9 (1978): 39-46;

Fraser, *The Novels of Ayi Kwei Armah: A Study in Polemical Fiction* (London: Heinemann, 1980);

Bodil Folke Frederiksen, " 'The Loved Ones': Racial and Sexual Relations in Ayi Kwei Armah's *Why Are We So Blest?*," *Kunapipi*, 9, no. 2 (1987): 40-49;

Shatto Arthur Gakwandi, *The Novel and Contemporary Experience in Africa* (London: Heinemann, 1977);

Terry Goldie, "A Connection of Images: The Structure of Symbols in *The Beautyful Ones Are Not Yet Born*," *Kunapipi*, 1, no. 1 (1979): 94-107;

Gareth Griffiths, "Structure and Image in Armah's *The Beautyful Ones Are Not Yet Born*," *Studies in Black Literature*, 2, no. 2 (1971): 1-9;

B. M. Ibitokun, "Binary Aesthetics in Armah's Novels," *Commonwealth Essays and Studies*, 9 (Spring 1987): 109-112;

Solomon O. Iyasere, "Cultural Formalism and the Criticism of Modern African Literature," *Journal of Modern African Studies*, 14 (June 1976): 322-330;

D. S. Izevbaye, "Ayi Kwei Armah and the 'I' of the Beholder," in *A Celebration of Black and African Writing*, edited by Bruce King and Kolawole Ogungbesan (Oxford: Oxford University Press, 1975), pp. 232-244;

Izevbaye, "Time in the African Novel," *Journal of Commonwealth Literature*, 17 (August 1982): 74-89;

Joyce Johnson, "The Promethean 'Factor' in Ayi Kwei Armah's *Fragments* and *Why Are We So Blest?*," *World Literature Written in English*, 21 (Autumn 1982): 497-510;

Leonard Kibera, "Pessimism and the African Novelist: Ayi Kwei Armah's *The Beautyful Ones*

Are Not Yet Born," *Journal of Commonwealth Literature*, 14 (August 1979): 64-72;

George Lang, "Text, Identity, and Difference: Yambo Ouologuem's *Le Devoir de violence* and Ayi Kwei Armah's *Two Thousand Seasons*," *Comparative Literature Studies*, 24 (1987): 387-402;

Charles R. Larson, *The Emergence of African Fiction* (Bloomington: Indiana University Press, 1971);

Neil Lazarus, "The Implications of Technique in *The Healers*," *Research in African Literatures*, 13 (Winter 1982): 488-498;

Lazarus, "Pessimism of the Intellect, Optimism of the Will: A Reading of Ayi Kwei Armah's *The Beautyful Ones Are Not Yet Born*," *Research in African Literatures*, 18 (Summer 1987): 137-175;

Lazarus, *Resistance in Postcolonial African Fiction* (New Haven: Yale University Press, 1990);

Bernth Lindfors, "Armah's Histories," *African Literature Today*, 11 (1980): 85-96;

Ken Lipenga, "Malignant Readings: The Case of Armah's Critics," *Journal of Humanities*, 1, no. 1 (1987): 1-19;

Edward Lobb, "Armah's *Fragments* and the Vision of the Whole," *Ariel*, 10 (January 1979): 25-38;

Joseph Lurie, "*Fragments*: Between the Loved Ones and the Community," *Ba Shiru*, 5, no. 1 (1973): 31-41;

Obi Maduakor, "Symbolism in Armah's *Two Thousand Seasons*," *Commonwealth Essays and Studies*, 10 (Spring 1988): 75-79;

Gerald Moore, *Twelve African Writers* (London: Hutchinson, 1980);

Charles Nama, "Ayi Kwei Armah's Utopian World," *World Literature Written in English*, 28 (Spring 1988): 25-35;

Charles Nnolim, "Dialectic as Form: Pejorism in the Novels of Armah," *African Literature Today*, 10 (1979): 207-223;

Emmanuel Obiechina, *Culture, Tradition and Society in the West African Novel* (Cambridge: Cambridge University Press, 1975);

Ode S. Ogede, "Armah as a Literary Critic," *Savanna*, 10, no. 1 (1989): 84-92;

Ogede, "Ayi Kwei Armah in America: The Question of Identity in *Why Are We So Blest?*," *Ariel*, 21 (October 1990): 49-66;

Kolawole Ogungbesan, "Symbol and Meaning in *The Beautyful Ones Are Not Yet Born*," *African Literature Today*, 7 (1975): 93-110;

Isidore Okpewho, "Myth and Modern Fiction: Armah's *Two Thousand Seasons*," *African Literature Today*, 13 (1983): 1-23;

Kofi Owusu, "Armah's F-R-A-G-M-E-N-T-S: Madness as Artistic Paradigm," *Callaloo*, 11, no. 2 (1988): 361-370;

Eustace Palmer, *The Growth of the African Novel* (London: Heinemann, 1979);

Palmer, *An Introduction to the African Novel* (London: Heinemann, 1972);

Richard Priebe, "Demonic Imagery and the Apocalyptic Vision in the Novels of Ayi Kwei Armah," *Yale French Studies*, 53 (1976): 102-136;

Ahmed Saber, "Ayi Kwei Armah's Myth-Making in *The Healers*," in *Literature of Africa and the African Continuum*, edited by Jonathan A. Peters, Mildred P. Mortimer, and Russell V. Linnemann (Washington, D.C.: Three Continents/African Literature Association, 1989), pp. 5-14;

Ato Sekyi-Otu, "Towards Anoa . . . Not Back to Anoa: The Grammar of Revolutionary Homecoming in *Two Thousand Seasons*," *Research in African Literatures*, 18 (Summer 1987): 192-214;

Wole Soyinka, *Myth, Literature and the African World* (Cambridge: Cambridge University Press, 1976);

Taban lo Liyong, "Ayi Kwei Armah in Two Moods," in *Crisis and Creativity in the New Literatures in English*, edited by Geoffrey V. Davis and Hena Maes-Jelinek (Amsterdam: Rodopi, 1990), pp. 171-189;

Derek Wright, "Ayi Kwei Armah and the Significance of His Novels and Histories," *International Fiction Review*, 17 (Winter 1990): 29-40;

Wright, *Ayi Kwei Armah's Africa: The Sources of His Fiction* (London, Munich & New York: Zell, 1989);

Wright, "Critical and Historical Fictions: Robert Fraser's Reading of Ayi Kwei Armah's *The Healers*," *English in Africa*, 15 (May 1988): 71-82;

Wright, "The Early Writings of Ayi Kwei Armah," *Research in African Literatures*, 16 (Winter 1985): 487-513;

Wright, "*Fragments*: The Akan Background," *Research in African Literatures*, 18 (Summer 1987): 176-191;

Wright, "The Metaphysical and Material Worlds: Ayi Kwei Armah's Ritual Cycle," *World Literature Today*, 59 (Summer 1985): 337-342;

Wright, "Orality in the African Historical Novel: Yambo Ouologuem's *Bound to Violence* and Ayi Kwei Armah's *Two Thousand Seasons*," *Journal of Commonwealth Literature*, 23 (August 1988): 91-101;

Wright, "Ritual Modes and Social Models in African Fiction: The Case of Ayi Kwei Armah," *World Literature Written in English*, 27 (Autumn 1987): 195-207;

Wright, "Time and Community: 'Ritual Moments' in *The Beautyful Ones Are Not Yet Born*," *Commonwealth Essays and Studies*, 12 (Spring 1990): 101-114;

Wright, "Totalitarian Rhetoric: Some Aspects of Metaphor in *The Beautyful Ones Are Not Yet Born*," *Critique*, 30 (Spring 1989): 210-220;

Wright, ed., *Critical Perspectives on Ayi Kwei Armah* (Washington, D.C.: Three Continents, 1992).

Kofi Awoonor
(13 March 1935 -)

Kofi Anyidoho
University of Ghana—Legon

BOOKS: *Rediscovery, and Other Poems* (Ibadan: Mbari, 1964);

Night of My Blood (Garden City, N.Y.: Doubleday, 1971);

This Earth, My Brother . . . An Allegorical Tale of Africa (Garden City, N.Y.: Doubleday, 1971; London: Heinemann, 1972);

Come Back, Ghana (Accra: Awoonor, 1972);

Ride Me, Memory (Greenfield Center, N.Y.: Greenfield Review, 1973);

The Breast of the Earth: A Survey of the History, Culture and Literature of Africa South of the Sahara (Garden City, N.Y.: Anchor, 1975);

The House by the Sea (Greenfield Center, N.Y.: Greenfield Review, 1978);

The Ghana Revolution: A Background Account from a Personal Perspective (New York: Oases, 1984);

Until the Morning After: Collected Poems (Greenfield Center, N.Y.: Greenfield Review, 1987; London: Heinemann, 1987; Accra: Woeli, 1987);

Ghana: A Political History from Pre-European to Modern Times (Accra: Sedco, 1990).

OTHER: "Reminiscences of Earlier Days," in *The Writer in Modern Africa*, edited by Per Wästberg (Uppsala, Sweden: Scandinavian Institute of African Studies, 1968; New York: Africana, 1969), pp. 112-118;

Messages: Poems from Ghana, edited by Awoonor and G. Adali-Mortty (London: Heinemann, 1971 [i.e., 1970]);

Ancestral Power and *Lament*, in *Short African Plays*, edited by Cosmo Pieterse (London: Heinemann, 1972);

Guardians of the Sacred Word: Ewe Poetry, translated and edited, with an introduction and notes, by Awoonor (New York: Nok, 1974);

"Tradition and Continuity in African Literature," in *In Person: Achebe, Awoonor, and Soyinka*, edited by Karen L. Morell (Seattle: African Studies Program, Institute for Comparative and Foreign Area Studies, University of Washington, 1975), pp. 133-145; reprinted in *Exile and Tradition: Studies in African and Caribbean Literature*, edited by Rowland Smith (London: Longman & Dalhousie University Press, 1976), pp. 166-172;

"The Writer and Politics in Africa," in *African Cultural and Intellectual Leaders and the Development of the New African Nations*, edited by Robert W. July and Peter Benson (New York & Ibadan: Rockefeller Foundation & Ibadan University Press, 1982).

SELECTED PERIODICAL PUBLICATIONS—
UNCOLLECTED: "Modern African Literature" [series], *Eastern Horizon*, 3 (August 1964): 5-10; *Ghana Radio Review and TV Times* (23

Kofi Awoonor

October 1964): 8; (30 October 1964): 9; (13 November 1964): 10; (20 November 1964): 4; (27 November 1964): 14;

"Fresh Vistas for African Literature," *African Review*, 1 (May 1965): 35-38;

"Changing Role of the African Writer," *Ghana Guardian*, 1 (October 1966): 9-14;

"Culture, Literature and Arts in Africa," *New Time*, 2 (September 1967): 17-26;

"Sources of Ghanaian Literature," *New Time*, 3 (October 1967): 29-30;

"Nationalism: Masks and Consciousness," *Books Abroad*, 45 (Spring 1971): 207-211;

"Africa's Literature Beyond Politics," *Worldview*, 15 (March 1972): 21-25;

"Voyager and the Earth," *New Letters*, 40 (Autumn 1973): 85-93;

"Comes the Voyager at Last" [excerpt], *Okike*, 7 (1975): 31-56;

"The Poem, the Poet and the Human Condi-

tion," *Asemka*, 5 (September 1979): 1-23;

"Caliban Answers Prospero: The Dialogue between Western and African Literature," *Obsidian*, 7 (Summer-Winter 1981): 75-98;

"The Imagery of Fire: A Critical Assessment of the Poetry of Joe de Graft," *Okike*, 18 (1981): 70-79;

"A Servant of the Ghanaian Dream," *South* (June 1985): 97.

Kofi Awoonor (formerly George Awoonor-Williams) has written something noteworthy in almost all the major literary genres. As a poet his name is to be found high on the list of the best contemporary African poets. His novel *This Earth, My Brother* (1971) continues to attract critical attention. His major critical work, *The Breast of the Earth* (1975), is widely used as a standard introductory text on African literature and is frequently cited in African literature scholarship. All in all, his work as a creative writer, critic, and translator provides a clear demonstration of the enduring power and beauty of the African oral-poetic tradition.

Awoonor, born to Atsu E. and Kosiwo Nyidevu Awoonor on 13 March 1935, spent his earliest years in Wheta, Ghana, his birthplace, before moving with his family to Dzodze, some eleven miles away, where in 1939 he enrolled at the Roman Catholic Mission School. In 1943 he was transferred to the Presbyterian Mission School in the sea-and-lagoon town of Keta, where Awoonor spent the greater part of his youth. He had his secondary-school education there, at the Zion College of West Africa (1951-1954), before moving on to Achimota College in Accra for his so-called sixth form year (1955-1956). During these early years, he developed a strong attachment to the land, exploring its physical and human geography with an intimacy that was to leave an enduring mark on his sense of place. In much of his work Awoonor evokes these scenes of childhood with a tenderness so lyrical that its echoes remain with the reader for a long time. But there was something there more than the landscape, deeper than the lagoon and the sea, larger even than the people, a special factor that was to play a central role in Awoonor's creative universe, as he makes clear in the essay "Reminiscences of Earlier Days" (in *The Writer in Modern Africa*, 1968):

Their world was my real world of consciousness, of growth. It was formed in mysteries about life;

it had to do with invisible living phenomena that pertained to everyday existence. I do not rationalize this world now, because I have returned to it, to the underlying energy that sustained it. The principle that I believe was at its base was *continuity*. . . .

The magical and the mysterious relationships defining only the very simple and mundane have, beyond time and place, their anchorage in *words*. Our people say the mouth that eats salt cannot utter falsehood. For the mouth is the source of sacred words, of oaths, promises, prayer and assertions of our being. When the mouth says it, then it must be true. Truth is *being*, presence, affirmation. This is the source of my poetry, the origin of my commitment—the magic of the word in the true poetic sense.

The recurring pleasure of reading and hearing Awoonor's best poetry is that of listening to a voice deeply rooted in the secret pains and pleasures of the earth. His poetry constantly seeks out the magic of the word. It is primarily a poetry of the speaking voice, taking readers into its confidence, sometimes gently stirring troubled mental rivers, and sometimes complaining of neglect and waywardness, provoking shame out of hiding places, or soothing hurt with wisdom as ancient as the origins of death and life. The poet laments, complains, praises, blames, curses, and laughs, almost always in a voice whose musical rhythms crisscross with the heart's beatings and the sea's motions.

The constant search for new beginnings that is so much a part of Awoonor's creative universe may be an inevitable factor of the special circumstances in which his literary career began. Awoonor entered the University College of the Gold Coast, now the University of Ghana—Legon, in 1957 on the eve of Ghana's independence. He earned a B.A. with honors in English in 1960, the year in which Ghana became a full republic. After graduation he first worked as a lecturer in English at the University of Ghana from 1960 to 1963, then began work as a research fellow at the Institute of African Studies, Legon. The institute had opened a few years earlier, but it was not formally dedicated until 1963. On that occasion, Kwame Nkrumah, first president of the new first African republic, gave specific directives to the fellows, such as Awoonor, as to what their pursuits ought to be:

In studying the arts . . . you must not be content with the accumulation of knowledge about the arts. Your researches must stimulate creative activity; they must contribute to the development of the arts in Ghana and in other parts of Africa; they must stimulate the birth of a specifically African literature, which, exploring African themes and the depth of the African soul, will become an integral portion of a general world literature. It would be wrong to make this a mere appendage of world literature. . . .

In this way the Institute can serve the needs of the people by helping to develop new forms of dance and drama, of music and creative writing, that are at the same time closely related to our Ghanaian traditions and express the ideas and aspirations of our people at this critical stage in our history. This should lead to new strides in our cultural development.

Awoonor's direct participation in the artistic traditions of his people was given great impetus by the vigorous national cultural programs that came with the general independence movement in Ghana. Nkrumah was a great lover of the arts and took personal interest in several artistic programs and projects. In an old issue of the *Ghana Cultural Review* (July-September 1965) there is a picture of Nkrumah chatting with Awoonor, Kwesi Brew, and others at the newly built Ghana Drama Studio following the performance of a play. The president was the patron of the theater group in which both Awoonor and Brew played key roles. It was perhaps inevitable that Awoonor's preoccupations as an artist should be infused with a deep commitment to cultural nationalism. He was part of a generation of people of artistic talent and skill who rose to meet the cultural challenges of Ghana's independence movement with its clear emphasis on what came to be known as "African personality." Other creative writers who were part of that movement include Efua Sutherland, G. Adali-Mortty, and Joe de Graft.

In a way, Awoonor was doubly prepared for his task: the national cultural movement helped define his concerns and provided a supportive climate for his creativity, and his family background and childhood cultural experiences had mapped out the paths he could most fruitfully follow. "I grew up," he writes, "on the lap of my grandmother Afedomeshi, a great singer of dirge songs. . . . Born into a community of drummers, dancers, and singers, my earliest recollections of Ewe oral poetry became the basic inspiration of my earliest writings" (*The Breast of the*

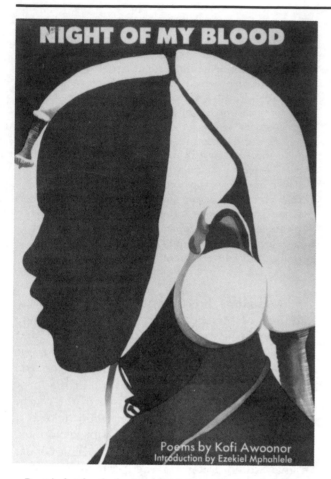

Dust jacket for the book in which Awoonor introduced his "collage" technique

Earth). For Awoonor, then, poetry became an old family heirloom that could be re-created and fed into Ghana's and Africa's cultural heritage. Awoonor began with Ewe oral tradition, but he did not end there. It was a point of departure, to other places, other people, and other times, though there is almost always in his poems a return to his primal origins and sources of inspiration.

The most clearly recognized specific point of departure for Awoonor's poetic career, one that he has himself frequently acknowledged and even analyzed, is the dirge tradition, especially the songs of Vinoko Akpalu, the greatest of all dirge composers among the Anlo Ewe. Indeed, Awoonor explains that many of his early poems are built around central thematic lines directly translated from Akpalu. The best known of these poems is Awoonor's "Songs of Sorrow," in which not just a line or two but whole segments are drawn from more than one Akpalu song and worked into the core of especially the first part of Awoonor's poem.

The poem opens with a complaint against Dzogbese Lisa, the Ewe equivalent of the Igbo's Chi, a personal god of destiny and dispenser of life's fortunes and misfortunes, made familiar to students of African literature by Chinua Achebe. The poet-persona's life road has taken him among thorns, "the sharps of the forest." The first stanza closes with an almost direct translation of lines from Akpalu: "The affairs of this world are like the chameleon faeces / Into which I have stepped / When I clean it cannot go." The first of these lines slightly alters Akpalu's original statement "Xexeamenyawo zu ganami mefa," where he sings not of chameleon (*agama*) but of hyena (*ganami*) feces. Ewe observation of the natural environment holds that the hyena's feces carries a stench that outlasts the fragrance of all perfumes. Awoonor's slight alteration endows the lines with an added sense of mystery, a state of almost mythical defilement.

The second stanza opens with yet another Akpalu original: "Xexeame fe dzogui dzie mele," translated as "I am on the world's extreme corner," offering the ultimate image of loneliness and personal misery. Later in the poem the persona's misfortunes are carefully itemized, among them a situation that is generally acknowledged in the tradition as the most severe of all calamities: no sons to give him a decent burial; no daughters to wail over his dead body. Akpalu's particular sense of loss and loneliness, which informs many of his laments, derives from the claim that he had no child of his own. He could not expect his individual line of descent to survive his death. This sense of desolation is captured in what has become a central Awoonor motif: the image of a fallen homestead surrounded by termite-eaten fences.

A dramatic change occurs in the second half of "Songs of Sorrow." The poet personalizes his lament by directly invoking deceased members of his own family, and the tone of lament finally gives way to a burst of angry pleas to his ancestors, including his maternal grandfather, whose last name is Awoonor's middle name, Nyidevu. The rest of the poem reminds one of the content and style of the traditional Ewe libation-prayer text, often part plea and part complaint with occasional threats. The speaker does not only ask for blessings from the ancestral spirits but also accuses them of neglecting their offspring, and he demands to know "Why they idle there / While we suffer / and eat sand." One special power of traditional oral poetry so well captured here is Awoonor's use of a series of evocative images and proverbial statements that strike home with the sharpness of anger and pain.

While "Songs of Sorrow" may best illustrate the tendency in Awoonor's early phase of borrowing liberally from Akpalu and other traditional sources, there are few other poems in which there is such extensive use of traditional lines. Significantly Awoonor omits "Songs of Sorrow" from all his poetry collections published to date, despite the poem's great popularity among students of African poetry. It remains an anthology piece of disputed authorship (among certain critics).

Poems such as "Songs of Sorrow" are directly and closely worked out from their traditional models, but others take off from the dirge form and mode and then move on into new areas of experience; in the process, they define those imaginative extensions of the traditional medium that have allowed Awoonor's voice to provide the peculiar experience of listening to several voices coalesce into a harmonious sensation of echoes of various times and places. Such is the overall impression left by even his first collection, *Rediscovery, and Other Poems* (1964).

For a first book *Rediscovery* is remarkable for its confident handling of metaphor, thematic consistency, and pure lyricism. The title piece sums up the basic thematic thrust of the volume, the theme of tradition and continuity that has so far remained a constant and central factor in Awoonor's work. A poem of great evocative beauty, "Rediscovery" is at once nostalgic for the warmth and security of childhood joys, and self-assured with the solemn wisdom of knowing that life changes only to bring one back to one's various points of departure. The speaker dries his tears on the shores of childhood, shores that can exist in memory only, because they have been eaten away by the sea. He recalls the fishermen carrying their nets home, the sea gulls returning to their island, and the laughter of children receding at night. Suddenly his voice offers the pleasant realization that "there shall still linger here the communion we forged / the feast of oneness whose ritual we partook of." The eternal gateman closes the cemetery doors and sends the late mourners away, away from death and back to life, to "the new chorus of our forgotten comrades / and the halleluyahs of our second selves."

"Desire," the opening piece in *Rediscovery*, presents the poet in the image of a diviner; this is a culturally and biographically relevant point,

since the name Awoonor is generally reserved for diviners. In "Desire" Awoonor Bokor, the diviner character, begins to probe the mysteries of the herb pot, pursuing his calling in the direction of the single quest that simultaneously leads into the past and into the future as a way of coming to terms with the present. His findings contradict those who see the past only in terms of travails and the future as filled with promised glories. In the end, the unfathomable mysteries usher readers into "the place of skulls," where the speaker finds himself reclining in an armchair, supervising the ceremony of the lost souls that would presume to be his pallbearers.

The quest motif and the diviner's revelations recur in several other poems in *Rediscovery*. In "Salvation" the speaker sets out by lantern light, past the "narrow strip / That is now the shores of childhood," past the sea and the funeral drums with their sounds of "Doom, Doom, Doom" still ringing in his ears, until he lands on far-off shores. But he has to return and "find . . . salvation here on the shore, asleep." There is a familiar revelation awaiting all "Exiles" stranded on alien shores (in the poem of that name): the ultimate need for return, tedious, pain-filled return to "the dunghill that has mounted on their birth place":

> They committed the impiety of self-deceit
> Slashed, cut and wounded their souls
> And left the mangled remainders in manacles . . .
> Lost souls, lost souls, lost souls that are still at the
> gate.

In most of these poems about the eternal quest for recovery from disastrous adventures in alien and hostile worlds, the tone is often a mixture of pity, muted sorrow, and gentle humor. In some cases, however, the humor yields to an ironic, subversive use of biblical language to debunk the alien system that seems to exercise such strong but generally injurious influence on the traditional culture for which this poet is a self-elected spokesman. "Easter Dawn" illustrates this tendency. In "We Have Found a New Land" Awoonor's sense of humor becomes a sharp, pointed weapon directed with devastating effect at the blundering self-deception of the "smart professionals in three piece / Sweating their humanity away in driblets." In their anxiety to be seen "in the best company," these lost souls have become ghosts walking through limbo toward hell's gate to plead for admission, having effectively "abjured the magic of being themselves." The two final lines of this poem represent a carefully balanced metaphorical statement and definition of Awoonor's poetic quest and its fundamental guiding principle: "Reaching for the Stars we stop at the house of Moon / And pause to relearn the wisdom of our fathers." The determination is to forge new paths into the future, but always firmly guided by a clear knowledge of the achievements and failures of the past. For Awoonor the poet, this is no abstract principle. It must find immediate realization in the true, original, creative, poetic voice, such as in "What Song Shall We Sing?," "My God of Songs Was Ill," and "The Return," where he seeks "the promise of a rebirth." That rebirth of the true poetic self must come not through a mere sentimental or nostalgic wish but by full participation in the rituals of the ancestral tradition, enacted in "My God of Songs Was Ill," at the end of which the poet's god bursts into "new strong songs."

Though a first book, *Rediscovery* is not the work of a novice. It offers the strong, self-confident voice of an artist who had realized at the outset of his career that he might be about to make a false start, so he took the precaution of serving his apprenticeship by drawing on the experts in the arts of eloquence in his own tradition.

Though much is made of Awoonor's tendency toward the elegiac, mainly because of the influence of Akpalu and the dirge tradition, the tone and mood of his laments are not necessarily of the heavy, brooding kind. Even in the work of Akpalu, the voice of sorrow frequently is superseded by that of critical denunciation and satirical comment. There are many of these qualities in Awoonor's poetry, even the early work.

"The Weaver Bird" (in *Rediscovery*) probably his most popular anthology piece, moves away from the strict lament over lost scenes of childhood, neglected gods, and homesteads into the contemporary historical reality of Europe's assault on Africa's treasures of the land and the mind. In the image of the weaver bird, notorious for its colonizing crusades, Europe's presence in Africa is sketched in sharp outline as a sinister despoiler of homesteads and sacred grounds. Africa also comes in for blame, because of its bemused indulgence of the arrogant visitors. Too late Africa realizes the tragic error when "the weaver returns in the guise of the owner / Preaching salvation to us who owned the house." Awoonor's use of the past tense for the African people's ownership of the house alerts one to the

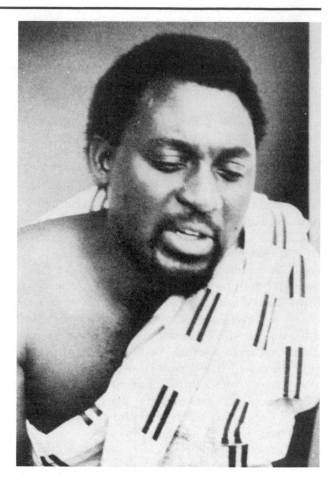

Awoonor in 1971 (photograph by Willis Bell)

dilemma of a people reduced to servitude on their own soil. But the tragedy is seen as only a passing moment. The people are not to be dispossessed so easily; they could not be permanently persuaded into accepting false salvation from an ungrateful visitor. They would not join the communion of lost souls:

> Its sermon is the divination of ourselves
> And our horizons limit at its nest
> But we cannot join the prayers and answers of the
>   communicants.
> We look for new homes every day,
> For new altars we strive to re-build
> The old shrines defiled from the weaver's excrement.

This denunciation of Europe's presumptions and impositions on the will of Africa is remarkably calm but nonetheless biting. Its total effect is that of presenting a person of confidence whose anger refuses to yield to screams and hysteria. Later, in Awoonor's "Songs of Abuse" (from *Ride Me, Memory*, 1973), gently biting satire gives way to direct verbal assault of the most provocative kind.

In 1965 Awoonor quit his research fellowship at the Institute of African Studies to become the managing director of the Ghana Film Industries Corporation, a post he held until 1967, when he left on a Longman Fellowship to study for an M.A. in English at the University of London. He left Britain for the United States in 1968, taking an assistant professorship at the State University of New York at Stony Brook. While teaching at Stony Brook, he also enrolled for the Ph.D. in comparative literature, completing the program in 1972. He served until 1975 as chairman of the comparative literature program at Stony Brook and also held visiting professorships at the University of Texas at Austin; Queens College, New York; and the New School of Social Research, New York.

Awoonor's return to Ghana in 1975 brought to an end the most productive years of his literary career to date. His time in the United States not only furthered his distinguished academic career but was a period of vigorous and varied creativity, with several books published and at least three other manuscripts completed.

The harvest of these American years began with the publication of *Messages: Poems from Ghana*, a 1970 anthology he coedited with Adali-Mortty (with 1971 on the title page); *Night of My Blood* (1971); and *This Earth, My Brother*. *Messages* remains the only major anthology of Ghanaian poetry, although it omits all the older poets of the early days of the independence movement, such as Michael Dei Anang and Raphael G. Armattoe. However, this limitation is somewhat compensated for by the full representation the book gives to the generation of literary talent that emerged as the cultural voices of independence. Several went on to become major talents in contemporary African literature: Joe de Graft, A. Kayper Mensah, Ayi Kwei Armah, Kwesi Brew, Amu Djoleto, Cameron Duodu, and Efua Sutherland.

Night of My Blood deserves its reputation as Awoonor's most important collection of poems so far. It incorporates most of the poems of *Rediscovery*. This means that one needs only to read *Night of My Blood* to have a good grasp of Awoonor's poetic development up to that point. The major thematic preoccupations remain unchanged. However, a firmer grasp of style and technique has entered his poetry. The general impression is that of a poet who has digested the work of older poets enough to sing in a strong, clear voice rooted in tradition and yet with unexpected variations and changes in mood and tone.

The voice of lament is still evident in *Night of My Blood*, but the lament is no longer so much for neglected gods as it is for the short-lived joys of the independence dream. The language itself is no longer under the heavy and direct influence of Akpalu's style, though the imprint of the traditional models is in evidence. "More Messages," for instance, is cast in the lament mode, retaining much of the authentic mood and proverbial style of the traditional dirge, yet exploring the idiom of new as well as old experiences. The eternal search for the "lonely miracle of redemption" finds the speaker crawling and sitting by the roadside,

> breaking
> the palm kernel, eating of the white
> with the visiting mice
> throwing the chaff to the easterly wind.

Unlike the traditional dirge singer, however, this speaker would not look to death as the end of his sorrow. Despite the countless agonies of the journey, the ferrymen with their heavy cargoes of flesh, and the hunter "beaten by desert rain and thistle" returning home with an empty gun, regardless of past failures and present doubts, the aim is not the quiet and loneliness of the grave but a firm rededication to life and its promise of new seasons of good harvest. This is no time for unending tears.

A sense of increasing urgency has entered Awoonor's poetry at this point, even in poems cast in the dirge mode, such as "At the Gates," and especially in sections of the longer poems that dominate the second half of the collection. To register the correct effect and set the right mood and pace, he begins to explore more consciously the rhythms of the drums and the dance. He has become a choreographer, a mover; readers seem to work out the dance sequence with him:

> No, no your hands must encircle the invisible.
> Your hips must harmonize with your feet.
> Your chest must beat the time.
> Yes, my dance, my movement,
> They must tell the primal story
> of birth waters, blood, umbilical cords
> in defiance of moon marks at every turn.
> Yes, my dance, my movement
> They are not steps, no:

Dust jacket for Awoonor's only novel, which he calls a "prose poem"

they are journeys, roads, avenues, boulevards
Dream boulevards of life incarnate.

In the rhythms of the dance, he explores the regions of mystery beyond the physical world and the self in search of the sustaining energy that governs continuity in a universe forever threatened by fragmentation and disintegration.

Another significant development that enters Awoonor's poetry in *Night of My Blood* is the technique of the collage. Ezekiel Mphahlele, in his introduction to the original Doubleday edition of the collection, describes such a style in terms of a musical medley. The technique operates in two main ways. At one level, Awoonor pulls together themes, images, lines, and line sequences from several of his earlier poems. At another level, he draws on a baffling range of apparently disparate and fragmentary experiences, historical, mythical, or purely symbolic. All these scattered bits are then pasted onto a wide canvas and are held together by a coherent rhythm and movement, the essential unity of which is sometimes registered in certain basic thematic lines repeated in a carefully regulated pattern. The poems in which this technique is best seen are necessarily long, among them "Night of My Blood," "I Heard a Bird Cry," "This Earth, My Brother," and "Hymn to My Dumb Earth." The title piece takes for its canvas the history of the migratory journeys of the Ewe, recounting the terrors of that journey, the rituals and unfailing endurance of the trekkers, and their eventual triumph over all the tribulations of that search for a new home. This basic model is, however, re-created as the history of all the people of the land in its new geopolitical arrangement, embracing all of modern Ghana at one level and all of Africa at another level of poetic symbolism.

"Night of My Blood" recounts much precolonial history, and "Hymn to My Dumb Earth" presents the terrors, triumphs, and lessons of postindependence experience. This hymn bursts out suddenly, then calms down into the rather plaintive sounds of George Frideric Handel's *Messiah* (1742) and the Ghanaian national anthem. The various contradictions built into the independence experience are effectively captured in the various voices, tunes, and rhythms. The Christian, biblical voice blends into an uneasy harmony with the rhythms of jazz, dirge, and political demagoguery. Names, sounds, events, poetic lines, and passages are freely evoked from the en-

84

tire range of African and Western experience. There is a tone of irreverence lurking behind some of the biblical invocations: "O, Come all ye faithless"; "Our Father who art in heaven / do whatever that pleases you." The satiric tone foregrounds fundamental contradictions and blunders:

A new Constitution is drawn up
filled with webs of brilliant arguments
and quotations from Plato's Republic.
Africans know about such Grecian matters.

Everything comes from God.

In the end readers are compelled to query the truth of this last statement, which runs as a disturbing refrain throughout the entire hymn. Perhaps God does not have to take the blame for it all. The collage technique becomes an appropriate metaphor for a bewildering experience that failed to produce an expected harmony.

This technique is also the central idiom for the narrative discourse of *This Earth, My Brother*. Of all his creative writing outside of poetry, Awoonor is best known for this novel. Described by the author as a "prose poem" and subtitled *An Allegorical Tale of Africa*, this work has a complex structure, and although it is generally considered a novel, none of the conventional terms of classification fits it perfectly. The discourse unfolds at two levels, each representing a different kind of consciousness, a different kind of reality. The first level is that of the narrative proper, the story of Amamu, the protagonist. It is also the story of the society that makes and unmakes Amamu. This is the level of everyday, mundane reality, a reality in which the individual and society are both threatened by physical and psychic disintegration. At this level the narrative is carried by a normal prose style.

It is on the second level that this work is probably more interesting to the analyst and certainly more challenging. Made up of the prologue and the "(a)" segments of each chapter up to 12, this level draws readers into the world of dream and myth from which one can look back on and make better sense of the disturbing reality of the first level. The "(a)" segments are poetic interludes that draw upon a variety of images and powerful symbols of myth and ritual to provide a running commentary and a larger vision concerning the "revolting malevolence" of the main narrative. Chapter 2, for instance, follows Amamu through a typical working day of despair, among helpless crowds of citizens whose rights the makers of laws seem determined to ignore or frustrate, among an army of beggars and the unemployed, and among the negligent and decadent elite into whose hands the fate of the independent state of Ghana has fallen. At the end of it all, he parks his car "near a forgotten refuse dump" and disappears into the darkness of a house "painted in a dim blue."

Then comes the poetic interlude and commentary of "Chapter 2 (a)," sketching in carefully selected images the building of the nation and structural weaknesses that clearly portend its imminent collapse:

Bricks cement mortars pounding. A nation is building. Fart-filled respectable people toiling in moth-eaten files to continue where the colonialists and imperialists left off. . . .
Woman, behold thy son; son, behold thy mother. This revolting malevolence is thy mother. She begat thee from her womb after a pregnancy of a hundred and thirteen years. She begat thee after a long parturition, she begat you into her dust, and you woke up after the eighth day screaming on a dunghill.

The pregnancy of 113 years represents the period of formal British rule over the Gold Coast. It began with the signing of Commander Hill's "Bond of 1844" and ended with Nkrumah's declaration of independence on 6 March 1957. Newly independent Ghana, then, is that baby screaming on the dunghill. But the dunghill that appears again and again throughout this work is more than a symbol of death and decay. It is a fertile patch, transforming rot into manure. The dunghill is the paradoxical symbol of life through death, of regeneration through degeneration. This paradox is central to the theme of *This Earth, My Brother*. The basic picture of Amamu's society is one of rapid degeneration of the dreams of independence, but the poetic interludes lift readers above the decay of dunghills, offering lavender mists and other colors of beauty seen in the eternal butterfly of rainbow seasons, in the regenerative capacity of even the dunghill and, above all, of the mythical woman of the sea.

The central myth of *This Earth, My Brother* is the myth of the mermaid. Known in West African mythology as Mammy Water, she is the magic woman, healer, lover, and spiritual guardian who takes the men she befriends into the depths and mysteries of the sea, prepares them to be strong, endows them with spiritual healing powers, and then sends them back into society to offer hope and a cure for the society and the individual's various ailments. The mythical woman of the sea first enters the story early in the prologue; she is sitting on the protagonist's lap, dripping water, with her eyes rolling in circles of little fires. She is also breathing gold and cinnamon pollen and shedding tears of moon dust.

It is within the context of this myth that Amamu's career falls into a coherent, meaningful pattern. His despair and sudden disintegration have not often received favorable analysis among critics. A typical objection is raised by Atukwei Okai, who puts him in the same corner with the unnamed protagonist of Ayi Kwei Armah's *The Beautyful Ones Are Not Yet Born* (1968) and accuses them both of having a special disease called "Amamuosis," moral impotence. However, seen against the background of the woman-of-the-sea legend, Amamu's career suddenly begins to assume a more positive significance. His lonely, though haughty, initial stand against the general corruption and lack of energy in the ruling elite offers some hope for the future, however bleak and uncertain. Even his ultimate despair, madness, and death by suicide become necessary stages of a regenerative process of nature that turns the dunghill into a fertile patch and death into a gateway to new beginnings. Amamu's death at the scene of his childhood dreams is a return to his eternal woman of the sea, the mythical principle of creativity and healing that must come to refertilize a despoiled earth.

The regenerative capacities of the feminine principle, fully established in Awoonor's novel, contrast sharply with the satirical evocation of the potentially destructive masculine principle in one of the two short plays Awoonor contributed to Cosmo Pieterse's *Short African Plays* (1972). *Ancestral Power* is remarkable for its striking use of metaphorical and proverbial language, and for the brief but powerful sketch of its main character. Akoto is typical of the domineering male with criminal tendencies, and he hides behind frequent and possibly empty invocations of mystical ancestral powers, a mere cover for an unacceptable aggressive display of manliness against his family and the community. His elaborate boasting of how he called lightning down on his father-in-law's house is brought to an abrupt end when the police arrest and charge him with "arson, assault and battery." His final plea is not deserving even of a frightened child, let alone of ancestral power: "I have taken purgative; I drank it this morning. Please."

Awoonor's second play, *Lament*, is a short piece of poetic drama in which three voices speak in passages from some of Awoonor's poems. The First Voice, female, is assigned segments of "Lament of the Silent Sister," the poem dedicated to the distinguished poet Christopher Okigbo in *Night of My Blood*. The sudden, violent end to Okigbo's brief career is captured in sharp, startling imagery: "He was erect like the totem pole of his household / He burned and blazed for an ending." The two male voices in the play draw mostly on passages from "I Heard a Bird Cry," a long poem of which Awoonor has written in *The Breast of the Earth*, "I tried to capture a total mood of the Ewe lament, its stock images, its flow and direction, its ability to digress . . . and above all its persistent preoccupation with the human condition."

A remarkable change occurs in Awoonor's poetry in his third collection, *Ride Me, Memory*, mainly through the widening of the thematic and stylistic range of his poetry. There is no clean break with earlier preoccupations. The dirge mode and style, for instance, continue in the final section, "African Memories." The poem "To Those Gone Ahead" is one of the most lyrical laments in the entire Awoonor corpus. But *Ride Me, Memory*, as a whole, moves away from the lament into other areas of the oral-poetry tradition and into artistic traditions outside Awoonor's immediate ancestral heritage. The collection, significantly, is dedicated to "Herbert Weisinger, Frank Platt, Calvin Canton, and all messengers of love and peace." The work is a testimony to the commonality of human suffering, struggle, and aspiration, compelling a celebration of various successes, however small. Quite understandably, Awoonor displays deep sympathy for the experiences of the African people of the diaspora, incorporating several lines and themes from African-American literature and music into his poetic sketches. A particularly dramatic dimension of the poetry of *Ride Me, Memory* is Awoonor's use of the hilarious poetry of abuse. In "Songs of Abuse" he draws directly on the techniques of traditional Ewe *halo*, a special type of poetic insult organized as a contest involving two sections of the same town or neighboring villages. A musical-poetry group on each side composes and publicly performs songs of insult directed against members of the opposing group. The public performance is often attended by some of those being as-

Awoonor circa 1972, the year he published his political essay Come Back, Ghana

saulted in the songs, whose turn to perform will fall on another day.

Following the example of the *halo* poets, Awoonor begins "To Stanislaus the Renegade" with an open address. This is no satire or indirect attack. The subject of the verbal attack must be identified and made known to all. Before launching into his streams of insult, Awoonor, like his ancestral masters, attempts to justify his use of insult, his *maledicta*, by recounting how Stanislaus has provoked him with shameless behavior and ingratitude. Three types of insult commonly encountered in *halo* are all used by Awoonor. First there is insult directed at physical ugliness and lack of personal hygiene. Stanislaus, readers are told, stinks so badly that "The jail [he] occupied in Poonaville, Tennessee / was burnt down after [he] escaped; / They could not eradicate the smell." The second type of insult, that directed at immoral behavior, is scattered throughout the poem. Stanislaus is a frequenter of brothels, a thief, a cheat, and a drug trafficker. The third and probably most hilarious and pleasantly shocking type of abuse is the use of obscenities. The poet concludes his song of abuse with another usual feature of *halo*, the boast or the challenge, challenging his renegade

comrade to single combat, and boasting of how he, too, has come of age.

To place this kind of poetry, as well as Awoonor's laments, in their proper context, one needs to look at his work as a critic and translator of the Ewe oral-poetry tradition. In *Guardians of the Sacred Word: Ewe Poetry* (1974) Awoonor presents translations of dirge and *halo* poetry by three major oral poets. His twenty-five-page introduction is rich in its grasp of the essentials of the Ewe oral tradition and the natural and human environment in which this poetry thrives. Of the three poets, the oldest and best known, Akpalu, Awoonor's primary model, stands out as a man whose creative industry is credited by the Anlo Ewes with the establishment of the traditional funeral songs performed at almost all funerals in the area. His preeminence, even after his death, confounds the long-held notion that oral tradition does not leave much room for the flowering of individual creativity. The other two poets, Komi Ekpe and Amega Dunyo, are representatives of *halo*. They are also equally gifted in the lament, ably balancing their devastating vitriolic compositions against the somber, reflective, and philosophically deep mood of songs of sorrow. Literature in translation is often a poor substitution for the original, but the songs in *Guardians of the Sacred Word* often come across with freshness and power.

In *The Breast of the Earth* Awoonor makes a substantial contribution to the critical evaluation of Africa's vast literary heritage. Subtitled *A Survey of the History, Culture and Literature of Africa South of the Sahara*, this 387-page study (based on Awoonor's doctoral dissertation) makes a largely successful attempt at providing a unified view of Africa's varied forms and traditions of literary expression. It demonstrates an important principle that has informed most of Awoonor's own work, the principle of creative continuity between oral forms and written literature. Unlike most other surveys of African literature, Awoonor's study goes beyond a mere mentioning or brief sketch of oral tradition as the major origin of written African literature. In seeking to establish how literature in Africa is a creatively continuous art beginning with the oral narrative, Awoonor dwells at length on oral tradition in its various manifestations, then moves on to literature written in African languages, before finally turning to contemporary literature written in European languages that were imposed by the colonial order. Probably the richest part of the book is chapter 12, where Awoonor discusses "contemporary samples of English-speaking African poetry," citing Mazisi Kunene, Okigbo, and himself as examples of poets writing in an English that speaks with a voice grounded in the fertile soil of Africa's cultural heritage.

With all these achievements behind him, Awoonor returned to Ghana in 1975 to a senior lectureship in the English department of the University of Cape Coast. The confused political situation in Ghana soon engulfed him. He was arrested for suspected subversion on New Year's Eve 1975 and detained in solitary confinement without any charges or immediate trial. Eight months later he was finally brought to trial and charged with allegedly aiding Brig. Alf Kattah to escape lawful arrest for alleged involvement in a coup plot. In a trial that lasted two months, the prosecution failed to prove Awoonor knew that his friend was a fugitive from justice when he drove him to the Togo border town of Aflao. He was nevertheless found guilty and sentenced to twelve months. He was released on bail the same evening, ten months after his arrest, and never returned to jail. His sentence was formally rescinded in April 1979. Awoonor tells the full story of that experience in *The Ghana Revolution*

(1984), and the experience of political detention inspired several of the poems in *The House by the Sea* (1978), the house in the title being the Ussher Fort Prison in Accra, the old slave fort in which he served his term.

The House by the Sea suffers from a lack of the usual lyrical evenness associated with Awoonor at his best. It does, however, contain several pieces of great lyrical power, among them the two poems dedicated to Pablo Neruda, as well as "Departure and Prospect," "On Being Told of Torture," and the final piece, "The Wayfarer Comes Home." But too many of the poems in the collection are fragmentary. This is especially true of those in part 2, "Homecoming," which are poems that were originally written on toilet paper in prison and hurriedly smuggled out. In any case, even in their fragmentary state, the poems make a significant statement on the creative mind under extreme conditions of repression. They are a testimony to the spirit of endurance.

The House by the Sea presents poems in which Awoonor's political vision obtains a sense of urgency. Almost absent are poems in which he chooses only to reflect with a sense of detachment on politics, history, and culture. Words seem inspired by a larger vision, an experience of political repression and cultural genocide as contemporary, global realities, so pressing that the poet must not only reflect and complain but also must define and urge action, in word and deed. In the face of the brutal experience of Neruda and his contemporaries in Latin America, Awoonor sees the need to celebrate the revolutionary creative spirit that has the courage to defy political repression, even to the death. In the face of such repression and assassination squads, the greatest thing is for the human spirit to endure and identify itself with that global "octopus of this undying liberty." The call for perseverance in the face of death reaches a climactic moment in "On Being Told of Torture," one of Awoonor's most successful attempts at confronting the raw brutality of political torture. It is easy for the spirit to break once the body is beaten into submission, but he calls for the determination to "make a reckoning in the red bright book / of history." Political justice can only come by the miracle of one's own hands. Awoonor, like Wole Soyinka and Ngugi wa Thiong'o, two other African writers with personal testimonies of political detention without trial, has provided, in *The House by the Sea*, a record of the need for even the poet to transform his dreams into visions and his visions

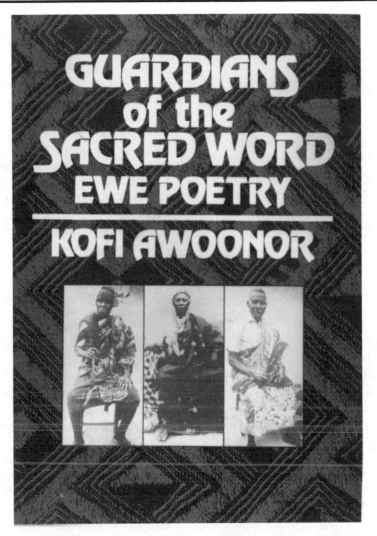

Dust jacket for Awoonor's translation of works by three poets of the Ewe oral-poetry tradition

into the courage to wake his society with warning shots fired through "the barrel of the pen."

Awoonor's recent book of poems *Until the Morning After* (1987), which won the 1988 Commonwealth Poetry Prize for the African area, consists in part of selections from his earlier work, and in part of new poems, some of which are translations of works originally composed in Ewe. The nine works in the section titled "New Poems," in theme, subject matter, style, technique, and language, reiterate many of Awoonor's basic preoccupations. The first few are in part laments over "life's tears" or "life's winds and fate." But as always with Awoonor and the Ewe dirge tradition, there is hope beyond death. Life itself is seen as an "act of faith" in the eternal miracle of the seeding time that must come even after the fires of life have raged over the houses, reducing them all to stump walls:

Along a hope hill and fields
when dreams crush like petals
in a protective foil
against our fate
We move on, carrying I say
a singular faith in death
the only companion in this valley.

The poem "Act of Faith" makes a sudden transition from the lament to satire and poetry of abuse when the land's miseries are laid at the door of the "professional acrobats" who, believing they are "destined rulers," goad the young men to their deaths in attempted seizures of power:

these hypocritical tax dodgers
and their fraudulent briefs and lies
these leeches who live on the fat
of a lean country

devourers of corpses in foetal state
whose claim is supported by an ecclesiastical
    order. . . .

There is much of Ghana's recent political history
written into these metaphors.

The final poem, "For Ezeki," dedicated to
Ezekiel Mphahlele, opens with a salute to "the
homestead and the ancestors," then moves into
an evocation of all the joys and sorrows of the
exile in his perpetual search for a home and a
hope, and the final return to the land of birth:

to seek memories along the goat paths, home
to those lingering shrubs of childhood
denuded by exile tears.

We say
the snake that dies on the tree
returns home to the earth.

Readers follow Mphahlele, the elder South African
poet, in his travels and struggles against oppression
and alienation. His brave, irrevocable return
to life among his own people to share with
them "their meagre meals . . . in freedom's
name" provides the ultimate poetic image: "to
postpone dying until / the morning after freedom."

Between the publication of *The House by the
Sea* and that of *Until the Morning After* almost ten
years elapsed. At least part of the explanation for
the paucity of Awoonor's creative writing since
his release from prison must be sought in a decisive
change in his life, leading increasingly to direct
participation in national politics. Following
his release he went back to his job at the University
of Cape Coast, where he became a professor
and the head of the Department of English, and
later dean of the Faculty of Arts. But he was no
longer content to play the regular academic, observing
his nation's political life from the false security
of what he calls "the outlaws' hill."

As a first step, he became a founding member
of the Action Congress party, one of the
many political parties that contested elections to establish
a civilian government to replace the military
rulers who had locked him up. For a time he
contemplated running for a parliamentary seat,
but he finally settled for the position of general
secretary of the party. His party won only a handful
of seats and was relegated to the background.
He later joined a group of intellectuals who decided
to offer intellectual support to the military
government of Jerry John Rawlings, the young
air force officer who first seized power in June
1979 and launched a program aimed at the revolutionary
transformation of Ghanaian society.
Awoonor still backs that program, and after serving
for several years as Ghana's ambassador extraordinary
and plenipotentiary to Brazil, with accreditation
to five other countries in the Central
American region, he was appointed Ghana's ambassador
to Cuba and then to the United Nations.
He was also a key member of the National
Commission on Democracy, a body charged with
the task of researching and formulating a program
of action leading to a new kind of democracy,
one based on the special conditions and traditions
of Ghanaian society.

To all these direct political activities Awoonor
brings the special gift of the power of the
word. He has become a major political essayist.
This branch of his career began in 1972 with the
small pamphlet *Come Back, Ghana*, privately
printed and circulated to all those involved in the
task of rebuilding Ghana, including members of
the new military junta of Col. I. K. Acheampong.
This twenty-three-page pamphlet, dedicated to
"Kwame Nkrumah who died to show us the
way," is a brief political analysis of Ghana's problems,
with suggestions on how they could be
solved. Awoonor's next major work in this direction
was *The Ghana Revolution*, a work that has
drawn mixed reactions. His latest, *Ghana: A Political
History from Pre-European to Modern Times*
(1990), is an intellectual's gift to a nation in
search of solid foundations for popular and just
structures and principles of self-rule, firmly placing
Ghana's current problems within the context
of political and cultural history.

Whether Kofi Awoonor returns to his earlier
preoccupation with imaginative writing or
not, he has already secured a safe place within
the canon of African literature, both for the quantity
and the quality of his work. In particular his
poetry is notable for its intense lyricism. He is
classed with a select group of African poets who
have been most successful in bringing African aesthetic
norms to bear on their writing in English,
a group that invariably includes Mazisi Kunene,
Okot p'Bitek, and Christopher Okigbo. The contribution
of these poets to world literature lies in
the great poise and power with which they can
take a second language with its own literary heritage
and peculiar linguistic structures and yet use
it so as to capture effectively the rhythms, the essential
imagery, and the often elusive thought patterns
of their first language and culture.

Dust jacket for Awoonor's best-known critical work, often used as a textbook in African-literature courses

Awoonor's career demonstrates that such an achievement does not come through chance or through a cursory encounter with primary sources of literary sustenance. It is not enough to be born African. It is essential that the writer serve his apprenticeship with African experts in the art of eloquence. Awoonor's researches into African oral culture have played a crucial, formative role in giving shape and direction to his own creative skills.

Interviews:

Dennis Duerden and Cosmo Pieterse, eds., *African Writers Talking: A Collection of Radio Interviews* (London: Heinemann, 1972; New York: Africana, 1972), pp. 29-50;

John Goldblatt, "Kofi Awoonor: An Interview," *Transition*, 41 (1972): 42-44;

Bernth Lindfors, Ian Munro, Richard Priebe, and Reinhard Sander, eds., *Palaver: Interviews with Five African Writers in Texas* (Austin: African and Afro-American Research Institute, University of Texas, 1972), pp. 47-64;

Karen Morell, ed., *In Person: Achebe, Awoonor, and Soyinka at the University of Washington* (Seat-

tle: African Studies Program, Institute for Comparative and Foreign Area Studies, University of Washington, 1975);

"Kofi Awoonor on Poetry and Prison," *West Africa* (17 April 1978): 750-751;

Ian H. Munro and Wayne Kamin, "Kofi Awoonor: Interview," *Kunapipi*, 1, no. 2 (1979): 76-83;

Ben Ephson, "Historical Forces," *West Africa* (4 November 1985): 2304-2306.

Bibliography:

Kwaku Amoabeng and Carrol Lasker, "Kofi Awoonor: An Annotated Bibliography," *Africana Journal*, 13 (1982): 173-214.

References:

Chinua Achebe, Introduction to Awoonor's *This Earth, My Brother* (Garden City, N.Y.: Anchor/Doubleday, 1972), pp. vii-xii;

Kofi Anyidoho, "Kofi Awoonor and the Ewe Tradition of Songs of Abuse (*Halo*)," in *Toward Defining the African Aesthetic*, edited by Lemuel A. Johnson, Bernadette Cailler, Russell Hamilton, and Mildred Hill-Lubin

(Washington, D.C.: Three Continents, 1982), pp. 17-29;

Rosemary Colmer, "Kofi Awoonor: Critical Prescriptions and Creative Practice," *ACLALS Bulletin*, 5, no. 1 (1978): 22-31;

Colmer, "The Restorative Cycle: Kofi Awoonor's Theory of African Literature," *New Literature Review*, 3 (1977): 23-28;

Jocelyn-Robert Duclos, " 'The Butterfly and the Pile of Manure': A Study of Kofi Awoonor's Novel, *This Earth, My Brother*," *Canadian Journal of African Studies*, 9 (1975): 511-521;

L. R. Early, "Kofi Awoonor's Poetry," *Ariel*, 6 (January 1975): 51-67;

R. N. Egudu, *Four Modern West African Poets* (New York: Nok, 1977);

Egudu, *Modern African Poetry and the African Predicament* (London & Basingstoke, U.K.: Macmillan, 1978; New York: Barnes & Noble, 1978);

Robert Fraser, *West African Poetry: A Critical History* (Cambridge: Cambridge University Press, 1986);

Ken Goodwin, *Understanding African Poetry: A Study of Ten Poets* (London: Heinemann, 1982);

John Haynes, "Song and Copy: The Relation between Oral and Printed in Kofi Awoonor's 'Dirge,' " *Journal of Commonwealth Literature*, 20, no. 1 (1985): 118-129;

G. D. Killam, "Kofi Awoonor: *The Breast of the Earth*," *Dalhousie Review*, 56 (1976): 143-156;

Thomas R. Knipp, "Myth, History and the Poetry of Kofi Awoonor," *African Literature Today*, 11 (1980): 39-61;

Ayo Mamudu, "Kofi Awoonor as Poet," *Lagos Review of English Studies*, 3-5 (1981-1983): 112-125;

Gerald Moore, *The Chosen Tongue: English Writing in the Tropical World* (London: Longmans, 1969);

Moore, *Twelve African Writers* (London: Hutchinson, 1980; Bloomington: Indiana University Press, 1980);

Felix Morrisseau-Leroy, "The Ghana Theatre Movement," *Ghana Cultural Review*, 1 (July-September 1965): 10, 14;

Ezekiel Mphahlele, Introduction to Awoonor's *Night of My Blood* (Garden City, N.Y.: Doubleday, 1971);

Olatubosun Ogunsanwo, "Awoonor's *This Earth, My Brother* . . . : A Personal Memoir," *Kunapipi*, 9, no. 1 (1987): 74-87;

Femi Ojo-Ade, "Madness in the African Novel: Awoonor's *This Earth, My Brother* . . . ," *African Literature Today*, 10 (1979): 134-152;

Richard Priebe, "Kofi Awoonor's *This Earth, My Brother* as an African Dirge," *Benin Review*, 1 (1974): 95-106;

Priebe, *Myth, Realism and the West African Writer* (Trenton, N.J.: Africa World, 1988);

Martin Tucker, "Kofi Awoonor: Restraint and Release," *English in Africa*, 6 (March 1979): 46-51;

Elaine Saint-André Utudjian, "Aspects of Myth in Two Ghanaian Novels," *Commonwealth Essays and Studies*, 10, no. 1 (1987): 22-25;

Utudjian, "Rites of Passage in the Poetry of Kofi Awoonor," *Commonwealth Essays and Studies*, 8, no. 2 (1986): 67-74;

Derek Wright, "Ritual and Reality in the Novels of Wole Soyinka, Gabriel Okara and Kofi Awoonor," *Kunapipi*, 9, no. 1 (1987): 65-74;

Wright, "Scatology and Eschatology in Kofi Awoonor's *This Earth, My Brother* . . . ," *International Fiction Review*, 15, no. 1 (1988): 23-26.

Louise Bennett

(7 September 1919 -)

Michael E. Hoenisch
Freie Universität Berlin

BOOKS: *Jamaica Dialect Verses*, compiled by George R. Bowen (Kingston, Jamaica: Herald, 1942);

Jamaican Humor in Dialect (Kingston, Jamaica: Gleaner, 1943);

Anancy Stories and Poems in Dialect (Kingston, Jamaica: Gleaner, 1944);

Jamaican Dialect Poems (Kingston, Jamaica: Gleaner, 1949);

Anancy Stories and Dialect Verse, by Bennett and others (Kingston, Jamaica: Pioneer, 1950);

Anancy Stories and Dialect Verse, new series (Kingston, Jamaica: Pioneer, 1957);

Laugh with Louise: A Pot-Pourri of Jamaican Folklore, Stories, Songs, Verses, with music by Lois Kelly-Barrow (Kingston, Jamaica: City Printery, 1961);

Jamaica Labrish, edited by Rex Nettleford (Kingston, Jamaica: Sangster's Book Stores, 1966);

Anancy and Miss Lou (Kingston, Jamaica: Sangster's Book Stores, 1979);

Selected Poems, edited by Mervyn Morris (Kingston, Jamaica: Sangster's Book Stores, 1982; revised, 1983).

RECORDINGS: *Jamaican Singing Games*, New York, Folkways, 1954;

Jamaican Folk Songs, New York, Folkways, FT 6846, 1954;

Children's Jamaican Songs & Games, New York, Folkways, FC 7250, 1957;

The Honourable Miss Lou, Kingston, Jamaica, Boonoonoonoos, 1981;

"Yes M'Dear": Miss Lou Live, London, Island Records, ILTS 9740, 1983;

Anancy Stories, Kingston, Jamaica, Federal Records, FRM-129, n.d.;

Carifesta Ring Ding, Kingston, Jamaica, Record Specialists, n.d.;

Listen to Louise, Kingston, Jamaica, Federal Records, 212, n.d.;

Miss Lou's Views, Kingston, Jamaica, Federal Records, 204, n.d.

OTHER: *Mother Goose / Jamaica Maddah Goose*, edited by Bennett (Kingston, Jamaica: Friends of the Jamaica School of Art Association, 1981).

Louise Bennett has been popular since she began to write poems and read them in public in Jamaica in the late 1930s, and her fame continues to grow. Her poetry, as well as her prose monologues on radio and the Anancy tales she published, are rooted firmly in the oral-culture tradition of Jamaica. The creole language of this tradition, its folk material, and its forms of perception delayed her recognition as a serious artist during the first part of her career. However, she was awarded an M.B.E. in 1960, and, after the cultural reorientation of the 1960s and 1970s, her commitment to the tradition was no longer perceived as a limitation but as an asset, which won her continued popular appeal, a central position in Jamaican literature, institutional recognition (the Order of Jamaica in 1974 and an honorary D.Litt. from the University of the West Indies in 1983), and international fame.

On the surface, her background does not seem very close to the tradition of folk culture and the literary creativity that characterizes her development. She grew up in the city of Kingston and was the daughter of Cornelius A. Bennett, a baker, and Kerene Robinson Bennett, a dressmaker. School years in St. Simon's College (1933-1936) and Excelsior High School (1936-1938) provided the young Bennett with a colonial education characterized by the split between the dominant culture of the "motherland" and the "subcultural" tradition of colonial people. Her reaction to this cultural dichotomy resulted neither in paralysis nor overadjustment or regression, but in a continuing creative effort to represent and legitimize the culture of the Jamaican people. Interviewed by Dennis Scott in 1968, she remembered an experience on a streetcar as a schoolgirl in Kingston: the lively comments of the passengers about her middle-class appear-

Dust jacket for a 1966 collection of Louise Bennett's creole poetry

ance made her aware of the beauty and vitality of the creole language, to which she would dedicate her life and her literary efforts. After successful performances at free concerts, she was sponsored by promoter Eric Coverley and appeared in one of his shows in 1938. Performances on the radio then increased her popularity.

When the *Gleaner* newspaper in Kingston, after earlier rejections, began to publish her poems every Sunday, starting in May 1943, she gained a national audience and a certain kind of recognition by the educated middle class, although not yet as a serious poet. Her first book of poetry (in creole) had been published in 1942: *Jamaica Dialect Verses*. She continued her formal education by taking correspondence courses in journalism in the late 1930s and began to do social work in 1943. Like so many other Caribbean artists and intellectuals of this period, she felt she could not continue her development at home and went to England in 1945, after receiving a Brit-

ish Council scholarship to attend the Royal Academy of Dramatic Art in London. While there she also worked for the BBC, one of the centers of anglophone Caribbean culture at the time. At the BBC she had a weekly variety show, "Caribbean Carnival" (1945-1946), and later a program called "West Indian Guest Night" (1950-1953). Through her work on radio and as an actress in English theater companies, she continued to develop her talent for oral communication. She also spent two years in New York City (1953-1955), where she sang folk songs at the Village Vanguard in Greenwich Village, did radio work, and performed in places such as St. Martin's Little Theater in Harlem. With Coverley she directed *Day in Jamaica*, a folk musical. On 30 May 1954 she and Coverley were married; they have two children, Fabian and Christine. Altogether Bennett spent almost a decade abroad, with the exception of the years from 1947 to 1950, when she tried unsuccessfully to make a living in Jamaica.

After she returned with her family to Jamaica in 1955, Bennett used all the opportunities open to her to continue her studies of oral culture, to write poetry, and to perform for a widening public. Her work for the Jamaica Social Welfare Commission, as drama officer from 1955 until 1959 and as director until 1963, allowed her to travel all over the island and add to her knowledge of Jamaican folklore. She also taught drama and Jamaican folklore at the University College of the West Indies from 1955 to 1969. Since 1963 she has performed frequently on radio, television, and the stage. She has delivered regular prose monologues on radio, and from 1970 to 1982 she had a children's television show called "Ring Ding." She continues to perform in Jamaica and abroad. Major collections of her poetry were published in 1966, when Rex Nettleford edited *Jamaica Labrish*, and in 1982, when Mervyn Morris edited her *Selected Poems*. For those who have not been able to see or hear a performance by Bennett, the record *"Yes M'Dear": Miss Lou Live* (1983) gives an excellent impression of the vitality, power, and skill of her performance.

When Bennett refers to her poetry as "dialect verse," she seems to accept a very modest literary position. With its implication of a local language variety, used by only a limited number of people, and lacking the social prestige of the standard language of the educated elite, the term *dialect* seems to confine her to a narrow poetic field. In Jamaica at one time, dialect was frequently associated with illiteracy and lack of formal education. Therefore "dialect verse" signified popular entertainment, not serious art. Bennett was, of course, perfectly aware of this situation. In her interview with Scott she spoke frankly about the fact that for a long time she was not considered a creative writer, or even a writer at all. But it is characteristic of her poetry that she maintains this modest position with great tenacity and at the same time turns it into a position of strength.

Laughter and entertainment are evident in her poetry, but they are masks behind which the careful reader or listener will detect self-confidence, criticism, and defiance. The big words of prominent people, or of those striving for prominence, are deflated. The confrontation with traditional folk experience, often condensed in the form of creole proverbs, reveals the element of fakery in the pretensions of the would-be elites. Satire, sometimes hidden in the rhythm of the language or the tone of voice, is the cutting edge of her poetical confrontation with the dominant culture. From the perspective of the creole tradition, which she accepts with self-confident identification, English appears, as in her poem "Bans a Killin" (in *Selected Poems*, 1983 edition) as one dialect among many. The culture of the motherland does not command the respect of a norm: it is taken down from its elevated position, democratized, and incorporated in the pluralistic vision of fraternal, almost equal cultures.

Bennett's poetic declaration of independence from Great Britain took place in the context of powerful upheavals in the Caribbean in the late 1930s. Profound changes seemed imminent, accompanied by a strong thrust toward cultural nationalism. The journal *Public Opinion* and the literary magazine *Focus* demonstrated to a middle-class public the creative possibilities of indigenous Jamaican culture. Roger Mais, who was closely associated with this process of cultural transformation, introduced the Kingston ghetto as the collective protagonist of two of his novels; creole appears occasionally in the form of quoted direct speech, competing with English and American language models. The writers close to *Focus* and *Public Opinion* expressed their position of cultural independence in language and thought patterns similar to those of their English contemporaries. Bennett, who shared their position in many ways, was isolated at that time by her commitment to the oral tradition and the creole language. The poem "Strike Day" (in *Jamaica Labrish*) is characteristic of her approach in several ways. Its reference to social unrest, as it occurred in the late 1930s, relates a topical event to the experience of one of the participants. Public life is seen through a representative personal perspective: "We drive pon tram car free of cos' / Dis like is fe we own, / An wen we tiad o' de drive / We block de line wid stone."

The theme of the poem and its verbal strategy are exactly parallel: the appropriation of public transportation by the poor—in opposition to the dominant—and the appropriation by the people of communication about the strike both express the temporary breakthrough of a suppressed culture. Against an initial moderating voice, the poem unfolds as the oral report of an unemployed black woman about her liberating experience:

Shet up yuh mout mah meck me talk,
How nayga reign teday,

How we lick wite man till dem beg
An shout an start fe pray.
. . . .
Soh me gwan bad jus like de res,
An never fraid at all,
For nayga was a-reign today,
An wite man got a fall!

By appearing to quote the woman striker herself, who participated in a momentary reversal of her powerlessness, the poem reverses the printed versions of the strike events and asserts the experience of those usually excluded from public discourse. The point of view of the poor is given substance in the form of a persona whose narrative develops as a dramatic monologue seemingly without authorial intrusion, producing an effect of realism. The monologue reveals not so much the event as the perspective of the speaker. Although a great variety of personae are dramatized in Bennett's poetry, reflecting the wide spectrum of folk experience, the point of view is always that of the oral tradition of creole culture. Within the loose structure of the traditional English ballad meter, modified and shaped by creole rhythms, Bennett dramatizes a situation of oral communication within the poem as well as in the process of reception. When the fictive persona reveals more to the listener/reader than she is aware of, a dialogue between poem and responding audience is initiated, which can be enhanced by the live performance of the poem.

Bennett's poetry comments on a great variety of topical events and everyday experiences, ranging from World War II to the introduction of buses, in place of streetcars, in Kingston; and from governors, self-government, and elections to the street cries of peddlers and the gossip in the lanes. However, of the typical features, unifying the great variety within her literary work, three deserve special emphasis. In the first place, her poetry does not simply reproduce an existing creole culture but uses elements from the creole tradition to strengthen black cultural self-confidence and mediate between the people's subculture and the dominant culture. Bennett's poetry, remarkably free of black self-hatred, represents pride in the black tradition. It is characteristic of her work that this stance is often achieved indirectly: in a self-reflective turn, language, the medium of this process, becomes the theme of some of her best poems. The affectation of an English accent appears as a symptom of cultural alienation in the poem "Dry-Foot Bwoy" (*Selected*

Poems). Laughter does not deny but dissolves the false assumption of cultural superiority and reverses the perspective of inauthenticity: "Wha wrong wid Mary dry-foot bwoy?" Similarly, in the poem "Noh Lickle Twang" (*Selected Poems*) the ironic complaint about the lack of an American accent satirizes the effects of Americanization from a position of creole self-confidence.

Second, it is characteristic that the laughing chorus in "Dry-Foot Bwoy" consists of women, and the experience in the poem "Strike Day" is recreated by a female speaker. Bennett's poetry is based on the strength and verbal skill of a women's tradition—not "Oman Lib," which "bruck out / Over foreign lan," as she says in the poem "Jamaica Oman" (*Selected Poems*). Rather it is a tradition of survival that black women have achieved since slavery through open rebellion, symbolized by Nanny the Maroon, or through proud independence behind a mask of laughter and stoicism. The women's everyday communication was essential in this tradition: it created some form of community and helped to transmit values of female identity; it also provided one of the models for Bennett's poetry.

Finally, her works have a political dimension much more significant than the explicit and often dated topical commentary. The oral quality of her poetry evokes the talk of local communities, where events and people can be judged by personal observation. The public discourse of this critical subculture is constantly brought into play against public discourse of the dominant culture and erodes the latter's claim to universal validity. Her poetry, therefore, poses a challenge to the cultural hegemony of the established elite.

The laughing subversiveness of Bennett's poetry was hidden behind the image of the entertainer until Caribbean poets began to relate to her as a literary ancestor. Poets such as Linton Kwesi Johnson, Mutabaruka, Oku Onuora, and Michael Smith transform her poetic structure and the oral creole tradition on which it is based by invoking a context of conflict and radical change. Louise Bennett, in contrast, has maintained an optimistic trust in a national culture of the whole of the Jamaican people, a pluralistic culture characterized not by harsh antagonisms but by great diversity and common roots in folk traditions. This vision of Jamaican culture has sustained her popular success and, since the 1960s, her growing recognition by literary critics including Mervyn Morris and others. Recent changes in the cultural context of Jamaica are unlikely to diminish her stature.

Interviews:

Dennis Scott, "Bennett on Bennett," *Caribbean Quarterly*, 14 (March-June 1968): 97-101;

Barbara Gloudon, "Fifty Years of Laughter: The Hon. Louise Bennett, O.J.," *Jamaica Journal*, 19 (August-October 1986): 2-10.

References:

Peta-Anne Baker, "Louise Bennett-Coverley: A Poet of Utterance," *Caribbean Contact*, 1 (August 1973): 6;

Edward K. Brathwaite, *History of the Voice: The Development of Nation Language in Anglophone Caribbean Poetry* (London: New Beacon, 1984), pp. 26-30;

Lloyd Brown, "The Oral Tradition: Sparrow and Louise Bennett," in his *West Indian Poetry* (Boston: Twayne, 1978), pp. 100-117;

Rhonda Cobham-Sander, *The Creative Writer and West Indian Society: Jamaica 1900-1950* (Ann Arbor, Mich.: University Microfilms International, 1983), pp. 158-168, 241-244;

Carolyn Cooper, "Noh Lickle Twang: An Introduction to the Poetry of Louise Bennett," *World Literature Written in English*, 17 (April 1978): 317-327;

Cooper, "Proverb as Metaphor in the Poetry of Louise Bennett," *Jamaica Journal*, 17 (May 1984): 21-24;

Cooper, " 'That Cunny Jamma Oman': The Female Sensibility in the Poetry of Louise Bennett," *Jamaica Journal*, 18 (November 1985 - January 1986): 2-9;

Louis James, *The Islands in Between* (London: Oxford University Press, 1968), pp. 15-21;

Mervyn Morris, Introduction, notes, commentary, and teaching questions, in Bennett's *Selected Poems*, edited by Morris (Kingston, Jamaica: Sangster's Book Stores, 1983), pp. iii-xix, 120-164;

Morris, "Louise Bennett in Print," *Caribbean Quarterly*, 28 (March-June 1982): 44-56;

Morris, "On Reading Louise Bennett, Seriously," in *Critics on Caribbean Literature*, edited by Edward Baugh (London: Allen & Unwin, 1978), pp. 137-148;

Rex Nettleford, Introduction to Bennett's *Jamaica Labrish*, edited by Nettleford (Kingston, Jamaica: Sangster's Book Stores, 1966), pp. 9-24;

George Panton, "Our Well-Known Well-Loved Poet," *Sunday Gleaner* (Kingston, Jamaica), 11 August 1974, p. 23;

Gordon Rohlehr, "The Folk in Caribbean Literature," *Tapia*, 2 (17 & 24 December 1972): 8-9, 15.

Dennis Brutus
(28 November 1924 -   )

Abdul R. JanMohamed
University of California, Berkeley

BOOKS: *Sirens, Knuckles, Boots* (Ibadan: Mbari, 1963);

Letters to Martha, and Other Poems from a South African Prison (London, Nairobi & Ibadan: Heinemann, 1968 [i.e., 1969]);

Poems from Algiers (Austin: African and Afro-American Research Center, University of Texas, 1970);

A Simple Lust (New York: Hill & Wang, 1973; London: Heinemann, 1973);

Thoughts Abroad, as John Bruin (Del Valle, Tex.: Troubadour, 1975);

Strains (Austin, Tex.: Troubadour, 1975);

China Poems (Austin: African and Afro-American Studies and Research Center, University of Texas, 1975);

Stubborn Hope (Washington, D.C.: Three Continents, 1978; London: Heinemann, 1978);

Salutes and Censures (Enugu, Nigeria: Fourth Dimension, 1984);

Airs and Tributes, edited by Gil Ott (Camden, N.J.: Whirlwind, 1989).

RECORDING: *Informal Discussion in Third World Culture Class*, Ames, Media Resources Center, Iowa State University of Science and Technology, 1975.

OTHER: *African Literature, 1988*, edited by Brutus, Hal Wylie, and Juris Silenieks (Washington, D.C.: Three Continents/African Literature Association, 1990).

One of the foremost South African poets, Dennis Brutus is a prime example of Third World writers whose work is particularly striking because they are successful at combining Western literary structures and traditions with indigenous forms and experiences. Brutus's poetry evinces a remarkable range of poetic influences: from William Shakespeare and, particularly, John Donne to Pablo Neruda and some Japanese Haiku masters. Nevertheless, his most outstanding achievement consists of his political lyrics, intensely per-

Dennis Brutus (photograph from African Network)

sonal poems that focus on fundamental political topics.

Dennis Brutus was born in Zimbabwe (then Rhodesia) on 28 November 1924 to South African parents, both teachers: Francis Henry and Margaret Winifred Bloemetjie Brutus. He returned to South Africa with them shortly after his birth and lived there until he went into exile in 1966. He received his B.A. from Fort Hare University College in 1947, and for the next fourteen years he taught English and Afrikaans in various high schools in Port Elizabeth and (illegally) in Johannesburg. On 14 May 1950 he married

May Jaggers, a factory worker, and they have eight children. After a short time in Great Britain he has spent most of his exile (with his family) in the United States and has taught at various universities, including Northwestern, Swarthmore, and Texas. From 1986 to 1991 he was chairman of the Department of Black Community Education Research and Development at the University of Pittsburgh, where he is a professor of African literature.

While technically proficient and aesthetically masterful, his verse is deeply political in that he is uncompromisingly opposed to the apartheid regime of South Africa and committed to articulating the feelings of his oppressed countrymen. The manner in which racism permeates every facet of life in South Africa and how it affected Brutus's education is seen in his early poetry. However, Brutus's first major encounter with the politics of racism and apartheid came through his interest in sports, an activity that should be entirely free of political considerations. Attracted to track-and-field events at an early age, Brutus was frustrated by the racial segregation of sports, which allocated the better facilities and opportunities to whites. Brutus founded the South African Sports Association in 1959 in an attempt to overcome this discrimination. The government ignored his activities for a while; however, when Brutus attempted to organize a "Coloured National Convention" in 1961, the government banned him from writing or taking part in politics and dismissed him from his teaching position. Brutus studied law for two years at the University of the Witwatersrand but was banned from practicing as a lawyer. This confrontation was part of a larger conflict at a time when the government was legislating increasingly repressive measures, annulling the few civil liberties that remained, and consolidating its own totalitarian power. A series of laws legalized the government's power to arrest and imprison without charges or trials.

Refusing to be intimidated, Brutus attended a meeting of the South African Olympic Committee in Johannesburg in 1963. He was promptly arrested for violating his banning order. Released on bail, he attempted to flee South Africa through Mozambique, for he realized that life would be too restricted for him in South Africa. However, when the Portuguese colonial authorities who then controlled Mozambique captured and returned him to the apartheid police, Brutus was faced with a complex dilemma. Since his re-

Brutus in Port Elizabeth, 1966 (photograph from African Network). He was exiled from South Africa later that year.

capture was never announced, and his friends and relatives believed him to be safely out of the country, the South African Bureau of State Security (BOSS) could do with him whatever it wanted without anyone knowing about it. He could only announce his presence in the country by attempting to escape once again, hoping either to get away or to create an altercation in the streets of Johannesburg that would publicize his return. While attempting to dash from his captors in the streets of the city, Brutus was shot in the back, the bullet exiting through his chest. Fortunately he did manage to attract international support and publicity for his predicament. After his partial recovery, he was sentenced to eighteen months imprisonment on the notorious Robben Island, off Cape Town.

In the midst of the events leading to his imprisonment, Mbari Press in Nigeria published his first book of poems, *Sirens, Knuckles, Boots* (1963)—which, as one would expect, is severely critical of the apartheid regime. The manuscript had been sent out secretly because of Brutus being "banned." Though the ban continued upon his release from prison, Brutus was able to take ingenious advantage of the clause that permitted personal correspondence: he wrote a series of verse letters about his prison experience to his sister-in-law, Martha Jaggers. In 1969, during his exile, these were published in *Letters to Martha, and Other Poems from a South African Prison*.

Out of prison in 1965, Brutus was still confined under house arrest and unable to work. His desire to escape from this confinement coincided with a strategy chosen by the government to get rid of politically undesirable people. The government offered to issue a "canceled" exit permit to Brutus; after accepting and using this illegal permit, he would be automatically imprisoned if he ever returned to South Africa. Under the pressure of this mad logic, Brutus went into exile in 1966.

At that time the apartheid government's response to those who would not bow before its fascist will was relatively simple and monolithic. It tried to eliminate them in one of two ways: either by imprisonment, torture, and murder; or by stifling them into silence and oblivion. Brutus experienced both strategies. Preventing him from teaching or becoming a lawyer and thus from earning a living; holding him under house arrest and barring him from attending any gatherings; placing him under constant surveillance; and, finally, forbidding him to write or publish his statements—all these constituted an attempt to deny the very existence of the man: it was, in fact, an attempt to murder his spirit after his body had survived their guns and prisons. If a government thus tries to murder the spirit of a poet because he will not accept the distribution and justification of political and economic power based on skin color and if a government prevents him from writing poems ultimately because the color of his skin is not white, how then can anyone expect his poetry to divorce and compartmentalize the questions of race, politics, and imprisonment from aesthetic and lyric considerations? The division between literature and politics is perhaps viable in cultures that have constitutional guarantees safeguarding the civil liberties of individuals. But even in such societies one would have to consider how issues of race and politics are relevant to the literature of those minority groups that are disfranchised because of race, class, or gender. In examining the poetry of Brutus, then, not only must one avoid such compartmentalization, but,

Cover for a book Brutus wrote and published under a pseudonym at his Troubadour Press, which he founded while teaching at the University of Texas at Austin

on the contrary, one must appreciate that the South African society—where the public cannot be separated from the private, the political from the aesthetic, or the prisoner from the poet—is precisely the appropriate ground for the growth of the political lyric.

Brutus's poetry is varied and evolving, the changes and varieties produced by internal, personal shifts in his sensibility and preoccupations as well as by his response to the forms and attitudes of other poets. As John Povey has pointed out, the poems written prior to Brutus's imprisonment are significantly different from those written during his incarceration and from those composed in exile, which also can be grouped according to various phases and preoccupations. An alternative organization of Brutus's work, into complex, simple, and balanced poems, has been suggested by Bernth Lindfors. However, the political lyric is at the center of the diverse experiences that find appropriately varied forms in

Brutus's canon. The genesis, tone, and structure of his political lyrics are clearly visible in those poems that thematize the fusion of politics and the lyric voice.

Political oppression and aesthetic experience are presented in poem 18 of the "Letters to Martha" sequence. The imprisoned persona of the poem, overwhelmed by an urge to see the stars clearly through his prison window, dares to turn off the corridor light that interferes with his view. This immediately arouses the wrath of the guards, who descend upon him with threats: "And it is the brusque inquiry / and threat / that I remember of that night / rather than the stars." This poem, which emblematizes the incarceration of the entire nonwhite population of South Africa, implies that the brutality of the apartheid regime can permanently occlude all potentiality of aesthetic or sublime experience. Yet Brutus does not succumb. Another poem, "Tenderness" (in *Sirens, Knuckles, Boots*), begins, "Somehow we survive / and tenderness, frustrated, does not wither," then goes on to catalogue and characterize various kinds of oppression unleashed by apartheid, and concludes with a variation of the opening line: "but somehow tenderness survives." Tenderness, an emotion that recurs in Brutus's poetry, symbolizes the emotional quality essential to lyric poetry. The stoic calm, mild surprise, and sense of gratitude expressed in the last line of this poem characterize the typical attitude in Brutus's poetry toward the survival of a human voice in South Africa; the parallelism between the first and last lines suggests that individuals and communities survive *because* tenderness survives.

In "A Common Hate Enriched Our Love and Us" (also in *Sirens, Knuckles, Boots*) Brutus rejects the easy and comfortable life because "In draughty angles of concrete stairs / or seared by salt winds under brittle stars / we found a poignant edge to tenderness." The implication that deprivation somehow nourishes lyric sensibility is spelled out by the last two lines of the poem: "hate gouged out deeper levels of our passion— / a common hate enriched our love and us." The political brutality that had threatened to occlude aesthetic experience is gradually subordinated so that the latter is enriched.

This process of internalizing and sublimating not only a personal but a communal experience of social, economic, and political oppression and transforming it into a lyric expression is best exemplified in the title poem of *Sirens, Knuckles, Boots*:

> The sounds begin again;
> the siren in the night
> the thunder at the door
> the shriek of nerves in pain.
>
> Then the keening crescendo
> of faces split by pain
> the wordless, endless wail
> only the unfree know.
>
> Importunate as rain
> the wraiths exhale their woe
> over the sirens, knuckles, boots;
> my sounds begin again.

In this poem the internalization of sociopolitical oppression is mirrored by a metonymic chain of sounds that move fairly rapidly from the periphery to the center of the self: the sirens lead to the thunder at the door, which suddenly engulfs the entire self in that the "shriek" of nerves in pain excludes, at that moment, all other experience. The focus on sounds—for instance, the manner in which the poem presents a powerful physical blow as a crescendo, a final explosion of sounds—stresses the transformation of physical torture into a lyric cry that is being articulated by the poem. Finally, the minor but significant variation between the first and the last lines, characteristic of many of Brutus's poems, completes the transformation: "The sounds" become, after the internalization, "my sounds." This process whereby objective political conditions are appropriated through personal, physical suffering and eventually turned into a lyric poem defines the fundamental strategy and structure of Brutus's political lyrics.

The lyrical appropriation of the political world is designed not only to sublimate apartheid brutality but also to re-create the community that the Afrikaner government attempts to destroy. The poetic self consistently articulates the unspoken experience of others, thereby defining the efficacy of the self as being inherently dependent on its integration with others, as in the title poem of *A Simple Lust* (1973):

> A simple lust is all my woe:
> the thin thread of agony
> that runs through the reins
> after the flesh is overspent
> in over-taxing acts of love:

Brutus during the trip to China that inspired his China Poems, *published in 1975 (African and Afro-American Studies and Research Center, University of Texas at Austin)*

Only I speak the other's woe:
those congealed in concrete
or rotting in rusted ghetto-shacks;
only I speak their wordless woe,
their unarticulated simple lust.

Such a movement of incorporation fuses sexual love with patriotism, turns the lyric cry of the self into that of the community, transforms pain into sexual/political desire, and presents a complex, contradictory transformation in the oxymoronic tension of a "simple lust." In the desire to counteract the disintegration produced by apartheid, to weld a community back together again, the sentiment of the political lyric is even capable of compassion for the oppressors. As R. N. Egudu has pointed out, in the poem "The Mob" (in *Sirens, Knuckles, Boots*) Brutus's appropriation even includes a brutal white mob that attacked a group of black protesters and subsequently peopled the nightmares of the poet. It is Brutus's desire to bind his community by transforming hate and bru-

tality into passion and tenderness that leads him repeatedly to characterize himself as a roving troubadour who disdains political dangers in order to sing about his people and his land. The irony involved in this characterization of the self as a troubadour, who sings love songs to his country rather than to his mistress, contains and acknowledges the paradox of the political lyric. The last two lines of a troubadour poem in his first book run as follows: "—no mistress favour has adorned my breast / only the shadow of an arrowbrand." The troubadour's songs have not set in motion a Cupid's arrow but have instead earned him the prisoner's arrow-brand; the poet is a captive of his country and its captors. Brutus's political lyrics are as resonant as a metaphysical conceit.

A significant subset of this political genre comprises those poems that transform the implied conjunction between sexual love and patriotism into a bold metaphysical conceit. The poems in this category, varying from light and humorous to serious, and from the explicitly political to those that gradually fade into the purely erotic, are numerous. A brief (untitled) example is in Brutus's first book:

> I might be a better lover I believe
> my own, if you could truly be my own:
> trafficked and raddled as you are by gross
> undiscerning, occupying feet,
> how can I, the dispossessed, achieve
> the absolute possession that we seek?
> How can we speak of infidelity
> when, forced apart, we guess each other's woe?
> My land, my love, be generous to forgive
> my nomad rovings down the vagrant streets:
> return to me, sometime be wholly my own
> so you secure me entire, entirely your own.

Here the conceit, turning on the idea of sexual/military possession, invokes the foreign occupation of the country and the resultant separateness, the poet's passionate surrender to his land, and the reciprocal absorption of the poet by the country. The self is again defined by an experience that obliterates the "normal" boundaries of the self, and the intimacy of the political engagement is indicated by its equation with the intimacy of sexual and emotional love.

While this subset is characterized by ornate conceits and relatively complex imagery and diction, the other poems that together form the corpus of Brutus's political lyrics tend to be exquisitely simple and austere in diction, syntax, and imagery. Brutus defensively describes them as prosaic, but their strategy is more accurately described by poem 14 in the "Letters to Martha" sequence:

> How fortunate we were
> not to have been exposed
> to rhetoric
>
> —it would have falsified
> a simple experience;
> living grimly,
> grimly enduring
>
> Oh there was occasional heroic posturing
> mainly from the immature
> —and a dash of demagogic blood thirstiness
>
> But generally
> we were simply prisoners
> of a system we had fought
> and still opposed.

Cover for the second printing (1990) of Brutus's 1989 collection

The unadorned language, the rhythm, and the virtual lack of imagery in all the "Letters to Martha" poems, and other such works, match perfectly the meditative, stoic, reflexive voice of the speaker, thereby revealing the process of the political lyric. These poems derive their power from the lack of artifice, the honesty that the style imparts to the experience of political struggle and to the endurance necessitated by stubborn hope. The quiet, honest, intensely lyric voice better communicates a commitment to political liberation than would a vitriolic characterization of the oppressor or a rhetoric full of heroic bravado. These poems constitute the best part of Brutus's poetry.

His poetry has changed and evolved a great deal over the span of three decades. While firmly centered around the political lyric, his poetry radiates out to other forms and at times shows a marked influence of and a dialogue with other poets from Western and non-Western traditions. Much of his early poetry, what Brutus has characterized as his preprison poetry, is deeply influenced by the metaphysical poets, particularly

John Donne, as can be seen clearly in Brutus's poem that begins "I might be a better lover I believe." The controlling conceit of his lyric poems, a conceit that becomes the structural metaphor of many poems in *Sirens, Knuckles, Boots*, is the equation of the love between a man and a woman to that between a man and his country. The influence of Alfred, Lord Tennyson can be seen in the language and imagery of chivalry, particularly in the persona of the troubadour, which is not only featured in many of Brutus's poems, both early and late ones, but also furnished the name for the publishing firm founded by Brutus in Texas, the Troubadour Press. The presence of a Keatsian "negative capability" can be seen in the relentless quest to experience, merge with, and understand fully the oppressed condition of black South Africans—to digest thoroughly the "status of the prisoner," "savouring to the full its bitterness / and seeking to escape nothing." Strains of T. S. Eliot's "The Love Song of J. Alfred Prufrock" (1916) can be heard in poems such as "I Could Be Dead."

Interaction with a non-Western literary form is evident in Brutus's use of the Chinese *chueh chu*, after which the works in his *China Poems* (1975) are patterned. In his poems in *Salutes and Censures* (1984) Brutus returns to the African oral tradition of blame-and-praise poetry, which seems to have experienced a curious and ingenious revival in South Africa, where, in response to the government's banning of most literature written by black South Africans, oral poetry conveniently circumvents censorship and prohibition.

These influences in no way render Brutus's poetry derivative; rather, they indicate the richness and variety of his verse, which needs to be examined in the context of world literature rather than being dismissively confined to the ill-defined critical category of "protest literature" that so often prevents an adequate appreciation of black South African writing.

Interviews:
Dennis Duerden and Cosmo Pieterse, eds., *African Writers Talking: A Collection of Radio Interviews* (London: Heinemann / New York: Africana, 1972), pp. 53-61;
Bernth Lindfors, Ian Munro, Richard Priebe, and Reinhard Sander, eds., *Palaver: Interviews with Five African Writers in Texas* (Austin: African and Afro-American Research In-

stitute, University of Texas, 1972), pp. 25-36;
Lindfors, " 'Somehow Tenderness Survives': Dennis Brutus Talks about His Life and Poetry," *Benin Review*, 1 (1974): 44-55;
E. Ethelbert Miller, "An Interview with Dennis Brutus," *Obsidian*, 1, no. 2 (1975): 42-55;
Renato Berger, "Interview with Dennis Brutus," *Genève-Afrique*, 18, no. 2 (1980): 73-78;
William E. Thompson, "Dennis Brutus: An Interview," *Ufahamu*, 12, no. 2 (1983): 69-77.

References:
Ria de Meester, "An Introduction to Dennis Brutus' Prison Poems," *Restant*, 8, no. 2 (1980): 47-56;
R. N. Egudu, "Pictures of Pain: The Poetry of Dennis Brutus," in *Aspects of South African Literature*, edited by Christopher Heywood (London: Heinemann / New York: Africana, 1971), pp. 131-144;
Issac Elimimian, "Form and Meaning in the Poetry of Dennis Brutus," *Literary Half-Yearly*, 28 (January 1987): 70-78;
Colin Gardner, "Brutus and Shakespeare," *Research in African Literatures*, 15 (Fall 1984): 354-364;
Bernth Lindfors, "Dennis Brutus and His Critics," *West African Journal of Modern Languages*, 1, no. 2 (1975): 137-144;
Lindfors, "Dialectical Development in the Poetry of Dennis Brutus," in *The Commonwealth Writer Overseas: Themes of Exile and Expatriation*, edited by Alastair Niven (Brussels: Didier, 1975), pp. 219-229;
Gessler Moses Nkondo, "Dennis Brutus and the Revolutionary Idea," *Ufahamu*, 10 (Spring 1981): 79-91;
Nkondo, "Dennis Brutus: The Domestication of Tradition," *World Literature Today*, 55 (Winter 1981): 32-40;
Wole Ogundele, "The Exile's Progress: Dennis Brutus' Poetry in the First Phase of His Exile," *Commonwealth Essays and Studies*, 10, no. 2 (1988): 88-97;
Chikwenye Okonjo Ogunyemi, "The Song of the Caged Bird: Contemporary African Prison Poetry," *Ariel*, 13 (October 1982): 65-84;
Tanure Ojaide, "The Troubadour: The Poet's Persona in the Poetry of Dennis Brutus," *Ariel*, 17 (January 1986): 55-69;
Jasper A. Onuekwusi, "Pain and Anguish of an African Poet: Dennis Brutus and South Afri-

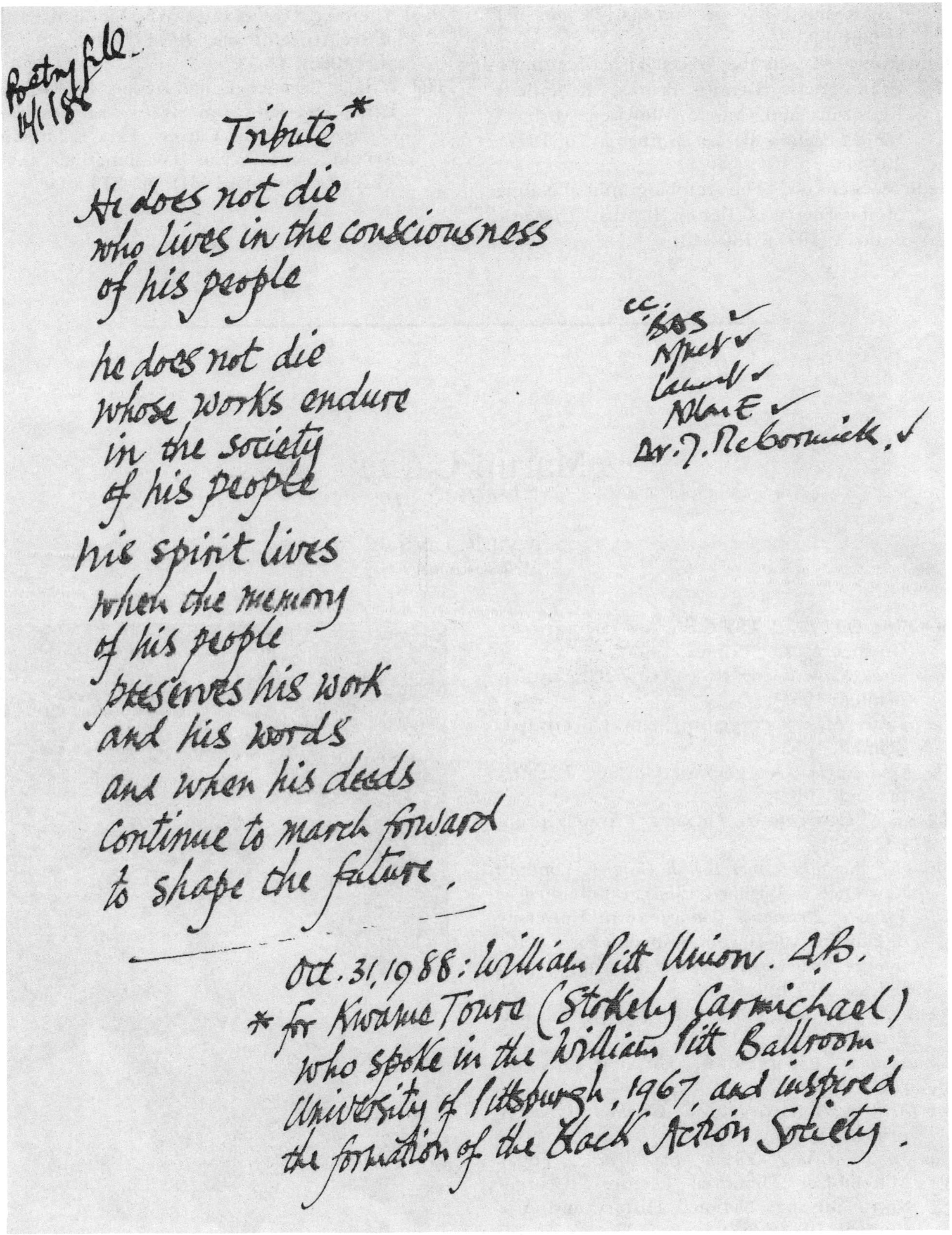

Poetry file
14/1/89

Tribute *
___

He does not die
who lives in the consciousness
of his people

he does not die
whose works endure
in the society
of his people

his spirit lives
when the memory
of his people
preserves his work
and his words
and when his deeds
continue to march forward
to shape the future.

cc:
SAS
NPU
Laura
Alan E
Dr. J. Reborwick

_____

Oct. 31, 1988: William Pitt Union. A.B.

* for Kwame Toure (Stokely Carmichael)
who spoke in the William Pitt Ballroom
University of Pittsburgh, 1967, and inspired
the formation of the Black Action Society.

Manuscript for a poem published in Airs and Tributes *(by permission of Dennis Brutus)*

can Reality," *Literary Criterion*, 23, nos. 1-2 (1988): 59-68;

John Povey, "I Am the Voice: Three South African Poets: Dennis Brutus, Keorapetse Kgositsile, and Oswald Mbuyiseni Mtshali," *World Literature Written in English*, 16 (1977): 263-280;

Bede M. Ssensalo, "The Autobiographical Nature of the Poetry of Dennis Brutus," *Ufahamu*, 8, no. 1 (1977): 130-142;

Paul Theroux, "Voices out of the Skull: A Study of Six African Poets," *Black Orpheus*, 20 (August 1966): 41-58;

Hal Wylie, "Creative Exile: Dennis Brutus and René Depestre," in *When the Drumbeat Changes*, edited by Carolyn Parker, Stephen Arnold, and Wylie (Washington, D.C.: Three Continents, 1981), pp. 279-293.

Martin Carter
(7 June 1927 -)

Selwyn R. Cudjoe
Wellesley College

BOOKS: *The Hill of Fire Glows Red* (Georgetown, Guyana: Master Printer, 1951);

To a Dead Slave (Georgetown, Guyana: Privately printed, 1951);

The Hidden Man (Georgetown, Guyana: Privately printed, 1952);

The Kind Eagle (Georgetown, Guyana: Privately printed, 1952);

Returning (Georgetown, Guyana: Privately printed, 1953);

Poems of Resistance from British Guiana (London: Lawrence & Wishart, 1954); republished as *Poems of Resistance* (Georgetown: University of Guyana, 1964); republished as *Poems of Resistance from Guyana* (Georgetown, Guyana: Release, 1979);

Poems of Shape and Motion (Georgetown, Guyana: Privately printed, 1955);

Conversations (Georgetown, Guyana: Privately printed, 1961);

Jail Me Quickly (Georgetown, Guyana: Privately printed, 1963);

Man and Making—Victim and Vehicle, Edgar Mittelholzer Memorial Lectures (Georgetown, Guyana: National History and Arts Council, 1971);

Poems of Succession (London: New Beacon, 1977);

Poems of Affinity, 1978-1980 (Georgetown, Guyana: Release, 1980);

Martin Carter circa 1977

Selected Poems (Georgetown, Guyana: Demerara, 1989).

OTHER: *New World: Guyana Independence Issue*, edited by Carter and George Lamming (Georgetown, Guyana: New World, 1966).

Martin Carter, a Guyanese, is one of the most important poets of the Caribbean in the post-World War II era. Writing out of what has come to be known as the "protest tradition" in West Indian poetry, Carter made an indelible mark on West Indian verse when he published his *Poems of Resistance from British Guiana* during the violent days of 1954, when British troops had moved into his country, suspended its constitution, and deposed the legitimately elected government of Cheddi Jagan. Along with Derek Walcott and Edward Kamau Brathwaite, Carter is a leading Caribbean poet.

Born in Georgetown on 7 June 1927 and educated at Queens College, Martin Wylde Carter joined the British Guiana Civil Service and soon became the secretary to the superintendent of prisons. By 1950, however, he began to take his writing and politics more seriously. When the British entered Guyana in 1953, Carter's involvement in radical politics led to his detainment at Atkinson Field (now Timehri) for three months. In 1954 Carter's fierce denunciation of the emergency regulations led to his being imprisoned once more. Out of his second stay in prison came his politically inspired *Poems of Resistance from British Guiana*, which led critic Paul Singh to note that Carter was "jailed into poetic eminence." On his release from prison he found a job teaching at a local school. He joined the Booker Group of Companies in 1959 as the chief information officer and remained there until 1966, when he became a U.N. representative for Guyana. From 1967 to 1971 he was the Guyanese minister of information and culture. Carter spent the 1975-1976 academic year lecturing at Essex University in the United Kingdom (his longest continuous stay outside Guyana), and from 1977 to 1981 he was writer in residence at the University of Guyana. Since 1981 he has been a senior research fellow at that university.

Carter's poems reflect his political involvement with the fortunes of his country. Because he believes that politics and poetry are interrelated, he feels that the committed poet should be involved in social and political activities. As he noted in a 1978 interview with Bill Carr, "Politics

... is a part of life and poets are interested in life ... [;] if politics is a part of life, we shall become involved in politics, if death is a part of life we shall become involved with death, like the butterfly who is not afraid to be ephemeral." In his Edgar Mittelholzer Memorial Lectures (*Man and Making—Victim and Vehicle*, 1971) Carter casts the relationship in a more philosophical light by pronouncing that "the creations of the artist are the creation of a culture. The artist thereby is a means through which the culture expresses itself." The artist and the society are merged into an indivisible whole.

It is no wonder, then, that Carter's poetical development followed the political evolution of his society. Thus the fiery responses contained in *Poems of Resistance from British Guiana*, formed in the furnace of the political turmoil of the 1950s, gave way to the uncertainties of the 1960s and early 1970s, followed by the disappointment and failed hopes of the late 1970s and early 1980s. In his 1974 address to the Eighth Convocation Ceremony of the University of Guyana, he noted,

> Something seems to have gone awry with the process of metamorphosis, which if we are to accept what our leaders tell us should work to transform us from what we function as—an aggregation of begging, tricking, bluffing, cheating subsistence-seekers and assorted hustlers—into a free community of valid persons; each of whom has existence in a way we have come to conceptualize, as at least one among other higher modes of being where the essence of staying alive means the fulfillment of self and self-realization.

The inability of Guyanese society to shape a "free community of valid persons" led to a diminution in the power of Carter's verse and eloquence: the defiance and anger seen in *Jail Me Quickly* (1963) fade into the silence and oblivion of *Poems of Affinity* (1980).

In the Mittelholzer Lectures, Carter states that there are certain "historic spaces in Commonwealth Caribbean society which only political leaders and obeahmen can and do fill." However, he believed that even though the politician has taken over the part the obeahman (sorcerer) played during slavery, the politician differs in that he manipulates social relations at the expense of the community's welfare. This is one reason why Carter ended his convocation address by warning Guyanese against a "paralysis of spirit," which occurs when an "individual person is confronted with the sometimes inscrutable workings of political and bureaucratic power." Carter is a poet who would be politician, and vice versa.

His first volume of poetry, *The Hill of Fire Glows Red* (1951), shows, in "Looking at Your Hands" and "Listening to the Land," intimations of the radical themes that would come to characterize Carter's more substantial work. In "The Kind Eagle" readers begin to see his characteristic preoccupation with the freedom of his country, his use of certain potent symbols of resistance, and a hint of the kind of consciousness with which his poetry has come to be associated:

> I dance on the wall of prison!
> It is not easy to be free and bold!
> It is not easy to be poised and bound!
> It is not easy to endure the spike!
> So river flood, drown not my pillar feet!
> So river flood, collapse to estuary!
> Only the heart's life, the kind eagle, soars
> and wheels in flight.

In *Poems of Resistance from British Guiana* Carter realized his fullest power as a poet. Readers get a feel for the sentiments that occupied the minds of the ordinary Guyanese during a terrible time of violation. Perhaps the poem that best captures the emotions of the period is "This Is the Dark Time My Love." In a staccato outburst Carter invokes the violence in the country and the people's response to it:

> This is the dark time my love.
> It is the season of oppression, dark metal, and
> tears.
> It is the festival of guns, the carnival of misery.
> Everywhere the faces of men are strained and anx-
> ious.

Further on, the persona asks: "Who comes walking in the dark night time? / Whose boot of steel tramps down the slender grass?" The answer comes: "It is the man of death, my love, the strange invader / watching you sleep and aiming at your dream." The nationality of the "strange invader" is provided in "I Clench My Fist." He is the "British soldier, man in khaki" who should be careful lest he provokes "My dead ancestor Accabreh / [who] is groaning in his grave." In spite of the invader's guns and ammunition, the poet asserts, "I clench my fist above my head; I sing my song of FREEDOM!" Such is the defiance, rage, and pride that one finds in this early volume of Carter's poetry.

In "I Come from the Nigger Yard," one of his most powerful and best-known poems, readers discover Carter's capacity for sustaining and developing a complex emotional response in poetry. The subtle blend of aesthetic control and political content embodies the best of his work. While violent outbursts against the naked oppression of the British government capture the anger of the Guyanese people, the tight poetic structure demonstrates the poet's ability to exert aesthetic control over anger, and the poem reminds one of the discipline Guyanese people displayed during the time of their greatest national violation. More than any single work of Carter, "I Come from the Nigger Yard" shows his strengths as a poet:

> I come from the nigger yard of yesterday
> leaping from the oppressor's hate
> and the scorn of myself;
> from the agony of the dark hut in the shadow
> and the hurt of things;
> from the long days of cruelty and the long nights of
> pain
> down to the wide streets of tomorrow, of the next
> day
> leaping I come, who cannot see will hear.

From a sense of cultural resistance and defiance against colonial oppression, the poem, through its rhythmic cadences, builds up to express the righteous indignation of a people. Hence one sees the repetition of certain key phrases:

> I come from the nigger yard of yesterday
> leaping from the oppressor's hate
> and the scorn of myself.
> I come to the world with scars upon my soul
> wounds on my body, fury in my hands
> I turn to the histories of men and the lives of the peo-
> ples
> I examine the shower of sparks the wealth of the
> dreams
> I am pleased with the glories and sad with the sor-
> rows
> rich with the riches, poor with the loss
> From the nigger yard of yesterday I come with my
> burden.
> To the world of tomorrow I turn with my strength.

It is within the poles of those paired sentiments (sadness and loss, pride and defiance) that the best poetry of Carter is constructed and wherein he reaches his apogee as a poet.

There is another dimension of Carter's verse that is seldom examined. Beyond its violence and spirit of defiance, his work articulates a particularity of landscape as well as the specificity of an emotional and spiritual history that is part of his aesthetic vision. "University of Hunger" is a pastoral poem that captures the physical and spiritual hunger of Guyanese people without the romanticism or idealization of the common folk that is associated with this traditional form. Overwhelmed by a brooding anxiety about life, and overcome and seemingly defeated by the apparent monotony and ruthlessness of history, the folk Carter celebrates seem to exert every nerve and sinew to keep on living and to face up to the burdens of their lives: "O long is the march of men and long is the life / And wide is the span. / O cold is the cruel wind blowing / O cold is the hoe in the ground." Earlier in the poem Carter's persona reminds readers of how "The print of hunger wanders the land / . . . The roofs of men are fused in misery." Yet the people keep plodding along the weary road of life even if there seems to be little hope at its end. The poem concludes:

The long streets of night move up and down
baring the thighs of a woman
and the cavern of generation.
The beating drum returns and dies away
the bearded men fall down and go to sleep
. . . .
Is they who rose early in the morning
watching the moon die in the dawn
is they who heard the shell blow and the iron clang
is they who had no voice in the emptiness
. . . .
O long is the march of men and long is the life
And wide is the span.

The end of the poem is ambiguous. Is it that these people merely cast their voices into emptiness without any hope of redemption? Or is it that they only come to realize their powerlessness and spiritual hunger as they trudge along life's weary road? At any rate, through a series of vigorous symbols, Carter is able to capture the ambiguity of colonial life as he methodically enumerates the obstacles barring the peoples' path toward liberation.

In the poetry of this early period, Carter describes his role as that of a comrade in arms ("I am no soldier hunting in a jungle / I am this poem like a sacrifice"); a comrade singing in international solidarity with his brothers and sisters in Kenya, Malaya, and Korea ("But wherever you fall comrade I shall arise"); a comrade ever vigi-

lant about his freedom ("Death must not find us thinking that we die"); and a black man who "drank from the calabash of his ancestors . . . climb[ing] toward the hole of heaven / and my hands are stretched to the altar of god / O wonder of all the stars departed."

Carter's next major group of poems, *Jail Me Quickly*, reflects the turmoil that continued to beset Guyanese political evolution at the beginning of the 1960s. Out of this fierceness and brutality came the poem "Black Friday, 1962":

were some who ran one way.
were some who ran another way.
were some who did not run at all.
were some who will not run again.
And I was with them all,
when the sun and streets exploded
and a city of clerks
turned a city of men!
Was a day that had to come,
ever since the whole of the morning sky,
glowed red like glory,
over the tops of houses.

At one level the sentiments of the poem are immediately accessible to the reader. At another level the work suggests a profound sense of identification with all factions in the struggle and articulates the multifarious meanings of their desire to be free. In this sequence there is still hope and a possibility that things will turn out all right. Such sentiments are also present in "After One Year":

I know this city much as well as you do,
the ways leading to brothels and those dooms
dwelling in them, as in our lives they dwell.
So jail me quickly, clang the illiterate door
if freedom writes no happier alphabet.

In "The When Time," a group of poems in *Poems of Succession* (1977), there seems a weakening of poetic force and only a residual sense of future sociopolitical possibilities. In fact most of the poems composed between 1964 and 1975 (contained in *Poems of Succession*) are not as powerful or as immediate as Carter's earlier poetry. The subtle play of poetic sentiments and political commentary are missing. *Jail Me Quickly* apparently brought to an end the defiance and anger that characterized Carter's early poems. Thus, with two exceptions, the poems in "The When Time" tend to be brooding and idealistic (as in "On a Pavement" and "The Leaves of the Canna Lily") and somewhat paradoxical (as in "Endless Moment World"). They are more reflective and absorbed in the constant defeats of the past and the tragic political reversals of the era.

By the time *Poems of Affinity* was published in 1980, the revolutionary fervor of Carter's early poems had been replaced by philosophical ruminations. Apart from the clear note of denunciation in "Bastille Day" (written on the occasion of the cold-blooded murder of the political activist and Catholic priest Father Drake, which Carter witnessed on 14 July 1979), there is a sense of nostalgia for the past, a longing for the clear-cut causes of earlier revolutionary days, and a pervasive sense of despair. In "Bastille Day" Carter seems to suggest that little has changed with time and that time itself has become a chimera:

> Every day is as old
> as a new day is. Time
> represents itself. . . .
> . . . .
>   I
> unapologetic, remember why every
> day was once a new day. As new
> and as old as my childhood roaming
> among grass. The world is a cold
> wind. It is a glass of sweet water
> in a grim place of thirst.
> Farewell rain. . . .

Most of the images in this collection are those of defeat and despair. Carter's terse structure and intensely painful lyrics reflect the sensibilities of a disillusioned person. Perhaps "Being Always" captures this sense of defeat and disillusionment more than any other poem:

>   Why,
> I have to ask, do I have to
> arrange anything, when every
> thing is already arranged
> by love's and death's inscrutable
> laws, mortal judiciary, time's
> doll house of replaceable heads,
> arms and legs? In another
> house, not time's, time itself arranges
> mine and the world's replacement.

Carr claims that Carter accomplished "the rare feat of writing tragic lyric poetry" in *Poems of Affinity*.

To get a sense of how Carter's poems changed during the course of his career, however, one only has to compare the hope and optimism of the glad woman in "Human Guide" (1952; in *Poems of Resistance from British Guiana*) to the pessimism and grief of the old woman in

Cover for the 1964 edition of the poems Carter wrote while he was a political prisoner in Guyana in 1954

"Bent" (1980; in *Poems of Affinity*), where one is left with the vision of "the crushed cloud / of an incredible want." Unquestionably, for Carter at least, the revolutionary fervor of the 1950s gave way to the unrealized dreams of the 1970s and a sense of having been manipulated by radical rhetoric. His association with the WPA (Working People's Party) in the late 1970s and early 1980s suggests that he hoped the promise of the 1950s could be realized once more. However, the tragic murder in 1979 of Walter Rodney, one of the leaders of the WPA, thrust Carter (and his work) back into the cycle of despair and uncertainty with which the 1960s and 1970s had ended.

Carter is one of the finest Caribbean poets. He has captured in a vigorous and original manner the sentiments of a period that remains indelibly printed on the minds of Caribbean people—a period in which a serious attempt was made by the people of Guyana to transform their social and political reality. Carter will always be remembered for the sustained bursts of poetical illumination through which he captured the possibilities of that period.

Interviews:

Bill Carr, " 'In Contradiction': Bill Carr Raps with Martin Carter," *Release*, 1 (First Quarter 1978): 5-24;

Rovin Deodat, "Interview with Martin Carter," *Kyk-over-al*, 40 (December 1989): 80-83;

Peter Trevis, "Interview with Martin Carter," in *Hinterland: Caribbean Poetry from the West Indies and Britain*, edited by E. A. Markham (Newcastle upon Tyne, U.K.: Bloodaxe, 1989), pp. 66-71.

Bibliography:

Joan Swamy, "Martin Carter: A Select Bibliography," in Carter's *Selected Poems* (Georgetown, Guyana: Demerara, 1989), pp. 179-192.

References:

S. O. Asein, "The Protest Tradition in West Indian Poetry from George Campbell to Martin Carter," *Jamaica Journal*, 6 (June 1972): 40-45;

Edward Brathwaite, "Martin Carter's Poetry of the Negative Yes," *Caliban*, 4 (Fall-Winter 1981): 30-47;

Brathwaite, "Resistance Poems: The Voice of Martin Carter," *Caribbean Quarterly*, 23 (June-September 1977): 7-23;

Stewart Brown, "All Are Involved: The Poetry and Politics of Martin Carter," *New Literature Review*, 7 (1979): 66-72;

Brown, "Martin Carter: The Poet as Guerilla," *New Voices*, 9 (August 1981): 50-61;

Syl Lowhar, "Carter's Resistance and Succession," *Caribbean Contact*, 5 (August 1977): 7;

Alan Persico, "A Note on Martin Carter's 'Bent,' " *Kyk-over-al*, 37 (December 1987): 59-65;

Jeffrey Robinson, "The Root and the Stone: The Rhetoric of Martin Carter's *Poems of Succession*," *Journal of West Indian Literature*, 1 (October 1986): 1-12;

Rupert Roopnaraine, *Web of October: Rereading Martin Carter* (Leeds, U.K.: Peepal Tree, 1988);

Paul Singh, "Martin Carter's Poetic Struggles for a New Day," *Release*, 1 (First Quarter 1979): 37-41;

Stephanos Stephanides, "Language and Identity in the Poetry of Martin Carter," *Kyk-over-al*, 39 (December 1988): 76-81.

J. P. Clark
(John Pepper Clark-Bekederemo)
(6 April 1935 -   )

Robert M. Wren
University of Houston

BOOKS: *Song of a Goat* (Ibadan: Mbari, 1961);
Poems (Ibadan: Mbari, 1962);
Three Plays (London & Ibadan: Oxford University Press, 1964);
America, Their America (London: Deutsch, 1964; New York: Africana, 1969);
A Reed in the Tide (London: Longmans, 1965);
Ozidi (London & Ibadan: Oxford University Press, 1966);
Casualties: Poems 1966-68 (Harlow, U.K.: Longmans, 1970; New York: Africana, 1970);
The Example of Shakespeare (Harlow, U.K.: Longmans, 1970; Evanston, Ill.: Northwestern University Press, 1970);
The Ozidi Saga, by Clark and Okabou Ojobolo (Ibadan: Ibadan University Press & Oxford University Press, 1977);
The Hero as a Villain (Lagos: University of Lagos Press, 1978);
A Decade of Tongues: Selected Poems, 1958-1968 (London: Longman, 1981);
State of the Union (London: Longman, 1985);
The Bikoroa Plays (Oxford & New York: Oxford University Press, 1985);
Mandela and Other Poems (Ikeja: Longman Nigeria, 1988);
Collected Plays and Poems, 1958-1988 (Washington, D.C.: Howard University Press, 1991).

MOTION PICTURE: *Tides of the Delta: The Saga of Ozidi*, commentary by Clark and Frank Speed, Colour Film Services, London, 1975.

PLAY PRODUCTIONS: *The Raft*, Ibadan, University of Ibadan Arts Theatre, 1964;
The Boat, Lagos, University of Lagos Auditorium, 29 April 1981;
The Wives' Revolt, Lagos, PEC Repertory Theatre, March 1984;
The Return Home, Lagos, PEC Repertory Theatre, 6 April 1985.

J. P. Clark, 1973 (photograph by Bernth Lindfors)

Poet and playwright J. P. Clark is one of Nigeria's foremost literary artists. Along with two other Nigerians, the novelist Chinua Achebe and the playwright Wole Soyinka, Clark is generally accorded a place in the first rank among writers of the British Commonwealth. His *A Reed in the Tide* (1965) was the first collection of poems by a black writer in Africa to be published by a major overseas company (Longmans). Some of his works have produced some controversy (in particular, his poems in *Casualties*, 1970), but his poetic diction is unrivaled for precision and rhythmic control while retaining the patterns of common speech.

Born on 6 April 1935, he was one of many sons of the Ijaw chief Clark Fuludu Bekederemo of Kiagbodo in the western Niger delta region of Nigeria. Perhaps due to the influence of his mother, the former Poro Adomi, Clark and two elder brothers (Edwin Kiagbodo Clark and B. Akporode Clark) had educational opportunities unusual for Kiagbodo children, who did not have a local grammar school. All three Clark brothers have had distinguished careers. J. P. Clark was christened Johnson Pepper Clark Bekederemo, but upon the publication of *Song of a Goat* (1961) this was shortened to John Pepper Clark by the designer of the cover, as part of a pleasing design. Clark's subsequent publications used "John Pepper" and "J. P." somewhat indiscriminately, until the publication of *State of the Union*, by "J. P. Clark Bekederemo" in 1985. In his preface to that volume, Clark wrote, "these works mark for me my assumption of my full family name, after waiting several years to do so jointly with my elder brothers. It is time to identify the man behind the mask so often misunderstood and speculated about."

Clark's first school was the Native Administration School of Okrika, on the Forcados River in the Burutu Local Government Area. He continued to attend there until 1948, then enrolled in the Native Administration School of Jeremi, in the Ughelli Local Government Area. Later that year he entered Government College, Ughelli, receiving the Cambridge School Leaving Certificate in 1954. He worked for a year as clerk for the chief secretary to the government of Nigeria, thus getting close to the center of power in colonial Nigeria, and then he matriculated at University College, Ibadan. UCI was then part of the University of London, which awarded him his B.A. (with honors) in English in 1960.

His inclinations led him back toward the center of power, and he became a feature writer and editor for the *Express* newspapers in Lagos. This work led to his being awarded a Parvin Fellowship at Princeton University, a scholarship designed to teach young and promising leaders of third world countries about American democracy. He was unresponsive and was required to leave the Parvin program early. He did not return to journalism but instead, back in Nigeria, began research into the traditions of the Ijaw peo-

Cover for Clark's first book (1961), a play he wrote while a student at University College, Ibadan

ple of the western Niger delta, and he also wrote a book about his experience in America (*America, Their America*, 1964). Then he accepted an academic position at the University of Lagos, where he became professor of English and then head of the department, until his retirement in 1980.

Since his undergraduate years at UCI, a dominant theme in Clark's work has been the vitality of traditional life and art, to which he has devoted many years recording, translating, adapting, and celebrating, while at the same time he has persisted as a critic of colonial and postcolonial circumstances and influences in Nigerian politics and affairs. Throughout, however, his has been an acutely personal art, expressive of a personal pain. His apparent detachment arises from an ironic poetic mode. In his earliest, most naive poetry, the personal was often obvious, leading Romanus N. Egudu to call "Grief, chaos, insecurity, and irredeemable loss" Clark's "hallmarks" (in *Four Modern West African Poets*, 1977). In Clark's later work those nouns continue to be meaningful, although their relevance is often more difficult to see.

Intellectually a central concern of his art has been the use of an alien language, English, as a means of expressing indigenous African speech and thought. Like others of his generation, he has found himself constricted by his education in English. While still an undergraduate, he characterized himself in his poem "Ivbie" as the "bastard child" of two cultures (in *Poems*, 1962). To write as he and others similarly situated have done has required adaptation, a reconceptualization of the function of the artist. In an essay titled "The Legacy of Caliban" (in *The Example of Shakespeare*, 1970) Clark defines the issue for the African writer abstractly. First asking if "Caliban [has] acquired just the right dose of language and technique to cope with his trade, to practise the art of Prospero?" he replies,

> Fidelity towards the demands of a particular experience being ordered anew by the artist means that he must recognize immediately, indeed instinctively, the true nature and substance of the material and subject at his disposal. As the erector or assembler of an outfit that should act upon the reader as a catalyst, is [the artist] himself serving as the medium to the experiment, or should he merely describe the process, or wholly leave the exercise to independent demonstrators to carry out? The first course entails the projection of the subject upon the screen of himself and consequently the production of a lyric piece. The second makes him something of a commentary man supplying a narrative. And the third leaves him completely out of the show, for then, having formulated what may be called a theoretical truth, the artist makes way for other experts to put it to the test, and the result is drama.

As Clark goes on to imply, he has opted for all three courses, which are by no means discrete: "No work," he says, "is so impersonal that it does not at some point carry upon it the pressure of the personality of the author and none is so personal that it does not possess an independent life of its own." More personally, in "Aspects of Nigerian Drama" (in *The Example of Shakespeare*), he says of play writing that "the task for the Ijaw ... artist, writing in ... English, is one of finding the verbal equivalent for his characters created in their original and native context." The same principle, quite obviously, applies when Clark's poetry aims to reproduce the Ijaw voice, as in the lyric "Streamside Exchange" (in *Poems*):

Child: River bird, river bird,
　　　Sitting all day long
　　　On hook over grass
　　　River bird, river bird,
　　　Sing me a song
　　　Of all that pass
　　　And say,
　　　Will mother come back today?

Bird: You cannot know
　　　And should not bother;
　　　Tide and market come and go
　　　And so has your mother.

The poem recalls the songs that children of the Niger delta sing to the objects of their attention, whether the ships that ply the Forcados branch of the Niger River or the birds that visit and pass on. Because of their range the ships and birds seem to know the world beyond the boundaries of the child's experience.

Of the notable Nigerian authors, Clark was surely the most precocious. Both his first volume of poetry, *Poems*, and his first play, *Song of a Goat*, were written while he was an undergraduate. A novel he wrote while still in secondary school has never been published, and some undergraduate fiction he wrote for newspaper publication has proved ephemeral. He abandoned fiction, apparently not because of a lack of talent but rather because of an intellectual belief that the novel, unlike poetry and drama, is alien to the African experience, as is the Western short story; only the folktale, perhaps, may be called indigenous fiction. So poetry and drama have been his arts, and it is these forms that have earned him high critical distinction.

His earliest serious publication was in a journal called the *Horn*, which he and a small group of fellow students began in late 1957. Clark was the first editor. In the poems that Clark has chosen to preserve from this early period (he has declined to republish many), three factors recur: a structure based on occasion (as, for example, the illness of his grandmother, or a photograph in a magazine); imagery drawn from his home country or from a traditional story or belief; and some intense fear or dissatisfaction. The imagery, of course, is not limited to the river country or mythology, nor is each occasion of each poem equally clear. But the dissatisfaction is virtually omnipresent, sometimes as anxiety, sometimes as anger. His early, extended major poem "Ivbie" is at times an outright cry of rage. It originally was published in *Poems*, was excerpted in *A Reed in the*

Wole Soyinka as Kengide (seated) with an unidentified actor in Clark's play The Raft, *University of Ibadan Arts Theatre, 1964*

Tide, and then reappeared complete in *A Decade of Tongues* (1981).

Ivbie is an Urhobo word. Clark's grandmother was Urhobo; Kiagbodo is an Ijaw town in the Ijaw/Urhobo borderland, and many of its people are bilingual from childhood. The title, Clark has said, alludes to the "hands above head" gesture of women lamenting the "great loss or wrong for which there can be no remedy or justice." The poem is a negritudist attack on the colonial past and is an equally negritudist appreciation of African identity. Negritude is a literary philosophy that Clark called (in the first issue of the *Horn*) "perhaps . . . sentimental and moonish." It celebrates the special characteristics that Africans (and blacks of the diaspora) share as a racial heritage. The idea, according to Clark, is one of "the dark Africa, careless of sputniks and missiles, and enjoying the . . . wise direction of her ancient rulers, teachers, and prophets." Further, Clark has written, Westernization is killing "that sense of deep calm and flow, mystery and rhythm which for ages has been [Africa's] peculiar grace." To him, at that time, the founding of

the *Horn* was a blow against the "subtle imperialism" of European intellect.

Clark was writing "Ivbie" virtually on the eve of Nigeria's independence from British colonial rule and, by analogy, from British cultural rule. "Pass on," he wrote to the West:

> in mad headlong flight
> O pass on, your ears right
> Full of throttle sound,
> So winding up your kaleidoscope
> Leave behind unhaunted
> An innocent in sleep of the ages.

The poem has five movements. The first shows colonial ignorance and arrogance, tempered by the discovery of the glorious African art unearthed in such places as Benin, revealing that Benvenuto "Cellini / Dwelt among cannibals." The second movement compares the exploitation of Africa to the (quite literal) rape of African women. The third movement points to the paradox of European civilization in Africa, marked by "Austin Herefords" (British automobiles) going "toot" and "Blazing wide trails of gold / Through the forests of the night." When the indictment is complete, Clark uses the fourth movement to look inward, asking the "communal gods at the gate / Has that whiff of carrion crept / Past your bars as you slept?" Oyin, the supreme deity and mother, gives the poem's key warning:

> Fear him, children, O fear the stranger
> That comes upon you
> When fowls have gone to roost.
> . . . .
> O fear the dragon smoke cloud
> That hangs bloated, floating over
> Roof-thatch mangoes and lime.

She was not heeded. Rather (in a voice recalling that of Tiresias in T. S. Eliot's *The Waste Land* [1922]—clearly Clark's model) she, in the form of an owl, regrets the failure of the first generation of Africans:

> I the white bearded woman
> Of night fame saw all
> But men heeded not my hooting
> Placed instead penalty in warning
> And finality in brief omen.

The succeeding generation, Clark warns in the final movement, may be already "more white than white," and all too ready, "well-fed on sweet quotations and wine," to say that forgiveness is "divine." No, the poet says, he cannot sleep in the ancestral house; the present generation must not rest, though drugged with colonial comfort just as their fathers were drunk on colonial gin. Worse, after thoughts of suicide, faith, and simple indecision, the speaker senses that he is himself Oyin's enemy, against whom her children should be warned. He is without certainty or place: "I cannot sleep or act / And here I pace her bastard child / A top twirling out of complexity. . . ." The "bastard child" is no one's child, and if he is to have an identity it will be something new, ambiguous, and doubtful. Still, the poem does not end in total pessimism. Some may find that the romantic hope is a serious flaw, unworthy of the rest. Yet it is not unique in Clark's poetry. An odd optimism mars several of Clark's better political poems, but on occasion the hopefulness is personal and, consequently, deeply felt.

One of Clark's best poems from the undergraduate period is a good example and has been frequently anthologized. "Night Rain" (in *Poems*) might be a companion piece to "Ivbie," so striking is the contrast. The locale, in time and place, is Clark's childhood, an evocation of the purity preceding the deculturation of the bastard child. The home is, by European standards, impoverished, but the poem shows no regret. The rain is idealized, not threatening. It falls

> through sheaves slit open
> to lightning and rafters
> I cannot quite make out overhead
> Great water drops are dribbling
> Falling like orange or mango
> Fruits showered forth in the wind[.]

The child seems to take comfortably the fact that the rain is being caught "In wooden bowls and earthenware / Mother is busy now deploying / About our roomlet and floor," and with "practised step" she moves stored goods to dry safety. With quiet economy Clark then elevates the circumstance to a universalizing calm, telling his "brothers,"

> We have drunk tonight of a spell
> Deeper than the owl's or bat's
> That wet of wings may not fly.
> . . . .
> So let us roll to the beat
> Of drumming all over the land
> And under its ample soothing hand
> Joined to that of the sea
> We will settle to our sleep of the innocent and free.

Romantic, certainly, but the rhymes are unfailing and life is precisely observed to create the ideal negritudist poem, an allegory of traditional life. No other poem by Clark matches its tenderness, for tenderness is generally alien to Clark's poetry, the exceptions (like "Night Rain" and the also-popular "Abiku") being successful aberrations.

There is heartlessness to "Streamside Exchange," in which the bird shows no sympathy for human loss, and to "Fulani Cattle" (also in *Poems*), focusing on animals that may welcome the slaughter awaiting them at the end of their "drunken journey / From desert, through grass and forest, / To the hungry towns by the sea. . . ." Romantic, but hardly tender, is "Agbor Dancer" (in *Poems*), imaged from a photograph in *Nigeria* magazine: she dances in "trance . . . rippling crest after crest / To meet the green clouds of the forest." She evokes from the young poet the regret of a bastard child:

> Could I, early sequestered from my tribe,
> Free a lead-tethered scribe
> I should answer her communal call

Lose myself in her warm caress
Intervolving earth, sky and flesh.

Poems is a volume of highly uneven quality, as might be expected. Much of the work is experimental and imitative, and Clark, wisely, declined to republish much of it when he had the opportunity in *A Reed in the Tide*, which includes only seventeen pieces from *Poems* (including those already mentioned) and sixteen new poems. The new poems were largely written in the United States, and several of them were printed as occasional pieces in Clark's one book of journalism, *America, Their America*. In "A Personal Note" to *A Reed in the Tide*, Clark says, "What to cut, and what to save out of a body of poems that has come to represent more or less part of my own self, will always remain with me an unsettled issue." He cut all of what might be called "love poems," thus depriving the volume of the autobiographical completeness it might otherwise have had, but he may justly be said to have preserved the poems whose richness best transcends the personal.

The range can be indicated by the first and last poems. "To Granny (from Hospital)" opens the collection. Awaiting "the ferryman's return" (evoking both Clark's delta and the Greek myth of death), the poet in his fear recalls a night "fifteen floods" ago, "When upon a dugout / Mid pilgrim lettuce on the Niger, / You with a start strained me to breast . . . ." Was the cause for fear "the loud note of quarrels / And endless dark nights of intrigue" among the many wives?

> Or was it wonder at those footless stars
> Who in their long translucent fall,
> Make shallow silten floors
> Beyond the pale of muddy waters
> Appear more plumbless than the skies?

The evocation of his lost childhood world is a profound contrast to the political anger motivating "The Leader," the final poem. Unnamed, but certainly identified, is Chief Obafemi Awolowo, whom "They have felled . . . to the ground." Awolowo had been tried from November 1962 to June 1963 and convicted for treason; the accusation and the evidence were certainly questionable, and the case aroused grave partisan emotions. When Clark republished the poem in *A Decade of Tongues*, he placed it between two other poems that appeared earlier in *A Reed in the Tide*, "Emergency Commission" and "His Excellency the Masquerader." In the latter, Awolowo's old rival, Dr. Nnamdi Azikiwe, who was the ceremo-

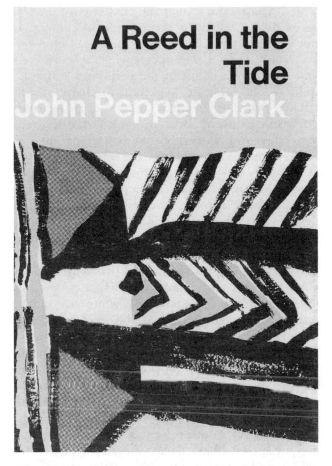

A Reed in the Tide
John Pepper Clark

Dust jacket for the first collection of poems by a black writer living in Africa to be published by a major overseas company (Longmans, 1965)

nial president of Nigeria, is seen behind the "masks": "What wind! What straw!" "The Leader" (Awolowo) is said to have been so strong that "No iguana during a decade of tongues / Could throw or twist him round / While he rallied the race and clan." Yet now "like an alligator he lies / Trussed up in a house without eyes / And ears. . . ." Clark never resumes the naive passion of his undergraduate verse, relatively free of the bitterness of partisan politics.

Yet it would not be wise to say that the early poetry was nonpolitical. Clark in a personal communication has said, "When you wrote about a girl bathing in a stream, you were making a statement. They were all political poems. You were asserting what you have. We didn't cry about it. How else could we speak to our ancestors? Or to the workers? If we spoke to them again, how could we communicate, if we didn't take this kind of stance? So we have been political from the beginning, I would say, in saying what we want, and what we don't like."

Perhaps the American experience had a great deal to do with the change of content, if not of character. Clark himself has said that *America, Their America* was, perhaps, "the jaundiced and unsavory account of the responses and reactions of one difficult, hypercritical character and palate, who, presented with unusually rich grapes in a dish of silver and gold, took deprecatory bites, and churlishly spat everything out and in the face of all." Certainly the book tells at least as much about Clark (in his youth) as it does about the United States, where he was lavishly cared for at Princeton University on a fellowship designed to display American democratic institutions in an idealistic way. He may have wished to keep an open mind about America, but he has said that he "must have felt and probably shall remain bitter at and jealous of all that passes and sells so loudly as Western and white civilization, achieved as likely as not at the expense of the dark [peoples]." Certainly no reader of the book would guess that Clark had a happy time in the United States, though he probably did. The book hardly allows any except the dreadful experiences to show. Yet, in an artlessness that gives the book an odd charm, he reveals again and again that whatever unpleasantness occurred was as much his own doing as anyone else's. Clark simply refused to play by any of the rules and as a result alienated many well-disposed people. On one occasion he abused a host for the inability to find an African text on his own bookshelf—only to hear "a week afterwards . . . that my professor friend had gone stone-blind . . . and that short day of our meeting had been the tail end of a twilight fast fading into complete darkness. And I had taunted him for trying to be smart with me. I felt rotten for days. . . ."

The primary interest of the book is not likely to be the prevailing unpleasantness (though, at Princeton University's Woodrow Wilson School, it was long remembered with extreme distaste and often anger) but rather the changes America caused in Clark. The Cuban Missile Crisis made him sharply aware of the dimensions of world conflicts. In the third part of "Three Moods of Princeton" (first published in *America, Their America*, then in *A Reed in the Tide*), he links the novelty of life in North America with the danger of nuclear catastrophe:

Snow,
  Away
From my window

By the time of waking,
  What deft, gentle hands spread
  You over this bed
Of bile, while we slept? And say,
Nurse, when shall the corpse lie?
  There, ding, dong, ding—
When all the world is a mushroom pie.

Clark returned to Nigeria, after being dismissed from the Princeton program, to a nation sliding into a protracted political crisis. In 1963 he began work in a one-year research fellowship at the University of Ibadan's Institute for African Studies. The product of that research eventually appeared in several forms, all relating to the legend of Ozidi, a tale Clark had first heard while still a schoolboy. If he wrote poetry (other than "The Leader"), it has not been published. In 1964 he married Ebun Odutola, and they eventually had four children. After publishing his book about America, he began his service in the English department of the University of Lagos. Nigeria's political crises intensified until, in January 1966, a group of young military officers brought the civilian government to an end, assassinating most of the national political leadership. One of the young officers was Clark's classmate and friend, Maj. Emmanuel A. Ifeajuna. In the aftermath of the coup, Ifeajuna became a fugitive, and was assisted in his escape to Ghana by the poet Christopher Okigbo. Later Clark and Okigbo together went to Ghana and escorted Ifeajuna back to Lagos and, unexpectedly, to jail. Later in the same year a countercoup led to further crises, climaxing in a civil war (1967-1970) in which Okigbo was killed. Clark, responding to the anguish of the period, wrote the poems in *Casualties*. The volume includes twenty-eight numbered poems, plus eleven "Incidental Poems for Several Persons."

The twenty-eight numbered poems are the lyric expression of an unstated narrative. The lyrics themselves are simple, for the most part. Their simplicity, which has deceived some critics, is made possible through symbolic representations of persons and events. For example, the second poem, "Skulls and Cups," was said by Kolawole Ogungbesan to be "tepid poetry" in which Clark is "singing (one can hardly say lamenting) the death of his most intimate friends." The critic is correct only in one point: three of the characters are Clark's friends who died during the civil war, two by execution (Ifeajuna and Sam Agbam) for treason against the rebel Biafran government, and the third, Okigbo, killed earlier fighting for that same government, at the start of the civil war. In the poem a speaker named Obi—patterned on Obiajuna Wali, who defected from the Biafran cause—asks, "Look, J. P. / How do you tell a skull / From another?" Obi compares the skulls of "Chris," "Sam," and "Emman" to cups: "How does one tell a cup on the floor / From another, when the spirit is emptied?" Far from lamenting, Clark is distancing himself from the horror: "And the goblets are legion / Broken upon the fields after Nsukka." The poem—as do all the poems in the book—demands that the war and its waste of lives be seen in context. Each participant has a long history, each event a circumstance, and each decision a conflict. If Okigbo, Agbam, and Ifeajuna had all died the same way, the poem would have no point; if Clark's feelings were less intimate, he might (like John Milton regarding Edward King) have composed a lament. The twenty-eight poems, read with sympathy often denied them, become a cumulative experience, a single work of art.

The experience is not precisely Clark's. The poems are the public expression of private emotion, and they were doubtless shaped in part by the poet's perception of the public for which he wrote. They were surely also shaped by the time in which they were written, a time when uncertainty and death were large in the land. It is likely that the "friends" in the opening poem, "Song," and the "faces" in the closing poem, "Night Song," are the collective dead, including those friends who were or might be dead. "Song" begins, "I can look the sun in the face / But the friends that I have lost / I dare not look at any." It is a kind of confession. Clark is not innocent, and the state of mind that produced the poems is not innocence. The poems are an apologia. In the patterned structure of *Casualties*, the friends in "Song" are joined in "Night Song" by "The strange and young I never met" who "intercept the faces I loved" and blot out the sun "that I / believe should ripen the land anew." This expansion shows the transformation of experience that lies between the two poems, inherent in the submerged narrative. The poems in between tell why the poet dares not look, and they imaginatively widen the scope of the poetry beyond his own predicament to the circumstances of the whole state.

In *Casualties* Clark greatly expanded his use of the animal folktale as metaphor. Most of the poems, in one way or another, use animals as representations or symbols for actual persons. The

Clark on location in Orwa, Nigeria, during the filming of Tides of the Delta: The Saga of Ozidi *(photograph by Frank Speed)*

contents of the poems are like folktales or fabulous stories that, like the main, overarching narrative, are often unstated or only partially stated. In the tales the animals are active participants in political conflict. In this use of the tale, Clark expanded folk tradition, in which satirical application of tale themes to current village affairs is ancient custom. That the form is naturally ironic suited Clark's purpose well.

The interconnection of Clark, Okigbo, and Ifeajuna is central to the poems. Clark has said, "I got so close to a number of the actors after the curtain rose ... that I came to be identified by some as playing in the show." In the nineteenth poem, "The Flood," Clark expresses his relationship to the others: "I flounder in my nest, a kingfisher, / Whose flockmates would play / At eagles and hawks, but like / Chickens are swept away." The flockmates have set in motion a chain of events that they were too weak to control. Clark shares in the effects they set in motion, but, still in his nest, he has not yet been swept away. The poem is the pivot upon which *Casualties* turns: it is a poem of disillusion, failure, and lost hopes.

"The rain of events pours down," it begins—suggesting the mindlessness that seemed to govern political change—introducing, not for the first time, the water imagery so marked in Clark's poetry. Against this rain, Clark, "Like a million other parakeets," puts on a brilliant coat, "the finest silver and / Song can acquire." When the coat does not suffice, "I unfurl my umbrella, resplendent as any / That covers a chief / At a durbar." Ogungbesan sees the lines as "narcissistic indulgence in the midst of a national disaster," but the judgment is invalidated by the tone, so ironic as to approach self-satire, and by the lines that follow (which Ogungbesan does not quote): the umbrella "buckles, and will / Fly out of my hand." The point is that art—surely the meaning of "coat" and "umbrella"—has no role in the events; instead there are "grief / Gusts of rain," continuing relentlessly. The anguish is almost hidden. The punning "grief" disguises meaning but makes it more poignant, especially as, in the lines that follow, the kingfisher and the chickens "are swept away / By flood fed from septic tanks, till / Together, we drift and drown, / Who were at home on sea, air, and land." They are together filthily caught in the flood of events, deprived now of their common freedom of art and imagination.

To the reader not a participant in the events, Clark's metaphor of "flockmates" who "play / At eagles and hawks" may be offensive: surely Ifeajuna, Okigbo, and the others did not "play" at killing and being killed. In context, however, in the ironic distancing and understatement that mark these poems, the tone is appropriate. Clark, who dares "not look at" friends in "Song," does not look at them in "The Flood." Instead, all "drift and drown," a painful image for uncertainty and violent death.

The earlier poems in *Casualties* include two stages: opening poems in the time after the events, with the poet looking back; then an extended series of responses to increasingly dangerous circumstances, experienced during or near the events. After "The Flood" the poems show an acceptance of circumstances, however terrible, beyond the poet's control. The war comes inevitably. Okigbo dies, as do Ifeajuna and other "faces." Clark and others survive but are transformed. The tragedy of *Casualties* lies not in the fact of death but in the chill isolation that makes death permanent. It is not the living Clark dare not look at, but the dead. The dead are those with whom Clark shared "bath and bed . . . dish

. . . tea . . . wine . . . " (as he writes in "Song"). The "casualties," Clark says in the twenty-seventh poem, "are not only those who are dead; / They are well out of it." In the divided Nigeria, where Clark's surviving friends are his enemies,

> We fall,
> All casualties of the war,
> Because we cannot hear each other speak
> Because eyes have ceased to see the face from the
>   crowd,
> Because whether we know or
> Do not know the extent of wrong on all sides,
> We are characters now other than before
> The war began. . . [.]

In *Casualties* Clark is the protagonist in his own poetic drama; his antagonist is the flood (always his favorite image), a deluge of events beyond the control of man, poet, or state.

The poem "Casualties" is dedicated to Chinua Achebe, the most distinguished of Nigeria's novelists and another of Clark's friends who sided with the Biafrans. In *A Decade of Tongues*, which includes most of the poems from *A Reed in the Tide* as well as from *Casualties*, Clark added a twenty-ninth poem to the *Casualties* series "Epilogue . . . to Michael Echeruo." It was written several years after the war to another friend who had been an enemy. In the poem, Clark revisits places he knew because of having been there with friends now dead "or gone to their own homesteads." His central image is of the once-great market town of Onitsha:

> Here houses, scalped and scarred past surgery,
> Stared at me, sightless in their sockets, like
> The relics of shell-shock that they are.
> One, so mutilated, it is a miracle
> The parts hung together at all,
> Called to me in the crush, in it one
> Plump woman, careless of her bare breast
> And brood, pounding yam up on a balcony,
> Tilted in the face of gravity.

Clark evokes the persistence of life in the ruins of war. So, too, friendships persisted: Clark became reconciled with Achebe and Echeruo, whom he had thought "would never forgive, never forget."

However, Clark's artistic impulse seemed to lose vitality. He entered into a period—more than a decade—during which he wrote virtually no poetry. He has said (in a personal communication), "You see, I feel some of us respond better if we are together. And when we are scattered,

A group of writers and educators at a meeting in Nigeria, 1973: Michael Echeruo, Gabriel Okara, Elechi Amadi, John Updike, Cyprian Ekwensi, Clark, Kole Omotoso, Ime Ikiddeh, Abiola Irele, Theo Vincent, and Dan Izevbaye (photograph by Bernth Lindfors)

like the war did us, some of us cease to be as active as we should have been. . . . I like to believe that the absence of the kind of community that we enjoyed in Ibadan twenty years ago—no, more—which the war, the crisis brought to a close violently by separating all of us, was like the scattering atoms that should have collided to make a nuclear charge. It would be quite absurd trying to rebuild today that part of our lives." What Clark was saying was clearly painful: "I'm not saying that one wrote by committee or conference, but you will not believe—for a long time, through the war years, so long—I mean, who did I have to relate to in Lagos? Between Lagos and Ibadan, who could I discuss my poetry with, who would I discuss my plays with? Who would do them? [Wole] Soyinka, who did, who could have done—the war split us. Achebe was across there [in the United States] . . . Chris [Okigbo] was dead."

Clark's long silence was broken when a volume of poems titled *State of the Union* was given to Longman for publication in 1981 (internal problems delayed publication four years). Although a process of artistic change had already begun for Clark, it was accelerated when he retired as professor of English at the University of Lagos. He says in a poem titled "Out of the Tower" that he had left so "That air and light may come again / Clean and free into the chambers / of my heart. . . ." The poem, which calls his academic role "standing in the cesspool," shows that Clark's bitter irony, his earthy imagery, and his political interest had not waned during his silence. The collection also, Clark states in the preface, "signals for me a new phase in my career, a phase I regard as my middle period, assuming there is a later one to come." Four new plays were also part of the phase.

Nothing could be clearer in *State of the Union* than the fact that Clark had abandoned negritude. In the opening poem, "Here Nothing Works," he asks,

What is it in ourselves or in our soil
That things which connect so well elsewhere,
Like the telephone, the motorway, the airways,
Dislocate our lives so much that we all
Begin to doubt our own intelligence?

This is direct, rhythmic speech—natural, angry, and impatient with the African slumber, though not denying something similarly fundamental:

> So something there must
> Be in ourselves or in our times that all
> Things working for good elsewhere do not work
> In our expert hands, when introduced
> To our soil that is no different from other lands.

The second poem, "Progress," metaphorically links the wind to modern technology, and links "sandboats on the lagoon" to Nigeria: "The wind / Stalling in their sails, / Has travelled a thousand miles / Since they set out at dawn." But the twenty-fifth (and last) poem of the series, "The Sovereign" (dedicated to Echeruo), is, in its way, an explanation: if Nigeria has failed to satisfy Clark's aspirations, the answer to the question, what is the state of the union, is simple: "It never was a union"—

> Four hundred and twenty-three disparate
> Elements by the latest count, all spread
> Between desert and sea . . .
>   how can any smith out
> Of fable fashion from such a bundle
> An alloy known to man?

The new coin that is finally forged, the "sovereign," Clark says, is "counterfeit."

Between poems 1 and 25, he comments on a wide range of difficulties, choices, shames, faults, and crimes in the society and in the nation. He asks, in "Sacrifice" for example, how will he tell his children the sacrifice they must make for "her," when she has sent out so many, "in hope / Though nothing but mounds, weeds / And thorns have sprung up in the field." In "Election Report" he details the census with its fraud, the registration lies, and the election, which needed no "prophet or fortune-teller to see" the outcome; he specifies the protections of a "free and fair" process, overseen by "a child of the soil," the "polling officer" who called the numbers "as pleased his purse and people." The result, mathematically formulated, "argued / By lawyers to the last decimal point," eventually "Confirmed the winners, announced by officials / And generals, discreetly out of sight. / It was, by all accounts, a numbers game." As seen by Clark, Nigeria was not a nation, and the result has been dismaying.

A "Postscript" includes a twenty-sixth poem, "The Playwright and the Colonels / To Wole

Soyinka." The poem alludes back to *Casualties*, to the civil war, early in which a colonel, Emeka Ojukwu, was head of the Biafran state, and another colonel, V. A. Banjo, led a Biafran invasion of what Clark calls "the bridge state," the midwestern region. Soyinka visited with both colonels briefly, just before the invasion, and some say that he was a courier for a plot to displace Ojukwu and the then head of state, Yakubu Gowon. Clark, it seems, accepts that version, in contrast to the one Soyinka himself gives in his autobiography, *The Man Died* (1972). Clark says,

>   the playwright,
> When picked up like a rabbit on the road
> In daytime, enroute to principals,
> All set to proclaim another kingdom,
> Swore between tears in the toilet

(where Soyinka got the paper for his writing in prison) that he'd write so that "All who read my tale // Will forget in our war / Much more than the man died." This bitter attack on Soyinka, more severe, taken in context of the conflict, than a brief discussion can show, is vitriolic irony in Clark's best rhetoric. The rhythms are natural, the diction precise, and the tone exactly intended.

The fourteen poems grouped as "Other Songs on Other States" complete the volume. Some, like "Birthday at Welseyan [*sic*], Middletown," are drawn from the year (1976-1977) that he spent teaching at Wesleyan College in Connecticut. Several allude to the possibility of new growth and others to lost opportunities. They are simple and autobiographical, anticipating Clark's new life, as in "Translation (from the Urhobo)": "The orange tree bears fruit, / Bears fruit: / If it does not / Fall, there is food for thought."

Throughout his career Clark has written drama as well as poetry. *Song of a Goat*, his first successful play, was published by the same Ibadan group that published *Poems*, and it was later reprinted, with his *The Masquerade* and *The Raft*, in *Three Plays* (1964).

Song of a Goat, while suggesting the origin of the Greek word for tragedy—*tragos* (goat) combined with *aeidein* (to sing)—also reflects the action of the play, in which the climactic moment is the ritual slaughtering of a goat. Structurally the play is almost a classic tragedy. Zifa, the protagonist, is a man of substance who bears the twofold burden of a family curse and sexual impotence. His aunt Orukorere anticipates the consequences,

Scenes from a 1981 performance of Clark's play The Boat, *at the University of Lagos: (top) the brothers Bradide and Biowa quarrel as their mother intervenes; (bottom) in the climactic trial scene, Biowa is convicted of murdering Bradide.*

but her gift of prophecy (granted by the sea god) has the same limitation as Cassandra's: she is not believed. Zifa's wife, Ebiere, takes her husband's younger brother, Tonye, as her lover, and the infidelity puts Zifa into a proud rage. The slaughter of the goat (which has cried through the night) exposes the lovers, as they are heard in the sudden silence. Tonye hangs himself offstage, Ebiere collapses, and Zifa walks into the sea (a neighbor, as messenger, reports the death). Three neighbors function as a chorus, and the Masseur, who acts as adviser and confidant, is like the choral leader in Greek drama.

The play's less obvious antecedents are John Millington Synge and W. B. Yeats, who used dramatic forms to celebrate tradition, or transform it for the modern theater. Like Synge, Clark has placed his rural drama in the present time, in which the modern, industrial, commercial world is incidental, present at the edges. Clark's rhetoric—always his distinctive mark—is far from the Irish, as might be expected, but it is also quite different from that in his lyric poetry. The play (like the other two in *Three Plays*) is in verse, but the mode is dominated by figures such as the parable/aphorism, which is often also a riddle, as when a neighbor explains Ebiere's strangeness: "Bring up a chicken among hawks / And if she is not eaten she will eat." Another facet is a metaphorical use of traditional concepts in a prosaic way, as when the Masseur informs Ebiere that her childlessness is neither rare nor incurable:

> Why even leopards go lame.
> And let me tell you, my child, for
> Every ailment in man there is
> A leaf in the forest. If both families
> Cherish each other so much, a good proposition
> Would be for your husband to make you over
> To another in his family.

The distinction among metaphors, riddles, aphorisms, and parables in Clark's plays is often difficult to draw, as in the Masseur's warning to Ebiere: "An empty house, my daughter, is a thing / Of danger. If men will not live in it / Bats or grass will, and that is enough / Signal for worse things to come in." The technique allows Clark to preserve a sense of traditional life, escaping the absurdity that might attach to an audience hearing native speakers of African languages conversing in English. He has not translated African languages, but rather he has found the verbal equivalents in English to represent characters (in Clark's words) "in their origi-

nal and native context." This is what Clark, in "The Legacy of Caliban," calls "the Shakespearean solution." The technique "makes it possible to tell Caliban from Othello simply by comparing the imagery and themes predominant in their language. In the same way it should be possible to tell the Ibo farmer Okonkwo in Mr. Achebe's *Things Fall Apart* [1958] from the Ijaw fisherman, Zifa, in my *Song of a Goat*: references of the one naturally incline more to barnyards and harvests as those of the other to fishlines and tides."

The characterizations in the play are generally well defined, but the reader of the play might well overlook the fact that in the performance Orukorere is the most powerful role. This suggests that the principals are not as strongly written as they should be, Zifa rising not to any splendor but only to an almost sullen anger, and Ebiere being limited to frustration and a sometimes foolish aggressiveness toward Tonye. Tonye himself is a cipher, and Dode, the child, serves only to accentuate Orukorere. The Masseur, however, is witty and philosophical, as a choral leader should be—though some lines are overly literary, derived from William Shakespeare or John Milton.

A sequel to *Song of a Goat*, *The Masquerade*, which was written, or at least finished, while Clark was in the United States, borrows from the Nigerian folk novelist Amos Tutuola's *Palm-Wine Drinkard* (1952), in which a girl who rejects her suitors follows a "complete gentleman" to his home, where he becomes quite incomplete—a "skull"—and holds her captive. It is a warning to young women that they should accept appropriate suitors and not go shopping for strangers, however handsome they may be. In Clark's play the monster is simply an attractive young man, Tufa. *The Masquerade* only alludes to *Song of a Goat* indirectly, but it is clear that Tufa is the son of Ebiere and Tonye, reared by Orukorere after his mother's death in childbirth. He does not know that he has inherited the curse brought on by infidelity, but gossipy neighbors (again as chorus) find out and expose him. Titi is the beauty he innocently entices and marries, enraging her jealous father, Diribi. Diribi kills both his daughter and her husband, the latter by accident in a struggle.

Although *The Masquerade* has received less attention (and fewer performances) than *Song of a Goat*, it is in several respects the better play. Less of the later play's tragic force depends on the young. Clark gives the lovers a bright, delicate courtship scene; thereafter they are largely passive, save for Titi's refusal to give up Tufa, and Tufa's bitter and fatal quest for revenge at the end of the play. Umuko, Titi's mother, is slightly comic until the events are beyond her understanding, and she then becomes a simple, mad market woman. The most splendid character is Diribi, and though he lives on at the play's end, his death can be foreseen, as he asks who can take him to the hangman to be punished. Diribi is complex. He is a great man, easily greater than Zifa in *Song of the Goat*, and his anger upon discovery of the danger that the cursed Tufa presents is both understandable and excessive. It is all the more affecting since his passion for Titi verges on the incestuous. In killing her he is fully in character, since he is shown to be quick to wrath and to action, while kinglike in his defense of his family line. Caught among fear of the gods, his pride in family, his love for Titi, and his hatred of her seducer, he offends the gods, wrecks the family, kills his daughter, and is so overcome by self-hatred that only by accident does his second victim (Tufa) die by the gun brought for the killing. In the end Diribi is helpless. A second chorus, made up of three priests, concludes the play:

> The hand of thunder, so sudden not even
> The double-visioned saw it, has battered
> Him down, boughs, bole and straight past pith.
> Let us help to pick up his scattered
> Scotched pieces, and oh, hurry, hurry
> For before the tide turns again we must
> For Forcados [the seat of government to which he
>   asks to be taken for execution].

The verse is more certain, the rhetoric less self-conscious, and the music harsher, while Clark fully exploits the imagery and riddling quality developed in his first play.

The Masquerade shows the variety and style of Niger delta life: the hard labor of fishing (seen in the neighbors), the rites of marriage, the taboos and gods of family life, and the role of women in the compound of a great man. It reveals the reverence and duty of such men as priests, as well as the comic irreverence of poor townsmen in a great house. And it shows that romantic love is an aberration in such a society, and the consequences it may have. These factors are present, too, in *Song of a Goat*, so that the two plays together are a celebration and validation of traditional life, its emotions, its dignity, and its suffering. Clark's use of operative, valid concerns in present-day delta life and his transformation of them into an English-language medium brought together his image of Africa and a vast potential audience. Properly seen, or read, the plays can bridge the cultural gap that divides the worlds of the delta and the people beyond.

The Raft, the second play Clark wrote in America, is a radical change from its predecessors. The characters are laborers rather than people of significance; they are neither cursed nor responsible. Although they are doomed, their deaths lack tragic significance. While the play has dramatic energy, it lacks a plot in the conventional sense, derived as it is from absurdist concepts of the world as an indefinite, problematic realm, without guiding fate or justice. In *The Raft* four men are adrift, after starting out with tethered logs being floated by them to market downriver. One of the men is lost when the log raft divides; another seeks safety from a passing ship and dies under its stern wheel. The remaining two drift out to sea. The play is a pessimistic, unheroic, negative parable of modern civilization, European and African, in a time of disillusion and collapsing faith. In particular, it is more than a hint of Clark's sense of the disintegration of postindependence Nigeria.

The play can be understood only through its characters, representatives and victims of their society. Kengide, the dominant one, condemns the corruption he practices, a zero-sum game: "In this game / Of getting rich, it is eat me or I eat / You." He derides the illusions of others. Olotu, the nominal leader, says he "hired" Kengide, but Kengide replies, "Slime and entrails! / And every fool that ever set foot on this raft / Are on the same payroll, and the man / With the purse is wining away at Warri." To him government and business are "two faces to one counterfeit coin." And women are no better: his own wife is both barren and promiscuous, "A reed in the tide," he calls her (invoking the name Clark soon gave to his next collection of poems). Olotu is more sophisticated, a townsman who knows great cities (Lagos, Kaduna, and Onitsha)—but he cannot swim. He is too loyal to his masters to leave the logs when the raft splits, he is not wise enough to lower his sail, and he drowns. Ogro, the most attractive, a man of goodwill, is a "blundering bullock," though the best sailor—he knows the river best. His death is pathetic, because he remembers how, as a boy, he'd played games with the ships, climbing on and jumping off again, for cheers and gifts. In a bitter irony sailors on a passing ship beat off his grasping hands,

Clark receiving the Solidra Award for Excellence, presented by the government of Nigeria, 1985

and the stern wheel of the boat captures his body. Ibobo is a priest: "the boy from the bush full of taboos," Kengide calls him (for doubting that male homosexuality exists). Ibobo fruitlessly promises the sacrifice of a goat for their successful landing. Fog binds the two survivors (Ibobo and Kengide), who are "adrift and lost" as their craft floats out to sea. If the play is allegorical (and to some extent it undoubtedly is), the allegory is unobtrusive. Clark has said that he "was trying to create a human condition which I knew existed not only in Nigeria but elsewhere."

The play *Ozidi* (1966) was the first published product of the research Clark undertook upon his return from America in the early 1960s. That he wrote the play at all—rather than only the translation of the native tale that he originally projected and did publish much later (*The Ozidi Saga*, 1977)—may be the result of one of his American experiences. As part of the Parvin program, the fellows were taken to Washington,

and a special arrangement permitted Clark, whose interests were different from most of the others, to visit that city's new Arena Stage. The experience was exciting. He wrote in *America, Their America* that the picture-frame stage had "become the image of the theatre fixed in my mind." At the Arena, he recognized that the arrangement was similar to his childhood experience of village "festivals and performances at the town square or market place." One such village performance was part of the research, and Clark, with Frank Speed and others, made a film of it, the full title of which is *Tides of the Delta: The Saga of Ozidi as Recreated by the Ijo People of Toro-Orua and Bulou-Orua in the Bendel State of Nigeria, and Recorded by J. P. Clark and Frank Speed* (1975). The film helps to clarify Clark's intent in the play.

Tides of the Delta opens with several minutes of introduction to the people of the river and their environment. Then the performance begins. As in Clark's play, the action starts with a ritual procession to the river with gifts for the water spirits. Throughout the film, the spectator sees the narrator, who is also the protagonist (as in the play), speaking, moving, and acting, often to the accompaniment of instrumental music, song, and chant. He wears (as described in the play's directions) "a white flowing shirt and tunic," and he is assisted in the performance by a great variety of men and women, often spectacularly costumed, who in dance and pantomime augment the narrator's performance. An audience is always present in the film, as in the play, surrounding the action on three sides, with the river as a backdrop. It is clear to the viewer of the film that the stage directions in the play are not to be taken literally (which very often would be impossible, involving magic of various sorts) but rather are to be danced or mimed, and indicated with costume, music, and narration. In the second act, the stage directions say that the monster Bouakarakarabiri is seen asleep, standing on his head, feet in the air. When spoken to by Ozidi he somersaults and grabs Ozidi by the neck, using his feet to throttle him. Later the monster puts into pots three huge animals, a lizard, an eagle hornbill, and a monkey, from which he makes a charm that Ozidi drinks. Productions of the play have been, understandably, few.

The Ozidi story is one that is very old, concerning a prince of Ado, the legendary name for the city of Benin. Clark substitutes the Ijaw town Orua for Ado. Ozidi defies his fellow warriors for their failure to do homage to his idiot brother, whom they have named their king. Using magic, they kill Ozidi, whereupon his grandmother, the witch Oreame, takes her daughter, who is pregnant, home. There, the new, reincarnated Ozidi is reared with one objective, revenge. He achieves the revenge and proceeds on to other terrible deeds. Making the legend available to a worldwide audience was clearly Clark's motive in writing the play in English, again using the techniques of English rhetoric to give the language a quality equivalent to Ijaw. The technique of indirect speech, riddling or aphoristic, intensifies the reader's sense of place and culture, as in a citizen's fearful remark about making the idiot a king: "You all know a god is / A god once you make him so. After / The ceremony, he ceases to be mere wood. Give him / Palm oil then, and he'll insist on blood." At one point, Clark ingeniously introduces pidgin English: while Ozidi and the other characters speak standard English (rhetorically modified), Ozidi's servant Omoni

shows the difference in class and origin through the lingua franca of the modern Nigerian markets, as in the question "Massa, papa kuku leaf shed for market sef?" (meaning, "Master, did your father leave you a market shed?"). It is less important that the reader understand the meaning perfectly than that the relationship between servant and master, and its understated comedy, should be clear.

Another of Clark's inventions is the introduction of an old fable character, Ewiri, the trickster tortoise, as the *amananaowei* (mayor) of Orua. Ewiri lightheartedly brings to the murderers of the elder Ozidi riddling news that the avenging Ozidi has come: "Many years ago several / Of you here present planted a champion yam. / Well, that yam you sowed several seasons gone by, / Has now grown beyond arm's span." When the killers figure out what he means, they answer with a similar riddle: "Did you say the cock has laid an egg?" Later he falsely reports to Ozidi that Tebesonoma of the Seven Heads has challenged him, and then takes a similar message to Tebesonoma, just as in a common folktale.

That battle leads to Ozidi's worst excess. The dying Tebesonoma warns that his sister's son will seek revenge for his death, so Ozidi must also kill the mother and child. Ozidi resists murdering the innocent, but his grandmother, relentless, forces the crime. That justifies the death of Orcame at the end of act 4, when Ozidi, berserk, slaughters both his enemy Odogu and his own grandmother. Act 5 is a kind of reconciliation, when the so-called Smallpox King visits and strikes down Ozidi, whose mother treats him for the disease, known as yaws. The Smallpox King, indignant, declares he will never return after such an insult:

> let no member of our train
> Set foot again on this shore where men see
> A royal python and call it worm of the earth, where
> They hold a goblet of wine between their hands
> And think it rainwater.

Upon his departure, a procession begins, with all the performers, Ozidi at the head, leading the spectators in a dance.

The play is somewhat forced and awkward, an intractable blending of dramatic action, special effects, Ijaw concepts, and English language. It does not lend itself to the stage. Yet it is nevertheless good reading.

After *Ozidi*, Clark did not write again for the stage, apparently, for many years. Then, on

Clark in 1986 with Douglas Turner Ward, director of the Negro Ensemble Company (New York), at the PEC Repertory Theatre in Lagos (photograph from USIS)

29 April 1981 the University of Lagos Centre for Cultural Studies and the Nigerian National Council for Arts and Culture jointly presented a new play, *The Boat*, at the University of Lagos Auditorium (with additional performances there and at the National Theatre, Lagos), directed by Bode Osanyin. Four years later, on 6 April 1985, a second new play by Clark opened, *The Return Home*. This production was under his own direction, in association with Jab Adu, at the PEC (Pepper and Ebun Clark) Repertory Theatre, which Clark and his wife, Ebun, had founded in 1982 at J. K. Randle Hall, Onikan, Lagos. Both plays were published in 1985, along with *Full Circle*, which completes the trilogy under the overall title of *The Bikoroa Plays*. A fourth play, a comedy titled *The Wives' Revolt* that he had written earlier, was produced in 1984 and again in 1986. Thus the new creative period that was first marked by his poems in *State of the Union* has meant a return to the theater as well.

The Bikoroa Plays embrace a half-century of Niger-delta history, along the eastern arm of the river Forcados, below Kiagbodo. The opening play, *The Boat*, the most substantial of the three, is set at the turn of the century. It concerns two brothers who share the ownership of a boat. The younger, Biowa, uses his time of possession to trade at the lagoon markets to the west, all the way to Lagos. The elder, Bradide, trades along the more traditional water paths, north on the Niger to Aboh, Onitsha, and Lokoja. When they dispute, as with their mother's goading they often do, bitter feelings arise, leading to Biowa's rash decision to cut the boat in half, and, at last, to commit homicide: Biowa kills Bradide. This astonishing fratricide is adjudicated by a Bikoroa government panel that includes, among the judges, a character called Ambakaderemo of Kiagbodo, based on Clark's great-grandfather who died in 1926.

While lacking in suspense, the play moves through the energy, enthusiasm, and concern of the family and the townspeople. It is not written in verse, but the rhetoric is imagistic, in keeping with Clark's concern for creating in English the quality of Ijaw culture. However, it rarely rises to the figurative energy of his early plays. One passage of three speeches anticipates the third play of the trilogy; citizens comment on the evil favoritism of the mother in more than usually energetic language:

ESENI: The witch, has she got the teeth to sample anything except the brains of new-born babies?

PELETUA: Oh, she is the fierce mother-hen who'll fight owner and hawk alike, protecting her brood, while trampling on the chicks in the process.

BURUBO: I hear Bradide was brought into the world as a result of forceful entry by his father. She has never forgiven him for that.

The conclusion of *The Boat* sends the murderer, Biowa, to death at the urging of his sister, Emonemua. The trial itself is something of a spectacle in performance, beyond the indications of the text—though the text itself is at least momentarily sensational. It is most of all so when Biowa, the favorite son, bites off his mother's ear, an act of poetic justice. Ambakederemo justifies the act: "By mouth she fed him the poison of her pap, and by ear she poured the venom of her tongue against his brother."

In the contemporary Western theater tradition, *The Boat* must be seen as conservative, and it further lacks the mystery of Clark's earlier productions. The same can be said of the other plays of the trilogy, though the mysticism of *The Return Home* permits two intriguing scenes. One of these is a consultation with a ladder named Obebe, which has mystic suffering and knowledge. Asked to identify the guilty, it searches onstage and, in a kind of desperation, invades the audience, only at last to conclude that no guilt is to be found among those present. The other is a celebration, at the end of the play, of the "return home" of Biowa and Bradide, in the form of effigies created for ritual and sacrifice. The action of the play is otherwise rather trivial: Egbeibo, the son of Biowa, attacks Fregene, the son of Bradide, slaps him twice, and is restrained from a third slap only by fierce wrestling. The quarrel is quickly resolved. It is, however, the pretext for calling home the dead and for the associated performances. Clark also finds an occasion to set the play in time by an allusion to the death of Bekederemo and the assumption of authority at Kiagbodo by Clark's grandfather Fuludu, who "could barely walk for the strings of coral beads round his neck, hands, and feet. They say it was more than you ever saw on the Oba of Benin."

Full Circle is a short play in which again a brother kills his brother; both are grandsons of Bradide. The younger, Kari, has had ill fortune in his work as a seaman out of Lagos. False prophets have convinced him that his loving and affectionate mother, Tibo, is the witch who has troubled him. The elder, Ojoboro, comes home just as Kari is beating Tibo; Ojoboro hurls Kari aside, causing his death more by accident than intent. Once again, Bikoroa must decide the case, but this time no great council is assembled. The family is allowed to decide, the authorities recognizing that the earlier decision, designed to end the trouble, was evidently a failure. They call upon Tibo's brother, who is not of Bikoroa, to take responsibility, since Tibo was a "free-born daughter" of another place, to which she returns. Ojoboro's fine is only a token—five shillings—and the case is closed.

In *Full Circle* the most expressive speech is directed against policemen. Eferemua, a cousin, for a full page of text, warns against calling in the regional police:

> Oh, yes, they will insist on eating fried eggs with boiled yam in the morning, and if there are not hens laying in the town, then goodbye to all the brood. . . . In the afternoon . . . the fattest pig . . . for the masters to feast on, and what they don't tuck into those pot-bellies of theirs must be penned or pickled for them to take home. . . . Oh, yes, you cannot cope with police palaver and wahala, for after they have stripped you of all you possess, they will drive you like common goats . . . to their station out there in Forcados or Warri.

Police intervention is more briefly rejected in *The Boat*:

> Good fellow, shall we also ask the white man permission before we sleep with our wives tonight? . . . Oh, tell me how did we live before he came among us? And how shall we live when he leaves us, for leave he must, considering how he yellows all over and dies on our shores like a mango leaf even when not touched by anybody.

Both speeches reflect ironically on the external changes over the half-century that, except for Biowa's trade and Kari's seaman life, seem to affect the internal life of Bikoroa very little. The lesson of *The Return Home* might seem to be that danger lies in traveling too far, since in that play the dispute is easily settled among cousins who have stayed at home.

The Wives' Revolt is an economical comedy, with only three characters: Okoro; his wife, Koko; and Idama, his friend. At issue is money paid to the town Erhuwaren by "the oil company operating our land." One-third has been paid to the town elders, one-third to the other men in their age groups, and one-third similarly to the women. But the women object that the elders are

Manuscript for a poem Clark published as "The Order of the Dead" in Mandela and Other Poems *(Collection of the Author)*

all male, and the women desert the town. Okoro tries comically to contend with all the problems Koko has left behind, until she returns suffering from some sort of venereal infection. Okoro will not hear any explanation, while he assumes the worst. As hard as Idama tries to intervene, Okoro will not stop talking long enough to hear, while Koko infuriates him with comments from the side. At last he swears to be silent: "There, I won't talk again. Yes; see I have stitched my lips from end to end. From now on, I'm the eunuch in service at the palace of the Oba of Benin— tongue pulled out by the root, eardrums punctured to the base, and therefore deaf, dumb from birth, and as the women will have it, completely without pestle." He is not silent of course, no more than a character in a medieval English interlude, or Hotspur. The interest of the play is not the novelty of the situation but Clark's witty display of Ijaw family and communal life through the old plot.

Ijaw life had long been Clark's great interest. In personal communication, Clark remarked that he did not know an uncle of his was a great poet until he began researching Urhobo poetry; "The point is that the poetry was already there. It was being sung and danced all around us. But we didn't know!"

Partly to correct this ignorance, Clark undertook to preserve the Ozidi saga, the hero tale he first published in dramatic form and then translated at length, in a volume that reproduces a transcription of an Ijaw recital of the story with Clark's translation in parallel columns. His research had found three versions, the festival performance that Clark and Speed filmed, a tale recited by the poet Afoluwa, and a full epic recited by another poet, Okabu Ojobolo. The third one was the version that Clark translated and published as *The Ozidi Saga*.

The saga was recorded in the sitting room of a lady in Ibadan, with an audience of enthusiastic listener-participants, mostly women, and with drumbeats as instrumental support. The saga is marked by repetition, prolixity, lapses of memory, and as Clark says in his introduction, "faults crying aloud in the frequent paratactic constructions." These very faults certify that the saga is, in the highest oral tradition, a unique thing, derived from but not identical with its predecessor renditions. Okabou learned the story from a professional storyteller, Atazi, for whom Okabou worked, apparently as a servant. That was many years earlier than the mid 1960s, when Okabou

was already over seventy years old. *The Ozidi Saga* is a tale of Ado, the legendary city of Benin (not the real imperial city).

The water imagery shows that the saga is an indigenous work, though set in fictitious Ado. In the canon of Clark's work *The Ozidi Saga* is unusual in that it is so purely Ijaw. Clark labored to re-create, so far as the English language permitted, the Ijaw text. There is no verbal trickery, no oblique or cryptic allusion, no use of surprising rhythm, and no flamboyant imagery. Even Clark's wit and irony are reserved for the preface, the introductory essay, and the notes. The reader of the English text senses that he is as near the performance as print is likely to bring him.

The saga was told over the course of seven nights, each representing several hours of recitation, interspersed with songs, chants, comments, and responses. The alert reader can imagine Okabou's vigor at the start, his miming of the character Temugedege's cowardice, the spectator's delight and encouragement, the conscious directing of attention to the recorder, then the entry of the drumbeats and the mocking antiphonal song, followed by Temugedege's quavering fear and the laughter it provokes, and finally the teller describing and miming Ozidi's hyperbolic sword stroke. What makes this so important is that such liveliness has customarily been edited out of scholarly transcriptions of oral performances, making them more Homeric than alive. Clark is faithful to the tape recorder, not academic tradition. The result is both interesting and demanding—some would say too demanding. It is a work of literature more for study than entertainment.

The saga has much that Clark put into the play *Ozidi*, including the killing of Oreame by Ozidi. But one should not take this as seriously as Clark does; he sees it as retributive justice, but Okabou has the old witch appear to Ozidi in a dream and advise him how to bring her back to life.

The saga, taken in conjunction with the film and the play, makes for a grand, if sometimes ambiguous, achievement. The variety of forms provides an unprecedented sense of the whole. Nowhere else can the layman find so rounded and fully dimensioned a record of what is now a lost experience of epic. Not that Clark has been without his critics. Serious questions regarding the transcription and the translation have been raised. Clark, as an anthropologist and as a linguist, is but a talented amateur, and this fact shows.

He is more at home in literary criticism, his major work in this field being five essays that were collected as *The Example of Shakespeare*. "Themes of African Poetry of English Expression," for example, is an early (1964) review of the corpus of poetry from West, East, and South Africa. Clark takes into account the historical circumstances and the social context of African poets, while seeing the weaknesses of clichéd negritudist and resistance poetry and praising the successes of better poets. His point in the essay, however, is to refute the strictures of committed critics and anthologizers of bad poetry, such as some living in the West. In "The Communication Line between Poet and Public" (1966) he contrasts the immediate connection between writer and reader in the easy, often bombastic, old poetry celebrating Africa, with more interesting but difficult work of Okigbo. He sets himself (and Gabriel Okara) between the two extremes, noting, however, that some of his work gives readers trouble, as does the poetry of Soyinka. A gap, he says rightly, exists between poets and their public, widened by the training of some teachers, who appreciate only traditional English poetry and cannot accommodate modern poetry, whether Nigerian or British.

Clark's inaugural lecture as professor of English, *The Hero as a Villain*, was delivered and published in 1978—six years late. In it Clark examines the great warrior-heroes of classical and English traditions—Achilles, Oedipus, Richard III, Othello, and Macbeth—along with Nigeria's Ozidi, to make a mild, ironic attack on recent Nigerian leadership. The warrior-hero often falls into error and wickedness, Clark says, and as a result needs cleansing. In Nigeria, "peace and justice" will not be possible, he suggests, until "society and the hero are purified of the villain within."

Interviews:

Bernth Lindfors, Ian Munro, Richard Priebe, and Reinhard Sander, eds., *Palaver: Interviews with Five African Writers in Texas* (Austin: African and Afro-American Research Institute, University of Texas, 1972), pp. 14-22;

Dennis Duerden and Cosmo Pieterse, eds., *African Writers Talking: A Collection of Radio Interviews* (London: Heinemann, 1972), pp. 63-74;

"The Lagos Scene," *West Africa* (16 December 1985): 2642-2643.

References:

J. A. Adedeji, "Some Notes on *Song of a Goat* by J. P. Clark," *Ibadan*, 28 (July 1970): 99-101;

Z. A. Adejumo, "Language in the Plays of J. P. Clark," *Nigeria Magazine*, 130-131 (1980): 56-74;

Dapo Adelugba, "Trance and Theatre: The Nigerian Experience," *Ufahamu*, 6, no. 2 (1976): 47-61;

Albert Olu Ashaolu, "J. P. Clark: His Significance as a Dramatist," in *Theatre in Africa*, edited by Oyin Ogunba and Abiola Irele (Ibadan: Ibadan University Press, 1978), pp. 177-199;

Ashaolu, "The Tragic Vision of Life in *The Raft*," *Obsidian*, 3 (Winter 1977): 20-25;

Anthony Astrachan, "Like Goats to the Slaughter: Three Plays by John Pepper Clark," *Black Orpheus*, 16 (October 1964): 21-24;

Lloyd W. Brown, "The American Image in African Literature," *Conch*, 4 (March 1972): 55-70;

Wilfred Cartey, *Whispers from a Continent* (New York: Random House, 1969), pp. 340-350;

William Connor, "Diribi's Incest: The Key to J. P. Clark's *The Masquerade*," *World Literature Written in English*, 18 (November 1979): 278-286;

M. J. C. Echeruo, "Traditional and Borrowed Elements in Nigerian Poetry," *Nigeria Magazine*, 89 (June 1966): 142-155;

J. B. Egberike, "J. P. Clark's Izon-English Translation of the Ozidi Saga," *Kiabara*, 2 (1979): 7-35;

Romanus N. Egudu, *Four Modern West African Poets* (New York: Nok, 1977);

Egudu, "J. P. Clark as a Bastard Child: A Study of 'Ivbie,'" *Journal of the New African Literature and the Arts*, 13-14 (1973): 21-26;

Egudu, "J. P. Clark's *The Raft*: The Tragedy of Economic Impotence," *World Literature Written in English*, 15 (November 1976): 297-304;

Isaac I. Elimimian, "J. P. Clark as a Poet," *Literary Criterion*, 23, nos. 1-2 (1988): 30-58;

Elimimian, "The Rhetoric of J. P. Clark's *Ivbie*," *World Literature Written in English*, 27 (Autumn 1987): 161-173;

Elimimian, "The Theme of Violence and Protest in J. P. Clark's Poetry," *Concerning Poetry*, 17 (Fall 1984): 73-87;

Martin Esslin, "Two African Playwrights," *Black Orpheus*, 19 (March 1966): 33-39;

John Ferguson, "Nigerian Drama in English," *Modern Drama*, 11 (May 1968): 10-26;

Robert Fraser, *West African Poetry: A Critical History* (Cambridge: Cambridge University Press, 1986);

Ken Goodwin, *Understanding African Poetry: A Study of Ten Poets* (London: Heinemann, 1982);

Paul O. Iheakaram, "John Pepper Clark and Stephen Crane: An Investigation of Source and Influence," *Research in African Literatures*, 13 (Spring 1982): 53-59;

Abiola Irele, Introduction to Clark's *Collected Plays and Poems, 1958-1988* (Washington, D.C.: Howard University Press, 1991), pp. xi-liv;

Dan Izevbaye, "The Poetry and Drama of John Pepper Clark," in *Introduction to African Literature*, edited by Bruce King (Lagos: University of Lagos & Evans, 1971), pp. 152-172;

Thomas R. Knipp, " 'Ivbie': The Developing Moods of John Pepper Clark's Poetry," *Journal of Commonwealth Literature*, 17, no. 1 (1982): 123-144;

Obi Maduakor, "On the Poetry of War: Yeats and J. P. Clark," *African Literature Today*, 14 (1984): 68-76;

Chidi T. Maduka, "African Religious Beliefs in Literary Imagination: Ogbanje and Abiku in Chinua Achebe, J. P. Clark and Wole Soyinka," *Journal of Commonwealth Literature*, 22, no. 1 (1987): 17-30;

T. O. McLoughlin, "The Plays of John Pepper Clark," *English Studies in Africa*, 18 (March 1975): 31-40;

Barbara Grant Nnoka, "Authenticity in John Pepper Clark's Early Poems and Plays," *Literature East & West*, 12 (March 1968): 56-67;

P. Emeka Nwabueze, "J. P. Clark's *Song of a Goat*: An Example of Nigerian Bourgeois Drama," *World Literature Written in English*, 28 (Spring 1988): 35-40;

Kolawole Ogungbesan, "Nigerian Writers and Political Commitment," *Ufahamu*, 5, no. 2 (1974): 20-50;

Emeka Okeke-Ezigbo, "The 'Sharp and Sided Hail': Hopkins and His Nigerian Imitators and Detractors," in *Hopkins among the Poets: Studies in Modern Responses to Gerard Manley Hopkins*, edited by Richard F. Giles (Hamilton, Ontario: International Hopkins Association, 1985), pp. 114-123;

Patrick O'Malley, "J. P. Clark and *The Example of Shakespeare*," *Odi*, 3, no. 1 (1978): 4-15;

Kirsten Holst Petersen, *John Pepper Clark, Selected Poems: A Critical View* (London: Rex Collings in assoc. with the British Council, 1981);

John Povey, " 'Two hands a man has': The Poetry of J. P. Clark," *African Literature Today*, 1 (1968): 36-47;

Paul Theroux, "Voices Out of the Skull: A Study of Six African Poets," *Black Orpheus*, 20 (August 1966): 41-58;

Edwin Thumboo, "An Ibadan Dawn: The Poetry of J. P. Clark," *Books Abroad*, 44 (Summer 1970): 387-392;

Nyong J. Udoeyop, *Three Nigerian Poets: A Critical Study of Soyinka, Clark and Okigbo* (Ibadan: Ibadan University Press, 1973);

Theo Vincent, "The Modern Inheritance: Studies in Clark's *The Raft* and Soyinka's *The Road*," *Oduma*, 2 (August 1974): 38-41, 44-49;

Robert M. Wren, *J. P. Clark* (Boston: G. K. Hall, 1984).

Joe de Graft

(2 April 1924 - 1 November 1978)

Kofi Ermeleh Agovi
University of Ghana—Legon

BOOKS: *Sons and Daughters* (London & New York: Oxford University Press, 1964);

Visitor from the Past (Accra: Anowuo, 1968);

Through a Film Darkly (London: Oxford University Press, 1970);

Beneath the Jazz and Brass (London: Heinemann, 1975);

Muntu (London & Nairobi: Heinemann, 1977).

PLAY PRODUCTIONS: *Village Investment*, Accra, Ghana Drama Studio, 1962;

Visitor from the Past, Accra, Ghana Drama Studio, September 1962;

Ananse and the Gum Man, Accra, Ghana Drama Studio, 1965;

Muntu, Nairobi, University of Nairobi Free Travelling Theatre, 24 November 1975;

Mambo, adapted from *Macbeth* by William Shakespeare, Legon, School of Performing Arts, October 1978.

MOTION PICTURES: *No Tears for Ananse*, adapted by de Graft from his play *Ananse and the Gum Man*, Ghana Film Production, 1965;

Hamile, adapted by de Graft from *Hamlet* by William Shakespeare, Ghana Film Production, 1965.

OTHER: Kofi Awoonor and G. Adali-Mortty, eds., *Messages: Poems from Ghana*, includes poems by de Graft (London: Heinemann, 1970).

SELECTED PERIODICAL PUBLICATIONS—UNCOLLECTED: "Drama Workshop, 1963," *Okyeame*, 2, no. 1 (1964): 48-56;

"*The Catechist* by J. W. Abruquah," *Okyeame*, 3 (December 1966): 63-64;

"Roots in African Drama and Theatre," *African Literature Today*, 8 (1981): 1-25.

Joe de Graft (courtesy of Mrs. Leone de Graft)

Soon after his death Joe de Graft was acclaimed an "elder statesman of Ghanaian letters . . . a pillar in the theatre movement of Ghana [and] a creative genius of stature" (obituary, *West Africa*, 1979). He was also seen as "a man with a consuming passion for drama," who led "a life fully committed and devoted to the performing arts of music and drama." De Graft established himself in the eyes of the younger generation of Ghanaian writers and lovers of theater arts as a "monumental figure, teacher and practitioner in one."

Joseph Coleman de Graft, playwright, poet, novelist, and educator, was born in Cape Coast, Ghana, on 2 April 1924. His father, also named Joseph, was one of the elite coastal merchants; his mother was Janet Acquaye de Graft, a housewife. He was educated at Mfantsipim School (1939-1943), Achimota College (1944-1946), and the University College of the Gold Coast (1950-1953). The same year he graduated from the university, he married Leone Buckle, a Ghanaian professional accountant from Osu, Accra; they eventually had a daughter (Carol) and two sons (Joseph and Dave). In the course of de Graft's career, he ultimately became an associate professor of drama and the director of the School of Performing Arts, University of Ghana, Legon, in 1977. In 1955 he taught at Mfantsipim School, where as head of the English department he initiated and developed drama as a subject in the curriculum; this eventually led to the founding of the Mfantsipim Drama Laboratory. He was also instrumental in building up a program of annual staff productions in the school.

A UNESCO fellowship in 1960 enabled him to travel to Great Britain and the United States to observe both amateur and professional theater and university work in drama. Nine years later a similar UNESCO grant took him to the University of Nairobi, Kenya, where he spent almost eight years building up and teaching drama courses at both the undergraduate and postgraduate levels. It was at the University of Nairobi, observed Adzei Bekoe, former vice-chancellor of the University of Ghana, in a eulogy in 1978, that de Graft's "talents as a playwright, actor and poet blossomed." He directed and produced several plays on stage, radio, and television, "half of which were from the works of Shakespeare." His fondness for Shakespeare was later to become a significant factor in his career, first because it prevented him from a total allegiance to the African theater, and second because it represented his desire to "internationalize" the African theater.

When de Graft left the University College of the Gold Coast in 1953, the changes in Africa had become exciting and momentous. The First Congress of Negro Writers and Artists, to be held in Paris, was only three years away. In the meantime there was a gathering momentum of two complementary forces: African nationalism and its attendant cultural revival. Inside Ghana, around 1953, Kwame Nkrumah had broken away from the "gradualism" of the United Gold Coast Convention (UGCC) and formed the Convention

People's Party (CPP), whose agitation had put the country on a firm course toward independence. The tradition of political journalism in the country, established by men such as S. R. B. Atto-Ahuma, J. E. Casely-Hayford, J. B. Danquah, and Kobina Sekyi, was given a completely new twist in popularity by the CPP, which used its party newspapers to raise the consciousness of the people to support the nationalist cause. Through its agitation, the CPP also created a mood of nationalism in the country, which encouraged creative artists such as Ephraim Amu (musician), Michael Dei-Anang (poet), and J. Benibengor Blay (fiction writer) to provide, in their own individual ways, leadership in the early stages of the cultural revival. Later they were to be joined by Kofi Antubam (artist), Efua Sutherland (playwright), and J. H. Kwabena Nketia (traditional poet and musician), all of whom helped Nkrumah in diverse ways to set up the cultural institutions of postindependence Ghana.

The emergent theater of the country in the 1950s was dominated entirely by the performances and activities of itinerant concert-party troupes whose existence dates back to the 1930s. Thus, long before Nkrumah launched the nationalist struggle in 1949, these troupes had established a tradition of direct and widespread appeal to the masses, a factor the nationalists exploited. Concert-party groups such as Ghana Trio and Bob Cole's Dynamic Ghana Trio, which were current by 1954, had anticipated the new name for the independent Gold Coast (Ghana). In the context of the cultural nationalism of the time the concert-party theater groups culminated in the National Theatre Movement of the 1960s. In all these developments the literary theater of the 1950s was, by comparison, still asleep, content to produce only the occasional adaptation of a foreign text, musical, or cantata play.

As a teacher of English and the initiator and director of the Mfantsipim Drama Laboratory from 1955 to 1960, de Graft appeared completely unaffected by the strong nationalist aspirations of the popular theater. He was also unmoved in his love for Shakespeare's plays, since he was still active in producing and acting in plays of the English classics, and School Certificate set plays. Later, in the early 1960s, he started to develop a sympathy for the aspirations of cultural nationalism in Africa. Nevertheless, he did so with caution and circumspection. In a review of J. W. Abruquah's novel *The Catechist* in 1966, he decried the "almost paranoiac search

De Graft (with unidentified actresses) in the University of Nairobi Free Travelling Theatre production of his Muntu, November 1975 (courtesy of Mrs. Leone de Graft)

for distinctively Ghanaian forms of expression." He also contended later, in *African Literature Today* (1981), that "modern dramatists are fundamentally individualists with a fierce pride in their individual effort, their unique ideas, their artistic integrity, and their achievement." In his view, therefore, nothing should be done to reverse the trend. In an era of mass political parties, mass movements, and the dominance of collective traditions, including obsolete family traditions, it was necessary, from de Graft's point of view, to assert a freedom of choice and an individual claim to responsibility in the conduct of life. One must be able to come to terms with human life from one's own distinctive perception of it. This concept, in effect, is the theme of his first published play, *Sons and Daughters* (1964).

James Ofosu, the central character in the play, has a wealthy and aspiring middle-class household; two of his sons are already overseas, one a medical officer and the other "a fully qualified chartered accountant." Ofosu also has firm plans for two other children: Maanan, his daughter, to become "Ghana's first lady lawyer"; and a son, Aaron, to be an engineer. Unfortunately for him, these two children have their own plans and

ambitions in life, Maanan aspiring to be a dancer and Aaron wishing to be a painter. These artistic inclinations upset Ofosu. Sometime later, in the course of Maanan's apprenticeship, Lawyer Bonu, an elderly friend to the family who had promised to secure her admission to a law school in London, decides to make amorous advances toward Maanan. This incident shocks Ofosu out of his "folly," and he grants his children the right to a free choice of their own careers.

Sons and Daughters appears to be little more than an exploratory statement about rapid departures from accepted traditions. Everything is either being knocked down or is collapsing under its own weight. Such a focus on social change was common in the African poetry and novels of the 1950s. It also became the theme of Ene Henshaw's plays of the early 1960s, plays which de Graft helped to introduce into Ghanaian schools. Moreover, as the director of the Ghana Drama Studio, a research fellow at the Institute of African Studies, and head of the Drama Division of the School of Music and Drama from 1961 to 1969, de Graft was in a position to appreciate the effects of social change on African institutions. He was also well placed, as a poet and budding playwright, to record it for the theater in a much more authoritative way.

Sons and Daughters was his first attempt to achieve a creative correspondence between his personal convictions and the outer realities of contemporary Africa. Unfortunately, this attempt failed because he was unable to integrate the two fundamental concerns in the play—individualism and social change—within a common frame of reference. The themes stand out as two separate convictions. While other African writers were reasonably clear about the need to assert the collective consciousness of the African past, de Graft remains undecided in this play, unable to define clearly where his loyalty should lie. This uncertainty undermines the play's integrity, originality, and moral vision.

The Ghana Drama Studio, opened in 1961 by Nkrumah, was designed to resemble a traditional Ghanaian household. Part of Nkrumah's conscious nationalistic policy was to create relevant artistic and cultural institutions to meet the demands of the new state of Ghana. Bodies such as the Arts Council, the Institute of African Studies, Ghana Film Production, GBC-TV, and the Bureau of Ghana Languages were therefore either created or given new orientations and emphases. All of them had complimentary roles and objectives. The Institute of African Studies, for example, was to develop the arts of Ghana and other parts of Africa in close relation to Ghanaian traditions, while expressing "the ideas and aspirations of our people in our contemporary era." The School of Music and Drama was to build up knowledge through research in order to train students "to develop vital theatre traditions in our own image." The Arts Council of Ghana also had the mandate to create a National Theatre Movement, whose central objective was "to stimulate the growth of new artistic idioms, new forms or new styles of music, dance and drama that have their roots in African tradition, but which also express the contemporary Ghanaian experience."

All these policies influenced the work of de Graft. As he admitted in an interview with Bernth Lindfors, the "amorphous program" in all these institutions gave him "a lot of scope" and ushered in a period of intense experimentation and active involvement with leading creative ideas. His first play at the Drama Studio was produced in 1962. In Village Investment, a one-act play, a young boy from the village is purposely sent to the city with the hope that after he has become sufficiently enlightened in the ways of the city, he would return and help the villagers improve and develop. Unfortunately city life proves too attractive and too seductive, thus dissuading him from going back to the village, a theme resembling those in Cyprian Ekwensi's People of the City (1954) and Jagua Nana (1961).

De Graft soon followed Village Investment with Visitor from the Past, also performed in 1962, later retitled Through a Film Darkly (1970). He adapted the play, with its original title, as a novel in 1968. Two unfortunate love affairs in the past coexist uneasily in the memory of John, the main character—one with Rebecca, his former Ghanaian girlfriend, and the other with Molly, an English girl he met in London in the course of his studies. Then two incidents bring the affairs to the surface: the first is the appearance in John's house of his friend Feyinka's white wife, and the second is the reappearance of Rebecca. These two incidents eventually bring him emotional ruin and destroy him. Although much has been made of the theme of racial hatred in the play, John's mere refusal to shake hands with Feyinka's white wife (the only actual scene of racial hatred in the play) cannot be the center of de Graft's intentions.

John has tried to banish Rebecca's love from his memory after meeting Molly in London. In turn Molly has betrayed John's total surrender of his love to her, and in bitterness John has returned to Ghana and married Serwah, a local girl. At this point Rebecca suddenly reappears to remind him of his perfidy. On learning that John is now married—not to Molly whom she knows, but to Serwah, a fellow Ghanaian—Rebecca walks off in utter frustration only to meet her death in a car crash on her way home. Unable to live with Rebecca's memory and the perfidy of Molly, John seeks refuge in suicide. It appears that the symbolism of John's emotional burdens and his fate is intended to be similar to the bewildering experience of contemporary Africa: the continent, suggests de Graft, cannot harbor two irreconcilable historical burdens—its cultural traditions and Western experience—at the same time. This is bound to lead to disaster, particularly where these "burdens" are full of bitter memories.

Ananse and the Gum Man (1965) is based on a traditional folktale that de Graft adapted for the stage, film, and radio. Kweku Ananse, the Spider, a symbol of shrewdness and cunning in Akan mythology, contrives his death so he will be buried on a huge family farm where he can con-

Cover for the 1977 publication of the play that, according to de Graft, "spans the whole of African man's existence"

sume all the harvest alone. This bizarre robbery, discovered soon after Ananse's funeral, shocks his son, Kweku Tsin, who decides to erect a "Gum Man" to trap the culprit. Ananse is trapped, and the whole village confronts his unbridled gluttony. The stage version makes use of folktale elements such as a narrator, mime, and drumming and singing, but the film version, *No Tears for Ananse* (also 1965), effectively emphasized the central drive of humor, fun, and sheer entertainment, coupled with a lesson for humankind. After de Graft's death, the play was once again returned to the stage in Kenya in 1979.

In the same year that the film *No Tears for Ananse* was released, de Graft's *Hamile* (a Tongo version of *Hamlet*) also became a Ghana Film product, directed by Terry Bishop. It was produced specifically for presentation at the 1965 Commonwealth Arts Festival in London. The film was based on the original stage production performed earlier in the same year by students of the School of Music and Drama at the University

of Ghana. Although de Graft admired and directed many of Shakespeare's plays throughout his drama career, *Hamile* was his first experiment in adapting a major Shakespearean play to a Ghanaian setting and audience. De Graft was attempting to extend the dimensions of the Ghanaian theater to accommodate a universal experience in a distinctively Ghanaian setting, an experiment in line with the aspirations of the National Theatre Movement. However, while the costumes, props, decorations, and sets were recognizable as being rooted in the northern Ghanaian culture of the Frafra people, the play remained unaltered, except where it did not make sense in a Frafra community or where archaic words would obscure the meaning. The relevance of *Hamlet* to a contemporary Ghanaian audience is achieved through the skillful deployment of cultural symbols, including those in the setting and costumes.

But while de Graft's works seemed to support the aspirations of the National Theatre Movement, his stated personal convictions and ideas were completely at odds with the ideology of the movement. In an interview with Cosmo Pieterse he declared that he did not believe playwrights "must evolve any one form of popular theatre for everybody." He added, "to me, the important thing is not coming in solidly on the side of any particular movement."

Similarly, for de Graft the poet, the result of the African record of amalgamation, of reconciling with European values, has been particularly unfortunate and negative. The continent seems to abound with violence and disintegration. *Beneath the Jazz and Brass* (1975), which has been described as de Graft's "inner autobiography," records an increasingly personal and intimate disillusionment with the political problems of the continent. De Graft's sensitivity and forthrightness shine throughout the collection, compelling attention and obliging the reader to make a choice on each subject treated. But it is the total atmosphere of unremitting pessimism and disillusionment, powerfully rendered, which seems to dominate the poems. De Graft's profound awareness and presentation of the African environment start in Ghana in the mid 1960s; he records the betrayals, recklessness, and violence of the post-Nkrumah era.

However, it was in Kenya, at the request of the World Council of Churches in 1975, that his awareness matured into a full artistic statement, an extended creative metaphor. *Muntu* (performed, 1975; published, 1977) was that achievement, one he considered "a major breakthrough" in his creative writing. In his interview with Lindfors, de Graft pointed out that *Muntu* "spans the whole of African man's existence, from the beginning to the latest political murders and military coups in Africa." The broad sweep of the history of the African continent and the destabilizing effects of alien contact and influences make *Muntu* ambitious and thought-provoking theater. Its absolute concentration on ideas, in the tradition of Bertolt Brecht and Samuel Beckett, provides eloquent testimony on the contemporary African predicament.

A significant development in this work is de Graft's total affirmation of African culture in the play. Whereas, in his earlier adaptations and original plays, he had experimented with forms and techniques of African expression, including settings and cultural symbols that seem extraneous to his thematic concerns, in contrast the framework of *Muntu* is Akan creation mythology, which is effectively employed from the beginning to the end. God's nearness to his creation and his subsequent withdrawal from human beings as a result of their greediness become symbolic parallels of the Muntu family's inner closeness to each other and their dispersal and disintegration when greed sets in during their contacts with the "water people" and the "desert people." Moreover, the African costumes, background, songs, and mimes, as observed by the reviewer for the *Sunday Nation* at the premier production in Nairobi, "were so naturally incorporated into the play that they were a part of it, and not as usually happens, a mere interlude" (30 November 1975). The integration of African culture and expression into the thematic design of the play marks a significant shift in de Graft's perception of African culture. He comes to terms with his roots in a reconciliation that strengthens his contribution to the mainstream of the New Theatre Movement in Africa.

It is also significant that, soon after *Muntu*, his last work was an adaptation of Shakespeare's *Macbeth. Mambo* (1978), as his version was called, finally consolidates de Graft's vision of contemporary African politics as the locus of the "latest political murders and military coups." De Graft's dramatic work was becoming increasingly political just before his untimely death on 1 November 1978.

According to the *West Africa* obituary, Joe de Graft "fought doggedly to resist any tendency towards insularity in African literature, which he wished to integrate into a lively and varied world tradition." While this was true of his critical essays and most of his adaptations of Shakespearean plays, de Graft increasingly came to realize that it was by helping to create a distinct national literature that one could talk meaningfully about integrating it into a world literature. For the world tradition of literature is made up of collective national literatures including works of the stature of *Muntu*. In this sense *Muntu* may be regarded as a culmination of de Graft's consistent admiration for his roots in African culture and his desire to mold it effectively for artistic purposes. However, it should also be added that his works embody a profound ambivalence, which in effect reveals a certain unwillingness to be wholly loyal to the cultural assumptions of either Africa or Europe. His apparent need to distance himself from any commitment to a culture system reflects a weakness that goes beyond his works. Certainly, in recording similar turbulent transitions in their societies, great artists all over the world have reflected deep-seated ambiguities and ambivalences in their attitudes and presentations. Yet there is usually a "moral center" to their works—a firm impression of an inner resilience, an inner coherence, and a strength of artistic integrity that is hard to find in the works of de Graft outside *Muntu*. Since he carefully divorced his personal convictions from the convictions embodied in his works, one is unable to understand the whole man either through his works alone or through his critical utterances. However, de Graft's contributions as a playwright, poet, novelist, actor, teacher, and administrator of the arts in Ghana and elsewhere will long remain an inspiring legacy, for his works have become a part of the struggle of contemporary Africa to attain full identity, maturity, and worldwide acceptance.

Interviews:

Cosmo Pieterse, "Joe de Graft interviewed by Pieterse," *Cultural Events in Africa*, 46 (1968): i-v;

Bernth Lindfors, "Interview with Joe de Graft," *World Literature Written in English*, 18 (November 1979): 314-331.

References:

Charles Angmor, "Drama in Ghana," in *Theatre in Africa*, edited by Oyin Ogunba and Abiola Irele (Ibadan: Ibadan University Press, 1978), pp. 55-72;

MAMBO

PROLOGUE

The speaker is an itinerant musician, and he enters singing to some stringed instrument. Could it be a cora, or a lyre, or perhaps an ordinary guitar? As we look more closely, we realize that he is blind; maybe that is why he is preceded by a little boy holding a stick, a cloth bag slung over one shoulder.

The blind man continues to sing and play until the audience falls silent, as if under some compulsion from his voice and strings. Then he speaks, addressing himself to the audience as if to one person — a casual acquaintance with whom he has been carrying on a broken conversation.

... I heard your question, my good friend, if I did not answer you, it was because my mind was on this temperamental instrument... At this point, and whenever possible during the rest of his delivery, he slips in a few bars on his strings...

Now let us imagine, my good friend, that you were stopped in your tracks suddenly, as by a flash of lightning on a dark night, and that you saw, reflected in a mirror miraculously before you at the moment of the flash, yourself not as you are but as you have always wished to be:

Obscure tally clerk in a dingy customs office
        Instead of a gangster chief,
Goatherd with little care and no worries
        Instead of a business tycoon,
Simple village fish monger
        Instead of the first emancipated lady of the land,

P.T.O.

Page from the manuscript for de Graft's last play, an adaptation of Macbeth *(by permission of Mrs. Leone de Graft)*

Jawa Apronti, "Ghanaian Poetry in the 1970s," in *New West African Literature*, edited by Kolawole Ogungbesan (London: Heinemann, 1979), pp. 31-44;

Kofi Awoonor, "The Imagery of Fire: A Critical Assessment of the Poetry of Joe de Graft," *Okike*, 19 (September 1981): 70-79;

Robert Fraser, *West African Poetry: A Critical History* (Cambridge: Cambridge University Press, 1986), pp. 139-146;

Jochen R. Klicker, "The School of Performing Arts: Joe C. de Graft, *Mambo*," in *Horizonte-Magazin 79*, edited by Ulrich Eckhardt (Berlin: Berliner Festspiele GmbH, 1979), pp. 28-29;

Reinhard Sander, "Joe de Graft's 'Two Views from a Window,'" *Greenfield Review*, 2 (Fall 1972): 23-30.

H. G. de Lisser

(9 December 1878 - 18 May 1944)

Frank M. Birbalsingh
York University

BOOKS: *In Jamaica and Cuba* (Kingston, Jamaica: Gleaner, 1910);

Twentieth Century Jamaica (Kingston, Jamaica: Jamaica Times, 1913);

Jane: A Story of Jamaica (Kingston, Jamaica: Gleaner, 1913); republished as *Jane's Career: A Story of Jamaica* (London: Methuen, 1914; New York: Africana, 1971);

Susan Proudleigh (London: Methuen, 1915);

Triumphant Squalitone: A Tropical Extravaganza (Kingston, Jamaica: Gleaner, 1916);

Jamaica and the Great War (Kingston, Jamaica: Gleaner, 1917);

Revenge: A Tale of Old Jamaica (Kingston, Jamaica: Gleaner, 1919);

The White Witch of Rosehall (London: Benn, 1929);

Under the Sun: A Jamaica Comedy (London: Benn, 1937);

Psyche (London: Benn, 1952);

Morgan's Daughter (London: Benn, 1953);

The Cup and the Lip: A Romance (London: Benn, 1956);

The Arawak Girl (Kingston, Jamaica: Pioneer, 1958).

OTHER: *Planters' Punch*, 4 volumes, edited by de Lisser (Kingston, Jamaica, 1920-1944).

SELECTED PERIODICAL PUBLICATIONS— UNCOLLECTED: "Christina's Dream," *Planters' Punch*, 1, no. 1 (1920);

"The Rivals," *Planters' Punch*, 1, no. 2 (1921);

"The Devil's Mountain," *Planters' Punch*, 1, no. 3 (1922-1923);

"The Defence of Jamaica," *Planters' Punch*, 1, no. 4 (1923-1924);

"The Adventures Abroad of Mr. Jenkins," *Planters' Punch*, 1, no. 5 (1924-1925);

"The Jamaica Nobility," *Planters' Punch*, 1, no. 6 (1925-1926);

"The Sins of the Children," *Planters' Punch*, 2, no. 2 (1928);

"The Jamaica Bandits," *Planters' Punch*, 2, no. 4 (1929-1930);

"The Crocodiles," *Planters' Punch*, 3, no. 1 (1932-1933);

"Poltergeist," *Planters' Punch*, 3, no. 2 (1933-1934); no. 3 (1934-1935);

"Conquest," *Planters' Punch*, 3, no. 6 (1937-1938);

"The White Maroon," *Planters' Punch*, 4, no. 1 (1938-1939);

"Haunted," *Planters' Punch*, 4, no. 2 (1939-1940);

"Myrtle and Money," *Planters' Punch*, 4, no. 4 (1941-1942);

"The Return," *Planters' Punch*, 4, no. 6 (1943-1944).

H. G. de Lisser in 1944, the year of his death (photograph courtesy of the National Library of Jamaica)

Herbert George de Lisser was active as a journalist, editor, novelist, and man of letters during the first half of the twentieth century. For much of this period, de Lisser also gave unstinting service to public institutions, and, together with his literary achievements, this made him a distinguished figure in Jamaican intellectual, artistic, political, and social circles. Although his distinction has faded as a result of sociopolitical changes that have inevitably overtaken Jamaica, de Lisser still retains a notable position in literary history as the first important novelist of the English-speaking Caribbean.

De Lisser was born in Falmouth, Jamaica, on 9 December 1878, at a time when the island was still a British colony and when slavery had been abolished for almost fifty years, but manners were still largely determined by factors of race, color, and class—a system that had flourished in the rigidly feudalistic structure of slave society. De Lisser's father, also named H. G. de Lisser, owned and edited the *Trelawny*, a paper

published in Falmouth; his mother was a Miss Isaacs, who came from a well-known Kingston family. Since he was of mixed (mainly Portuguese and Jewish) blood, de Lisser escaped the social and economic disadvantages endured by the more obviously black descendants of the African slaves, who formed the mass of the Jamaican people. He began his education at a private school in Falmouth, before entering a secondary school in the capital city of Kingston, where his family had moved. But the premature death of his father curtailed de Lisser's education when he was only fourteen, and he was forced into menial jobs for a time. His first significant job was as an assistant in the library of the Institute of Jamaica, and de Lisser grasped the opportunity to read widely and educate himself. Later he joined the *Daily Gleaner* as proofreader, then the *Jamaica Times*, and the *Daily Telegraph*, before finally rejoining the *Daily Gleaner* as associate editor in 1903. He became chief editor of the paper the next year and held the post until 1942, when he retired because of ill health. De Lisser was married to the former Ellen Guenther. He died on 18 May 1944.

De Lisser's role as editor of what became Jamaica's chief newspaper gave him a vantage point from which to observe Jamaican affairs. These observations nourished both his journalism and fiction, and provided material for his first two books, *In Jamaica and Cuba* (1910) and *Twentieth Century Jamaica* (1913). The first was written after a trip de Lisser made to Cuba in 1909, and it includes his impressions of that island along with a commentary on Jamaican affairs. The second book provides as authoritative and wide-ranging an account of Jamaican history and current affairs as existed at the time. These two books established de Lisser's reputation as an informed and reliable commentator on Jamaica. His step from national commentator to novelist benefited from the help of Sir Sydney Olivier, the British governor of Jamaica from 1907 to 1913. In his book *Jamaica the Blessed Island* (1936) Olivier claims that he encouraged de Lisser "to write some stories out of his knowledge of the everyday life of the common Jamaican people." De Lisser's first novel, *Jane: A Story of Jamaica* (1913), better known as *Jane's Career* (its later title), was apparently composed in response to this encouragement and was dedicated to Olivier.

Jane's Career tells the story of a black girl, Jane Burrell, who leaves the Jamaican countryside to improve herself—socially and economically—in Kingston. At first she lives with Mrs. Mason and her family, who are members of the affluent, colored middle class. The contrast between Mrs. Mason's family and Jane and her friends highlights the post-slavery social stratification based on race and color in early-twentieth-century Jamaica. Mrs. Mason and her nieces are brown (mulatto), educated, affluent, and supposedly genteel in manners and virtuous in conduct, whereas black characters such as Jane, Sarah—the former Mason maid—and Jane's friend Sathyra are poor and expected to be vulgar in manners, ribald in speech, and venal in morals. Yet de Lisser describes Mrs. Mason's family as hypocritical, snobbish, and venal, whereas in Jane and her friends he perceives independence, ambition, and a will to survive. In a scene in which Mrs. Mason hits Jane and quarrels with Sarah, Jane is terrified but not Sarah, who says: "I know I am black, an' I know God meck two colour, black an' white, but it must be the devil meck brown people, for dem is neider black nor

white." Sarah's outburst illustrates both the aggrieved feelings of the black Jamaican majority and the ambivalence of the brown middle class, which are important themes running throughout de Lisser's fiction.

It is going too far perhaps to regard *Jane's Career* as a plea for radical social change that would satisfy both black and brown people, although the heroine does grow in confidence and experience, and by her success she represents the need for more democratic rights in Jamaica. What the novel achieves is an objective presentation of Jamaican social attitudes at the turn of the century, including feelings of oppression and resistance. It is not only black labor that is shown to be exploited: black women are easy prey for men who use money, color, and social prestige to buy sexual favors. Jane has to resist the advances of Mrs. Mason's nephew Cecil as well as those of her subsequent boss Mr. Curden. Whether Jane survives through luck or strength of will, her story vividly evokes Jamaica as it really was less than a hundred years ago, and it is because of this lifelike, realistic evocation that *Jane's Career* has proved the most enduring of de Lisser's novels.

In de Lisser's next novel, *Susan Proudleigh* (1915), the Jamaican heroine is deserted by her lover, who migrates to Panama at the time the Panama Canal was being dug. There is much intrigue later on, when Susan goes to Panama with another lover and becomes the central figure in complicated love affairs before her return to Jamaica. *Susan Proudleigh* presents realistic social vignettes of Jamaica as authentic as those in *Jane's Career*. The victimized condition of women is particularly evident in both novels, together with the extraordinary survival skills that de Lisser's women characters seem to muster. But the complicated intrigue of the second novel seems a little contrived and introduces a strain of melodrama that becomes a regular feature in subsequent de Lisser novels. However, *Susan Proudleigh* was popular in its day, was successfully dramatized by E. M. Cupidon, and was produced in Kingston in 1931—it opened on 7 January at the Ward Theatre.

The plot of *Triumphant Squalitone* (1916) is the result of a fanciful declaration during World War I by the king of England, proclaiming Jamaica a republic (though any thoughts of true independence were impractical). Presidential elections were held featuring rival candidates. But in the novel the frivolity of the whole exercise is obvious from the humor that emerges out of the elec-

Dust jacket for the Heinemann edition (1972) of de Lisser's first and best-known novel, originally published in 1913

tion campaign. A policeman, for example, betrays his own ignorance when he mistakes a Latin quotation for obscene language and threatens to arrest the speaker. At the end of the campaign, before the president-elect can take office, the governor announces "that the old order which had never changed for an instant" is to be restored. No one is surprised when the president-elect agrees "with hearty readiness"; for, one feels, a change in the status quo had never been seriously contemplated. *Triumphant Squalitone* conveys sentiments of fervent loyalty to the British Empire, and, despite its unrealistic elements of fantasy, it indicates de Lisser's own faith in imperialism.

De Lisser's first three novels show that his chief subject is Jamaican history and society. His main themes are oppression and resistance, and his technique consists of the realistic evocation seen in *Jane's Career* and less realistic elements of melodrama and fantasy in *Susan Proudleigh* and

Triumphant Squalitone. In his fourth novel, *Revenge: A Tale of Old Jamaica* (1919), realism, romance, and fantasy are mixed into a blend that appears in all his subsequent novels. *Revenge* is set in the period of the so-called Morant Bay Rebellion, which occurred in Jamaica in 1865. Seventeen whites were killed and thirty-one wounded by black Jamaicans in a riot (rather than rebellion) that provoked the British governor into having 435 blacks shot, about 600 more flogged, and about one thousand buildings destroyed. Curiously the horror and destructiveness of these events do not come to the fore in de Lisser's account. Not that they are ignored, but their full significance is hidden behind an imaginary story involving the Carlton family—in particular, their son Richard and his cousin Joyce Graham.

Richard and another gentleman, Solway of Cranebook, vie for the love of Joyce. The Morant Bay Rebellion provides a suitably dangerous and threatening background to heighten this lovers' conflict. When Solway disguises himself as a Negro to win Joyce's love by rescuing her during the riot, his disguise makes it more plausible that British soldiers shoot him during their reprisal against the rebels. Richard also has an affair with Rachel Bogle, the daughter of Deacon Bogle, a historical figure who did play a prominent role in the uprising, but this minor affair merely thickens the plot by adding intrigue and complicating the major conflict among Joyce and her two lovers. Certainly Richard's liaison with Rachel cannot be taken as an attempt to investigate or probe the circumstances of the rebellion or to illuminate history. In the treatment of the same event, for example, in the novel *New Day* (1949) de Lisser's countryman Vic Reid brings out the heroism of the Jamaican people's struggle to reduce or modify the injustice of colonial government. In *Revenge*, however, de Lisser's interest seems at least equally divided between history and romance, and his novel is remembered more for its romantic twists and turns than for its accurate reconstruction of the general social background and atmosphere in Jamaica at the time of the Morant Bay Rebellion.

The literary model de Lisser fashions in *Revenge*, which mixes the reconstruction of a historical period with melodramatic elements, consisting of adventure, violence, romance, mystery, intrigue, and suspense, carries over to *The White Witch of Rosehall* (1929), which is set in Jamaica in the early 1830s, when emancipation was approaching and there was much unrest among slaves who sensed freedom in the air. The general background of unrest, threats of plots, and severe punishments dealt out to suspected slaves is historically accurate, and the protagonist of the novel, Annie Palmer, is based on the biography of an actual plantation owner who had a reputation for cruelty, necromancy, and the murders of her husbands. She herself was killed by her slaves. De Lisser's Annie is an extraordinary portrait of unrelieved cunning, malignance, and cruelty: "Annie ruled her people by terror, white and black alike. She had witnessed whippings for years and years, and her appetite had grown with what it fed on." The story of dark suspicions, secret threats, brutal beatings, murder, and necromancy ends with Annie being throttled by the black *obeahman* (sorcerer), who, in fact, was her former ally and had killed one of her three husbands in the same way.

Annie's earlier sobbing, choking, crying, and gasping add to the Gothic excesses in the novel, which serves as a good text for examining stylistic models that may have influenced de Lisser's fiction. If de Lisser did not have direct knowledge of the Gothic romances of Horace Walpole and Ann Radcliffe, he may have encountered similarly Gothic elements in the work of many popular Victorian writers, including Charles Reade and Wilkie Collins, who also traded in romantic incidents, complicated twists and turns of plot, and violent or sensational incidents. Such writing was probably popular in Jamaica during much of de Lisser's life, although it now appears dated and obsolete. This would explain both why *The White Witch of Rosehall* was the most popular of his novels during his lifetime and why it seems almost unreadable today.

The White Witch of Rosehall was first published in an annual magazine, *Planters' Punch*, started by de Lisser in 1920 as the unofficial organ of the Jamaica Imperial Association. De Lisser edited the periodical, which usually carried one of his long stories or novels. *Planters' Punch* died only with de Lisser and only after it had afforded a trial run to several of his works that were later republished in book form in London. Fifteen of these periodical stories were never republished as books, although they contain the same blend of historical or contemporary social reproductions mixed with elements of adventure, suspense, and mystery—as suggested by titles such as "The Rivals," "The Devil's Mountain," "Poltergeist," and "Haunted."

Under the Sun (1937), de Lisser's sixth novel, is set in Jamaica in the period between the two world wars, and gives as authentic a picture of society as *Jane's Career*, except that his observations are entirely concentrated on the upper classes. Through the story of Amy Brown, an English girl whose colored husband is snubbed by her white friends, de Lisser illustrates the injustice of the same social code, based on race and color, that he first examined in *Jane's Career*. In *Under the Sun* the economic implications of the code are less damaging, because Amy's husband, Christopher, belongs to the well-to-do middle class. But the psychological damage caused by color snobbery and racial prejudice is just as severe. Amy eventually divorces him and enters into marriage with a member of the local white establishment, and Christopher reunites with an old girlfriend. As in *Jane's Career*, while the injustices of post-slavery Jamaican society are recognized, and although a need for reform is implied, there is no strength in de Lisser's instinct for reform. The suffering of the victimized characters in both novels is overcome or endured with relative ease, and there is no tragic sense in their victimization. In both cases romantic and exotic aspects seem to predominate. No wonder de Lisser's fiction was admired by writers such as W. Somerset Maugham and Rudyard Kipling who, in some of their fiction, presented other areas of the world merely as exotic outposts of the empire.

Under the Sun is the last of de Lisser's novels that was published as a book during his lifetime. Between 1937 and 1944 he continued to write and serialize stories and novels for *Planters' Punch*, and one of these, "Psyche," became the first of four to be republished as books after his death. *Psyche* (1952) has the same emancipation setting seen in *Revenge*. As always de Lisser demonstrates his considerable grasp of facts and details about Jamaica's historical and social development. The administration, economy, and general day-to-day domestic and field routine of a West Indian plantation are comprehensively and authoritatively evoked. Burning issues of the day are accurately and vividly dramatized, in particular, the debate about emancipation, problems in its practical implementation, and the resistance of some planters to it. De Lisser's knowledge of history and his skill in lucid commentary are again impressive.

But the interest in history is overshadowed by a story of passion and violence in which Psyche, an African slave, schemes, plots, and maneuvers to secure the affection of her master, Charles Huntingdon. The uncanny success of her nefarious maneuvering continues until her daughter (by Huntingdon) is grown up and engaged to marry another plantation owner, Frederick O'Brian. In a typically Gothic denouement, O'Brian is killed by rebel slaves while his fiancée (Psyche's daughter, also named Psyche) poisons herself, and with her dying breath she reminds her mother that it was the same poison she (the mother) had used to remove a rival many years before. The novel neither argues strongly against the injustice of slavery nor strongly for its validity. Slave owners and slaves are both capable of cruelty as well as kindness. The circumstances of Psyche's career are presented objectively, but it is the objectivity of a journalist interested mainly in reporting the facts, unaccompanied by any strong emotional reaction or feeling. Whether this is true objectivity or deep-seated ambivalence is a central question in evaluating de Lisser's fiction. In historical novels such as *Psyche*, where the issues surrounding emancipation and slavery are now obsolete, it is perhaps easier to acknowledge his objectivity. At the same time, this objectivity reduces the impact of themes concerning oppression by plantation owners and resistance by rebellious slaves, ideas that have continuing significance as the results of race and color prejudice in Jamaica in de Lisser's lifetime.

Morgan's Daughter (1953) falls in the same historical mold as *Psyche*. Set in the nineteenth century, it vividly and accurately re-creates the period with its routine of plantation life and relationships, threats of slave uprisings, and collusion with the Maroons—slaves who had escaped former Spanish rule in Jamaica. But these historically authentic circumstances simply form the background for another story of adventure and romance. The heroine is Elizabeth Morgan, a descendant of the well-known pirate and politician Sir Henry Morgan. Elizabeth's lover is John Huntly Seymour, a gambler, robber, and adventurer who has deserted from the British navy. The relationship between two such spirited and flamboyant characters is as stormy as one would expect, and when Elizabeth reports him to the authorities because she feels betrayed, she prompts a denouement worthy of Hollywood: the two lovers become reconciled and die together in a shoot-out with soldiers. As in previous de Lisser novels the historical events in *Morgan's Daughter* are gathered behind an attractive embroidery of romance. The style itself, in employing labored and sometimes repetitive means to promote suspense, betrays de Lisser's aim to tell an entertaining and dramatic story rather than investigate history. This is why de Lisser creates larger-than-life characters such as Annie Palmer, Psyche, and Elizabeth Morgan, who dominate the action in which they are involved. Such characters are memorable for their exaggerated, eccentric, or extraordinary qualities rather than for their reflection of "normal" human behavior. In the case of each protagonist her dominant emotion is revenge, while her principal activity involves some form of cruel, deceptive, or violent behavior.

In *The Cup and the Lip* (1956) de Lisser returns to twentieth-century Jamaica and the upper class, whose weaknesses he exposed so skillfully in *Under the Sun*. The prejudices, rivalries, snobbery, and hypocrisy of this group are again portrayed with forthrightness, yet with matter-of-fact detachment. The main story of Gladys Ludford's social climbing is effective at a satirical though not an emotional level. Her emotional reactions are glib. She first has a liaison with Arthur Norris, then marries his rich, aging uncle, and when the uncle conveniently dies, she resumes her relationship with Arthur. *The Cup and the Lip* has a subplot in which Arthur has an affair with his East Indian servant Marie Ramsingh. This affair is as perfunctory as those of Gladys with Arthur and his uncle, except that it ends in a scene of grotesque brutality, when Marie's jealous husband attacks her with a machete and virtually severs her head from her body. The subplot in *The Cup and the Lip* is particularly interesting for its portrait of manners and relationships in plantation society. De Lisser's description of East Indian laborers, for example, is an original contribution to Jamaican literature, confirming the breadth and exhaustiveness of his observations and his comprehensive knowledge of Jamaican society. Moreover, in exactness of detail, fluency of expression, and absolute authenticity, the passage on banana reaping given in chapter 11 remains one of the best presentations of an agricultural scene in West Indian literature.

De Lisser's last published novel *The Arawak Girl* (1958) is the republication of "Anacanoa," which appeared in *Planters' Punch* twenty-two years before. In this novel de Lisser extends the scope of his historical survey to consider Jamaica in the earliest period of European settlement, when Christopher Columbus landed on the island on his fourth voyage to the New World. Attention is focused mostly on the Spanish sailors

Cover for an issue of the annual that de Lisser founded in 1920 and presided over until his death

and specifically on one of Columbus's captains, Diego Mendez, who falls in love with Anacanoa, the daughter of an Arawak chief. Diego has to leave Jamaica for Cuba and Spain, and when Anacanoa is later killed, news of her death is sent to him in Spain. This romantic story is interwoven with events of Spanish and Indian rivalries and the bravery of Anacanoa, who behaves like an Arawak Joan of Arc. Because of the remoteness of the period and paucity of historical records, *The Arawak Girl* displays de Lisser's powers of imaginative reconstruction and invention. It also illustrates his scholarship and industrious research in supplying details about Columbus's enforced stop in Jamaica more than four centuries ago, about the mutiny that followed, and the eclipse of the sun on 29 February 1504. The final

impression of this novel and of de Lisser's fiction as a whole is most likely admiration for his tenacious interest in the manifold affairs of his native land, for his lifelong study of these affairs, and for the prodigious literary skills he displayed in transferring into the medium of fiction what he had discovered about Jamaican history and society.

As a public figure de Lisser achieved great eminence in Jamaica, where his career as a journalist and writer lasted from 1903 to 1944. While he edited the *Daily Gleaner*, de Lisser wrote a regular column, "Random Jottings," for the paper, commenting humorously or satirically on current affairs and events. Walter Adolphe Roberts, in his book *Six Great Jamaicans* (1952) notes that de Lisser attended the Imperial Press Conference held in Canada in 1920 and another held in London in 1930: "Praise was heaped on de Lisser at these gatherings; he was regarded as being at least the peer of any newspaper editor in the Empire." For his writing achievements de Lisser was awarded the Silver Musgrave Medal in 1919 and the C.M.G. (Companion of the Order of St. Michael and St. George) in 1920. But de Lisser's eminence extended beyond his reputation as a writer. He was on the Board of Governors of the Institute of Jamaica for twenty-two years and served as chairman for fifteen. The institute was established for the encouragement of literature, science, and art. For twenty-seven years de Lisser was also the secretary of the Jamaica Imperial Association, which fostered trade and social links with Great Britain. In his work for this association de Lisser became a sort of agent for Jamaican and British trade, especially in matters dealing with sugar, rum, and bananas. De Lisser's service to the sugar and rum industries of Jamaica was recognized in 1938, when he received a silver bowl and a check for five hundred guineas from the Sugar Manufacturers Association.

De Lisser's eminence has declined over the years as the importance of issues he championed has decreased or disappeared. His literary reputation, however, survives and flourishes; for he is not only the first notable Jamaican writer but the first writer of substance produced by the English-speaking Caribbean. Up to the period just before World War I, when de Lisser began writing, West Indian literature consisted largely of writing by English people who viewed the region as simply a part of the empire. De Lisser was the first West Indian novelist to present Jamaica from an insider's point of view. No English novelist could have written *Jane's Career*, or any of de Lisser's novels with a contemporary setting. At the same time, de Lisser does present his main themes of oppression and resistance with an objectivity that cannot easily be distinguished from a detached, Eurocentric point of view. In *Under the Sun*, for example, de Lisser gives this description of the English heroine: "But now, in a new environment entirely, in a land where most of the faces were dark, where a beautiful white woman moved like a kind of goddess amongst plainer-looking people and against a romantic background, here indeed such a one, given strength of character, ambition, a goal to pursue, might make something of her life." This is a very detached attitude for a Jamaican to take toward his native island. But one has to remember that de Lisser's conservative political views brought him very close to the position of liberal Englishmen at the time. Lord Olivier, for example, was a Fabian associate of George Bernard Shaw, and Olivier's liberal paternalistic view toward British colonies probably influenced de Lisser.

Nevertheless, de Lisser's fiction contains the first extensive and reliable portrait of Jamaica in imaginative literature. His accounts of threatened slave rebellions, for example in *Revenge* and *The White Witch of Rosehall*, can be linked with Jane's rebellion against oppression in *Jane's Career*. De Lisser's novels illustrate the natural evolution of an oppressive class of Jamaican plantation slave-owners into the upper classes described in *Under the Sun* and *The Cup and the Lip*. The resistance of black slaves against their white masters in his historical novels leads to the resistance of de Lisser's twentieth-century black characters against the injustices of a social code based on values of race and color. This fundamental feature of Jamaican society as presented by de Lisser served as a model for Jamaican writers who succeeded him, for example, Vic Reid, Roger Mais, and John Hearne. Hearne's novels in particular offer an almost identical mixture of realistic aspects of Jamaican society with romantic elements of escapist fantasy. The novels of the Guyanese Edgar Mittelholzer, including his Kaywana trilogy, also examine West Indian history in a manner similar to those of de Lisser. Although present-day West Indian readers may regard de Lisser's treatment of oppression and resistance as too conservative, ambivalent, or unemotionally matter-of-fact, he must be credited at least with journalistic objectivity; for de Lisser was, above all else, a highly experienced career journalist. Even if he did not approve of liberalizing trends and social changes that were taking place in Jamaica during his lifetime, he had the training and skill of a practiced journalist to record them faithfully and accurately in his novels.

References:

Frank M. Birbalsingh, "Jamaican Indians: A Novelist's View," in *Indenture and Exile: The Indo-Caribbean Experience*, edited by Birbalsingh (Toronto: TSAR, 1989), pp. 91-99;

Birbalsingh, "The Novels of H. G. de Lisser," *International Fiction Review*, 9 (Winter 1982): pp. 41-46;

Victor L. Chang, "The Historical Novels of Herbert G. de Lisser," in *West Indian Literature and Its Social Context*, edited by Mark A.

McWatt (Cave Hill, Barbados: University of the West Indies, 1985), pp. 12-17;

Rhonda Cobham, "Cuba and Panama in the Writings of Herbert G. de Lisser," in *El Caribe y América Latina*, edited by Ulrich Fleischmann and Ineke Phaf (Berlin: Vervuert, 1987), pp. 173-181;

Cobham, "The Literary Side of H. G. de Lisser (1878-1944)," *Jamaica Journal*, 17 (November 1984 - January 1985): 2-9;

Michael G. Cooke, "West Indian Picaresque," *Novel*, 7 (Fall 1973): 93-96;

J. J. Figueroa, "*Jane's Career* by H. G. de Lisser," *World Literature Written in English*, 12 (April 1973): 97-105;

Mervyn Morris, "H. G. de Lisser: The First Competent Caribbean Novelist in English," *Carib*, 1 (1979): 18-26;

Lizabeth Paravisini-Gebert, "*The White Witch of Rosehall* and the Legitimacy of Female Power in the Caribbean Plantation," *Journal of West Indian Literature*, 4 (November 1990): 25-45;

Kenneth Ramchand, "*Jane's Career*," in his *An Introduction to the Study of West Indian Literature* (Sunbury-on-Thames, U.K.: Nelson, 1976), pp. 1-10;

Walter Adolphe Roberts, "Herbert George de Lisser," in his *Six Great Jamaicans* (Kingston, Jamaica: Pioneer, 1952), pp. 104-122;

Amon S. Saakana, "Trauma and Bourgeois Nationalism: Buckra's Perspectives," in his *The Colonial Legacy in Caribbean Literature* (Trenton, N.J.: Africa World, 1987), I: 54-58.

Cyprian Ekwensi

(26 September 1921 -)

Ernest N. Emenyonu
Alvan Ikoku College of Education, Owerri, Nigeria

BOOKS: *Ikolo the Wrestler, and Other Ibo Tales* (London: Nelson, 1947);

When Love Whispers (Onitsha, Nigeria: Tabansi, 1947);

The Leopard's Claw (London: Longmans, Green, 1950);

People of the City (London: Dakers, 1954; revised edition, London: Heinemann, 1963; Evanston, Ill.: Northwestern University Press, 1967);

The Passport of Mallam Ilia (Cambridge: Cambridge University Press, 1960);

The Drummer Boy (Cambridge: Cambridge University Press, 1960);

Jagua Nana (London: Hutchinson, 1961; New York: Fawcett, 1969);

Burning Grass (London: Heinemann, 1962);

An African Night's Entertainment (Lagos: African Universities Press, 1962; London: Ginn, 1971);

Yaba Roundabout Murder (Lagos: Tortoise Series, 1962);

Beautiful Feathers (London: Hutchinson, 1963);

The Great Elephant-Bird (London: Nelson, 1965);

The Rainmaker and Other Stories (Lagos: African Universities Press, 1965; London: Ginn, 1971);

The Boa Suitor (London: Nelson, 1966);

Iska (London: Hutchinson, 1966);

Juju Rock (Lagos: African Universities Press, 1966; London: Ginn, 1966);

Trouble in Form Six (Cambridge: Cambridge University Press, 1966);

Lokotown, and Other Stories (London: Heinemann, 1966);

Coal Camp Boy (Ibadan: Longman, Nigeria, 1973);

Samankwe in the Strange Forest (Ibadan: Longman, Nigeria, 1973);

Samankwe and the Highway Robbers (London: Evans, 1975);

Restless City and Christmas Gold, with Other Stories (London: Heinemann, 1975);

Cyprian Ekwensi (photograph by Bernth Lindfors)

The Rainbow-Tinted Scarf and Other Stories (London: Evans, 1975);

Survive the Peace (London: Heinemann, 1976);

Divided We Stand (Enugu, Nigeria: Fourth Dimension, 1980);

Motherless Baby (Enugu, Nigeria: Fourth Dimension, 1980);

For a Roll of Parchment (Ibadan: Heinemann, 1986);

Jagua Nana's Daughter (Ibadan: Spectrum, 1986);

The Masquerade (London: Heinemann, 1991);

Gone to Mecca (Ibadan: Heinemann, 1991).

RECORDINGS: *The African Novelist and His Society*, Ames, Iowa State University of Science and Technology, University Lecture Series, 1975;

Cyprian Ekwensi of Nigeria, Washington, D.C., Voice of America, 1978.

OTHER: *African New Writing*, includes five short stories by Ekwensi (London: Lutterworth Press, 1947);

Festac Anthology of Nigerian New Writing, edited by Ekwensi (Lagos: Ministry of Information/ Nigeria Magazine, 1977).

SELECTED PERIODICAL PUBLICATIONS—
UNCOLLECTED: "Outlook for African Writers," *West African Review* (January 1950): 19;

"Challenge to West African Writers," *West African Review* (March 1952): 255 +;

"West African Voices," *West African Review* (May 1952): 430-431;

"The Dilemma of the African Writer," *West African Review* (July 1956): 701-704;

"Three Weeks Among the Fulani," *Nigeria Magazine* (October 1960);

"Problems of Nigerian Writers," *Nigeria Magazine*, 78 (September 1963): 217-219;

"Literary Influences on a Young Nigerian," *Times Literary Supplement*, 4 June 1964, pp. 475-476;

"African Literature," *Nigeria Magazine*, 83 (December 1964): 294-299.

Cyprian Ekwensi is a Nigerian writer who deserves patient reading and careful review. He is frequently relegated to the background by critics, spurned by some and ignored by a few. Many a critic has made his debut by "shooting down" Ekwensi. It is quite easy to criticize a popular writer such as Ekwensi, yet whatever his faults (and there are many of them), he cannot be ig-

Dust jacket for Ekwensi's novel about a middle-aged prostitute in Lagos. This novel is his most popular book with both readers and critics.

nored by any serious student of African literature, for he has an undeniably important place in the historical development of the West African novel in English, and he is truly the father of the modern Nigerian novel. No matter how offensive some of his adult novels may be to moralists, no parent or teacher who has young children yearning for exciting literature can afford to overlook Ekwensi's stories for young readers. No matter how uneven the quality of his novels may be, Ekwensi remains one of Africa's best short-story writers. The key word to his art as a creative writer is *versatility*.

Born in Minna, Nigeria, on 26 September 1921, Cyprian Odiatu Duaka Ekwensi, an Igbo, is the son of Ogbuefi David Duaka Ekwensi and Agnes Uso Ekwensi. He has published novels and short stories, and he has written plays for radio and scripts for television and the screen. His works focus on love, infatuation, infidelity, war,

adventure, fantasy, politics, childhood, marriage, death, and ritual sacrifice. He has also collected folktales and written about life in various Nigerian ethnic groups: Yoruba, Hausa, Igbo, Ijaw, Efik, and Urhobo. Ekwensi has traversed rural and urban landscapes of Nigeria, recording them in his fiction. He married Eunice Anyiwo, and they have five children.

Perhaps if he had stuck to one genre, focused on one major theme, or concentrated on one segment of Nigerian society, Ekwensi could have commanded a greater following among literary critics. But he has chosen to cover many situations, themes, and types of characters. Most readers have no knowledge of the full range of his extraordinary literary output in the last forty years: it includes nine major novels; five short novels; nine children's books; seven collections of short stories; many stories in journals and magazines; and several unpublished, book-length manuscripts. He is one of the most prolific writers in Nigeria.

Ekwensi's career has been as varied and widespread as his fiction. Ekwensi received his secondary education at the Higher College in Yaba and in Ibadan at Government College, his postsecondary education at Achimota College in Ghana, the School of Forestry in Ibadan, and the Chelsea School of Pharmacy at London University. In 1919 his family had moved to northern Nigeria from their Nkwelle homeland near Ogidi in eastern Nigeria and only returned to Nkwelle in 1966 on the eve of the Nigerian civil war, ten years before Ekwensi's father's death on 19 November 1976. Ekwensi was already mature before he first encountered the village life in Nkwelle. As a teacher at Igbobi College, near Lagos, in the 1940s he taught English, biology, and chemistry. At the Lagos School of Pharmacy in 1949, he began teaching pharmacognosy and pharmaceutics. Although he had professional qualifications in forestry and pharmacy, he joined the news media in 1951, working for the Nigerian Broadcasting Corporation; studied broadcasting in England; and has remained in media work of one form or another since then. In 1961 he was named federal director of information, in which capacity he controlled all Nigerian media, including films, radio, television, printing, newspapers, and public relations. In 1967 he joined the Biafran secession as the chairman of the Bureau for External Publicity and director of Biafra Radio. Ekwensi has continued his various interests, as a teacher, journalist, pharmacist, diplomat, businessman, company director, public relations consultant, photographer, artist, information consultant, writer, and molder of public opinion. In 1991 he was made chairman of the Federal Radio Corporation of Nigeria. In his fiction he reflects this diversity, producing a kind of hodgepodge that has amused many, excited some, and irritated a few.

Ekwensi had begun writing as early as the end of World War II. His first stories were about his father, eulogizing his unequaled bravery as an adventurous elephant hunter and his skill as a carpenter. Ekwensi's first collection of short stories, *Ikolo the Wrestler, and Other Ibo Tales*, was published in 1947. Also in 1947 he published what was probably the first pamphlet in the Onitsha market-literature tradition, *When Love Whispers*. It is a lighthearted romance but with a heavy didactic message. In 1954 he published *People of the City*, his first major novel, which ranks as the first West African English novel written in a modern style.

All the rest of his major novels with one exception, *Burning Grass* (1962), have followed the tradition of *People of the City* in their blunt depiction of the realities of modern urban environments. They read like indictments of city inhabitants. Ekwensi's subject is people, and his thematic preoccupation is to confront city dwellers with the revolting social injustices and outrageous, immoral practices that seem to have become part of their way of life. The picture he presents is unattractive to the eye and mind, and it has often been remarked that he has a predilection for focusing only on the ugly and repugnant in new African cities. Ekwensi has insisted that the work of the novelist is to hold a mirror up to life and describe it truthfully regardless of the feelings of his public. Ekwensi maintains that much of what he writes is true of his life and of the lives of others in these urban settings. In the last forty years he has continued in this vein with varying degrees of both success and acceptance.

People of the City is of major significance in the literary career of Ekwensi. It got him started as a "city chronicler." He was writing at a time when nationalist movements and the struggle for independence were gaining ground in Nigeria. Many people had started to anticipate the golden era of freedom and emancipation. Many others, however, perceived this freedom from a purely selfish standpoint. The society was at a point of transition from the old order to the new. The new order, associated with the emerging urban

Ekwensi in 1965, just after returning to Nigeria from his first visit to the United States

centers, was colorful and vigorous, but it was also socially crowded, multiracial, and complex. Moral values were in a state of turmoil, and the social pace was fast and gripping. The "heroes" of the new age were torn apart by attempts at personal aggrandizement. Despite calls to share in the development of their new nation, they remained self-centered and wasted themselves in frivolities and the desire for sensual excitements. Ekwensi was disenchanted with this euphoria and saw the new urban environments as bewitched with "terribly corrupting influences . . . a den for Ali Baba and the forty thieves." It is this milieu Ekwensi sought to reflect in his first novel and in subsequent works set in the city. He chose Lagos as the social base for displaying the confused priorities and emotions of the new Africa—on the eve of political independence.

People of the City did not originate as a novel, nor as a single story written consistently from beginning to end. Instead it is a stringing together of thirteen different stories written at different times for different purposes. The plot was built on a series of separate episodes Ekwensi had broadcast in his weekly short-story program on Radio Nigeria in the 1940s. Each story was set in a different city location and had its own message and style. In 1951 Ekwensi had won his government scholarship for further studies in pharmacy at London University. It was on the ship that took him from Nigeria to England that Ekwensi wrote *People of the City*, stringing together those stories he had broadcast on Radio Nigeria and uniting them into one long story originally entitled "Lajide of Lagos." Lajide was an obnoxious character in a story about extortionist landlords. At the end of the fourteen days in which Ekwensi had secluded himself inside his lonely cabin, he had completed his first major literary creation. In 1954 Andrew Dakers published it as *People of the City*. This novel brought him international visibility as a novelist, but it also earned him the disfavor of literary critics.

The people in the novel are forced to choose between the picturesque rural life of the village, which is tradition-bound, and life in the more recently established urban centers, which is devoid of personal and familial ties and any continuity of custom. In the latter setting the characters evolve and grow. They are in a cold, alien atmosphere; alone and rejected, they seek life and self-fulfillment in this barren wasteland, where businessmen are dishonest, politicians corrupt, neighbors hostile, and friends conniving. They meet few people they can trust or love. Instead, they are daily confronted with wretched filth, decadence, and hopelessness. The greedy, the ambitious, and the licentious surround their every movement. The people of the city possess a synthetic self-importance and a plastic sense of glory. Despite immediate superficial attractions, the characters' hopes for a successful life in the city remain illusory. Yet they are not disillusioned. Instead they pursue their search energetically, believing that the city must eventually have something positive to offer them. They remain adamant in this misguided determination despite the advice and forewarnings of parents and elders outside the city. This element of search is a unifying theme in all Ekwensi's city novels.

People seem lured to the city. Sango, the main character, is one such person. He thinks he knows exactly why he is in the city: "Sango had his own life to lead, his name to make as a bandleader and journalist." He is there to seek success and become a celebrity. His goals are self-oriented, his search a personal quest. He wants

Dust jacket for one of the many books Ekwensi wrote about urban life in Nigeria. This novel, published in 1966, forecast the civil war that began the following year.

his road toward self-fulfillment to be clear of interference, and when it is not, he is greatly disturbed. For instance when Aina, a young girl Sango had professed to love, goes to jail for stealing, Sango almost tells her he does not care for her in the least, because such emotional relationships, based on brief encounters, are fleeting and within a day are already past and forgotten.

The other characters in the story are not delineated as fully as Sango. They are stereotyped figures and appear to have been created as means to preconceived ends. These ends—the moral purpose of the book—help to throw more light on Ekwensi's attitude toward the perverted values of his urban society.

Ekwensi knows Lagos very well. He also knows the idiosyncrasies of his characters, who are symptomatic of the moral depravities of the city. The strongest quality of the novel is the effective delineation of urban realities in Africa.

Ekwensi ponders why things happen the way they do and why no one seems to care, or care enough. He is attempting to confront his society with its evils. The picture is one of squalor, bribery, corruption, and mercenary values presented by one who has an inside knowledge of the situation. In the end it is the city that emerges as the villain: "The city eats many an innocent life every year. . . . It is a waste of our youth. . . ."

Perhaps Ekwensi's close proximity to his setting and his compassionate reactions to its problems have produced some of the weaknesses noted by critics of the novel. His didacticism and sense of retribution are always in evidence. Often he oversteps his role of mirroring society to that of standing in judgment of it. He is both the plaintiff and jury, and he sometimes resolves conflicts in the novel by deploying a deus ex machina that kills off the characters for whom he has no more use. This leads to contrivances that are melodramatic and unconvincing. The looseness at the end of each subplot makes the novel read like day-to-day records of events, sometimes interconnected but more often than not just thrown together haphazardly.

Nonetheless, *People of the City*, as the first modern West African novel in English, remains of major importance. It is the picture of Lagos in all its squalor—the infectious corruption, the grab-and-keep mania—that confers on *People of the City* its lasting value as a work of fiction.

Ekwensi's second major city novel, *Jagua Nana*, published in 1961, is remarkable in many ways and has drawn conflicting responses from critics. To many it is a masterpiece and may well be his most lasting contribution to the art of the African novel. Certainly it is his most popular novel. To some, however, all the praise it has attracted is misplaced and misdirected, for its value as a work of art is questionable. Right from the date it was published, a year after Nigerian independence, some church organizations and women's unions attacked the novel and demanded that it be banned from circulation among the young. Even the Nigerian parliament was not detached from the controversy. Before finally rejecting the idea, it debated several times a proposed filming of the novel in Nigeria by an Italian company. At the center of the whole controversy was Jagua, the heroine of the novel, whose uninhibited sexual life was said to have turned the novel into a mere exercise in pornography. But those who admire the novel have described Jagua as Ekwensi's most fully realized character and one of the most memorable heroines in fiction anywhere.

Jagua Nana, like *People of the City*, is set in Lagos, but, unlike the latter, it is a post-independence novel. The life-style of the people in the novel reflects this newly won freedom. Nigerians confidently speak Pidgin English without feeling the need to apologize to British expatriates. They compete boldly with white men for sexual favors from the best of the glamorous women found in the foyers of prestigious hotels and elsewhere. The heroine of the novel takes her name from the famous British car, the Jaguar, to emphasize the elegance and magnificence of her physical appearance. Jagua, a fashionable prostitute in her mid forties, embodies in her own passionate, colorful, and inconsistent personality the very life of the modern city, reflecting its variety and vibrance.

Everything in the novel—the Tropicana nightclub, Lagos politics, British Council lectures, electric lights, and the hustle and bustle of the city—is portrayed in relation to the life of Jagua. They become important only to the extent that they help the reader to understand this city woman. Jagua's physical presence is conveyed with remarkable intensity, and eventually she becomes a familiar feature of Lagos nightlife. With her as the center of the novel, the author has scope to explore all the facets of life in modern Nigeria, because by virtue of her chosen profession she becomes involved in the affairs of a series of partners. She therefore automatically supplies the cohesion lacking in *People of the City*. It would seem that in choosing Jagua as his major character, Ekwensi intended to emphasize the influence women wield in Nigeria, and in this light Jagua can be seen as the symbol of women's power and versatility. In this sense it could be said that the novel is written from a woman's point of view. It tells a story of agony and joy, hope and despair, dream and reality, and inner innocence and outward sinfulness.

Jagua is a character with many contradictions, and Ekwensi makes her complex yet consistent. At times she appears a heartless bitch, and at other times she seems a tender and soft-hearted woman. She can be cruel and selfish no matter how altruistic some of her motives may be on the surface, yet she is never entirely devoid of sensitivity, love, and generosity. She does many things for her own good, but she helps others, too. Jagua is both the proud city whore and the humble village girl. The former is a character con-

Ekwensi in 1970, at the end of the Biafran War

emerges the victor, and this can be seen as the triumph of good over evil.

Yet Ekwensi's real purpose in the novel is to show the corruption in Nigerian political, social, and economic life, masked by the veneer of glamorous sex. The political story in *Jagua Nana* is one of exploitation of the people, fraudulent abuse of power, reckless embezzlement of public money, and the ultimate forfeiture of the public trust. The electoral process is full of corrupt distortions: elections are rigged, opponents are murdered, election campaigns are violently disrupted, opinions are muzzled, and the masses suffer in silence.

Jagua Nana is Ekwensi's most successful novel to date. Subsequent artistic creations by Ekwensi are judged and accepted or rejected according to the standards of *Jagua Nana*. Nothing before it brought him so squarely into the literary limelight, and nothing after it has done so much to establish Ekwensi's reputation as a serious writer. It remains his greatest contribution to the growth and development of the novel in Africa.

Ekwensi's third major novel, *Burning Grass*, published in 1962, came as a result of his personal experiences with a special cultural group in northern Nigeria in the 1940s. While Ekwensi was training as a forestry officer, he lived with a Fulani family for three weeks as part of his fieldwork, and he became particularly interested in the Fulani culture, learning about their ways of life. In an article entitled "Three Weeks Among the Fulani," published in *Nigeria Magazine* in October 1960, Ekwensi recalled with nostalgia his interactions with the Fulani in that brief period. He was so fascinated by those experiences that he was inspired to re-create them imaginatively in *Burning Grass*. The story tells of the cultural peculiarities and life-styles of the Fulani nomadic herdsmen. This was the first novel by a Nigerian to deal with the Cattle Fulani group of northern Nigeria.

The hero is Mai Sunsaye, the popular chief of the village of Dokan Toro, the setting of the story. Sunsaye, unlike other protagonists in Ekwensi's novels, is not a modern man of the city with gilded hopes and unreasonable expectations. As a cattle rearer he moves from place to place with the seasons to keep himself and his cattle alive. He is free from the brutish, bestial city, but he knows and fears its evils.

The theme of the novel is the quest for a lost identity. The plot traces the wanderings and

trolled by raw emotions—lust, greed, power, and hatred. When these feelings are in control, Jagua is like a wild animal, unpredictable, cunning, and dangerous. Then there is her other side, the woman with a motherly disposition. In this role she is nothing like her alter ego. By turns she plays the part of the aging, almost maternal lover of youth—the woman who loves children and has feelings for others. She wants to look beautiful, get married, bear children, and have a home of her own. In this frame of mind she is tender, soft, understanding, and wise, and can make peace between two warring camps and settle long-standing feuds between families. This is the Jagua who visits Krinameh and offers to sacrifice herself in order to prevent the death of many men. Jagua the whore and Jagua the mother are constantly contending with one another throughout the novel. In the end Jagua the mother

Ekwensi with John Updike at a literary gathering in Nigeria, 1973 (photograph by Bernth Lindfors)

attendant ordeals of the Sunsaye family from the moment a slave girl, Fatimeh, enters the family and, by her presence, upsets the relationship between Hodio and Rikku, Sunsaye's two younger sons. Ekwensi exploits the natural characteristics of the Cattle Fulani in the development of the story. Such people are always on the move in search of green pastures for their cattle. In the course of the novel Sunsaye is struck with the much-dreaded disease "sokugo," which makes its victim wander ceaselessly and aimlessly. Ekwensi manipulates the events in Sunsaye's "lost" life and turns his wandering and that of his family into an allegorical search in which every action has symbolic significance. In this way *Burning Grass* is linked to Ekwensi's earlier major novels, which have as their focus the search for the meaning of existence.

Burning Grass reveals a new dimension of Ekwensi's artistic skills. Love is a dominant theme, but it is a different kind of love from that in *Jagua Nana* or *People of the City*. The Cattle Fulani are known for their magic and superstition, and all emotions are kept under rational control. Ekwensi's style in the book is a faithful reflection of the strict discipline that characterizes the behavior of the nomadic Fulani.

In spite of the success of this pastoral novel, Ekwensi has never tried anything again of that nature in his adult fiction. His subsequent major novels—*Beautiful Feathers* (1963), *Iska* (1966), *Survive the Peace* (1976), *Divided We Stand* (1980), *For a Roll of Parchment* (1986), and *Jagua Nana's Daughter* (1986)—all take the reader back to Ekwensi's familiar canvas: the city with its upheavals, madness, and orderly disorder. *Beautiful Feathers, Iska, Survive the Peace,* and *Divided We Stand* are daring attempts to distill committed political messages in fiction. *Beautiful Feathers* satirizes the noble dreams of Pan-African unity, subverted by sectionalism and acrimony. *Survive the Peace, Iska,* and *Divided We Stand* are based on the civil disorder that engulfed Nigeria from 1967 to 1970. Despite Ekwensi's efforts at making lofty political statements, what comes across most vividly in each of these novels is still his fascination with the city, particularly with the single girl, the wayward seductress, and the indiscreet young man who never thinks before he acts.

Ekwensi's two other major novels (*For a Roll of Parchment* and *Jagua Nana's Daughter*) may have been published in the same year (1986) to coincide with his sixty-fifth birthday. *For a Roll of Parchment* was published thirty years after it was written. Set largely in England, it is the story of an elderly Nigerian, Kola Aliz, who forsakes a promising heritage in order to pursue an elusive "Golden Fleece," the symbolic "roll of parchment" (a law degree), in England. The plot tells of mental torture, disorientation, unrequited love, and the degradation to which the hero is subjected in the British social and political environment because of his skin color. It is a revealing imaginative documentary of race relations and color prejudice in England during the 1950s. It is also an evocative tale filled with pathos and narrated with candor, its acrimonious undertones notwithstanding.

Jagua Nana's Daughter is more spectacular in its artistic effects. It was conceived in 1981, twenty years after the publication of *Jagua Nana*, and took Ekwensi five years to write. A sequel to the controversial *Jagua Nana*, the story in *Jagua Nana's Daughter* includes both a prelude to and is contemporary with its precursor, leaving the reader lost in a jigsaw puzzle. *Jagua Nana* ends on a note of resignation for the aging heroine, whose desperate aspirations for motherhood yield no fruits. Childlessness for her is a nagging regret. By its title, therefore, *Jagua Nana's Daughter* offers an enigma, and it is the resolution of this mystery that provides the justification for the story. Jagua was born in Jos to God-fearing parents, but, unknown to them, she had at an early age come under the influence of a lascivious and loose-living neighbor, Auntie Kate, who manipulated her into a complex love affair with a Greek tin miner. Lizza, Jagua Nana's daughter, was the product of that liaison, but her existence was concealed from her grandparents. Jagua leaves Jos in the wake of the Nigerian civil war, and when she comes back for her daughter years later, she is led to believe that Lizza has since died. Later events reveal that Lizza is alive and prosperous.

Jagua Nana's Daughter begins as the story of a dual search—daughter for mother, and mother for daughter—and later develops into a moving account of international border clashes and migrant labor. Adult Lizza, true to type, is sexy almost to the point of being promiscuous, but as a trained legal practitioner she is bound by ethics, unlike her mother. She has to have love as a basis for relationships with men. *Jagua Nana's Daughter* is an action-packed novel rich with lively dialogue and suspense. It has all the ingredients of a gripping film thriller.

Ekwensi has earned the reputation of being a sensational writer, a novelist perpetually preoc-

Dust jacket for one of Ekwensi's fictional treatments of political and social problems in post-civil-war Nigeria

cupied with the city and its disastrous impact on morality. He has not been generally acclaimed as an artistically disciplined writer. Attention is often drawn to his haphazard plots with their contrived and unconvincing endings. His moral crusades are said to overwhelm his artistic vision, particularly in his fast-paced tales of the city. The result is a concentration of attention on characters moving quickly through a series of congested episodes, a technique that tends to submerge any serious concerns.

However, Ekwensi won the Dag Hammarskjöld International Prize for Literary Merit in 1969. His success with young readers is incontrovertible, and his skill as a short-story writer is widely acknowledged. In addition, some of his most recent writings show evidence of a more mature handling of complex plots. Of all Nigerian writers, Ekwensi remains the novelist whose work is most likely to be picked up and read by the person on the street; he is one of Africa's most popular authors.

Ekwensi's greatest contribution to Nigerian literature is undoubtedly his success as a social realist and commentator on current events. *Jagua Nana* was one of the first novels to expose the corruption within the Nigerian political system. *Beautiful Feathers* was among the first to address itself to the subterfuge in Pan-Africanism. *Iska* forecast civil war in Nigeria. *Survive the Peace*, a postwar novel, drew timely attention to the enormity of refugee problems, the tragic fate of scattered families, and the fragility of peace. *Divided We Stand* was one of the first fictional documentaries on the war and its aftermath. *For a Roll of Parchment* was at the time of its conception one of the earliest exposés of the indignities suffered by African students in England. And *Jagua Nana's Daughter* revealed some of Nigeria's international problems, border clashes having become an increasingly common phenomenon. Ekwensi's choice of topical subjects has added to his unrivaled popularity. Cyprian Ekwensi has contributed immensely to the development of Nigerian literature in the past four decades, and he remains prolific, showing increasing confidence in his mastery of the novel form.

Interviews:

Dennis Duerden and Cosmo Pieterse, eds., *African Writers Talking: A Collection of Radio Interviews* (London: Heinemann, 1972; New York: Africana, 1972), pp. 77-83;

Bernth Lindfors, "Interview with Cyprian Ekwensi," *World Literature Written in English*, 13 (1974): 141-154;

Lee Nichols, ed., *Conversations with African Writers: Interviews with Twenty-Six African Authors* (Washington, D.C.: Voice of America, 1981), pp. 36-47;

Raoul Granqvist, "Cyprian Ekwensi: Interview," *Kunapipi*, 4, no. 1 (1982): 124-129;

B. Nganga, "An Interview with Cyprian Ekwensi, Enugu, March 15, 1980," *Studia Anglica Posnaniensia*, 17 (1984): 279-284.

References:

Umar Abdurrahman, "Cyprian Ekwensi's *Burning Grass*: A Critical Assessment," *Ufahamu*, 16, no. 1 (1987-1988): 78-100;

Eckhard Breitinger, "Literature for Younger Readers and Education in Multicultural Contexts," in *Language and Literature in Multicultural Contexts*, edited by Satendra Nandan (Suva, Fiji: University of the South Pacific, 1983), pp. 79-88;

Rosemary Colmer, "Cyprian Ekwensi," in *Essays on Contemporary Post-Colonial Fiction*, edited by Hedwig Bock and Albert Wertheim (Munich: Hueber, 1986), pp. 47-66;

Donald Cosentino, "Jagua Nana: Culture Heroine," *Ba Shiru*, 8, no. 1 (1977): 11-17;

J. de Grandsaigne, "A Narrative Grammar of Cyprian Ekwensi's Short Stories," *Research in African Literatures*, 16 (1985): 541-555;

Michael J. C. Echeruo, "The Fiction of Cyprian Ekwensi," *Nigeria Magazine*, 75 (1962): 63-66;

Ernest Emenyonu, *Cyprian Ekwensi* (London: Evans, 1974);

Emenyonu, *The Rise of the Igbo Novel* (Ibadan: Oxford University Press, 1978);

Emenyonu, ed., *The Essential Ekwensi* (Ibadan: Heinemann, 1987);

Albert Gérard, "Cyprian Ekwensi: Romancier de la ville africain," *Revue Générale Belge*, 99 (October 1963): 91-105;

Susan M. Greenstein, "Cyprian Ekwensi and Onitsha Market Literature," in *Essays on African Literature*, edited by W. L. Ballard (Atlanta: Georgia State University, School of Arts and Sciences, 1973), pp. 175-191;

Loretta A. Hawkins, "The Free Spirit of Ekwensi's Jagua Nana," *African Literature Today*, 10 (1979): 202-206;

Paul O. Iheakaram, "The City as Metaphor: The Short Stories of Cyprian Ekwensi," *International Fiction Review*, 6 (1979): 71-72;

Bernth Lindfors, "C. O. D. Ekwensi's First Stories," in his *Early Nigerian Literature* (New York & London: Africana, 1982), pp. 35-66;

Lindfors, "Cyprian Ekwensi: An African Popular Novelist," *African Literature Today*, 3 (1969): 2-14;

Russell J. Linnemann, "Structural Weakness in Ekwensi's *Jagua Nana*," *English in Africa*, 4, no. 1 (1977): 32-39;

Jamile Morsiani, "Cyprian Ekwensi: Una narrativa 'scritta,'" *Spicilegio Moderno*, 11 (1979): 123-155;

Peter Nazareth, "*Survive the Peace*: Cyprian Ekwensi as a Political Novelist," in *Marxism and African Literature*, edited by Georg M. Gugelberger (London: Currey, 1986; Trenton, N.J.: Africa World, 1986), pp. 165-177;

Emmanuel N. Obiechina, "Ekwensi as Novelist," *Presence Africaine*, 86 (1973): 152-164;

Juliet I. Okonkwo, "Ekwensi and Modern Nigerian Culture," *Ariel*, 7, no. 2 (1976): 32-45;

Okonkwo, "Ekwensi and the 'Something New and Unstable' in Modern Nigerian Culture," in *Literature and Modern West African Culture*, edited by Donatus Nwoga (Benin City: Ethiope, 1978), pp. 130-143;

Okonkwo, "Popular Urban Fiction and Cyprian Ekwensi," in *European-Language Writing in Sub-Saharan Africa*, edited by Gérard (Budapest: Akadémiai Kiado, 1986), II: 650-658;

Femi Osofisan, "Domestication of an Opiate: Western Paraesthetics and the Growth of the Ekwensi Tradition," *Positive Review*, 1, no. 4 (1981): 1-12;

Eustace Palmer, "Cyprian Ekwensi," in his *The Growth of the African Novel* (London: Heinemann, 1979), pp. 36-62;

Dennis R. Passmore, "Camp Style in the Novels of Cyprian O. D. Ekwensi," *Journal of Popular Culture*, 4 (1971): 705-716;

John F. Povey, "Cyprian Ekwensi: The Novelist and the Pressure of the City," in *The Critical Evaluation of African Literature*, edited by Edgar Wright (London: Heinemann, 1973), pp. 73-94;

Austin J. Shelton, " 'Rebushing' or Ontological Recession to Africanism: Jagua's Return to the Village," *Presence Africaine*, 46 (1963): 49-60;

Neil Skinner, "From Hausa to English: A Study in Paraphrase," *Research in African Literatures*, 4 (1973): 154-164;

Joseph Ukoyen, "Emile Zola's *Nana* and Cyprian Ekwensi's *Jagua Nana*," in *Comparative Approaches to Modern African Literature*, edited by S. O. Asein (Ibadan: Department of English, University of Ibadan, n.d.), pp. 65-76.

Buchi Emecheta

(21 July 1944 -)

Kirsten Holst Petersen
Aarhus, Denmark

BOOKS: *In the Ditch* (London: Barrie & Jenkins, 1972; New York: Schocken, 1980);

Second Class Citizen (London: Allison & Busby, 1974; New York: Braziller, 1975);

The Bride Price (London: Allison & Busby, 1976; New York: Braziller, 1976);

The Slave Girl (London: Allison & Busby, 1977; New York: Braziller, 1977);

The Joys of Motherhood (London: Allison & Busby, 1979; New York: Braziller, 1979);

Titch the Cat (London: Allison & Busby, 1979);

Nowhere to Play (London: Allison & Busby / New York: Schocken, 1980);

The Moonlight Bride (Oxford: Oxford University Press, 1980; New York: Braziller, 1983);

The Wrestling Match (Oxford & New York: Oxford University Press, 1980; New York: Braziller, 1983);

Our Own Freedom, by Emecheta and Maggie Murray (London: Sheba Feminist, 1981);

Destination Biafra (London: Allison & Busby / New York: Schocken, 1982);

Naira Power (London: Macmillan, 1982);

Double Yoke (London & Ibuza, Nigeria: Ogwugwu Afor, 1982 [i.e., 1983]; New York: Braziller 1983);

The Rape of Shavi (London & Ibuza, Nigeria: Ogwugwu Afor, 1983; New York: Braziller, 1985);

Adah's Story (London: Allison & Busby, 1983);

Head Above Water (London: Fontana, 1986);

A Kind of Marriage (London: Macmillan, 1986);

Family Bargain (London: BBC, 1987);

Gwendolen (London: Collins, 1989; New York: Braziller, 1990).

OTHER: "Feminism with a Small 'f'!," in *Criticism and Ideology: Second African Writers' Conference, Stockholm 1986*, edited by Kirsten Holst Petersen (Uppsala, Sweden: Scandinavian Institute of African Studies, 1988), pp. 173-185.

Buchi Emecheta (photograph by Anna Rutherford)

SELECTED PERIODICAL PUBLICATIONS—
UNCOLLECTED: "Head Above Water," *Kuna-
    pipi*, 3, no. 1 (1981): 81-90;
"That First Novel," *Kunapipi*, 3, no. 2 (1981):
    115-123;
"A Nigerian Writer Living in London," *Kunapipi*,
    4, no. 1 (1982): 114-123.

Buchi Emecheta is to date the most important female African writer. The extent of her out-

put and the centrality of her subject matter—the
role of women in present-day Africa—have put
her in this position. In her fiction she shows courage in challenging traditional male attitudes
about gender roles; anger and iconoclastic contempt for unjust institutions, no matter how time-
honored or revered they are; and a willingness
to seek new ways to break what she sees as the unjust subjugation of women in the name of tradition.

Emecheta was born on 21 July 1944 in Yaba
near Lagos, Nigeria, to Jeremy Nwabudike
Emecheta (a railway worker and molder) and
Alice Okwuekwu Emecheta, both Igbos. The
young Emecheta was orphaned early on and educated at a missionary school until she was sixteen,
when she married and moved to London. Her
first two books, *In the Ditch* (1972) and *Second-
Class Citizen* (1974), are heavily autobiographical.
They describe her childhood in Lagos; her 1960
marriage to Sylvester Onwordi, a student to
whom she had been betrothed since she was
eleven; and their subsequent move to England.
But the novels concentrate on her struggle to support and bring up her five children in London.
(She and Onwordi separated in 1966.) *In the
Ditch* begins at the point when she has left her husband and is living on her own with her children
in a slum, supporting them by working in the
library at the British Museum. The book is a collection of "observations" that Emecheta sent to
the *New Statesman*, which published them and
thereby effectively launched her writing career.

The story follows Emecheta's slightly fictionalized self, Adah, in her descent into the "Ditch,"
which is living on the dole on a council housing estate set aside for problem families. Despite the pre-
dictably negative framework of appalling conditions, the book hovers between acceptance and
rejection of the slum world. Problem families are
defined by officialdom as single parent and possibly colored families; the estate named Pussy Cat
Mansions is very much a world of women. With
as much dignity as they can salvage, they scratch
around for whatever warmth life might offer.
Adah feels both compassion for and solidarity
with the women, but she cannot fully identify
with them. Her pride is hurt by the charity she is
reduced to accept, and she has an ambivalent attitude both toward the authorities and toward her
fellow dwellers. She survives racial prejudice by reminding herself of her superior education, her
current studies, and her former civil-service job.
The emphasis is increasingly on the values of ini-

tiative and determination, with the help of which Adah eventually climbs out of the ditch.

Those qualities had been part of Adah from childhood. *Second Class Citizen* portrays the young Adah as an unusually determined little girl whose mind is firmly set on getting a Western education, from which she has been effectively barred because she was "only a girl." This sets a basic theme that runs through Emecheta's entire oeuvre: an intense anger at the sexual discrimination at the core of the culture of her people and a concomitant contempt for the men who perpetrate it. In England Adah is oppressed because of sex, race, and class, but the aspect she finds most difficult to overcome is the sexual discrimination, embedded in her marriage. She is the property of her husband, Francis, and he treats her as such. The injustice is spelled out: she supports them and is responsible for the children while he studies and keeps failing exams. The book narrows down to a battle between the spouses, centered on domestic issues vital to the survival and self-preservation of the woman: sex, motherhood, birth control, economic independence, and a sense of personal value. Through painful experience Adah works out her own solutions to the problems. Marital sex is increasingly felt as rape, and motherhood becomes the focus of her emotional attachment. The birth of each child alienates her further from her husband, but strengthens her ties with English society and its value system and hardens her determination to succeed. Her desire for birth control is seen by Francis as an attempt to steal rights of control over her body, which rightly belong to him, and she receives a severe beating. The final blow is when he burns the manuscript of a book she has written. When she finally leaves him, there is a strong sense of relief, and the move is seen as the result of increasing self-awareness and growing maturity on the part of Adah. She has moments of loneliness and longing for affection, but she emerges victorious, vindicated in her belief that success is a matter of willpower.

The autobiography in the first two novels is updated in *Head Above Water* (1986). It describes Emecheta's continued struggle to bring up her family as a single parent, gain a degree in sociology, find jobs, and continue to write. It ends with the achievement of two major goals, the purchase of a house of her own and her settling down to become a full-time writer. In between it explores social conditions in black London and sheds interesting light on Emecheta's develop-

Dust jacket for Emecheta's second autobiographical novel, which describes events that took place before those recounted in the first

ment as a writer, as it describes her involvement with each of her novels as they emerge.

It comes as no surprise that the manuscript Francis burned in *Second Class Citizen* surfaces as Emecheta's 1976 book, *The Bride Price*. With this book, set in the early 1950s in Lagos and Ibuza, she departs from her own life story. Despite this radical shift in subject matter, *The Bride Price* is a logical development of her writing. She continues to explore the injustices of caste, one of her main concerns in the first two books, but the emphasis is somewhat different. Whereas in her autobiographical books Emecheta stresses the possibility of overcoming the restrictions of caste or castelike conditions through personal initiative, in *The Bride Price* and the following novels set in Nigeria she stresses the destructive potential of rigid caste structures, which persist in the otherwise rapidly changing Igbo society. Her main preoccupation continues to be the role of women.

Aku-nna, her name significantly meaning "father's wealth," is a young girl of thirteen when her father dies, and she is forced to move from Lagos with her mother and brother back to their village. Her desire to continue school is frowned upon but accepted, as educated girls fetch higher bride prices. Aku-nna is alienated from the village youth and falls in love with the schoolteacher. He, however, is the victim of another caste structure: he is a descendant of slaves and thus not allowed to marry a freeborn. True love runs its course—they elope under dramatic circumstances, get married, and settle down to a good life, supported by the oil boom, education, and Western values, but tradition takes its revenge. The bride price is not paid, and according to tradition the bride must die in childbirth, which is what Aku-nna does. Emecheta's explanation for this hovers uneasily between either presenting it as a psychological effect of a strongly held belief—resulting in fear and fatalistic surrender—or using modern medical terminology. The book thus ends with the defeat of what is clearly portrayed as progressive forces, but this somewhat surprising defeat only helps to highlight the injustice of the situation.

In *The Slave Girl* (1977), published while Emecheta was a social worker in London, the situation is not only unjust, it is also completely rigid. Objeta is sold into slavery when her parents die in the 1916 influenza epidemic in eastern Nigeria. She becomes a domestic slave with no rights whatsoever. Much of the book is devoted to a description of this kind of slavery, which persisted long after slavery was outlawed, and this necessitates both historical and ethnographical explanations. *The Slave Girl* is therefore closer to the genre of "village novels" written by Chinua Achebe, T. M. Aluko, and others, but the ideological content is different. Domestic slavery is seen as part and parcel of the society, and it is described as unjust and cruel, but with certain ameliorating features: Objeta's move from the village to the thriving market town ushers her into the modern world, and as a slave she is among the first to be sent to the missionaries to become a Christian and learn to read and write. This is a reversal of the usual pattern of "village novels." "From tradition to church" is seen in *The Slave Girl* as a positive move, not a destructive one. Objeta eventually marries an educated man, who sets her free by repaying her former owner the eight pounds originally paid for her. She is now free—to belong to him. The parallel between domestic slavery and marriage is made very explicit: "Slave, obey your master, wife, honour your husband." As a wife Objeta has no more power over her person than she did as a slave. She has simply, as the last line of the novel states, changed masters. Progress has eliminated one caste structure but kept another.

The theme of the slavelike conditions of marriage for a woman is further developed in *The Joys of Motherhood* (1979), Emecheta's most accomplished book so far. It is set in a period in the history of Nigeria (from the 1930s to just before independence) during which time enormous political and economic changes took place, but the Igbo immigrant society in Lagos, the focus of the book, refuses to make any allowances for change; as the men experience defeat and humiliation in the new society, they cling even more tenaciously to the power they have over the women and children within their group. The final sufferers become the women who, like the protagonist, Nnu Ego, are caught between economic necessity on the one hand and cultural taboos and aspirations on the other. Nnu Ego struggles hard against appalling poverty and a cruel and irresponsible husband to reach her objective, which is to give her sons an education and to marry off her daughters, so their bride price can help toward the boys' school fees. She reaches her goal but dies a lonely and disillusioned woman. The moral is obvious: by clinging to her traditional role as wife, or first wife, after her husband inherits a second wife from his deceased brother, she is destroyed and in turn tries to destroy her daughters' chances for a happier life. In contrast, her cowife, Adaku, leaves the home and becomes a prostitute in order to be able to give her daughters an education, denied to them within the traditional family structure. She has Emecheta's blessing, and the novel is a testimony to its author's growing radicalization and willingness to consider unorthodox means of change.

After an interlude of four pleasant children's books, Emecheta's authorship took a new turn with *Destination Biafra* (1982). Since the subject matter is war, the imaginative backdrop of the book is on a larger scale than the previous, mainly domestic settings, and Emecheta widens her scope as she tries to include army movements, war atrocities, and political deliberations and deceptions. The result is a mixed bag. With regard to plot, the novel follows the buildup and the actual events of the Nigerian Civil War so closely that it is easy to identify all the main

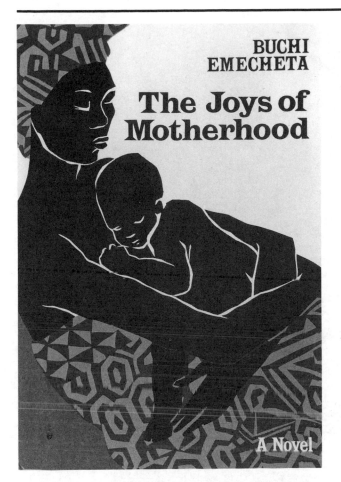

BUCHI
EMECHETA

The Joys of Motherhood

A Novel

Dust jacket for the American edition of Emecheta's fictional examination of the social position of married women in Nigeria until just before Nigerian independence in 1960

agents, despite their fictional names. Into this framework is inserted the story of Debbie, the English-educated daughter of a rich Nigerian businessman who was killed when the civilian government was overthrown in 1966. Debbie chooses to join the Federal army not because she is bloodthirsty but as yet another unorthodox way of breaking out of the female role of passive suffering. The burden of the book, however, is to sort out the confusing ideologies of the war. In this it does not quite succeed. In the foreword Emecheta states, "Yet it is time to forgive, though only a fool will forget." The ambiguity of this statement permeates the novel. Debbie is "a neutral Itsekiri woman" with personal ties to leaders on both sides of the war. She seems both to believe in a united Nigeria and in the ideals for which Biafra stands. There are, however, some clear ideological goals: one is to criticize the role of the British in the war and another is to bring to the world's attention the plight of the Nigerian Midwest, which is Emecheta's homeland. The area

was successively occupied by Biafran and Nigerian troops, and both sides carried out widespread killings of civilians. It is the description of this somewhat neglected aspect of the war that is the most convincing part of the book.

With her next novel Emecheta returned to a smaller and more familiar setting. *Double Yoke* (1983), a campus novel, confronts directly the prejudices surrounding the educated woman in Nigeria. (Emecheta was a visiting professor at the University of Calabar from 1980 to 1981.) The story is an attack on Nigerian men. Nko, the heroine, sets out with the aim of being "an academician and a quiet, nice and obedient wife." The latter part of her wish is also what her boyfriend wants, but as a result of her experiences Nko changes her mind. After having faced her boyfriend's scorn because she has allowed him to make love to her, and after having been forced into a choice of prostituting herself to her professor or not getting her degree, some of the obedience has worn off. At the conclusion of the novel, she is pregnant by the professor, but her boyfriend is considering accepting her, "growing up," as Emecheta mercilessly suggests. Independence for women in Nigeria, according to this novel, has to be a leap, with much burning of bridges, and the relationship between the sexes resembles most of all a war.

After lecturing at various universities in the United States, England, and Nigeria from 1972 through 1982, Emecheta began to run the Ogwugwu Afor Publishing Company, which has branches in London and Ibuza, Nigeria. *Double Yoke* and her next book carry that imprint.

The Rape of Shavi (1983) represents yet another new departure in her writing. It is an allegory about the relationship between Europe and Africa. The plot begins in an unknown place, set sometime in the future after a rumored nuclear holocaust, but in the course of the book the story moves into the present time, with known localities, and it is also a summing-up of the history of the European conquest of Africa. A small group of Englishmen flee the threat of a nuclear war in a homemade airplane and crash in an unknown spot in the middle of a desert, where they are surprised to find a thriving community of cattle-rearing desert people. Shavian society has had no contact with the West, and the Shavians live a prelapsarian life of peace, justice, dignity, and hospitality; the latter becomes their downfall. They take in the refugee group and with it the contradictions, greed, and destructiveness of Western civili-

Buchi Emecheta (photograph by George Hallett)

zation. One of the refugees rapes the prince's future bride, and the newcomers discover diamond-like stones. When they have repaired their plane, they take the stones and the Shavian prince with them back to England. This ends the Shavian time of innocence. The prince returns with guns and knowledge, and he starts plundering neighboring desert communities. But the whites suddenly do not need the stones anymore, and the Shavians then starve. Their society is devastated by war, drought, and famine, and the surviving heir-apparent is faced with the task of picking up the tattered ends. The idealization of precontact African society is a countercurrent in Emecheta's writing. In her previous books the emphasis is on the negative aspects of traditional African (Igbo) culture (especially gender roles and slavery), and Britain, despite its racism, is seen as offering the freedom of social mobility through individual initi-

ative and effort. *The Rape of Shavi* cannot be said to moderate this view, as it is in too sharp a contrast to it. Emecheta seems to be searching for the best values in the worldviews of her two civilizations, and as they appear stubbornly incompatible, she lands, so to speak, between them.

With her next novel, *Gwendolen* (1989), Emecheta returns to the London black-immigrant milieu that she knows so well, but for the first time the main character is not a Nigerian but a West Indian. The theme is incest, and although this is new in Emecheta's work, it lends itself to the well-known scenario of girls and women oppressed by men and fighting for self-respect. The book starts off in Jamaica. Gwendolen is left behind with Granny, as first her father and later her mother leave for the "Moder Kontry" and settle in London. While in Granny's care, Gwendolen is sexually assaulted by Uncle

Johnny, who misuses his position as old family friend. The village blames Gwendolen, but luckily her family sends for her, and she goes to London. Her arrival in London gives Emecheta the opportunity to describe immigrant slum conditions through eyes that are innocent of the social meaning of such observations. Gwendolen's family is at the bottom of the social scale, illiterate and unable to cope with the complexities of British society, but they are surviving and gaining pleasure and support from a primitive church community. Granny dies and Mother goes back to Jamaica; during her absence the father starts an incestuous relationship with Gwendolen, who is sixteen. She becomes pregnant, but she also meets a white boy and starts a sexual relationship with him. The outcome of all this is optimistic if slightly confusing. The father commits suicide; the mother is partially reconciled with her daughter. Gwendolen lives with the baby in a council flat and is happy, and the boyfriend remains a friend, despite the shame of the paternity of the baby. This modern ending rests on a new set of relationships formed on the basis of personal choice rather than on blind acceptance of the established pattern of race and family relationships. There seems to be an implicit suggestion that this alternative mode of social organization might avoid a repeat of the experiences of the main character.

Despite variations and contradictions in Emecheta's work, critics—both approving and disapproving—tend to be drawn to her novels for their ideological content. Her criticism of aspects of African cultural tradition invites the charge of being a traitor to her culture, and her feminism, though mild in Western eyes (she refuses to be called a feminist), has enraged some male African critics to a vitriolic attack on her books, which they claim misrepresent Igbo society. Some of that criticism makes one suspect that her books are, indeed, of vital importance. She insists on education and middle-class values as means of female emancipation, and she has summed up her philosophy in an interview in *West Africa*: "I believe in the power of the Will, with the help of that man upstairs, of course, but one can always achieve one's goal, if one is determined enough." As a role model for other women she is important, and, despite certain stylistic limitations, she represents a new and vigorous departure in fiction about women in and from Africa.

Interview:
West Africa (3 April 1978): 671.

Bibliography:
B. F. Berrian, "Bibliographies of Nine Female African Writers," *Research in African Literatures*, 12 (1981): 214-236.

References:
Anthony Barthelemy, "Western Time, African Lives: Time in the Novels of Buchi Emecheta," *Callaloo*, 12, no. 3 (1989): 559-574;

Charlotte Bruner, "The Other Audience: Children and the Example of Buchi Emecheta," *African Studies Review*, 29, no. 3 (1986): 129-140;

Charlotte and David Bruner, "Buchi Emecheta and Maryse Condé: Contemporary Writing from Africa and the Caribbean," *World Literature Today*, 59 (1985): 9-13;

Christina Davis, "Mother and Writer: Means of Empowerment in the Work of Buchi Emecheta," *Commonwealth Essays and Studies*, 13, no. 1 (1990): 13-21;

Afam Ebeogu, "Enter the Iconoclast: Buchi Emecheta and the Igbo Culture," *Commonwealth Essays and Studies*, 7, no. 2 (1985): 83-94;

Ernest Emenyonu, "Technique and Language in Buchi Emecheta's *The Bride Price, The Slave Girl*, and *The Joys of Motherhood*," *Journal of Commonwealth Literature*, 23, no. 1 (1988): 130-141;

Katherine Frank, "The Death of the Slave Girl: African Womanhood in the Novels of Buchi Emecheta," *World Literature Written in English*, 21 (1982): 476-497;

Alastair Niven, "The Family in Modern African Literature," *Ariel*, 12, no. 3 (1981): 81-91;

Chikwenye Okonjo Ogunyemi, "Buchi Emecheta: The Shaping of a Self," *Komparatistische Hefte*, 8 (1983): 65-77;

Femi Ojo-Ade, "Female Writers, Male Critics," *African Literature Today*, 13 (1983): 158-179;

Eustace Palmer, "The Feminine Point of View: Buchi Emecheta's *The Joys of Motherhood*," *African Literature Today*, 13 (1983): 38-55;

Palmer, "A Powerful Female Voice in the African Novel: Introducing the Novels of Buchi Emecheta," *New Literature Review*, 11 (November 1982): 21-33;

Kirsten H. Petersen, "Unpopular Opinions: Some African Women Writers," *Kunapipi*, 7, nos. 2-3 (1985): 107-120;

Rolf Solberg, "The Woman of Black Africa, Buchi Emecheta: The Woman's Voice in the New Nigerian Novel," *English Studies*, 64 (1983): 247-262;

Omar Sougou, "The Experience of an African Woman in Britain: A Reading of Buchi Emecheta's *Second Class Citizen*," in *Crisis and Creativity in the New Literatures in English*, edited by Geoffrey V. Davis and Hena Maes-Jelinek (Amsterdam: Rodopi, 1990); pp. 511-522;

Oladele Taiwo, *Female Novelists of Modern Africa* (London & Basingstoke, U.K.: Macmillan, 1984), pp. 100-127;

Marie Umeh, "African Women in Transition in the Novels of Buchi Emecheta," *Presence Africaine*, 116 (1980): 190-201;

Umeh, "*The Joys of Motherhood*: Myth or Reality," *Colby Library Quarterly*, 18, no. 1 (1982): 39-46;

Umeh, "Reintegration with the Lost Self: A Study of Buchi Emecheta's *Double Yoke*," in *Ngambika: Studies of Women in African Literature*, edited by Carole Boyce Davies and Anne Adams (Trenton, N.J.: Africa World, 1986), pp. 173-180;

Cynthia Ward, "What They Told Buchi Emecheta: Oral Subjectivity and the Joys of 'Otherhood,'" *PMLA*, 105 (1990): 83-97.

Wilson Harris

(24 March 1921 -   )

Jean-Pierre Durix
Université de Dijon

BOOKS: *Fetish*, as Kona Waruk (Georgetown, Guyana: Miniature Poets Series, 1951);

Eternity to Season, as Waruk (Georgetown, Guyana: Privately printed, 1954; revised edition, London: New Beacon, 1978 [i.e., 1979]);

Palace of the Peacock (London: Faber & Faber, 1960);

The Far Journey of Oudin (London: Faber & Faber, 1961);

The Whole Armour (London: Faber & Faber, 1962);

The Secret Ladder (London: Faber & Faber, 1963);

Heartland (London: Faber & Faber, 1964);

The Eye of the Scarecrow (London: Faber & Faber, 1965);

The Waiting Room (London: Faber & Faber, 1967);

Tradition, the Writer and Society: Critical Essays (London & Port of Spain: New Beacon, 1967);

Tumatumari (London: Faber & Faber, 1968);

History, Fable & Myth in the Caribbean & Guianas, Edgar Mittelholzer Memorial Lectures (Georgetown, Guyana: National History and Arts Council, 1970);

Ascent to Omai (London: Faber & Faber, 1970);

The Sleepers of Roraima: A Carib Trilogy (London: Faber & Faber, 1970);

The Age of the Rainmakers (London: Faber & Faber, 1971);

Black Marsden: A Tabula Rasa Comedy (London: Faber & Faber, 1972);

Fossil and Psyche (Austin: African and Afro-American Studies and Research Center, University of Texas, 1974);

Companions of the Day and Night (London: Faber & Faber, 1975);

Da Silva da Silva's Cultivated Wilderness; and, Genesis of the Clowns (London: Faber & Faber, 1977);

The Tree of the Sun (London: Faber & Faber, 1978);

Explorations: A Selection of Talks and Articles, 1966-1981, edited by Hena Maes-Jelinek (Mundelstrup, Denmark: Dangaroo, 1981);

Wilson Harris (photograph by Helen Tiffin)

The Angel at the Gate (London: Faber & Faber, 1982);

The Womb of Space: The Cross-Cultural Imagination (Westport, Conn. & London: Greenwood, 1983);

Carnival (London & Boston: Faber & Faber, 1985);

The Infinite Rehearsal (London: Faber & Faber, 1987);

The Four Banks of the River of Space (London & Boston: Faber & Faber, 1990).

Wilson Harris is a modern version of the Renaissance humanist: his concern as an artist bears on all aspects of life, and, in his style of expression, he transcends all notions of genre. The main bulk of his work is in fiction, but his novels have also been interpreted as long poems in prose or as philosophical reflections. His experi-

mentation with language makes him one of the most original and powerful writers of the twentieth century. He has often been called a "difficult" novelist. This comes from his unfailing dedication to the truth of his vision, the complexity and richness of which demands all the reader's attention and power of imagination. Harris never oversimplifies issues for the sake of clarity. His respect for the complexity of his art is only equalled by his faith in the reader's intelligence. He has frequently been compared with such visionary writers as Dante, William Blake, and Arthur Rimbaud. In Harris's search for new forms, he is also close to William Faulkner and T. S. Eliot. His concepts, though original, owe a debt to Martin Buber and Carl G. Jung. Gentleness, distinction, loyalty, dedication to art, and unfailing optimism are features that Harris's friends associate with him. His capacity for listening to other people's opinions is well illustrated by the enthusiastic response of his students in the creative-writing classes he has taught for many years.

The son of Theodore W. (an insurance agent) and Millicent Glasford Harris, Theodore Wilson Harris was born on 24 March 1921 in New Amsterdam, in what was then British Guiana. He was educated at Queen's College, Georgetown. As a government surveyor from 1942 to 1958, he led many expeditions into the interior of the country. Several of his early novels are suffused by the brooding atmosphere of the Amazonian forest. Born in a country torn by ethnic rivalries, Harris considers his mixed ancestry (Amerindian, African, and European) as symbolic of a possible synthesis to overcome polarization, which is his aim in life.

His early collections of poetry, *Fetish* (1951) and *Eternity to Season* (1954), were followed by "The Sun: Fourteen Poems in a Cycle" (1955), which was published, together with prose sketches, in *Kyk-over-al*, the literary journal edited by A. J. Seymour in Georgetown (some of the poems are also in *Eternity to Season*). These early works contain many of the themes of his later fiction, including the relationship between seasons and eternity, destruction leading to new creation, and the metaphor of the voyage between two worlds (also a symbol for the movement from surface reality to deeper layers of consciousness).

In 1945 Harris had married Cecily Carew. After divorcing her, he moved to London in 1959 to concentrate on writing. On 2 April of that year he married Margaret Burns, a Scottish writer. Once settled in London, Harris began to focus on creating fiction. He soon produced his first masterpiece, *Palace of the Peacock*, published by Faber and Faber in 1960. The manuscripts had been rewritten several times under different titles (including "Almanac of a Jumbi" and "Horseman Pass By"). Unfortunately nothing remains of these early versions. The book is an attempt in fiction to achieve what Rimbaud did with his long poem "Le Bateau ivre" (The Drunken Boat, 1871). Harris's novel opens with a series of nightmarish tableaux from which the first-person narrator seems to wake up, only to discover that he has merely dreamt he was emerging from sleep. This situation illustrates Harris's desire to uncover the various layers of material reality and prejudices in order to avoid illusion and come closer to the roots of being. The unnamed narrator-protagonist says, "I dreamt I awoke with one dead seeing eye and one living closed eye."

Professed vision is presented as a form of blindness, whereas the acceptance of limited possibilities is a prelude to increased awareness. This type of paradox, which Harris uses in common with many other metaphysical writers (including John Donne) is not a gimmick; paradoxes are one of the privileged ways of access to modes of understanding that do not rest on simple premises. If language is meant to signify more than appears at first sight, then it, too, must be tampered with and exploded.

In *Palace of the Peacock* the protagonist and his brother, called simply Donne, a tyrannical farmer in the interior of Guyana, start on a journey upriver, with several companions, to catch up with the Amerindian workers (the "folk") who have left Donne's plantation because of his dictatorial methods. Donne, a prototype of the pioneer (his name with Elizabethan resonances may evoke the conquistadors in search of El Dorado), is cruel and ruthless. For him, the protagonist is a dreamer, a man who lacks practical sense, energy, and ambition. Still, as the plot develops, readers discover that it is precisely these "dreaming" qualities that enable him to break the harsh surface of reality and probe deeper. The two brothers have radically different characteristics; and yet, in some ways, they are complementary. They both feel strangely fascinated by Mariella, Donne's much-abused female companion, who later develops into the figure of the muse. She becomes their guide and interpreter along the journey back to their origins. The narrator clearly hints that the quest is possibly into a land that is the territory of the self. Their journey brings them closer to the realization that they know nothing about the world and their own consciousnesses.

In allegorical fashion each member of the group represents one section of the Guyanese nation: the da Silva twins, of Portuguese stock, come from Sorrow Hill; Schomburgh, the oldest in the group, bears the name of a nineteenth-century German explorer who wrote one of the first accounts of life in the interior of Guyana; an Amerindian, Vigilance, is the lookout for dangerous rocks in the river. He is also a spiritual watcher and a member of the "lost tribe" whom the crew tries to rejoin. Carroll, the black man in the group, paddles superbly and possesses musical gifts that are revealed in the final vision of the novel. The crew also includes Cameron, who has Scottish ancestors; Jennings, the mechanic; and Wishrop, the assistant bowman.

As the boat falls into the grips of rapids, the narrator suddenly sees Donne as a projection of himself and a complementary figure: "he was myself standing out of me while I stood inside of him." This splitting process undergone by the individual is one step in the progression toward self-discovery. When the narrator sets foot on land, he suddenly falls prey to a fit of dizziness during which directions, including up and down, become confused. All conventional frames of reference disintegrate.

At the beginning of book 2 the crew arrives at the Mission of Mariella and causes panic because they exactly resemble another crew that met tragic deaths on the river. Doubts concerning what is dream and what is reality, and what belongs to life and what belongs to death, are carefully maintained so that the reader also loses the usual points of reference in fiction. Instead of resorting to clear-cut systems of opposition, one must learn to be carried away by the particular logic of the novel. Networks of images are woven; concepts become more fluid.

As the crew passes through the Straits of Memory and negotiates War Office—a series of dangerous rapids—the psychic nature of their journey becomes more evident. They will have to be physically destroyed before they can be reborn to a new form of identity. Gradually these men with their separate ethnic origins appear as part of a great unity that they must endeavor to restore: Vigilance is Carroll's stepbrother. At one point, his father took Carroll's mother as his wife. Carroll's father, who, officially, remains unknown, may well be Schomburgh. Thus the journey also involves the rediscovery of their common links and an exploration of their identities.

Some of the members of the crew suffer accidental deaths one after the other. The survivors eventually have to abandon their boat when they arrive at a great cliff that bars their progression. They start to ascend, and along their way they have a series of visions: first, Donne sees a carpenter in a room through a window in the rock. This Joseph-like figure is carving a human figure, but when Donne tries to attract his attention, the "craftsman of God" remains absolutely indifferent. It seems that Donne has become transparent or nonexistent. Then the carpenter turns to a picture of a bounding animal, wounded by a spear in its side. The shape of the spear twists, resembling a horn of plenty or the crescent of the moon. The poetic transformation hints at the kind of liberation that results from a use of lan-

Harris in Georgetown, Guyana, circa 1957-1958, when he was a government surveyor

guage based on a system of associations that break down conventional barriers. In a second window, Donne perceives a woman holding a child on her knees. This nativity figure becomes an image of creative frailty when the narrator discovers that her threadbare dress is her hair, which joins with the straw in the cradle, becoming a "melting essence." This symbol of universal communication is radically different from Donne's old desire to be all-powerful and to dominate.

The seventh day of the trip marks the completion of the crew's genesis. The whole landscape becomes fluid. The first-person narrator, who significantly has vanished during some parts of the annihilating process of the journey (being replaced by a third-person narrator), reappears and merges with a "we-narrator," an indication of the process of relationships being established. A bare tree in the savannahs turns into the "palace of the peacock," a starry dress with peacock's eyes. Harris introduces the Jungian *cauda pavonis* (peacock's tail) symbol as an image of constantly changeable reality, which seems to revolve round a mysterious and invisible center of genesis and whose elements merge into one another like the colors of the rainbow. This image represents an advanced stage of awareness at which fixed polarizations have been destroyed. The whistling that issues from Vigilance's lips becomes pure music, frail and yet always renascent, engulfing the whole universe. Metaphoric correspondences are established between these diverse forms of perception. The apotheosis at the end of the novel is the closest Harris ever comes to a formal vision of perfection.

The Far Journey of Oudin (1961), the second volume of the "Guiana Quartet" (as Harris calls his first four novels), is set in the East Indian community of the Berbice area of Guyana. The plot, following a circular pattern, starts with a paradoxical scene presented through the point of view of Oudin, the dead hero of the novel. Soon after the funeral, Ram, Oudin's old, miserly employer, begins to pester Beti, the hero's wife, concerning the contract Ram and Oudin signed. The nature of the covenant—a major theme in the book—only becomes clear at the end. Beti has actually swallowed the document, fearing that the agreement might prove dangerous to her.

The second part of the novel retraces the history of the family. Beti, who is in the care of her uncle Mohammed, is the object of Ram's lecherous desires. After Ram has asked Oudin, his servant, to abduct her on his behalf, Oudin makes off with the girl. When Oudin and Beti finally come back after a long flight through the swamps, Ram demands Beti's child-to-come in exchange for their financial independence. Such are the terms of the dreaded covenant.

The plot of this novel, which also focuses on the problems of inheritance, is far more realistic and intricate than that of *Palace of the Peacock*. No one knows anything about Oudin's origins. Yet he closely resembles Mohammed's illegitimate half brother, whom Mohammed and his brothers killed because their father had chosen him as rightful heir. Harris suggests that true roots are often problematic, but that brutality alone cannot give legitimacy to a transgression of the lawful transmission of inheritance.

Beti and Oudin's flight is a journey of initiation that forces them to face their limits and the reality of death. Unlike Ram, who merely wishes to possess Beti, Oudin considers the woman with compassion, a quality that enables him to value the beauty of frailty and envision possibilities of genuine communication. The first stage of their journey takes the two lovers across a river where they meet a fisherman described as a John the Baptist figure. This meeting, which symbolizes the death of the lovers' old selves and the beginning of their new existence, initiates them into the extreme dangers associated with any form of revelation. In this archetypal landscape, the old man also acts as Charon to ferry them from the known land to the unknown. Oudin and Beti make love near a dead tree. Their act symbolizes the fertility that emerges out of apparent destruction.

Without the poetic richness of *Palace of the Peacock*, the narration seems at times flawed by the excessive intricacy of the plot, by a jerky pace in the progression, and by the presence of some clumsy prolonged metaphors. Yet the novel shows that true vision is not reserved for only sophisticated people.

The Whole Armour (1962) is set along the Pomeroon River, an area of western Guyana with impenetrable forests and a shore easily eroded. The center of the action is the house where Magda, a formidable prostitute, entertains her customers. Cristo, her son, has just been accused of killing a rival in a brawl for Sharon, a local beauty; and Magda asks Abram, an older solitary patriarch (whose name bears apt biblical connotations), to hide the boy, who, she says, could be his son. Abram disappears after the boy has been staying with him for a while, and again Cristo is suspected of murder. Magda takes her son back to Abram's house; they find nothing there and follow the tracks left by a tiger who has dragged the maimed body into the jungle. Cristo and Magda are guided by circling vultures who feed on the man's remains. In a devilish attempt to save her son, Magda forces Cristo, at gunpoint, to put on the dead man's clothes, and she buries the body, later telling others that it is Cristo's. Meanwhile the boy escapes in the forest. During the wake organized by Magda, Mattias, Sharon's new fiancé, is killed by Peet, the girl's father. Magda has convinced Sharon to go and meet Cristo in the jungle. At the end of the novel, the police are closing in on the couple. There is hope for the future in Cristo's child that Sharon carries in her womb. Cristo is ready to face his accusers.

On one level *The Whole Armour* is mostly realistic. The narration contains no elements indicating flights into the world of dreams. Yet events take strange turns. In a sort of carnival process—a theme taken up again by Harris nearly twenty-five years later—characters have to assume other personae. Cristo "becomes" the dead man, Abram, but also has traits of the tiger that roams the area and is reputed to have taken several lives; ironically the "innocent" boy in some ways has the external appearance of the beast. Harris suggests that one has to face the destructive forces within and outside oneself. When Cristo finally decides to give himself up, he may appear as a scapegoat (Christ, the crucified victim). But he is also the lucid hero, who has come to terms with guilt and death. Christian allusions are also present in Magda's name (which evokes Mary Magdalene). The redoubtable harlot at the beginning, she is ready to sacrifice all her material interests to save her son's life.

In the course of the plot, polarities are blurred. Innocence and guilt no longer correspond to simple categories. "Sinful" characters such as Magda surpass themselves, and "innocent" people such as the virgin Sharon cause deaths. In order to face the whole complexity of existence and be able to conceive the child of the future, Sharon must make her own journey into the jungle, abandon the safety of a rich marriage with Mattias, the businessman's son, and venture near the tiger's claws. The novel significantly starts on Jigsaw Bay, where the elements encroach upon one another and where certainties vanish. During his flight in the jungle, Cristo also meets a fleeing tribe of Amerindians; because of his long sojourn in mud and forest, he is taken for one of them by the tribe, which wears ceremonial markings. Cristo fails to follow them but is rejuvenated by their meeting.

The Whole Armour can be interpreted as a shamanistic novel in that it involves the restoring of the dead. Cristo descends into the jaws of the beast to be fragmented and reborn in a new guise (probably through his baby, whose existence is prefigured in an anticipatory passage just before the close of the novel).

The Secret Ladder (1963) closes the cycle of the Guiana Quartet and is much more straightforward than any other Harris novel: Russell Fenwick, a surveyor, has gone to the Canje River to take hydrological measurements with a view to regulating the seasonal flow of what is an essential fresh water supply to an area threatened by the advance of brackish currents. But the setting up of the scheme will flood the poor farming land occupied by the descendants of runaway slaves led by Old Poseidon. Conflict is inevitable between the two groups. While Fenwick favors peaceful discussions, some members of his crew, led by Jordan, are in favor of laying down the law ruthlessly. Events take a tragic turn when Poseidon is accidentally killed by Bryant, an African member of Fenwick's party who adores the old man.

Fenwick is different from Donne, the leader of the expedition in *Palace of the Peacock*. Whereas Donne is ruthless, Fenwick is permeable to "nonscientific" truths. His task is to gauge the river, but he soon realizes that the nature of his assignment is closer to the biblical Jacob's ladder of dreams. He abandons the tyranny of science and becomes aware of the importance of understanding and compassion. Even though Poseidon's land is considered worthless, agriculturally speaking, its spiritual value must be taken into account. Fenwick discovers that his apparently simple mission arouses a mass of historical, sociological, and metaphysical problems that he had not suspected. What town dwellers call "progress" cannot be imposed tyrannically on a population to the detriment of its spiritual values.

Weng the Amerindian, Chiung the Chinese, Perez the Portuguese, Bryant the African, Stoll the mulatto, and Van Brock, a tall black man, represent the various ethnic groups that make up Guyana. Fenwick, their leader, has African, Amerindian, and European ancestors (like Harris). This party, like the country itself, is torn by internal dissension. The improvement of their relationships can only rest on an awareness of their deep bond of community. Poseidon cannot be seen as a mere backward opponent of technology; he is also part of the crew's past and inheritance. In imposing their will on him, they run the risk of violently suppressing an important part of themselves. This difficult situation causes the characters to reexamine their premises radically.

The plot abounds in catastrophes: Chiung is nearly struck dead while keeping his night watch, dressed in Fenwick's coat. The blow he receives on his head, meant for Fenwick, is a physical reminder of the powers of death. Directly or vicariously all the characters suffer a reduction to a skeletal stage, to the very minimal framework of life akin to death. An allusion to the seven days of creation shows that the process is a genesis. The threefold organization of the novel (Book I: The Day Readers; Book II: The Night Readers; Book III: The Reading) mirrors a process of creation that starts from polarization and finally dissolves opposing groups into the dynamic force of their interaction.

The relatively straightforward story is told by a third-person narrator who frequently interprets the characters' thoughts. But the reader soon discovers that it is impossible to know anything for sure. Following a conscious strategy of disorientation, the narrative voice imperceptibly switches from one character to the next.

The functioning of the narrator's apparently "omniscient" stance proves that omniscience is impossible. Thoughts are fragmented and linked with the thoughts of others. *The Secret Ladder* may be the easiest door into Harris's complex world. Yet the surface simplicity must be penetrated in order to appreciate the craftsmanship that characterizes his work.

Heartland (1964), his next novel, has long been out of print. Yet it is one of the most interesting books in Harris's oeuvre. It is really a continuation of the Guiana Quartet and includes several characters from *Palace of the Peacock*. An evocation of the first novel is made by da Silva, the pork knocker (gold digger), who announces that he has remained in the jungle since the catastrophe at the bottom of the falls. Similarly, Petra, the protagonist Stevenson's "muse," is linked with Mariella. The narrator even suggests that she might be the same woman, since Amerindians have a habit of calling themselves different names. She has been excluded from her tribe because it is rumored that she might be pregnant by Donne.

The theme of guilt, which is one of the main points in *The Whole Armour*, is presented in *Heartland* through Stevenson. He has taken up a job in the jungle to make up for a disaster he has indirectly caused: his father committed suicide after discovering that his accountant, Camacho, had made off with the money of the firm, while Camacho's wife was having an affair with Stevenson. His stay in the interior leads him to come to terms with the implications of physical decay. Da Silva, who had come to collect his supplies, is found dead between the boulders on the Kamaria Falls. Stevenson learns that one cannot possess anything or anyone for sure: the Amerindian Petra gives birth to her child with Stevenson's help. When he comes back after leaving her for some time, he discovers that Petra has gone with her baby, and he has to accept the fact that the one he was hoping to have as a replacement for Camacho's wife is equally elusive. The "flight of the muse" is a ruling metaphor in this novel. Women have a destructive role, yet their reluctance to be possessed evokes the shaman's flight when he abstracts himself from his concrete environment to have intercourse with the spirits.

Da Silva is one of the first "scarecrow" characters in Harris's fiction: his fragile frame and ragged clothes may symbolize the rich potentialities of apparent drabness and deprivation. Stevenson goes astray in a borderline country on the edges of Guyana, Brazil, and Venezuela. Points of reference vanish, and he loses his bearings. This environment is conducive to visions, which, in Harris's novels, usually take place in the "directionless depth of the forest." In such conditions history is resurrected. The fluidity of the past contrasts with the solidity of the present. Stevenson learns to see himself in all his strangeness. This may arouse panic because, in such situations, the rigid barriers between inside and outside, between above and below, lose clarity. These experiences of transitional stages lead the character to search for a "center" that holds all the disparate pieces of his experience together. This "heartland" is the zone where certainties fade but where polarities and tyranny lose their substance.

When Stevenson discovers that his boat has been carried away by the current, he suddenly thinks of the letter (to a woman named Maria) that lies crumpled at the bottom of the dinghy. This message to an unseen correspondent may be a metaphor for the art of fiction. Significantly the novel closes with the discovery of Stevenson's disappearance in the forest. In the charred remains of a resthouse where he once stopped, fragments of poems are discovered: "Troy," "Behring Straits," and "Amazon" (published by Harris in complete form in *Eternity to Season*) strike the essential themes of the novel: the individual "must die first to be free. . . . Who blazes a trail / is overtaken by a labyrinth / leading to many conclusions." This quotation illustrates the greatness and the risks involved in Harris's artistic quest. The reader may feel lost in the maze of images and situations, but this is, according to Harris, the only way to gain access to a fuller type of perception, opening out onto visionary prospects.

The Eye of the Scarecrow (1965) marks a turning point in Harris's career. It is the first time a narrator (in this case a letter writer) alludes to Edinburgh and to the London environment in which, at that time, Harris had lived for about six years. Still, the setting of the novel is Georgetown, Guyana, and the Amazonian forest. The style is deliberately nonrealistic. The story concerns the functioning of memory and, mingled with fantasies, the reconstruction of past events in broken chronological order. Much of the interest of the plot lies in the echoes triggered by episodes: the narrator remembers his youth in an East Street house built on the site of an old plantation. In the background there are evocations of the great British Guiana strike of 1948, a prelude to the independence of the country. The young boy has lost his father and lives with his mother's parents. He is very friendly with L—, who subsequently becomes an engineer and travels with the narrator into the jungle to find a lost settlement called Raven's Head. The goal of their search is a mythic four-gated city.

Written in the form of a diary, the novel opens on "25th-26th December 1963" and closes on "25th September 1964," a nine-month period that evokes the gestation of a baby and offers a link with the birth of Christ, though the process is inverted, as if seen in a mirror. The conventional diary soon turns into a journey of associations that break the realistic convention of the genre. This shows that memory reconstructs more than reproduces what actually happened, because that is where the possibilities of creation are.

Characters are organized in twin patterns, as the reader realizes with the narrator and L—, who appear as two complementary personalities reminiscent of the couple formed by Donne and his dreamer of a brother in *Palace of the Peacock*. L— serves to test dangerous grounds when, on an impulse, the narrator pushes him into the canal to be his own "gauge of extremity." Dramatic reversals take place during the journey to Raven's Head, so that, especially in book 3, it is impossible to tell who has experienced what. This illustrates Harris's conception of one's identity, which is made up of many unknown and suppressed elements. Although on the surface the trip into the jungle reminds the reader of *Palace of the Peacock*, the fragmentation of characters, time, and place is carried much further and is an indication of Harris's integration of theory into literary practice.

Harris also applies the process of disorientation to the narration. Not content with the conventional third and first person, he introduces a third element, which he calls "It." It, the scarecrow of the title, is identified with the frailest, most elusive elements in the novel. Nevertheless,

It transcends systems of oppositions and polarities and dynamizes the search for otherness that is the goal of one of the characters. It is a catalytic agent that originally sends the narrator and his companion on their search for Raven's Head. It is inside and outside them. It is the spark that keeps the novel alight with metamorphic possibilities.

At the end a section entitled "Manifesto of the Unborn State of Exile" includes what is apparently Harris's *ars poetica*. Creation aims at reaching—and yet always fails to reach—the original Word, "the Well of Silence . . . Which is concerned with . . . a fluid logic of image." Vision is a striving for unity, but it forces the seer to acknowledge the radical otherness of his own experience. Language, the writer's privileged means of access to reality, can never be taken for granted. For the author, a plunge into the dark at the bottom of the well of silence is a necessary prelude to creation. In this novel, which has important metafictional connotations, Harris uses paradoxes and echoes: events, characters, and ideas mirror one another while sending back a slightly altered version of the original. Behind every shape lies a shadow. Behind traditional consonance lies a kind of dissonance that must be uncovered before more truly harmonious links can be established on new premises. The elusive image of the scarecrow, which has been earlier developed with da Silva, turns into a metaphoric representation of language and writing.

The Waiting Room (1967) pushes one step further the disintegration of characters and time. One of the most complex works in the Harris canon, it develops largely on a metaphoric level. It is the story of Susan Forrestal, who has become blind after several eye operations. She was deeply in love with a man who subsequently left her after a violent argument and disappeared into the jungle. Though she married someone else after becoming blind, her memory is still full of her former lover. The narration is supposedly based on Susan's diary, which was found in the remains of her house after an explosion killed her and her husband. Harris experiments with a direct "Author's Note," signed "W. H." (a technique he also uses in several later novels), in which he explains the background of the characters and his desire to write fiction that is a "living construction of events." He sees himself merely as an agent through which the plot develops. Past events are reshaped by means of free association. The difficulty of the novel is that the reader

First page of the manuscript for Ascent to Omai *(Harry Ransom Humanities Research Center, University of Texas at Austin; by permission of Wilson Harris)*

can take very little for granted: characters fuse, not only with others but also with clusters of images. The action is constantly situated on margins between identity and namelessness, between vision and blindness, and between life and death. Fragments of notations that bring the novel back to the primary reality of events alternate with metaphors.

The nature of relationships—as seen in Susan's original love affair—takes on cosmic values: the novel starts with "The Void" (title of book 1) and moves on to "The Vortex." The text develops through a drift of images centered on the idea of the operation (Susan's eye surgery but also the sexual intercourse with her lover, an evocation of the awakening of consciousness). Harris also alludes to the episode of the flight of Ulysses from Circe. Ulysses, the creative individual, is apparently a prisoner, tied to his mast, abandoned. And yet, to Harris, he remains paradoxically freer to confront the singing of the sirens, an image of self-indulgence and sterility.

The narrative weaves in and out of various layers of consciousness and imagination, entering each one in turn and modifying the whole structure in the process. The development is poetic and musical in its broken fluidity. Out of the disjointed diary that supposedly forms the basis for the narration emerges a potential for regeneration.

Tumutumari (1968) blends the radical technique of *The Waiting Room* with a more conventional form of narrative. Prudence, the heroine, through whose mind the story is filtered, lives near waterfalls in the heartland of Guyana with her Amerindian servant, Rakka. Rakka has been the mistress of Prudence's husband, Roi, an engineer in charge of gauging the water discharge of the river. Roi has dug a well at a certain distance from the river, to which the well is connected by a shaft. This device, which technically is meant to improve the precision of the measurements, becomes a central metaphor in the novel. Roi is "accident prone" and suffers a crashing fall down the well while he is digging it. Later on, his canoe is carried downriver when the shear pin snaps and he crashes down the rapids. Prudence, who at the beginning of the novel has just lost a child she was carrying in her womb, relives the death of her husband, who was beheaded by the "sleeping rocks" (the English meaning of *tumatumari*). She has suffered a mental breakdown after the series of catastrophes, and she is being nursed by Rakka. Gradually a series of half-dreaming, half-real thoughts reconstruct the past in Prudence's mind.

A thematic strand that runs throughout this novel is the history of Guyana, which soon appears to be an example of the relationships between people anywhere. Henry Tenby, Prudence's father, was a historian. The daughter recaptures the mood of her father's research and explores the submerged past of her family and ancestors. Some of her forebears were black. This element was suppressed in the context of the British Guianese middle classes. Much of Prudence's reconstructive work aims at recapturing the value of this slave past in her. Her father and her husband have a problem with accepting the Amerindian genes in them. Roi, like Donne in *Palace of the Peacock*, tends to exploit Amerindian workers and to abuse Rakka, his mistress. Her barrenness as a result of a bad fall and the tribes' propensity for flight and disappearance in the face of the modern world are symptoms of a malaise whose extent Prudence begins to grasp. The importance of the Amerindian past in the buildup of the Guyanese personality is a problem more fully developed in *The Sleepers of Roraima* (1970) and *The Age of the Rainmakers* (1971). In *Tumutumari* "the folk," as Harris calls them in *Palace of the Peacock*, are seen as an unjustly rejected part of a national and personal heritage.

As Prudence sits in the "Chair of the Well" (the well becomes the pit at the bottom of which the past is reflected in a visionary form), she brings back to life fragments of memories compounded of her own as well as her father's experience. In book 3, entitled "The Chair of the Well," she follows her father's footsteps through Marseilles and London, where her father traveled and met Isabella, a woman he lived with before he met a prostitute in the so-called Brothel of Masks. These are sterile encounters because they do not involve any deep understanding between the man and the woman. Interspersed within her father's story are pieces of Prudence's own relationship with her husband and with Rakka, a story of misunderstandings and misconceptions.

In book 4, titled "The Brothel of Masks," the novel is turned into a free-associative pattern similar to the one in *The Waiting Room*. The narration is several times removed from the original reality: the various chapters reconstruct Prudence's and her father's stories in various guises; at one point Prudence resumes her father's conversation with a waif of the streets he met thirty-three years before; later she writes a script based on an unfinished play by her father. The interpenetration of the various people and situations shows the intimate community of problems. All these destructions and fissures point to a "game" of conception, which Prudence only discovers in the final chapter. She becomes aware of all the masks she has lived with in her explorations of history, of her own ancestry, and of her relationships with others. The game, playful at first, becomes deadly serious when the masks splinter, and everything points toward catastrophe (represented by the Tumatumari Falls). Yet, curiously, antagonism is replaced by a genuine thread of compassion. Self-centered initiatives lead to reciprocal exchanges.

Ascent to Omai (1970) internalizes the quest themes present since *Palace of the Peacock*, the paradoxical movements of ascent-descent central in *Tumatumari*, and the idea that vision can only emerge after a catastrophe shattering the materialistic blinders of the characters. Victor is in the jungle, searching for traces of the land claim his father, Adam, had near Omai. On the way, he is bitten by a tarantula, which makes him unconscious and triggers memories about his past: his mother died while giving birth to him; his father, a welder, one day ran berserk and set fire to his factory and home. Fragmentary events of his youth complement and echo these early memories: Victor sees himself on the floor of the hovel where he lived when his father brought a woman in and made love to her on the floor, while the boy hid behind his mother's petticoat. In an initiative imitating his own father's acts of arson, Victor burned a hole in a copybook at school and was caned. Later on he went to sea.

The threefold movement ("Book I: Omai Chasm"; "Book II: Ascent"; and "Book III: Omai") charts an evolution that starts from a fairly conventional story, develops into a complex journey of associations, and finally brings together some key strands to form a meaningful pattern of genesis. The originality of this novel lies in the depth to which its second book goes: based on the theme of judgment, it presents itself as Adam's trial but actually develops into the trial of humanity's propensity for clear-cut (and sterile) solutions. Starting with the incident of the burning factory, it moves into all layers of human guilt. The proceedings take the form of a comedy in which different characters, whose identities remain fluid, discuss the predicament of the protagonist. The fictional nature of the process is emphasized by the different actors appearing on a game of cards shuffled by the judge.

The novel, like *The Eye of the Scarecrow*, has metafictional connotations. For Harris, language must be made to bring back the past with a new reality, thanks to a free association of images. The judge professes his desire to write a novel in which the "spectre of time" would be the protagonist, a kind of "drama of community" unlike the limited scope of the traditional comedy of manners. This involves a medium free from any desire to "conscript time" in any preformed mold. Time assumes the same fluidity and capacity for metamorphosis as other elements in the creative process. The judge also declares that—like Harris himself—he refuses to sacrifice depth of experience on the altar of clarity. The reader must accept the same burden of difficulty, not for its own sake, but because it is the only way to reach profundity. Disintegration is not cultivated per se. It is only the necessary passage through which one can gain a vision of the frail seeds of authentic reconstruction.

Book 3 picks up tableaux from earlier parts of the novel and sets them to face and echo one another. Similarly the narrator offers a graphic representation of his creative technique in the form of concentric circles that correspond to various levels of perception and images, each one materialized as an area of ripples that fan outward and inward, merging with and dynamizing the others, the whole movement being initiated by the original "wound" or "chasm" caused by the stone that hits Victor at the beginning. Trains of associations break the various entrenched layers of narrative and initiate a dance of the elements, an echo of what the creative process aims to achieve. At the end, only a very frail vision of a star remains to guide Victor. But this frailness is of immense value for the re-creation of a sense of community.

At the beginning of the 1970s Harris became increasingly interested in retrieving long-forgotten mythic representations belonging to his Amerindian forebears as part of a global Caribbean heritage, which also includes voodoo, limbo dancing, and various folk traditions (for example, see the first three essays collected in his *Explorations*, 1981). Pursuing his revision of history in an imaginative way, he took fragments of memories left by the decimated tribes and argued that in their legends lie the seeds of genuine vision, despite the crushing weight of fear and oppression that forced the native people to escape and disintegrate as a major social group.

In *The Age of the Rainmakers*, a collection of four stories, Harris starts with the myth of *Couvade*, which, according to his prefatory note, is a dream through which the legacy of the tribe is handed down to every newborn child. In the first story Couvade is the name of a young boy who tries to find traces of his vanished parents with only the help of his aged grandfather. The old man tells of the sickness that affected the tribe and from which they could only be cured if they accepted the rules of fasting and seclusion imposed on them by tradition. But their failure to observe the law led to the destruction of some of the group by their enemies and the flight of the remaining individuals. Couvade, abandoned at the mouth of a cave, dreams that he goes back to the paintings in the cave and relives the drama inscribed in them. The boy gives new life to the pictorial representations and becomes the artist who dreams myths alive and bears hope for the future.

The four stories composing *The Age of the Rainmakers* culminate in "Arawak Horizon," in some ways the most experimental piece of fiction Harris has ever written. Starting with a succession of numbers from one to nine, the narrator rebuilds a whole world in which the various representations symbolized by the basic numbers are made to correspond to various pieces of furniture in a room and to the main themes of the last two volumes of fiction. Thus the problems of vision, cannibalism, escape, hunting, oppression, and flight, as well as the sun, moon, and stars, are brought together into an evolutionary dance of creation.

After the complexity of "Arawak Horizon," *Black Marsden: A Tabula Rasa Comedy* (1972) seems based on a much more realistic plot. For the first time in Harris's work, the setting is clearly outside Guyana. He has moved from the country of his parents to that of his wife, Margaret, and of part of his own Celtic ancestors: Scotland. This novel is also the first of a new, third phase in Harris's career—after the Guiana Quartet and the increasingly complex and interiorized "middle novels." In *Wilson Harris* (1982) Hena Macs-Jelinek underlines the importance of the theme of creation-as-painting in the next phase. Certainly visual elements are uppermost. But there is also a clearly discernible story: Clive Goodrich, who has won a fortune in the soccer pools, meets a beggarlike character called Doctor Marsden in the ruins of Dunfermline Abbey in Scotland. This conjurer-cum-hypnotist figure is supposed to put on a play at the Edinburgh Festival in which Jennifer Gorgon, a beautiful woman, will play the part of a chaste Salomé. Goodrich offers to take Marsden, Jennifer, and Knife, their comrade, into his house, kept by the dutiful Mrs. Glenwearie. These ambiguous characters soon take hold of Goodrich's imagination, fill the reflections he consigns to his diaries, and people his dreams.

The plot becomes an alternation of referential notes telling of Marsden's wanderings through Edinburgh and of dreamlike excursions that culminate in the journey to Namless (the name echoes Idiot Nameless in *The Eye of the Scarecrow*). This voyage into an Eliotic wasteland is "revisioned" as Goodrich is taking a walk through the Botanical Garden. The country revisited in some ways resembles contemporary Guyana: it is torn by strikes, endless dissension, and a tyrannical government that rules with the help of the secret police. But it also becomes a prototype for almost any country. It is a landscape alternately composed of snow and desert, cold and heat, and it seems cruelly devoid of population, as if all the inhabitants had fled in fear of some unexpressed threat. The scene is a sort of tabula rasa (one of the main themes of the novel), a reduction to essentials to lay bare the springs of oppression and prejudice and to reveal the possibility of another "black" reality (Marsden is sometimes referred to as Black Marsden), an invisible shadowy existence that a visionary quest can bring to light.

Namless is clearly a landscape of the mind. Everything there is bare and polarized. Knife, Goodrich's "taxi-driver" and guide, takes him through this journey in a theaterlike decor whose tableaux change constantly. The drama brings the protagonist into contact with "death-dealing masks and gods." The world he discovers during the trip and his connection with Knife parallel his relationship with Marsden (who resembles in some ways the Director-General who rules over Namless). Goodrich gains a certain insight into the fascination of beauty and masks, and he becomes aware of the dangers of any institutionalized form of dependence. The theater, camera, clowns, and harlequins play a major thematic role, as if to suggest that an exploration in depth always involves the uncovering of disguises. At the end, when Goodrich discovers that Jennifer and Marsden are taking advantage of him, he throws them out. He feels terribly lonely and lost without their presence. But it may be the beginning of his own freedom.

Companions of the Day and Night (1975) is intimately linked with *Black Marsden*: the pieces that are rearranged into the novel are supposed to have been collected by Clive Goodrich, who, in an introduction, professes to be the editor of papers, diaries, "paintings," and "sculptures" belonging to Idiot Nameless and sent on, after their owner's fatal fall from the Teotihuacán pyramid, by Black Marsden. These different levels of enunciation reflect Harris's desire never to forget that pieces of information or objects can never be totally separated from their owner or from the one who reports them. The complicated network leading to the narration itself is only an image of the intricate process of extricating meaning out of reality. Goodrich declares that he, too, had to "translate" these pieces of information into a novel. The translation involves a reactivation of passive details pertaining to history. Marsden's intervention also proves that he is not as negative as a cursory examination of the end of *Black Marsden* might have indicated. This type of correspondence weaves a network of threads between Harris's novels, which can only be truly understood in relation to each other. This chamber of reflections implies a constant movement from one to the next, the model undergoing a subtle transformation as it collides with its reflection.

Goodrich proves sensitive to "objects" that bring back to life the essence of different historical eras. The process of comprehension does not involve a reduction of the object to some apparently logical, finite definition. Understanding implies establishing metaphoric links that throw a different light on the original topic of examination.

The journey undertaken by Idiot Nameless in the novel takes him to Mexico at Easter, a fit symbol for the process of re-creation at work in the novel. The structure is based on a particular feature of the ancient pre-Columbian calendar, which was composed of a nine-day cycle (companions of the night) and a thirteen-day cycle (companions of the day). Days eight and nine of the first cycle were called Dateless Days. In the novel days one to seven correspond to different stages of Nameless's journey through Mexico, whereas days eight and nine refer to events anterior to that trip. This organization suggests the whole movement of the exploration, which starts in a relatively linear temporal manner and then digs deeper into history. In his introduction, Goodrich talks of the "absorption" of the remaining

four days in the thirteen-day cycle through the medium of the "dateless" days. This "digestion" of time and events is facilitated by the editor's plunge back to the provider of information.

In Nameless's journey to Mexico different events draw the attention of the protagonist: first, in Mexico City, he meets a fire-eater who fascinates him with the capacity to absorb the "sun" into his mouth and then to disgorge fire, in the same way as a writer first wolfs down material, revises it, and then presents it in a new shape. The fire-eater also sculpts religious figures. He has already made a triumphant image of Christ that is used in processions. But his sculpture of the Virgin has been refused because he took a prostitute as his model. This girl happens to be the granddaughter of a nun who was chased out of her convent after the revolution and was raped by several men in the crowd. This prostitute, born out of the rape of a religious person, is the anonymous woman with whom Nameless sleeps at the beginning of his stay in Mexico. Searching for this ever-elusive girl, he is drawn to the ruined convent whose remains symbolize religious persecution in the name of politics. This theme also evokes the ritual of the Aztecs who made offerings of human hearts to the gods on their altars because they were afraid that time would not regenerate itself at the end of the cycle. Nameless's death at the bottom of the great pyramid resembles these sacrifices of old. The novel opens bridges among "great" moments of history (including the Aztec era, the Mexican revolution, and the present time with its scientific discoveries, such as black holes of gravity). It also suggests that their greatness lies in their apparent flaws. The book is an evolutionary sculpture or canvas, which leads to other, less frozen aspects of experience.

The name of the protagonist in *Da Silva da Silva's Cultivated Wilderness* (published with *Genesis of the Clowns* in 1977) evokes one of Donne's companions in *Palace of the Peacock* and the pork knocker in *Heartland*. But here the character is far more developed and only keeps vague family links with South America: born in Brazil of Spanish and Portuguese parents with black ancestors, he became an orphan and was adopted by a British ambassador, Sir Giles Marsden-Prince (another meaningful name in Harris's canon), after the orphanage collapsed during a cyclone and flood. Da Silva's wife, Jen, a distant relation to Paul Gauguin, was born in Peru. Jen and da Silva live near Holland Park—the part of London

Harris in Austin during the early 1980s, when he taught creative writing at the University of Texas

where Harris himself lived until 1986, when he moved to Chelmsford in Essex. The plot develops out of da Silva's paintings. The novel starts with a strange dream of an aircraft crashing into a lake (a reminder of similar happenings in *Ascent to Omai*), a thematic echo of catastrophe, which, in Harris's works, usually heralds renewal.

Another essential concern in the novel is the problem of love, which goes hand in hand with the process of resurrection. In da Silva and Jen's relationship, exploitation is nearly absent. There is a warm and understanding feeling between husband and wife. Similarly motherly love in the face of external obstacles characterizes the struggle of Manya, a girl who sits for da Silva as a model (she also comes from South America). She fights to keep her child Paul, whom Kate and other welfare workers want to place in an institution because of Manya's mother's alleged inability as an educator. Paul was born out of a temporary union with a leukemia patient who wanted to leave some of himself on earth and who, after

the child was born, was miraculously cured of his disease. The power of love to create life and to transcend appalling conditions is not treated sentimentally. On the contrary, the paradoxical destructive-constructive elements inherent in such a relationship are explored in depth through the use of highly charged metaphoric associations that give this novel a particularly poetic tone.

Harris pursues the possibilities of visual images through the sketches he includes in the middle of his novel—a technique inaugurated in *The Waiting Room* and pursued in *Ascent to Omai* and "Arawak Horizon." Here a painting of the London Commonwealth Institute, with its characteristic marqueelike architecture, becomes a graph representing a sort of tent held by a central pole that separates visible (institutional tone) colors, materials, and shapes on the right-hand side from the invisible (universal nontone) transparency evoking genuine beauty and compassion on the left. Thus painting becomes a threshold of vision.

When, at the end, Jen comes back from work to announce that she is at last pregnant after many years of marriage, da Silva is filled with a mixture of extraordinary joy and fear because of all the new responsibilities he cannot yet fathom. Jen's fertility reminds readers of the "foetus" subtly contained in each of da Silva's paintings.

Genesis of the Clowns is very different in tone and subject. The story starts with a letter Frank Wellington receives in London from an anonymous correspondent who announces the death of Frank Hope, a man who used to work for Wellington when he was a surveyor in Guyana. The novel is reminiscent of *The Secret Ladder*. One of the characters, a Chinese called Chung, bears almost the same name as another Chinese in *The Secret Ladder*. Chung succumbs to psychological disorder after a long exposure to the bush country. Despite the resemblances with several characters or situations in earlier novels, *Genesis of the Clowns* is much more a novel of personal memories. It has no linear plot like *The Secret Ladder* but is rather a meditation on Wellington's past association with the different members of the crew, whom he tended to see as merely workers who had to be given their meager pay every fortnight. Hope, Chung, Marti Frederick the East Indian, and Reddy the Amerindian are mentally resurrected in a new guise and take on a complexity that was not there originally. Wellington learns to judge the quality of his relationship with them and sees it as an example of the way in which the old empire and the new nations can consider each other. Although he was on the side of the colonial administration, he can see that his understanding of the workers now goes much deeper and that he can identify with many of their prejudices, fears, and hopes. The resemblance becomes more disturbing when the anonymous correspondent adds that, before taking his life, Hope killed a man who was in bed with his girl and whose name was also Frank Wellington. This meaningful coincidence brings back to the protagonist's mind the different moments when he, too, had desired his men's female companions and when he had considered these women merely as commodities to be consumed. He feels that he is one of the "clowns." He has worn many masks, some tyrannical, some profoundly affectionate. And the journey back into the past has reopened a precious line of connection in his life.

The Tree of the Sun (1978) takes up the themes of painting, birth, and resurrection also present in *Da Silva da Silva's Cultivated Wilderness*

of which this novel can be considered a continuation. *The Tree of the Sun* begins where the other novel stops: Jen has discovered that she is pregnant; da Silva had started his big painting called "The Tree of the Sun" the same morning the child was conceived. In the process of creation the artist discovered an unfinished book and letters left by Francis and Julia Cortez, who occupied the flat previously. Da Silva's retelling of their stories is the plot of the later novel and part of his picture. The tree becomes a metaphor for his art, whose branches bear strange fruit. Thus creation serves to link the dead and the living. The evocation of these characters with conquistadorial names reveals a family tree with surprising branches: it is as if Jen were expecting the child that Julia could never have after her aborted attempts. In the strange mutual relationship that is established between painter and models, the creator is created by them as much as he creates them. His search for a principle of unity between all the diverse moments of time and characters leads him to remark that "unity is the mystery of otherness." The artist subsists on other people, "cannibalizes" them to a certain extent. But this act of violence is counterbalanced by his compassion and desire to establish deep connections with them.

The Angel at the Gate (1982) begins with a preliminary note signed "W. H.," saying that the text is a transcription of Mary Stella Holiday's automatic writing that took place while she was undergoing treatment and receiving guidance from Father Joseph Marsden, a priest-cum-hypnotist living at Angel Inn, an old house in London. In the automatic writing, the protagonist is split into two personae: Mary, Marsden's secretary and patient, lives with her brother Sebastian, an unemployed drug addict. Stella, Sebastian's wife, has been rushed to the hospital after absorbing a massive quantity of Valium. Father Marsden is later nearly crushed by a bale that falls from a lorry in the street. His accident and "little death" are the occasion for Khublall, a Hindu, and his friend Jackson, a Jamaican, to join the plot. Through Mack, Stella's father, they are linked with the family. Personal parallels grow deeper when it is discovered that one of Marsden's ancestors in the eighteenth century sold Mary's black ancestor, a slave, in his auction room.

The familiar Holland Park setting takes on unusual aspects when it opens onto imaginary locales, such as Paradise Park and Planet Bale. Harris also creates characters out of a song Stella has loved since childhood. Mack the Knife, Sukey Tawdrey, Jenny Diver, and Lucy Brown, of course, originate in the modern song (by Kurt Weill and Marc Blitzstein) inspired by John Gay's *Beggar's Opera* (1728) and Bertolt Brecht's *Dreigroschenoper* (1928), but they also illustrate Harris's thematic preoccupations with the nature of cruelty and love. The different "angels," such as Marsden, Khublall, and Jackson, are characters who can reach out to other people and help them to achieve a higher degree of relationship with them. The narrative can be compared to the automatic writing described by W. B. Yeats in *A Vision* (1925). The web of the novel is made of an elaborate system of related opposites. Artificial paradises and political or personal utopias have no place here. Sebastian's drug haven leads only to irresponsibility and violence. This novel may appear simpler than others in its use of language. Yet, in its exploration of memory, in its mixture of the familiar and the disorienting, it shines a new light on disturbing aspects of reality.

Jonathan Weyl, the memorialist narrator of *Carnival* (1985), reconstructs the life of Everyman Masters, who has just died in London in the summer of 1982. As a young man, Masters was raised on a South American plantation. His death takes place just after his meeting in a London flat with a striking woman named Jane Fisher. This encounter is reminiscent of Master's "first death" in New Forest (the fictional name of his native country), where he was stabbed by a fisherman's spouse. The story then goes back to another "catastrophe," when Masters and his cousin Thomas run away in fright from what they think is a rapist on the foreshore. Scampering along East Street, Thomas runs into a woman carrying eggs to market, and he breaks her load. He goes back to the woman's hovel to find out where to take the compensation money. But Czar Johny, the woman's lover, taking him for a rival, begins to threaten her. Thomas seizes a knife and stabs Johny.

In the course of Masters's years at Brickdam College, he is reunited with his biological father, Martin Weyl, a lawyer whom public gossip subsequently forces to marry Jennifer, the narrator's mother. Martin dies after failing to win the acquittal of an Amerindian client accused of ritually killing his terminally ill mother. Masters takes charge of the narrator's family after Martin's death. But Jennifer dies soon after. Masters and Jonathan Weyl cross over to England on the same boat in 1957. Masters, the former overseer, abandons all his properties to work in a refrigerator factory in London. The narrator ultimately marries Amaryllis, the daughter of an anthropologist shot by Amerindians in a boat journey organized by Masters in New Forest.

Memory serves to revive material the narrator may have thought dead. Instead of being a simple exercise in remembering, the narrator recreates past relationships in an attempt to unlock blocked situations. This novel also reexamines the problem of the exploitation of women by men, which was essential in *Palace of the Peacock*.

Carnival, lengthy in comparison to previous Harris novels, is a thematic summary of much of his earlier fiction. With the emphasis on the powers of love and vision to redeem past errors, *Carnival* seems more serenely positive than any other novel in the Harris canon. The creator is still as conscious of his limits as ever: he knows that he is fathered by his fiction as much as he fathers it. He lets himself be carried by different, apparently unrelated clusters of images, which constitute many lenses through which reality is refracted. *Carnival* pushes this journey of exploration to the limits of the abyss. This possibly accounts for the difficulties it presents to the reader. Yet great merit lies in the relentless unveiling of different masks—through which people perceive reality—in order to reach the common thread of unity Harris hopes to find in all of them.

The Infinite Rehearsal (1987) also returns to the shores of childhood. Events or scenes mentioned in his previous novels are fused with reflections on metafiction; more than ever in Harris's work, the relations between characters and author or his representations in the novels are probed and exposed in all their complexity. The fictional text progresses through metaphoric echoes, side plots, and paradoxes in a constant revisionary process that precludes the possibility of any final statement. But this does not lead to despair; on the contrary, Harris believes in the possibility of the resurrection of the spirit despite and through the apparent deadlocks and catastrophes of human experience. Strands of narration emerge out of numerous literary memories woven into the primary plot and give birth to new developments. The novel "rehearses" fragments by Walter de La Mare, T. S. Eliot, Jessie Weston, James Joyce, Wilfrid Owen, William Shakespeare, Robert Louis Stevenson, Samuel Beckett, Robert Burns, Johann Wolfgang von Goethe, Christopher Marlowe, Joseph Conrad, Dylan

Wilson Harris (photograph copyright by Erich Malter)

Thomas, and others. Harris does not merely duplicate an Eliotic experience: he integrates this intertextual dimension in his general theory, which aims at untiringly revising all premises in order to explore the possibilities of rebirth in any apparently sterile system. *The Infinite Rehearsal*, which, together with *Carnival* and *The Four Banks of the River of Space* (1990), forms a trilogy, includes a humorous element that has never appeared so clearly before: in chapter 7 the narrator quotes "W. H." (same initials as the author), the person who, according to Robin Redbreast Glass, the narrator, has "put his name to [his] fictional autobiography." Robin playfully remarks that "W. H. says we are becoming literate imaginations," thus parodying one of Harris's sometimes elliptic formulations.

The Four Banks of the River of Space returns to the geographical and metaphorical landscapes of the past: Anselm, a former Guyanese "engineer, sculptor, painter, architect, composer" is visited one evening in Essex by Lucius Canaima

whom he used to know when he worked in the Amazonian forest of his native land. This dreamlike meeting sends Anselm back on a journey to rediscover his past connections with various characters. Through his protagonist, Harris pursues a parallel with Ulysses in the *Odyssey*. In themes and situations, this novel is also the reworking of several passages from *Palace of the Peacock*, *The Secret Ladder*, *Heartland*, *The Waiting Room*, *Tumatumari*, and *Ascent to Omai*, which are blended into a new imaginary structure.

Critics took time to appreciate fully the extent of Harris's originality. But now adjectives such as "hermetic" or "unreadable" no longer appear in reviews. Younger Caribbean writers generally regard Harris with reverence. International scholars ready to follow him in his radical questioning of language, of the realistic illusion, and of ready-made definitions have realized that he stands in the same category as William Blake, Arthur Rimbaud, or Dante Alighieri. Besides stressing parallels with these writers, Michael Gilkes also suggests resemblances with Swedenborg and the esoteric Christian mystics. One might add Martin Buber and the authors of most important metaphysical texts in the world's great religions (the *Tao Te Ching, The Secret of the Golden Flower, The Cloud of Unknowing . . .*). Besides the obvious parallel with T. S. Eliot, Joyce Adler convincingly outlines the influence of Herman Melville on Harris. Gilkes rightly shows the author's borrowing from the alchemical tradition, notably vehicled by C. G. Jung's works. Harris's broad sense of culture, which ranges from the classics to recent scientific theories such as that underpinning quantum physics, has encouraged Nathaniel Mackey, Russel McDougall, and Stephen Slemon (all represented in Hena Maes-Jelinek's *Wilson Harris: The Uncompromising Imagination*) to follow comparative or theoretical approaches to his work. Maes-Jelinek has contributed most to the thorough examination of Harris's novels in their own terms. Indeed the reader who wishes to take part in Harris's revolutionary quest must agree to follow his radical restructuring of language and meaning. Helen Tiffin (also in Maes-Jelinek's volume) rightly considers Harris's novels as an example of "counter-discourse," which is concerned with "the exposure of the strategies of conquest and the creative retrieval of what [Harris] refers to as 'eclipsed cultures.' " Such enterprise "requires the destruction of monolithic codes and familiar patterns of binary opposition, and the recognition of the provisionality of all authority." Maes-Jelinek believes that Harris's importance transcends by far the context of postcolonial literatures. To her, he is one of the world's boldest imaginative creators. She admires his language's "endless capacity of metamorphosis," which plays an essential part in the genesis of his rich fictional and philosophical oeuvre.

In recent years Harris has taught creative-writing courses at Austin, Santa Cruz (California), and in Australia. This activity has helped to bridge the gap between the novelist and the critic. His most important essays on the role of art in society, which take up many of the issues approached in his fiction, are collected in *Tradition, the Writer and Society* (1967) as well as in *Explorations* (1981). He has also applied his particular vision of literature to such works as those by William Faulkner, Edgar Allan Poe, Ralph Ellison, Jean Toomer, Juan Rulfo, Jean Rhys, Patrick White, Paule Marshall, Raja Rao, Mervyn Peake, Claude Simon, and others. These essays are collected in *The Womb of Space* (1983). Harris has re-

ceived many awards, including honorary doctorates from the University of the West Indies (1984) and the University of Kent at Canterbury (1988); he won the Guyana National Prize for Fiction in 1987.

Wilson Harris is definitely avant-garde in his approach to art. Yet his practice does not stem from any fashionable literary theory. He was a "deconstructionist" before Jacques Derrida. He has been prolific without repeating himself. Admittedly his desire to probe under the surface, to bring out the grains of life in apparent sterility, and to stretch language to its limits are always present. Yet these premises have proven so fecund that each new novel, while extending the same canvas of fiction, brings in a design definitely its own.

Interviews:

"Interview with Wilson Harris," in *Kas-Kas: Interviews with Three Caribbean Writers in Texas*, edited by Ian Munro and Reinhard Sander (Austin: African and Afro-American Research Institute, University of Texas, 1972), pp. 43-56;

Kalu Ogbaa, "Exile, Philosophic Myth, Creative Truth, Thrust and Necessity: An Interview with Wilson Harris," *Caribbean Quarterly*, 29 (June 1983): 54-62;

Jane Wilkinson, "Wilson Harris: Interview," *Kunapipi*, 8, no. 2 (1986): 30-45;

André Dommergues, "An Interview with Wilson Harris," *Commonwealth Essays and Studies*, 9 (Autumn 1986): 91-97;

"Wilson Harris: In Conversation with Fred D'Aguiar," *Wasafiri*, 5 (Autumn 1986): 22-25;

Stephen Slemon, "Interview with Wilson Harris," *Ariel*, 19 (July 1988): 47-56;

"Extract from an Interview with Rovin Deodat," *Kyk-over-al*, 39 (December 1988): 82-87.

References:

Ian Adam, "Marginality and the Tradition: Earle Birney and Wilson Harris," *Journal of Commonwealth Literature*, 24, no. 1 (1989): 88-102;

Rolstan Adams, "Wilson Harris: The Pre-Novel Poet," *Journal of Commonwealth Literature*, 13 (April 1979): 71-85;

Joyce Adler, "The Art of Wilson Harris," *New Beacon Reviews*, 1 (1968): 22-30;

Adler, "Attitudes Towards 'Race' in Guyanese Literature," *Caribbean Studies*, 8 (July 1968): 23-63;

Adler, "Melville and Harris," in *Commonwealth Literature and the Modern World*, edited by Hena Maes-Jelinek (Brussels: Didier, 1975), pp. 33-41;

Adler, "*Tumatumari* and the Imagination of Wilson Harris," *Journal of Commonwealth Literature*, 7 (July 1969): 20-31;

Gary Crew, "The Eternal Present in Wilson Harris's *The Sleepers of Roraima* and *The Age of the Rainmakers*," *World Literature Written in English*, 19 (Autumn 1980): 218-227;

Crew, "Wilson Harris's Da Silva Quartet," *New Literature Review*, 7 (1979): 43-52;

Sandra E. Drake, *Wilson Harris and the Modern Tradition: A New Architecture of the World* (Westport, Conn.: Greenwood, 1986);

Jean-Pierre Durix, "Along Jigsaw Trail: An Interpretation of *Heartland*," *Commonwealth Novel in English*, 1 (July 1982): 127-146;

Durix, "Crossing the Arawak Horizon," *Literary Half-Yearly*, 20 (January 1979): 83-92;

Durix, "*The Eye of the Scarecrow* by William Harris," in his *The Writer Written: The Artist and Creation in the New Literatures in English* (Westport, Conn.: Greenwood, 1987), pp. 87-105;

Durix, "An Introduction to Wilson Harris's Discursive Strategies," in *A Sense of Place*, edited by Britta Olinder (Göteborg: Göteborg University, 1982), pp. 131-141;

Durix, "Paradoxes of Creation: Wilson Harris's *The Secret Ladder*," *Ariel*, 15 (April 1984): 27-38;

Durix, "A Reading of 'Paling of Ancestors,'" *Commonwealth Newsletter*, 9 (January 1976): 32-41;

Durix, "Through Tension to Metamorphosis: *The Angel at the Gate* . . . ," *World Literature Written in English*, 24 (Summer 1984): 120-127;

Durix, "The Visionary Art of Wilson Harris," *World Literature Today*, 58 (Winter 1984): 19-23;

Durix, "Wilson Harris: From the Void into the Unknown," in *Essays on Contemporary Post-Colonial Fiction*, edited by Hedwig Bock and Albert Wertheim (Munich: Hueber, 1986), pp. 275-294;

Durix, ed., "Symposium on Wilson Harris," *World Literature Written in English*, 22 (Spring 1983): 1-106;

Michael Gilkes, "The Art of Extremity: A Reading of Wilson Harris's *Ascent to Omai*," *Caribbean Quarterly*, 17 (September-December 1971): 83-90;

Gilkes, "*Da Silva da Silva's Cultivated Wilderness* and *Genesis of the Clowns*," *World Literature Written in English*, 16 (November 1977): 462-470;

Gilkes, *Wilson Harris and the Caribbean Novel* (London: Longman, 1975);

Gilkes, ed., *The Literate Imagination: Essays on the Novels of Wilson Harris* (London: Macmillan, 1989);

Glyne Griffith, "*Ascent to Omai*: Towards a Novel-History," *Journal of West Indian Literature*, 2 (December 1987): 67-75;

Gareth Griffiths, *A Double Exile* (London: Boyars, 1978), pp. 171-192;

J. J. Healy, "Wilson Harris at Work: The Texas Manuscripts with Special Reference to the Mayakovsky Resonance in *Ascent to Omai*," *Ariel*, 15 (October 1984): 89-107;

John Hearne, "The Fugitive in the Forest," *Journal of Commonwealth Literature*, 4 (December 1967): 99-112;

W. J. Howard, "Shaping a New Voice: The Poetry of Wilson Harris," *Commonwealth Newsletter*, 9 (January 1976): 26-31;

Howard, "Wilson Harris and the 'Alchemical Imagination,'" *Literary Half-Yearly*, 11 (July 1970): 17-26;

Howard, "Wilson Harris's 'Guiana Quartet,'" *Ariel*, 1 (January 1970): 46-60;

Graham Huggan, "Anxieties of Influence: Conrad in the Caribbean," *Commonwealth Essays and Studies*, 11 (Autumn 1988): 1-12;

C. L. R. James, *Wilson Harris—A Philosophical Approach* (Port of Spain: University of the West Indies, 1965);

Louis James, "Wilson Harris and the 'Guyanese Quartet,'" in *A Celebration of Black and African Writing*, edited by Bruce King and Kolawole Ogungbesan (Zaria, Nigeria: Ahmadu Bello/Oxford University Press, 1975), pp. 164-174;

Joyce Jonas, "Anancy Strategies in *The Whole Armour*," *Kyk-over-al*, 31 (June 1985): 52-56;

Jonas, "Wilson Harris and the Concept of Threshold Art," *Journal of West Indian Literature*, 1 (June 1987): 29-34;

Nathaniel Mackey, "Limbo, Dislocation, Phantom Limb: Wilson Harris and the Caribbean Occasion," *Criticism*, 22 (Winter 1980): 57-86;

Mackey, "The Unruly Pivot: Wilson Harris's *The Eye of the Scarecrow*," *Texas Studies in Literature and Language*, 20 (Winter 1978): 633-659;

Hena Maes-Jelinek, "Ambivalent Clio: J. M. Coetzee's *In the Heart of the Country* and Wilson Harris's *Carnival*," *Journal of Commonwealth Literature*, 22, no. 1 (1987): 87-98;

Maes-Jelinek, "Ascent to Omai," *Literary Half-Yearly*, 13 (January 1972): 1-8;

Maes-Jelinek, " 'Inimitable Painting' . . . ," *Ariel*, 8 (July 1977): 63-80;

Maes-Jelinek, "The Myth of El Dorado in the Caribbean Novel," *Journal of Commonwealth Literature*, 6 (June 1971): 113-127;

Maes-Jelinek, *The Naked Design: A Reading of Palace of the Peacock* (Aarhus, Denmark: Dangaroo, 1976);

Maes-Jelinek, "The True Substance of Life: Wilson Harris's *Palace of the Peacock*," in *Common Wealth*, edited by Anna Rutherford (Aarhus, Denmark: Akademisk Boghandel, 1971), pp. 151-159;

Maes-Jelinek, "The 'Unborn State of Exile' in Wilson Harris's Novels," in *Commonwealth Writers Overseas*, edited by Alastair Niven (Brussels: Didier, 1976), pp. 195-205;

Maes-Jelinek, *Wilson Harris* (Boston: Twayne, 1982);

Maes-Jelinek, "The Writer as Alchemist," *Language and Literature*, 1 (Autumn 1971): 25-34;

Maes-Jelinek, ed., *Wilson Harris: The Uncompromising Imagination* (Aarhus, Denmark: Dangaroo, 1991);

Russell McDougall, "Music in the Body of the Book of *Carnival*," *Journal of West Indian Literature*, 4 (November 1990): 1-24;

McDougall, "Wilson Harris and the Art of Carnival Revolution," *Commonwealth Essays and Studies*, 10 (Autumn 1987): 77-90;

Mark McWatt, "Form and Originality: The Amerindian Fables of Wilson Harris," *Journal of West Indian Literature*, 1 (June 1987): 35-49;

Gerald Moore, *The Chosen Tongue* (London: Longman, 1969), pp. 63-73, 76-82;

Kirsten Holst Petersen and Anna Rutherford, eds., *Enigma of Values* (Aarhus: Denmark, Dangaroo, 1975);

Kenneth Ramchand, Preface to Harris's *Palace of the Peacock* (London: Faber & Faber, 1968);

Ramchand, "The Secret Ladder," in his *An Introduction to the Study of West Indian Literature* (Sunbury-on-Thames, U.K.: Nelson, 1976);

Ramchand, "The Significance of the Aborigine in Wilson Harris's Fiction," *Literary Half-Yearly*, 11 (July 1970): 7-16;

Jeffrey Robinson, "The Aboriginal Enigma: *Heart of Darkness, Voss*, and *Palace of the Peacock*," *Journal of Commonwealth Literature*, 20, no. 1 (1985): 148-155;

Robinson, "The White Goddess and *Palace of the Peacock*," *Journal of West Indian Literature*, 2 (October 1988): 15-22;

D. W. Russell, "The Dislocating Act of Memory: An Analysis of Wilson Harris's *Tumatumari*," *World Literature Written in English*, 13 (November 1974): 237-249;

Eva Searl, "T. S. Eliot's *Four Quartets* and Wilson Harris's *The Waiting Room*," in *Commonwealth Literature and the Modern World*, pp. 51-59;

Paul Sharrad, "*Palace of the Peacock* and the Tragic Muse," *Literary Criterion*, 16, no. 4 (1981): 44-58;

Gregory Shaw, "Art and Dialectic in the Work of Wilson Harris," *New Left Review*, 153 (September-October 1985): 121-128;

Stephen Slemon, "*Carnival* and the Canon," *Ariel*, 19 (July 1988): 59-75;

Slemon, "Revisioning Allegory: Wilson Harris's *Carnival*," *Kunapipi*, 8, no. 2 (1986): 45-55;

Ivan van Sertima, "Into the Black Hole: A Study of Wilson Harris's *Companions of the Day and Night*," *ACLALS Bulletin*, 4, no. 4 (1976): 65-77;

Mark Williams, "Containing Continents: The Moralized Landscape of Conrad, Greene, White and Harris," *Kunapipi*, 7, no. 1 (1985): 34-45;

Williams, "Why We Should Read Wilson Harris," *Landfall*, 39 (June 1985): 144-151.

Bessie Head
(6 July 1937 - 17 April 1986)

Greta D. Little
University of South Carolina

BOOKS: *When Rain Clouds Gather* (London: Gollancz, 1968; New York: Simon & Schuster, 1968);

Maru (London: Gollancz, 1971; New York: McCall, 1971);

A Question of Power (London: Davis-Poynter, 1973; New York: Pantheon, 1973);

The Collector of Treasures, and Other Botswana Village Tales (London: Heinemann, 1977; Cape Town: Philip, 1977);

Serowe: Village of the Rain Wind (London: Heinemann, 1981);

A Bewitched Crossroad: An African Saga (Craighall, South Africa: Donker, 1984; New York: Paragon House, 1986);

Tales of Tenderness and Power (Johannesburg: Donker, 1989; London: Heinemann, 1990);

A Woman Alone: Autobiographical Writings, selected and edited by Craig MacKenzie (London: Heinemann, 1990).

RECORDING: *Bessie Head of Botswana*, Washington, D.C., Voice of America, 1978.

OTHER: Sol Plaatje, *Native Life in South Africa*, foreword by Head (Johannesburg: Ravan, 1982), pp. ix-xiii;

"A Search for Historical Continuity and Roots," in *Momentum: On Recent South African Writing*, edited by M. J. Daymond, J. V. Jacobs, and Margaret Lenta (Natal, South Africa: University of Natal Press, 1984), pp. 278-280;

Ellen Kuzwayo, *Call Me Woman*, foreword by Head (Johannesburg: Ravan, 1985; London: Women's Press, 1985), pp. xiii-xv;

"Some Happy Memories of Iowa," in *The World Comes to Iowa: Iowa International Anthology*, edited by P. Engle, R. Torrevillas, and H. E. Engle (Ames: Iowa State University Press, 1987), pp. 86-88.

SELECTED PERIODICAL PUBLICATIONS— UNCOLLECTED: "Some Notes on Novel Writing," *New Classic*, 5 (November 1979): 30-32;

"Social and Political Pressures that Shape Literature in Southern Africa," *World Literature Written in English*, 18 (November 1979): 20-26.

When Bessie Head died in 1986 at the age of forty-nine, she left a legacy of diverse writings including three novels, a volume of short stories, an oral history, a reconstructed history of nineteenth-century southern Africa, and two volumes of collected writings published after her death. Her first works show the influence of her own experience in South Africa, focusing on themes of refugeeism and racism. Despite the parallels between her personal life and her story lines, Head transcended the specific setting of southern Africa to address patterns of evil that can be found in the minds of people everywhere. In her later works she shifted the focus from an individual's struggle for dignity to helping preserve the cultural and historical heritage that a people needs to achieve dignity.

Bessie Emery Head was born on 6 July 1937 in a mental hospital in Pietermaritzburg, where her white mother, Bessie Amilia Emery, had been committed because the father of her child was a black stable hand. The child was handed over to colored foster parents, who cared for her until she was thirteen. Because her natural mother had provided money for Bessie's education, she was placed in a mission orphanage, where she earned a high-school diploma and was trained to be a teacher. She taught elementary school and then wrote for the African magazine *Drum*. On 1 September 1961 she married Harold Head, a journalist with whom she later had a son, Howard. The marriage ended in divorce, and in 1964 she accepted a teaching position in Botswana, then the British Bechuanaland Protector-

Bessie Head (photograph by George Hallett)

ate. When she left South Africa she was given a canceled exit visa, depriving her of citizenship and making her a refugee. Fifteen years later, in 1979, she was granted citizenship by the government of Botswana. There she found an African past with depth and dignity she could be proud to claim as her own. She died of hepatitis in 1986 in Serowe, where she had made her home.

When Rain Clouds Gather (1968), Head's first novel, is the story of Makhaya Maseko, a political refugee from South Africa who escapes to Botswana after serving a prison term for sabotage. He is taken to the village Golema Mmidi (its name meaning "to grow crops") by Dinorego, a village elder, who introduces him to people who, like him, are seeking to make new and better lives for themselves in the harsh, drought-stricken land. Gilbert Balfour, for example, is a British expatriate setting up a cattle cooperative. He sees in Makhaya an ally for helping the villagers to learn greater self-sufficiency, and he recruits him to teach the women how to grow to-

bacco as a cash crop. Dinorego, his daughter Maria, Mma Millipede, and the young widow Paulina Sebeso share Gilbert's hopes for the future of Golema Mmidi, and they, too, accept Makhaya into their community. The local chief, Matenge, and his African nationalist friend Joas Tsepe seek to have Makhaya barred from the village, but a British district police official allows him to stay. Although welcomed to the village by most, he retains an aloofness, a separateness from the villagers and their problems. Events, however, pull him into the center of village life as the drought worsens, killing Paulina's young son and all her cattle. When the power-hungry Matenge tries to implicate Paulina in the boy's death, the whole village responds, challenging Matenge and his tyranny over them for the first time. Through these experiences and because of his growing involvement with Paulina, Makhaya's alienation is overcome. He discovers the love and goodwill in Golema Mmidi and accepts the new and hopeful life that the village offers, marrying

Paulina and settling down to a quiet, apolitical revolution.

When Rain Clouds Gather was widely acclaimed as a surprisingly mature first novel. British audiences especially responded to it, perhaps because it is a traditional romance with factual details about the society neatly interwoven into a fast-moving plot. The potential personal conflict between Makhaya's public and private self is not fully developed, which has often been cited as a shortcoming of the novel. However, Head demonstrates her ability to capture the African landscape and its impact, teaching her readers about the regional customs while she creates finely drawn individual personalities.

The theme of Head's second novel, *Maru* (1971), is racism, not of whites against blacks as might be expected, but the prejudice of the Tswana people against the Masarwas, the bushmen. An infant found beside her dead Masarwa mother is taken in by a female British missionary, who gives the child her own name, Margaret Cadmore. As a lone Masarwa in the mission school, young Margaret quickly comes to understand and accept her separateness when the other students torment her because of her background.

After she completes her teacher-training course, Margaret takes a teaching post in a small rural village, Dilepe. There she meets Dikeledi, Moleka, and Maru. Dikeledi, a young woman, teaches at the same school and intercedes for her when the children discover Margaret is a Masarwa and disrupt her class. Moleka, the local playboy, falls in love with Margaret when they first meet, but his love is never fulfilled because of Maru. Maru, brother of Dikeledi and best friend of Moleka, also loves Margaret. Believed destined to be the next paramount chief, he is admired for his wisdom and sensitivity. The entire village looks to him for leadership, but it is a burden Maru refuses to take up, always finding excuses to delay accepting his role as chief. In Margaret, Maru sees the ideal partner and a way out of his dilemma since the people would never accept his marrying a Masarwa. However, Margaret loves Moleka. Using three henchmen, Maru prevents Moleka from approaching Margaret and engineers Moleka's seduction of Dikeledi, who has always loved him. What makes such scheming acceptable in a character of Maru's nobility and integrity is Margaret's mystical ability to share Maru's dreams and record them in her paintings. Because of this supernatural closeness between

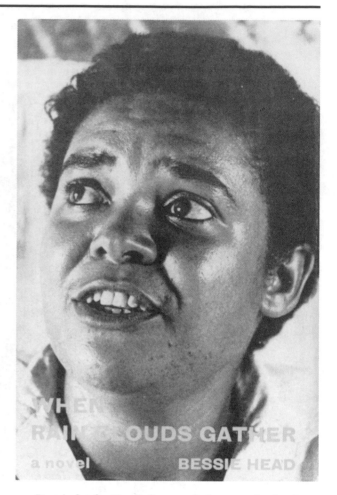

Dust jacket for Head's first novel, the story of a South African exile who finds a home in Botswana

the two, their union seems right, and readers can believe with Maru that Moleka would make Margaret miserable because of his inability to overcome the prejudice against the Masarwas.

Critical reaction to *Maru* has been diverse, ranging from Lewis Nkosi's view, that it is "as nearly perfect a piece of writing as one is ever likely to find in contemporary African literature" to Cecil Abrahams's dismissal of it as "a rather weak vapoury study on the theme of racial prejudice." *Maru* is Head's attempt to universalize racial hatred, pointing out that victims seek other victims lower in power and prestige than themselves. As in *When Rain Clouds Gather*, she examines how one feels alienation and copes with it. She once again raises the question of an individual's political responsibility to a larger society. Maru, unlike Makhaya, leaves his village for an isolated existence with Margaret, allowing his act of abdication "to pull down the old structures" and leaving Dikeledi and Moleka to change society. In

Maru Head's strength lies in giving her characters a subtle depth that takes them beyond the limitations of a fairly simple plot and obvious didactic message.

A Question of Power (1973), Head's most important work, is a dramatic departure from her earlier writing. It is an autobiographical account of mental disintegration, encompassing a classic battle between good and evil. The primary character is Elizabeth, a teacher who has come to Botswana from South Africa and settled in Motabeng at an agricultural cooperative. Like Head herself, she is colored, the daughter of a white woman and a black stable hand. Warned that she may be insane like her mother, and unprepared for the isolation she feels in her new home, Elizabeth finds herself losing control as she is nightly visited by terrifying hallucinations that ultimately lead her to a complete mental breakdown when she cannot distinguish reality from her phantom world.

Her nightmares are dominated by two men whose real counterparts in the village Elizabeth has never met—Sello and Dan. The first section of the book is devoted to Sello's invasion of her mind. Although Sello represents goodness and compassion, he also introduces Elizabeth to the power of absolute evil and to his own weakness. After surviving the hell of Sello's world, Elizabeth still lacks complete understanding. Thus she can be seduced and then coerced by Dan to experience his satanic power. She is subjected to a constant parade of sexual depravity and filthy stories about people in the village. As Elizabeth loses touch with reality, she is sent to a mental hospital, where she is finally able to recognize the existence of evil without being overcome by it. Dan has shown her the full power of evil, and in her quiet passive way Elizabeth has resisted, hanging onto the simple realities of her son and her work in the co-op garden. In the end she responds to Sello's reminder, "love is two people mutually feeding each other"; she embraces the brotherhood of man and at last finds a place to belong.

The symbolic richness in *A Question of Power* invites a wide range of critical interpretation. The extensive sexual content and dominant concern about insanity have prompted readings, including that of Adetokunbo Pearse, drawing heavily on psychology and arguing that the sexual negativism expressed in the book is the result of the negative self-image projected on black Africans by the South African government.

Dust jacket for the Heinemann African Writers Series edition (1972) of Head's second novel, which examines the Tswana people's prejudice against the Masarwas, the bushmen

Elizabeth's work on the cooperative being presented as a resolution of the conflict and the implicit political overtones throughout the novel have appealed to Marxist critics such as Kolawole Ogungbesan, even though Head's approach to social problems was meager and frustratingly slow. Readers who seek in her work metaphorical statements about the future of Africa find a picture of enduring hope touched by a cynical mistrust of politics. Feminists, including Femi Ojo-Ade, have been attracted by the female protagonist of *A Question of Power* and the nature of the battle she wages. The threatening male images of power in Elizabeth's inner world contrast with the positive, nurturing personalities of men such as her friend Tom and the co-op leader Eugene. Yet it is by defeating these male forces that she gains her place in the world. Religious interpretations (such as those of Linda Susan Beard and Joanna Chase) are also common, fed by the Christian symbolism of Elizabeth as a messianic figure who redeems herself and the world through her suffering. These readings are not incompatible with Head's overriding humanistic message that God and goodness are to be found in man: "There is only one God and his name is Man. And Elizabeth is his prophet." Such affirmation is present, although less obvious in her earlier books, just as the predominant themes of those books are present in *A Question of Power*. The alienation of the refugee is opened for intense psychological exploration, whereas she before examined it superficially from a distance. The racial prejudice under attack is her own, born of the self-hatred engendered particularly among coloreds by the separatist policies of South Africa. However, she does not allow readers to focus solely on South Africa; part of Head's achievement is her ability to transcend her South African context and speak of all people.

The Collector of Treasures, and Other Botswana Village Tales (1977) is a collection of thirteen finely constructed short stories, in which Head continues to explore good and evil, paying special attention to tribal witchcraft and the mistreatment of women in village life. These are dramatic, poignant stories where the distinction between right and wrong is never clear. "The Deep River: A Story of Ancient Tribal Migration," for example, displays a new historical orientation that characterizes Head's later works. "The Deep River" explains how the Botalaote tribe came to be separated from their parent tribe because a man refused to deny the woman he loved and their son. The account is fictionalized, but in its telling Head captures the tone and scope of mythic folklore. She maintains a traditional style in all the tales and imbues them with a strong sense of cultural integrity.

Short stories are not likely to draw significant critical attention, and Head's are no exception. Most of them bear a definite feminist bias, exploring the place of women within traditional society, and question the significance of religion, whether tribal witchcraft or Western Christianity. However, more important, the stories represent Head's deepening commitment to her new home in Botswana and to its cultural heritage.

In *Serowe: Village of the Rain Wind* (1981) Head shares the roots she has discovered by means of an oral history of the people of Serowe and their efforts for progress. The book is not a coherent, plotted narrative. Head has structured her history around three prominent men whose lives and achievements are intimately interwoven with the life of the village: Khama the Great, his son Tshekedi Khama, and Patrick van Rensburg. She presents interviews with people who knew and worked with these men, allowing the people to tell the stories in their own way. Thus she traces the village's notion of self-help through its evolution in the individual vision of each leader. The result is an unusual, innovative book—historical yet immediate.

A Bewitched Crossroad: An African Saga (1984) is a loosely organized novel tracing the migrations of the Sebina clan during the nineteenth century. As in *Serowe*, Head's focus is more on discovering and publicizing the history of blacks in southern Africa than on writing a novel in the traditional sense. Consequently the book can be confusing, appearing to lack coherence. Individual characters do not come to life as they do in her early novels. However, it could be argued that no character is as important as the land. Head's purpose is not to tell the story of individual characters but to portray a time in history when decisive steps were taken by the British and Afrikaners, which determined the future of the southern part of the continent. She celebrates the African role in that history and juxtaposes its humanity against Boer exploitation in South Africa. For Head, the historical direction of her last two works is a natural development of her life as a South African exile. In *A Bewitched Crossroad* she undertakes the task of reviving a history for the people of southern Africa "that is not sick with the need to exploit and abuse people."

Two volumes of Head's writings have been published posthumously: *Tales of Tenderness and Power* (1989) and *A Woman Alone: Autobiographical Writings* (1990). Each collection begins with a substantial biographical introduction and ends with Head's observations about the role of storytellers in South Africa. Seven stories appear in both collections, despite the difference in focus of the two books. *Tales* includes twenty-one stories, all but one grounded in real events. Three of the stories are previously unpublished. Although Head claims no interest in politics, her fears about the misuse of power and her implicit humanistic teachings are much in evidence. *A Woman Alone* contains twenty-nine reprinted essays and stories, which combine fictional narrative, journalistic reporting, cultural comment, and personal introspection; these selections are divided into three periods—"Beginnings, 1937-1964"; "In Exile, 1964-1979"; and "Retrospect, 1979-1986." Both collections reflect Head's evolution as a writer

Page 44

SEROWE: THE VILLAGE OF THE RAIN-WIND
(era of Khama -- introduction)

Where can one encounter a situation of such vivid contrast?
In Sekgoma 1, the old order died a complete death. In Khama, a new
order was born that was a blending of all that was compassionate
and good in his culture and in the traditions of Christianity. A
historian, Douglas Mackenzie, writing during the nineteen twenties
has/written of Khama, that he produced a history as yet unsurpassed
                   observed
anywhere in Africa. The reformer at village level was only one aspect
of his complicated career. His life did not only benefit the Bamangwato.
It reached out and benefitted Botswana as a whole, for he was the
founder of the/Bechuanaland Protectorate, which, so people firmly
                British
maintain, prevented Botswana from becoming another South Africa or
Rhodesia and resulted in independence for the country in 1966.

In 1885, Khama drew up a preliminary and lengthy document
for British protection. There had been threats from the Boers and
other enemies like Cecil John Rhodes' British South Africa Company,
to seize his land. Initially, the principles outlined in the document,
concerned only the Bamangwato. They were later to apply to the whole
country, in so far as the/British felt inclined to honour the
document. I quote a short extract:

"I, Khama, Chief of the Bamangwato, with my younger brothers
and heads of my town, express my gratitude at the coming of
the messenger of the Queen of England, and for the announcement
to me of the Protectorate, which has been established by the
desire of the Queen, and which has come to help the land of the
Bamangwato also. I give thanks for the word of the Queen which
I have heard, and accept the friendship and protection of the
government of England within the Bamangwato country.

I am not baffled in the government of my town, or in deciding

Page from the typescript for Head's history of her Botswana village (Mugar Memorial Library, Boston University; by permission of the Estate of Bessie Head)

and citizen of Africa and the world.

Although she left South Africa, Bessie Head, unlike her fellow exiles, remained in Africa, and in Botswana she found roots. What began in her early novels as a search for freedom and dignity ended as an affirmation of her African heritage and an attempt to make that heritage available for others.

Letters:

Randolph Vigne, ed., *A Gesture of Belonging: Letters from Bessie Head, 1965-1979* (London: SA Writers / Portsmouth, N.H.: Heinemann, 1991).

Interviews:

Betty McGinnis Fradkin, "Conversations with Bessie," *World Literature Written in English*, 17 (November 1978): 427-434;

Jean Marquand, "Bessie Head: Exile and Community in Southern Africa," *London Magazine*, 18 (December 1978-January 1979): 48-61;

Lee Nichols, "Bessie Head, South Africa," in his *Conversations with African Writers* (Washington, D.C.: Voice of America, 1981), pp. 49-57;

Linda Susan Beard, "Bessie Head in Gaborone, Botswana: An Interview," *Sage*, 3, no. 2 (1986): 44-47;

Michelle Adler, Susan Gardner, Tobeka Mda, and Patricia Sandler, "Bessie Head," in *Between the Lines: Interviews with Bessie Head, Sheila Roberts, Ellen Kuzwayo, Miriam Tlali*, edited by Craig MacKenzie and Cherry Clayton, (Grahamstown, South Africa: National English Literary Museum, 1989).

Bibliography:

Susan Gardner and Patrick E. Scott, *Bessie Head: A Bibliography* (Grahamstown, South Africa: National English Literary Museum, 1986).

Biography:

Susan Gardner, " 'Don't Ask for the True Story': A Memoir of Bessie Head," *Hecate*, 12 (1986): 110-129.

References:

Cecil Abrahams, "The Tyranny of Place: The Context of Bessie Head's Fiction," *World Literature Written in English*, 17 (November 1978): 30-37;

Abrahams, ed., *The Tragic Life: Bessie Head and Literature in Southern Africa* (Trenton, N.J.: Africa World, 1990);

Ursula A. Barnett, *A Vision of Order: A Study of Black South African Literature in English (1914-1980)* (London: Sinclair Browne / Amherst: University of Massachusetts Press, 1983), pp. 119-126, 198-203;

Nancy Topping Bazin, "Venturing into Feminist Consciousness: Protagonists from the Fiction of Buchi Emecheta and Bessie Head," *Sage*, 2 (Fall 1985): 32-36;

Linda Susan Beard, "Bessie Head's *A Question of Power*: The Journey through Disintegration to Wholeness," *Colby Library Quarterly*, 15 (1979): 267-274;

Lloyd W. Brown, "Creating New Worlds in Southern Africa: Bessie Head and the Question of Power," *Umoja*, 3 (Spring 1979): 43-53;

Brown, *Women Writers in Black Africa* (Westport, Conn.: Greenwood, 1981), pp. 158-179;

Charlotte H. Bruner, "Bessie Head: Restless in a Distant Land," in *When the Drumbeat Changes*, edited by Carolyn Parker and Stephen Arnold (Washington, D.C.: Three Continents, 1981), pp. 261-277;

Bruner, "Child Africa as Depicted by Bessie Head and Ama Ata Aidoo," *Studies in the Humanities*, 7, no. 2 (1979): 5-12;

Joanna Chase, "Bessie Head's *A Question of Power*: Romance or Rhetoric?," *ACLALS Bulletin*, 6 (November 1982): 67-75;

Sara Chetin, "Myth, Exile, and the Female Condition: Bessie Head's *The Collector of Treasures*," *Journal of Commonwealth Literature*, 24, no. 1 (1989): 114-137;

Cherry Clayton, "A World Elsewhere: Bessie Head as Historian," *English in Africa*, 15 (May 1988): 55-70;

M. J. Daymond, "Bessie Head, *Maru* and a Problem in Her Visionary Fable," in *Short Fiction in the New Literatures in English*, edited by Jacqueline Bardolph (Nice: Faculté des Lettres & Sciences Humaines, Université de Nice, 1989), pp. 247-252;

Teresa Dovey, "A Question of Power: Susan Gardner's Biography versus Bessie Head's Autobiography," *English in Africa*, 16 (May 1989): 29-38;

Elizabeth N. Evasdaughter, "Bessie Head's *A Question of Power* Read as a Mariner's Guide to Paranoia," *Research in African Literatures*, 20 (Spring 1989): 72-83;

Susan Gardner, "Bessie Head: Production under Drought Conditions," in her *Women and Writing in South Africa: A Critical Anthology* (Marshalltown, South Africa: Heinemann, 1989), pp. 225-235;

Kathryn Geurts, "Personal Politics in the Novels of Bessie Head," *Presence Africaine*, 140 (1986): 47-74;

Christopher Heywood, "Traditional Values in the Novels of Bessie Head," in *Individual and Community in Commonwealth Literature*, edited by Daniel Massa (Msida: Malta University Press, 1979), pp. 12-19;

Joyce Johnson, "Metaphor, Myth and Meaning in Bessie Head's *A Question of Power*," *World Literature Written in English*, 25 (February 1985): 198-211;

Johnson, "Proper Names and Thematic Concerns in Bessie Head's Novels," *World Literature Written in English*, 30, no. 1 (1990): 132-140;

Johnson, "Structures of Meaning in the Novels of Bessie Head," *Kunapipi*, 8, no. 1 (1986): 56-69;

Ketu H. Katrak, "From Pauline to Dikeledi: The Philosophical and Political Vision of Bessie Head's Protagonists," *Ba Shiru*, 12, no. 2 (1985): 26-35;

Charles R. Larson, *The Novel in the Third World* (Washington, D.C.: INSCAPE, 1976), pp. 164-173;

Craig MacKenzie, *Bessie Head: An Introduction* (Grahamstown, South Africa: National English Literary Museum, 1989);

MacKenzie, "Bessie Head's *The Collector of Treasures*: Modern Story-Telling in a Traditional Botswanan Village," *World Literature Written in English*, 29, no. 2 (1989): 139-148;

MacKenzie, "Short Fiction in the Making: The Case of Bessie Head," *English in Africa*, 16 (May 1989): 17-28;

Isabella P. Matsikidze, "Toward a Redemptive Political Philosophy: Bessie Head's *Maru*," *World Literature Written in English*, 30, no. 2 (1990): 105-109;

Lewis Nkosi, *Tasks and Masks: Styles and Themes in African Literature* (London: Longman, 1981), pp. 100-102;

Kolawole Ogungbesan, "The Cape Gooseberry Also Grows in Botswana: Alienation and Commitment in the Writings of Bessie Head," *Presence Africaine*, 109 (1979): 92-106;

Femi Ojo-Ade, "Bessie Head's Alienated Heroine: Victim or Villain?," *Ba Shiru*, 8, no. 2 (1977): 13-26;

Adetokunbo Pearse, "Apartheid and Madness: Bessie Head's *A Question of Power*," *Kunapipi*, 5, no. 2 (1984): 81-93;

Andrew Peek, "Bessie Head and the African Novel," *Span*, 21 (1985): 121-136;

Arthur Ravenscroft, "The Novels of Bessie Head," in *Aspects of South African Literature*, edited by Christopher Heywood (London: Heinemann, 1976), pp. 174-186;

Charles Ponnuthurai Sarvan, "Bessie Head: *A Question of Power* and Identity," in *Women in African Literature Today*, edited by Eldred Durosimi Jones (Trenton, N.J.: African World, 1987), pp. 82-88;

Alain Séverac, "Beyond Identity: Bessie Head's Spiritual Quest in *Maru*," *Commonwealth Essays and Studies*, 14 (Autumn 1991): 58-64;

Oladele Taiwo, *Female Novelists in Modern Africa* (New York: St. Martin's Press, 1985), pp. 185-214;

Michael Thorpe, "'Treasures of the Heart': The Short Stories of Bessie Head," *World Literature Today*, 57 (Summer 1983): 414-416;

Margaret E. Tucker, "A 'Nice-time Girl' Strikes Back: An Essay on Bessie Head's *A Question of Power*," *Research in African Literatures*, 19 (Summer 1988): 170-181;

Brighton Uledi-Kamanga, "Alienation and Affirmation: The Humanistic Vision of Bessie Head," *Journal of Humanities*, 1 (1987): 21-35;

Rukmini Vanamali, "Bessie Head's *A Question of Power*: The Mythic Dimension," *Literary Criterion*, 23, nos. 1-2 (1988): 154-171;

Robin Visel, "'We Bear the World and We Make It': Bessie Head and Olive Schreiner," *Research in African Literatures*, 21 (Fall 1990): 115-124;

Cherry Wilhelm, "Bessie Head: The Face of Africa," *English in Africa*, 10 (May 1983): 1-13.

Papers:

The Bessie Head Papers are in the Khama III Memorial Museum, Serowe, Botswana. Some of her other papers are in the Manuscript Collection at Mugar Memorial Library, Boston University.

John Hearne

(4 February 1926 -   )

Wolfgang Binder
Universität Erlangen-Nürnberg

BOOKS: *Voices Under the Window* (London: Faber & Faber, 1955; London & Boston: Faber & Faber, 1985);

Stranger at the Gate (London: Faber & Faber, 1956);

The Faces of Love (London: Faber & Faber, 1957); republished as *The Eye of the Storm* (Boston: Little, Brown, 1958);

The Autumn Equinox (London: Faber & Faber, 1959); republished as *Autumn Equinox* (New York: Vanguard, 1961);

Land of the Living (London: Faber & Faber, 1961; New York: Harper & Row, 1962);

Our Heritage, by Hearne and Rex Nettleford (Mona, Jamaica: Department of Extra-Mural Studies, UWI, 1963);

Fever Grass, by Hearne and Morris Cargill, together as John Morris (Kingston, Jamaica: Collins & Sangster, 1969; London: Collins, 1969; New York: Putnam's, 1969);

The Candywine Development, by Hearne and Cargill, together as Morris (London: Collins, 1970; New York: Citadel, 1970);

The Checkerboard Caper, by Hearne and Cargill, together as Morris (New York: Citadel, 1975);

The Sure Salvation (London & Boston: Faber & Faber, 1981; New York: St. Martin's Press, 1982);

Testing Democracy Through Elections, by Hearne, Lawrence Coote, and Lynden Facey, edited by Marie Gregory (Kingston, Jamaica: Bustamante Institute, 1985).

TELEVISION: *Freedom Man*, teleplay by Hearne, BBC, 1957;

Soldier in the Snow, teleplay by Hearne and James Mitchell, BBC, 1960;

A World Inside, teleplay by Hearne, BBC, 1962.

OTHER: "Landscape with Faces," in *Ian Fleming Introduces Jamaica*, edited by Morris Cargill (London: Deutsch, 1965), pp. 41-70;

"The Fugitive in the Forest—A Study of Four Novels by Wilson Harris," *Journal of Common-*

John Hearne (photograph by Erich Malter)

wealth Literature, 4 (December 1967): 99-112;

Carifesta Forum: An Anthology of 20 Caribbean Voices, edited, with an introduction, by Hearne (Kingston, Jamaica: Carifesta 76, 1976);

The Search for Solutions: Selections from the Speeches and Writings of Michael Manley, edited, with notes and an introduction, by Hearne (Oshawa, Ontario: Maple House, 1976).

John Hearne belongs to the generation of Jamaican novelists who produced a substantial body of their work in the 1950s. With five novels published between 1955 and 1961, and his last one to date (*The Sure Salvation*) in 1981, Hearne's position among Caribbean writers seems secure, even if certain critics attribute to him a peculiar place somewhat outside mainstream Jamaican writing.

John E. C. Hearne was born on 4 February 1926 in Montreal, Canada, to Jamaican parents (Maurice V. and Doris May Hearne), who returned with him to Jamaica two years after his birth. He lived in Jamaica until age seventeen and attended Jamaica College. During World War II he joined the Royal Canadian Air Force, a venture about which he is reluctant to talk. On 3 September 1947 he married Joyce Veitch; they were later divorced. The studies in education he undertook at the University of Edinburgh (1947-1949) and London University (1949-1950) marked him profoundly. A great esteem for European "high culture" and a rather hesitant admittance of the value of Caribbean culture seem to stem from his extended stay in European cities. More than a Caribbean writer, Hearne would like to be thought of as western-hemispheric. He spent most of the 1950s living in London and Paris, teaching and struggling to establish himself as a writer. Most of his novels and teleplays were produced during this period. In the early 1950s he shared lodgings with another Jamaican writer, Roger Mais. The two remained close friends until Mais's death from cancer in 1955. Hearne married Leeta Mary Hopkinson, a teacher, on 12 April 1955; they have two children.

After years of studying, teaching, and writing in Great Britain and on the Continent, Hearne returned to live permanently in Jamaica in 1962. He has worked as resident tutor in the Department of Extra-Mural Studies (1962-1967) and as head of the Creative Arts Center (1968-1974) at the University of the West Indies in Mona, and he has also served as the chairman of the Institute of Jamaica. In the 1960s and early 1970s he was a close collaborator with and assistant to Jamaican politician and prime minister Michael Manley, from whose ideas Hearne later dissociated himself. Since the 1960s he has been an astute, if increasingly conservative, observer of sociopolitical events in his country and in the world, and he has authored many columns in the *Kingston Daily Gleaner*. Now retired, he is writing a new novel. He sees one of the functions of writers, as he commented in a 1984 interview with Wolfgang Binder, as the necessity "of having to create institutions as he or she lives out his or her life. By institutions I mean those impalpable social institutions and relationships, the resolutions that we are arriving at as we try to identify our singularity as a people, as a culture."

Hearne's fiction, with the exception of *The Sure Salvation*, deals mainly with the Jamaican middle class. He is interested in individual character, in love, and in ethical values. One of the themes running through his work centers on betrayal and pain. In the interview with Binder, Hearne stated one of the central ideas of his philosophy:

I think that we are a species that was very definitely given a mandate to salvage ourselves or to destroy ourselves. I have no evidence at the moment that we will fulfill that mandate. My real hope is that having been given that by God we may yet salvage ourselves. In all honesty, in most of the relationships that one must emphasize is an appalling pain that is central to all great literature that I know. That is why we love the musicians, the Mozarts, the Raphaels, even the Picasso of *Guernica* so much, because at least we don't have to live so intimately with pain that has often been portrayed with the betrayal, with the cruelty and most of all with the lack of comprehension ... that we bring into our relationships with each other.

Hearne's first novel, *Voices Under the Window* (1955), which was written in 1953, found a congenial editor in Charles Monteith of Faber and Faber. Monteith was to remain his editor for all his books under that imprint. Hearne was determined to have all his fiction published outside Jamaica; he wanted to compete with the best authors who were getting published in major cosmopolitan cities.

Voices Under the Window is the successful portrait of Mark Lattimer, a lawyer of mixed blood, who must come to grips with the disturbing fact that he is not white. Lattimer, who is dying after being attacked by a mulatto man during a riot, remembers crucial moments of his life with regret, in a series of flashbacks. Cherishing ideals such as integrity, friendship, and courage, he is acutely aware of his failure as a politician, as a leader in a predominantly black society, and as a man loving Brysie, a warmhearted black woman.

All Hearne's other novels, except *The Sure Salvation*, have as their setting the fictitious island of Cayuna, which closely resembles Jamaica. The middle-class protagonist in *Stranger at the Gate* (1956), Roy McKenzie, is the last character in Hearne's work who sees politics as the center of

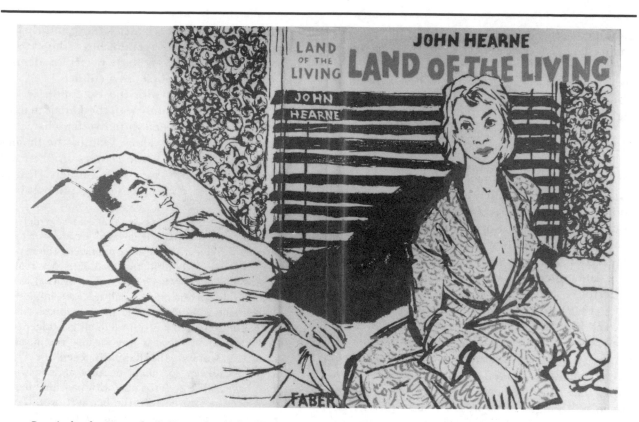

Dust jacket for Hearne's 1961 novel, which—like most of his novels—is set on Cayuna, a fictional island that closely resembles Jamaica

his efforts in life. McKenzie, a Communist, attempts to bring about radical political change on Cayuna, quite in contrast to his friend Carl Brandt, who, without being a detestable character, favors a stratified society.

With Hearne's next novel, *The Faces of Love* (1957), his vital interest, and that of his protagonists, moves away from sociopolitical involvement and toward more private, if not less passionate, feelings. The search for love and fulfillment in relationships becomes, in the framework of a rather introverted worldview, the main thrust of Hearne's work. Both *The Faces of Love* and *The Autumn Equinox* (1959) are marred by this prevailing sense of the importance of the personal over the urgent political questions the reader expects to find in works dealing with preindependence Cayuna-Jamaica. The family closeness, which Hearne himself experienced in his childhood and youth, and which he cherishes in retrospect, is presented in the depiction of the life of planter Nichols Stacey, who is stoic and cynical.

Land of the Living (1961) is more complex; the crucial issues of rapprochement and understanding between the Jamaican middle class and the underprivileged are taken up again. The lack

of a secure place in a country and in one's life assumes racial and philosophical dimensions in the portrayal of the Jewish narrator, Stefan Mahler, and the black character Markus Heneky, who advocates the Back-to-Africa movement. The solutions for the two characters—departure for Mahler and death for Heneky—reinforce Hearne's benign, static, and rather pessimistic outlook on Cayuna life. The redeeming force of love, represented by Bernice and Joan, is given importance but not victory.

The idea for *The Sure Salvation*, which Hearne published after a silence of twenty years as a novelist, was conceived in 1962 but only began to be realized after 1977. Hearne felt that Jamaican society was changing too quickly for him to paint another canvas of contemporary life. His tendency to reach for principles—for general, philosophical statements—became strong enough to lead him into another historical period, the nineteenth century. Nevertheless, the life he describes on a slave ship is given unavoidable symbolic and allegorical attributes. Betrayal, fatal flaws of character, sexuality as a means of power and estrangement, and deep racial differences are parts of a dehumanized world in which

Dust jacket for Hearne's only historical novel, which focuses on life aboard a slave ship

no reconciliation seems possible. Hogarth, the captain, goes to prison; Alex, his former black ally, sets out with his slaves to found a kingdom on the mainland. Harmony—societal, racial, or sexual—seems no longer possible. *The Sure Salvation* is a powerful, harrowing text that raises disturbing questions.

Hearne has not published any novels since *The Sure Salvation*. His reputation as a serious Jamaican artist rests mostly on his first novel, *Voices Under the Window*, on his fifth, *Land of the Living*, and on *The Sure Salvation*.

Surprisingly there is no substantial body of criticism on Hearne's work; there exists neither a book-length study on him nor an article that analyzes the complete evolution of his art. Critics such as Barrie Davies and Wilfred Cartey, and even more so Sylvia Wynter and Frank M. Birbalsingh, have taken exception to Hearne's conservative sociopolitical and racial ideas as they find

them expressed in his novels. They do not share what they conceive as his idealization of middle-class life and values; they demand solutions, not laconic comments or philosophical statements. Davies mentions Hearne's tendency to overwrite. As a rule, *Voices Under the Window* remains, at least partially due to the lack of criticism on *The Sure Salvation*, his most acclaimed work.

Interviews:

Wolfgang Binder, " 'Subtleties of Enslavement': An Interview with the Jamaican Writer John Hearne," *Komparatistische Hefte*, 9-10 (1984): 101-113;

"Interview with John Hearne," in *A Common Tongue*, edited by Horace I. Goddard (Saint-Laurent, Quebec: A.F.O. Enterprises, 1987), pp. 35-45.

References:

Frank M. Birbalsingh, "Escapism in the Novels of John Hearne," *Caribbean Quarterly*, 16 (March 1970): 28-38;

Wilfred Cartey, "The Novels of John Hearne," *Journal of Commonwealth Literature*, 7 (July 1969): 45-58;

Barrie Davies, "The Seekers: The Novels of John Hearne," in *The Islands in Between*, edited by Louis James (London: Oxford University Press, 1968), pp. 109-120;

Arthur D. Drayton, "West Indian Fiction and West Indian Society," *Kenyon Review*, 25 (Winter 1963): 129-141;

John Figueroa, " 'Too Sharp Distinctions' or 'Caught in Between'?," *Revista Interamericana*, 2 (Spring 1972): 72-79;

Reinhardt Küsgen, "John Hearne's 'The Lost Country': A Caribbean Version of the American Dream," in *The Story Must Be Told*, edited by Peter O. Stummer (Würzburg, Germany: Königshausen & Neumann, 1986), pp. 77-85;

Roberto Márquez, "The Stoic and the Sisyphean: John Hearne and the Angel of History," *Anales del Caribe*, 3 (1983): 240-277;

Mervyn Morris, "Pattern and Meaning in *Voices Under the Window*," *Jamaica Journal*, 5 (March 1971): 53-56;

Sandra Pouchet Paquet, "The Fifties," in *West Indian Literature*, edited by Bruce King (Hamden, Conn.: Archon, 1979), pp. 69-72;

Kenneth Ramchand, *The West Indian Novel and Its Background* (London: Faber & Faber, 1970), pp. 45-50;

Daizal R. Samad, "Arise the West Indian: Marcus Heneky's Racial Awakening in John Hearne's *Land of the Living*," *Journal of West Indian Literature*, 4 (November 1990): 66-79;

Samad, "In Quest of the Dialogue of Self: Racial Duality in John Hearne's *Voices Under the Window*," *Journal of Commonwealth Literature*, 25, no. 1 (1990): 109-119;

Samad, "In Search of the Chrysalis of the Voice:

The Language of the Slaves in John Hearne's *The Sure Salvation*," *World Literature Written in English*, 30 (Spring 1990): 11-16;

Sylvia Wynter, "We Must Learn to Sit down Together and Talk About a Little Culture: Reflections on West Indian Writing and Criticism, Part 2," *Jamaica Journal*, 3 (March 1969): 27-42.

Roy A. K. Heath

(13 August 1926 -   )

Ian H. Munro
William Jewell College

BOOKS: *A Man Come Home* (Port of Spain: Longman Caribbean, 1974);

The Murderer (London: Allison & Busby, 1978; New York: Persea, 1992);

From the Heat of the Day (London: Allison & Busby, 1979);

One Generation (London & New York: Allison & Busby, 1981);

Genetha (London & New York: Allison & Busby, 1981);

Kwaku; or, The Man Who Could Not Keep His Mouth Shut (London: Allison & Busby, 1982);

Art and Experience, Edgar Mittelholzer Memorial Lectures (Georgetown, Guyana: Ministry of Education, 1983);

Orealla (London: Allison & Busby, 1984);

The Shadow Bride (London: Collins, 1988);

Shadows Round the Moon: Caribbean Memoirs (London: Collins, 1990).

PLAY PRODUCTION: *Inez Combray*, Georgetown, Guyana, 1972.

SELECTED PERIODICAL PUBLICATIONS—
UNCOLLECTED: "The Function of Myth," *Kaie*, 8 (December 1971): 19-23;

"The Wind and the Sun," *Savacou*, 9/10 (1974): 55-64.

Roy A. K. Heath (photograph by Valerie Wilmer)

Though Roy A. K. Heath has lived in London since 1951, his eight published novels are set in Guyana (to which he frequently returns during holidays) and especially in Georgetown. For Heath, Georgetown life is a source of fascination and inspiration. A passage in his novel *Orealla* (1984) describes vividly the city's beauty and ugliness: "its inequalities, its prison, its avenues of jacaranda and flamboyant, its stretch of river and ocean" are side by side with reminders of its long colonial history, and reminders, too, of other traditions: "its drummers, who had never lost the art of summoning up the spirits of departed ancestors." Heath's intensely detailed, naturalistic rendering of the life, sights, sounds, and talk of Georgetown streets, slums, rum shops, brothels, and middle-class suburbs is often praised by his reviewers. His reference to ancestors illustrates a vital aspect of Heath's vision as a novelist, for though the surface of his work is naturalistic, his narrative technique relentlessly probes the hidden realities of Guyanese life, the complex web of myths, dreams, customs, and prejudices arising from the aboriginal, African, and East Indian legacies.

In his autobiography, *Shadows Round the Moon* (1990), Heath suggests that his fascination with the hidden and the grotesque arose as a reaction against the prohibitions of a Creole society riddled with "secrets and secret places." His protagonists characteristically pursue restless dreams of freedom and independence, but their quest leads them in an ironic cycle, into themselves and the patterns of their past. Heath's employment of a constantly shifting viewpoint suggests the impossibility of an individual seeing himself clearly or comprehending his relation to others. The greatest strength of Heath as a writer, perhaps, is his ability to convey the complexity of the individual, through a loose, episodic narrative strategy that conceals as much as it reveals. His style, occasionally florid and artificial in the earlier novels, has grown increasingly controlled and ironic: it is a style, comments another contemporary Guyanese writer, Wilson Harris, "that truncates emotion."

Roy Aubrey Kelvin Heath was born in Georgetown, Guyana (then British Guiana), on 13 August 1926 to Melrose A. and Jessie R. Heath, both teachers. His father died before Heath's second birthday, and Heath was raised in genteel poverty by his mother. After attending Central High School and Queen's College in Georgetown and working as a government treasury clerk, he moved to England and entered the University of London the following year, 1952, eventually receiving his B.A. in French, having

studied modern languages. Subsequently he studied law and was called to the bar in 1964 but has never practiced law. Since 1959 he has taught French and German at public schools in London. He is married to Aemilia Oberli Heath, and they have three children.

Heath's first published novel, *A Man Come Home* (1974), got warm reviews from English and West Indian critics, who commented especially on its realism. The *Times Literary Supplement* reviewer (Frank Pike, 27 December 1974) noted the "intimate and convincing evocation of the texture and quality of daily life in Georgetown" but confessed to discomfort with Heath's use of the "Fair Maid" myth. More recently, however, Louis James referred to Heath's "daring" challenge to the reader "to share in a world balanced between materialism and superstition, and lapsing into the latter." In Heath's work, the abnormal and bizarre prowl just beneath the surface of the everyday.

In *A Man Come Home*, Bird Foster is an easygoing layabout, dependent for his living on his mistress, Stephanie, until he is seized by a sudden desire for wealth and a house of his own. He disappears upriver, returning with enough money to realize his dream. Gossip has it that he made a pact with Fair Maid, a riverine spirit who, in the manner of the Nigerian "Mammy Wota," grants favors in return for the sexual allegiance of human lovers. Bird's wealth does not make him happy, though, and when Stephanie throws away the gold chain given him by Fair Maid, the vengeful spirit materializes and causes a car accident in which Bird dies.

Bird Foster is only one of the characters in this multilayered novel who are bound to their conditions and seeking escape. His father, Egbert Foster, has spent his life waiting to raise the flag of an independent Guyana over his house, a symbol of independence and permanence for both Egbert and his son, only to witness helplessly the ensuing disintegration of his large family as each member pursues his own version of independence. Egbert has dreamed of "heroic children," but he is unprepared for the violent dreams of the new generation, forged in the "great fires and political upheavals" of contemporary Guyana. Egbert's lusty, live-in mistress, Christine, takes out her frustrations by beating their pregnant daughter, Melda, so severely she is braindamaged, and Christine and Melda are in turn seduced and victimized by Bird's friend Gee, who only wants to escape from the poverty of the range yard (slums). The occasional allusions to Guyana's tormented history are reminders that the explosive, unexamined emotions of Bird, Christine, and Gee have counterparts in the larger world.

Heath's second novel, *The Murderer* (1978), seems at first a contrast to *A Man Come Home*. A dark, haunting work set in the slums of Georgetown, it is a psychological study of the protagonist, Galton Flood, who murders his wife after discovering she had an affair before their marriage. The murder of Gemma—her name suggests her goodness—is essentially a replay of Bird's death, however, as both victims had resisted the web of domination and subservience lying at the heart of Guyanese society as Heath perceives it. Galton Flood, whose name suggests the fury of his repressed emotions, is as much victim as agent. His fear of moral impurity and compromise and his obsession with the boundaries of "propriety, of pride, of privacy, of love" are the products of his mother's middle-class repudiation of his father's village ways, a repudiation visited on Galton, a surrogate, in the form of endless humiliations. Galton's obsessions make him unable to penetrate other people's motives or to understand his own desire to escape from love by dominating Gemma. The flood of repressed emotion he feels when he kills her is his one moment of emotional truth. Galton, a reflective, even generous man, is a stranger to himself.

The Murderer won the *Guardian* fiction prize in 1978 and was well received by critics at British newspapers and weeklies, who praised its realistic penetration of a troubled psyche. Writing in the *Times Literary Supplement* (19 May 1978), Homi Bhabha commented on the ironic significance of Heath's dedication of the novel to "wife, mother and sister—the endlessly forbearing," in the context of the novel's conclusion, in which the police, Gemma's former lover, and even her father conspire to cover up the murder.

The so-called Georgetown Trilogy, beginning with Heath's third novel, *From the Heat of the Day* (1979), traces the history of the Armstrong family from the marriage of Sonny Armstrong and Gladys Davis through the lives of their children, Rohan (in *One Generation*, 1981) and Genetha (in *Genetha*, also 1981). The trilogy, based in part on the story of Heath's own parents and siblings, is a stunning depiction of the panorama of Guyanese life from the 1920s through the 1950s. Its common theme is social

prejudice in all its uniquely Guyanese dimensions.

The marriage of Sonny and Gladys in *From the Heat of the Day* is ill-fated from the start. Gladys's very proper family, for whom "breeding," "background," and money are all-important, looks down on Sonny, a minor civil servant from the countryside. Sonny, tormented by feelings of social inadequacy, responds by treating Gladys brutally, though he is innately compassionate. Like Galton Flood, Sonny is hardly conscious of the reasons for the uncontrollable passions animating him; he wavers perpetually between an irritable need to humiliate Gladys and a desire to show how much he cares for her.

The gulf of incomprehension between Gladys and Sonny is paralleled by Gladys's distrust of their servant, Esther, a country girl who idolizes her mistress's refined ways, and by Sonny's admiration of his friend Doc for the unconventional life he lives with his illiterate mistress, even as Doc envies Sonny his family life. Each character, isolated in half-articulated feelings, is unable to communicate with those closest to him.

One Generation traces the history of Sonny Armstrong and his two children after his wife's death. Heath shifts the focus from Sonny, a lonely figure still pursuing his guilt-ridden passions, to Rohan, his generous, confusedly ambitious son. Sonny remains a country man at heart—his hometown of Agricola is his hinterland—while Rohan seeks his own hinterland, away from Georgetown gossip and his incestuous desire for his sister, in the exotic world of the rural East Indian community of Suddie, where he pursues a beautiful East Indian girl, Indrani Mohammed. *One Generation* is essentially a study of the contrast between Rohan's middle-class, urban values and the conservatism of Indrani's relatives, represented principally by Mr. Ali. Ali sees Rohan as a threat to the community's ancient control over its women, as the wartime infusion of American cash into Guyana, making "all the work people dissatisfied," threatens Ali's control over his workers.

While *One Generation* widens the scope of Heath's fiction beyond the familiar world of Georgetown, the strange, exotic world of the East Indians tilts the novel toward the melodramatic. The murder of Rohan and Indrani, at the hands of one of Rohan's underlings in the civil service, is unsatisfactorily motivated, with the novel thereafter taking on some of the qualities of a detective thriller. Reviewers nonetheless found strength in the novel's depiction of Guyanese life, John Naughton of the *Listener* (16 April 1981) commenting on Heath's "narrative skill, ingenuity of plot and marvellous, vibrant dialogue." The *Times Literary Supplement* reviewer (Holly Eley, 17 July 1981) found ominous political portents in Rohan's "emotionally strong but directionless" character, as a portrait of those "in whose hands power will continue to rest."

As Heath's work has become more familiar to English reviewers, their comments have made less of its superficial exoticism and more of its underlying social and psychological dimensions. Eley, writing in the *Times Literary Supplement* (1 January 1982) of Heath's fourth novel, *Genetha*, drew a parallel between Heath's Guyana, a "fragmented, post-colonial society with no real history," and Joseph Conrad's "land without memories" (in *Heart of Darkness*, 1899), from which characters struggle only to escape. Alone among Heath's prior protagonists, however, Genetha is able to complete her journey.

Initially Genetha's quest is hedged about by her own class prejudices and family background. Her father's passionate ways cause her to fear her own sexuality, yet she is drawn from a boring relationship with the respectable Michael into a passionate affair with Fingers, a snooker ace, who eventually bilks her out of her property and abandons her. Drifting aimlessly in pursuit of "Freedom and the secret of a settled mind," Genetha is stripped of her vanity, her desire for men, and even her religion after she is seduced by her confessor. She finds peace not in a remote village but, ironically, at a brothel run by Esther, the Armstrong family's former servant. Genetha finally achieves a quiet emptiness, without the confusing codes of social responsibility. In her "knowledge of death, the mystery of time and insights into the unexplored countries of the heart," Genetha's fate anticipates that of the protagonists in Heath's next two novels, who undergo a similar process of having illusions stripped away.

The Guyana of Heath's sixth novel, *Kwaku; or, The Man Who Could Not Keep His Mouth Shut* (1982), is a country in a state of collapse, with rampant "choke-an'-rob," a tottering rural economy, and the omnipresent governing party. For Kwaku Cholmondley, a shoemaker in the village of "C," the only defense is an air of idiocy, though Kwaku is privately convinced of his special mission in life, "a journey to be undertaken." Pursuing respectability, he marries Miss Gwen-

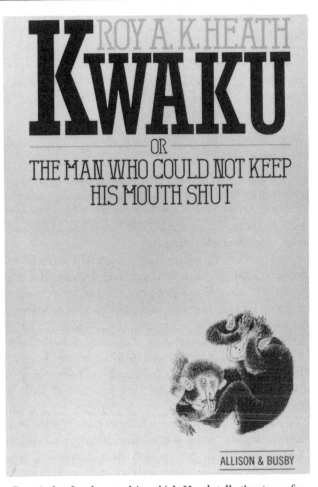

Dust jacket for the novel in which Heath tells the story of a Guyanese shoemaker who becomes a healer

doline, who bears him eight children, yet Kwaku gains no reputation until—forced to leave the village after a plague of locusts destroys its one cash crop—he attains success as a healer in New Amsterdam.

There Kwaku has little more going for him than a few garlic concoctions, a sense of ritual, and the common touch. He is convinced of his worthlessness, though to the villagers in "C" he has become a man of reputation. His insecure need to command respect leads to his downfall: he fails to fulfill a rash promise made to a fisherman, who retaliates by blinding Miss Gwendoline with an obeah curse. Back in New Amsterdam, Kwaku's herbal practice languishes, he is beaten up by his own sons, and he ends up touring the rum shops, capering for dollar bills. The narrative tone of *Kwaku* passes skillfully, almost imperceptibly, from comic to tragic, yet Kwaku is, finally, a heroic character, loyal to his family to the end and able to cope with misfortune by accepting it, even as his country "seemed to be sinking under its weight of debt and ambitions." The reviewer for the *Times Literary Supplement* (Alan Bold, 12 November 1982) commented on the combination of "considerable skills—of narration, characterization and description" with a "comic vision . . . wisdom as well as wit."

Heath's seventh novel, *Orealla* (1984), is set in the Georgetown of the 1920s. The aura of gas lamps, shadows, burning sun, and horses passing on rain-sodden streets provides a haunting background to this most disturbing of Heath's novels, the troubling story of Ben, a free-lance writer and unenthusiastic chauffeur, who has a compulsive avocation as a burglar.

For Ben, burglarizing houses is a form of rebellion against "a life regulated by the munificence of work-shop proprietors and the coming of long rains." His life includes violent, confused attacks against the class and racial prejudices of his society. He is black in a country where "only red people can get a good job on the paper." Ben is a typical Heath protagonist, complex and contradictory: he seeks independence, yet is forced into virtual servitude as driver for an overbearing "brownskin civil servant," Schwartz. Ben admires those, like his aboriginal friend Carl, who are at peace, yet Ben despises Edna, Schwartz's cook, for passively accepting her condition. Ben's wife, Tina, is from a respectable middle-class family, but his mistress, Mabel, is violent, passionate, and lower-class; the two women are always at one another's throats. Ben's rare, uplifting moments of insight are mixed with hours of foreboding and distress. Like Kwaku, Ben is adrift, driven only by his search for "the certainty of happiness."

Ben is protected from Schwartz's malevolence only by his knowledge of Schwartz's marital infidelities, and once the latter's wife dies, Ben promptly finds himself framed for robbery and sent to prison. There he is able at last to see his personal struggle in some wider context, that of the other prisoners and even of Violet, Carl's vengeful erstwhile lover, who expresses her revolt through "the society of women." Like all of Heath's heroes, Ben has dreamed of a refuge, like Carl's home village of Orealla, but realizes no refuge except in action. His final act of rebellion is to kill Schwartz, giving Ben the first sense of freedom he has known. As Paul Binding in the *Listener* (2 August 1984) pointed out, Ben is a complex, authentic individual: the truth of the novel is that "the self is multiple and defies label-

ing." Even Schwartz and Carl, who embody social types, become individuals through Heath's deft shifting of viewpoint. Ben is perhaps Heath's most complex, multisided fictional creation, Guyanese in habit and prejudice, yet intensely human in his struggles.

The bride in Heath's *The Shadow Bride* (1988) is Mrs. Singh, who has come to Guyana from South India as bride to a wealthy, if disreputable, Guyanese. Once free of her husband—gossip has it she poisoned him—she becomes an authoritarian figure in her household, determined to control her son, Betta, and the assortment of servants and "hangers-on." Like many of Heath's characters, Mrs. Singh is trapped in images of the past: her nostalgia for her Indian home is so strong she raises Betta apart from other children, until he complains that he knows more of Kerala than Guyana.

Respected by the community for her outward strength, Mrs. Singh has an inner weakness that is seized upon by the Pujaree, a Hindu priest, who succeeds in having her expel all her household so he can create in its place an image of the India of her imagination. Mrs. Singh and the Pujaree live not in Guyana, where all is change, but construct a static "house of illusion."

Betta attempts to live in the world as he finds it, though even he must discover how much the past has shaped his present. After completing his medical degree in England, he dedicates himself to serving East Indian estate workers but finds that his quest cannot conceal a deeper self-doubt about his motivations. His devotion to the distressed is, he suspects, egotism in disguise. Betta's preoccupation with discovering an absolute purity of motive identifies him with earlier Heath heroes such as Galton Flood; like them, he yearns for some absolute, a communal faith.

Betta's journal, which he has begun in order to record his medical studies, becomes a means of self-exploration, through which he understands the way he is intricately bound not only to the East Indian community at its point of crisis, as thousands of East Indians desert the estates for the city with the end of indenture, but to his mother, whose crisis he had failed to recognize: "he had seen fit to ignore his mother's plea for help, he, who did not hesitate to speak of ideals." If mother and son are both confined by their past, Betta, fortified by a disintegrating but still powerful communal tradition, is able to recognize and accept the irony of his motivations without submitting to despair: "He could not," the novel concludes, "have acted otherwise."

Heath's *Shadows Round the Moon* (1990), the first volume of his autobiography, tells of his upbringing prior to his departure for London and of the tensions of growing up in torpid, colonial British Guiana. It reveals the roots of his distinctive imagination.

Roy A. K. Heath's eight novels have added a new dimension to the literary map of Guyana, complementing Wilson Harris's fantastic journeys into the Guyanese hinterland. Heath has become a novelist of international stature by remaining in compassionate contact with the world he knows best. British and West Indian reviewers have almost unanimously praised his writing, and his novels are circulated worldwide—Louis James reports them selling well as far afield as Singapore and Australia. It is therefore surprising that his innovative work has attracted only a scattering of serious commentary from critics of Caribbean literature to date. Perhaps, as James suggests, it is because his work does not fit the "established categories for Caribbean writing." His work may be "indelibly Guyanese," but it belongs also to "the small group of works that make the reader understand more about the nature of human suffering and violence."

References:

Anthony Boxill, "Penetrating the Hinterland: Roy Heath's Guyana Trilogy," *World Literature Written in English*, 29 (Spring 1989): 103-110;

Wilson Harris, "Roy Heath, *The Murderer*," *World Literature Written in English*, 17 (November 1978): 656-658;

Louis James, "Dark Muse: The Early Fiction of Roy A. K. Heath," *Wasafiri*, 5 (Autumn 1986): 26-27;

Mark A. McWatt, "Tragic Irony—The Hero as Victim: Three Novels of Roy A. K. Heath," in *Critical Issues in West Indian Literature*, edited by Erika Sollish Smilowitz and Roberta Quarles Knowles (Parkersburg, Iowa: Caribbean, 1984), pp. 54-64;

McWatt, "Wives and Other Victims: Women in the Novels of Roy A. K. Heath," in *Out of the Kumbla: Caribbean Women and Literature*, edited by Carole Boyce Davies and Elaine Savory Fido (Trenton, N.J.: Africa World, 1990), pp. 223-235.

Mazisi Kunene
(12 May 1930 -   )

Ernest Mathabela
University of Texas at Austin

BOOKS: *Zulu Poems* (London: Deutsch, 1970; New York: Africana, 1970);
Emperor Shaka the Great: A Zulu Epic (London: Heinemann, 1979);
Anthem of the Decades: A Zulu Epic (London: Heinemann, 1981);
The Ancestors & the Sacred Mountain (London & Exeter, N.H.: Heinemann, 1982).

OTHER: Aimé Césaire, *Return to My Native Land*, translated by John Berger and Anna Bostock, introduction by Kunene (Baltimore: Penguin, 1969).

Mazisi Kunene

Mazisi Kunene believes that the function of literature is "not entertainment but primarily to teach social values and serious philosophical concepts." In his introduction to Aimé Césaire's *Return to My Native Land* (1969), Kunene also states unapologetically that "the black man must find a new definition of man, i.e., he must redefine reality in his own terms rather than in the role allocated to him by the white man." And to redefine reality in his own African terms is exactly what Kunene is doing. Although his endorsement of negritude is clear, Kunene's poetry conspicuously reflects his allegiance to a Pan-African worldview. Kunene's vision extends beyond his continental affiliation to encompass "the general experience of mankind" and "emphasize the oneness and unity of man." He elaborates, "I think the important thing in doing this [writing] is that you in fact release the energies of the particular community, and its expression in general, realizing its content in the whole history of mankind." In Zulu or in English, Kunene's poetry illustrates this vision.

Mazisi kaMdabuli Kunene was born in Durban, Natal, South Africa, on 12 May 1930. He began writing poetry as a boy and by the age of ten or eleven was submitting poems to newspapers and magazines. A small collection of his poems in Zulu, "Idlozi Elingenantethelelo," won the Bantu Literary Competition in 1956, and some of his poems were published in *Ilanga laseNatal* and the *Native Teacher's Journal*. Since then Kunene's poetic output has been prolific. Kunene's achievement as a poet is paralleled by his extensive academic, cultural, and political accomplishments. Formerly head of the Department of African Studies at Pius XII College (now the National University of Lesotho) and director of education for the South African United Front, Kunene is presently a professor of African literature and languages at the University of California, Los Angeles.

Kunene left South Africa for England in 1959, having earned a B.A., B.A. Honors, and

204

M.A. from the University of Natal; his M.A. thesis was "An Analytical Survey of Zulu Poetry Both Traditional and Modern." His aim in England was to conduct research in comparative literature and to complete a doctoral dissertation on Zulu literature in the School of Oriental and African Studies at London University. But he got involved in politics, becoming in 1962 the United Nations representative for the African National Congress and later its director of finance (in 1972). These activities took him to Europe and the United States, where he lectured and traveled widely. In addition, he held office in the Anti-Apartheid and Boycott Movement (1959-1968), Committee of African Organizations (1960-1966), Pan-African Youth Movement (1964), and Afro-Asian Literature Organization (1966-1970). On 7 October 1973 he married Mabowe Mathabo, and they have four children.

Kunene is best known for his Zulu poetry that he has translated into English. But he feels that "writers who do not write in African languages have come to represent African writing," and he doubts that African writers can "expect to create a literature of excellence in the very language of their former (colonial) master." He argues, "The claim by exponents of this literature that writing in the former colonial languages widens the writer's audience ignores the fact of quality for quantity. . . . The question of the writer's responsibility becomes crucial here. A writer, it would seem, should avoid the temporary attractions of cheap popularity and make a contribution to the community that gave birth to his genius. This way he/she is able to grasp its deepest traditions. Such literature can then be translated (both literally and philosophically) into various languages and cultures of the world."

It should be clear, then, why Kunene has not ceased to write in Zulu, although it is equally clear why South African black writers of the present generation, with H. I. E. Dhlomo as the forerunner, started writing in English. They wanted to transcend tribal, and therefore linguistic, distinctions that no longer had any meaning in spite of the efforts of the South African government to maintain them. However, Kunene and his compatriots do not necessarily contradict each other, and by translating some of his poetry into English, he has, in a way, supported their cause. In translating his works, Kunene cherished "particularly the thought of sharing our history and literature with many people of Africa and also other parts of the world." However, his fellow country-

men cannot legally share his poetry. Along with forty-five other authors, he was banned by a government order issued in 1966. Thus his own country has tried to silence him, and its move might have silenced him for the rest of the world had he not translated his poetry into English.

Kunene is particularly indebted to the traditional Zulu literature, which has survived, he notes, "in spite of the brutal assault made upon Bantu societies of Southern Africa by white supremacist regimes." In his master's thesis, he explains how this literature changed from personal expression to a powerful vehicle for social and political ideas. He attributes its maturity during Shaka's reign to the efforts of the national poet Magolwane, whom he admires and tries to emulate. Kunene distinguishes three periods of the development of this literature: the pre-Shakan (1780-1800), the Shakan (1800-1850), and the post-Shakan (1850-1900). His poetry draws largely from the last two periods.

Kunene's first collected poems, *Zulu Poems* (1970), consisting mainly of elegiac, lyrical, epic, and African resistance poems, demonstrate fully Kunene's indebtedness to Zulu literature. "These are not English poems," Kunene says, "but poems directly evolved from a Zulu literary tradition. . . . Zulu literature, like most African literature, is communal. This has fundamental stylistic and philosophical implications. The common organization in Africa is not just a matter of individuals clinging together to eke out an existence. . . . In brief, it is a communal structure which has affirmed its particularity through forms of religion and thought arising directly out of its organization. It believes, for instance, that the highest virtue is not justice. . . but heroism, that is, self-sacrifice on behalf of the community. . . ." Here lies the crux of difference, the critic Ursula Barnett concludes, between Western poetry of the past two centuries and African poetry.

Kunene's poetry goes back to the foundations of traditional Zulu literature. His images and symbols reflect the Zulu cultural experience and environment. In "The Night," for example, hopes and fears evoked by cosmic forces are expressed in symbols and images of pastoral Zululand:

> The heart of the earth is covered with weeds,
> Darkness descends from the path of the skies.
> The black tails of cows shake against the wind,
> Beating the sea with the fence of dusk.

"This," Jacques Alvarez-Péreyre remarks, "was in no sense an urban poetry like that which was to be written in the middle of the sixties. It did not reflect the African's confrontation with the white city and its restrictedness; it contained no descriptions of the ghettos or of the humiliating contact with the whites. Several of the poems have a pastoral setting; they are concerned with nature, love, friendship, with the cycle of the seasons and generations. Yet Kunene is not at all indifferent to what is going on in the world, especially in his country."

In traditional Zulu poetry the effectiveness of the images may be increased by the judicious use of repetition, particularly in the form of parallelism. Predominant in Kunene's poetry is not only perfect parallelism but also parallelism by initial linking, as in "Peace": "*Sing* again the great song / *Sing* it with the winds that are shaking the reeds / *Sing* it until the whole earth is shaken by the song"; and parallelism by final linking. Repetition enhances the aesthetic unity of form and theme.

The traditional naming device, or *eulogue*, is also common in Kunene's poetry. *Eulogues* often carry meanings expressive of events. Thus, in "A Poem," the deverbative *mpindelele*, which means "recurrent," is the name of a fountain and at the same time a description of recurrent yearnings:

> May I when I awake
> Take from all men
> The yearnings of their souls
> And turn them into the fountain of Mpindelele
> Which will explode in oceans[.]

Kunene's poetry also owes much to the traditional elegy, in which feelings are sometimes understated. For example, in "An Elegy to an Unknown Man Nicknamed Donda," death is described as a journey on a path "to the place of the setting sun," a path that the "elephant" (a symbol of death) gestures for the poet to follow. "The understatement," Kunene comments, "produces its own horror by the sudden realization it creates that however 'frivolous' the treatment of the subject, the loss is intense."

Kunene's poetry also adopts certain traditional forms of address or formulas that emphasize its communal nature. In "Elegy," for example, the poet prefers the traditional "we" to the individualistic "I" to convey shared sentiments: "We have come to mourn the bleeding sun / We are the children of Ndungunya of the Dlamini

Dust jacket for Kunene's first book-length poem, about the chief who founded the Zulu Empire in the early nineteenth century

clan." And frequently "I," wherever it is used, implies "I on behalf of."

One of the most important contributions of the Shakan period—the stanza capable of expressing an episode—is also used by Kunene, as in "The Day of Treachery":

> Do not be like people of Ngoneni
> Who rushed with arms
> To embrace the man at the gates
> And did likewise on the day of treachery
> Embracing the sharp end of the short spears.

"In the Shakan stanza," Kunene explains, "we see how thought is completed: the poet introduces the theme, treats it and concludes with the consequence of such an activity."

In short, Kunene's poetry displays a wide range of culture-specific devices. These enhance its expressive power, which draws from elements of praise, persuasion, and performance, giving his poems the force of the spoken word, reminiscent of the *imbongi* (national poet) in action.

True to its tradition, Kunene's poetry focuses mainly on concepts and values that define the moral and intellectual consciousness of the African (Zulu) world. It is didactic, stressing communal rather than personal issues. Poems such as "From the Ravages of Life We Create" and "In Praise of the Earth" reflect not only on the grandeur of creation but also on the paradoxes of life. Some of them, such as "Man's Power over Things," stress human centrality in the world, which gives meaning to raw nature, and they assert the value of humanity over the value of things. These epic poems are based on the myths that provide Zulus with a context in which to live and interpret their lives. Many of Kunene's poems also embrace and emphasize the role ancestors have in holding the community together and acting as the custodians of its morality. In "Cycle" he writes: "We too shall follow their footsteps / Our dust shall arise at the gathering place."

As Barnett points out, "there is no question in Kunene's mind about the right of a poet to make his protest, or, as he calls it, to write resistance poems. Like the oral poet in precolonial times, Kunene sees it as his duty to uphold an unchanging set of values and attack those who would destroy it." The protest poems in his first book include "Europe," "The Civilization of Iron," "Thought on June 26," "The Spectacle of Youth," and "The Political Prisoner," which range in mood from a thirst for vengeance through bitter invective to awareness of the problems of political belief and action. A just cause, he contends in "Other," can only be served when the primary intent of everyone in the community is to serve not only his own needs but also those of the next generation:

When I have filled my desire
Let me take these grain baskets,
And fill them with other men's desires.
So that whoever crosses the desert
May never starve.

Although these are Zulu poems, Kunene hopes they will "stimulate thought and some understanding of African thought and literature," thus confirming his allegiance to an African worldview rather than to a particular language.

However, Kunene's two long Zulu epics are his major contributions to African poetry. The first to be published, *Emperor Shaka the Great*

(1979), is, according to Kunene, "an attempt to present an honest view of the achievements of Shaka." Shaka has long stood in the center of African literature but has seldom been positively represented outside negritude or Pan-African writing. Kunene's epic is supposed to amend that situation and "cut through the forest of propaganda and misrepresentations that have been submitted by colonial historians." But ultimately he hopes it "will stimulate more extensive interest in the varied innovations of this African genius. Through knowledge of his vision, many may understand the dreams and realities that have shaped the destinies of the people of Africa."

Containing seventeen hundred lines, seventeen books in all, this epic is an impressive work. Book 1 traces Shaka's ancestry, focusing on Jama, his grandfather, whose heroic path he is supposed to follow. Shaka must live in exile because of discord between his parents. From books 2 to 10, because of his mother's determination to make him the greatest of all kings and because of Dingiswayo's support, Shaka emerges from exile a most remarkable military and social organizer who builds the great Zulu empire. He also meets the "white strangers from overseas" with great confidence. From book 11 onward tragic events crash into Shaka's life. Close friends and relatives, including his mother, die; dissension and jealousy creep in; and in book 17 Shaka is assassinated by his half brothers Dingane and Mhlangana, aided by Mbopha, his court councillor. The epic concludes with a "Dirge of the Palm Race," which laments the loss of Shaka and other deceased heroes and exults in Shaka's glory, urging "his children" (the nation he built), imbued with his spirit, to "rise like locusts," "scatter the dust of our enemies," and "make the world free for the Palm Race."

Kunene's Shaka is not the brutal, ruthless autocrat portrayed by A. T. Bryant and other colonial historians. He is *ilembe* (hero of heroes), whose untimely death is tragic because he would have pushed African history in a different direction and prevented colonial domination by uniting the "Palm Race" and bargaining with the "white strangers" for an international alliance. Blacks and whites, Kunene's Shaka prudently realizes, are bound by a common fate:

I have a thought which obsesses me about our nation.
Often I see your fate tied up with that of the Palm Race.

Our nation and yours must grow in bonds of friend
  ship.
Not only have I heard of your courage and wisdom,
I want to send to your king, George, my messen-
  gers
So that in all your visits you may hold an honour.
This way two nations shall strengthen an alliance.
I want you to convey this to my brother, George.
There is, too, a point of strategy,
Since he must unite the White Race as I have
  united the Palm Race.

Kunene's Shaka is a Pan-Africanist. Most significant to the poet, more than Shaka's conquests
and other actions, is the grand vision he has of
"an all-embracing (African) nationhood" and a
world free of "bandit" rulers that rob humankind
of its freedom and dignity. Kunene attributes
Shaka's fall to a tragic flaw in his character. As
Barnett notes, Shaka "allows a personal
relationship—that with his mother—to violate the
nation's great ancestral heritage by forbidding all
ploughing, reaping, milking, and sexual relations
between men and women for a year after his mother's death. Shaka has tried to pit himself against
the community and must suffer the consequences." The epic is a bold but genuine projection of African historical realities. It is a noble attempt to balance facts and let the world hear the
African side of historicizing.

Kunene's second epic to be published, *Anthem of the Decades* (1981), proceeds along the
lines of the Zulu creation myth and reflects on
the philosophy of contradiction, by which certain
ethical standards are examined. The epic is divided into three parts of five books each. It demonstrates how a whole set of opposite pairs (creation and destruction, good and evil, triumph
and defeat, pleasure and pain, and so on) eternally blend in shaping human reality. Readers
are told in part 1 that without man, "who must
bind all things in creation / A shepherd who ex-
cels in wisdom," the task of the gods is incomplete. However, the question is: "What will this
creature do / With the knowledge that dwarfs all
created things?" The gods, who represent different qualities in heaven and earth, cannot agree
about what must distinguish man from beasts, on
the one hand, and from the gods themselves, on
the other. The gods are torn between the interests of Sodume's group, who are for a wise, intellectually free, and immortal man; and those of
Somazwi's followers, who ridicule all this and afterward meddle in man's life, always plotting its destruction. Man's life on earth becomes restless, as

*Cover for the long poem in which Kunene examines the Zulu
creation myth and the philosophy of contradiction*

opposite forces of creation ceaselessly interfere
with it.

Whereas at the end of part 1 the gods have
sent the chameleon to earth to grant man immor-
tality, in part 2 the salamander is racing to over-
take the slow chameleon because the gods have re-
versed their decision. Consequently man is
divided into two opposite races locked in mortal
battle. The only hope for man's survival is to har-
monize or achieve balance between opposite factions. The epic, quite appropriately, is dedicated
to the women of Africa because it celebrates
Nomkhubulwane, "the princess of life," or the female power that, after several attempts in the
epic, finally in part 3 brings about balance. In
Zulu culture she is the model of beauty and balance of mind and character, especially for young
women. Sodume comments: "True wisdom is
only of a woman / She alone holds the balance between two opposites / She nourishes the forces

that bind day and night together." In part 3 there is the emergence of the Ancestors, who offer a balance between life now and life after, which relieves man of the fear of mortality.

The epic emphasizes the importance of reconciliation and synthesis of contradictions in things and in man's mind. Opposition, struggle, and conflict must be seen not only as inevitable but also as a necessary condition for all progress and development. Confronted, for example, by the dogs of heaven, man takes the initiative to combat them and capture the fire of heaven. Selfishness and blind individualism are condemned for encouraging a one-sided outlook. For example, the Thusis are banned from society for failing to share. And Somazwi is punished for making unilateral decisions. The search for collective wisdom, demonstrated by the consultative councils of the gods and the ancestors, is necessary to assure harmony and balance.

The Creator, the epic emphasizes, did not fashion the world in the image of idealized notions. All things, irrespective of their opposite designations, contribute to the beauty and ultimate good of the cosmos. They emerge from the same hidden universal force, which Mvelingqangi signifies. The philosophy of contradictions, championed, for example, by Georg Wilhelm Friedrich Hegel and also known to Islam, is worldwide. But is treated in the *Anthem* as a specimen of Zulu culture.

Art cannot ignore the goals and directions of the present society, but according to Kunene it must draw its deepest meaning from the ethical ideals that have guided all past generations (ancestors). Although he is preoccupied with this thought in almost every one of his works, he pays particular attention to it in the poetry collection titled *The Ancestors & the Sacred Mountain* (1982). African society, which traditionally separates clearly social from material progress, is in danger of losing its ethical grounds if it forgets the role of the past in the evolution of its social and material philosophies. It is essential, Kunene maintains, that the present African society recognize the importance of continuity in which the present is linked with the past and both guide decisions affecting the future. And he sees the ancestors, who have made their contribution to human welfare and progress, as having a key role in survival and continuity. This is the main focus of almost all the poems in *The Ancestors & the Sacred Mountain*. Kunene insists that

the present generation and all subsequent generations must revere the Ancestors for the alternative is reverence of the tool as the measurement of human progress. The tool focuses on only one aspect of human activity. By featuring it as the primary instrument defining human progress we run the risk of putting the social purpose into second place. Yet by the example of courage and personal sacrifice of the past communities man is able to create and maintain a civilization. Achievements of the Ancestors are not isolated acts of individual heroism, but describe the collective effort of all those who make up our history. . . . Collectively, they are the heroes and heroines of the human race. It is these assumptions which make African society unique.

Although some of the poems in *The Ancestors & the Sacred Mountain* have no obvious connection with ancestors, the collection as a whole is about them. Many poems pay tribute to ancestors collectively (for example, "My Forefathers") or individually ("Tribute to Mshongweni"). The bulk of the poems, however, deal with the role of ancestors in the current struggle for liberation in South Africa. For Kunene the goal of liberation is humanization, aiming at the replacement of the selfish, barbaric materialism that dominates the institutions of the oppressors with a humane system that separates social and material progress and reaffirms the peace and cooperative character of human societies.

He considers struggle for liberation on three levels: the war, the peace, and the celebration of freedom. Equipped with the ancestors' "vision of life" and "weapons" of liberation, as seen in the poem "A Heritage of Liberation," the young generation, profiled in "The Rise of the Angry Generation," will unleash retribution. But the great transition and transformation that accompany the dawn of a new era of freedom will occur in the millennium after the war. In "Brave People" he writes, "All things are free for joy"; in "Anthem of Fruitfulness," "Friendships long forgotten are rekindled"; and in "Awakening," "We run down the valley embracing almost everyone." In each of these poems there are images of the ecstasy of peace, joy, reconciliation, and humankind's full communion with nature. Following this will be the celebration of freedom, which is the theme of poems such as "Sun of Beautiful Ones." In all these poems there is a sense of the ancestors presiding over the succession of generations and rejoicing in the new era of freedom

Mazisi Kunene (photograph by George Hallett)

and peace. According to "In Praise of the Ancestors,"

> They are the mystery that envelopes our dream.
> They are the power that shall unite us.
> They are the strange truth of the earth.
> They come from the womb of the universe.

In spite of living in exile, Kunene does not seem to have lost communion with his people. In fact, K. L. Goodwin maintains, "Kunene has the confidence of the poet who speaks on behalf of the clan rather than as an individual agonized voice. His work thus stands in sharp contrast to the sense of romantic isolation and alienation expressed by most African poets writing in English." In spite of geographical separation from his people, Kunene still shares a common vision with them and the same sense of destiny. Alvarez-Péreyre thinks Kunene has foreshadowed the tendencies that will emerge fully into the open with "Black Consciousness." Kunene, he maintains, "is not concerned with a love for the past or a re-

turn to a parochial view of culture harmful to the political battle of the present but with the urge to regain his dignity and force the white man to acknowledge the African, the 'Other,' he has long ignored and humiliated."

"More importantly, however," Goodwin concludes, Kunene "has written the two most ambitious poems to come out of modern Africa. With modest confidence in face of much discouragement, he has created from his Zulu inheritance two epics (and others that have not been translated or published yet) that are both thoroughly African and at the same time of international significance. His achievement may mark the end of the period when African poetry in English turned to Britain and America for its style and allusions." In "speaking poetically and imaginatively for the significance of African literature and thought" Kunene remains unparalleled.

Interviews:
Dennis Duerden and Cosmo Pieterse, eds., *African Writers Talking: A Collection of Radio Inter-*

views (London: Heinemann, 1972), pp. 88-89;

Chipasha Luchembe, "An Interview with Mazisi Kunene on African Philosophy," *Ufahamu*, 7, no. 2 (1977): 3-27;

Jane Wilkinson, "An Interview with Mazisi Kunene," *Commonwealth Essays and Studies*, 10, no. 2 (1988): 34-42.

References:

Jacques Alvarez-Péreyre, *The Poetry of Commitment in South Africa*, translated by Clive Wake (London: Heinemann, 1979), pp. 117-129;

Kofi Awoonor, *The Breast of the Earth: A Survey of the History, Culture, and Literature of Africa South of the Sahara* (Garden City, N.Y.: Anchor/Doubleday, 1975), pp. 193-201;

Ursula Barnett, *A Vision of Order: A Study of Black South African Literature in English (1914-1980)* (Amherst: University of Massachusetts Press / London: Sinclair Browne, 1983), pp. 43-44, 103-109;

K. L. Goodwin, *Understanding Poetry: A Study of Ten Poets* (London: Heinemann, 1982), pp. 173-201;

John Haynes, "Kunene's Shaka and the Idea of a Poet as Teacher," *Ariel*, 18, no. 1 (1987): 39-50;

Chidi Maduka, "Poetry, Humanism and Apartheid: A Study of Mazisi Kunene's *Zulu Poems*," *Griot*, 4, nos. 1-2 (1985): 57-72;

Mbongeni Z. Malaba, "Super-Shaka: Mazisi Kunene's *Emperor Shaka the Great*," *Research in African Literatures*, 19 (1988): 477-488.

Alex La Guma
(20 February 1925 - 11 October 1985)

Cecil A. Abrahams
Brock University

BOOKS: *A Walk in the Night* (Ibadan: Mbari, 1962); enlarged as *A Walk in the Night, and Other Stories* (London: Heinemann, 1967; Evanston, Ill.: Northwestern University Press, 1967 [i.e., 1968]);

And a Threefold Cord (Berlin: Seven Seas, 1964; London: Kliptown, 1988);

The Stone Country (Berlin: Seven Seas, 1967; London: Heinemann, 1974);

In the Fog of the Seasons' End (London: Heinemann, 1972; New York: Third Press, 1973);

A Soviet Journey (Moscow: Progress, 1978);

Time of the Butcherbird (London: Heinemann, 1979);

Memories of Home: The Writings of Alex La Guma, edited by Cecil A. Abrahams (Trenton, N.J.: Africa World, 1991).

OTHER: "Nocturne," "Out of Darkness," "A Glass of Wine," and "Slipper Satin," in *Quar-tet*, edited by Richard Rive (London: Heinemann, 1963);

"Coffee for the Road," in *Modern African Stories*, edited by E. A. Komey and Ezekiel Mphahlele (London: Faber & Faber, 1964), pp. 85-94;

Apartheid: A Collection of Writings on South African Racism by South Africans, edited by La Guma (New York: International, 1971; London: Lawrence & Wishart, 1972).

SELECTED PERIODICAL PUBLICATIONS—
UNCOLLECTED: "A Christmas Story," *Fighting Talk*, 10 (December 1956 - January 1957): 6;

"The Machine," *Fighting Talk*, 12 (October 1958): 8-9;

"Battle for Honour," *Drum* (November 1958): 85-90;

"A Matter of Honour," *New African*, 4, no. 7 (1965): 167-170;

"Thang's Bicycle," *Lotus: Afro-Asian Writings*, 29 (1976): 42-47.

Alex La Guma and his sons, Bartholomew and Eugene (photograph by George Hallett)

Between 1956 and 1985 Alex La Guma published more than a dozen short stories, five novels, and a travel book on the Soviet Union (1978). In addition he wrote many essays on the political struggles in South Africa and edited a collection of writings on apartheid (1971). His work has been translated into twenty languages. As a creative writer and political activist he was honored by several national governments, and as a writer who addressed the central questions of life in South Africa, he established himself as an important literary figure both in Africa and in the rest of the world.

Alex La Guma was born on 20 February 1925 in Cape Town. He was the son of Jimmy La Guma, president of the South African Coloured People's Congress and member of the Central Committee of the Communist party, and Wilhelmina Alexander La Guma, who worked in a ciga-

rette factory. In a country tragically plagued by racism, he grew up in the "Cape coloured" (mixed race) District Six. Not only did he learn of racism early in his life (at a segregated circus when he was eight) but he also grew accustomed to the poverty most children of his race experienced. Since his father was active both in the fledgling union movement and the newly founded South African Communist party, the young Alex was introduced early to the important political issues of the day and learned to do without his father's presence at home. He attended Upper Ashley primary school, Trafalgar High School, and Cape Technical College (1941-1942). He did not complete his studies because he was interested in either joining the fight against fascism in Spain or in seeing combat in World War II. Rejected as a volunteer because he was too young and underweight, he found jobs in a furniture factory and at Metal Box Company. He also became active in the union movement and helped to organize a strike. Dismissal from Metal Box only made him more militant, so that by 1947 he had joined the Young Communist League. When the Afrikaner Nationalist party won the 1948 South African election on the platform of apartheid, La Guma decided to become a full member of the Communist party. When the party was banned in 1950, he was listed under the Suppression of Communism Act. On 13 November 1954 he married Blanche Valerie Herman, a midwife and office manager; they later had two sons. La Guma was active with the South African Coloured Peoples Organization, and he and 155 other antiracist leaders were put on trial in 1956 for treason. In December of that same year La Guma published his first short fiction, "A Christmas Story," in the journal *Fighting Talk*.

La Guma was already more than thirty years old when his stories began to be published in Cape Town newspapers. In 1955 he had started a job with one of those papers, *New Age*, as a journalist reporting especially on his community. It is not surprising, therefore, that most of his stories and novels deal with people and situations in that same oppressed community. All but two of his stories were published between 1956 and 1966, while he was still living in South Africa. Often stories were written while he was busy on a novel, so story material is at times expanded on in the novel. Most of his stories deal with the conflict of the races inside South Africa and are derived from incidents told to him or from actual events.

"Nocturne" (in *Quartet*, 1963; originally published as "Etude," *New Age*, 24 January 1957) refers to Chopin's music, but it is also a reminder of La Guma's own love of classical music and his frequent visits to Cape Town City Hall to hear the orchestra play. In the story the protagonist, Harry, is part of a trio planning to rob a factory. While he and his compatriots are discussing their plans for the robbery, Harry's attention is caught by music emanating from a piano across the street. When the discussion is over, Harry follows the sound of the music and finds himself in a dilapidated building where an attractive girl is playing a nocturne. Although he is transported into a world of loveliness, he remembers his date with the other robbers and has to leave. He is, however, invited back by the girl, and he departs with his head full of the notion that "it would be real smart to have a goose [girl] that played the piano like that."

In "Nocturne" La Guma portrays the world of music in an exquisite and enchanting manner. This beauty is contrasted with the ugly reality of the racist world that Harry survives in, the hopeless poverty of the people who inhabit the building from which the music originates, and the awful-looking building itself. Yet, among these ruins, La Guma shows that Harry is capable of absorbing good music and living a life free of crime. Although La Guma places heavy blame on the unjust sociopolitical environment, he also insists that his characters should do everything possible to transcend this environment in a manner more positive than indulging in crime.

Harry would rather dream of a life without sin than do anything positive about it. This escapist view is also found in another of La Guma's early stories, "Out of Darkness" (in *Quartet*). According to La Guma, this is a true story of a man he met in prison. The story deals with the theme of playing white and the tragic consequences of this practice. The narrator, Old Cockroach, is in a prison cell telling how he landed in jail for killing his best friend, Joey. Old Cockroach had been "a teacher at a junior school and was doing a varsity course in his spare time" when he met and fell in love with the "beautiful" Cora. All his life plans, including marriage, were centered on Cora. But Cora "was almost white" and realized that in an absurd racist country such as South Africa one can benefit from one's light skin. Hence, she frequented "white places, bioscopes, cafes." Old Cockroach is black and was therefore unable to take Cora to these places. Cora "drifted away" from him, but he "kept loving her." Cora finally told him "to go to hell" and called him "a black nigger." Instead of revenging himself on Cora, Old Cockroach surprisingly killed his friend Joey, who had called him "a damn fool for going off over a damn play-white bitch."

In this story La Guma shows a remarkable ability to pace his narrative and to introduce the surprise twist at the right moment, and his penchant for creation of dialogue and vivid description is also apparent. His themes remain relevant to the concerns of his community, as they do in further stories about the colored community's dealings with whites and blacks. To pass themselves off as white in the white community, coloreds have to live their lives literally in darkness. As a "play white" Cora must leave her colored suburb for work before dawn and arrive home after nightfall. And her social life with whites must occur far away from the prying eyes of other coloreds. This anxiety-ridden, clandestine life of stealth is referred to again in the stories "A Glass of Wine" and "Slipper Satin" (both also in *Quartet*). In "A Glass of Wine" a young white boy is in love with the shebeen queen Charlette, Ma Schrikker's brown daughter. The courtship has taken place in secret, but the narrator and his drunken friend Arthur are suddenly witnesses to it. Arthur's drunken state allows him to question the young couple about their courtship and marriage plans. Since his questions are illogical and embarrassing in South Africa's world of racism, he is finally banished from the shebeen. The ending of the story reveals South Africa's cruel absurdity. When Arthur wonders aloud why he was ejected from the shebeen, the narrator answers: "You and your wedding. . . . You know that white boy can't marry the girl, even though he may love her. It isn't allowed." Arthur responds to this revelation by uttering, "Jesus. What the hell." The use of both "Jesus" and "hell" in one breath sums up in a devastating way one aspect of racism in South Africa.

In "Slipper Satin" it is not only the government-enforced law forbidding love encounters between whites and blacks that condemns the protagonist Myra; it is also the colored community itself, which acts as a vigilante force against such meetings. Myra, a colored girl, is in love with Tommy, a white boy. One evening at Tommy's house their privacy is invaded by the police. Aware that he has violated the "Immorality Act" and fearful of exposure to the white populace, Tommy shoots himself before he can be taken to the police station. For her part in the affair, Myra spends four months in jail. In the main, "Slipper Satin" deals with Myra's return from jail and with the violent reaction of her mother and community to her so-called crime. Myra has left prison with a determination to pick up her life and to begin again. After badgering from her mother and community, she decides to become a prostitute.

Interracial arrogance is also the theme of "The Gladiators" (in *A Walk in the Night, and Other Stories*, 1967). Though the story appears to be about a boxing match between a black and a colored South African, the "play white" phenomenon crops up again. Furthermore, La Guma shows that racism exists in the black community, too. Because blacks with lighter pigmentation receive a greater largesse from the apartheid system, they consider themselves superior to those with darker skins.

Dust jacket for the enlarged edition of La Guma's first book. The manuscript for the title story, which is critical of the South African police, was held by South African postal authorities for more than a year, after La Guma's wife tried to mail it to a publisher in Nigeria.

The colored boxer, Kenny, who "just missed being white," has only contempt for his black opponent. He considers the black boxer to be a "bastard," a "tsotsi" (street thug), and not one of "our kind." While Kenny is in control of the fight, the colored boxing fans share his racist views. But in keeping with crowd behavior, they shift their loyalty to the black boxer as soon as he takes command of the fight. La Guma deals deftly with the racist overtones and also makes skillful use of boxing language and description.

Often the cruel aspects of racism are reinforced by class behavior. This is especially true in the story "At the Portagee's" (in *A Walk in the Night, and Other Stories*), in which an immigrant from Portugal owns a café in the colored District Six. Because Portuguese immigrants are often

214

dark in pigmentation and Catholic in religion, they are barely tolerated among the Afrikaners. They tend, therefore, to live in lower-middle-class white suburbs that border colored districts and to own cheap shops in the colored areas, selling mostly steak and chips, egg rolls, coffee, fish, and Coca Cola. Although in the story the café owner's appearance is in keeping with the sweaty shabbiness of his establishment, and he is dependent on the nonwhite consumers, he displays utter contempt toward them. As an immigrant, he regards it as his duty to be loyal to the racist policies of the country. However, since he is not fully accepted into the white community, he shows his frustration (and supposed superiority) by being rude to all his colored customers, especially those who give him reason to react.

"The Lemon Orchard" (in *A Walk in the Night, and Other Stories*) and "Coffee for the Road" (in *Modern African Stories*, 1964) deal with events that actually occurred in South Africa during racial violence when members of the oppressed groups finally refused to accept the injustices of the apartheid system. "The Lemon Orchard" is based on the savage beating of a colored teacher in the rural town of Calvinia in the Cape. The teacher had charged the minister of the Calvinia Dutch Reformed Church with assault, "and as this was regarded by the Afrikaner community as an unheard of affront to God's servant by a Hotnot [colored person]," the teacher was taken at night from his home and "beaten up savagely." La Guma's story keeps the main outline of the actual event; but instead of simply concentrating on the bloodthirsty act that is to occur, he emphasizes more subtly the atmosphere of sterile, brutal racism tinged with the fertile, fragrant growth of a lemon orchard. As earlier, in "Nocturne," he displays an impressive ability to contrast human ugliness with nature's beauty, creating an authentic climate in which a terrible deed is to be enacted.

"The Lemon Orchard" gives the reader an excellent demonstration of how La Guma portrays the brutality of South Africa. In ironical, understated language, tone, and action, ominous hints are given of the fate that the teacher is about to suffer at the hands of five white men. The title itself is clouded in irony. The lemon fruit is a bittersweet citrus variety, and the smell it gives off is sharp and pungent. The beating the teacher is to receive is to occur in the lemon orchard, where the "fragrant growth" and "the pleasant scent of the lemons" contrast sharply

with the bitterness of the human deed. Pleasant as the orchard may be, it is also "a small amphitheatre" where the human hyenas are to victimize the black man to ensure that apartheid's authority is not challenged.

"Coffee for the Road" demonstrates well how La Guma used his personal experiences and those of other people in his work. According to La Guma, "this true story was narrated to me by an East Indian South African woman. I, of course, created the atmosphere, dialogue and so on." As in most of La Guma's stories, the climactic moment is short and intense, as the tired, harried protagonist of the story, in frustration, hurls a thermos flask at a white serving woman. But to arrive at this point, La Guma provides the reader with many intimate and informative details of geography, racial division, and human frustration.

The protagonist, a "dark, handsome, Indian [woman]," is driving the family automobile from Johannesburg to Cape Town, roughly one thousand miles. The three-day journey is in its second day when the chief incident occurs. Accompanying the woman is her whining and restless six-year-old daughter, Zaida, and her slightly older son, Ray. She has driven throughout the night because in racist South Africa there are no hotels open to them. At the insistence of Zaida, she decides finally to pull up outside a café on the main street of a rural Karoo town to seek coffee. As in the case of hotels, the Afrikaner-dominated rural areas have no cafés where nonwhites can sit down to enjoy food and refreshment. All that is available is "a foot-square hole" in "the wall facing the vacant space" of the café, where, at the point of the woman's arrival, "a group of ragged Coloured and African people stood in the dust and tried to peer into it, their heads together, waiting with forced patience."

The woman refuses to join the humiliating line and proceeds to walk confidently into the café, where the only customer present is "a small white boy with tow-coloured hair, a face like a near-ripe apple and a running nose." The serving woman, who is described as having "a round-shouldered, thick body and reddish-complexioned face that looked as if it had been sandblasted into its components parts," is surprised and stunned by the presence of a nonwhite person inside the whites-only café and screams in disgust at the woman when she asks that her flask be filled with coffee. Although startled by this screeching, insulting outburst by the white serving woman, the Indian woman's years of suffering humiliation at the hands of whites suddenly reaches the breaking point, and while accusing the white woman of being "bloody white trash," she hurls her thermos in disgust at the white woman, striking her forehead and causing her to bleed. As she storms angrily out of the café, her actions and brisk movements are stared at in disbelief by the ragged collection of nonwhites on the outside. She leaves the depressing town, vaguely aware that repercussions will follow. White policemen, complete with "riot-truck" and "holstered pistols," are given orders to set up a roadblock on the highway and to arrest the woman.

In "A Matter of Taste" (in *A Walk in the Night, and Other Stories*) La Guma shows that regardless of the racist laws in South Africa, which seek to destroy harmonious communication between the races, there is a natural propensity among human beings to share their joy and despair. This gives reason for both hope and pessimism: hope reveals itself in the fact that the races can cooperate and aid each other; but this hope threatens the racist governors of the system and causes them to create more laws that can prevent cooperation. The story deals with two black men who have "just finished a job for the railways" and a scruffy, hungry white man who harbors dreams of working on a boat that will take him to the United States. The black men are poor and are unable to afford supper—all they possess is some coffee, which they are in the process of boiling "some distance from the ruins of a onetime siding." When they are ready to serve the coffee, they are surprised by the arrival of the white man, who is "thin and short and had a pale white face covered with a fine golden stubble." His shabby appearance indicates that he is among the discarded of white society and that he has not had food for some time. His physical condition is clearly worse than that of the black men. But since he is also a victim of hunger he becomes one with them.

However, before a bond can be established among the three men, there are certain practices of the racist system that must be overcome. Chinaboy, the black who first observes the arrival of the white man from "the plantation," is suddenly and uneasily interrupted in his task of pouring the coffee. Chinaboy's unease stems from the fact that although he and his friend are "camped out" near an abandoned railway siding, whites are generally suspicious of such occurrences and respond by arming themselves and then forcibly ejecting the blacks from the land. Second, his un-

ease reflects his indoctrinated belief that whites are far too privileged to appear in such shabby dress. The white man is also uneasy: he is not accustomed to seeking aid from blacks, but his hunger forces him "hesitantly" and hopefully to remark, "I smelled the coffee. Hope you don' min'."

In a lesser writer the opportunity to exploit this delicate moment in a propagandistic way would be ideal. La Guma, however, weaves his tale so that he may hint at the unusualness of the encounter but still continue with his chief purpose: to show that at certain levels the racist system is also a class system affecting both white and black. Hence the focus of the story becomes the common desire of the three men to have a proper meal rather than the meager offering of a cup of coffee. The difference in race becomes secondary to their culinary needs, and even when they refer to each other in usually contemptuous racist terms such as "Whitey" and "boys," they do it more in a friendly than in a pernicious manner. In a bantering tone Chinaboy invites the new "table boarder" to eat, and the narrator jokingly refers to the "sparing" of "some of the turkey and green peas." Chinaboy, after indicating to the "white boy" that they are not "exactly [at] the mayor's garden party," begins to long for "a piece of bake bread with [the] cawfee." This longing by Chinaboy gives rise to a discussion of foods that are not then available to the poverty-stricken threesome and, once again, suggests the parameters of their world.

The stories "A Matter of Honour" (*New African*, 1965), "Tattoo Marks and Nails," and "Blankets" (the latter two in *A Walk in the Night, and Other Stories*) are anecdotes of individual interest rather than being in the tradition of seriously examining race relations in South Africa. These vignettes of life in District Six and in the Roeland Street jail are considered by La Guma to be an "exercise of the imagination and the testing of my ability to observe and to report interesting anecdotes." In "A Matter of Honour," a slight story about a bragging former boxer and a jilted husband, the narrator's sensitivity and kindheartedness, and the surprise ending, seem to preoccupy La Guma. "Tattoo Marks and Nails" also ends in a surprising way, when the narrator, Ahmed the Turk, prepares to disrobe and in so doing demonstrate that he is not the cheating, imprisoned World War II soldier, also named Ahmed, who had been humiliated by his fellow prisoners with a shameful tattoo (the phrase "A CHEAT AND

216

A COWARD" on his chest). In "Blankets" La Guma deals to some extent with the life of the unfortunate drunk and bully Choker. By highlighting moments when Choker uses certain types of blankets to create different moods, La Guma offers insights into the bully's life.

"Thang's Bicycle," written in 1975 when La Guma first visited Vietnam, near the end of the Vietnam War, shows that it is not difficult for him to write stories of interest and concern about situations that are different from those in South Africa. His characteristic qualities of creating atmosphere, portraying character, designing realistic dialogue, and fashioning an interesting and imaginative tale are all very much present. The reader finishes the story more aware of the devastation in Vietnam and appreciating the roles that both humans and machines played in the struggle.

La Guma's first novel, *A Walk in the Night,* was published in 1962. He completed the short novel in 1960 but was arrested under the state of emergency the government declared immediately after the massacre of sixty-nine blacks at Sharpeville and the unsuccessful assassination attempt on Prime Minister Hendrik Frensch Verwoerd. From his cell La Guma instructed his wife to mail the manuscript to Mbari Publications in Nigeria. The manuscript, however, was kept deliberately by authorities at a South African post office for more than a year, and his wife was fortunate to retrieve it. She eventually handed it to Ulli Beier of Mbari when he made a personal visit to South Africa in 1961.

As a reporter and columnist for *New Age,* and as an active opponent of the apartheid regime, La Guma had written extensively about the plight of colored people. *A Walk in the Night* both embodies and extends the work he was doing as a journalist and political activist. In it he demonstrates that the colored community is "struggling to see the light, to see the dawn, to see something new." The novel concerns the social, economic, and political purpose of the colored community. The developing consciousness of the community is depicted through the development of major and minor characters and through the setting of District Six. First there is Michael Adonis's gradual movement from being a law-abiding citizen to the desperate position of being a "skollie," or local thug. Second, the novel studies the development of the lives of Willieboy and the "skollies" and shows how inevitably Adonis will either become like Willieboy or the "skollies."

Third, through the study of the perverse police work of Constable Raalt, the reader is given an insight into the objectives and modus operandi of the South African white police. Last, La Guma describes the conditions of living in District Six and clearly demonstrates why the lives of the various characters develop as they do.

The development of consciousness in Adonis is closely tied to the racial problems in South Africa and the social environment that exists in District Six. Adonis lost his job because he refused to cower to the cheap insults of a white worker. In his anger he confronts Willieboy, who escapes the pressures of Adonis's work experience because he refuses to work at all. He prefers to live parasitically off his friends and strangers. In a way Adonis envies Willieboy's nonchalant attitude, but he is too defiant and vengeful to accept slothfulness. At this stage Adonis makes contact with the "skollies" as well, but since they live violently off others, he shies away from joining their group.

Upon returning to his shabby room in a dilapidated building, he confronts the aging, discarded, poor-white Uncle Doughty. At the invitation of Doughty he enters the old man's room and shares some cheap wine with him. When Doughty begins to identify Adonis's troubles with his own, and when he describes the two of them as ghosts like "Hamlet's father's ghost," Adonis recognizes the race difference between them and sees in the old man all the racist sins of the white society. In his anger he strikes Uncle Doughty dead. Fearful of the consequences of his crime, he joins the underworld gang of "skollies."

Willieboy's life is pathetic throughout. He is the product of a home where his father was a drunk and a wife-beater. In turn, Willieboy's mother beat him mercilessly. As a child, he found escape from his cruel life by going to the movies and imagining himself "a big shot." As an adult, Willieboy refuses to work and lives off the generosity of others. Soon after Adonis kills Doughty, Willieboy enters the dead man's room. He quickly retreats but is spotted by one of the other tenants, who accuses him of murder. Like Adonis, Willieboy, knowing that his innocence will not be accepted by an unjust society, now begins to walk the night. He is, however, apprehended and shot by Constable Raalt, and his life ends in the back of a police van.

Adonis chooses to join the "skollies" instead of Willieboy because a life of sloth was sooner or later to end pathetically. Through policemen

Dust jacket for La Guma's most successful and most autobiographical novel, based on his experiences in the struggle to abolish the system of apartheid in South Africa

such as Raalt, the system of injustice is perpetuated. Since La Guma spent a considerable part of his life in jail or house detention, he knew the work of the police. Some of his most remarkable characters are policemen. In depicting Raalt he provides the police with a human face.

Raalt is completely contemptuous of the colored community. He encourages gambling and prostitution among the colored people because he is able to obtain "protection money." Raalt's investigation of the murder of Doughty shows the contempt that he has for coloreds and the hatred the people have for him. When Willieboy is accused, Raalt begins a determined, relentless pursuit, which does not end until he shoots his prey. Raalt's behaving without conscience is hard for the reader to accept. La Guma, therefore, shows Raalt's marital problems as a possible explanation for his brutality.

A Walk in the Night was well received from its inception, and La Guma was considered to be a writer of great promise and talent. The novel has been translated into twenty languages and continues to be read widely. For people interested in

knowing something about South Africa, La Guma strives to provide information and graphic evidence of injustice and oppression; he handles the elements of plot, character, and imagery very well.

La Guma's second novel, *And a Threefold Cord*, was published in 1964 in Berlin. The novel was written while he was a prisoner in the Cape Town jail on Roeland Street. On this particular occasion (in October 1963) he and many others were jailed because the government feared a mass insurrection after Nelson Mandela and several major figures of the Congress movement were arrested. La Guma spent five months in prison, three in solitary confinement. The negotiations for the publication of the book were carried out in prison between him and his attorney, and La Guma literally signed the contract there.

The chief focus of *And a Threefold Cord*, as in *A Walk in the Night*, is the socioeconomic and political environment of the Cape Town slum where the action occurs. The dreadful lives of the victims of this environment are shown at a time when the Cape winter has set in and rain has fallen continuously for days. The reader is made aware of the woeful slum situation at the beginning of the novel when La Guma describes the misery and shabby conditions of those who inhabit the crowded "pondokkie cabins" and who must now face the cold rain. The world of the South African slum is one of bare survival, where corrugated cardboard cartons, rusted sheets of iron and tin, bitumen, and old sacking are stuffed into the cracks and joints of shacks. In his meticulous manner La Guma surveys the dismal conditions of the slum. He focuses in particular on the Pauls family shack, which had been built in a hurry so as to prepare shelter for Ma Pauls, who was at the time pregnant with her third child, Caroline. The shack is typical of the other structures in the slum, a place of squalor, decay, and poverty.

What poverty does to the slum inhabitants preoccupies La Guma in the novel. The shacks in their varying stages of collapse house inhabitants who, because of their crowded, poverty-stricken, and frustrating lives, resort to cheap liquor, prostitution, family quarrels, and violence. Their already miserable lives are dogged further by sickness, police raids, and the strong among them exploiting the weak ones. The inhabitants of the slum are trapped in the same manner as the fly whose actions are described in painstaking detail by La Guma. They have been unconcernedly knocked down by the racist and class system of South Africa, and in their struggling, collapsing positions they are frantically attempting to save themselves from complete destruction. But the more they flail and thrash to survive, the more hopeless it seems. And instead of forming a community to console each other, shack dwellers turn inward to seek solace and satisfaction and to rebuild their destroyed egos. Some of the shack dwellers see their poverty-stricken state as God-made and believe that, by trusting in God, things in time will be set right. Many drink themselves into a stupor so as to forget their miserable condition. Others, as in the case of Roman, indulge in cheap wine not only to forget the pain of their condition but to fire themselves up with so-called courage to take out their frustration through violent acts on others. Poverty drives attractive young women such as Susie Meyer to prostitution.

Poverty also causes severe illness and infectious diseases among the inhabitants. Already undernourished, they are unable to obtain medical help because they are too poor to pay for it. The case of Dad Pauls is an example. The almost unbearable misery of the slum dwellers is further compounded by regular police raids. Instead of building a proper settlement for the impoverished, the South African authorities employ large numbers of police, who, under the name of "law and order," brutalize the already wretched slum dwellers. Although *And a Threefold Cord* powerfully exposes the cruelty of the apartheid-dominated state, it was not reprinted until 1988, and hence it is the least known of La Guma's work.

The Stone Country was first published in Berlin in 1967, a year after La Guma had gone into exile from South Africa. The novel, however, was written inside South Africa immediately after La Guma spent five months in jail for being a member of an "illegal political organization." He was already under a twenty-four-hour, five-year house arrest order.

The Stone Country is based on La Guma's experiences and the experiences of other prisoners in South African prisons. As in the previous novels, the center of attention is the socioeconomic and political environment of South Africa, which creates conditions of brutality for the major and minor characters of the novel. The prison is a "stone country" where guards and prisoners are "enforced inhabitants of another country, another world." The prison is the last line of defense for the racist system.

The discrimination against peoples of color, inhumanity against others, cruel authority, and general brutality in the stone prison is an extension of the "stone country" that is South Africa. The black population cowers before the rigorous imposition of the apartheid system. Again, La Guma is searching for a character who can demonstrate to the other oppressed people that it is possible to oppose monsters such as the prison guard called Fatso; hence, he invests George Adams with ideas of human dignity that he himself held. From the moment that Adams enters the jail, he argues for his rights as an awaiting-trial prisoner, and he urges every prisoner that he comes into contact with to do the same. But Adams's defiant spirit is curbed somewhat by the reality in prison. Here he discovers, as he did in the nonprison world of South Africa, that rights may exist but they are ignored. The prison, like South Africa, is conceived by both the oppressed and the oppressor as a world of survival of the fittest. Thus Adams's attempt to win over the other prisoners to his side is unsuccessful. The prison is ruled permanently by types such as Fatso and Butcherboy.

Once more La Guma shows the sad reality of South Africa—a country where most inhabitants have willingly or unwillingly accepted the fact that merely to exist one must either become a bully or find alternative means of survival that are not any more honorable. The extended metaphor that La Guma employs in *The Stone Country*, in which a mouse has been brutally clubbed and clawed by the prison cat, also applies to the inmates of the prison. The sullen, young Casbah Kid has earlier taken his frustrations out by killing another oppressed innocent person, and in prison he delivers the death blow to Butcherboy. The Casbah Kid accepts his fate—life is a jungle where the fittest alone survives. Butcherboy is the head man of the jungle killing squad. He terrorizes everyone in prison, and his immense energy is employed in a negative manner. Alone in defying the prison officials, Adams almost in a resigned manner accepts the escape attempt of Gus, Morgan, and Koppe, seeing it as at least a sign of defiance by some prisoners. But for the majority of the inmates life in prison is a defeatist extension of what life is like outside prison. La Guma sheds his reporter's garb of the earlier books, and in the guise of political prisoner George Adams he tries to influence his readers. The prisoners are generally the same people who created so much pain and havoc in their slum settlements and who continue to behave in a selfish and monstrous manner. Again, as in the earlier books, the apartheid system stands unchallenged, and the oppressed "ghosts" continue to walk the night.

The Stone Country was, from the beginning, well received by the reading public. Parts of the novel have been anthologized. It has also been translated into several languages. Although the book gives an authentic account of happenings in South African jails, it is not La Guma's most memorable work.

In the Fog of the Seasons' End was published in 1972 in London, six years after La Guma had left South Africa, but it had been conceived and substantially written while he was still there and is his most explicitly autobiographical novel. Not only is it dedicated to one of his closest friends, Basil February, who died on the battlefield as a guerrilla activist, but, as La Guma observes, "everyone mentioned in the novel and every incident come from my lived past." The depiction of the chief character, Beukes, and his arduous

work is largely a portrait of La Guma and his political activities. The places in the novel are colored suburbs of Cape Town, with the exception of the black township Langa, where Elias Tekwane is arrested and Beukes wounded, and the "expensive" white Cape Town suburb where Beukes wanders around and witnesses a carefree social gathering.

The characters are based on real figures who worked with La Guma in the resistance struggle. Tekwane's name is fictitious, and so are the names of Flotman, Polsky, Abdullah, Isaac, Tommy, Henny April, Halima, and Beatie Adams. But the roles they play in the novel are the actual ones they performed and, in some cases, are still performing. La Guma refuses to reveal their real names for security reasons. He refers in the novel to several incidents that occurred in his own life: his first, personal experience with race discrimination at the circus; the school concert where blacks prepare themselves to sing at a white school; his experience as a factory worker; his stint at the American oil company (where the character Isaac works); and the meeting and courting of a character he calls Frances, although he did not marry this girl in real life. But the father of Frances in the novel has an interest in rugby, and this is true of the father of Blanche Herman, whom he did marry. Beukes's frequent absences from his home to carry on his political work and to escape the dragnet of the security police are directly from La Guma's life experience. Although La Guma was never wounded, the doctor who treats Beukes is, says La Guma, "still very much alive in Cape Town." La Guma also says that the despair, joy, fear, and hope that Beukes expresses "are straight out of my own life history."

The emphasis of *In the Fog of the Seasons' End* is on the South African resistance-and-liberation movement. But to help readers appreciate the new, defiant response of some of the oppressed, La Guma returns to the theme of his earlier work to show how the protest arose. Hence the novel develops the familiar theme of the devastating effects that the socioeconomic and political situation has on the oppressed people. Once again the reader is taken on a slow, painful tour through the human destruction that the apartheid regime and its system have caused. In the first chapter of the novel the municipal park that Beukes is resting in has segregated benches for "Whites" and "Non-Whites." Behind the "maze of pathways" leading to the museum is an "open-air restaurant" reserved for "Whites

Only." A sign near the top of the statue of Cecil John Rhodes points toward "the segregated lavatories." The museum that Beukes finally enters once had separate "Whites" and "Non-Whites" entrances.

The beaches of South Africa are divided along racial lines, with the inferior places being set aside for the nonwhites. Discrimination exists at the railway station as well. Apart from the separate entrances to the station and the different compartments and seats for different races, nonwhites are also forbidden to cross the "White footbridge." When Beukes circumvents the security-police network, he considers the use of the footbridge, but he is deterred by the forceful reminder that "a Coloured man had recently been sentenced to twenty pounds or ten days" for using the "White bridge." The magistrate had further warned the fined person that "sterner measures would be taken if the practice continued. . . ." As Beukes discovers at the age of seven, the schools are also divided rigidly along color lines: "They had been told that they would be giving a special performance of their concert for a White school. That was really the first time that the little boy had realized that children called 'White' attended separate schools."

Perhaps the most serious indignity and injustice the apartheid system perpetrates is to force all blacks over the age of sixteen years to carry the hated pass book. In depicting what occurs countless times every day in South Africa, La Guma makes the reader vividly aware of the total power that the regime wields over the oppressed. He goes on to depict a discussion between an aggressive white South African policeman and a black man who, although his credentials are impeccable, is subjected to abusive treatment. The black man is humiliated by the officer's use of the derogatory denotation of "kaffir," by his insolent and absurd questioning, by his contempt and brutality, and by the laws of the country that allow a citizen to be subjected to so much indignity. Without the pass, the black person is not permitted to live in his township, to travel from one place to another, to work, or, in fact, to exist, as indicated by the policeman. But, even with the pass, the black man is not permitted to have his family visit or live with him without prior permission, or he stands to have "the wrath of the Devil and all his minions" invoked against him. The policeman also reminds the man that he is "not allowed to leave" his job with his present employer without permission, nor can he leave his present

place of abode for another without consent. It is the similar humiliation that Tekwane suffers at the pass office that spurs him on to revolt against the racist system.

In the face of an environment dominated by a brutal police force with their cohorts of "informers" and by members of an oppressed community who are selfish, class-oriented, wrapped in unreality, and who turn their frustration on each other, it seems difficult and at times impossible to organize a resistance-and-liberation movement against the racist regime. In moments of despair and longing to be with Frances and his child, Beukes wonders, "Why the hell am I doing this?" Fortunately he abandons "the thought a little reluctantly, discarding it like a favourite coat, and [goes] along the road, carrying the cheap case packed with illegal handbills." Beukes knows that he is a tiny but necessary part of a struggle that began with the Bushman warriors at the beginning of the Dutch invasion of South Africa in 1652. He knows that he is part of a just struggle that has had its moments of victory in the early wars between the blacks and whites and that must once again and finally triumph. Hence, although the task of defeating an "ignoble regime" is very difficult, and even though the help needed is "as shaky as hell," it is necessary to persevere because "sometimes . . . you understand why, often because there was nothing else to do. You couldn't say, the hell with it, I'm going home."

The successful departure to the north (Botswana) by Peter, Michael, and Paul is a short moment of triumph for the resistance work carried out by Tekwane, Beukes, and others. But it is an essential moment that people such as Beukes, Tekwane, Flotman, and Abdullah must have in order to carry on their uplifting but difficult task. When one of Beukes's protégés, Isaac, turns up at Henny April's place near the Botswana border disguised as the guerrilla activist Paul, Beukes can hardly restrain his joy. Isaac is based on Basil February, to whom the novel is dedicated, and also symbolizes the warrior past of the oppressed, the future victory of the just struggle for liberation, and the chief reason for Beukes's task of preparing and awakening the people for the battle at hand. Hence, unlike the first three books, *In the Fog of the Seasons' End* concludes with the knowledge that the foggy night with its walking ghosts is about to be burned away. The final, triumphant vision is of a liberated South Africa.

From the street came the sounds of motor engines being started up, gears changing, the sounds of traffic leaving the little dorp, as people headed back ~~towards~~ to the forms. Others would stay on a little longer, go visiting, gossip over melktert, on the ~~stoops~~-stoops ~~or~~ or talk about the Dominee's sermon, the weather, creaking in their best clothes and fanning perspiring faces with newly-pressed handkerchiefs. Relenting parents would allow the children to take off the uncomfortable shoes so they could ~~to~~ wiggle their toes in the hot dust of the garden lots. On the whole it would be a visiting day, the special church service had provided fringe amenities. But those who ran the town's business had to resume their functions at the little cafes, the garage, the grocers, ~~grocery stores~~, the offices of local authority, the grain store.

Pages from two drafts for Time of the Butcherbird *(by permission of Blanche La Guma and Cecil A. Abrahams, Estate of Alex La Guma)*

(70)

Now there was this ~~redfaxed~~ bungalow of orange brick, ~~like~~ which,
with its ~~iron~~ corrugated ~~iron~~ roof and ~~features~~ twin front windows,
gave the impression of a flushed face angry/under an iron vizor. They
lived in the ~~oldest~~ part of the ~~town~~ [city], a sort of no-man's-land between
the concrete towers of ~~progress~~ [adulthood] and the ~~tumbled~~ [flaking] ruins of ~~days~~. (The
jacarandas lining the streets did not ~~exixxix~~ relieve the atmosphere
of ~~history~~ [embattlement], which metal guards—ornate in places but still protective—
gave the ~~street~~. Bungalows ~~built for~~ [where] ~~tenanted~~ [nervous] old ladies ~~who feared~~
~~the~~ viewed the black houseboys and kitchenmaids as potential ~~hordes~~ [members of hordes]
of rampaging barbarians. ~~Fearxxx~~ Apprehension ~~xxxxxx~~ [scuttled] like ~~mice~~ [pets] ~~the fax mice~~
behind the decorative curtains and each creak of a floorboard, the
crack of loose parquet, ~~xxxxxxxxxxxxxx~~ [was the sound of] alarm-bells ~~xxxxx~~, the paranoia (?)
of perpetual seige. North, beyond the border, the lily-livered Portagees [had given]
~~were giving~~ in [to] the howling mobs; fear commenced to (itch in the [rag like an]
groin ~~below~~. [of the continent.]   was

But she ~~xxxxxxx~~ bored. ~~Inxxxfrightxxxxx~~ ~~Beyond~~ [Across the frontiers of the] her boredom, was
nothing. ~~It was boredom~~. The sullenness of life ~~that~~ made her itch.
God, all these years in that place with the fancy iron-work over every
~~p~~ aperture, like that what-~~do-you~~-call-it [you-ma], chastity belts she had read
about in a story full of handsome knights and swooning ladies. Errol
Flynn and Olivia DeHavilland. She remembered those films, years ago,
but now ~~a~~days it was Steve McQueen, Robert Redford, Ster Elite showing [the]
~~The~~ Revenge of the Mafia. She shared the native maid [jolly] (with)
Mrs. Muller next door [where she also left the spare key when the
girl had to clean.] At least she could do her own
ordering about when she was home.

223

In the Fog of the Seasons' End has proved to be La Guma's best-received work to date. Described by several critics as a major achievement in African literature, it has been translated into twenty languages and has outsold his other books.

La Guma's last published novel, *Time of the Butcherbird* (1979), is the first of his novels to be conceived and written in its entirety outside South Africa. Free of constant harassment and surveillance by the South African security police and able to place all his energies behind the struggle of the liberation movement in exile, he was able to address a central question of South African society in a more revolutionary way. In his characteristic manner La Guma has succinctly packed together in *Time of the Butcherbird* two major stories and some shorter ones. The major stories are tied integrally to the theme of the time of the butcherbird (a period of natural "cleansing") and deal with the personal revenge of Shilling Murile, the forced mass removal of the blacks by Afrikaners in the Karoo region, and their resistance to this removal. The minor stories, and in some cases more personal portraits, deal with the failed marriage of Edgar Stopes and Maisie Barends, the history of Oupa Meulen, the struggle between Hlangeni and Mma-Tau, and the dismal failure to establish harmonious and just relationships between blacks and whites on both the personal and collective levels. All of these stories, major and minor, are held together by the metaphor of the butcherbird. The butcherbird is common in South Africa and is found especially in areas where there are cattle, sheep, and pigs. These livestock are generally molested by bloodsucking ticks. The butcherbird preys on these parasites, and in performing this useful task it is considered by rural dwellers as a bird of good omen that cleanses nature of negative influences. The book, therefore, reflects La Guma's belief that the time of cleansing South Africa's negative ways has come.

Murile's revenge for his brother Timi's death occupies a large part of the novel. The stalking and killing of Hannes Meulen, who had been instrumental in the death of Timi, exemplify the role of the butcherbird. But the butcherbird's destruction of parasites aids the entire population that lives off the livestock. Murile, on the other hand, first seeks personal revenge, and even though his action brings to an end the cruel and ignoble life of Meulen, he does not see his task as benefiting all those who have suffered at the hands of Meulen. When he finally joins forces with the collective struggle, he becomes an integral part of the butcherbirdlike work of cleansing the society of parasites. La Guma traces Meulen's ancestral roots and shows how his family had robbed blacks of their ancestral land. This gives the reader an intimate and authentic view of some Afrikaner people. La Guma sees in Meulen a modern Afrikaner but one who continues to treat blacks with contempt.

A part of the black community, led by Chief Hlangeni's militant sister, Mma-Tau, follows Murile's example by refusing to leave their ancestral land and instead challenging those who have come to remove them. Used to meek and resigned blacks, the sergeant in charge refuses at first to accept Mma-Tau's authority or the decision to disobey "the orders from the government." Annoyed at the songs of resistance, the sergeant "unbuttons his pistol holster," and this causes a black youth to throw a stone at him. The stone misses the sergeant, but his clerk panics and begins to flee, creating fear and confusion among the drivers of the government convoy, who decide to drive away from the scene. Embarrassed, the sergeant wonders "who would have thought that these bloody kaffirs would start something like this?" Not convinced as yet by the militant action of the blacks, he views the resistance as "a lot of baboons in jumble-sale clothing." The blacks, to confirm their determination not to permit the "ticks" to continue to suck their blood without resistance, throw stones at the sergeant and his convoy.

The sergeant returns to the town to seek reinforcements, while the black people, led by Mma-Tau, move into the hills to continue their resistance. The final three paragraphs contrast sharply with the opening of the book: gone is the hopelessness of the opening scene, in which Hlangeni and the remnant of his followers await their death as they succumb to the cruel laws of the white society. As the "yellowing afternoon light puts a golden colour on the land," a "flight of birds swoop overhead towards a water-hole." The symbolism is clear: the drought of human destruction and unjust dispossession of land has ended, and the butcherbird will smell out the sorcerer, hunt him down, and cleanse the society of his bloodsucking, negative nature.

Time of the Butcherbird relies heavily on symbolism and historical narrative and less on the immediate experiences so characteristic in La Guma's South Africa-based novels. As a consequence, readers have not shown the same enthusiasm for it as for the other books. However, it is still widely read.

Before La Guma died he was busy on several projects. First, his sixth novel, "Crowns of Battle," had been planned extensively and two rough chapters had been written. This novel concerns the nineteenth-century battle at Rorke's Drift in Natal, where Zulu warriors inflicted a heavy defeat on the white settler forces. La Guma had also sketched, in some detail, material for two short stories. And, finally, he had started to collect data for an autobiography.

Throughout his life La Guma succeeded in combining his political and literary activities. His task was always that of supporting the forces that were to bring the liberation of men, women, and children in South Africa and in the world at large. To this end, he created memorable fictional characters and situations based on harsh reality. He was an articulate spokesperson for his society, one who has left his mark as an important writer.

Interview:

Dennis Duerden and Cosmo Pieterse, eds., *African Writers Talking: A Collection of Radio Interviews* (London: Heinemann, 1972; New York: Africana, 1972), pp. 91-93.

Bibliography:

Robert Green and Agnes Lonje, "Alex La Guma: A Selected Bibliography," *World Literature Written in English*, 20 (Spring 1981): 16-22.

Biography:

Samuel O. Asein, *Alex La Guma: The Man and His Work* (Ibadan: New Horn/Heinemann, 1987).

References:

Cecil A. Abrahams, *Alex La Guma* (Boston: Twayne, 1985);

Abrahams, "The Context of Black South African Literature," *World Literature Written in English*, 18 (April 1979): 8-19;

Abrahams, "The Writings of Alex La Guma," in *Essays on Contemporary Post-Colonial Fiction*, edited by Hedwig Bock and Albert Wertheim (Munich: Hueber, 1986), pp. 149-172;

Samuel O. Asein, "The Revolutionary Vision in Alex La Guma's Novels," *Black Image*, 3 (Summer 1974): 17-27;

Ursula A. Barnett, *A Vision of Order: A Study of Black South African Literature in English (1914-1980)* (London: Sinclair Browne, 1983; Amherst: University of Massachusetts Press, 1983);

Anthony Chennels, "Pastoral and Anti-pastoral Elements in Alex La Guma's Later Novels," in *Literature, Language and the Nation*, edited by Emmanuel Ngara and Andrew Morrison (Harare, Zimbabwe: Atoll & Baobab, 1989), pp. 39-49;

J. M. Coetzee, "Alex La Guma and the Responsibilities of the South African Writer," *Journal of the New African Literature and the Arts*, 9-10 (1971): 5-11;

Coetzee, "Man's Fate in the Novels of Alex La Guma," *Studies in Black Literature*, 4 (Winter 1974): 16-23;

Ebele O. Eko, "From Vagrancy to Concerted Action: Progressive Commitment in Three Novels of Alex La Guma," *Journal of the Literary Society of Nigeria*, 2 (1982): 46-56;

V. A. February, *Mind Your Colour: The 'Coloured' Stereotype in South African Literature* (London & Boston: Kegan Paul, 1981);

Shatto Arthur Gakwandi, *The Novel and Contemporary Experience in Africa* (London: Heinemann, 1977; New York: Africana, 1977), pp. 21-26;

Robert Green, "Chopin in the Ghetto: The Short Stories of Alex La Guma," *World Literature Written in English*, 20 (Spring 1981): 5-16;

Green, "The Politics of Subversion: Alex La Guma's *In the Fog of the Seasons' End*," in *Studies in the African Novel*, edited by Asein and Albert Olu Ashaolu (Ibadan: Ibadan University Press, 1986), pp. 241-251;

Abdul R. JanMohamed, *Manichean Aesthetics: The Politics of Literature in Colonial Africa* (Amherst: University of Massachusetts Press, 1983);

S. P. Kartuzov, *Alex La Guma* (Moscow: Nauka, 1978);

Leonard Kibera, "A Critical Appreciation of Alex La Guma's *In the Fog of the Seasons' End*," *Busara*, 8, no. 1 (1976): 59-66;

Vladimír Klíma, *South African Prose Writing in English* (Prague: Oriental Institute in Academia, Publishing House of the Czechoslovak Academy of Sciences, 1969);

André Lefevere, "Alex La Guma: Exile, Protest, Procedure," *Comparison*, 13 (1982): 68-97;

Cover for La Guma's last published book, the first novel he conceived and wrote in its entirety after he was exiled from South Africa in 1965

Adewale Maja-Pearce, "The Victim as Hero: Alex La Guma's Short Stories," *London Magazine*, 24, no. 3 (1984): 71-74;

Felix Mnthali, "Common Grounds in the Literatures of Black America and Southern Africa," in *American Studies in Africa*, edited by Andrew Horn and George E. Carter (Rome: University Press of Lesotho/Ford Foundation, 1984), pp. 37-54;

Gerald Moore, *Twelve African Writers* (London: Hutchinson / Bloomington: Indiana University Press, 1980);

Ezekiel Mphahlele, *The African Image* (London: Faber, 1962);

Emmanuel Ngara, *Art and Ideology in the African Novel: A Study of the Influence of Marxism on African Writing* (London: Heinemann, 1985);

Lewis Nkosi, *Home and Exile* (London: Longmans, 1965);

Nkosi, *Tasks and Masks: Themes and Styles of African Literature* (Harlow, U.K.: Longman, 1981);

J. Okpure Obuke, "The Structure of Commitment: A Study of Alex La Guma," *Ba Shiru*, 5, no. 1 (1973): 14-20;

David Rabkin, "La Guma and Reality in South Africa," *Journal of Commonwealth Literature*, 8 (June 1973): 54-62;

Dieter Riemenschneider, "The Prisoner in South African Fiction: Alex La Guma's *The Stone Country* and *In the Fog of the Seasons' End*," in *Individual and Community in Commonwealth Literature*, edited by Daniel Massa (Msida: University of Malta Press, 1979), pp. 51-58;

Adrian Roscoe, *Uhuru's Fire: African Literature East to South* (Cambridge: Cambridge University Press, 1977);

Richard Samin, "Aspects de la satire dans quelques écrits d'Alex La Guma," *Revue de Littérature et d'Esthetique Nègro-africaines*, 4 (1982): 89-106;

Samin, "L'image de l'homme blanc dans les romans d'Alex La Guma," *Annales de l'Université d'Abidjan*, 15D (1982): 81-100;

Samin, "La Situation n'est pas eternelle," *Europe*, 708 (1988): 35-39;

Paul A. Scanlon, "Alex La Guma's Novels of Protest: The Growth of the Revolutionary," *Okike*, 16 (1979): 39-47;

John Updike, "Books: Shades of Black," *New Yorker*, 49 (21 January 1974): 84-94;

Michael Wade, "Art and Morality in Alex La Guma's *A Walk in the Night*," in his *The South African Novel in English: Essays in Criticism and Society* (London: Macmillan / New York: Africana, 1978), pp. 164-191.

Claude McKay

(15 September 1889 - 22 May 1948)

Alan L. McLeod
Rider College

See also the McKay entries in *DLB 4: American Writers in Paris, 1920-1939; DLB 45: American Poets, 1880-1945;* and *DLB 51: Afro-American Writers from the Harlem Renaissance to 1940.*

BOOKS: *Songs of Jamaica* (Kingston, Jamaica: Gardner / London: Jamaica Agency, 1912, Miami: Mnemosyne, 1969);

Constab Balluls (London: Watts, 1912);

Spring in New Hampshire, and Other Poems (London: Richards, 1920);

Harlem Shadows (New York: Harcourt, Brace, 1922);

Negry v Amerike, translated (into Russian) by P. Okrimenko (Moscow: Gosudarstvennoe, 1923); retranslated into English by Robert J. Winter and edited by Alan L. McLeod as *The Negroes in America* (Port Washington, N.Y. & London: Kennikat, 1979);

Sudom Lincha, translated (into Russian) by A. M. and P. Okrimenko (Moscow: Ogonek, 1925); retranslated into English by Winter and edited by McLeod as *Trial by Lynching: Stories about Negro Life in North America* (Mysore: Centre for Commonwealth Literature and Research, University of Mysore, 1977);

Home to Harlem (New York & London: Harper, 1928);

Banjo: A Story Without a Plot (New York & London: Harper, 1929);

Gingertown (New York & London: Harper, 1932);

Banana Bottom (New York & London: Harper, 1933);

Claude McKay

A Long Way from Home (New York: Furman, 1937; London: Pluto, 1985);

Harlem: Negro Metropolis (New York: Dutton, 1940);

Selected Poems (New York: Bookman, 1953);

The Passion of Claude McKay: Selected Poetry and Prose, 1912-1948, edited by Wayne F. Cooper (New York: Schocken, 1973);

My Green Hills of Jamaica, and Five Jamaican Short Stories, edited by Mervyn Morris (Washington, D.C.: Howard University Press, 1975; Kingston, Jamaica: Heinemann, 1979);

Harlem Glory: A Fragment of Aframerican Life (Chicago: Kerr, 1990).

Collection: *The Dialect Poetry of Claude McKay: Two Volumes in One*—volume 1: *Songs of Jamaica*; volume 2: *Constab Ballads* (Freeport, N.Y.: Books for Libraries, 1972).

What is generally termed the Harlem Renaissance, a decade of black self-awareness and racial pride, is frequently dated from the appearance in print of Claude McKay's great sonnet "If We Must Die," which commemorated the cataclysmic race riots in the United States during the second half of 1919. So great was the effect of that poem that McKay has been proposed as the founder of the Harlem Renaissance and as the prototype of the modern black social-realist contributor to American culture. When in 1925 Alain Locke (the Howard University philosopher and recorder of black literary and artistic achievement) wrote about the "New Negro," he was thinking about those who, in effect, followed in McKay's path in taking pride in African culture, in Negro racial self-consciousness, and in black folkways. After achieving international renown as a poet, McKay experimented with the realist short story; became a professional journalist and editor; wrote novels, an autobiography, and a popular sociological study of Harlem; and thereby attained major stature as a black author. However, his absence from Europe and North Africa from 1922 to 1934, his changing political and religious positions, and his often strained relationships with his friends and supporters resulted in a diminished reputation by the time of his death. The development of black studies, Commonwealth literature, and Jamaican nationalism in the 1960s redirected attention to McKay and resulted in a series of analytic studies that have identified his strengths and weaknesses and reestablished his literary reputation in both the United States and the Caribbean. In 1977 he was posthumously awarded the Order of Jamaica and declared the national poet.

McKay in 1920, when his Spring in New Hampshire *was published*

Festus Claudius McKay, the youngest of the eleven children of peasant farmers Thomas Francis McKay and Ann Elizabeth Edwards McKay, was born at Sunny Ville, Clarendon Parish, in the south-central section of Jamaica. His father claimed Ashanti ancestors; his mother, Madagascan. Though the family attended Baptist services, McKay was influenced by the rationalism of his brother Uriah Theophilus (U'Theo), an elementary-school teacher with whom young McKay lived for ten years, and of Walter Jekyll, a British expatriate freethinker and folklorist who befriended McKay after the latter moved to Kingston at age nineteen; Jekyll became his mentor and benefactor. In 1912 Jekyll arranged publication of *Songs of Jamaica* and *Constab Ballads* and made it possible for McKay, then a Kingston policeman, to leave Jamaica to study in the United States at Tuskegee Institute, and subsequently at Kansas State College. From there, in 1914, he went to New York City. On 30 July 1914 he married Eulalie Imelda Edwards; they were divorced six months later. McKay never returned to his native country, though it inspired much of his poetry and his best fiction, the novel *Banana Bottom* (1933). Jamaica represented the Edenic antithesis to the urban culture of America.

The dialect poems that established McKay as the "Robert Burns of Jamaica" have little to recommend them: most perpetuate the racial attitudes of Victorian colonialism in language that is almost incomprehensible to readers unacquainted with West Indian vernacular. However, some (such as "Hard Times" and "Out of Debt") reveal a genuine sympathy for the less fortunate, and others (such as "My Native Land, My Home" and "My Mountain Home") are informed by emotional attachments to places and persons. After leaving Jamaica, McKay eschewed dialect except for caricature or special effect in establishing social hierarchy or regional verisimilitude.

The poems written in the United States (many in sonnet forms and almost all in iambic pentameter) are of two broad types: lyrical responses to environment ("Dawn in New York," "On Broadway," and "The Harlem Dancer," for example), and what might be called poems of protest, which reveal a strong social commitment and a desire to ameliorate the situation of blacks, women, and all others who are differentiated or discriminated against. Examples of these poems are "The Lynching," with its horrendous concluding couplet— "And little lads, lynchers that were to be, / Danced round the dreadful thing in fiendish glee"—"The Negro's Tragedy," "The Tired Worker," "Alfonso, Dressing to Wait at Table," and "Outcast." The poems that were written in response to life in foreign cities (especially "St. Isaac's Church, Petrograd" and "Tetuan") capture the spirit of each place with great exactitude and felicity, and suggest that McKay's claim that he was essentially a troubadour has merit: he could see things from the outsider's viewpoint, appreciate the insider's attachment and reverence, and compare the present with the absent.

It is this reflection upon distant and past events that makes *The Negroes in America* (1979; originally published in Russian as *Negry v Amerike*, 1923) and *Trial by Lynching* (1977; originally *Sudom Lincha*, 1925) interesting artifacts. Without being maudlin, overemotional, or too complaisant, McKay was able to write about race, religion, politics, and cultural assimilation for a foreign audience that was officially supportive of the black struggle and of the black writer. And in *The Negroes in America* he clearly states the case for regarding the fight for Negro rights as part of the struggle for woman's rights, and the case

against the trade union movement for excluding black workers. With somewhat greater application and development, this booklet might have become a major critique of the treatment of blacks in the United States. Perhaps because of his subsequent disillusionment with communism, McKay never alluded publicly to the two books published as a result of his protracted stay in the Soviet Union as a guest of the government (1922-1923).

After leaving the Soviet Union, where he had met Leon Trotsky, acknowledged membership in the Communist party, and addressed the Fourth Communist Congress, McKay lived in Germany, France, Spain, and Morocco and commenced writing fiction seriously. "Color Scheme," his first novel, was written in Toulon in 1925, but he destroyed the manuscript after a publisher rejected it. A series of short stories on Harlem life then took McKay's writing time, and on the advice of a publisher's reader he developed one into *Home to Harlem* (1928), which was an immediate financial and popular success—though it was censured by W. E. B. Du Bois for being too prurient and for stressing the low-culture rather than the high-culture aspects of black life. *Home to Harlem* depicts the life of the majority of American blacks in the urban ghetto—rather than the old, rural life of the South that had been chronicled by Jean Toomer in *Cane* (1923). McKay celebrates Harlem's vitality.

Home to Harlem opens with Jake Brown working as a stoker aboard a freighter en route from Cardiff to New York. He had joined the army with patriotic motives but went AWOL when assigned to noncombat duties. Back in Harlem, which he refers to as "back home," Jake engages a prostitute, Felice, who returns his money and disappears; the remainder of the novel is an account of the adventures of Jake in his search for Felice. He meets Zeddy Plummer, "a razor-flashing nigger" who had been Felice's lover; Congo Rose, a nightclub "entertainer" who keeps him; and Ray, "a book fellah"/railroad waiter from Haiti who has become an antimaterialist, an advocate of black racial self-consciousness, and a believer in responsible sexual ethics. But when Ray meets Agatha, "a rich-brown girl with soft, amorous eyes" who wants to marry him, he ships off to Europe as a mess boy; and when Jake reencounters Felice, they decide to leave Harlem for Chicago—where they believe they will be free of the overcrowding and crime of Harlem and will be able to start a new life.

McKay and Max Eastman in Moscow, 1922. While in Russia, McKay wrote two booklets about racism in America.

In this novel (as in all his fiction, essentially) McKay develops characters who represent the two polarities he wanted to bridge: the intellectual, responsible type and the emotional, picaresque type. Ray is a version of McKay himself; Jake is McKay's alter ego; together they reveal the constant antagonisms that have to be controlled by the black who finds himself belonging to neither the urban, industrial North nor the rural, agricultural South. It is the conflict of loyalties described in his poem "North and South"; it is the conflict of present and past, of philosopher and folk. Yet neither Jake nor Ray is a role model for modern American blacks: Ray, while observing that "Civilization is rotten," is unable to cope with reality, with Harlem, and leaves the United States; Jake, who has led a life of "rude contacts and swift satisfactions," is both streetwise and principled but is nonetheless unrealistic in believing that by migrating to Chicago he can escape the denigration of Harlem. Neither man seems able to cope with life in the "black belt," yet Jake is the more appealing character: he tries to cope with adversity; he espouses moderation, optimism, and stability; and he adheres to those principles (such as not being a strikebreaker) that he has learned to respect. Whereas Ray places

the blame for the plight of blacks on society, Jake accepts individual responsibility for his fate, whether in romance, housing, employment, or life.

With McKay's depiction of promiscuity, drug and alcohol abuse, numbers rackets, and similar unsavory aspects of New York black life, *Home to Harlem* impressed many readers as a work of vivid social realism, yet McKay stressed that he aimed at emotional realism—he wanted to highlight his characters' feelings rather than their social circumstances. Nevertheless, Du Bois and Locke attacked the book—principally because it did not show the "better" side of black life to advantage. The novel was a great success, however, and was awarded the medal of the Jamaica Institute of Arts and Sciences.

Banjo (1929), McKay's second novel, is essentially a sequel to *Home to Harlem* set in Marseilles. Lincoln Agrippa (Banjo) Daily and Ray (now a beachboy and still a would-be writer) lead hand-to-mouth lives in the port city; they enjoy the music, sex, and alcohol of cheap nightspots; and in conversations with blacks from various countries, they come to understand something of their racial heritage and realize that the folk rather than the intelligentsia represent the heart of blackness. Yet the drifting, purposeless lives of the characters (principally interested in momentary hedonism) are hardly an acceptable alternative to the commercialism, nationalism, and individualism of the white world they denounce. The main character's banjo—a clear symbol of the mythical, Edenic life of the American South—is a wry reminder that there is little advantage to be gained from an expensive, sophisticated musical instrument when there is neither regular employment and income nor rest and achievement to be celebrated. The Ditch (the area in which Ray and Banjo have lived) proves as inhospitable as Harlem, and the two friends abandon their women and continue their peripatetic existence—never considering Africa as a destination, however. As with *Home to Harlem*, *Banjo* received acclaim, though it was apparent to critics that McKay's imagination had been somewhat strained and that the novel was essentially an autobiographical exercise.

Gingertown (1932), a collection of twelve short stories, continues to develop a theme that absorbed McKay: the role of a black person in a fundamentally white society—even if (as in Jamaica) the white population is numerically small. The first six stories are set in Harlem and might, without difficulty, have been included in *Home to Harlem*. Again readers see the dichotomies that McKay explored: New York/West Indies, expression/repression, and emotion/reason. The four Jamaican stories imply that white mores are hypocritical and that white morality is desiccated; by contrast, the black folk are warm, supportive, forgiving, and realistic. The final stories (one set in Marseilles, one in Tangier) explore intercultural sexual relationships.

With *Banana Bottom* McKay achieved his peak as a fictionist. Bita Plant, the female protagonist, is his most skillfully drawn character, the themes are treated without obvious propagandistic didacticism, and the plot is eminently credible within the then-contemporary Jamaican context. Bita, after having been raped as a child, is raised by white missionaries, Malcolm and Priscilla Craig, who provide her with an English education and Christian morals in the expectation that she will become, in effect, a black-skinned white person. The Craigs encourage Bita's engagement to Herald Newton Day, a theological student who has been "transformed" by them to the point that he abhors his own blackness and folk sensuality; ironically he is discovered copulating with a goat and is sent abroad. Bita, attracted to folk reli-gion, freed from Christian sexual repression, and made financially independent by an inheritance, ultimately marries her father's drayman, Jubban. Reconnected with her peasant roots, she raises their child in an environment that represents the best of the West Indian folk culture, modified by some Western elements. Bita has pride in blackness, is free of hypocrisy, and is independent and discerning in her values. She synthesizes the values of Jake/Banjo and Ray in a fundamentally Edenic setting. Praise for *Banana Bottom* has been unanimous.

Considering the artistic achievement of *Banana Bottom*, it is easy to understand why McKay's *Harlem Glory* (published in 1990) and "Romance in Marseilles" (unpublished), short novels written later on, have been found disappointing by those who have read them. Instead of building on Jamaican material, they revert to Harlem and Marseilles and replicate characters, events, and themes of *Home to Harlem* and *Banjo*.

McKay's autobiography, *A Long Way from Home* (1937), provides glimpses of his "public" life, offers many terse judgments of his friends and enemies, and is enriched by anecdotal material. It is not wholly reliable, however: for example, in it he denies that he ever belonged to the Communist party. The book provides a highly selective account of his European and North African stays, and it offers no account of his early years—a deficiency made good, in part, by the posthumously published *My Green Hills of Jamaica* (1975). On the other hand, *A Long Way from Home* offers a succinct review of his main beliefs: American blacks should lead the struggle against colonialism, segregation, and oppression; and American blacks must unite (urban and rural, men and women, intellectuals and the majority). Unity, organization, and racial self-consciousness are essential to progress.

Harlem: Negro Metropolis (1940), described by the publisher as "an account of the world's largest black community during the eventful years of the twenties and thirties," is an impressionistic, quasi-sociological study of Father Divine, occultists, cultists, Harlem businessmen, the numbers and other entertainment racketeers, black politicians, Marcus Garvey, and Sufi Abdul Hamid and organized labor. For most of the period covered, McKay was overseas, and when he returned in 1934, he was unfamiliar with much that had transpired during his absence. The book has been superseded by many more-scholarly studies, yet it retains value as a reexamination of Harlem

32 Morningside Ave
NYC. March 23

Dear Max: There is nothing more to be done through the Naturalization Bureau. That was the first quarter I appealed to when I was informed of the new ruling. I was told that there were so many names, it would take at least 3 months or more before I was called and that my number could not be put ahead of others. Only the local administration could have found a loophole for me to escape (as I was told they did in certain cases) but they were glad of the chance at last legally to get rid of an embarrassing person like me. The only hope would be intervention by an influential government official, but I don't have access to any and there is the official fear of investigation and charges of favoritism to reckon with.

Also I have just discovered that the new ruling has a joker, which makes aliens who apply for relief again liable to deportation. It has started already. The clause says that aliens who arrived in the country during the last 5 years and have held a WPA job for more than 2 years may be deported as public charges if they ask relief. That perfectly covers my case! I don't want to be sent to the little island of Jamaica or back to Tangier. So many would be glad to have me out of the way,

So I have already sold some books, including

A 1939 letter from McKay to Eastman, who had been instrumental in getting McKay's poetry published in the United States (Manuscripts Department, Lilly Library, Indiana University)

my Georg Grosz. I got 7.50 for the little Figs & Thistles, which St. Vincent Millay autographed for me & was very disgusted parting with it. Now I am trying to dispose of Hemingway. If Stackpole or somebody doesn't come through, so that I may sell myself too, I don't know what next. Wish I could discover a capitalist to invest in a Harlem magazine; there is enough original & rich stuff to exploit. Life's Negro number was a huge success. What a job I could do if any magazine would employ me to do a Harlem number.

Last evening, a Jewish acquaintance dropped in with a copy of the current issue of Lovestone's Worker Age, which carries my, "If We Must Die". He remarked that the poem may have been written for the persecuted Jewish group and that someone should read it to Hitler! I replied I was happy he was moved by the universal appeal and told him about Frank Harris's reaction to it & how you first published in the Liberator. I also told him that it was being whispered around that I was anti-Semitic, because I had expressed my opinion on the Zionist problem in Palestine & I considered myself not only a Negro but also a worker. He said people should identify themselves more with their own groups & less with the workingclass movements for it had failed to protect minorities! Churchill is in Florida

& when it returns, I shall contract get you involved—Claude

by one who had established a necessary critical distance.

In the course of a writing career of thirty years, Claude McKay was able to establish his reputation as a master of the dialect poetry of the Jamaican folk; as a sonnet writer of merit, able to treat subjects as diverse as West Indian flora, European cities, and racial conflicts; as a journalist, reviewer, and essayist of the Left; as a short-story writer of some force; and as a picaresque novelist whose forte was social and emotional realism. That he was able to capture a universality of sentiment in "If We Must Die" has been fully demonstrated; that he was able to show new directions for the black novel is now acknowledged; and that he is rightly regarded as one of the harbingers of (if not one of the participants in) the Harlem Renaissance is undisputed. On 22 May 1948 McKay died of heart failure in Chicago, where he had moved in 1944 to work with the National Catholic Youth Organization. He was buried in New York City, after his funeral was held in Harlem.

Biography:

Wayne F. Cooper, *Claude McKay: Rebel Sojourner in the Harlem Renaissance: A Biography* (Baton Rouge: Louisiana State University Press, 1987).

References:

Richard K. Barksdale, "Symbolism and Irony in McKay's *Home to Harlem*," *CLA Journal*, 15 (March 1972): 338-344;

Robert Bone, "Claude McKay," in his *The Negro Novel in America*, revised edition (New Haven: Yale University Press, 1965);

Lloyd W. Brown, "The Contribution of Claude McKay," in his *West Indian Poetry* (Boston: Twayne, 1978), pp. 39-62;

Elaine Campbell, "Two West Indian Heroines: Bita Plant and Fola Piggott," *Caribbean Quarterly*, 29 (June 1983): 22-29;

Eugenia W. Collier, "The Four-Way Dilemma of Claude McKay," *CLA Journal*, 15 (March 1972): 345-353;

Mary James Conroy, *Claude McKay: Negro Poet and Novelist* (Ann Arbor: University Microfilms, 1968);

Conroy, "The Vagabond Motif in the Writings of Claude McKay," *Negro American Literature Forum*, 5 (Spring 1971): 15-23;

Claude McKay

Wayne F. Cooper, "Claude McKay and the New Negro of the 1920s," *Phylon*, 25 (Fall 1964): 297-306;

Cooper and Robert C. Reinder, "A Black Briton Comes 'Home': Claude McKay in England, 1920," *Race*, 9 (November 1970): 37-51;

Arthur D. Drayton, "McKay's Human Pity: A Note on His Protest Poetry," *Black Orpheus*, 17 (June 1965): 39-48;

Addison Gayle, Jr., *Claude McKay: The Black Poet at War* (Detroit: Broadside, 1972);

James R. Giles, *Claude McKay* (Boston: Twayne, 1976);

Jacqueline Kaye, "Claude McKay's 'Banjo,'" *Presence Africaine*, 73 (First Quarter 1970): 165-169;

George E. Kent, "The Soulful Way of Claude McKay," in his *Blackness and the Adventure of Western Culture* (Chicago: Third World, 1972), pp. 36-52;

Phyllis Martin Lang, *Claude McKay: The Later Years, 1934-48* (Ann Arbor: University Microfilms, 1973);

Geta J. LeSeur, "Claude McKay's Marxism," in *The Harlem Renaissance: Revaluations* (New York: Garland, 1989), pp. 219-231;

LeSeur, "Claude McKay's Romanticism," *CLA Journal*, 32 (March 1989): 296-308;

Clarence Major, "Dear Jake and Ray," *American Poetry Review*, 4 (1975): 40-42;

Alan L. McLeod, "Claude McKay, Alain Locke, and the Harlem Renaissance," *Literary Half-Yearly*, 27 (July 1986): 65-75;

McLeod, "Memory and the Edenic Myth: Claude McKay's Green Hills of Jamaica," in *Individual and Community in Commonwealth Literature*, edited by Daniel Massa (Valletta: University of Malta, 1979), pp. 75-83;

Marian B. McLeod, "Claude McKay's Russian Interpretation: *The Negroes in America*," *CLA Journal*, 23 (March 1980): 336-351;

Mervyn Morris, "Another Claude McKay: A Poet of Love," *Jamaica Journal*, 19 (May-July 1986): 46-48;

Kenneth Ramchand, "Claude McKay and *Banana Bottom*," *Southern Review*, 1, no. 1 (1970): 53-66;

Lewis Rupert, "Claude McKay's Political Views," *Jamaica Journal*, 19 (May-July 1986): 39-45;

Wilfred D. Samuels, "Claude McKay, Harlem's Radical Poet," in his *Five Afro-Caribbean Voices in American Culture, 1917-1929* (Boulder, Colo.: Belmont, 1977), pp. 61-82;

Robert P. Smith, Jr., "Rereading *Banjo*: Claude McKay and the French Connection," *CLA Journal*, 30 (September 1986): 46-58;

Tyrone Tillery, *Claude McKay: A Black Poet's Struggle for Identity* (Amherst: University of Massachusetts Press, 1992);

Melvin B. Tolson, "Claude McKay's Art," *Poetry*, 83 (February 1954): 287-290;

Jean Wagner, "Claude McKay," in his *Black Poets of the United States: From Paul Laurence Dunbar to Langston Hughes*, translated by Kenneth Douglas (Urbana: University of Illinois Press, 1973), pp. 197-257.

Papers:

The principal collection of McKay's papers is in the James Weldon Johnson Memorial Collection of Negro Arts and Letters at the Beinecke Library, Yale University. Additional material is in the Schomburg Collection of Negro Literature and History, housed in the Harlem Branch of the New York Public Library; in the Howard University and Harvard University collections; and among the Max Eastman papers in the Indiana University Library at Bloomington.

Edgar Mittelholzer

(16 December 1909 - 5 May 1965)

Frank M. Birbalsingh
York University

BOOKS: *Creole Chips* (New Amsterdam, Guyana: Lutheran Press, 1937);

Corentyne Thunder (London: Eyre & Spottiswoode, 1941; New York: Humanities Press, 1970);

A Morning at the Office (London: Hogarth Press, 1950); republished as *A Morning in Trinidad* (Garden City, N.Y.: Doubleday, 1950);

Shadows Move Among Them (London & New York: Nevill, 1951; Philadelphia: Lippincott, 1951);

Children of Kaywana (London: Nevill, 1952; New York: Day, 1952); republished as *Savage Destiny* (New York: Dell, 1965);

The Weather in Middenshot (London: Secker & Warburg, 1952; New York: Day, 1953);

The Life and Death of Sylvia (London: Secker & Warburg, 1953; New York: Day, 1954); republished as *Sylvia* (London: Four Square, 1963);

The Adding Machine (Kingston, Jamaica: Pioneer, 1954);

The Harrowing of Hubertus (London: Secker & Warburg, 1954); republished as *Hubertus* (New York: Day, 1955); republished again as *Kaywana Stock* (London: Secker & Warburg, 1959);

My Bones and My Flute: A Ghost Story in the Old-Fashioned Manner (London: Secker & Warburg, 1955);

Of Trees and the Sea (London: Secker & Warburg, 1956);

A Tale of Three Places (London: Secker & Warburg, 1957);

With a Carib Eye (London: Secker & Warburg, 1958);

Kaywana Blood (London: Secker & Warburg, 1958); republished as *The Old Blood* (New York: Doubleday, 1958);

The Weather Family (London: Secker & Warburg, 1958);

The Mad MacMullochs, as H. Austin Woodsley (London: Owen, 1959);

A Tinkling in the Twilight (London: Secker & Warburg, 1959);

Eltonsbrody (London: Secker & Warburg, 1960);

Edgar Mittelholzer (photograph by Mark Gerson)

Latticed Echoes (London: Secker & Warburg, 1960);

Thunder Returning (London: Secker & Warburg, 1961);

The Piling of Clouds (London: Putnam's, 1961);

The Wounded and the Worried (London: Putnam's, 1962);

A Swarthy Boy: A Childhood in British Guiana (London: Putnam's, 1963);

Uncle Paul (London: Macdonald, 1963; New York: Dell, 1965);

The Aloneness of Mrs. Chatham (London: Library 33, 1965);

The Jilkington Drama (London & New York: Abelard-Schuman, 1965).

Edgar Mittelholzer occupies a special place in the literary history of the English-speaking Caribbean. Although H. G. de Lisser is generally regarded as the first major novelist to emerge from the region, his achievement is divided between fiction, journalism, and public affairs. On the other hand, in a career lasting some three decades, Mittelholzer wrote virtually nothing but fiction and earned his living by it. He is thus the first professional novelist to come out of the English-speaking Caribbean. Some of Mittelholzer's novels include characters and situations from a variety of places within the Caribbean. They range in time from the earliest period of European settlement to the present day and deal with a cross section of ethnic groups and social classes, not to mention subjects of historical, political, psychological, and moral interest. In addition eight of Mittelholzer's novels are non-Caribbean in subject and setting. For all these reasons he deserves the title of "father" of the novel in the English-speaking Caribbean.

The society into which Edgar Austin Mittelholzer was born, on 16 December 1909 in British Guiana (now Guyana), is typical of the Caribbean as a whole. Although Guyana is situated on the northeast coast of South America, between Venezuela and Brazil, it shared common patterns of settlement, colonization, and history with most English-speaking islands in the Caribbean. As a direct product of British colonial rule, therefore, Guyana has inherited a social legacy in which African slavery and the plantation system play dominant roles. Guyana, or "the wild coast," was first settled by the Dutch in the early seventeenth century. It changed hands many times between European rulers before it finally became a British colony in the early nineteenth century. During this time, especially up to 1833 when slavery was abolished, the population of the colony became very mixed. It included the indigenous Amerindians, various European colonizers, and many Africans brought over as slaves, beginning in the seventeenth century. After the abolition of slavery, further groups of immigrants arrived, including Portuguese, Chinese, and East Indians, who today form more than 50 percent of the Guyanese population.

Mittelholzer was born in New Amsterdam, the second largest town in Guyana, to William Austin Mittelholzer and Rosamond Leblanc Mittelholzer; he was of mixed descent, with forebears from Switzerland, France, Great Britain, and Africa. In the feudalistic structure of colonial Caribbean societies, mixed-blood or colored families such as Mittelholzer's belonged to the well-to-do, or at least respectable, urban middle class.

The photograph of Mittelholzer that he selected as the frontispiece for his autobiography and captioned "A swarthy boy—scowling at the camera because he was forced to wear an effeminate silk bow instead of a tie"

Accordingly Mittelholzer attended Berbice High School, one of the best secondary schools in the colony. Even at this early stage, aspects of character emerged that marked him as resolutely single-minded and idealistic, if not highly idiosyncratic and self-destructive. By the account of fellow novelist Jan Carew, who also attended Berbice High School, Mittelholzer was expelled from school at the age of thirteen because he kicked a teacher—an Englishman—who had referred to Guyanese as "natives." The force of his reaction and his passion in confronting issues such as racial prejudice or political oppression appear in Mittelholzer's writing and, more tragically, in his personal life.

Mittelholzer's firm resolve to become a writer in colonial Guyana is nothing short of miraculous. In the 1920s he began submitting stories to British periodicals such as the *Strand, Pearson's,* the *Royal,* and the *Connoisseur.* Despite the continuous rejections of his early submissions, he never gave up. Since there were almost no publishing outlets in his homeland, Mittelholzer realized that his best hope lay in England, where he sent most of his manuscripts. Yet, ironically, success first came in a local paper, the *Daily Chronicle*, which published one of his stories in July 1928. The *Connoisseur* accepted another story in 1929, but his manuscripts for full-length books were all rejected. With typical defiance Mittelholzer published his first book, *Creole Chips* (1937), locally at his own expense and sold it door-to-door. Real success did not come until 1941, when his novel *Corentyne Thunder* was published by Eyre and Spottiswoode in London, marking the beginning of a career in which Mittelholzer produced more than twenty novels, a travel book—*With a Carib Eye* (1958)—and an autobiography, *A Swarthy Boy* (1963). In sheer volume his output has not been surpassed by any other Caribbean novelist.

Mittelholzer moved to Trinidad in December 1941 to join the Trinidad Royal Volunteer Naval Reserve; he received a medical discharge in 1942. In March of that year he had married Roma Halfhide, and they remained in Trinidad until 1948. Then, with their young daughter, they immigrated to England for the express purpose of advancing his literary career. Mittelholzer established a precedent to be followed by West Indian writers such as George Lamming, Samuel Selvon, and others who emigrated in the 1950s.

The London publication of *A Morning at the Office* in 1950 brought Mittelholzer more critical acclaim than he had previously received. *Shadows Move Among Them* (1951) was followed by *Children of Kaywana* in 1952. At this stage of his career Mittelholzer felt confident enough to give up his typist job with the British Council and try to earn a living by his writing alone. In May 1952 a Guggenheim Fellowship in creative writing took him to Montreal, Canada, but the frigid weather soon made him move to Barbados, where he stayed with his wife and growing family (four children) until returning to England in May 1956. The quick succession in which his four books from this period came out—*The Weather in Middenshot* (1952), *The Life and Death of Sylvia* (1953), *The Adding Machine* (1954), and *The Harrowing of Hubertus* (1954)—meant that Mittelholzer was producing one novel or more each year, a rate he maintained virtually uninterrupted until his death in 1965.

Mittelholzer's astonishing productivity was partly helped by a cordial relationship with the London publishing firm of Secker and Warburg, which produced thirteen books by Mittelholzer from 1952 to 1961. But he seemed inclined to include bizarre or gratuitous references to sexual deviation, abnormal psychological states, physical cruelty, and supernatural or occult practices. In 1961 such references caused Secker and Warburg to object to "pornographic elements" in the manuscript for *The Piling of Clouds* and break off their long-standing relationship with Mittelholzer. Once again, as in the 1920s and 1930s, Mittelholzer had great difficulty getting his work published, though Putnam's produced *The Piling of Clouds* later in 1961. Now, however, he also had to cope with negative reviews and personal problems. He had divorced his first wife in May 1959, and after he married Jacqueline Pointer in April of the following year, he found it increasingly difficult to support two families. It was about this time (1960) that Mittelholzer made a second attempt at suicide (his first having been in the 1930s). Although he recovered enough to reestablish his literary career, he remained troubled. Five years later, when he was only fifty-five years old, Mittelholzer ended his life by dousing himself with kerosene at his Surrey, England, home and setting himself afire.

Mittelholzer's novels can be grouped by their subjects, themes, or genres. The novels of the Kaywana trilogy, for example, form a distinct group dealing primarily with one family and the history of Guyana. Other groups of novels are concerned with experimental political theories, abnormal forms of psychology, sexual deviation, the supernatural, and the occult. Inevitably these subjects and themes overlap. In *Corentyne Thunder* Mittelholzer discusses theories of political order, heredity, and sexual behavior, but his main achievement in the book is his vivid portrayal of Indian peasant life in colonial Guyana. For example the main character, Ramgolall, is a miser who prefers to hoard the meager earnings from his agricultural and dairy farming rather than pay for medical help when he is sick. The impoverished living conditions of Ramgolall and his family contrast with the more affluent life-style of a middle-class, colored family, the Weldons. *Corentyne Thunder* also displays Mittelholzer's remarkable sensitivity to variations of weather and the beauty of the landscape, features of all his novels, especially those set in the Caribbean.

Mittelholzer's skill as a perceptive observer of people and landscapes is deployed even more effectively in *A Morning at the Office*, which offers insights into a broader cross section of Caribbean society through the presentation of the lives of members of the office staff of a trading company

Dust jacket for the last novel in the Kaywana trilogy, historical novels about Guyana and the fictional van Groenwegel family

in Port of Spain, Trinidad. Apart from the lowly office boy Xavier, who is of African descent, there are Indian characters, such as Edna Bisnauth and Mr. Jagabir; Olga Ten Yip, who is Chinese; Nanette Hinckson, who is colored; and the Creole Laura Laballe, a local white of French extraction. In fleshing out these characters, Mittelholzer reveals a finely nuanced understanding of the subtle interrelationships among factors of race, color, class, and economics in Caribbean society. White characters form an essential feature of this social fabric. There are Everard Murrain, who is the chief accountant and assistant manager, and George Waley, the manager; their superior social, economic, and professional status is based less on ability than on their skin color. This point is underlined in a bitter outburst from Sidney Whitmer, an idealistic young Englishman who feels disappointed by the ease with which "my white skin alone was sufficient to give me entrée into the best circles." The pervasiveness of racial distinctions in Caribbean society is represented throughout Mittelholzer's Caribbean novels. In a later novel, *Latticed Echoes* (1960), for example, the colored hero, Richard Lehrer, expresses curiously racist views about Africans to a black American journalist. Race was a factor in

Mittelholzer's own life: he describes his father as a "confirmed negrophobe" in *A Swarthy Boy* and refers to his father's "momentous disappointment" when he—Edgar—was born with a "swarthy" complexion.

As a composite portrait of West Indian society, illustrating typical conditions, issues, and concerns, *A Morning at the Office* was more popular and critically successful than *Corentyne Thunder*: it established Mittelholzer's reputation as a writer and probably encouraged him to move away from strict social realism into a type of fiction he evidently found more to his liking. By setting his novels in imaginary social milieus, he allowed himself the freedom for speculation and often extravagant theorizing about his most deeply felt preoccupations. To some extent these preoccupations appear in all his novels, but they predominate in *Shadows Move Among Them*, *The Weather in Middenshot*, *The Mad MacMullochs* (1959), *A Tinkling in the Twilight* (also 1959), and *The Wounded and the Worried* (1962), which are set in generic locations in the Caribbean or in Britain but portray eccentric behavior and bizarre situations that would strain credulity were it not for the extraordinary narrative power and convincing vividness of the writing.

The location of *Shadows Move Among Them* is Berkelhoost, an imaginary Guyana jungle settlement, which is run by the Reverend Gerald Harmston who has power of life and death over the largely Amerindian inhabitants. Essential public services are carried out by squads of citizens organized in paramilitary fashion; antisocial acts such as stealing are brutally punished and, if repeated, can lead to execution; and although free love is advocated and practiced, the inhabitants must also use contraceptives so that their birthrate can be controlled by Harmston, who selects special couples, at suitable intervals, for procreation. Although Berkelhoost is ostensibly designed to allow maximum individual freedom, paradoxically it denies as much freedom as it allows. Harmston's utopian ideas seem inspired by a strong dislike for bourgeois morality based on conventional Christian beliefs and ethics; but while Berkelhoost effectively does away with some of the more hypocritical conventions that prevailed in Western societies during the first half of the twentieth century, it does not implement alternative conventions with equal effect or plausibility. Instead Harmston is portrayed as a dictator who runs Berkelhoost with rigid, authoritarian ethics that border on fascism.

The forms of social and political organization practiced in Berkelhoost are probably influenced by Clive Bell's *Civilization* (1947), to which Mittelholzer frequently refers in his writings. Bell argues against what he calls "unqualified liberty" and suggests that antisocial behavior should be ruthlessly eliminated in order to safeguard civilized values. But the means employed to eliminate antisocial behavior in Berklehoost are themselves too rigid and brutal to be considered civilized. Thus, in *Shadows Move Among Them*, and in most of Mittelholzer's novels dealing with imaginary settings and eccentric behavior, whereas admittedly imperfect Western social conventions are shunned, they are replaced by customs and practices that are obviously too restrictive or cruel to be workable. These novels therefore contain elements of self-contradiction. At the same time, Mittelholzer creates entertaining situations and events.

Among other novels grouped with *Shadows Move Among Them*, *The Mad MacMullochs* is set on a plantation in Barbados. Two young men, Ronald Barkley and Albert Grahamstown, are gradually indoctrinated into the ways of the MacMulloch plantation, which are as permissive as those of Berkelhoost, at least in intention.

Once more the price for permissiveness is strict supervision, planning, and social control. Yet these self-contradictory ideas are interwoven into episodes of intrigue and embroidered with sexual complications that are immensely entertaining. Undoubtedly Mittelholzer's interest in political order and social planning was also influenced by his upbringing in a colonial environment with plantation mores that evolved out of a rigid, feudalistic, and hierarchical relationship between white masters and black slaves. Although slavery was long abolished, these mores survived in the postcolonial Caribbean well past the middle of the twentieth century. Certainly they flourished in Mittelholzer's lifetime, when they could be clearly seen as a historical inheritance of patterns of brutality and servility that came to be linked with social and economic status. In any case, as a keen student of history Mittelholzer was aware of these patterns at least as they existed in his homeland. His best fiction is the Kaywana trilogy, which provides a dramatized reconstruction of Guyanese history from the period of Dutch settlement in the early seventeenth century to 1953, when elections were held in Guyana for the first time under a system of universal adult suffrage.

The Kaywana trilogy consists of *Children of Kaywana, The Harrowing of Hubertus*—later republished as *Kaywana Stock* (1959)—and *Kaywana Blood* (1958). *Children of Kaywana* deals mainly with the early period of European settlement in Guyana and the establishment of colonial rule in the three counties of Essequibo, Demerara, and Berbice. Perhaps the most outstanding event in this first novel is the account of the slave rebellion in 1763. The second novel takes the historical record from 1763 to 1797, while the third novel is concerned with events from then until 1953, including a second slave rebellion in 1823. Although the Kaywana novels stick to the main facts of Guyanese history, they also contain much invention. The two slave rebellions, for example, are accurately described down to the names of slave leaders and government administrators, and the places where each incident happened; but the personalities, their speech, mannerisms, relationships, and idiosyncrasies are largely a matter of adaptation, embellishment, or invention. The imaginative and intellectual task involved in this process of reconstructing history is formidable, requiring not only an encyclopedic grasp of three and a half centuries of historical details but also their translation into a coherent narrative. Nothing illustrates Mittelholzer's skill as a novel-

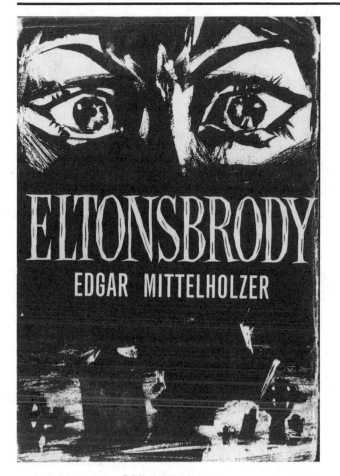

Dust jacket for one of Mittelholzer's Gothic novels, a story of black magic and necrophilia in Barbados

ist more than his successful accomplishment of this task. Two of his chief techniques are close adherence to the chronology of historical events and a focus on the biography of a single family, the van Groenwegels. The Kaywana novels may therefore be read as a family biography in which are interwoven significant episodes in the unfolding of Guyanese history.

The van Groenwegel family chronicles begin with a sexual liaison between Dutch settler Adriansen van Groenwegel and Kaywana, daughter of an Amerindian woman and an English sailor. The progeny of Adriansen and Kaywana, and of Kaywana and another Dutchman, August Vyfuis, form the principal characters in the three novels. Kaywana's great-granddaughter Hendrickje is ironically descended on her mother's side from Kaywana and Adriansen, and on her father's side from Kaywana and Vyfuis. Whether such inbreeding is simply a result of the author's invention or reconstruction of the actual sexual complexities of Caribbean plantation life,

it is one example of the varieties of sexual deviation found in the Kaywana novels. The list also includes rape, incest, flagellation, castration, fornication, adultery, and sadomasochism. In the process, Mittelholzer features characters who are either strong or weak, perverse or pure, good or evil, and two of the most outstanding are Hendrickje and Hubertus.

Hendrickje van Groenwegel (in *Kaywana Blood*) has been called a magnificent harridan, queen of the van Groenwegels. Her distinguishing quality is unwavering allegiance to jungle justice. She inherits an indomitable fighting spirit, or so she believes, from forebears who bravely resisted European raids on their plantations, and she is determined that this spirit should pass on to her descendants. She persecutes those of her children she considers weak and expresses openly atheistic views to her son, Adrian, for whom she harbors an ardent, incestuous passion. When she finally dies, hacked to death by rebellious slaves, it seems a vindication of her stern and cruel philosophy of life. Hendrickje's career may be taken as representative of her own family and of a whole class of plantation owners who treated their slaves with great savagery, sometimes even burying them alive. Her death and the torture and humiliation the rebellious slaves visit on their white captives are therefore typical aspects of the amoral code that, according to Mittelholzer, governed plantation ethics.

Hendrickje may seem utterly without pity, but Hubertus (in the second novel of the trilogy) struggles more sensitively with the contradictions inherent in plantation ethics. In 1763, at the age of thirty-six, Hubertus is plagued by religious doubt and skepticism, but he is more of an agnostic than an atheist. He is deeply conscious of a conflict between spiritual and sensual values, and even if he does not completely reconcile this conflict, he feels, by the age of seventy, that he can believe in both God and himself.

There is no doubt about the serious, moral interest of questions raised by Hendrickje and Hubertus. Yet Mittelholzer has often been accused of exploiting such issues for their titillation value. Thus it may be argued that the nonmoral code of ethics in the Kaywana novels serves largely as a convenient backdrop for unlimited sensuality. It is not that Mittelholzer was unaware of the unbalanced nature of this code and its potential for evil; rather, he exploited—in the interest of exciting storytelling—its equal potential for indulgent and unrestrained behavior. One never loses sight of the van Groenwegel biography. By the time of the third novel the family's survival is threatened by the fall in the price of sugar at the end of the eighteenth century and later by emancipation of the slaves. The threat is met by the heroic spirit of the van Groenwegels, seen in Dirk, eight generations removed from Adriansen. Dirk is inspired by old family letters that provide a link with the past. In this way the family spirit persists through the nineteenth and early twentieth centuries until its eclipse in 1953, when universal adult suffrage puts an end to the old planter-laborer, or master-slave, social structure on which the van Groenwegels had depended for over three centuries.

By the time *Kaywana Blood* was published, Mittelholzer had become known as a popular novelist to be reckoned with. Reviewers acknowledged the exotic scenery, vigorous action, flamboyant characters, and rich adventure in his books. If they did not fully grasp the significance of his themes, it was because these tended to be obscured by romantic action enlivened by excitement and sensuality. His main concern with the problem of a nonmoral world order had some validity in his historical novels dealing with West Indian planters, who felt disillusioned and powerless because their interests were constantly ignored by metropolitan decision makers in Europe.

In his travel book, *With a Carib Eye*, Mittelholzer suggests that West Indian plantation owners could not help feeling cynical when decisions were made about their lives by colonial overlords in Europe who either did not consider their needs or were forced to consider other, more pressing metropolitan needs. But a similar cynicism is evident in his novels dealing with early-twentieth-century or contemporary society. The story of the heroine in *The Life and Death of Sylvia*, for example, is one of unbroken adversity, until she loses her life in almost masochistic frenzy while still under thirty years of age. Sylvia's father is English, and her mother is of mixed Amerindian and African blood. Sylvia develops an Oedipus complex because she is constantly in the company of her father, while her illiterate mother leads the life of a recluse, sewing clothes in her room all day. After the death of the father, Sylvia faces poverty bravely, rejecting the lust of one of her employers and the temptation to become a prostitute. But she neglects her health and soon succumbs to pneumonia. Her death does arouse some degree of tragic feeling,

suggesting that her struggle against evil has not been completely predetermined to be lost. This tragic feeling, however small in degree, means that a code of amorality is not adopted with wholly cynical approval in *The Life and Death of Sylvia*. Implied questioning of this code is evidence of Mittelholzer's attempt to introduce serious aims alongside entertainment in his works.

As a professional writer with an exceptionally high rate of productivity, he may have been tempted to emphasize or favor entertainment. One may get a sense of Mittelholzer's own possible speculation on the genre of his writing from the comments of Colonel Heather, a minor character in *Of Trees and the Sea* (1956), who, when asked about the form his book on Barbados will take, replies: "What other form could a book on Barbados take but poetical comedy-fantasy? . . . With marine, botanical and religious overtones as a matter of course." This is a clue to the genre not only of Mittelholzer's Barbadian novels but to elements in several other novels.

Of Trees and the Sea illustrates the strong sense of entertainment, for the sake of itself, that plays such a frequent role in Mittelholzer's writing. Strange events occur in the Barbadian village of St. Stephen. There are mysterious sounds reputedly made by an "atomic" mule. This strand of the plot is combined with two affairs: between Mr. Drencher, a middle-aged eccentric, and Patricia Wert; and between Patricia's husband, Roger, and Daphne Sedge. Patricia and Daphne become pregnant. A whimsical denouement has Drencher marrying Daphne to give respectability to her pregnancy, while Roger is led to believe that he is the father of Patricia's child; Roger also discovers that he is the son of Drencher's deceased brother. When Drencher explains that he used an air-raid siren and a loudspeaker to produce the loud noises called "atomic" sounds, the reader may well wonder about the point of such prankish behavior and apparently nonsensical events; but Mittelholzer's skill as a storyteller, inventing a variety of characters and creating suspense, tends to hold the reader's interest.

Other novels in the category of "comedy-fantasy" contain Gothic elements related to necromancy and the occult. *My Bones and My Flute* (1955) carries the subtitle *A Ghost Story in the Old-Fashioned Manner* and has the haunting atmosphere of tales by Edgar Allan Poe. There is an old manuscript supposedly written by a Dutch planter who was murdered in the slave rebellion of 1763 in Guyana. The planter puts a curse on

Dust jackets for the first and second novels of an unfinished, erotic trilogy linking sexual and psychological deviance with death

anyone finding the manuscript, enjoining the finder to seek out the planter's remains and give them a Christian burial. The story focuses on the journey by the narrator and his friends through a jungle settlement in the upper reaches of the Berbice River in Guyana, nearly two hundred years after the manuscript was written. During their search they often hear the music of the planter's flute, experience nightmares, and encounter "spectral manifestations." Eventually they find the grave and give the planter's remains a Christian burial. *My Bones and My Flute* also supplies a good example of Mittelholzer's sensitive evocation of the Guyanese landscape, with its dense tropical growth and rich animal life and sounds:

> There was real fascination in the night. A dense aliveness and intelligence—a watching calm. The jungle, silhouetted like a ragged lace-edge against the starry sky, held an indigo smile in its wet depths, and the occasional chirp of a frog concealed a chuckle that might mean anything. The

river's soft sibilance now and then took on a derisive quality. From out of its secretive gloom it seemed deliberately to breathe up into our faces a humid vegetable miasma expressive of its deep antagonism towards us. The fireflies, engaged all the while in their deadly silent dance, heightened the vigilant aspect of the dark, as though within the core of their cool incandescence they knew the meaning of this night—the hidden motive behind the jungle's smile, the message the frog kept chirping at intervals, the reason for the river's sly animosity.

If *My Bones and My Flute* is a "comedy-fantasy," there is more fantasy than comedy in it. There is even less comedy in *Eltonsbrody* (1960), which is set in Barbados and is altogether more horrific, eerie, and macabre, dealing not simply with the supernatural but with black magic and necrophilia. But with typical expertise Mittelholzer engages the reader's interest in a series of mysterious events that are finally solved, however shocking the solution might be.

Novels such as *A Tinkling in the Twilight* and *The Wounded and the Worried* are more concerned with abnormal psychology. They can be classified as "comedy-fantasy," but they are set in England. There are elements of fantasy, for example in the experience of Brian Liddard, hero of *A Tinkling in the Twilight*. Liddard records the process of his apparent mental deterioration. The first stage, called "Doubt," shows him in a state of confusion and voluntary sexual abstinence. In the second stage, "Preparing," his sexual fantasies are overpowering, and he contemplates suicide. In the third stage, "Farewell Time," Liddard imagines himself in the future. Then he resumes normal sexual activity and is restored to sanity. The comic aspects of his experience are evident:

> The night before in bed, it was true, the temperature in the Labyrinth had risen a trifle and I had a spot of trouble with an old buzzard and a nymph. The old buzzard—a milky-bearded "deva" from the Upper Planes—had leant over my bed, his aura glowing blue and pink, and wheezed hoarsely: "See your mistake now, you fool! You should have gone the whole hog. When you employ half-way methods you turn half-spirit—and that's too bad. No wonder you've been having these howling hallucinations!" He coughed and capered back into the Astral World.

The combination of frivolity and vulgarity downplays the intensity of the hero's apparent mental illness, and like so much else in Mittelholzer's fiction, Liddard's strict, military routines and "astral" experiences do not live up to their promise of seriousness. The label of "comedy-fantasy" therefore seems appropriate.

Sexual liaisons are prominent in two novels that form part of an incomplete trilogy: *Latticed Echoes* and *Thunder Returning* (1961) are novels of technical experimentation employing a leitmotiv method taken from music. As in music certain descriptions or phrases are associated with certain characters and are used to introduce them or indicate their presence. But this new technique is less eye-catching than the intrigue in *Latticed Echoes* between Richard Lehrer and Tommy Rowleyson and their respective wives, Lydia and Lindy. Lehrer seduces his friend's wife, and she becomes pregnant. This leads to a fight between Lehrer and Rowleyson in which neither is seriously injured. The relationship between the two wives, however, is less tranquil and ends eventually with the suicide of Lydia Lehrer. Psychologi-

Dust jacket for Mittelholzer's novel about group therapy

cal illness, sexual permissiveness, and deviation are therefore linked with death in many of Mittelholzer's works, whether his subject is psychology, politics, history, racial matters, or the supernatural. The result is a potent and intoxicating fictional brew as notable for its erotic stimulation as for anything else.

The Wounded and the Worried is about psychologically damaged people who seek rehabilitation through group therapy. Mittelholzer's last two books published in his lifetime, *The Aloneness of Mrs. Chatham* (1965) and *The Jilkington Drama* (also 1965), are about complications produced by neurotic temperaments. An earlier novel, *Uncle Paul* (1963), introduces elements of espionage. But in all these novels, including two set in the Caribbean—*A Tale of Three Places* (1957) and *The Weather Family* (1958)—the action is replete with a wide variety of sexual liaisons, many of which could be considered perverted or at least unusual. These novels confirm Mittelholzer's success as an erotic writer of great power. Regardless of his themes, settings, or subject, eroticism is pervasive in all Mittelholzer's novels. Even if characters such as Hendrickje, Sylvia, and Garvin Jilkington are interesting because of their philosophical ideas, their sexual perversions prove more memorable. In many cases eroticism derives from sexual deviation, as in *The Piling of Clouds*, where forty-seven-year-old Pruthick, an inspector of taxes in London, who has a thoroughly respectable background, rapes and strangles a nine-year-old girl whose parents have come to regard him as a trusted friend.

Despite its large volume, Mittelholzer's work has not received the critical attention that some of the better-known West Indian writers can claim, not only in Great Britain and the United States but increasingly in Third World countries. Curiously no book-length study of Mittelholzer's work has yet been published. Shorter studies, however, acknowledge Mittelholzer's innovative contribution to Caribbean literature in establishing the novel as a medium for social criticism, philosophical speculation, and pure entertainment. Some critics also notice his penchant for airing pet theories about social evils and political organization, even to the extent of becoming dogmatic or sermonizing. There is some controversy about Mittelholzer's exact attitudes on race and color, no doubt due to his ambivalence on these subjects and his repeated, admiring comments within his novels on such well-known but not universally sympathetic figures as Nero, Adolf Hitler, and Benito Mussolini. In general, it is believed that his West Indian novels are more successful than those set abroad, and that they have greater social density and meaning. While most critics praise Mittelholzer's exceptional productivity, inventiveness, and narrative fluency, some admit that the seriousness of issues he raises is not always sustained but rather gets overlain by violent and sensational action. Nevertheless, the critical response to Mittelholzer's novels is generally positive, although more detailed studies, especially of his later works, are badly needed.

Mittelholzer was moved by powerful obsessions that enter his fiction. As some critics have claimed, *A Morning at the Office* may be artistically his most distinguished work because of its wit, ironic detachment, and objectivity. Yet, based on the relative paucity of similar works of social realism in Mittelholzer's output, this was not the genre he most liked. What he liked may be called

comedy-fantasy or erotic comedy-fantasy, a genre of fiction in which eccentric characters are driven by obsessions, even perversions, to engage in strange pursuits or outlandish activities invariably connected with some aspect of sexual permissiveness or deviation. Novels with such characters and activities poured out of him in a compulsive stream that ran virtually without a break for nearly twenty years; these are the works on which his reputation as a writer will finally rest. These novels contain much eroticism, violence, and perversion that might be considered sensational. But in the historical plantation context of the Kaywana novels, where such sensational activities seem appropriate, Mittelholzer's fiction achieves its greatest success. Similar success is also achieved in novels such as *The Life and Death of Sylvia*, where the more sensational aspects of Mittelholzer's action are tempered or reduced. Thus Sylvia emerges as the most sensitive and compassionate study of character in all Mittelholzer's novels. As a rule Mittelholzer's characters are obsessive or exaggerated, like Hendrickje, who protests a little too much about the virtues of a nonmoral universe. Although Sylvia exists in the same universe and is destroyed by its harsh, arbitrary ethics, she never celebrates these ethics or pays them lip service: she plays the victim's role with silent defiance and thereby wins more sympathy than Hendrickje.

Mittelholzer's achievement may be more fully understood if one considers two factors that appear to have strongly influenced his writing. The first has to do with his restrictive puritanical upbringing, which he describes in his autobiography. This upbringing, enforced by his mother and aunts, aroused a powerful and deep-seated resentment in him, which may explain the force of his rejection of bourgeois forms of social organization and morality based on Christian ethics. When this resentment is coupled with the obstinacy that built up in Mittelholzer in response to the constant rejection of his manuscripts in his early career, one has more insight into the iconoclasm that inspires the sweeping away of middle-class Western social conventions and ethics in so many of his novels. The other factor that influenced Mittelholzer is also autobiographical in the sense that it concerns the literary and cultural sources available to him in colonial Guyana. Apart from Clive Bell, Mittelholzer's reading consisted of the Bible, the ghost stories of M. R. James, tales of Buffalo Bill, Victorian penny dreadfuls about Nelson Lee and Sexton Blake, and the British periodicals to which Mittelholzer submitted his earliest manuscripts. In addition he was addicted to silent-film serials based on the novels of Sax Rohmer, with their racist stereotypes of Chinese and Jews and their morality of a dualistic universe in which good can only overcome evil by superior force and cunning, and often not at all. When all this is combined with the brutality and cynicism of Caribbean history in which Mittelholzer steeped himself, one can begin to understand the violence, eroticism, and comedy-fantasy of his fiction.

Biographies:

Frank A. Collymore, "Edgar Mittelholzer: A Biographical Sketch," *Bim*, 11 (June-December 1965): 23-26;

Arthur J. Seymour, *Edgar Mittelholzer: The Man and His Work* (Georgetown, Guyana: National History and Arts Council, 1968);

Jacqueline Mittelholzer, "My Husband Edgar Mittelholzer," *Bim*, 15 (June 1976): 303-309;

Jacqueline Mittelholzer, "The Idyll and the Warrior: Recollections of Edgar Mittelholzer," *Bim*, 17 (June 1983): 33-89.

References:

Frank M. Birbalsingh, "Edgar Mittelholzer: Moralist or Pornographer?," *Journal of Commonwealth Literature*, 7 (July 1969): 88-103;

Birbalsingh, "Indians in the Novels of Edgar Mittelholzer," *Caribbean Quarterly*, 32 (March-June 1986): 16-23;

Jan Carew, "An Artist in Exile—From the West Indies," *New World Forum*, 1 (12 November 1965): 23-30;

John Figueroa, Introduction to Mittelholzer's *A Morning at the Office* (London: Heinemann, 1974), pp. vii-xx;

Michael Gilkes, "Edgar Mittelholzer," in *West Indian Literature*, edited by Bruce King (London: Macmillan, 1979), pp. 95-110;

Gilkes, "The Spirit in the Bottle: A Reading of Mittelholzer's *A Morning at the Office*," *World Literature Written in English*, 14 (April 1975): 237-252;

Patrick Guckian, "The Balance of Colour: A Re-Assessment of the Work of Edgar Mittelholzer," *Jamaica Journal*, 4 (March 1970): 38-45;

William J. Howard, "Edgar Mittelholzer's Tragic Vision," *Caribbean Quarterly*, 16 (December 1970): 19-28;

Louis James, Introduction to Mittelholzer's *Corentyne Thunder* (London: Heinemann, 1970), pp. 1-6;

Colin Rickards, "A Tribute to Edgar Mittelholzer," *Bim*, 11 (January-June 1966): 98-105;

Roydon Salick, "The East Indian Female in Three West Indian Novels of Adolescence," *Caribbean Quarterly*, 32 (March-June 1986): 38-46;

Arthur J. Seymour, "An Introduction to the Novels of Edgar Mittelholzer," *Kyk-over-al*, 8 (December 1958): 60-74;

Geoffrey Wagner, "Edgar Mittelholzer: Symptoms and Shadows," *Bim*, 9 (July-December 1961): 29-34.

John Munonye

(28 April 1929 -   )

Charles E. Nnolim
University of Port Harcourt, Nigeria

BOOKS: *The Only Son* (London: Heinemann, 1966; London & Ibadan: Heinemann, 1980);
Obi (London, Ibadan & Nairobi: Heinemann, 1969);
Oil Man of Obange (London: Heinemann, 1971; London & Exeter, N.H.: Heinemann, 1983);
A Wreath for the Maidens (London: Heinemann, 1973);
A Dancer of Fortune (London: Heinemann, 1974);
Bridge to a Wedding (London: Heinemann, 1978).

John Munonye

Had there been no Chinua Achebe and no *Things Fall Apart*, John Munonye as a novelist would have occupied a different, more elevated niche in the annals of Nigerian literary history. Yet Munonye has not been eclipsed by Achebe as an Igbo writer. The point at which the two writers converge –the issue of culture conflict—is also the beginning of their divergence. For Achebe the conflict of cultures attendant on colonial intrusion into Africa could only result in a general sense of loss for Africa, and all Achebe's heroes—including Okonkwo, Ezeulu, and Obi Okonkwo—are losers in some ways, as African culture, clan unity, religion, and language suffered setbacks during the colonial period. But while Achebe's philosophical pessimism wears the face of tragedy, Munonye's novels of culture conflict ultimately wear the face of comedy, as they record the collective *gain* from Africa's contact with Europe. While for Achebe the Igbo encounter with Europe led to the death of several protagonists and to the death of the Igbo way of life, for Munonye the coming of Europeans with their new administrations, religions, and schools offers his protagonists new challenges, opens new vistas, and provides better alternatives that lead to progress. In Munonye's novels villagers move out to the new cities, form social clubs and cooperatives, and change backward-sounding village names to more modern prototypes in order to attain modern amenities such as pipe-borne water, electricity, and good roads for their villages. To effect these changes, old men who are regarded suspiciously as antagonistic to progress are ignored, and young men, iconoclasts eager for a definite break with the past, are appointed to committees that transform their communities. These are optimistic village novels focusing on the plight of the common man and on his efforts to improve his lot in life.

Munonye agrees that the predicament of the common man in society is the central theme of his novels. And society for him is not just an abstract idea but a living body that in many cases hinders rather than helps the individual who is weak, lonely, and neglected. Traditional societies were sometimes indifferent to their members, exploiting the talents of an individual for their own selfish ends but making no arrangement for his welfare. Nor are modern societies any better; especially if they have no welfare schemes, no social services, no insurance coverage, no free education, and no free health-care services. Munonye complains, "Nigeria sends millions of Naira [dollars] to the liberation movements outside Nigeria. This is not wrong in itself. But this altruism is not matched by similar concern for the downtrodden in Nigerian society who need to be liberated from the slavery of poverty, ignorance and disease."

Munonye was born on 28 April 1929 in Akokwa, in eastern Nigeria, and was the fourth of seven children. His education began in his hometown, then continued at Christ the King College in Onitsha, where he graduated in 1948. Going on to University College, Ibadan, he studied history, Latin, and Greek, earning his B.A. in 1952. He moved to England for his postgraduate work, attending the Institute of Education at the University of London. After returning home, he took a job with the Nigerian Ministry of Education in 1954, later becoming principal of the Advanced Teacher Training College at Owerri. He has now retired. Munonye is married and has two children.

One cannot read Munonye for long without being struck by his abiding interest in family relationships. He revels in depicting boys and girls living in a close-knit family, with their parents anxiously watching them grow up, fall in love, and get married. Munonye extols happy marriages and happy family life within the nuclear household. Of this interest in the family he says:

> One wonders if it could be otherwise. We grew up in the village and we knew how closely knit families, even on an extended scale, had to be. Life wasn't terribly secure then. Everybody knew everybody, and everybody came to everybody's defence or rescue, when anything threatened or happened from outside.... I must also admit that the family has a fascination for me as an individual—a happy family—Maybe because I came from a large family.... But the man-woman relationship, the husband-wife, the mother-son, it has a fascination for me. It is poetic and—let me add a word—pure.

Often this interest in the family centers on the welfare of children. In *The Only Son* (1966) it

Dust jacket for the first novel in Munonye's tragicomic trilogy about colonialism, Christianity, and changing family relationships

is the delicate relationship between a troubled widow and her only son that supremely matters. *Obi* (1969) focuses on the temptations that beset a young, childless, Christian family under pressure from society. In *Oil Man of Obange* (1971) excessive parental love and concern for the welfare and educational progress of the children lead to disaster. Munonye admits his interest in young people: "I think my books have been of particular relevance to the young in Nigeria. I just have a feeling for young people; they can really absorb things. I always tell my colleagues ... that the best thing we can do for the country is to produce good teachers who will go out and teach the young."

Munonye's novels are set at definite periods in Nigerian history. He says that the "mental span" of his novels is fifty years—from the early days of colonial administration in Nigeria (as in *The Only Son* and *Obi*) through independence, to the Nigerian civil war (in *A Wreath for the Maidens*,

1973), to post-civil-war events in the 1970s, with attention to the political, cultural, and religious climate. *Bridge to a Wedding* (1978), he asserts, "attempts a dialogue between the old and the new, traditional and modern. We do need the bridge."

In his first novel, *The Only Son*, the major issue is culture conflict, which was in vogue then. Munonye acts as a miniaturist and confines the conflict to the delicate relationship between a widowed mother, Chiaku, and her only son, Nnanna, for whose welfare she has denied herself everything, including remarriage, until Nnanna disappoints her by becoming a Christian and going away to live with a white missionary, Father Smith, at distant Ossa. *The Only Son* is the beginning of a trilogy that includes *Obi* and *Bridge to a Wedding*. Therefore those who discuss *The Only Son* in isolation, as a tragedy, forget the open-endedness of this work. Chiaku, disappointed in her son's "apostasy," remarries to begin a new connubial life for herself (she is already expecting a baby), while Nnanna charts a new life of adventure full of promises under the tutelage of Father Smith.

In the trilogy the position of Munonye as a writer of comic vision emerges clearly. Nnanna's double exile ends in a triumphant return for him as the protagonist in *Bridge to a Wedding*. He becomes the perfect example of the hero of myth coming back home with a boon and with a more enhanced status than when he left. Munonye's optimism, his belief in the efficacy of the new order—Christianity and the new civilization—is most clearly stated within the trilogy. Embracing Christianity fully, without looking back, has stood the Kafo family, for example, in good stead. Their daughter Rose, convent educated and a role model for the younger ones, marries Ebeneto Junior, one of the first graduates from the new university, "a disciplined one [who] had never been associated with any of the excesses by which many of the young men from the university are known." Thus Munonye's optimism about the new order includes a belief that modernity need not necessarily spoil the young. Colonialism, which causes such tragic consequences for Africans in the novels of Achebe, becomes the leverage for progress in Munonye's fiction.

Oil Man of Obange, which may eventually earn stature as Munonye's most artistically constructed novel in the timelessness of its tale and the leanness of its narrative, is a novel conceived in irony with a touch of Molière: love of one's children, a great virtue in itself, when indulged in in-

ordinately, leads to the ruin of parents; and the brilliance of all six of Jeri's children in school, a great blessing for many a parent, goads Jeri on to disaster in his effort to cater simultaneously to the welfare of all the children with his meager resources. Jeri's ambition for the success of his children at school is the kernel of his failure as a father.

In *Oil Man of Obange* the major theme is hidden in Mica's school motto: "*Da nobis recta sapere*" (Give us the right discernment), which implies that had Jeri the oilman had the wisdom to train only those children he could afford to support with his meager resources, he might have succeeded. The unstated social vision is an indictment of Nigerian society, which has no social welfare system that could come to the aid of Jeri and his children. The novel highlights the pathetic sense of loss, the wasted efforts, the indifference of society, and the feeling that the orphaned children of Jeri will sink into an abyss of poverty and neglect after his death—that all his efforts have been in vain.

A Wreath for the Maidens, Munonye's most complex and ambitious novel, is a roman à clef regarding the Nigerian civil war. It could easily rank as Munonye's least successful novel in its lack of thematic focus and lack of artistic distance. It is part experience, part biography, and part fiction, full of undigested bits of political philosophy and boiling like a stew into which a potpourri of Nigerian history has been thrown. The subject matter is familiar: the story begins with the struggle for independence by corrupt politicians in Nigeria and ends with the civil war, catching in its sweep both the activities of acid-throwing politicians before independence and the bombing and strafing of the former Biafran territory during the internecine, fratricidal warfare.

The three major political divisions of Nigeria before the civil war are depicted in conflict before Bokenu (Biafra) broke away. In the novel Sakure State represents the North, where Bokenu citizens were massacred, and Doda State is the West, which aided and abetted the aggressive military in subduing Bokenu State. Munonye insists that this novel is a dialogue on the moral issues involved in the Nigeria-Biafra War. The title of the novel was suggested by a quotation from *Iphigenia in Aulis* by Aeschylus: "By the blood of the maidens slain thou shalt pacify the winds." The youths slain during the conflict were sacrificial lambs, as people in positions of power used the op-

Dust jacket for Munonye's novel about a dancer who is also a successful con man

portunity to exploit fellow citizens and precipitate sufferings and privations. For the two idealists in Munonye's book—Roland Medo and Biere Ekonte—the original war they came to fight has abandoned them: "It wasn't . . . a war between the righteous Biafran side and the oppressive Federal side. In fact, it was no longer between Nigeria and Biafra, but corrupt Biafrans versus idealist Biafrans."

A Dancer of Fortune (1974) is unusual in Munonye's canon. The dancer Ayasko is also a mercenary con man who exploits his talents as a dancer to ruin one patent-medicine dealer after another until he establishes a monopoly. Those who argue that, in Munonye's works, society is the victimizer while the individual is the victim, agree that Ayasko turns society's weapons against itself and emerges successful. Because a trickster succeeds and evil triumphs over good, moralists might chide Munonye for teaching the youth that evil pays.

Munonye's *Bridge to a Wedding*, which celebrates the triumphant return of Joseph Kafo, was published in 1978. An unpublished novel written after 1978, "House of Enoch," is about the place of religion and religious affiliations in the lives of Nigerians. Since then, Munonye has turned his attention to short stories, mostly on religious themes. In "Horn of Salvation," "Land of Prophecy," and "The Missing Treasure" he concerns himself with the proliferation in Nigeria of religious groups including Anglicans, Catholics, the Salvation Army, Brotherhood of the Holy Cross, True Sabbath Spiritual Church, Mount Zion Spiritual Fraternity, Divine Fellowship Congregation, Holy Evangelist Assembly, Christ Apostle Healing Sabbath Church, and the Supreme Sabbath Church of the Most Holy Spirit. In these stories Munonye wonders why the same Christian seems as ready to embrace the idol as the cross, why this rush to "ride in a Freudian truck," why this "orgiastic bewildering emotionalism." The escape by Nigerians into religion, Munonye thinks, is an effort "to dwell close to the frontiers of lunacy," to avoid the rigors of "rational, logical or constructive thinking," thus allowing "others to come in to do the thinking for us . . . to think and research and invent and manufacture for us."

One of the paradoxes in Munonye's life after his early retirement from the civil service is the inverse proportion of his literary output to the amount of time he has on his hands. He obviously retired to devote his time to writing, but to his consternation the muse seems to have fled with regular employment. In a mild lament in "Letters from Retirement" he writes:

> I must confess that in my own case I had assumed I would soft-land on retirement and then set out immediately writing, producing wonderful things. But then, it didn't quite work out that way. . . . I felt there was now all the time, limitless time, at my disposal—so why hurry. Next, my very sweet assumptions of the past concerning the environment into which I would be retiring, came in for some very severe tests. In those circumstances, it became almost impossible to settle down to creativity. . . . And my instincts began to blunt. Put precisely, I could no longer see with my usual eyes. Green leaves whose mid-morning sheen had been food for my heart became ordinary to the sight. My perceptions and creative response had dulled. Men, women, boys and girls had changed terribly too. Were they not now too busy, intense, over-ambitious, blustering. In fact, I need to adjust to this new ambience.

John Munonye

Given the serious critical attention his novels are attracting, Munonye can be said to have already earned a secure place among African novelists of the twentieth century. And Munonye will be better known as the years go by.

Interviews:

Bernth Lindfors, "An Interview with John Munonye," in *Dem-Say: Interviews with Eight Nigerian Writers*, edited by Lindfors (Austin: African and Afro-American Studies and Research Center, University of Texas, 1974), pp. 35-40;

Charles Nnolim, "An Interview with John Munonye," *Okike*, 24 (1983): 77-90;

Don Burness, "John Munonye," in *Wanasema: Conversations with African Writers*, edited by Don and Mary-Lou Burness (Athens: Ohio University Center for International Studies, African Studies Program, 1985), pp. 35-39.

References:

Azubike Festus Iloeje, "Optimism in John Munonye's *Bridge to a Wedding*: The Anatomy of a Viewpoint," *Research in African Literatures*, 16 (1985): 525-534;

Iloeje, "From Folk to Formal: Education and Adjustment in John Munonye's *The Only Son*," *World Literature Written in English*, 29 (1989): 7-18;

Charles E. Nnolim, "Structure and Theme in Munonye's *Oil Man of Obange*," *African Literature Today*, 12 (1982): 163-173;

Julius N. Ogu, "The Individual and Society: A Study of John Munonye's Early Novels," *International Fiction Review*, 11 (1984): 90-93;

Benaiah E. C. Oguzie, "Fate in Man's Struggle for Survival: *Oil Man of Obange*," in *African Literature for Secondary Schools*, edited by Oguzie and Ernest Emenyonu (Ibadan: University Press, 1985), pp. 14-24;

Virginia Ola, "The Christian Wives of John Munonye's Novels," *Okike*, 21 (1982): 78-88;

'Bayo Williams, "A Critical Survey of John Munonye's Novels," *Obsidian II*, 2, no. 1 (1987): 74-81.

Lenrie Peters

(1 September 1932 -   )

Thomas R. Knipp
Saint Louis University

BOOKS: *Poems* (Ibadan: Mbari, 1964);
The Second Round (London: Heinemann, 1965);
Satellites (London & Ibadan: Heinemann, 1967);
Katchikali (London: Heinemann, 1971);
Selected Poetry (London: Heinemann, 1981).

The Second Round (1965) is Lenrie Peters's only published novel, perhaps because he realized early that his great literary gift was not for fiction but for poetry, a craft at which he has worked steadily. The results of this labor have been four collections of verse beginning with *Poems* (1964) and continuing through *Satellites* (1967) and *Katchikali* (1971) to *Selected Poetry* (1981). Because Peters lives and works in Banjul, Gambia, at a great distance from the literary centers of Ibadan, Lagos, and Accra, he has not received the attention he deserves; but he has earned critical respect as a thoughtful, intellectual poet. O. R. Dathorne, in *African Literature in the Twentieth Century* (1975), attributes to him "a wider range of ideas than any other African poet." There was an early attempt by critics and reviewers to deracinate and internationalize Peters's verse, but more recent criticism has tended to emphasize his African qualities and themes. As Dathorne points out, "certain qualities of his verse and the selective nature of his experiences identify him as an African poet." Romanus N. Egudu (in *Four Modern West African Poets*, 1977) confirms this view: "The psychology portrayed cannot be other than that of an African."

Lenrie (Wilfred Leopold) Peters was born in Bathurst (now Banjul), Gambia, on 1 September 1932. After primary school in Gambia and secondary school in Sierra Leone, in 1952 Peters began to study medicine at Trinity College, Cambridge University, and trained in surgery at University College Hospital, London, earning his M.D. in 1959. He practiced at hospitals in Guildford and Northampton until the mid 1960s. Since returning to Africa, he has worked as a surgeon in Sierra Leone and Gambia. His chief recreation has always been music, and he is a fine singer. As he

makes clear in some autobiographical poems, from his undergraduate days onward he has felt compelled to pursue his literary avocation in the face of a demanding professional schedule.

One early product of this compulsion is *The Second Round*. Initially well received, it was praised, for example, by Gerald Moore (*East Africa Journal*, November 1965), who called it "a distinguished and memorable work of the imagination." But it has subsequently fallen into neglect. Set in Freetown, Sierra Leone, just before independence, it tells of the return to Africa of Dr. Kawa, a British-trained physician. Kawa is a somewhat autobiographical character possessed of a "subdued temperament and tendency to reflection" and of "noble ideas about progress in Africa." He is quickly caught up in the lives and trials of his Krio family, neighbors, and friends. A series of conventional plot elements are handled without great distinction—including an unfortunate love affair and a neighbor's unhappy marriage. The chief weakness is that this material is not Africanized; it could happen anywhere. In one passage Peters says that "political events flared across Africa like a trail of gunpowder," but he deals neither with these events nor with the problems of tradition and the hearth under the stress of change. The most interesting element in the novel is Kawa's sense of doubleness—of being both a Western physician and an African. The story ends with Kawa preparing to immerse himself more deeply in Africa by accepting a post in a lonely bush hospital.

Poems, published by Mbari Publications of Ibadan, is a slim volume of thirty-three poems. These were written for the most part when Peters was still in his twenties. Collectively they communicate an excessive youthful melancholy mostly unrestrained by the irony and anger that give bite to his later collections. They are marked by expressions of grief, loneliness, suffering, hopelessness, and futility—emotions presented as responses to specifically African problems, the most important of which are the disconnected-

Lenrie Peters

ness between the present and the past in Africa, the cultural clash between traditional Africa and the West, and the disoriented psyche of the Westernized African. Those poems Peters considered the best in this initial volume were incorporated into *Satellites*, the first of the three major collections.

In *Satellites* the speaker is standing in the harsh African present reacting to nature, to history, and to the contemporary human condition, especially in Africa. Most of the nature images in these numbered, untitled poems are violent or decadent. For instance, in the first poem, he sees a "skyflood of locusts." When it descends,

> A bleeding earth
> ferments in agony
> success goes up in smoke,
> returns a deluge of ruin.

Elsewhere the destructive violence is "a sabre shark / [that] lifts and plunges / cutting the emerald / sea." In the poet's response to such a world the affirmations are infrequent, and they come as a demand for faith in a faithless world: "I believe / shout; I believe."

In this natural setting the images of human life are bleak. Futile youth "burns out its fuel";

maturation brings "the panic / of growing older." Hands fumble and shake. Thus as one reads through *Satellites*, one senses an attitude toward the human condition more akin to the despair of the existential pessimists than to the aggressively confident rhetoric of the political leaders of newly independent Africa. In Peters this attitude is made specifically African because it is linked tropologically to experience that is historically African—to cold hearthstones and crumbling huts.

In some of the best poems in the collection Peters portrays the African as the victim of history, bereft and adrift, as in poem 25:

> Bartered birthrite
> Like the chaste membrane
> Is lost for good
> . . . .
> Early strength never returns
> to oppose the grinding artificialities.

In several densely structured ironic poems the persona is located in a shattered present from which he contemplates the past, the process of change, and the present point to which both the person and the continent have come. Speaking for all Westernized Africans, he says in poem 16,

Dust jacket for Peters's only published novel, the story of a British-educated African doctor who has returned to his native country

We have come home
From the bloodless wars
With sunken hearts
Our boots full of pride
From the true massacre of the soul.

As a result of the "massacre" of Westernization, he comes back alienated to a confused moment "when the dawn falters / Singing songs of other lands." And the Africa to which he returns is a "house without a shadow / Lived in by new skeletons."

This is a grim picture sketched by a realist who will not blink or turn away. Near the end of the volume, in the longest poem in the collection, the realist turns satirist. Peters was one of the first African anglophone poets to use satire, and he uses it to accuse the new black leadership of perpetuating the "massacre" of the African soul and expropriating the shadowless house of the modern African state. The guilty are the politicians who "came and went / Meteors about the sky," learning "to beg in style."

Katchikali, a volume of sixty-nine numbered poems, is one of a half-dozen important collections by West African poets to appear in the early 1970s. It is not a happy or hopeful book: its predominant theme is the painful isolation of the individual. But again Peters speaks of this isolation as an African would. To the degree that one can judge these things, a great deal of Peters's personality has gone into *Katchikali*. In different poems, he writes as an artist, a parent, a physician, and an African. This last appellation is the most important and is seen in the design of the book. He places the specifically African poems at the beginning and the end of the volume, creating a parenthesis of Africanness within which the other poems are enclosed.

He depicts the isolation of the spirit in several poems through references to the transitory character of an interracial love affair, but most of the poems focus on the uprooted mind rather than the broken heart, as in poem 4:

The mind
Is like the desert winds
Ploughing the empty spaces
Listless, fastidiously laying down the dust.

In a later poem he personalizes this pain by lamenting his inability to impose meaning on experience: "There where all the opposites arrive / to plague the inner senses, but do not fuse / I hold my head." In another poem this personal feeling has its counterpart in nature itself: "Around me / dead winter trees / wolves howling." This alternating between the internalizing and generalizing of the theme of isolation is important in Peters's poetry. As Edwin Thumboo points out in a 1973 essay, Peters is "mainly concerned with the dissociated sensibility as a contemporary problem" in ways that are speculative, personal, intellectual, and existential.

In "Katchikali," the title poem, Peters examines the possibility of a return to African tradition as a solution to existential isolation. He uses Katchikali, a sacred pond in Gambia, to symbolize an indigenous past in which crocodiles are "as tame as pumpkins." But the pond and the past are defiled by colonial intruders who force press-gangs into the labor of desecration. The result is not that the African is transformed by a return to roots but that he finds himself almost hopelessly trapped in the rubble of the present when "all the institutions crumble." The uprooted men call in vain because the pond's "wisdom is silent." But if the conclusion of the poem is pessimistic because "there are no more answers," the form of the poem is hopeful with a hope signaled by a grammatical shift. Beginning by talking descriptively *about* Katchikali, the speaker ends by talking *to* Katchikali. What begins as a lament ends as an invocation. Like the poet Christopher Okigbo, Peters is "waiting on barefoot," learning perhaps that the most hopeful thing about prayer is not that one is answered but that one can pray at all.

The remaining poems of the collection alternate between cautious expressions of hope in an African future built on an African past, and cries wrung from the isolated heart and from the angry citizen. In the latter tone, with what Ezekiel Mphahlele calls Peters's "rejection of cant— honesty of purpose," he repudiates the political and manipulative exploitation of Africa, as seen in poem 63:

Octogenarian breasts at twenty
    enthroned in pools of urine
    after childbirth, whose future
is not theirs to mould or flirt with mirth

    There is your "self " crushed
    between the grinding wheel
    of ignorance and the centuries.

In 1981 Heinemann published a collection of Peters's verse under the title *Selected Poetry*. Along with selections from the previous volumes, it contains fifty-eight new poems. They are not always as good as the earlier poems: they exhibit less control of the brief, clear line, and there is less use of the vivid structural metaphor. But there are still fine lines and strong poems. As in the past, Peters writes of and out of the moment. The mood and subject shift from poem to poem, but there is a kind of weaving or pulsating of dominant concerns. The sense of discontinuity is always strong in Peters's work, but it is especially so in the new poems. And it is presented in terms of the African past, present, and future. The primary focus is again the present, depicted in the lives of individuals, in the clash of cultures, and in the exploitation of neocolonialism. Juxtaposed is an intense nostalgia expressed in pastoral images of the African past. A third concern is the future of Africa. Especially toward the end of the volume, Peters considers how it will happen and what it will be like.

Among the interwoven themes, the broken dream of the present prevails: a generalized reflection on political and economic life—the greed of the elite and the poverty of the people. Often Peters is compelled to simple, sad assertions: "It has been dismal / since the new freedom came." In one of the best of the new poems (poem 67) he depicts the painful present as the center of Africa's dilemma and his own poetic consciousness:

Sand castles on the beach
within easy reach
of the white tide's
menacing graces

I start in my dreams
calabash world in fragments
my pillow wet with tears
acid centuries of bitterness.

The first quatrain is a superb image of the vulnerability of traditional Africa. The second links the poet's consciousness to the torment of the continent through the dream of the broken "calabash world."

In some of the new poems his response to this broken world is an intense nostalgia—a longing to return to traditional Africa as depicted by pastoral and domestic images. He speaks longingly of "messages / from wood fires and the warm / pungency of cooking." But he, the modern African, is disconnected. This sense of separa-

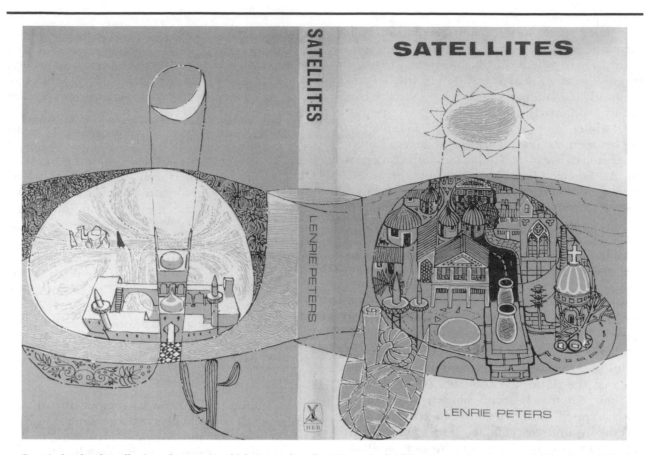

Dust jacket for the collection of poems in which Peters describes Westernized Africans returning home with "Our boots full of pride / From the true massacre of the soul" and finding a "house without a shadow / Lived in by new skeletons"

tion from the healing past is expressed in poem 93, one of the best poems in the collection:

Men are roasting nuts
on wood fires
their laughter like sheet lightning
in the night,
girls dancing by firelight
among green-flowing fields of rice crop.
I, always one removed
from their fun and laughter,
cannot reach them.
They know where sorrow ends,
and I, the broken bridge
across the estuary,
across worlds, cannot reach them.

The whole thrust of the new poems is an attempt to connect the traditional past to some bearable, livable future through the shattered present. Peters is ambivalent about the possibility of such a connection. In one poem he sees traditional Africa welcoming its lost children with singing, drumming, and dancing. In another he warns that "the nearness of nature / has not taught us self-reliance." But he is a realist as well as a humanist. In the final analysis, continental self-reliance is the only message the past *can* communicate to the present to create a future: "the tom-toms are saying / 'This is the time to know yourself.'" Self-knowledge will make possible a collective action, "a mass uprising / from the Atlas to the Cape / to ravage the puppets / perverts, iconoclasts." But as this harsh indictment of the new African elite makes clear, Peters offers no easy answers but only a slim hope and a stern warning, as in poem 85:

Ogun will not help us
Christ will not help us. . . .

We hold our destiny
in rugged palms.

In Peters's poetry what readers see over and over again is the interaction of a strong sense of negation and a rather desperate hope for the future. The center of his poetic vision is the African present with its grief, violence, oppression, loneliness, and death. From this he moves toward a past now lost and a future that is uncertain. In this center of the shattered present, even nature is filled with menace unless cleansed by association with an idealized past.

But there is a progression of feeling and focus from one volume to the next. *Satellites* contains many poems that explore the relation of the African past to the harsh present, "when the dawn falters," as well as poems that record Peters's involvement in the modern African's cyclical journey to the West and back. The untitled poems that begin "We have come home" and "The present reigned supreme" are among his best and most ironic. And running through the volume, providing a kind of figurative unity, are images of the indifferent harshness of nature. The poems in *Katchikali* are often less specifically African. In this collection, Peters writes more of the condition of modern man generally and of the problems facing the world. Even the political satire tends to be more generalized. But it also seems that the center from which he writes is the broken dream of the African present. This is made clear in those poems near the end of the collection in which he uses images of present suffering and future disaster to attack the rhetoric of African politicians. Although the pictures of the present in *Selected Poetry* are still harsh and bitter, the new poems express increased nostalgia for the pastoral African past as well as a cautious assertion of hope for the future. Like the other poets of his generation, Lenrie Peters has found that the conditions of life in contemporary Africa are tragic. As a poet he depicts this tragedy while trying to reclaim the past and point the way to a viable future.

References:

Wilfred Cartey, *Whispers from a Continent* (New York: Vintage, 1969), pp. 213-215;

O. R. Dathorne, *African Literature in the Twentieth Century* (Minneapolis: University of Minnesota Press, 1975), pp. 117-119, 201-202;

Romanus N. Egudu, *Four Modern West African Poets* (New York: Nok, 1977), pp. 93-120;

Egudu, *Modern African Poetry and the African Predicament* (New York: Barnes & Noble, 1978), pp. 85-89;

Ken Goodwin, *Understanding African Poetry* (London: Heinemann, 1982), pp. 48-60;

Thomas R. Knipp, "Lenric Peters: The Poet as Lonely African," *Studies in Black Literature*, 2 (Fall 1971): 9-13;

Ezekiel Mphahlele, *The African Image* (New York: Praeger, 1974);

Armando Pajalich, "Africa e Africanità nella poesia di Lenrie Peters," *Africa* (Rome), 33 (1978): 69-96;

Paul Theroux, "A Study of Six African Poets," in *Introduction to African Literature*, edited by Ulli Beier (Evanston, Ill.: Northwestern University Press, 1967), pp. 110-131;

Edwin Thumboo, "The Universe Is My Book: Lenrie Peters," *African Literature Today*, 6 (1973): 93-111.

Jean Rhys
(24 August 1890 - 14 May 1979)

Elaine Savory Fido
University of the West Indies, Barbados

See also the Rhys entry in *DLB 36: British Novelists, 1890-1929: Modernists.*

BOOKS: *The Left Bank, and Other Stories* (London: Cape, 1927; New York: Harper, 1927);

Postures (London: Chatto & Windus, 1928); republished as *Quartet* (New York: Simon & Schuster, 1929);

After Leaving Mr. Mackenzie (London: Cape, 1931; New York: Knopf, 1931);

Voyage in the Dark (London: Constable, 1934; New York: Morrow, 1935);

Good Morning, Midnight (London: Constable, 1939; New York & Evanston, Ill.: Harper & Row, 1970);

Wide Sargasso Sea (London: Deutsch, 1966; New York: Norton, 1967);

Tigers Are Better-Looking; with a Selection from The Left Bank (London: Deutsch, 1968; New York: Harper & Row, 1974);

My Day: Three Pieces (New York: Hallman, 1975);

Sleep It Off, Lady (London: Deutsch, 1976; New York: Harper & Row, 1976);

Smile Please: An Unfinished Autobiography (London: Deutsch, 1979; revised edition, New York: Harper & Row, 1979);

Tales of the Wide Caribbean, selected by Kenneth Ramchand (Portsmouth, N.H. & London: Heinemann, 1985);

The Collected Short Stories (New York & London: Norton, 1987).

Collections: *The Early Novels* (London: Deutsch, 1984)—comprises *Voyage in the Dark; Quartet; After Leaving Mr. Mackenzie;* and *Good Morning, Midnight;*

The Complete Novels (New York: Norton, 1985).

TRANSLATIONS: Francis Carco, *Perversity* [translation erroneously attributed to Ford Madox Ford] (Chicago: Pascal Covici, 1928);

Edouard de Nève [Jean Lenglet], *Barred* (London: Harmsworth, 1932).

Jean Rhys

Jean Rhys is a significant writer who lived a difficult life full of personal tragedies, setbacks, and self-doubts: three marriages, the loss of her first child and the absence of her second one for long periods, financial strain, and psychological conflict. Out of this, in two very productive phases, came her writing, but these creative years were separated by a long period of obscurity during which she virtually disappeared from the literary scene. She came to international prominence through the publication of *Wide Sargasso Sea* (1966) when she was in her seventies. Rhys's writing and her life story are closely intertwined. She said that she thought the only truth she knew was herself, and certainly most of what she wrote can be easily related to known experiences of hers. But she was separate from her work as well. The facts of her life are often confusingly vague (she herself contributed to the fact that her birth year is often given as 1894 rather than 1890). Yet one can perceive the main currents of her life and how these relate to her fiction, in which she gives shape and clarity to experience.

The issue of the placement of Jean Rhys as a writer has been raised often. Despite her Caribbean birth and upbringing, her move to live in England at the age of sixteen displaced her from direct, prolonged contact with Caribbean culture for the rest of her life. Her early work has a continuous subtext of reference to the Caribbean, and certainly her great work *Wide Sargasso Sea* is centered there, but critics have varied in their perception of her, often reflecting their own concerns in their readings. Feminist critics, such as Helen Nebeker, Nancy R. Harrison, and Deborah Kelly Kloepfer focus on Rhys's portrayal of the political frames around women, whereas Louis James and Teresa O'Connor focus on her identity as a Caribbean writer and the links between colonialism and the situation of women in her work. Poet and historian Edward Kamau Brathwaite writes, in his essay on Caribbean culture *Contradictory Omens* (1974), "White creoles in the English and French West Indies have separated themselves by too wide a gulf and have contributed too little culturally, as a group," to be identified with "the spiritual world on this side of the Sargasso Sea," a statement which can be read as excluding Rhys from full membership in Caribbean identity. However, he was responding to an affirmation of her Caribbean identity by Wally Look Lai, who said that Rhys's white Creole heroine, Antoinette, could legitimately long for a return to the spiritual world of the Caribbean.

Clearly Rhys was a child of two cultural inheritances, with her Creole mother and her Welsh father, but her formative experience was as an insider to Caribbean culture, albeit as a white Dominican. Whichever side of this debate one chooses, she cannot be understood without reference to the Caribbean, for her understanding of race, class, and gender was framed by her formative experience of Caribbean society at the beginning of the twentieth century, which markedly deepened her understanding of gender issues within European contexts. This construction of her identity has been helped somewhat by Carole Angier's useful *Jean Rhys: Life and Work* (1990), which shows Rhys's mental and emotional connection to the Caribbean to have been life-

long. Recent criticism has further stressed her themes of colonization and resistance, which place her fiction in the canon of postcolonial work.

Her placement within another canon, that of European women writers, has produced good critical work, however, despite its limitations. She was first claimed by British and American critics, who mostly remarked on her style. Her first book, *The Left Bank, and Other Stories* (1927), was praised for clarity and economy. A reviewer for the *New York Times* said of her second book, *Quartet* (1929; originally published as *Postures*, 1928), "The style, especially of the dialogue, belongs to the new tradition in prose, which shuns elaboration for sharpness and intensity of effect." Later, in the context of the growth of international awareness of women's issues, her treatment of the woman as victim drew attention. Recently, as a result of developing feminist critical interest in women writers, Rhys has become the subject of several book-length studies, such as Harrison's *Jean Rhys and the Novel as Women's Text* (1988), and the *Jean Rhys Review* publishes a regular bibliography. Within the Caribbean, Rhys has become identified as one who reveals strong connections to the French traditions of Dominica and other parts of the francophone Caribbean. In addition there has been some important work on the intertextuality of Rhys's *Wide Sargasso Sea* and Charlotte Brontë's *Jane Eyre* (1847). Carol Ann Howells's 1991 study of Rhys usefully interrelates modernism, gender issues, and postcolonial concerns. In the context of feminist discussion of the forms of female autobiographical writing, Rhys's autobiographical writing has also become important. There is also a growing interest in her relation with Phyllis Shand Allfrey, the Dominican novelist and political activist, and in the similarities and differences between these two white Creole writers.

Finally, it is important to note that Rhysian criticism is multicultural, reflecting Rhys's own cultural complexities and contradictions. Critics bring to her work their own cultural emphases and biases, emanating mainly from England, the United States, France, and the anglophone and francophone Caribbean.

Jean Rhys was born on 24 August 1890 in Roseau, Dominica, as Ella Gwendolen Rees Williams into the family of a Welsh doctor, William Rees Williams, who, according to Louis James (in *Jean Rhys*, 1978), had left his boyhood home in Caernarvon to try to run away to sea. Then his

Rhys's childhood home in Roseau, Dominica, in a photograph taken in 1970. The gallery has been enclosed, and the garden that once surrounded the house has disappeared.

Anglican-clergyman father allowed him to train on a sailing ship; ultimately he became a ship's doctor. He settled in Dominica toward the end of the nineteenth century. His wife, Rhys's mother, was Minna Lockhart Williams, who was related through her father to John Gibson Lockhart, the biographer of Sir Walter Scott. The Dominican Lockharts were slaveholders on the island, and they experienced the hostility of former slaves after emancipation, when an estate house was burned down in the 1830s. Antoinette Cosway's family has a similar experience in *Wide Sargasso Sea*.

Rhys (choosing the variant spelling of Rees for her professional name) was the fourth of five children and was often alienated from the others and even from herself. In her autobiography, *Smile Please* (1979), Rhys speaks of her unhappiness with the name Gwendolen, because it means *white* in Welsh, and she was convinced that her tall, thin body; her straight, fair hair; and her "huge staring eyes of no particular colour" were causes for despair. All her brothers and sisters had brown eyes and brown hair. Rhys suffered more than the usual physical self-rejection of young girls growing toward puberty because her mother once said (and the child took it to heart) that black babies were prettier than white ones.

After this Rhys "prayed so ardently to be black." As a child she envied black people and later experienced a lifelong ambivalence toward them, which caused her both to love and to hate them jealously. Rhys the writer defended and championed the underdog and thus empathized with black people and with women, both suffering in patriarchal white-dominated cultures. But just as there is a strong undertow of aggression underneath her heroines' passive demeanor, so there is clearly also a definite longing and resentment mixed together in her attitude to black culture. This comes out very clearly in her interviews with David Plante (included in his *Difficult Women: A Memoir of Three*, 1983).

Ironically Rhys's willingness to abandon the racist-supremacist position adopted by so many white West Indians of her day led her into a position of psychic vulnerability, and she herself acquired a feeling of being shut out from the black culture she had begun to love and admire more than her own. Her father was known in Dominica for his unusual racial ease, and within the strict and confined world of her family childhood, which her mother clearly controlled, Rhys grew to desire what she perceived as the greater happiness, the warmth and color of the black world. This desire grew despite some unpleasant experiences, such as her terror at the hands of Meta, the "very black" nanny, who created deep fear and distrust in Rhys with stories of the supernatural and of threats to the child from the insects and creatures that surrounded her, and who was sometimes simply unkind. Rhys would yell "Black Devil" at her when frustrated. That there was a serious racial-psychological stress in the young girl is revealed by her account in *Smile Please* of delightfully smashing with a stone the face of a white doll.

But Rhys was sensitive to the natural beauty and wildness of Dominica, even though in adult life she viewed the island as a place hostile to human beings. Reading was a great consolation to her, and she was drawn to literature as a magical source of escape. From early on she was responsive to color, an aspect of her environment that was to become a developed emotional and psychic code in her fiction. The Caribbean is stunningly colored, and Dominica particularly so. Years after leaving, Rhys was able to write of details of the environment in Dominica with an unusual vividness.

Spiritual matters were also a source of ambivalence in Rhys's early life, and perhaps this explains the sense of spiritual danger perceived by her heroines, especially Antoinette in *Wide Sargasso Sea*. Rhys's family had associations with Anglicanism and Catholicism: her great-grandmother was reputed in the family to be a Spanish countess from Cuba who was converted after her marriage to Protestantism, and therefore, according to the nuns who taught Rhys, was inevitably damned. The cults and beliefs of the African-based culture of black Dominicans, which mingled with such Christianity, also fascinated Rhys. From her warm and affectionate father, whose free and easy ways she liked, she got no clear spiritual guidance, since his offhand view of the whole thing was that "Buddhism is a far more beautiful religion than Christianity." Her mother went to church on Sunday but was not deeply religious. Rhys, however, was deeply involved in the world of the nuns who taught her, and she once wanted to become one of them.

The moral carelessness that characterizes Rhys's fictional characters seems at first quite un-Caribbean, as religion is still central to Caribbean culture, despite the strong threat from materialism, Western culture, and secular political philosophies. The kind of devil-may-care approach to life of which Rhys wrote so often still has behind it, however, an awareness of good and evil and of the spiritual risk taking that those who distrust the justice of the material world may embark upon. Despite the influence on her of the British/Parisian world of the twentieth century, with all its rationalism and lack of central commitment to spiritual values, Rhys remains a Caribbean writer in her awareness of the opposition of good and evil, and the misery of many of her characters after their moral risk taking shows her to be aware that such behavior is not likely to lead to any good result.

At the age of sixteen Rhys left Dominica for England, not to return for many years, and then only for a short visit in 1936. Perhaps her voluntary exile came partly out of a sense of being alone, even within her own family. Sibling rivalry shows up clearly in the story of the smashing of the doll: the fair doll, destroyed so gleefully, was given to Rhys, but she wanted the dark one given to her sister. Maternal ambivalence might also have been a factor—Rhys writes in *Smile Please* that her mother often said she did not know what would become of Rhys. The question of maternal images in Rhys's work and of the relation between her and her mother has provoked much critical discussion. O'Connor cites an important passage from Rhys's early "Black Exercise Book," describing an encounter between the child and her mother: the mother's arms are taken away, and the child thinks, "I knew no one would save me and I must do it." Kloepfer argues that textualization (the act of writing itself) enabled Rhys to come to terms with her mother, and Harrison discusses the idea of a "mother-text" in Rhys's work. Rhys says in *Smile Please* that, as a child, she had an image of two books as signifying God—a larger one and a smaller one, the latter of which she interprets, as an adult, as having been her mother's book, a sewing book with needles inside.

Rhys's first experiences of Great Britain, in 1907, almost inevitably caused some culture shock. Instead of being in Wales, her father's homeland, she had to deal with attending a strict school for girls in Cambridge (the Perse School). Despite her father's Anglican, middle-class origins, which might have cut him off from the Methodist, working-class, Welsh masses with their warm, clannish, ebullient, and creative culture, Wales would have been an easier place for a West Indian to start. Her account of reaching London—after an enjoyable voyage during which she gained some attention as a singer in a concert—is given in *Smile Please*. There is a constant aware-

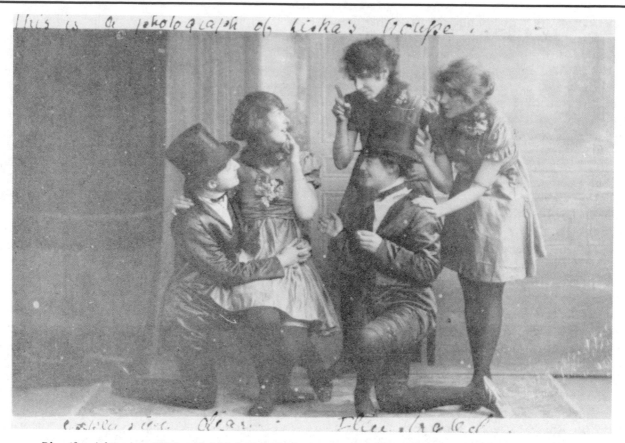

Rhys (far right), circa 1910, with Liska's Troupe, the British acting group with whom she toured for two years

ness of lack of color, warmth, and ease. Color is an important and subversive emotional code in Rhys's writings, both fictional and autobiographical. Soon Rhys rebelled against the life of school and asked to train for the stage. She got support from her father and passed the entrance examination for the Academy of Dramatic Art in London. The aunt, Clarice Rees Williams, who was supposed to be keeping an eye on her was disapproving. Actresses were thought of as little more than courtesans or worse. Unfortunately, on 19 June 1910, William Rees Williams died of a heart attack, and Rhys's financial support came to an end.

Her mother wrote, asking her to come home immediately, but Rhys refused, feeling, as she states in *Smile Please*, that "they didn't want me back." Instead she got a job in the chorus of a musical comedy titled *Our Miss Gibbs*. There followed a period of about two years during which she toured Britain and experienced life in a theatrical troupe: dingy boarding houses; cold, poor food; and the lively companionship of other girls in the same situation. By this time she was strikingly pretty and loved colorful, elegant clothes (a

love thwarted, while she was under her aunt's care, by the dictates of economy and propriety, and by limited financial resources when Rhys was taking care of herself).

This period led to the beginning of her writing career. The major event that concerned her at this time was the affair she had with Lancelot Hugh Smith, a wealthy but emotionally handicapped stockbroker, forty years old to her twenty, who had a house off Berkeley Square in London. According to Carole Angier (in *Jean Rhys*, 1985), Smith came from a well-established family of bankers, M.P.'s, and diplomats. His background was impeccably British upper class (Eton and Cambridge). Men of that group have often been taught a neurotic attitude to women and sexuality: sex is to be enjoyed with women of a lower class or of dubious reputation, or even with prostitutes; marriage is for making an alliance with a woman of one's own class and for the production of children. Smith was not the worst of his type, for rather than pick up his sexual pleasure in a brothel, he met Rhys (then calling herself Ella Gray) at a supper party and saw his role in her life as not simply exploiter but also as an opener of doors for her advancement. He wanted to help in her career and provided for her for about six years after she had an abortion, and long after the affair was finished. Rhys told Plante, "People say he was a villain. He wasn't. People don't understand. He was kind to me when I had no one else to help me. And if he left me after the abortion, well. . . ."

With her love of fine surfaces, comfort, color, and romantic dreams, "Ella Gray" was not very observant of reality, and when the ending of the affair came, it hurt her so traumatically that she apparently never loved again so fully and freely in her life, despite her three marriages. She lived in a world of theatrical illusion and continued to be attracted to surfaces. She had a concern with makeup, which was to go on all her life. Rhys the writer frequently dwells on details of makeup as a clue to character. Other aspects of her life at this time, which Rhys put into the lives of her heroines later on, included lack of financial security, passive-aggressive responses to other people and circumstances (often resulting in her own depression and inertia), bleak awareness of the injustices of the world, and a sense of having to go on alone, rather than return to her family or find a true companion. Alcohol became a way of coping with loneliness and despair. In *Smile Please* Rhys says she stopped loving books when she began to live in England, and that this lasted for several years, so an important and healthy way of escape was closed to her.

But another source of sanity and release became available. Living in a room in Fulham in 1914, with some financial support from Smith, she went for a walk one day and noticed some quill pens in a stationer's window in the colors she loved—red, blue, green, and yellow. She bought them to put in a glass and cheer up her room, but she also bought some black exercise books, with stiff covers and red edgings, and some nibs, a penholder, a bottle of ink, and a cheap inkstand. She recalls in *Smile Please*, "after supper that night . . . it happened. My fingers tingled, and the palms of my hands." She began to write and continued late into the night. Next day she continued, despite a threat from her landlady that she might have to leave because of disturbing the man below by walking about, crying, and laughing until three o'clock in the morning. Rhys dealt firmly with this problem and won the confrontation, although she promised to take off her shoes in the future. She did not look again at the notebooks produced then for seven years,

though in fact what she had done was to learn how to write the pain of her affair (and all other pains) out of her system. She also moved out of the room and went back to Bloomsbury. Her habit of writing a diary in emotionally tense or elated times was established.

However, there is more to a writer than a need to unburden the self of dangerously intense inner chaos. To be heard, noticed, and appreciated, a writer needs skill, a style, and a commitment to the craft and profession of writing. For an immature woman, such as Rhys clearly was—incapable of taking responsibility even for herself in an adult fashion—that style would take some time to come. For a while longer Rhys drifted, doing odd jobs as a model or in the theater and working in a wartime canteen in London as a volunteer. Then in 1917 she met her future husband Jean Lenglet, who was half-French and half-Dutch and said he was a journalist. He was far from the Anglo-Saxon element in British society to which she was hostile in life and in her work. She was looking for escape, fun, and comfort, and when Lenglet proposed after a few weeks, she accepted. She worked in a pensions office until 1918, when she joined him in Holland. Early in 1919 she told Smith she was getting married and thus would not need his allowance. According to Angier he tried to warn her off Lenglet, but she was determined. Perhaps, Angier suggests, he knew that Lenglet was a French spy. But for Rhys the marriage, which began on 30 April 1919, was a new beginning, a new life.

The couple did not settle in Holland but went to Paris not long after the marriage. They lived cheaply and were constantly on the move. Both of them worked, Lenglet somewhat mysteriously, Rhys as an English tutor to some children of a wealthy family. She became pregnant, but the baby, Owen, born on 29 December 1919, quickly sickened and died in the hospital. To Plante, Rhys said she did not know why—perhaps she had been a bad mother. Angier gives the cause of death as pneumonia. A devastating aspect of all this, beyond the death itself, was that Rhys and Lenglet were trying to cope by drinking champagne as their son was dying: they were not there at the time of death and did not know until the next day. Afterward Lenglet moved to Vienna and took a new job, Rhys joined him, and they seemed able to live more comfortably. But it soon became clear that Lenglet had been obtaining money by false pre-

Rhys's first husband, Jean Lenglet, and her daughter, Maryvonne, circa 1930, after the couple's separation

tenses, (selling stolen goods), and despite the fact that Rhys was pregnant again, they became fugitives, often moving. By the end of 1922 they returned to Paris, and Rhys tried to ease their poverty by offering to translate articles Lenglet would write for the English papers.

As a result of trying to sell these, she made a contact, a Mrs. Adams, who was impressed enough with her style to ask about her own writing. Rhys showed her the early diaries, which Mrs. Adams edited and sent to the well-known writer and publisher Ford Madox Ford, then living in Paris. He also thought the writing worth working on, but suggested "Jean Rhys" as a pen name. This occurred in 1923, the year Lenglet was finally arrested, tried, and sent to prison, leaving Rhys destitute. An important aspect of this time seems to be the absence of Maryvonne, their daughter, born in May 1922 in Belgium. Angier and Thomas Staley (in *Jean Rhys*, 1979) state that she was left until the age of six months in a nurs-

ery in Brussels, and after that she was not with her mother in Paris until she was three. Certainly, in Rhys's fiction that deals with these years in Paris, which reflects other important aspects of Rhys's life, there is no mention of the experience of single parenting. The absence of the maternal role at this time was perhaps what kept Rhys relatively immature and more vulnerable to Ford's quasi-paternal, manipulative interest, although, judging from Ford's novel *When the Wicked Man* (1932) and some other sources from the period, Rhys was also capable of causing others to view her as manipulative.

Through Ford she met writers in the Parisian literary set, including Ernest Hemingway and James Joyce. She was already writing the stories that were stimulated by her experiences in the Caribbean, Vienna, and Paris, stories that would eventually be published in 1927, with Ford's introduction, as *The Left Bank*. He helped her with these. His interest, like Hemingway's and that of many other writers of the time, was in the development of a precise, clear style. There was no thought of women and men writing differently: to be taken seriously a woman had to accomplish something similar to the prevailing male-dominated vision of literary excellence. Ford is witheringly explicit on the subject of women writers (in his introduction to *The Left Bank*): he says that his interest in Rhys's technique came from her "instinct for form," which he claims is possessed by "singularly few writers of English and by almost no English women writers." The book is "extraordinarily distinguished by the rendering of passion," but this rendering is done through a controlled, dispassionate narrative voice, which distances the reader from any untoward involvement in the emotional experiences being described. Thus Rhys's characteristic tone was established partly through the mentorship of Ford, and her lifelong writing voice of clarity, precision, and coolness—often applied to situations of appalling intensity and chaos—was developed.

Rhys had become sexually involved with Ford in the mid 1920s, and she became miserably dependent on him and his companion, the Australian painter Stella Bowen. The story of this ménage à trois became her first novel, *Quartet* (the title she preferred), a work turned down by Cape, the London publishers of *The Left Bank*, because they feared Ford might sue for libel. Chatto and Windus, who published it in 1928, changed the title to *Postures*. The novel was completed after the ending of the affair with Ford and after Lenglet's release from prison, while her marriage was still intact and she was with Lenglet in Amsterdam. Under the pen name Edouard de Nève, he wrote his own fictional version of the situation with Ford, a novel entitled *Barred* (published in 1932), and Rhys translated it for him, despite its relative hostility to herself. But by 1927 she was separated from Lenglet and back in England, where she met the man she would ultimately marry after her 1932 divorce, Leslie Tilden Smith, a literary agent and publisher's reader; their wedding came in 1934. She was about to settle down to some years of writing and seeing her work coming out. The 1930s saw her publish three novels, *After Leaving Mr. Mackenzie* (1931), *Voyage in the Dark* (1934), and *Good Morning, Midnight* (1939). She also wrote drafts (including something for her later novel *Wide Sargasso Sea*) and stories. She was clearly and finally a writer.

Leslie Tilden Smith, Rhys's second husband, whom she married in 1934

The Left Bank, though not uniformly impressive, contains elements so characteristic of Rhys's later work that it stands as an indication of how far her writing identity was developed at the beginning of her career. The opening story, "Illusion," is a succinct presentation of Miss Bruce, a rather masculine Englishwoman living in Paris, who has a wardrobe full of brilliantly colored, daringly designed clothes that are a complete contrast to the sensible, discreet clothes she wears. Her cheerful, pleasant nature and her admiration of feminine women are traits of a character who is always in control, never vulnerable in public. This kind of woman contrasts absolutely with Rhys's usual heroines—Fifi, for example, in "La Grosse Fifi"—who are needful of men to the point where they must become victims of them. Fifi supports a faithless gigolo who finally kills her, and her fat, overblown appearance and admission of being old and ugly are signs of the lack of self-respect and self-confidence that is the mark of the Rhysian female. The stories are told in a clear, very disciplined prose and are full of detail, particularly physical detail of characters and of colors.

Most of the stories can be linked to Rhys in some way: her life in Paris, in Vienna, in various bars; her time as a model or among the bohemian artists; her experiences with Lenglet—a husband on the run for theft, a prison story; and a story about the reality, as opposed to the romantic image, of being a mother. Some stories deal with the Caribbean—"Mixing Cocktails" and "Again the Antilles," for example—or with Caribbean characters in Paris. Some deal with genteel poverty, or with the rich who deal out charity to those they consider talented or amusing in some way.

One of the most slyly clever stories is "A Spiritualist," which shows a man visiting his dead mistress's apartment. Madeleine was a woman who never crossed him, and so he loved her. But her passivity in life seems suddenly changed after death, when a large block of marble crashes into her closed sitting room and terrifies both him and the housekeeper. A woman who knew the couple laughs when she hears this and says Madeleine must have been furious that she missed him. This story contains the depressing notion that all a man wants is a woman who never disturbs his comfort and his sense of his own centrality, but that under her apparently total willingness to accept his will is a strong and fierce aggression. This, too, is a characteristic of Rhys's women.

Reviewers understood that this book was a mature, accomplished beginning. The critic for the *Saturday Review of Literature* said, however, that although Rhys's vision was not yet clarified, her "tricks of the trade are already mastered." She was compared to Katherine Mansfield by the critic for *New York Times Book Review*, who also said Rhys gained her effects as much by what she omitted as by what she included.

Quartet has a more ambitious, carefully constructed plot, based on Rhys's experience with Ford and his companion, as well as Lenglet's term in prison. But for all its closeness to autobiography, the writing is crisp and controlled by the cool distance of the style. There is a relaxed narrative voice, which occasionally addresses the reader.

The analysis of the central character, Marya, is dispassionate and not particularly positive. She is "reckless, lazy, a vagabond by nature," she sees danger and moral chaos, and yet she still involves herself in them. The clarity with which she perceives the Heidlers, the intuition that tells her nothing good will come of her associ-

ation with them, the need she has to stand by her husband—none of these good impulses wins out against apathy, a love of comfort, and a willingness to abnegate responsibility. The novel is the first of Rhys's extended treatments of the amoral nature of passive femininity and is an indictment of it. On the other hand, the coldness and lack of scruples of Lois Heidler and the self-indulgent coarseness of her husband are hardly better, nor is the charming weakness, immorality, and fecklessness of Stephen, Marya's husband. Rhys's world is frequently one in which there is no clear good, but mainly there are predatory people, some better than others at obtaining victims. Even the weak are predatory, forever looking for someone else to bear their burdens.

Once again the familiar elements of Rhys's early experience surface: Paris; the poverty of a young woman; the artistic community (among whom the friendly and supportive are also sometimes without resources and disposed to borrow when funds are necessary); sensitivity to colors and to place; and acute awareness of the physical appearance of individuals. The style is very controlled, even when exploring, usually in a laconic way, intense emotional conflict, and Rhys often uses landscape, weather, or colors to denote a strong undertow of feeling. It is also clear by this stage of her work that Rhys was not interested in making her heroines completely like herself. When all was apparently lost for her, Rhys began to write, finding real autonomy when she struggled, as all artists must, to control her material. Marya, by contrast, like the women in most of the stories in *The Left Bank*, knows of no way to attain such freedom and space.

Quartet was discussed by reviewers and later critics both for its stylistic achievements and for its bleak, modernist perception of human nature, particularly that of females. The critic for the *Saturday Review of Literature* compared the novel to Ernest Hemingway's *The Sun Also Rises* (1926). Staley, in his study of Rhys's work and life, said the novel is "deeply suspicious of all human motivation."

Rhys's association with Leslie Smith, her second husband, began when he undertook to place her first novel with a publisher. According to Angier, Ford made the connection between these two, which is very ironic, for whereas Ford represented yet another controlling, needy, cruel, selfish male force in her life, Smith was gentle, unassuming, passive, not particularly successful, but nurturing and not at all destructive toward Rhys.

Dust jacket for the 1967 London edition of Rhys's 1934 novel, which is based on her early notebooks about her love affair with Lancelot Hugh Smith

However, he could not marry her until his father, who disapproved of the relationship, had died, and Smith had a little money left him. They finally married on 19 February 1934. But, as in the case of her other two husbands, he was never able to provide her with enough money to feel secure and comfortable, and Rhys's uncertain moods meant that she was not able to sustain housekeeping for long.

Angier makes an important point about this second marriage when she says that Rhys never wrote about a woman being taken care of, and yet Smith did look after her domestically (he often cooked, cleaned, and washed) and professionally (he typed her work; took it away from her when it was finished but when she was still agonizing over it; edited it; sold it; and handled her business affairs with publishers). Smith was not really much rewarded for this extraordinary degree of male support for a woman writer. It meant that the early years of this marriage saw Rhys producing three major works. But Rhys could also be destructive, especially when drunk, and was sometimes abusive and violent to Smith,

once tearing up his work and throwing his typewriter out of the window. Also during this period, in 1936, the couple paid a visit to her birthplace, Dominica; the trip was not a complete success. Jean evidently felt that her childhood there had been eradicated by history itself, by the changes in political power and the place of her people in society. But she wrote to her friend Evelyn Scott that she was enjoying the beauty of it and the relative isolation. She said she felt jealously protective of the island: "I don't want strangers to love it except very few whom I'd choose."

Despite the strains of genteel poverty, of not seeing much of her daughter, Maryvonne, and of Smith's ups and downs—having to give up his literary agency and return to being a publisher's reader—Rhys had enough stability and quiet during the 1930s to be productive. But her vision steadily became more pessimistic and destructive with each novel. *After Leaving Mr. Mackenzie* charts the desolate experiences of Julia Martin, living from hand to mouth by means of allowances from a former lover and, when that ends, by whatever she can cadge from friends, relatives and men she meets. The novel turns the blame on the woman herself, presenting the men as cold and self-contained but sensible and not particularly predatory, whereas Julia is openly indifferent to almost everyone and simply concerned with acquiring the means to eat and sleep another night in some cheap, dirty, dismal hotel. One important new facet of the recurrently depressive Rhysian heroine's life is sibling rivalry, for the relation between Norah, the "good, caring" daughter, and Julia, the "selfish, feckless" daughter, and their response to their dying, paralyzed mother are imaginative renditions of the kinds of family tension that can separate sisters and blight two lives by making each one crippled in some important way. Destructive as Julia is, with her excessive drinking, her lack of sexual self-respect, and her seemingly endless desire to sponge off other people as opposed to trying to be independent and self-sufficient, she is a figure to be understood and pitied more than condemned. The work ends with Julia having to return to Mr. Mackenzie briefly, to beg more cash under his uncertain but patronizing gaze: "Women go phut quite suddenly, he thought. A feeling of melancholy crept over him."

Once again the style is clear and controlled, with a devastating capacity to deliver horrifying aspects of Julia's life and feelings in an understated tone that makes the information more painful to read: "She was very tired, her muscles were relaxed, her eyes half shut. She was thinking: 'Nothing matters. Nothing can be worse than how I feel now, nothing.' It was like a clock ticking in her head, 'Nothing matters, nothing matters . . .' Goodnight, she said again, in a cold withdrawn voice." Appearances are once more an important aspect of character. Mr. Horsfield, who survives a sexual involvement with Julia well and can comment at one point that she has given him back his youth, is protected from emotional chaos by his orderly life, but Julia's physical being is slowly destroyed by her inner fragmentation and carelessness. She seems at times odd, crazy, old, and aggressive. Pathetically when she needs to regain some strength, she thinks of new clothes, alcohol, a meal, a change of scene—anything to give an illusion of comfort, freshness, and health. It is a drab novel, when compared to the normally colorful Rhysian palette, and this serves to reinforce the nihilistic vision it presents.

Voyage in the Dark is a revised and fictional version of the original notebooks Rhys wrote about her early love affair with Lancelot Smith. The pro-

tagonist, Anna Morgan, is a chorus girl, as Rhys was, falls in love with a wealthy Englishman of the upper-middle class, is pensioned off at the end of the affair, and drifts into a world of prostitution and despair. The novel ends with her getting an abortion. Anna originally comes from the West Indies, finds England cold and dismal, and thinks of her family and cultural background with nostalgia and some pain. Vivid Caribbean colors are opposed to drab, pale English tones. The novel charts the emotional ruin of a delicate girl, given to self-indulgences, to a love of superficial femininity, and to a desire that those she perceives as strong and possessed of resources will protect and support her. Her idealism and romanticism are flimsy bases for dealing with a hard, businesslike world, and when she is disappointed by her lover, she caves in, morally speaking, and gives up the battle to protect herself against amorality, exploitation, and despair. *Voyage* is written in the Rhysian clipped, understated, economical style, and yet it is a first-person narrative. This gives Anna a curiously detached, insightful manner of speech, slightly at odds with her failure to cope with life. She constantly (in the manner of Rhysian third-person narrators) realizes intelligently what is going on around her without being able to do anything to stop it or to rearrange her life to assure survival. The vivid, impressionistic style of the work struck Florence Haxton Britten (*New York Herald Tribune Books*, 17 March 1935) as relating to the style of the imagist poets. The psychoanalytic critic, Helen Nebeker, has examined the imagery of the voyage into the self in the novel.

The third of Rhys's 1930s novels, *Good Morning, Midnight*, is easily the most negative. Some elements of her previous fiction are reassembled into a more thoroughly negative portrait of the Rhysian woman—this time Sasha Jansen, another protagonist-narrator. Sasha goes to Paris on money lent her by a woman friend, for a rest. There she tries to deal with her past, her unhappy marriage, dead baby, and difficulties in supporting herself. She drinks, takes sleeping tablets, is concerned about her appearance (especially about aging), and knows she is dangerously adrift. Eventually she becomes involved with a friendly and mischievous gigolo who, because of her fur coat, ironically believes her to be someone from whom he can get some support. They are two of a kind. But the ending of the novel is truly horrific: Sasha surrenders sexually to a horrible, impersonal man who lives in the room next

Pages from the manuscript and notes for Wide Sargasso Sea *(British Library, Arts Council Collection of Literary Manuscripts,
Add. Ms. 57857, f. 119ᵛ, 120ʳ)*

to hers. This coupling has the force and meaning
of a giving of the self to the devil and of a total
abandonment of principle and self-regard. It is
the lowest point reached by any of Rhys's heroines yet.

Once again the style contributes much to
the shock of the reader's apprehension of the
scene. Sasha is concerned about which of his two
dressing gowns the man usually wears: "I must
find that out—it's very important." This is the ultimate end of taking surfaces seriously and marks
the damnation, so to speak, of the character. Importantly Rhys's first-manuscript version of this
ending has the line "And a ray of light came in
from under the door like the last flash of remembering before everything is blotted out and darkness comes." The editor at Constable who persuaded her to remove this was misguided, because it would have reinforced the sense of eternal perdition that is the feeling of the novel's
final moments. Kate O'Brien (*Spectator*, 16 June
1939) commented that the novel is "femininely
acute and painful, and the end very pitiful, very
bitter." Louis James, however, sees the novel as
bringing Sasha, in her involvement with the gigolo, to a moment of love and meaning, a "culmina-

tion of the search which has been passed through
in the four novels."

Good Morning, Midnight marked the end of
Rhys's run of major works for a long time, for
she disappeared after 1940 from the literary
scene so totally that many people thought she
was dead. Of course, World War II was an important element in this. Smith joined the RAF.
Maryvonne was not heard from for five years because of the war. (She was with Lenglet in Holland, was imprisoned, and joined the Resistance
after her release.) Rhys wrote some stories and evidently was working on an early draft of *Wide Sargasso Sea*, but life was a strain; then in late 1945,
just as she and Smith were hoping to take up
their quiet civilian life again, he died of a heart attack. Once again, someone was at hand to help:
Smith's cousin Max Hamer, in his early sixties
then. Hamer was a solicitor and the executor of
Smith's will. On 2 October 1947 he became
Rhys's third husband. Another gentle but hopelessly unworldly man, Hamer proved incapable
of fending for himself and his wife, despite his solicitor's training. Rhys was in her fifties, in a
shaky state, and she ended up in Holloway
Prison for a few days in 1949, after an assault on

a neighbor. But worse was to come. In 1950 Hamer was arrested for fraud. He spent two years in prison and lost his right to practice as a solicitor. He came out to rejoin Rhys, but their prospects were not good after that. By this time Maryvonne had been married for some years and was living in Holland.

Rhys's letters (published in 1984) illuminate her perceptive awareness of the nature of her difficulties, even while she continued to be relentlessly dependent and mostly unhappy. She remarked in 1946, in a letter to Peggy Kirkaldy, that she had wasted a lot of energy fighting physical ugliness and that this had been "my great mistake." In her fiction Rhys presents characters who never seem to act on any perception of a difference between surface ugliness and moral, or inner ugliness. Too often, the heroines end up missing the fact that the latter is the dangerous one, easily coexisting with pretty clothes, make-up, and a pleasant round of activities.

Rhys's letters show astute insight into her writing at the time, which in her opinion was not going well. Certain aspects of her character were, according to these private documents, very close to those of her fictional characters. She wrote to Maryvonne in 1949 that she would try to pull herself together, and one important aspect of this was to "buy a cheap dress"; there were "things like lovely colours to hang on to."

A break came in 1949, when Selma Vaz Dias adapted *Good Morning, Midnight* for theatrical presentation. Rhys was so lost to public view that Dias's husband had to place advertisements in the *New Statesman* and the *Nation* to find her for the permission; she responded positively. This contact led to a revitalization of Rhys, for, as she wrote to Dias on 9 November, "You've already lifted the numb hopeless feeling that stopped me writing for so long." Also in 1949, however, she blamed writing itself for making her miserable, saying in a letter to Kirkaldy on 6 December: "I never wanted to write. I wished to be happy and peaceful and obscure." But this is said in a letter that expresses her fear of being hated for being too "exalted." Like her heroines, Rhys seems scarcely ever to have felt a confident right to have a decent, comfortable life. One might perhaps trace this back to her sense of inferiority and rejection within the family in Dominica. Her denial of her own need for space, achievement, and happiness was perhaps the cause of the anger that turned inside and made her savagely depressed and often passive-aggressive, the psychological situation about which she writes so often and so revealingly in her work. This troubled attitude also separates her from the bulk of modern feminist writing, which seeks to find ways of increasing women's self-confidence, autonomy, strength, and capacity to be resourceful, in order to help them to be free of dependency, insecurity, and self-destructive behavior. Rhys diagnosed the problems of a certain prevalent kind of femininity in her work, but she never seems to have discovered, in her work or in her life, a more secure footing for personal happiness.

The patterns established during the earlier years continued during the 1950s and 1960s for Rhys. Included in *Smile Please* is a passage of self-analysis called "From a Diary: At the Ropemaker's Arms," which Rhys says was written in 1947 while she was separated from Hamer (Angier places the date in the early 1950s, during his prison sentence). The writing is terse, frank, and self-castigating: she "learnt everything too late," and she had to write—"If I stop writing my life will be an abject failure ... I will not have earned death." In the same piece she remarks, "all of a writer that matters is in the book or books." She lists mortal sins as "pride, anger, lust, drunkenness, despair, presumption (hubris), sloth, selfishness, vanity, there's no end to them, coolness of heart," and then comments, "But I'm not guilty of the last. All the others." The important personal events of the 1950s and 1960s were mostly sad: from 1957 both Hamer and Rhys were in poor health. Showing a rare maternal caring, she did try to act as his nurse, until he got too helpless to be cared for at home; he died in 1966.

In 1957 Dias's adaptation of *Good Morning, Midnight* was performed on BBC radio, and the editor and critic Francis Wyndham came into Rhys's life; he became the mentor who would encourage *Wide Sargasso Sea* into existence. The novel was published in 1966 and soon acclaimed. Rhys, at this point frail and in her late seventies, set to work again and wrote steadily until her death on 14 May 1979. Two more collections of stories were published in her lifetime, *Tigers Are Better-Looking* (1968) and *Sleep It Off, Lady* (1976), as well as a collection of nonfiction: *My Day* (1975). She received the CBE in 1978 for her service to literature.

The crowning glory of her career is indisputably *Wide Sargasso Sea*, although critical response to it has been by no means uniformly positive. It

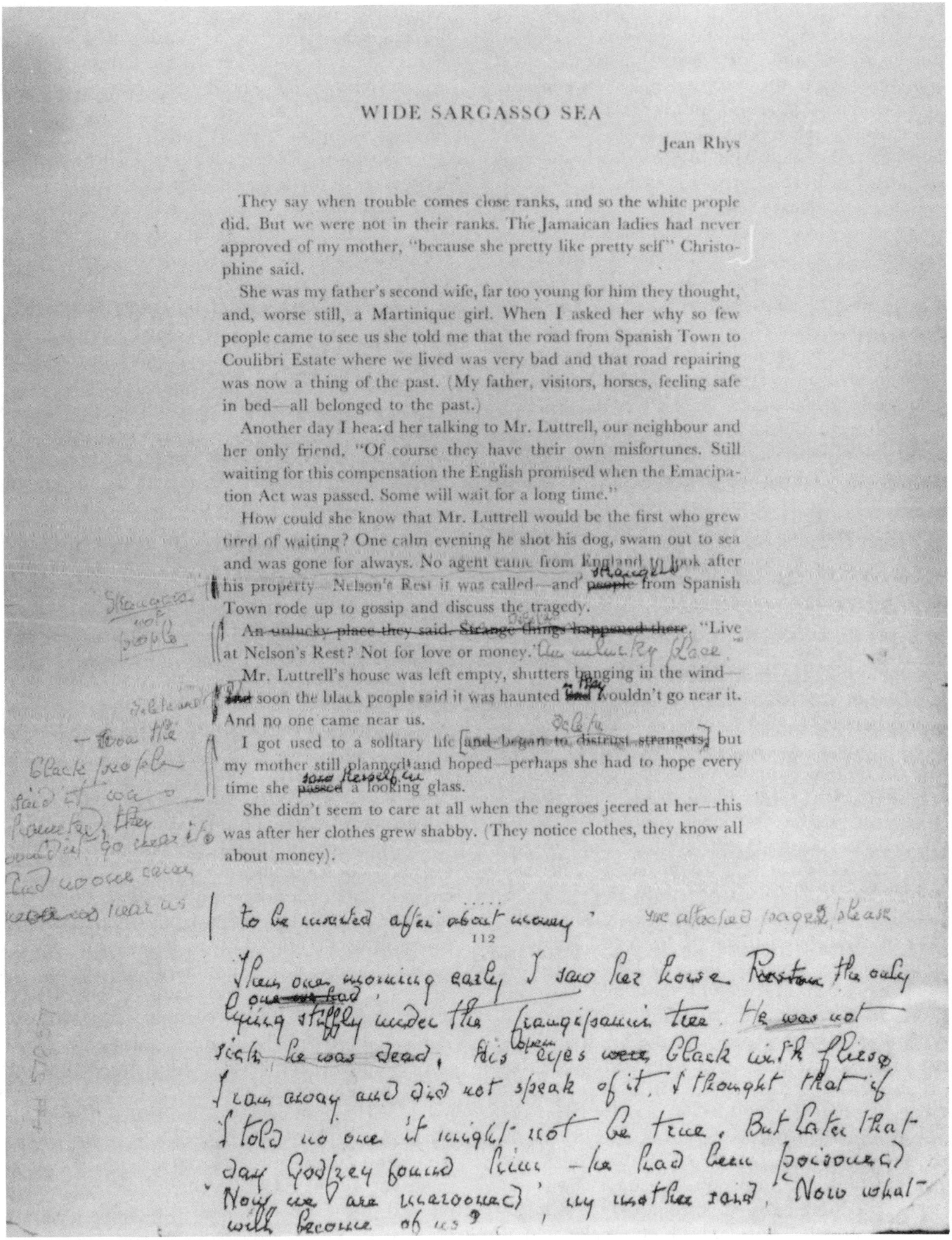

WIDE SARGASSO SEA

Jean Rhys

They say when trouble comes close ranks, and so the white people did. But we were not in their ranks. The Jamaican ladies had never approved of my mother, "because she pretty like pretty self" Christophine said.

She was my father's second wife, far too young for him they thought, and, worse still, a Martinique girl. When I asked her why so few people came to see us she told me that the road from Spanish Town to Coulibri Estate where we lived was very bad and that road repairing was now a thing of the past. (My father, visitors, horses, feeling safe in bed—all belonged to the past.)

Another day I heard her talking to Mr. Luttrell, our neighbour and her only friend, "Of course they have their own misfortunes. Still waiting for this compensation the English promised when the Emancipation Act was passed. Some will wait for a long time."

How could she know that Mr. Luttrell would be the first who grew tired of waiting? One calm evening he shot his dog, swam out to sea and was gone for always. No agent came from England to look after his property—Nelson's Rest it was called—and ~~people~~ *strangers* from Spanish Town rode up to gossip and discuss the tragedy.

~~An unlucky place they said. Strange things happened there.~~ "Live at Nelson's Rest? Not for love or money." *An unlucky place*

Mr. Luttrell's house was left empty, shutters banging in the wind—~~and~~ soon the black people said it was haunted ~~and~~ *They* wouldn't go near it. And no one came near us.

I got used to a solitary life [~~and began to distrust strangers~~] but my mother still planned and hoped—perhaps she had to hope every time she ~~saw herself in~~ ~~passed~~ a looking glass.

She didn't seem to care at all when the negroes jeered at her—this was after her clothes grew shabby. (They notice clothes, they know all about money).

(handwritten marginal and interlinear annotations)
Strangers not people
Solitary — How the Black people said it was haunted; they wouldn't go near it And no one came near us

(handwritten at bottom)
to be inserted after "about money" — see attached page 2 please

112

Then one morning early I saw her horse, Preston the only one we had, lying stiffly under the frangipanni tree. He was not sick, he was dead, his open eyes were black with flies. I ran away and did not speak of it. I thought that if I told no one it might not be true. But later that day Godfrey found him — he had been poisoned "Now we are marooned", my mother said, "Now what will become of us?"

Page from Rhys's proofs for her 1966 novel (British Library, Arts Council Collection of Literary Manuscripts, Add. Ms. 57857, f. 153)

takes its point of departure from *Jane Eyre*, and some critics have perceived the work as too dependent on the Brontë story. But whereas Brontë is concerned with the relationship between the plain governess Jane and her wild, difficult employer, Rochester, a relationship that ends in marriage after the mad Mrs. Bertha Rochester, his wife who has been kept in the attic, burns down his house and causes him injury and physical disfigurement, Rhys's story is of the mad wife in the attic herself and of her experiences with Rochester. Called Antoinette, she is first presented as a beautiful, emotional, childish woman who desperately needs her black mother figure, Christophine, particularly after Rochester's mind is poisoned against Antoinette by her vindictive and jealous half-brother, Daniel Cosway. Rochester, never actually named in the novel, but who can be identified from the intertextual relation between *Wide Sargasso Sea* and *Jane Eyre*, renames her Bertha, after her mad mother, who had become mentally deranged after her house was burned down by angry blacks, Antoinette's brother being killed in the fire, when Antoinette was a child. Thus, in a sense, Rhys's novel begins and ends with fire, symbolic of passionate feelings out of control, of the hate and intensity of human emotions warped by cruelty.

One of the most powerful aspects of Rhys's novel is her delving into the terrible depths of racial antagonisms in the West Indies, first through the vivid depiction of Antoinette's experiences as a child—as when her black friend Tia throws a stone during the traumatic time of the house fire and hits Antoinette's forehead, and as the blood runs down, it is Tia who cries—and then through Rochester's entry into Creole society. The novel does not, however, only show the world of Antoinette through her eyes. Rhys realized, with her usual need for writing controlled prose, that Rochester was the most self-possessed major character she had created and that he would need to carry some of the weight of the story. But, as Angier pointed out in 1985, this tack meant trying to understand the type of Englishman she had blamed for his coldness and rejection since her experience with Lancelot Smith. It also meant examining that coldness as a means of self-protection, a kind of armor a man might use to cover over his weakness, need, and fear of rejection and ridicule. That would not make him a noble character, but it would make him as human and as worthy of pity as Rhys's women heroines, who are patently full of shortcomings and

whom she neither spares nor condemns. Thus *Wide Sargasso Sea* has a balance that makes it deeper than her earlier works, although in the end it centers on Antoinette's consciousness as she makes her last walk along the corridors of Rochester's house with a lighted candle.

Woven into the novel are also Rhys's familiar themes of the confrontation of the warm Caribbean and cold England, the vividness of the emotions set against the pallor of an orderly and controlled life, the hurt of rejection (which runs like a theme through the novel, standing behind the unkindness, violence, and madness of various characters), and the willfulness and self-destructiveness of the outcast who has accepted blame for her condition. The language changes from Antoinette's emotional opening section to Rochester's cool prose to Antoinette's final confusions, but it never becomes uncharacteristic of Rhys's style: laconic, understated, terse, and charged with an undercurrent of feeling provided by the narrators' responses to color and to setting. When Rochester responds to the colors of the Caribbean landscape by saying "Too much blue, too much purple, too much green," this is a code for his inability to cope with the emotional spaces he encounters in the West Indies. Even Antoinette's mental agony is coolly described: "So there is still the sound of whispering that I have heard all my life, but these are different voices." Rhys understood very well that those with inner turbulence can develop a veneer of calm, a way of speaking that sounds perfectly logical and orderly but is totally at odds with reality.

Wide Sargasso Sea is often said to be her masterpiece, but Rhys found it difficult to finish, and critical views of it are not all positive. Staley says that Antoinette lacks the kind of insights that Rhys's other heroines possess. James is more sympathetic, saying that Antoinette "asserts the values of heat and light versus darkness." But Rhys's assertion is a passional one, not based on a symbolic pursuit of light in the sense of maturity, understanding, and revelation of truth but rather on an indulgence of passive-aggressive responses to life, of emotional chaos, and of selfhood that lacks proper strength and adult responsibility. The flames of the fire associated with Antoinette seem like the flames of hell, a further development of the damnation Sasha accepts at the end of *Good Morning, Midnight*. Wilson Harris, the Guyanese writer, has perceived Antoinette as a "subversive, religious spirit" (*Kunapipi*, 1980). Perhaps the interpretation of Rhys on a spiritual

Dust jacket for the novel in which Rhys told the story of "the madwoman in the attic," Rochester's wife in Charlotte Brontë's Jane Eyre

level comes more easily to a critic close to the Caribbean and its religious consciousness.

On this level the novel takes and develops the spiritual themes of the other major works to an unhappy but dramatic climax. But some British and American critics remain untouched in their responses to the book. Walter Allen (*New York Times Book Review*, 18 June 1967) said that *Wide Sargasso Sea* was not as impressive as *Jane Eyre* because Rochester was too shadowy. On the other hand, the reviewer for the *Times Literary Supplement* mentioned that Rhys's work clearly existed in its own right. The same reviewer said of Antoinette that she is a "Creole narcissus, she sees the world in terms of its beauty, but the only beauty she understands derives from the experiences and the fantasies of her own childhood; and with it belongs safety and happiness." The work clearly centers on the Caribbean world, and on women's consciousness. In these contexts it is a powerful postcolonial book. Howells comments that *Wide Sargasso Sea* is Rhys's "most rebellious text of all," and she says that, in dealing with colonialism and the white Creole woman, it goes to

"the heart of the matter." Helen Tiffin, an Australian critic, selects the master-servant/slave relations within the novel as important interpretations of the British-colonial relationship; the Indian poststructuralist critic Gayatri Spivak has examined *Jane Eyre* in relation to *Wide Sargasso Sea*. She comments that Christophine's story is the "tangent" to *Wide Sargasso Sea*, just as St. John River's story is to *Jane Eyre*.

After *Wide Sargasso Sea* was published, Rhys was able to find a publisher for a collection of stories she had finished years before and regarded as largely mediocre. Together with a selection from *The Left Bank*, these stories are collected in *Tigers Are Better-Looking*. They include "Till September Petronella," which had appeared in the *London Magazine* in 1959; it is a sharp, cynical piece about relations between men and women. "Let Them Call It Jazz," drawn from her Holloway Prison experience—and which she said was "A bit of a crazy story. For fun"—has an important place in her work, because in it she writes in a creolized English from the point of view of a black West Indian woman living in London. This is Rhys's alter ego, so to speak, and represents her somewhat naïve comprehension of black culture and identity (music as a source of strength in adversity, for example). The *Times Literary Supplement* review of the volume found it had "the slightly acid charm and poetic style" of Rhys's other, earlier writing. However, the novelist A. S. Byatt (*New Statesman*, 29 March 1968) commented that she was "moved by [Rhys's] prose, but a whole series of stories in which it is always Them against a Me seen with a very indulgent irony begins to seem limited."

Sleep It Off, Lady is a stronger collection than *Tigers*, and seems to follow a thread that chronologically reflects Rhys's residences and life—the Caribbean, London, Paris, chorus-girl work, and old age. The title story is a chilling account of an old woman who finds herself unable to move after a physical collapse, and spends a cold night up against a dustbin, rubbish spilled all over her, terrified of a large rat she has seen previously in the same place. She is ignored by a little girl who sees her there and who callously tells her to "sleep it off, lady," because the girl's mother has told her the old lady drinks too much. The last, short piece, "I Used to Live Here Once," is a curious little fragment presenting a spirit trying to make contact with two children. The little boy, showing no recognition of her, simply remarks that it has grown suddenly cold, and the children go inside. These pieces show Rhys had lost nothing of her precision with language or her capacity to face and depict the unpleasant, frightening aspects of life and imagination. Susanna Clapp, reviewing for the *New Statesman* (22 October 1976), speaks of Rhys seeming at times "on the point of self-parody" and "wistfulness" but says she is always capable of "springing bleak treats." Nick Totton, in the *Spectator* (30 October 1976), openly calls the collection "a kind of autobiography," saying that Rhys "treads the boundary between fiction . . . and history. . . ."

But the real autobiography was to come last in Rhys's career. Her unfinished *Smile Please* was published soon after her death. In it Rhys shows again her characteristic, carefully controlled style, her way of selecting detail and arranging it. The honest but fragmentary descriptions are quite different from the alcoholic talk she indulged in with Plante, and while revealing, they often show the savagely insecure, immature side of Rhys's personality, unleavened by her maturity and insight. Together with the selected, published letters (1984), the autobiography reveals an important as-

pect of Rhys's experience: the making of the writer. Her childlike self is very evident in those parts of life that are domestic and personal (her inability to take on long-term responsibility for others, her self-centeredness, and her love of pretty clothes and makeup), but this is balanced by her literary professionalism—her concern for accuracy, truth, and stylistic perfection.

Rhys's last years were the years of a well-established and recognized writer, and though there was pain, loneliness, memories of hurt, and suspicions of people (including Selma Vaz Dias, who tried to lay claim to a large portion of Rhys's royalties), she did have some evidence that important people close to her loved and respected her. The conflicts that characterized her life continued to the end, as Angier points out. Rhys was wry, in a May 1964 letter to Francis Wyndham, about the difficulty some people had in seeing her clearly: "I simply *cannot* understand why so many people imagine that I'm a bit of rather battered ivy waving around—looking for any old oak to cling to, because I'm really a Savage Individualist." But that was the writer talking. Rhys, the woman, was indeed likely to create an impression of failure to cope with the basic demands of life.

Yet, indisputably, Rhys was exceptionally talented—and was a Caribbean writer. The themes of alienation, exile, and displacement that are central in her work are also central to Caribbean writing as a whole. Her insights into power relations, and into racial identity as a central cornerstone of self-definition, developed out of her understanding of race and class in Dominica during her childhood, and these inform her portrayal of woman. Importantly, too, her sense of the English and of England was shaped by being a colonial person, and this sense she gives to her central characters, who exist in very definite relation to a cultural frame of English or European male power. Whereas it might be argued that Rhys is a cross-cultural writer, who draws on English and French literary styles and cultural contexts, as well as on her Caribbean origins, especially since her father was a British immigrant into Dominica, that identity itself is Caribbean: the majority of Caribbean peoples, whether they live within the region or outside, are particularly conscious of having to cope with bringing together disparate cultural influences. No one who knows the Caribbean well could deny that Rhys's work is grounded in a Caribbean consciousness, however her European experience altered or refracted it. Such refraction, after all, is common-

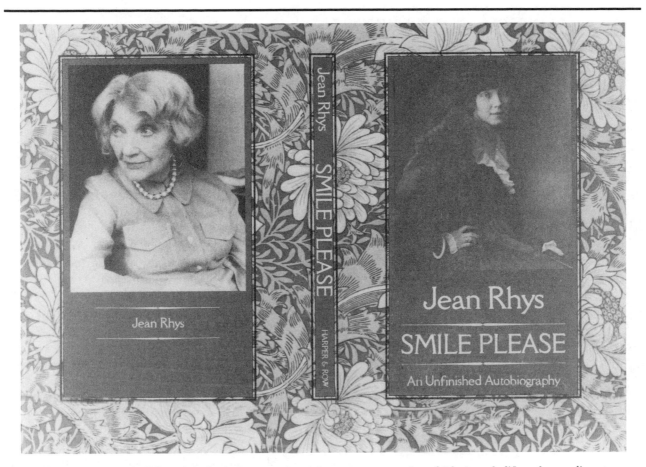

Dust jacket for the revised edition of the book that comprises a fragmentary narration of Rhys's early life and some diary passages from 1917

place in the work of other Caribbean writers of very different identities who have lived outside the region for much of their working lives, such as V. S. Naipaul, or, more recently, Paule Marshall, Michelle Cliff, Pauline Melville, and Marlene Nourbese Philip. It marks such writers as separate from the national literatures to which they may be affiliated (British, American, Canadian) and also sets them apart within Caribbean literature as a group of writers who bring a Caribbean consciousness to bear on an experience outside the Caribbean. Yet no one could deny their Caribbean identity, which is most essential to a full understanding of their work, and the same is true of Jean Rhys.

Her work has become somewhat dated in the light of the women's movement, especially in the West Indies, where young women, particularly black women, now look at their mothers and grandmothers as strong, surviving individuals and find Rhys's heroines alien to them, from a racial-cultural and a woman's point of view. Rhys could, however, as the Jamaican critic Betty

Wilson has said, be linked to the francophone-Caribbean women writers whose heroines are passive, willing to be abused by men, and yet carry internal hostility and aggression. Perhaps Rhys had more of a French-Caribbean consciousness, in the end, than an English one. But her work has lasted, despite all the changes of focus and approach critical and readerly response have shown, and it seems clearly able to transcend changing fashions of literary style and political interpretations of literary images of women. Rhys's clarity of vision and her passionate attention to the details of creating that vision in a supple, intelligent style make her work durable and a provocative source of important questions about gender, race, and class, questions that are raised unconventionally.

Letters:

Jean Rhys: Letters, 1931-1966, selected by Francis Wyndham and Diana Melly (London: Deutsch, 1984); republished as *The Letters of Jean Rhys* (New York: Viking, 1984).

Jean Rhys

Interview:

Mary Cantwell, "A Conversation with Jean Rhys," *Mademoiselle*, 79 (October 1974): 170-171, 206-213.

Bibliographies:

Elgin W. Mellown, *Jean Rhys: A Descriptive and Annotated Bibliography of Works and Criticism* (New York & London: Garland, 1984);

Nora Gaines, "Bibliography on Jean Rhys" [continuing feature], *Jean Rhys Review*, 1 (Fall 1986): 29-35; 2 (Fall 1987): 15-20; 3 (Fall 1988): 14-20; 4, no. 1 (1990): 15-27.

Biograpies:

David Plante, *Difficult Women: A Memoir of Three* (New York: Atheneum, 1983);

Carole Angier, *Jean Rhys* (Harmondsworth, U.K.: Penguin, 1985);

Angier, *Jean Rhys: Life and Work* (New York: Little, Brown, 1990).

References:

Elizabeth Abel, "Women and Schizophrenia: The Fiction of Jean Rhys," *Contemporary Literature*, 20 (1979): 155-177;

Phyllis Shand Allfrey, "Jean Rhys: A Tribute," *Kunapipi*, 1, no. 2 (1979): 23-25;

Paula Grace Anderson, "Jean Rhys' *Wide Sargasso Sea*: The Other Side," *Caribbean Quarterly*, 28, nos. 1-2 (1982): 57-65;

Elizabeth R. Baer, "The Sisterhood of Jane Eyre and Antoinette Cosway," in *The Voyage In: Fictions of Female Development*, edited by Abel (Hanover, N.H.: University Press of New England, 1983), pp. 131-148;

Patricia Barber-Williams, "Images of the Self: Jean Rhys and Her French West Indian Counterpart," *Journal of West Indian Literature*, 3 (September 1989): 9-19;

Wendy Brandmark, "The Power of the Victim: A Study of *Quartet, After Leaving Mr. Mackenzie,* and *Voyage in the Dark* by Jean Rhys," *Kunapipi*, 8, no. 2 (1986): 21-29;

Edward Kamau Brathwaite, *Contradictory Omens* (Mona, Jamaica: Savacou, 1974), pp. 33-38;

Nancy Hammond Brown, "England and the English in the Works of Jean Rhys," *Jean Rhys Review*, 1 (Spring 1987): 8-20;

Charlotte Bruner, "A Caribbean Madness: Half Slave and Half Free," *Canadian Review of Comparative Literature*, 11, no. 2 (1984): 236-248;

Elaine Campbell, "Reflections of Obeah in Jean Rhys' Fiction," *Kunapipi*, 4, no. 2 (1985): 42-50;

Nancy Casey, "Study in the Alienation of a Creole Woman," *Caribbean Quarterly*, 19 (September 1973): 95-102;

Maryse Condé, "Jean Rhys, la prisonnière des Sargasses," *Recherche, Pedagogie et Culture* (September-December 1981): 121-124;

Jan Curtis, "Jean Rhys's *Voyage in the Dark*: A Reassessment," *Journal of Commonwealth Literature*, 22, no. 1 (1987): 144-158;

Cheryl Dash, "Jean Rhys," in *West Indian Literature*, edited by Bruce King (London: Macmillan, 1979), pp. 196-209, 238;

Arnold E. Davidson, *Jean Rhys* (New York: Ungar, 1985);

Laura Niesen de Abruna, "Jean Rhys's Feminism: Theory against Practice," *World Literature Written in English*, 28 (Autumn 1988): 326-336;

Mary Lou Emery, *Jean Rhys at "World's End": Novels of Colonial and Sexual Exile* (Austin: University of Texas Press, 1990);

Emery, "The Politics of Form: Jean Rhys' Social Vision in *Voyage in the Dark* and *Wide Sargasso Sea*," *Twentieth Century Literature*, 28, no. 4 (1982): 418-430;

Mona Fayad, "Unquiet Ghosts: The Struggle for Representation in Rhys' *Wide Sargasso Sea*," *Modern Fiction Studies*, 34 (Autumn 1988): 437-452;

Elaine Savory Fido, "The Politics of Colours and the Politics of Writing," in *West Indian Literature and the Political Context* (Río Piedras: University of Puerto Rico, 1987), pp. 61-78; reprinted in the *Jean Rhys Review*, 2 (1990): 3-11;

Fido, "Woman on Woman: How Far to Disclose," *Bulletin of Eastern Caribbean Affairs*, 11 (March-April 1985): 35-44;

Judith Kegan Gardiner, *Rhys, Stead, Lessing, and the Politics of Empathy* (Bloomington: Indiana University Press, 1989);

Carol R. Hagley, "Aging in the Fiction of Jean Rhys," *World Literature Written in English*, 28 (Spring 1988): 115-125;

Wilson Harris, "Carnival of Psyche: Jean Rhys' *Wide Sargasso Sea*," *Kunapipi*, 2, no. 2 (1980): 142-150;

Harris, "Jean Rhys's 'Tree of Life,'" *Review of Contemporary Fiction*, special issue on B. S. Johnson and Jean Rhys, 5 (Summer 1985): 114-117;

Nancy R. Harrison, *Jean Rhys and the Novel as Women's Text* (Chapel Hill: University of North Carolina Press, 1988);

John Hearne, "The Wide Sargasso Sea: A West Indian Reflection," *Cornhill Magazine*, 1080 (Summer 1974): 323-333;

Kristien Hemmerechts, *A Plausible Story and a Plausible Way of Telling It: A Structural Analysis of Jean Rhys's Novels* (New York: Lang, 1987);

Molly Hite, *The Other Side of the Story: Structures and Strategies of Contemporary Feminist Narratives* (Ithaca, N.Y.: Cornell University Press, 1989);

Carol Ann Howells, *Jean Rhys* (New York: St. Martin's Press, 1991);

Louis James, *Jean Rhys* (London: Longman, 1978);

Selma James, *The Ladies and the Mammies* (Bristol, U.K.: Falling Wall, 1983);

Deborah Kelly Kloepfer, *The Unspeakable Mother: Forbidden Discourse in Jean Rhys and H. D.* (Ithaca, N.Y.: Cornell University Press, 1989);

Wally Look Lai, "The Road to Thornfield Hall," *New Beacon Reviews*, 1 (1968): 38-52;

Nancy J. Leigh, "Mirror, Mirror: The Development of Female Identity in Jean Rhys's Fiction," *World Literature Written in English*, 25 (Autumn 1985): 270-285;

James Lindroth, "Arrangements in Silver and Grey: The Whistlerian Moment in the Short Fiction of Jean Rhys," *Review of Contemporary Fiction*, special issue on B. S. Johnson and Jean Rhys, 5 (Summer 1985): 128-134;

Anthony Luengo, "*Wide Sargasso Sea* and the Gothic Mode," *World Literature Written in English*, 15 (April 1976): 229-245;

Helen Nebeker, *Jean Rhys: Woman in Passage* (Montreal: Eden, 1981);

Elizabeth Nunez-Harrell, "The Paradoxes of Belonging: The White West Indian Woman in Fiction," *Modern Fiction Studies*, 31, no. 2 (1985): 281-293;

Joyce Carol Oates, "Romance and Anti-Romance: From Brontë's *Jane Eyre* to Rhys' *Wide Sargasso Sea*," *Virginia Quarterly Review*, 61 (Winter 1985): 44-58;

Teresa O'Connor, *Jean Rhys: The West Indian Novels* (New York: New York University Press, 1986);

Kenneth Ramchand, "Terrified Consciousness," *Journal of Commonwealth Literature*, 7 (July 1969): 8-19;

Jeffrey Robinson, "Gender, Myth and the White West Indian: Rhys's *Wide Sargasso Sea* and Drayton's *Christopher*," *Commonwealth Essays and Studies*, 13 (Spring 1991): 22-30;

Ronnie Scharfman, "Mirroring and Mothering in Simone Schwartz-Bart's *Pluie et vent sur Télumée Miracle* and Jean Rhys' *Wide Sargasso Sea*," *Yale French Review*, 62 (1981): 88-106;

Erika Smilowitz, "Childlike Women and Paternal Men: Colonialism in Jean Rhys' Fiction," *Ariel*, 17 (October 1986): 93-103;

Gayatri Spivak, "Three Women's Texts and a Critique of Imperialism," *Critical Inquiry*, 12 (Autumn 1985): 243-261;

Thomas Staley, *Jean Rhys* (London: Macmillan, 1979);

Helen Tiffin, "Mirror and Mask: Colonial Motifs in the Novels of Jean Rhys," *World Literature Written in English*, 17 (April 1978): 328-341;

Robin Visel, "A Half-Colonization: The Problem of the White Colonial Woman Writer," *Kunapipi*, 10, no. 3 (1988): 39-45;

Ruth Webb, "Swimming the Wide Sargasso Sea: The Manuscripts of Jean Rhys's Novel," *British Library Journal*, 14, no. 2 (1988): 165-177;

Betty Wilson, "European or Caribbean: Jean Rhys and the Language of Exile," *Frontiers: A Journal of Women's Studies*, 10, no. 3 (1989): 68-72;

Wilson, " 'Women Must Have Spunks': Jean Rhys' West Indian Outcasts," *Modern Fiction Stud-*

ies, 32 (Autumn 1986): 439-448;

Peter Wolfe, *Jean Rhys* (Boston: Twayne, 1980).

Papers:

A large collection of Rhys's papers is at the University of Tulsa.

Garth St. Omer
(15 January 1931 -)

Elaine Campbell
Massachusetts Institute of Technology

BOOKS: *A Room on the Hill* (London: Faber & Faber, 1968);

Shades of Grey (London: Faber & Faber, 1968)—comprises *The Lights on the Hill* (separately published, London: Heinemann, 1986) and *Another Place Another Time*;

Nor Any Country (London: Faber & Faber, 1969);

J—, Black Bam and the Masqueraders (London: Faber & Faber, 1972).

OTHER: "Syrop," in *Introduction Two: Stories by New Writers* (London: Faber & Faber, 1964), pp. 139-187;

"The Colonial Novel: Studies in the Novels of Albert Camus, V. S. Naipaul, and Alejo Carpentier," Ph.D. thesis, Princeton University, 1975.

Garth St. Omer has adapted the usual elements of existential art to re-create fictionally his native Caribbean island (Saint Lucia). For example, in chapter 8 of *A Room on the Hill* (1968) the description of Castries, Saint Lucia, at midnight (although he never names the city) might just as well be of the Left Bank of Paris: "He walked uptown along the empty streets. Driven by the wind, a piece of paper passed him noisily. A cat crossed the street and disappeared into the darkness of the other side. The business houses stood shut, cold and remote. But it was Sunday and the town, at this hour, was a dead town." The wind-blown newspaper and the midnight cat are familiar icons of existential loneliness and alienation. When the reader continues, though, he discovers that St. Omer subsequently counterpoints these trite images with distinctly West Indian ones. The

protagonist, John Lestrade, walks on through the lingering smell of rum and fried foods, past decrepit wooden houses, into a world of freshly baked bread. Bare-chested black men sit on wooden boxes, and there is the "sharp, dry smell of fresh bread and the crackling of the cooling loaves in the baskets." The wooden houses, the black men, the rum smell, and the French bread belie the ennui expressed in the protagonist's words. St. Omer betrays himself. His is not a grand weltschmerz. It is instead a love-hate response to his native island. St. Omer writes to formulate his interior vision of Castries. He writes to express his disappointment with the less-than-perfect world from which he comes. His writing is best appreciated by those who have had the rare fortune of knowing Castries.

Not only does St. Omer draw Castries with a subtle touch, he also ably portrays the gifted young intellectuals who grew up there. More important than the backdrops of existentialism is his success in transcribing the environment that produced Saint Lucia's poets, painters, and teachers. The very Catholicism that concerns him was a factor that contributed to Saint Lucia's creativity. St. Mary's College provided the training ground for many of the young men who went on to study at the University of the West Indies or overseas, and the presence of the prolific Father Charles Jesse, who wrote and published Saint Lucian poetry, history, sermons, and essays, served as a catalyst for artistic creativity. St. Omer acknowledges Jesse through his fictional representation of a nameless old priest with whom Lestrade plays chess. In these and other aspects, universal

Cover for the separate, paperback edition (1986) of a novella that was first published with Another Place Another Time in Shades of Grey (1968)

themes are presented in decidedly Caribbean settings in St. Omer's fiction.

He was born in Castries on 15 January 1931, but information on his parents is unavailable (St. Omer guards his privacy). He graduated from St. Mary's College, which trained many of the young intellectuals of the island, then taught for seven years in various Caribbean high schools. Like Stephenson, the hero of *The Lights on the Hill* (in *Shades of Grey*, 1968), St. Omer entered a university after a long leave from formal study: he attended the University College of the West Indies in Kingston, Jamaica, from 1956 to 1959, when he earned a B.A. (honors) in French and Spanish. After teaching in France for two years, he moved to Ghana, where he taught French and English from 1961 to 1966.

Between 1966 and 1969 St. Omer wrote fiction in Saint Lucia and in London. From 1969 to 1971 he studied for a master's degree in fine arts at Columbia University in New York, then began work on his Ph.D. in comparative literature at Princeton University; his thesis (1975) is a study of Albert Camus, V. S. Naipaul, and Alejo Carpentier. Upon completion of his doctoral program, St. Omer joined the faculty of the University of California at Santa Barbara, rising to the rank of professor of English.

St. Omer's period of creative writing was concentrated in the years between his graduation from the University of the West Indies and his entry into graduate study at Columbia. Since his last novel was published by Faber and Faber in 1972, St. Omer has been virtually silent as a creative artist. However, he has apparently completed an unpublished novel with a North American rather than a West Indian setting.

St. Omer's first published fiction is in the 1964 collection *Introduction Two: Stories by New Writers*. "Syrop" is a long, carefully developed short story with strong classic elements, in which a worthy protagonist (the title character) suffers greatly amid scenes of violence and horror. Indeed, the zenith of horror in "Syrop" is such that its tragic nature is more Senecan than Sophoclean. "Syrop" ends quietly, however, in the manner of plays in the golden age of Pericles, with a chorus of citizens bearing witness to the tragic downfall of a well-known family. As in most modern tragedy the noteworthy family that St. Omer draws in "Syrop" is neither royal nor noble. Nor is it bourgeois or even proletarian. The mission

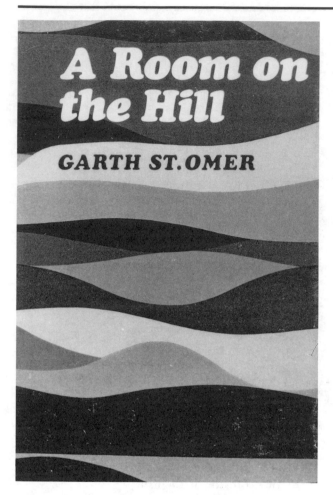

Dust jacket for St. Omer's roman à clef about intellectual life in Saint Lucia during the 1960s

unborn infant is killed, and St. Omer must work to shift responsibility for the killing from Syrop to Deaies. Despite the brutality of Syrop's action and its dreadful consequences, St. Omer preserves the reader's belief in Syrop's innate goodness, with his act of anger serving as the tragic flaw.

Ti-Son, Deaies's nephew, is the relative who vindicates the family. Ti-Son is respected, even revered, by the inhabitants of the blighted community. He is strong, manly, generous, and intelligent. He is morally unflawed, and for that reason Ti-Son does not function as a classic tragic hero. He is, perhaps, an example of what Syrop might have grown up to become. Ti-Son and his wife, Emillienne (a "small, thin, but durable woman"), invest Deaies's family with a dignity that is hard won in the social climate portrayed.

Echoes of the Theban plays reverberate in Deaies's blindness: the blindness of a very old, very poor West Indian Oedipus. This Third World Oedipus has a criminal son, Lescaut, and a prostitute daughter, Anne, unlike Sophocles's tragic protagonist who has his two good daughters, one of whom is uncommonly heroic. Deaies's life continues beyond Syrop's horrible death in the propeller blades of a ship, and, as the one who survives all losses—his wife, his children, his sight—Deaies marks St. Omer's movement away from ancient Greek tragedy toward modern existential angst.

A Room on the Hill was published by Faber and Faber in 1968. It is as if St. Omer made a categorical decision in the years between "Syrop" and his first novella to free himself from the classic mode in favor of a modern, existential one. In the early 1990s, existential angst seems a bit dated. In the 1960s, however, existentialism was fashionable. The derivative flavor of this first short novel, and, indeed, of those of his to follow, may account for the generally negative reception accorded St. Omer's fiction. However, there are special qualities that distinguish these novels from others written in emulation of the great masters of existentialism, notably St. Omer's concern about the influence of the Roman Catholic church.

The singular coterie of Saint Lucian artists—including the Walcott brothers and Dunstan and Garth St. Omer—is transfigured into the circle of friends surrounding John Lestrade in the novel. Lestrade, the musing, meditative intellectual, is in an excellent medium for observing and describing the set of young people who influenced one an-

St. Omer undertakes is to demonstrate that those inhabiting shacks without amenities, those siring children who live criminal lives, and those helpless in caring for their own physical needs can and do develop fine young men such as Syrop.

Irony of situation, another element linking "Syrop" with Sophoclean and Aeschylean tragic drama, occurs when Syrop, the most promising member of the afflicted family, is the one cut down in a senseless death, which expresses explicitly the theme that humans are merely the playthings of the gods. In this case the gods of pagan Greece are collected and focused, as it were, into the often-invoked monotheistic god in Deaies's (Syrop's father's) internal musings.

Syrop, the child Deaies sired in his old age, is sweet, as his name indicates, but his is not a sweetness of pure innocence. For example, he succumbs to anger when his sister, Anne, responds viciously to Deaies; Syrop strikes his pregnant sister's belly repeatedly with a wooden stick. The

other so profoundly. Stephen, Harold, Derek, Dennys, and their sweethearts Miriam, Anne-Marie, Sheila, and Rose move effortlessly through *A Room on the Hill*. St. Omer does not go to great pains to differentiate them, although certain characters such as Anne-Marie tend to stand out. Their lack of distinction is a reflection of Lestrade's peculiar temperament and the vague nature of his musings. There is, however, no doubt left in the reader's mind that these young people are gifted, albeit star-crossed. Their presence, their tragedies, and their special qualities mark them as latter-day versions of the noble men and women who peopled the world of Greek drama.

In 1968 Faber and Faber also published St. Omer's *Shades of Grey*, which comprises two novellas, *The Lights on the Hill* and *Another Place Another Time*. *The Lights on the Hill* is the longer of the two, and it has been republished alone in a paperback edition by Heinemann (1986) in the Caribbean Writers Series. This edition is enhanced by a short biography and an anonymous introduction. Why *The Lights on the Hill* was selected for reintroducing St. Omer is unclear. The novella lacks the coherence of *A Room on the Hill*, and it displays St. Omer's increasing engagement with his antihero, now named Stephenson.

Again, St. Omer through his protagonist Stephenson, evokes the circle of talented young men and women who were studying, teaching, and writing in St. Lucia during his own early manhood. This time, however, the characters are even less differentiated than in *A Room on the Hill*. More names are thrown at the reader: Val, Margaret, Moira, Ronald, Marie, Eddie, Thea, Peter, Rosa, Phyllis, Jeannine, Carlton—all members of the campus set. The reader struggles mightily to sort them out, because some of them do seem to have importance in Stephenson's life, his protestations to the contrary notwithstanding. Members of Stephenson's family are a bit more identifiable: Carl, a brother; a mother; a stepfather; and a woman called Meme, possibly a grandmother.

All these figures whirl about the egocentric Stephenson, who presents himself as a mysterious man of few words. When Stephenson emerges from his self-absorption, he throws out hints of a dark patch in his past that has turned him into the brooding creature he has become. The reader tends to bear with Stephenson, with perhaps as much patience as his friend Thea, until learning that the dreadful event in Stephenson's past is simply that as a young man

he was caught passing bribes to avoid paying duty on illegally imported rum and cigarettes.

The position presented, then, is that society has injured Stephenson by reacting negatively to his criminal behavior. When the judge fails to indulge Stephenson on the basis of past friendship, St. Omer condemns the judge. There are traces of the same sort of special pleading implanted in "Syrop." Despite acts of brutality or venality, St. Omer's protagonist must be indulged. St. Omer does not stand back and permit the reader to reach his own decision: sympathy for the protagonist—Syrop or Stephenson—is elicited at all costs. Perhaps it is this factor that provoked Jacqueline Kaye to fault St. Omer's "lack of objectivity."

A breakdown in structure further invalidates the credibility of *The Lights on the Hill*. The novella's tone is set by the opening staccato dialogue between Thea and Stephenson. Stephenson's terse rejoinders, many of which are empty of information, exhibit the failure in sharing that characterizes him throughout the story. A successful maintenance of the established mode and tone would have supported commitment to the protagonist as a type of modern tragic hero. However, when Stephenson finally unburdens himself to Thea in chapter 8, the prose assumes the manner of conventional narration. The teasing one-liners are replaced by solid blocks of description, and the narrator's air of alienation vanishes before the biographical impulse. In other words, the prose style itself suggests that the protagonist's specialness as an existential antihero is ephemeral.

Another Time Another Place, the companion novella to *The Lights on the Hill*, might well have been written earlier. It is closer to the style of "Syrop" possibly because the protagonist, like Syrop, is a young boy who has not yet taken up the role of alienated antihero. Derek Charles falls into the age bracket between Syrop and Stephenson. He has completed secondary school but has not yet entered the university. Still living on his home island, clearly Saint Lucia although not named, Derek is an observer and reporter of the peasant life about him. The novella is aptly named, because after reading *The Lights on the Hill* and *A Room on the Hill*, the St. Omer reader may feel as if he or she has indeed returned to an earlier and more refreshing era.

This is not to say that St. Omer's hero does not display his usual callous treatment of women and his taste for morbidity. The teenager Derek ruthlessly exploits his first girlfriend both sexually and psychologically. Another island woman, Babsy, dies from an abortion, which is bloodily depicted. And young Cecil dies from tuberculosis after a lingering illness. St. Omer relies on frequent deaths to bolster the general air of futility with which he surrounds his protagonist.

Such sensationalistic tactics notwithstanding, *Another Time Another Place* is successful in translating into fiction the realities of Saint Lucian life. There are amply developed scenes between Derek and his mother, between Derek and Cecil's mother, and between Derek and a little cousin, all of which convey graphically the sense of life on a Caribbean island not too small to satisfy a young boy's inquisitiveness. *Another Time Another Place* is a bridge between St. Omer's earliest writing and his later, more typical work.

Nor Any Country (1969) marks the full maturing of St. Omer's prose. Clive Jordan in the *New Statesman* said of this novella, "The quiet, flat honesty of his style tends to mislead. Its impact is frequently delayed . . . and it hides latent warmths." Honesty is a good word to apply to St. Omer's fourth novella. In it, the hero's posturings no longer dominate the story, although Peter remains remote and relatively dispassionate toward those around him—especially his wife, Phyllis, whom he has left behind for eight years while furthering his career in England. But Peter, in the last chapter, confronts his social responsibilities. All the while intending to leave Phyllis behind again after a week's visit to his Caribbean island, Peter surprises the reader and himself by deciding to take Phyllis back to England with him along with his orphaned nephew Michael. He reaches this decision with few histrionic statements.

This closeness to reality was prepared for by all St. Omer's preceding fiction. The large-scale tragedy of "Syrop," the experimentations in existential antiheroism of *The Lights on the Hill*, the social realities in *Another Time Another Place*, and the concern over Catholicism found in *A Room on the Hill* are all ingredients melded together in *Nor Any Country*. While it would be extreme to call *Nor Any Country* a work of reconciliation, the novella probably leaves the St. Omer reader with the impression that the author has finally gained control over his topic, his style, and his hero.

Peter is the familiar educated West Indian who has left his island for England and who returns home with the potential for reordering his values. St. Omer does not provide the reader

Dust jacket for the sequel to Nor Any Country

with any forewarning that, this time, he is creating an existential antihero with a difference. Peter is like his predecessors in many ways. He exploits the women with whom he lives; he watches others, rather like a scientist collecting specimens; and he is generally self-indulgent. He takes a greater interest in the members of his family, however, and his accounts of his father, his mother, his brother, and his wife are more sympathetic. Finally, Peter is able to listen to the fears and worries of a Roman Catholic clergyman. He allows Father Thomas to explain his own sense of alienation as a dark-skinned clergyman assigned to labor among parishioners on his home island. In short, Peter has outgrown his solipsism enough to hear another's anxieties.

Peter's ability to open himself to Father Thomas's anxieties might well be the crack through which compassion for Phyllis enters. Once he is able to accept her love and to recognize her need for him, Peter is able to extend his compassion to include Michael, his brother's little son. While Peter appears to be a stereotypical antihero, he has grown beyond the protagonists of St. Omer's earlier works. He has redefined tragedy to include the angst of those who share his world.

Having achieved the ability to participate in the angst of those around him, Peter in *J—, Black Bam and the Masqueraders* (1972) is able to empathize with his brother Paul's worldview. Paul, not unlike Hamlet, declares himself mad. Paul's antic disposition enables him to countenance the disappointing turn his life has taken. An earlier Peter would have been too self-centered to share space with his brother. Now, he and his brother become, as John Thieme notes, "fully-fledged doubles in the Dostoevskyan or Conradian sense."

Thieme believes that *J—, Black Bam and the Masqueraders* is St. Omer's most successful novel because the author is able to sustain the two parallel-but-separate points of view that Peter and Paul present. The point of view St. Omer elects is an interesting variant of the omniscient narrator. The St. Omer reader is so conditioned to accept the existential antihero's self-absorption that he assumes Paul's narration is filtered through Peter's sensibility. In fact, it is not. Each narrative line is distinct, enabling both Peter and Paul to delineate the details of their personal tragedies.

Whereas *Nor Any Country* offers the promise of reconciliation, St. Omer's *J—, Black Bam and the Masqueraders* plunges the reader back into the depths of modern alienation. This time, however, the degree of alienation is compounded by the doubling. Not one, but two promising young West Indians have succumbed to disillusionment and despair.

Garth St. Omer continues to guard his privacy at the University of California, Santa Barbara. He politely but firmly declines to comment on his life or writing. Although his philosophy might well have been changed by almost twenty years in California as the member of a prestigious university faculty, only a new publication would enable a critic to assess such an effect. Consequently it would be extremely interesting to read a future novel by St. Omer. He remains a singular voice in the burgeoning of West Indian literature that followed World War II. Further, his work is the literary representation of a highly productive period when all the arts flourished in Saint Lucia and when a small group of St. Mary's College colleagues created a world-class literature that is still growing today in the poetry of Derek Walcott.

References:

Elaine Campbell, "The Third Wave of St. Lucian Literature," in *Studies in Commonwealth Literature*, edited by Eckhard Breitinger and Reinhard Sander (Tübingen, Germany: Gunter Narr, 1985), pp. 115-121;

Jacqueline Cousins, "Symbol and Metaphor in the Early Fiction of Garth St. Omer," *Journal of West Indian Literature*, 3 (September 1989): 20-37;

Peter Dunwoodie, "Images of Self-Awareness in Garth St. Omer's *J—, Black Bam and the Masqueraders*," *Caribbean Quarterly*, 29 (June 1983): 30-43;

Michael Gilkes, "Garth St. Omer," in his *The West Indian Novel* (Boston: Twayne, 1981), pp. 102-115;

Patricia Ismond, "West Indian Literature as an Expression of National Cultures: The Literature of St. Lucia," *World Literature Written in English*, 29 (Autumn 1989): 104-115;

Jacqueline Kaye, "Anonymity and Subjectivism in the Novels of Garth St. Omer," *Journal of Commonwealth Literature*, 10 (August 1975): 45-52;

Bruce King, "Garth St. Omer: From Disorder to Order," *Commonwealth Essays and Studies*, 3 (1977-1978): 55-67;

Pamela C. Mordecai, "The West Indian Male Sensibility in Search of Itself: Some Comments on *Nor Any Country*, *The Mimic Men*, and *The Secret Ladder*," *World Literature Written in English*, 21 (Autumn 1982): 629-644;

Gordon Rohlehr, "Small Island Blues: A Short Review of the Novels of Garth St. Omer," *Voices*, 2 (September-December 1969): 22-28;

John Thieme, "Double Identity in the Novels of Garth St. Omer," *Ariel*, 8 (July 1977): 81-97;

David Williams, "Mixing Memory and Desire: St. Omer's *Nor Any Country*," *Journal of West Indian Literature*, 2 (October 1988): 36-41.

Efua Theodora Sutherland

(27 June 1924 -   )

Chikwenye Okonjo Ogunyemi
Sarah Lawrence College

BOOKS: *Playtime in Africa*, by Sutherland and Willis E. Bell (Accra: Aut, 1960; London: Brown, Knight & Truscott, 1960; New York: Atheneum, 1962);

The Roadmakers, by Sutherland and Bell (Accra: Ghana Information Services, 1961; London: Newman Neame, 1963);

Foriwa (Accra: State Publishing, 1967);

Odasani (Accra: Anowuo, 1967);

Edufa (London: Longmans, Green, 1967; Washington, D.C.: Three Continents, 1979);

Vulture! Vulture! [and *Tahinta*]: *Two Rhythm Plays* (Accra: Ghana Publishing, 1968);

The Original Bob: The Story of Bob Johnson, Ghana's Ace Comedian, by Sutherland and Bell (Accra: Anowuo, 1970);

Anansegoro: Story-Telling Drama in Ghana (Accra: Afram, 1975);

The Marriage of Anansewa (London: Longman, 1975);

The Voice in the Forest (New York: Philomel, 1983).

Collection: *The Marriage of Anansewa and Edufa* (Harlow, U.K.: Longman, 1987).

RECORDING: *Efua Sutherland of Ghana*, Washington, D.C., Voice of America, 1978.

OTHER: "The Redeemed," "Once Upon a Time," "The Dedication," and "Song of the Fishing Ghosts," in *Messages: Poems from Ghana*, edited by Kofi Awoonor and G. Adali-Mortty (London: Heinemann, 1971), pp. 158-169;

"Song of the Fishing Ghosts" and "Our Songs Are about It," in *Ghanaian Writing as Seen by Her Own Writers as well as by German Authors*, edited by A. Kayper-Mensah and Horst Wolff (Tübingen: Erdmann, 1972), pp. 127-128;

"A Professional Beggar's Lullaby," in *Aftermath: An Anthology of Poems in English from Africa, Asia, and the Caribbean*, edited by Robert Weaver and Joseph Bruchac (Greenfield, N.Y.: Greenfield Review, 1977), p. 23.

Efua Theodora Sutherland

SELECTED PERIODICAL PUBLICATIONS—
UNCOLLECTED: "Samataase Village," *Okyeame*, 1 (1961): 53-58;

"Venture into Theatre," *Okyeame*, 1 (1961): 47-48;

"You Swore an Oath: Anansegoro," *Présence Africaine*, 22 (Summer 1964): 231-247.

Efua Theodora Sutherland, the grande dame of the Ghanaian drama and theatrical world, is an Akan by birth and was trained in the folkways of her people. In her plays she utilizes local myths, folktales, and traditions to comment on the present, showing that human nature has not changed; she is, however, determined to change the inhuman situation in Ghana and, by extension, the African world. Sutherland has three children of her own, which has aroused her interest in writing and producing plays for educating children. She believes in engaging the young and the not-so-young for revolutionizing the country. A versatile, indefatigable visionary, she has produced works in different genres—drama (performed both in Ghana and abroad), poetry, biography, and fiction. Her pioneering work in Ghanaian theater has undoubtedly affected a whole generation of Ghanaian dramatists producing material in Akan and English. She helped to create a conducive atmosphere in which dramatists such as Ama Ata Aidoo, Patience Henaku Addo, and Joe de Graft thrived. Sutherland is a household name in Ghana, and her plays are studied in African universities. She has had some hostile reception, particularly from Ayi Kwei Armah, who lampooned her in his novel *Fragments* (1970) through a character named Aunt Efua.

Born Efua Theodora Morgue on 27 June 1924 in Cape Coast, Ghana, she completed her secondary education at St. Monica's Training College in Ashanti, then earned a B.A. in education at Teacher Training College, a part of Homerton College, Cambridge University. She also attended the School of Oriental and African Studies at the University of London. After returning to her homeland in 1951, she taught at a secondary school in Takoradi, Ghana, and at St. Monica's Training College. In 1954 she married an African-American, William Sutherland, with whom she later founded a school in the Trans-Volta Region in northern Ghana and established a theater for local productions in the Central Region.

She generated wide interest in 1958 when she founded the Ghana Experimental Theatre in Accra. Her approach was radical: she wanted to take the theater to both urban and rural areas. This experiment lasted until 1961. With funds from the Rockefeller Foundation and the Arts Council of Ghana, the ambitious Sutherland in 1960 founded the Ghana Drama Studio to try out plays that might culturally rouse people at a time when Nkrumahism was energizing the populace and driving them ideologically toward social-

ism. In 1963 the studio became part of the University of Ghana, housed in the Institute of African Studies, and Sutherland was granted a long-term research position. She had thus moved from performing plays experimentally in the streets of Ghana to the Ghanaian academy.

In her productions, she shows an interest in the nature of human power and a dedication to change, emphasizing the indispensable role of women in effecting the revolution. She has generated some moral awareness by using the oral traditional repertoire because of its familiarity to her audience. She is widely acclaimed for her three major plays—*Foriwa* (1967), *Edufa* (also 1967), and *The Marriage of Anansewa* (1975). She has also published some children's plays, notably *Vulture! Vulture!* [and *Tahinta*]: *Two Rhythm Plays* (1968). In addition she has written a biography (1970), short stories, and some poetry, though she is not distinguished for these.

Foriwa had a long gestation period. It first appeared as a short story, "New Life at Kyerefaso," in 1960 in Langston Hughes's *African Treasury*. As if bothered by the limited impact that a short story could have in an analphabetic population, Sutherland expanded the work into a three-act play. The core of the play emanated from Sutherland's experimental theater the Kodzidan, in the village of Atwia—an attempt to inject a fresh spirit into the community.

An autobiographical strain is discernible in *Foriwa* if one considers the Queen Mother as an alter ego for Sutherland, while Foriwa might represent Sutherland's eldest daughter, Esi Sutherland-Addy, who has followed in her mother's footsteps somewhat by working in the Institute of African Studies, and by being recently chosen by the Jerry Rawlings government to help in nation building. The mother-daughter bonding is well developed in *Foriwa* with its emphasis on female and communal solidarity. The Queen Mother and Foriwa are independent and dynamic, traits that benefit the society. The play was first performed in the Akan language in 1962 and comments fearlessly on the five years of little progress after Ghanaian independence in 1957. The play accentuates the women's voice to show what women can do to contribute to national development.

"Kyerefaso has long been asleep," the audience is told by Labaran, a new arrival in the country. (Kyerefaso represents Ghana in the play.) The outsider's interest and involvement reflect Ghana's ideological contacts, especially with

Dust jacket for Sutherland's first book (1960), a manifestation of her lifelong interest in the education of children

African-Americans. (Labaran could represent Sutherland's husband). In the play, Kyerefaso needs a prince and a princess (Labaran and Foriwa) to wake it up. The foundation on which they are to build has already been laid by their predecessors. In the play, Sutherland proposes that all the people—men and women, old and young, educated and illiterate, traditionally oriented and technologically minded, indigene and stranger—should be involved in community development. This play appeals for national unity, discarding gender, ethnic, and ideological differences.

To convey the idea of the social malaise, images of decadence proliferate. There is the foundation of a building that has not been completed; the "dilapidated royal house" a symbol of the condition of the country; the "camp" with its temporary nature; the "depressed condition" of the bookstore, which should help to disseminate knowledge; and vultures, those "birds of death." With Kyerefaso/Ghana in this terrible state, the sensitive Queen Mother calls for rethinking and for renewed commitment on the part of the people. The Queen Mother's unprecedented request for a rehearsal of the festival is not fortuitous. She uses the occasion to express herself before the entire population, thus giving them a new

sense of direction. Her speech is a challenge to the people: the chauvinists such as Sintim; the idlers, including the draughts players; and the uncommitted.

Foriwa rejects the marriage proposal of the "fly," Mr. Anipare, and accepts Labaran, the new man. This acceptance is indicative of the desired fusion of different parts of Ghana—Hausa and Akan, North and South—for the building of the nation. Some of Foriwa's friends' marriages have failed, a sign of the fragmentation of the society, but Foriwa's marriage will (symbolically) cement and improve relationships needed for growth.

The Magic of Dreams, an old book in the local bookstore, shows the dreams the Queen Mother and her supporters have for transforming their world. Foriwa, the symbol of the new woman, joins her mother; so also does Labaran, the man of the future with his technology, tape-recording present events as a catalyst for the future. Akan rather than English is spoken because the Scholars' Union finds English difficult, and one's own language should serve as the basis for scholarship. The Head Priest throws white powder in a ritual to cleanse the village. Thereafter the quarrelsome Sintim undergoes a change and provides the lamb that will be sacrificed to usher in a new era.

The radical mother and daughter thus unite on the occasion of the festival to effect a revival. Sutherland revises the source of the play, a folktale about a fussy girl who ends up with a horror for a husband. Foriwa, the so-called choosy bride, chooses propitiously by accepting Labaran, with whom she can build a home on a solid foundation. Foriwa, exquisitely dressed like a butterfly, represents social cross-pollination. She dances into the future, following in her mother's footsteps. The punctuation of the play with songs shows that Sutherland believes in the efficacy of the oral tradition.

The tragedy *Edufa* dramatizes the tensions in a sexist society in which women are assigned subservient roles. The audience sees the actions of Abena, Edufa's sister; Seguwa, a female member of Edufa's household; the chorus of women singing Edufa's praise; and, most important, Ampoma, Edufa's wife, who works herself to death so that Edufa might have life more abundantly. Sutherland depicts gender inequalities in a sexist Ghanaian society where women serve men for a pittance.

Instead of the female bonding in *Foriwa*, Sutherland portrays in *Edufa* an estranged father-son relationship where the old father, Kankam, stands for uprightness and the son, Edufa, for self-centeredness and greed. The strain in their relationship marks the divisiveness in society. Through the portrait of Edufa, Sutherland develops the theme of materialism with its amorality. The westernized Edufa uses people, particularly women, for his own selfish ends.

Once again an atmosphere of malaise predominates, especially with Ampoma's illness: the "near insanity" of a "doting woman," the victim of love. Her death serves as a warning to women about the dangers of loving too much. In marriage a woman can sacrifice her life for her man's progress. Kankam is the voice of sanity, upholding womanhood and upbraiding man's greed and destruction of the woman. He acknowledges Ampoma as the catalyst that brings about Edufa's fortune, which she will not live to enjoy.

Sutherland Africanizes Euripides' Alcestis myth while retaining the tragic gloom by introducing an owl, ominous and frightening. The use of African magic with its local color accentuates the aura of evil and uncertainty. The terror is occasionally relieved with local songs that involve the community. Edufa's dilemma over endangering his wife represents the degree of anomie in Africa. When his juju harms his wife, tragedy ensues: the house (or nation) is divided against itself on gender lines, and woman is the victim.

As Kankam's voice warns the young generation about overreaching, Ampoma's faint voice remains almost unheard as she sacrifices herself. The men, represented by the amoral Edufa and his friend the carefree, womanizing Senchi, are too selfish for the communal good. Through Edufa and Senchi—the first weighed down by his acquisitive nature, the other traveling light—Sutherland highlights the tragedy of the future.

Building on a folktale repertoire known as *Anansesem*, Sutherland in the comedy *The Marriage of Anansewa* uses the *anansegoro*, a "system of traditional theater" in which she can almost indefinitely keep weaving materials around Ananse, the trickster in Ghanaian folklore. According to Sutherland, he is an Everyman figure with didactic implications. *The Marriage of Anansewa* becomes steadily complicated as Sutherland brings in more subplots in her three-act play. She modernizes Ananse's trickster image, generating laughter as the play tackles the problems of marriage and the exploitative culture surrounding it. The ultimate victim is the young bride, Anansewa, who becomes enslaved to the bridegroom and his family through bonds effected during negotiations carried out by the males, including her father, Ananse.

The play is experimental in adapting the *Anansesem* for the modern stage while retaining the omniscient Storyteller to act as coordinator for the subplots. Sutherland skillfully uses the *mboguo*, or "musical performances," as curtain raisers and for demarcative purposes. She thus combines the demands of modern theater with the traditional need for communal participation. She employs "participating audience" characters within the regular audience to capture the atmosphere of a traditional storytelling session.

Sutherland attacks the mercenary culture in which the courtship and betrothal of a young woman become a nightmarish affair where the bride-to-be's father exploits and deceives his daughter's suitor(s). Instead of one suitor, Ananse secures four, and the trickster weaves webs to entangle everybody. The daughter will go to the highest bidder, though the four bidders remain unseen. The vocabulary is that of a business transaction, and Anansewa feebly rejects the idea of being sold, with all its repercussions.

Ananse represents every modern African man who exploits women and cultural traditions for his own ends by using the advantages of a West-

Cover for the 1987 book that brings together two of Sutherland's best and most popular plays

ther's request, she exchanges one male dominating figure (her father) for another (her husband), the Chief-Who-Is-Chief. It is noteworthy that he wants her put in a glass coffin, to become an object to be displayed for viewing—like father, like husband. Since the audience knows Anansewa is alive, Sutherland is obviously commenting on the reifying of Ghanaian women.

Laughing at the local custom of using the photograph as a mode of introducing a woman to her would-be husband, Sutherland ridicules tradition by presenting this four times as the basis of the marriage transaction. The use of the photograph, a mere image and a shadow of reality, demonstrates the way man views woman without her substance. Man sees woman as an object without solidity, an object that can be viewed (perhaps for entertainment) and can be easily put away.

In this most aggressively feminist of Sutherland's works, Ananse controls not only his daughter (that is, the younger generation) but also his mother and aunt (the older generation), whom he entangles in one of the branches of this story. He brainwashes them and makes fools of them by lying. They are depicted as stereotypes of the harebrained female, credulous and trusting. They remove themselves from the scene at a crucial time when they could establish a vital support network to save Anansewa from further humiliation.

Ironically, Christie, a contemporary woman with her eye on marrying Ananse, rather than give support in a meaningful way to a fellow woman, directs whatever help she can give to Ananse to bind Anansewa further in order to enrich Ananse and, indirectly, herself. Christie subordinates herself to Ananse, though they are equals as tricksters. His last words to her, "Rare helper! Supporter, your thanks await you," followed by a hug, show she has played her part adroitly. Ananse thus controls three generations of women besides the suitors.

Throughout this play, Sutherland shows how woman is used, in spite of herself, against herself. Why then does Sutherland not punish Ananse for his machinations? Some critics have reservations about the amoral ending of the play; one can also fault it on sexual-political grounds.

Sutherland's involvement with children includes writing and producing plays for their edification. She uses the chorus in *Vulture! Vulture!* and *Tahinta* for comment and moral instruction, as she does in her plays for adults. The music that accompanies these two children's plays is de-

ern education. Typically, Anansewa is studying to be a secretary-typist, a profession in which woman is controlled and dictated to while her contribution goes unacknowledged. The scene in which Ananse dictates letters to Anansewa for the suitors—and she ignorantly types the letters that will bind her to the four men—is significant. It underscores the hazards of the life of the female secretary with her dependence on the male. Furthermore, Anansewa's financial dependence on her father is indeed the source of her trouble, since she uses the proceeds of his sale of her for her tuition in secretarial studies. She is used and sold with her unwitting cooperation, and it does not come as a surprise when she supposedly dies. She has been one of the living dead, powerless like most Ghanaian women. Lying down as though dead, Anansewa becomes an object for pity and mourning. When she wakes up at her fa-

liberately employed to lighten and entertain and make general participation possible.

Vulture! Vulture! is a short play in three parts. Vulture, played by a boy, refuses to come to eat *fufu*, palm soup, and roasted chicken, yet he jumps at eating a rat that has been long dead. What is food for one is poison for another. Women remain in the background of the play, invisible. Mrs. Vulture, as mother and wife, is nurturing and long-suffering, cooking different meals until she is finally able to satisfy Vulture. The shortness of the play ensures that Sutherland does not at any point lose her juvenile audience, whose attention span is limited.

Tahinta is a play in five parts. It is the story of a boy's initiation into the male world, especially into the clan's fishing occupation. The boy is provided with a net and a fish trap. When the "Ghost" forcibly takes away his prize—the mud fish he has caught—the boy becomes acquainted with the problems of human existence, particularly its unpredictability. In his distress he calls his mother; as he has only just been initiated into the male world full of adventure, he still remembers woman's secure, if boring, domestic sphere, so he remains close to his mother. On failing to retrieve the fish, his father promptly informs him, "A ghost is a ghost": in other words, some difficulties in life have to be endured. Though directed to the male world, the play also leads girls to glean the fact that life is full of nets and traps, and so people must find ways to avoid them or somehow use them for survival.

Efua Theodora Sutherland has had a tremendous impact on Ghanaian theater because of her experiments in skillfully combining the African and Western aspects of her heritage. She takes from each tradition useful aspects for African progress, which, in her writing, includes woman's liberation. Recently Sutherland has been an adviser to the Ghanaian president, Jerry Rawlings. She has also acted as a consultant to the Du Bois Centre for African Culture, the Pan-African headquarters in Ghana, and has served two terms on the National Commission on Children, her early interest in children being actualized in the library complexes that cater to children.

The University of Ghana has awarded her an honorary doctorate. Further, with the Drama Studio rebuilt as the New Arts Centre on university grounds, her work is symbolically beginning to be accorded an aura of permanence. Her husband, William Sutherland, an ambassador-at-

large, whose interaction with George Padmore and others helped lay the foundations for African liberation, has helped continue his wife's progressive accomplishments. One must not forget the Sutherlands' educational activities in the ideological phase of Kwame Nkrumah's regime. In stature, therefore, she belongs to the first order of nationals who worked for the genuine liberation of Ghana. She was fortunate; unlike Kenya, which exiled Ngugi wa Thiong'o and Micere Mugo for using an indigenous language for their living theater, Ghana is more accommodating, even if Sutherland's political message is less Marxist than those of her Kenyan counterparts. Her distinction in the world of letters, her role as a model for women (and men), the space granted her for her activism, and the recognition of her contribution are signs of the beginning of a progressive Ghanaian dyarchy with committed men and women exercising different forms of power and control for the good of the country.

References:

J. N. Amankulor, "An Interpretation and Analysis of *The Marriage of Anansewa*," *Okike Educational Supplement*, 2 (1980): 149-171;

Lloyd W. Brown, *Women Writers in Black Africa* (Westport, Conn. & London: Greenwood, 1981), pp. 61-83;

John C. Hagan, "Influence of Folklore on *The Marriage of Anansewa*," *Okike*, 27-28 (1988): 19-30;

K. Muhindi, "L'apport d'Efua Theodora Sutherland à la dramaturgie contemporaine," *Presence Africaine*, 133-134 (1985): 75-85;

Chinyere Okafor, "Parallelism versus Influence in African Literature: The Case of Efua Sutherland's *Edufa*," *Kiabàrà*, 3, no. 1 (1980): 113-131;

Okafor, " 'A Woman is Not a Stone but a Human Being': Vision of Woman in the Plays of Aidoo and Sutherland," in *Medium and Message*, edited by Ernest Emenyonu and others (Calabar, Nigeria: Department of English and Literary Studies, University of Calabar, 1981), pp. 165-177;

Adetokunbo Pearce, "The Didactic Essence of Efua Sutherland's Plays," *Women in African Literature Today*, 15 (1987): 71-81;

Linda Lee Talbert, "*Alcestis* and *Edufa*: The Transitional Individual," *World Literature Written in English*, 22 (1983): 183-190;

Susanne Thies-Torkornoo, "Die Rolle der Frau in der afrikanischen Gesellschaft: Eine

Betrachtung von Ama Ata Aidoos *Anowa* und Efua T. Sutherlands *Foriwa*," *Matatu*, 1 (1987): 53-67;

Gay Wilentz, "Writing for the Children: Orature, Tradition, and Community in Efua Sutherland's *Foriwa*," *Research in African Literatures*, 19 (1988): 182-196.

Derek Walcott
(23 January 1930 -   )

Robert D. Hamner
Hardin-Simmons University

See also the Walcott entry in *DLB Yearbook: 1981*.

BOOKS: *25 Poems* (Port of Spain: Guardian, 1948);

Epitaph for the Young (Bridgetown, Barbados: Advocate, 1949);

Henri Christophe: A Chronicle in Seven Scenes (Bridgetown, Barbados: Advocate, 1950);

Poems (Kingston, Jamaica: City Printery, 1951);

Harry Dernier (Bridgetown, Barbados: Advocate, 1952);

The Sea at Dauphin (Mona, Jamaica: Extra-Mural Department, University College of the West Indies, 1954);

Ione: A Play with Music (Mona, Jamaica: Extra-Mural Department, University College of the West Indies, 1957);

Ti-Jean: A Play in One Act (Kingston, Jamaica: Extra-Mural Department, University College of the West Indies, 1958);

In a Green Night: Poems, 1948-1960 (London: Cape, 1962);

Selected Poems (New York: Farrar, Straus, 1964);

The Castaway and Other Poems (London: Cape, 1965);

Malcauchon; or, The Six in the Rain (Port of Spain: Extra-Mural Department, University of the West Indies, 1966);

The Charlatan (Mona, Jamaica: Extra-Mural Department, University College of the West Indies, 1967);

The Gulf, and Other Poems (London: Cape, 1969); republished as *The Gulf: Poems* (New York: Farrar, Straus & Giroux, 1970);

Dream on Monkey Mountain and Other Plays (New

Derek Walcott in 1989 (photograph copyright by Dr. Peter Stummer)

York: Farrar, Straus & Giroux, 1970; London: Cape, 1972);

Another Life (New York: Farrar, Straus & Giroux, 1973; London: Cape, 1973);

Sea Grapes (London: Cape, 1976; New York: Farrar, Straus & Giroux, 1976);

The Joker of Seville & O Babylon! (New York: Farrar, Straus & Giroux, 1978; London: Cape, 1979);

The Star-Apple Kingdom (New York: Farrar, Straus & Giroux, 1979; London: Cape, 1980);

Remembrance and Pantomime (New York: Farrar, Straus & Giroux, 1980);

The Fortunate Traveller (New York: Farrar, Straus & Giroux, 1981; London: Faber & Faber, 1982);

Selected Poetry, selected by Wayne Brown (London & Kingston, Jamaica: Heinemann, 1981);

The Caribbean Poetry of Derek Walcott, and the Art of Romare Bearden (New York: Limited Editions Club, 1983);

Midsummer (New York: Farrar, Straus & Giroux, 1984; London & Boston: Faber & Faber, 1984);

Three Plays: The Last Carnival; Beef, No Chicken; and A Branch of the Blue Nile (New York: Farrar, Straus & Giroux, 1986);

Collected Poems, 1948-1984 (New York: Farrar, Straus & Giroux, 1986; London: Faber & Faber, 1986);

The Arkansas Testament (New York: Farrar, Straus & Giroux, 1987; London: Faber & Faber, 1988);

The Poet in the Theatre (London: Poetry Book Society, 1990);

Omeros (New York: Farrar, Straus & Giroux, 1990; London: Faber & Faber, 1990).

PLAY PRODUCTIONS: *Henri Christophe*, Castries, St. Lucia, St. Joseph's Convent, 9 September 1950; London, 1951;

Paolo and Francesca, Castries, St. Lucia, St. Joseph's Convent, 1951;

Wine of the Country, Mona, Jamaica, Whitehall Players Theatre, 1953;

The Sea at Dauphin, Port of Spain, Whitehall Players Theatre, 13 August 1954; London, 1960;

Ione, Kingston, Jamaica, Ward Theatre, 16 March 1957;

Ti-Jean and His Brothers, Castries, St. Lucia, R. C. Boys Infant School, 16 December 1957; New York, Delacorte Theatre, 20 July 1972;

Drums and Colours, Kingston, Jamaica, Royal Botanical Gardens, 25 April 1958;

Malcauchon; or, Six in the Rain, Castries, St. Lucia, Castries Town Hall, 12 March 1959; produced again as *Six in the Rain*, London, 1960; produced again as *Malcochon*, in *An Evening of One Acts*, New York, 25 March 1969;

Dream on Monkey Mountain, Toronto, Central Library Theatre, 12 August 1967; New York: St. Mark's Playhouse, 9 March 1971;

In a Fine Castle, Port of Spain, Little Carib Theatre, 1971; revised as *The Last Carnival*, Port of Spain, Government Training Center, 1 July 1982;

Franklin, Port of Spain, Bishop's Auditorium, 14 April 1973;

The Charlatan, with music by Galt MacDermot, Los Angeles, Mark Taper Forum, June 1974;

The Joker of Seville, with music by MacDermot, Port of Spain, Little Carib Theatre, 28 November 1974;

O Babylon!, with music by MacDermot, Port of Spain, Little Carib Theatre, 19 March 1976;

Remembrance, St. Croix, U.S. V.I., Dorsch Centre, 22 April 1977; New York, Shakespeare Festival, 24 April 1979;

Pantomime, Port of Spain, Little Carib Theatre, 12 April 1978; London, BBC, 25 January 1979;

Beef, No Chicken, Port of Spain, Little Carib Theatre, 30 April 1981;

A Branch of the Blue Nile, Bridgetown, Barbados, Stage One, 25 November 1983;

Steel, Cambridge, Mass., American Repertory Theatre, 3 April 1991.

OTHER: "The Muse of History," in *Is Massa Day Dead?*, edited by Orde Coombs (Garden City, N.Y.: Doubleday, 1974), pp. 1-28.

SELECTED PERIODICAL PUBLICATIONS—
UNCOLLECTED: *Drums and Colours*, *Caribbean Quarterly*, special issue, 7 (March-June 1961);

"Young Trinidadian Poets," *Trinidad Sunday Guardian*, 19 June 1966, p. 5;

"What the Lower House Demands," *Trinidad Guardian*, 6 July 1966, p. 5;

"Meanings," *Savacou*, 2 (1970): 45-51;

"The Caribbean: Culture or Mimicry?," *Journal of Interamerican Studies and World Affairs*, 16 (February 1974): 3-13;

"Soul Brother to 'The Joker of Seville,' " *Trinidad Guardian*, 6 November 1974, p. 4;

"Cafe Martinique," *House and Garden*, 157 (March 1985): 140, 222-228.

For some forty years Derek Walcott has been the preeminent poet and playwright of the West Indies. In spite of his international awards (including an O.B.E. in 1972) and the accolades of such peers as Robert Graves, Selden Rodman, and Seamus Heaney, Walcott has had to contend with the charge that he is so deeply influenced by Western tradition that he has yet to achieve his own voice. Yet this scion of African and European heritage embodies the cultural matrix of the New World. Thus inevitable questions of origins, identity, and the creation of meaningful order in a chaotic world lead Walcott to themes that transcend race, place, and time.

Derek Alton Walcott was born on 23 January 1930 in Castries, Saint Lucia, to Warwick and Alix Walcott. Warwick Walcott was a civil servant, poet, and visual artist who died at thirty-five, when Derek and his twin brother, Roderick, were only one year old. Their mother was a schoolteacher and encouraged their early education and love for reading; she was also involved in a community cultural group and got her sons involved in local theater. Roderick, along with his brother, was to become a well-known playwright. Derek Walcott published his first poem at fourteen and his first book at eighteen (*25 Poems*, 1948); his first play, *Henri Christophe*, was staged in 1950. He earned his B.A. in 1953 in English, French, and Latin, while on a British government scholarship at the University College of the West Indies in Mona, Jamaica, and he then studied for one more year in the Department of Education. In 1954 he married Fay Moyston, and they later had a son, Peter, but the marriage ended in divorce in 1959. From 1954 until 1957 Walcott taught in various West Indian schools; he soon began to devote more and more time to writing and the theater. On a Rockefeller Foundation Fellowship in 1958 he studied theater in New York City. In 1959 he moved to Trinidad and founded the Little Carib Theatre Workshop, which he ran until 1976.

Ambition and talent showed early in Walcott's career. In 1948, with two hundred dollars borrowed from his mother, he had published and then sold on street corners his *25 Poems*. Frank A. Collymore, doyen of West Indian letters, quickly hailed it as the work "of an accomplished poet." Strange as it may seem for a mulatto boy to dream of becoming a poet on an

Dust jacket for the 1964 volume in which Walcott included twenty-three poems from In a Green Night *(1962) with sixteen previously uncollected poems*

obscure island where there was no precedent for a serious career in writing, Walcott turned his unpromising situation to advantage. His father's friend Saint Lucian painter Harold Simmons nurtured his powers of observation.

While he has remained true to his roots in the Caribbean, Walcott began at an early age to appreciate the traditional European heritage provided in colonial education. "The writers of my generation," he asserts in introducing his *Dream on Monkey Mountain and Other Plays* (1970), "were natural assimilators. We knew the literature of Empires, Greek, Roman, British, through their essential classics; and both the patois of the street and the language of the classroom hid the elation of discovery. If there was nothing, there was everything to be made. With this prodigious ambition one began." For this reason, the poetry and drama preceding publication of his first major book, *In a Green Night* (1962), contain disparate elements that only later would be woven into more cohesive, mature works.

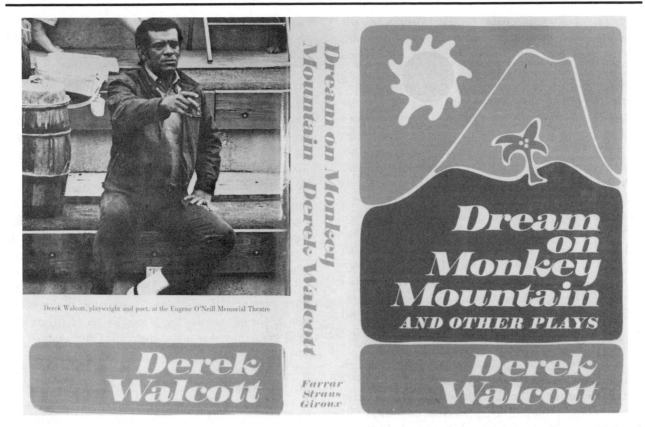

Dust jacket for the 1970 collection whose title play was inspired more than a decade earlier by Walcott's discovery of Bertolt Brecht's "epic theater" and classic Oriental drama

"A City's Death by Fire," from *25 Poems* and later reprinted in *In a Green Night*, illustrates the influence of Dylan Thomas and the intellectual play of metaphysical poetry. Another poem from the late 1940s, *Epitaph for the Young* (1949), is even more significant, not because it is a pastiche of James Joyce's style but because it became what Walcott calls the "urtext" for *Another Life* (1973). Leopold Bloom, Buck Mulligan, Stephen Daedalus, and Icarus are mentioned as *Epitaph*, this portrait of a young West Indian artist, recounts the voyage of self-discovery from one "island" to the next—from art, to first love, to foreign culture, to shipwreck on the shoals of reason. In the twelfth canto, a wiser, purged man (having come full circle) can hang up his oars, pray, and fall asleep. Important as the poem may be for understanding Walcott's early linguistic dexterity, the resolution is too facile, its cyclical voyage motif predictable, and the narrative too full of allusions, puns, myths, and set scenes to be sustained.

From this same period, Walcott's drama reflects a similar frenetic mix. The subject matter of *Henri Christophe* comes from Haitian history. The title character, based on a former slave who betrayed Toussaint-Louverture, became a king, and used his power to build a palace and fortress to rival European splendor, only to be overthrown by his own people, could have been part of a manifesto on Negro dignity and human tragedy. Instead Walcott's Jacobean poetic style and occasional lapses of dramatic control seem to obscure the expression of the feelings of the characters.

Walcott's enthusiasm for impressive styles and literary classics may have been detrimental to his writing, but it also impelled him to pursue drama further—as well as poetry and painting. In the same year that *Henri Christophe* was produced (1950), he and Roderick established the Saint Lucia Arts Guild. For the first time, Derek could cast, direct, and produce plays as he wrote them. The event is fortuitous because Walcott's creativity is evolutionary. His normal practice is to improvise and revise material even while it is in the middle of a production run. Soon after founding the Guild, Walcott was recipient of a Commonwealth Development Scholarship to study at the University of the West Indies in Jamaica.

The Sea at Dauphin (1954), produced the year after his university graduation, was Walcott's first successful early drama. While it is modeled on John Millington Synge's *Riders to the Sea* (1904), there is a progressive step beyond Walcott's other juvenilia. What distinguishes *The Sea at Dauphin* is the cohesion of theme and manner of expression. A cycle of generations continues in the play as old Afa reluctantly agrees to acquaint young Jules with the island fishermen's lore. In effect what Walcott gained from Synge is not another borrowed style but inspiration to record the actual patois of Saint Lucian fishermen struggling for existence. Walcott has often extolled the need for developing poets to learn from their predecessors. The advice in his *Trinidad Sunday Guardian* article "Young Trinidadian Poets" (19 June 1966) is typical: "The search eventually ends in the discovery of other voices, and yet at its end the poet, by acquiring all of these demons, becomes himself."

Walcott's next step toward acquiring his own voice can be seen in two plays from 1957 and 1958, which owe their inception to his early experiences in New York. His first visit there, in 1957, did not exactly inspire *Ti-Jean and His Brothers*, produced later that year; it did, however, drive Walcott into an isolation so intense that he was forced to write out of fear. The play is based on the West Indian folktale of three brothers who attempt to overcome the devil. Only Ti-Jean succeeds, by using wit rather than strength or erudition. Simple as the story appears, Walcott recognized in writing it the elements of the kind of West Indian play he wanted to create. He describes the discovery in "Meanings" (*Savacou*, 1970): "For the first time, I used songs and dances and a narrator in a text. Out of that play I knew what I wanted." The second valuable play, from 1958, is *Drums and Colours*. Commissioned for the opening of the first Federal Parliament of the West Indies, the play is a sequence of skits designed to chronicle West Indian history. There are different types of protagonists for the four major periods of development: Columbus for discovery, Raleigh for conquest, Toussaint for rebellion, and Gordon for independence. Linking the scenes are various motifs, such as a gold coin that passes from generation to generation; descendants of key characters; and, most relevant to Walcott's West Indian influence, carnival revelers dancing, singing, and joking during intervals. The explicitness and the didacticism of the play are necessary for its purpose. More noteworthy, however, is the introduction of carnival masks, mime, calypso music, frozen tableaux, and asides, which disrupt realistic illusions and draw the audience into the action. By 1958, then, Walcott had incorporated West Indian folk motifs, dialect, and local music into a dramatic form unique to the Caribbean. Also in 1958 Walcott discovered Bertolt Brecht and through Brecht, classic Oriental theater and film. Brecht's "epic theater" provided the theoretical foundation for Walcott's assimilated techniques. Neither the Oriental theater nor film, however, struck him as new, but they revived memories of life in Saint Lucia. In Akira Kurosawa's film *Rashomon* (1950) Walcott recognized familiar characters, topography, and superstitions involving mountains, mists, and forests. This led in 1959 to preliminary versions of what was to become his masterpiece, *Dream on Monkey Mountain*, first produced in 1967; the play won him an Obie Award in 1971.

Few plays appeared immediately, though, out of Walcott's rich experiences in New York; one reason may be his move to Port of Spain and the founding of the theatrical group that later became the Trinidad Theatre Workshop. He launched a seven-year program training amateur actors for the roles demanded by his type of West Indian drama. Another equally valid reason is that, in addition to writing a weekly arts column for the *Trinidad Guardian*, he gave much of his attention to poetry. Between his settling in Trinidad and his winning an Obie, he married Margaret Ruth Maillard in 1962, had two daughters, and published four books of verse.

One key to the first of these volumes, *In a Green Night*, may be found in one of its poems, "A Far Cry from Africa." The West Indian's dilemma is captured in Walcott's best-known lines: "The gorilla wrestles with the superman. / I who am poisoned with the blood of both, / Where shall I turn, divided to the vein?" It would be a mistake to assume that Walcott espouses one position. This first major collection testifies to his range of ideas and technical virtuosity. Concrete references identify his native island and scenes shift from there to northern Europe and America. Time is spanned from the anonymous past ("Bronze") to the personal present ("Letter from Brooklyn"); language runs from island patois ("Parang") to the rhetorical elegance of "Ruins of a Great House." Robert Graves was impressed enough to declare Walcott's understanding of English usage to excel most if not all contemporary English-born poets.

Given the multiplicity of this collection, no single poem is representative, yet "Ruins of a Great House" shows Walcott's technical artistry with its vivid picture of a fallen empire. All that remains of the "great" plantation are dislodged stones, a broken carriage wheel, and the acrid, rotting limes, the abandoned crop of past generations. The persona in the poem muses over the fact that former masters may have evaded guilt, but they could not avoid the grave. When it occurs to him that slaves' remains may be buried nearby, anger flares up briefly, only to be diluted with the thought that John Donne's England, too, was once a colony like his own. Compassion and intelligence intermingle to resolve that there is no easy forgiveness, no unalloyed guilt.

In his review of the book for the *Listener* (5 July 1962) P. N. Furbank noted that history has made Walcott a "citizen of the world"; therefore, Furbank accepts the echoes of François Villon, Dante, Catullus, the Metaphysicals, and various modern poets. In the *Trinidad Guardian* (10 December 1969) Gordon Rohlehr hailed *In a Green Night* as a landmark in West Indian poetry, freeing such poetry from "mindless romanticism," simple "historicism," overly rhetorical protest, and "sterile abstraction." This is high praise for a first book, but while there are strains of fine lyricism, sensuous imagery, and subtle turns with complex themes, the overall framework lacks purpose and direction. The utilization of so many different masks does not allow for a sense of unity.

Selected Poems (1964) suffers the same weakness because nearly two-thirds of its thirty-nine poems are reprinted from *In a Green Night*. Of the sixteen new poems only "Origins" was not republished in the next book, *The Castaway and Other Poems* (1965). "Origins" is Jungian in its utilization of racial memory, journeying back into the recesses of human history. Saint Lucia shares place with ancient Troy, Greece, Guinea, and Egypt. Significantly the point of origin is the sea, the inevitable but pathless link for islanders from lands to which they can never return. Precipitation derived from seas and rivers supplies the denouement in the closing stanza, consecrating exiles, their humble labor, and the soil of their adopted homes.

In *The Castaway and Other Poems* the typical nameless exile of "Origins" is represented by the protean castaway Walcott once described in an unpublished essay, "The Figure of Crusoe." Wal-

cott's Crusoe is multifaceted, embodying the functions of Adam, in having to name all the objects and animals in his New World Eden; of Columbus, as discoverer and conqueror; of God, because he rules his world as a figure of awe and worship, to his man Friday; and of Daniel Defoe, due to the record he creates based on such experiences. This restructured Crusoe becomes a more potent symbol for Walcott than Icarus and Daedalus had been in his previous poetry. From the opening, title poem, to "Crusoe's Journal" and "Crusoe's Island," near the end, this book has a central focus. With a few minor exceptions, the perspective is Crusoe's no matter where the poem is set and no matter how abstract or universal the implications. "Crusoe's Journal" focuses on accommodation to an alien environment, and "Codicil" brings the volume to a bitter conclusion. Walcott's personal and professional anguish over his divided heritage is apparent: feeling history disrupted, the best minds debased, and nothingness in his heart, he has an indifference that conceals a "different rage." Writing in the *London Magazine* (January 1966), Alan Ross perceived a more positive Walcott beneath such melancholy depression. Ross also detected greater clarity without loss of evocative power in *The Castaway*: less tropical density and fewer impenetrable trails of meaning turning back on themselves.

Just as Walcott seemed to be achieving greater control over his poetry in the middle and later 1960s, his theatrical project began to show progress as well. As Walcott explains in "Meanings," he abandoned New York to settle in Trinidad because there were few serious black actors in America in 1959, and there were no producers for the kind of West Indian plays he wished to write. Thus the workshop became an outlet for him and several other West Indian talents. It also served as an educational experience in which dancers, actors, mimes, musicians, choreographers, set designers, technicians, and directors could share in experimentation. Bringing all these technical disciplines to bear on the enthusiastic, talented members of his troupe, with Brecht as his guide, Walcott was shaping Afro-Caribbean content into European form.

While Walcott was guiding his drama group, he remained active as a writer. *Ti-Jean and His Brothers* had come to him almost spontaneously; *Malcauchon*, produced in 1959, was the result of his study of Brecht and Oriental theater, and is an imitation of *Rashomon*. Walcott's major borrowings are atmosphere, perspective, and character types. Just as in Kurosawa's film the deceptive quality of reality is the theme. *Malcauchon* opens, as does *Rashomon*, with peasants sheltering together from the rain. When Walcott's characters discover the legendary criminal Chantal in their midst, the tension mounts until Chantal's accidental death. There is irony not only in the fact that the murderer is victimized but also in that Chantal's killer is the defenseless creature he had taken into his protection. Chantal's dying words reveal the final irony. In spite of his irredeemable appearance, Chantal knows love and beauty, and in his way he reveres God. Only the audience and one old man witness this revelation. For everyone else, yet another truth remains hidden.

Educational as Walcott's imitation of *Rashomon* may be, the major gain is in the creation of Chantal, a social outcast who foreshadows Walcott's best-known protagonist, Makak, in *Dream on Monkey Mountain*. There is a clear connection among Kurosawa's Japanese peasants, Brecht's "alienated" characters, and Chantal and Makak. Yet there is an equally strong source within Walcott's childhood. In "Meanings" there is mention of a violent drunkard who used to terrorize children when he came into Castries each payday. Since the mythology of Africa had been adulterated through the middle passage and generations of slavery, West Indian folklore replaced lost heroic chiefs and warriors with devils and tricksters. Walcott wanted to recover the elemental warrior latent within the old Saint Lucian derelict. The meaning of *Dream on Monkey Mountain* centers on Makak's own recovery of that potential.

Since the play is offered within a dream framework, its irrational, contradictory, and stylized elements are accounted for. Walcott's introductory "Note on Production" warns that the source is metaphor and that the play may be best understood as "a physical poem." Versatile actors can play multiple roles, extend traits of the protagonist, and function as symbols. The plot unfolds as in a segmented dream.

With Lestrade's comic interrogation of Makak in the prologue, the audience sees Lestrade's Afro-Saxon prejudices and Makak's sincere confusion about his own identity and the meaning of his life. He cannot recall his legal name, says his religion is Catholic, and says his race is "tired." While Lestrade is questioning, complete with song-and-dance routines, Tigre and Souris mime a courtroom scene: hearing, seeing, and speaking no evil. Their reaction to Makak's vision, once he

is allowed to describe it, is open derision. When all is told, an apparition of a white woman has appeared, disclosing that he is descended from warrior kings and belongs to Africa.

Part 1 of the play is a flashback to events, antecedent to the prologue, which caused Makak's arrest for "drunk and disorderly" conduct. Makak awakens from a dream, and miracles occur when he begins to believe in his nobility and powers of healing. In scene 2 he prays not that Joseph, his dying patient, will be cured but that his people will believe in themselves. Upon Joseph's sudden recovery, word spreads that Makak is a savior. The only flaw in his messianic plan to lead his people back to Africa is that his disciple Moustique is caught exploiting the people for personal gain; Moustique is soon apprehended and beaten to death. Part 1 closes with Makak attempting to fathom the mysteries of death in Moustique's lifeless eyes.

At the beginning of part 2 Makak overpowers his jailer and leads an escape into the jungle. Unlike the single line of character exposition in previous scenes, this second part of the fable follows multiple levels of meaning. Lestrade begins pursuit, extolling the white man's rational laws and excuses for "putting down the natives." Political and social reality are unavoidable when Lestrade alludes to Sharpeville (to the police violence against demonstrators in this South African city in March 1960) and asserts that the most dangerous crime is men escaping from "the prison of their lives." Such a concept entertained by a racially mixed character such as Lestrade indicates the depth of his own delusion. Significantly when Corporal Lestrade takes to the jungle in pursuit of Makak, he "goes native," ultimately becoming Makak's staunchest convert to African "Zionism." Doing a radical turn, he sells out as completely to the black cause as he had previously to the white. In this respect Lestrade dramatizes a major philosophical point made by Walcott in his introductory essay, "What the Twilight Says": the West Indian suffers from a "schizophrenic daydream" of exile from an Edenic Africa. Therefore, Walcott contends, "Once we have lost our wish to be white, we develop a longing to become black, and these may be different, but are still careers."

Wrangling among Makak's ardent followers precipitates a rising level of violence, but, caught up in the frenzy for power and revenge, he loses control. There follows a comic Walpurgisnacht that Walcott has called an apotheosis, a dream within the larger dream. Settled in Africa, Makak

Dust jacket for Walcott's 1969 collection of poems that focus on distances between people and between cultures

presides over the judgment of all past racial discrimination. In addition to Noah, Robert E. Lee, and Al Jolson, who are patently guilty, Moustique is resurrected and damned for having perverted the original dream. Without offering any defense, Moustique countercharges that, despite the best intentions, Makak himself has been corrupted by racist power and revenge.

Makak's beheading of the white apparition concludes the bloodletting and paradoxically sets him free of his own delusions. The white goddess may have introduced blackness to replace a debilitating Anglophilia, but for the West Indian it is just as limiting to identify with distant Africa. The final step to personal liberty occurs when Makak no longer needs the racial crutch. In "What the Twilight Says" Walcott sees this release as essential to West Indian authenticity: "The depth of being rooted is related to the shallowness of racial despair." Obsession with ethnic purity can be counterproductive. In the epilogue

Makak transcends illusion to disclose his essential self. Immediately he recalls his legal name, Felix Hobain. Even Moustique recognizes that Makak is a new man. His aim is to return to his mountain home and claim the heritage he has earned as a West Indian.

Just as the play is rich in ambiguities, critical reaction has varied considerably. Errol Hill finds it tangled and incoherent; Theodore Colson appreciates the necessity of a vicarious journey to purge stereotypes that undermine humanity; and Denis Solomon notes the antithetical structuring of ideas in addition to black and white—"dream and reality, essence and substance, passivity and action, purity and corruption." Selden Rodman takes Walcott to task in a lengthy 1974 interview for permitting the Negro Ensemble to turn their New York production (1971) into an antiwhite vehicle. Walcott admits discomfort with their interpretation, since his intention was not confrontational: *Dream on Monkey Mountain* closes not with a beheading but with a man achieving accommodation with his environment.

The 1970 volume containing the play serves as a culmination of Walcott's theatrical search through the 1960s, and the multiple poetic voices and masks of the decade are brought together in *The Gulf* (1969). Rohlehr sees the central theme of *The Gulf* to be "the general chasm separating peoples, cultures and even individuals within the closed unit of a family." More often than not, the narrative persona views things through glass, detached, or passing by.

The title poem incorporates major ideas and motifs from the entire book. In an airplane over Texas, the speaker considers matters as disparate as tasteless coffee, Jorge Luis Borges's prose, John Kennedy's death, personal detachment, minority violence in the United States, and the gulfs (real and metaphorical) that separate men from all vestiges of home. The "catalogue" builds to a climax with the line "age after age, the uninstructing dead." As long as the living refuse to learn from them, the dead remain "uninstructing." The poetic voice is certainly not dispassionate. There may be distance between the observer and his subject, whether he is in England, North or South America, Europe, or his native Caribbean, but he is repressing his attachments.

"Mass Man" is a satirical probing of the carnival gaiety of clerks "making style" and of one forlorn child. The speaking persona looks ahead to

Ash Wednesday, feeling a different kind of abandonment: "my mania is a terrible calm."

The closing poems are more intimate, focusing on personal matters. "In the Kitchen" imagines a touching reunion between Walcott's mother and his deceased father. "Love in the Valley" and "Hic Jacet" concern love of life made more vivid by literature, great authors, and their heroines. In "Hic Jacet" Walcott gives his reasons for having rejected metropolitan exile to remain in the islands. Claiming that he actually sought more power and more fame than writers who emigrated, he says, "I pretend subtly to lose myself in crowds / knowing my passage would alter their reflection." The paradox of seeking fame through losing himself is not difficult to resolve: the line speaks of "pretending" to become one in the crowd. Blending in, he absorbs a kind of nourishment. Giving voice to his people defeats the forces that have driven other writers to seek their fortunes abroad.

The degree to which Walcott succeeds in *The Gulf* in balancing his aesthetic taste and the earthiness of raw experience is open to critical evaluation. Roy Fuller (*London Magazine*, November 1969) suggested that judicious revision could remedy obscurities of attitude and syntactical clumsiness in specific poems. Denis Donoghue (*New York Review of Books*, 6 May 1971) thought that a weakness for grandeur and the strain between public and private expression lead portions of *The Gulf* into rhetorical excesses. On the positive side Edward Baugh points out that the title poem is "a model of a firmly controlled blend of eloquence and rhythmic emphasis on the one hand and the plain-sounding and low-keyed on the other" (*Literary Half-Yearly*, July 1970).

Walcott put some of his hopes for the future into less metaphorical form during the 1970s. In the first decade following political independence for several West Indian nations and at the height of the black-power movement, great social pressures were at work. In introducing *Dream on Monkey Mountain*, he mentions the value of art and the artist as revolutionary weapons; however, he does not advocate revolution as an end in itself. In a 1973 interview with Raoul Pantin, "Any Revolution Based on Race Is Suicidal," Walcott complained about the failure of "radical" writers who are too concerned with extraliterary matters to serve the demands of their craft.

While he rejects the radical approach, he is not a reactionary. Elsewhere he explained to Rod-

man how the sophisticated author might provoke effective change. Using the label "colonial" as opposed to "revolutionary," Walcott defined a more mature writer. Because of the revolutionary's antagonistic approach, such a writer actually galvanizes and perpetuates the tradition he opposes. More subtly, by assimilating the time-tested aesthetics of his predecessors, the colonial artist confiscates what he wants and ultimately generates a tradition in his own image. By his special definition then, Walcott told Pantin that in respecting certain ideas he "is still revolutionary in the sense that he is saying that the preservation of these ideas is valid when the revolution is finished." This idea is consistent with his commitment to the West Indies and with his description of the audience he wishes to reach with his plays: "My audience is . . . the people we tend to have the most social contempt for. . . . It is our duty in the theatre to get to that person, not by any lowering of standards of literacy or anything like that, but by an intensity and a clarity of performance that will affect everybody in that audience from a Minister of Culture down to somebody who's somebody's maid." Walcott's article "What the Lower House Demands" (*Trinidad Guardian*, 6 July 1966) suggests how to reach them: with humanity, entertainment, and even proportionate vulgarity—the gifts of "geniuses from Shakespeare to Fellini."

More or less successful attempts to execute some of these concepts resulted in a few minor plays in the first half of the 1970s: *In a Fine Castle* (1971), *Franklin* (1973), and *The Charlatan* (1974). Themes common to the three have to do with social and racial conflict and problems of identity. As Walcott expected, the plays met with negative criticism because of the number of white roles in the scripts. Racially biased comments were occasionally made. In answer Walcott might well have repeated his words to Rodman: "My great desire is to make the scene I write about as *true* as possible regardless of the consequences." These three plays of the early 1970s are relatively minor, compared with Walcott's most accomplished dramas, but each reveals individuals coming to terms with life in an emerging society.

Walcott's next major publication, *Another Life*, his autobiographical poetic portrait of the West Indian artist, is based on personal experience, but there are universal implications rising out of the narrator's imaginative reflection. Not only does Walcott record the growth of an intelligence in *Another Life*, but a measure of his own artistic maturation will be evident through comparing the book with the poem he has called its urtext, *Epitaph for the Young*. In place of the earlier poem's allusiveness is a self-assured style, whether the mood is melancholy, humorous, or bitterly satirical.

Part 1 opens with a boy painting a landscape for his mentor (Harold Simmons) to inspect. Readers have the advantages of a dual perspective: the boy's feelings lend immediacy, but his seasoned insights as a man are also available to leaven naiveté with experience. The "Divided Child" indicated in the title of this section is then a subtle symbol for the many polarities that must be resolved before the long poem concludes. He begins by cataloguing the people and things nearest to him: domestic motifs of sewing, ironing, and washing clothes. The boy recalls laundry like "freshly ironed clouds," and the "iron hymn" on his mother's old sewing machine. Such metaphors are woven into the narrative fabric far more effectively than in *Epitaph for the Young*.

What the youth learns in the classroom is fused imaginatively with things he knows, turning Castries into his Troy, or his New Jerusalem. In his impressionable mind the juxtaposition of the Old World tradition and his neglected colony tends toward wild exaggeration. To restore balance, without undermining the pervasive sense of wonder, Walcott resorts to mild self-mockery: "Provincialism loves the pseudo-epic / so if these heroes have been given a stature / disproportionate to their cramped lives, / remember I beheld them at knee-height." Hindsight permits this editorial leveling. Lloyd W. Brown (*Journal of Commonwealth Literature*, December 1976) sees the child image as archetypal for the newness and the creative possibilities in the New World. As Walcott told Carl Jacobs in 1966, provincialism itself is not without certain advantages, giving him a "deeper communion with things that metropolitan writers no longer care about . . . attachments to family, earth and history."

Part 2, dedicated to "Gregorias" (an artist figure based on Dunstan St. Omer), concentrates on Walcott's teenage years and his valuable friendship with the aspiring young painter St. Omer, who becomes symbolic of all the "Gregoriases," struggling young artists of his generation. Their mutual aim, and the central objective of *Another Life*, is "Adam's task of giving things their names." Awed by the masters of Europe, they create, expressing their island's primeval past. Gregorias the painter "abandoned apprenticeship" to

Dust jacket for the long autobiographical poem in which Walcott chronicles his artistic development

risk the "errors of his own soul," while the poet is tied to "this sidewise crawling, this classic / condition of servitude"; and together the works are complementary, in style and medium: words and pictures, translating experience into art.

Part 3, "A Simple Flame," opens with the 1948 fire that devastated much of Castries. Reconstruction of the city in modern concrete reinforces the young narrator's sense of inexorable change. Walcott's first love, Anna (Andreuille Alcée), absorbs more and more of his attention and passes into his poetry. Conscious of the "noble treachery of art," he apologizes for the aesthetic urge to describe her even as they are holding hands.

The final segment of *Another Life* features severe social criticism before it rises to a lyrical conclusion. Titled "The Estranging Sea," this part seems bitter, for reasons both personal and professional. Experience has taught Walcott that, to the descendants of slaves, brotherhood means "spitting on their own poets / preferring their painters drunkards, / for their solemn catalogue of suicides." Closer to home he learns that Dunstan

St. Omer has tried killing himself and Harry Simmons has succeeded, his body lying undiscovered for two days. Venting frustrations, Walcott singles out government ministers, young radicals, and Uncle Toms alike as impediments to authentic development. Relenting slowly, he concedes that those who insist on dwelling on the cruelty of the past may have a point: that is, if the journey goes back to primal beginnings and wipes the slate clean.

From such a primal "nothing" (the word he repeats emphatically) a new beginning is possible. It is paradoxical that a poet who has assimilated such a wide variety of traditional influences should advocate forgetfulness. Nevertheless, measured, selective memory fits his practice. Obsession with the past is debilitating if it ends in bitterness, hatred, or self-contempt. As with Makak and as with the West Indian "intelligence" narrating *Another Life*, the individual must overcome the shackles that prevent his seeing himself as what he *is*, not simply as what he comes from (important as that may be). This is the basis of Walcott's revolution. Therefore the repetitive "nothing" near the conclusion of *Another Life* can be understood not as negative but as another beginning. Walcott ends on a note of exaltation, rejoicing in the Greek-sounding appellation "Gregorias" he has given Dunstan St. Omer. They are fulfilled in their self-appointed task— like that of the Mediterranean Greeks—naming a New World.

Criticism regarding *Another Life* has been generally favorable, even when not enthusiastic. Paul Smyth's assessment in *Poetry* (December 1973) speaks for several others, admiring lyrical passages while regretting the lack of sustained coherence. West Indian novelist George Lamming underscores the political and racial pressures that automatically make a writer with Walcott's open-mindedness unpopular with cultural nationalists (*New York Times Book Review*, 6 May 1973). Several leading writers and critics from the Caribbean have devoted articles to the book, but the most extensive coverage is Baugh's biographical *Derek Walcott: Memory as Vision* (1979). Baugh reaches the conclusion that "The Estranging Sea" fulfills the first sections of *Another Life* and provides "a frame and perspective" for viewing the entire poem. Despite questions of formal coherence or controversial ideas, the poetry alone bears repeated readings.

Following the publication of *Another Life*, Walcott accepted the commission of the Royal Shakespeare Company to write a modern version of Tirso de Molina's Spanish classic *El burlador de Sevilla* (1634). In his hands this Golden Age treatment of Spanish aristocracy, including the original Don Juan Tenorio, becomes *The Joker of Seville* (produced in 1974, published in 1978). A young West Indian poet-playwright may appear to be an unlikely choice for this adaptation, but Walcott saw himself as perfectly suited. Using the original plot as a rough map, Walcott said he strove to emulate the pace of scenes and the general pattern with an authentic re-creation rather than artificial imitation: "The wit, panache, the swift or boisterous elan of his period, or of the people in his play, are as alive to me as the flair and flourishes of Trinidad music and its public character. . . . Once its music entered my head naturally there was no artifice in relating the music and drama of the Spanish verse to what strongly survives in Spanish Trinidad." Perhaps it is this compatibility of cultures and expression that encouraged Walcott to change the setting of one major scene (the seduction of Tisbea) to the New World and to expand upon the original figure of Don Juan to dramatize several of Walcott's own principal themes.

The protagonist's inexorable quest and every other aspect of the play—music, humor, dialogue, and character revelation—push the action forward. Only shortly before his fatal encounter with the vengeful statue of Don Gonzalo does Juan come close to voicing his impulsive drive. Reminded of the church's call for penitence, he responds, "I serve one principle! That of / the generating earth." Farther on it becomes clear that Walcott's Juan embodies an irrational force—the human, Dionysian spirit that rebels against conscious prohibitions beginning in Eden. As an existential, post-Adamic man, he is alienated from institutional values. The terms of his existence require that he use every weapon in his arsenal to conquer each female and overmatch every man he meets.

Since Walcott's revision benefits from modern psychoanalytic insights, his characters are far more introspective. Juan's rival Octavio, for example, experiences vicarious wish fulfillment through Juan's exploits. While secretly admiring Juan's liberty, Octavio hates and represses the dark instincts in his own nature. He has a recurring nightmare involving a woman and a snake in a garden: he becomes the snake he fears, and the woman welcomes his violation. Guilt forces Octavio to suspect the motivations of even his

Poster for the first production of the musical Walcott and Galt MacDermot wrote about Rastafarian culture in Jamaica during the 1960s

most honorable intentions. There is ambivalence within the women Juan seduces as well. Instead of being ruined by Juan, they are liberated by his unlawful embrace. Each of them, because of a weakness in her spiritual armor, is partly responsible for her own seduction. She either accepts Juan disguised as the man she wants, or she is swayed by pride to be an accomplice in her own deception.

Walcott's depiction of women in this light is not to be seen as excusing the crime by blaming the victim. Far from it: he uses the opportunity to comment on the plight of women in a male-dominated society. His statement is cogent not merely because it coincides with the Western feminist movement but because it refers to humanity regardless of sex. Men as well as women are victimized by the conventional roles imposed by society. After Isabella, Juan's initial victim, has suffered months of forced seclusion in a nunnery,

she comes to regard the loss of her maidenhood in terms of the human responsibility purchased by Eve when she ate the fruit of knowledge in Eden. In consoling her fellow sufferers Ana and Aminta, Isabella does not offer sympathy but enlightenment. Their vaunted chastity, self-denial, and conformity to the dictates of propriety had made them marketable as wives only; at the same time it was antithetical to freedom and a full life. Her bitterly earned wisdom may console Ana and Aminta, but another woman, Tisbea, has committed suicide because Juan dashed her hopes of upward mobility through a noble marriage.

Juan disappoints people and sometimes causes death, as with Tisbea and Don Gonzalo, but for all his lies and chicanery he also discloses truth. Juan's tragic epitaph "sans humanité" becomes a choral refrain in the epilogue. As Juan remarks on various occasions, he is a principle, a force larger than life and therefore incapable of human emotions. Although others benefit from Juan's exploits, his flouting of maidenhood and all authority is fruitless for him. To compound the irony, the archliberator becomes trapped in the irreverent role he has chosen to play. In this respect, too, he assumes characteristics of Dionysus.

Yet, as is the case with Dionysus, Juan's death is not the final word. Death itself is cast in the joker's role as Juan's corpse is borne off to an insistent calypso beat: "If there is resurrection, Death is the Joker, / sans humanité!" Raphael's calypso band is appropriately costumed as other cards in the joker's deck. The island-flavored music is vibrant and sometimes as risqué as the native *kaiso* (popular songs ridiculing taboos and foibles). Thus, in spite of the serious theme, a lighter comic mood is an integral part of the overall drama. It is the kind of integrated theatrical performance Walcott considers necessary for the West Indies; it also radiates meaning in a form accessible to the world at large. A *Trinidad Guardian* reviewer, Victor Questel (6 December 1974), felt that the music and content enhance each other, and another critic, Patricia Ismond (in *Tapia*, 1 June 1975), attested to the fact that local audiences were elated with the "sensuous and aesthetic expression," which engenders a spirit of communal participation.

Walcott's next major play, *O Babylon!* (produced in 1976, published in 1978), is far removed from the Spanish aristocracy depicted in *The Joker of Seville*. He could hardly have selected a group less sympathetic to Western culture than the Rastafarians of Jamaica. The sect abstains from the material trappings of civilization, deifies Ethiopian leader Haile Selassie, and makes poverty a virtue until members can leave "Babylonian" exile to return to Africa. The dramatic tension in the story centers on the conflict between the temptations of fleshly comforts and the yearning for spiritual fulfillment. The primary antagonist is a North American corporation interested in acquiring a Rastafarian settlement as a site for a resort hotel. The corporation bribes officials, social workers, and Rude Bwoy, one of the slum dwellers who wants to become a "Big Black Star," but it cannot buy the consent of the protagonist, Aaron, and the community's spiritual leader, Sufferer. The particular era (the period of Emperor Selassie's 1966 visit to Jamaica) causes the pressure to mount rapidly. If the Rastafarians can reach an agreement with the government, many of them will be permitted to repatriate when the emperor returns to Ethiopia.

Unfortunately certain restrictions prevent former criminals, such as Aaron, and the elderly, including Sufferer, from being eligible. Striking out in frustration, Aaron commits arson. His rash act threatens to push Priscilla, the woman he loves, back into the city, but in the end they are reconciled. The long-range tragedy is that he gives the government the pretext it needs to deprive the Rastafarians of their land. As the various conflicts are resolved, the theme becomes clear. In this regard Rude Bwoy's changing outlook is especially instrumental. Cynicism permits him to grow successful, but he learns to respect and envy Aaron's resistance to the temptations that were too great for him. Aaron's defense in court is enlarged to include all the downtrodden people of the earth, and it praises the "unquenchable spark," the faith that preserves a man such as Aaron. When he is released from jail, his dreadlocks shorn, he still believes in the God he has not been permitted to see. Following days of walking among the Jamaican mountains, he learns to love his native land. His home, like Makak's "Africa of the mind," depends on the peace he makes within himself.

Since Rude Bwoy's nightclub act takes him from the slums to glittering foreign stages, there is motivation for the music (scored by Galt MacDermot). It ranges from throbbing reggae to soft, lyrical, moving spiritual numbers, and Walcott considers it to be so much a part of the play that he has called *O Babylon!* his first "real musical." His argument is that his previous plays do not integrate songs and dance so thoroughly into every aspect of the drama. He suggests that his cast be judged as closely for their singing and dancing as for their acting. The writer and director, too, of course, influence the theatrical production. Early presentations brought receptive audiences, but some critics complained of particular flaws. Questel found the play "too easily and glibly put together" for the "fierce integrity that the Rastafarian cult deserves" (*Tapia*, 28 March 1976). Sule Mombara (*Caribbean Contact*, April 1976) detected incompatibility between the sometimes-European musical form and the African content. Whether in reaction to such observations or for other reasons, Walcott made substantial revisions before *O Babylon!* and *The Joker of Seville* were published in a single volume in 1978.

Sea Grapes (1976), his next major poetry collection, revives familiar material, yet it seems fresher and more accomplished. Aside from *Another Life*, which conforms to an extended autobiographical thread, *Sea Grapes* is Walcott's first organically unified anthology. There is a subtle pattern in *Sea Grapes*, despite Richard Pevear's contention that there is too much diversity for the book to be rounded off completely (*Nation*, 12 February 1977). Whether Walcott consciously devised an overall substructure, it exists nonetheless. The initial sign that a metaphorical return voyage lies ahead appears in "Sea Grapes," the opening poem. The Caribbean schooner and the observer on the beach are linked with the Aegean and the archetypal wanderer Odysseus. Distances in time, space, and geography define the arrangement of the book.

The beginning section, containing twenty-one poems, culminates in a paean to Saint Lucia. Themes range from the desecrations caused by tourism in the U.S. Virgin Islands to meditations on painting and one of Walcott's favorite symbols, Adam and his progeny in the New World Eden. There follows a sequence of caustic poems on political machinations. The speaker shows his despair in "Dread Song": "let things be the same / forever and ever / the faith of my tribe." "Natural History" is milder in tone, and it reviews the evolution of man from his emergence as a "walking fish" through his arduous adaptation to the atomic age. The next poem, "Names," catalogues the broken shards of the Old World that have washed ashore in the Caribbean.

The earthy response of a child comparing stars to "fireflies caught in molasses" sets the stage for the volume's centerpiece. "Sainte Lucie," the longest poem in the collection, dramatically closes the first group of poems. Its final movement, entitled "For the Altar-piece of the Roseau Valley Church . . . ," has biographical interest because it centers on a mural painted by Walcott's friend St. Omer (the "Gregorias" of *Another Life*). In his mural St. Omer depicts not unearthly saints, but local people engaged in their accustomed duties. Walcott admits Roseau Valley is no Eden and its inhabitants no heavenly creatures, but he can see their spirits and the "real faces of angels."

In the next fourteen poems, from "Over Colorado" to "The Bright Field," he elaborates more on foreign places than he does in the poems ending with "Sainte Lucie." As Walcott's allusion to Walt Whitman in "Over Colorado" suggests, optimistic projections have gone wrong in places other than the West Indies. After touching numerous points on the circumference of his larger world, Walcott, with intermingled imagery of Lon-

Dust jacket for the volume in which Walcott defines poetry as "a phrase men can pass from hand to mouth . . . across the centuries"

don and Trinidad in "The Bright Field," returns attention to the West Indies. The conciliatory reflection in "The Bright Field" brings the voyage back to its beginning and provides an emotional close to the thus-far-accumulated poems.

Beginning with "Dark August," what may be considered the concluding group of eleven poems sets a more somber mood than has appeared earlier. Experience has taught the speaker to "love the dark days" and "to sip the medicine of bitterness." Gray comes to symbolize strength in "To Return to the Trees." Like these trees, he has sunk roots, "going under the sand / with this language slowly, / by sand grains, by centuries." In her review of *Sea Grapes* Valerie Trueblood (*American Poetry Review*, May-June 1978) reiterates the fact that Walcott has been "criticized at home for not making the break with the great tradition of English literature and writing in 'the language of the tribe.'" Trueblood detects the kind of originality he practices: "His way is to find what we didn't know was there in English, while keeping its excellences." What he has found derives from the spoken, as well as the written word, as is shown in the echoes of literary masterpieces and Saint Lucian patois.

In spite of two notable triumphs in 1976—publishing *Sea Grapes* to favorable reviews and bringing *O Babylon!* successfully to the stage—personal and professional factors led to Walcott's resignation from the Trinidad Theatre Workshop. Seventeen years of fruitful collaboration resulted in several plays with a distinctive West Indian style and an amateur theatrical troupe capable of going its own independent way. As a result of this break Walcott's next major play, *Remembrance*, while it starred Wilbert Holder, on loan from the workshop, had its 1977 premiere with the Courtyard Players in Saint Croix. Two years later, after Walcott's usual process of continual revision, the play premiered in New York at Joseph Papp's Shakespeare Festival, with Roscoe Lee Brown in the lead. By then Walcott had written *Pantomime* (produced in 1978), the play that was published together with *Remembrance* in 1980. In the meantime he began to accept visiting professorships at U.S. universities, including New York University, Yale, and Columbia. He was named an honorary member of the American Academy of Arts and Letters in 1979.

Following the large casts and exuberance of *The Joker of Seville* and *O Babylon!*, both *Remembrance* and *Pantomime* seem comparatively sedate. There is music in *Remembrance*, but its function is not so much to advance narrative as to support mood. The opening scene is in modern Port of Spain; then the body of the play is presented as a flashback to protagonist Albert Jordan's teaching career in preindependence Trinidad. Recalling his experiences, Jordan can remember at first only mistakes and failures. He is convinced that as a teacher, husband, parent, and occasional writer he has had no positive impact.

Inspired by Thomas Gray's "An Elegy Wrote in a Country Churchyard" (1751), Jordan's principal message, the theme of the play, is that the humble, seemingly insignificant individual is a valuable human being no matter what his provincial surroundings. Characteristically Jordan senses the damage of a lifetime of colonial subjugation. Had he been truly weak, however, he could have easily shifted with each political movement. Instead he has contained his anger and remained firm in his convictions, while nationalists and racists have spent their fury in slogans and gestures. Exposing these re-

pressed feelings proves therapeutic; in the closing scenes Jordan makes peace with his inner voices.

On a higher social plane, and with greater introspection, Jordan dramatizes the same journey to accommodation that brings a renewed Makak back to Monkey Mountain. Although there may be similarities in the conclusions of these two plays, Walcott is examining an altogether new facet of one of his most fundamental themes. Violence is not the only path back to self-discovery, and even the colonized intellectual contributes ultimately to the development of his country. As its title suggests, *Remembrance* is reflective, and the action is not carried so much by music and humor as it is in his other plays of the 1970s. Richard Eder found the New York production to grow tedious in later moments (*New York Times*, 10 May 1979). Edith Oliver, on the other hand, thought the slowly darkening action was quite effective (*New Yorker*, 21 May 1979).

Pantomime reclaims the archetypal Crusoe figure, who has been important in Walcott's poetry at least since *The Castaway*. The cast of only two male actors makes *Pantomime* an even more intimate play than *Remembrance*. Despite its scaled-down cast and time span, the play uses humor and ironic role reversal to delve into a complex subject. The primary plot follows a rambling argument between Harry Trewe, English manager of a small tourist hotel in Tobago, and his black assistant, Jackson Phillip. Their point of contention is the feasibility of staging a skit Harry has written for the entertainment of his seasonal patrons. Nothing out of the ordinary happens until Harry suggests adding humor to the Robinson Crusoe story by switching roles and improvising, Harry becoming Friday and Jackson taking on the part of Crusoe. Reluctantly Jackson plays along, but when he introduces serious points about the master-slave relationship, Harry demands that they forget the idea. Offering his resignation, Jackson insists that Harry face the implications of their colonial relationship; once again the specific grows into the universal.

When Harry tries to imagine himself in the situation of Friday, he is shocked at the irony of a black man's native culture being forcibly imposed on a Christian: "He'd have to be taught by this—African . . . that everything was wrong, that what he was doing . . . I mean, for nearly two thousand years . . . was wrong. That his civilization, his culture . . . *horrible*. Was all wrong." As Jackson is quick to point out, Harry has just summarized the history of European colonization, and what is happening between the two men repeats the pattern. Whenever the civilized native rises to the level of the ruling class, his master wants "to call the whole thing off, return things to normal." Tension is maintained because Jackson has determined to amplify that very point, while Harry wants to please tourists with light comedy.

In act 2 Harry has begun to see things more clearly, and the two men begin discussing in specific detail the terms of racial and social equality. With dramatic economy the exposition flows, on both individual and broader cultural levels. Thus Jackson addresses Harry's personal crises and simultaneously outlines the means whereby West Indians may authenticate their existence. Walcott's familiar castaway is resurrected in Jackson's description of what the real Crusoe would have been like. It is Jackson's contention that Crusoe was never the lonely romanticist Harry has imagined. Instead of pining over his distant family, Jackson's realist takes control of his environment and constructs a new life with the materials at hand. He stands as the first "true" Creole because of his practical faith. Jackson argues that if Harry is to survive on the island he, too, must cut his losses and adjust to circumstances in the present. After being forced to confront some of his misgivings about marital and professional failures, Harry begins to make progress. By the final curtain he is wiser, and he and Jackson have reached a more equitable relationship.

In print *Pantomime* seems to rely heavily on long passages of exposition. Nevertheless the play was staged at least nine times between 1978 and 1981 in the Caribbean, England, and the United States. Christopher Gunness (*People*, June 1978), reviewing a 1978 Trinidad production, was pleased with the lively verbal exchanges in the opening scene, with the slowly building seriousness, and with the emotional intensity packed into the conclusion. His sole reservation was that the conclusion appears ambiguous.

Whatever the ambiguity or ambivalence in this tragicomic drama, there is no such difficulty in the poetry collected in the same period. *The Star-Apple Kingdom* (1979) is self-assured, beginning vigorously and progressing to a satisfying conclusion. Walcott is at his lyrical best, ranging widely in language and emotion. The initial poem, "The Schooner *Flight*," is a brisk narrative in the patois of the seaman-poet-speaker Shabine. Shabine has tried many things in his life, but nothing has given him a sense of fulfill-

Walcott reading at Hardin-Simmons University in Abilene, Texas, 28 September 1981 (photograph by Charles Richardson)

ment. In the final portion of the poem he spells out his quest, the "vain search for one island that heals with its harbor / and a guiltless horizon." The poem does not allow for any nebulous grail quest; life has focused Shabine's world too realistically for that.

As with Walcott, Shabine's skin is not white enough to admit him among the ruling colonial class, and after independence he is not dark enough to benefit from black pride. In fact the revolution shows him political manipulation rather than effective change. He remarks cynically that "Progress is history's dirty joke." Among the accomplishments of civilization have been genocide, slavery, the fall of empires, and colonial neglect. Transcending the hard opinions, Shabine possesses a larger insight. He has learned, as had Samuel Taylor Coleridge's "ancient mariner," to respect the seemingly insignificant things in life. Drawing his story to a close, he can say, "I am satisfied / if my hand gave voice to one people's grief." Neither glossing over nor excusing the inequities of West Indian life, Shabine knows the role he has to play.

One following poem, "In the Virgins," may be an otherwise pleasant evocation of place, but it yields an example of Walcott's occasional tendency to overplay his context of reference: "Like neon lasers shot across the bars / discos blast out the music of the spheres, / and, one by one, science infects the stars." Neither idea nor mood necessitates such hyperbolic excess. Fortunately this is soon followed by "The Sea Is History" and "Egypt, Tobago," two poems closer to Walcott's rare skill in arranging words so that meanings evolve naturally and are motivated sufficiently. Judeo-Christian parallels to the story of slavery and emancipation in "The Sea Is History" are mirrored in "Egypt, Tobago" with Old World/ New World transpositions. Antony and Cleopatra recline on a Tobago beach while his ambitions expire. Among terms of veiled sexuality, the power of "All-humbling sleep" is the central focus. Burdened with sin, his world crumbling, Antony is purged of all concerns save "tenderness / for a woman not his mistress / but his sleeping child." The sentiment, understated, is timeless; their location and station in life become irrelevant.

That openness allows Walcott to introduce two non-West Indian poems into this predominantly Caribbean volume. Their appearance is explained in part by Walcott's personal friendship with the poets to whom they are dedicated: "R. T. S. L." for Robert Lowell and "Forest of Europe" for Joseph Brodsky. In a style more conversational than anything after "The Schooner Flight," Walcott asks in "Forest of Europe":

> What's poetry, if it is worth its salt,
> but a phrase men can pass from hand to mouth?
> From hand to mouth, across the centuries,
> the bread that lasts when systems have decayed.

The poetic line and the scene are relaxed. While snow drifts against their cottage, two men exchange experiences from two different worlds in the light of their winter fire.

The Star-Apple Kingdom is populated with individuals who respond imaginatively to their environments. The Jamaican narrator who provides the perspective in the final poem, "The Star-Apple Kingdom," has reached a point in life where he feels excluded from his heritage and his island home. His reverie, prompted by old photographs and other memorabilia, covers a sequence of mixed feelings. First he feels nostalgia over the tranquil plantation life now gone forever. As a child he had been excluded from the great house, but he was comfortable in a place where he knew he belonged. The mood is soon altered, however, as he contemplates the servants pushed to the background of a family picture. Since that scene, circumstances have permitted him to rise, and he now resides in that same great house. From his disquiet it is clear that his improved position has not brought happiness.

Entering a dream, he reviews his country's independence struggle. Next are satirical lines on the new exploiters of the people, giving way to nightmares of riots, martial law, and armed motorcades. Just before dawn, he sleeps peacefully, and when he awakens, like Shabine in "The Schooner Flight," he is refreshed. From his dream he retains a useful measure of anger and with it a reaffirmed commitment to his much-abused country. Glancing at a Caribbean map, he imagines the string of islands from west to east to be turtles, drawn like suicidal lemmings instinctively toward Africa. Crying out "with the anger of love," he seeks to warn them of their danger. With that gesture his tension breaks, and the poem descends to a tranquil close.

Through the window, he observes an ancient woman washing the cathedral steps, water dripping from her rag as "vinegar once dropped from a sponge." To his awakened mind she symbolizes possible new beginnings:

> and the woman's face, had a smile been decipher-
> able
> in that map of parchment so rivered with wrinkles,
> would have worn the same smile with which he now
> cracked the day open and began his egg.

The energetic thrust of that mixed metaphor concludes a great poem. A Times Literary Supplement reviewer (Vicki Feaver, 8 August 1980) suggested that to compare "The Star-Apple Kingdom" with its thematic predecessor "Ruins of a Great House," from In a Green Night, "is to recognize Walcott's development not only in terms of techniques but also in breadth of vision." This concluding poem and "The Schooner Flight" serve as bookends to a well-rounded selection.

Two years came between The Star-Apple Kingdom and The Fortunate Traveller (1981). Walcott's experiences in that time period influenced the poetry directly, because he was the "fortunate traveller," living part of each year in New England— teaching at Columbia, Harvard, or Boston University—and part of the year in the Caribbean. All Walcott's collections since *Sea Grapes* seem to be arranged according to some unifying principle. *The Fortunate Traveller* is polar in orientation, beginning and ending with sections labeled "North," with a longer central group entitled "South" framed between them.

In the title poem a petitioner from a developing country pleads for economic assistance in England. Told that "You are so fortunate, you get to see the world," he agrees, as befits his subordinate position. The next descriptive line, though, without commentary, describes ironically the angle of his economy-class, shipboard view: "Spray splashes the portholes and vision blurs." The dominant images of the northern locations have to do with unaccustomed seasonal changes and winter cold. "Upstate," "American Muse," and "Piano Practice" all include pity for the state of the American muse. In "Piano Practice" she pleads a headache when the poet asks her out; he suspects she is merely afraid to be seen "with someone who has only one climate." In the first section the major poem, "North and South," is transitional, moving not only toward the next part of the book but preparing readers for the greater intimacy that will be developed there. Walcott outlines his function as a colonial writer recording the postmortem on the empire. Looking through glass once again, he compares coral beds under a glass-bottomed boat to the detritus of sunken civilizations. Their language is his favored heritage, even when the American muse is reluctant, or when the prejudiced cashier in "North and South" winces from touching his dark hand.

"A Sea Change" begins the "South" section, maintaining the linkage with the North and with the past. The presence of U.S. marines is mentioned in the first two poems, including an allusion to war in the South Pacific in "Beachhead." In the third, "Map of the New World," Odysseus enters the picture. Due to the juxtaposition of such elements, X. J. Kennedy's principal complaint is that Walcott may strive to cover too broad a canvas, giving such longer poems as "North and South" the appearance of being disoriented (*Poetry*, March 1983). On the other hand, Mary Salter finds some metaphors cramped in too small a space or overexplained (*New Republic*, 17 March 1982). Writing in the West Indies, Jeremy Taylor is suspicious of Walcott's overly poetic craftsmanship. He suspects that Walcott is writing for "intellectuals rather than for me and you" (*Express*, 4 August 1982). Cogent as each of these

observations may be, they mostly speak of isolated points within a work of singular accomplishment. When the persona in the poems is back in the West Indies, in the "South" section, Walcott again sharpens his satirical pen. "The Spoiler's Return" resurrects a famous calypsonian to criticize graft, censorship, social decline, and fruitless causes. Spoiler sings about local scandals, international relations, and famous names from history and legend. Once again Walcott's vehicle of description and his subject matter are intricately bound together because of Trinidad's polyglot cultural matrix. Calypso and carnival bands draw upon issues ranging from the trivial to the sublime, using humor and extravagant theatrics to emphasize their points.

That basically critical stance and such broad references are but two features of this middle section. Beginning with "The Hotel Normandie Pool" and continuing to "Store Bay" at the end, Walcott turns confessional. Not only are his three children (Peter, Elizabeth, and Anna) and his wife (Norline Metivier Walcott) named, but his inner pain over divorce (from his second wife, Margaret), being alone, and the stillbirth of a daughter are disclosed. What could have been maudlin in inexperienced hands is delicately balanced between raw emotion and aesthetic distance. His brother poet Ovid and the mythical Narcissus enter the first of these poems, but, after that, literary allusions and face-saving humor give way to stark details of the observable scene.

The last section of the book is more detached once again. The title of the final poem, "The Season of Phantasmal Peace," is a benediction on all the cross-purposes and polar separations exemplified in the rest of the poetry. Moments of peace may be fleeting, as are the seasons, "but, for such as our earth is now it lasted long."

Three years passed before *Midsummer* was published in 1984, but there are connections between these two books, well beyond the facts that *The Fortunate Traveller* is dedicated to Brodsky and *Midsummer* addresses him directly in its first and last poems. The contrasts between temperate seasons and tropical stasis carry over from the earlier book, and *Midsummer* complements the polarities of *The Fortunate Traveller* by stressing correspondences. It is almost as though Walcott wishes to challenge those critics who continue to see his style as divided. The central focus of *Midsummer* is the unifying diversity of his personal Caribbean experience.

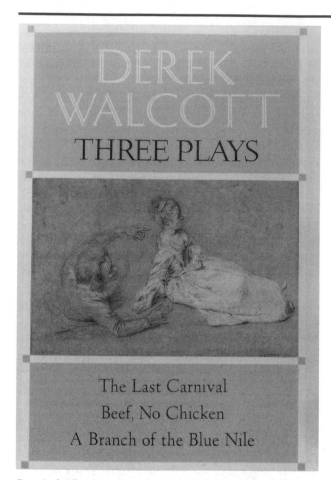

Dust jacket for the volume that includes a largely rewritten version of In a Fine Castle, *retitled* The Last Carnival

Although the volume is divided into two parts, the fifty-four (untitled) poems are numbered consecutively. Walcott's profession as colonial writer is the subject of many selections. In "IX" he describes the virtues of a writing style transparent as Chinese pictographics, "a tone colloquial and stiff," like the style of Li Po, "all synthesis is one heraldic stroke." In "XVII" Walcott weds his lifelong love of painting to his family tree: throughout the book he mentions names of artists, but in "XVII" he lays his rightful claim to the Dutch masters through his Dutch grandfather's bloodline. Elsewhere Walcott's autobiographical voice is emphasized by his naming relatives and places he has lived in New York, Brookline, Port of Spain, and Diego Martin. Beyond that, he describes small-town motel rooms, rainy days, the blistering heat of summer, and moments of dislocation that he recognizes as being almost universal.

As usual, critical opinion is divided and based on familiar criteria. R. W. Flint (*New York Times Book Review*, 8 April 1984) sees *Midsummer*

as a looser, more restful collection than some of Walcott's previous books, but he finds the Caribbean pieces more natural than the "Lowellian" poems on Boston. Both Flint and an anonymous *Yale Review* critic (Autumn 1984) admire the intense lyricism and the parallels with traditional sonnet sequences. The *Yale Review* article favors Walcott's leisurely journalistic style, "where digression is itself the matter of the journey." Steven Ratiner (*Christian Science Monitor*, 6 April 1984), on the other hand, despite praise for the brilliant language, longs for a controlling subject to provide balance and proportion, one that can sustain development beyond the myopic self-absorption of the poet himself.

There is hardly anything new here. Beginning in the 1960s, with Walcott's first books, there were reservations about the artificiality of a West Indian using such "eloquent English," and at the same time the disparity of Walcott's subject matter began drawing fire. Given the consistency of such remarks from a variety of critics, there is obviously substance to their concerns. Either Walcott has yet to rein in his unquestioned talent, or criticism is reluctant to grant license to his unprecedented oeuvre. It is Walcott's virtuoso performance as a lyricist that elicits admiration, while it simultaneously defies formal boundaries; it is his catholic ingestion of ideas and styles that enriches his subject matter, while it simultaneously taxes the very conventions it purports to assimilate.

Walcott's next publication was *Three Plays* (1986), which contains a vastly rewritten *In a Fine Castle*, retitled *The Last Carnival*, along with *Beef, No Chicken* and *A Branch of the Blue Nile*. The thematic focus in *The Last Carnival* has been shifted away from Brown, the uncommitted mulatto journalist of the 1971 version, to Agatha Willett, an immigrant English governess, and Clodia De-LaFontaine, her young Creole charge, who dedicate themselves to Trinidad's independence movement. Scenes in act 1 cover the time from 1948, when Agatha Willett arrives during carnival season, to Independence Day in 1962. Act 2 is set in the early 1970s. Carnival time is a recurrent motif, and different characters see each year's celebration as possibly the last "Mas": one character kills himself after the carnival; martial law threatens the carnival's continuation in another scene; and Clodia's exile means she has seen her last carnival. The situational irony concluding the play is that Brown, a cynical reporter for the *Guardian*, considers himself condemned to an island he spurns but cannot leave, while Clodia is forced out because she associates with rebellious guerrillas. Clodia's parting advice to Brown is to "Find a cause and love it."

The two white women appear exonerated in their choices because of their love and commitment, especially when Agatha's firebrand rhetoric evolves into practical assistance for officials learning to govern a fledgling nation. Since Walcott has been charged often enough with writing for white audiences, he may be accused of veiled racism in making Brown so negative while having an Englishwoman agitate for peasant awareness and later become an essential adviser to the new Trinidad government. Another interpretation may be closer to Walcott's message. For years he has insisted that good and bad are color-blind value judgments independent of race.

Beef, No Chicken treats with sensitive humor the personal tragedies that inevitably accompany "progress." Otto Hogan, his sister Euphony, and a circle of friends face the incursion of a new six-lane highway near the town of Couva. Despite their efforts to delay fate, their rural village will be lost to the traffic and a faster pace of life. As important as that theme may be, the sight gags and puns that provide entertainment throughout the play save it from becoming overly serious. Otto keeps reminding his friends of the values they are watching disappear. Knowledge of the expected death of his closest friend, Alwyn, darkens the horizon, but Alwyn's philosophy is that man should make the best of things even if they are short-lived. Through Otto and Alwyn, Walcott dramatizes two attitudes toward an uncertain future. Since he keeps the tone light and uplifting, this middle piece serves nicely as an interlude between the heavier burdens of *The Last Carnival* and *A Branch of the Blue Nile*.

A Branch of the Blue Nile begins as a play about an amateur acting troupe and grows into a compendium of all Walcott's theatrical experiences up to 1983. In this respect it may offer too many techniques and ideas for readers to digest well. From the outset the actors are rehearsing a West Indian version of William Shakespeare's *Antony and Cleopatra* (1606-1607). Without warning, rehearsals turn in on themselves and become improvised dramas about the cast. One of the themes, then, concerns the often-indistinguishable line between fact and fiction. After the unavoidable comparisons with Luigi Pirandello's *Six Characters in Search of an Author* (1921), Brechtian *verfremdungseffekten* (effects that main-

tain aesthetic distance), and stage confessionals such as Michael Bennett's *A Chorus Line* (1975), there remain internal echoes of Walcott's own career: play production as subject (*Pantomime*); the dream within a dream (*Dream on Monkey Mountain*); seeking fulfillment through a religious sect (*O Babylon!*); adaptation of a classic to West Indian terms (*The Joker of Seville*); and rifts between director and company, as happened between Walcott and the Trinidad Theatre Workshop. The list could be extended by recounting familiar themes.

The title of *A Branch of the Blue Nile* and the main theme derive from the English character Harvey St. Just's attempt to combine local dialect with Shakespearean lines in *Antony and Cleopatra*, while Trinidadian actor Chris Lewis is piecing together an impromptu play ("A Branch of the Blue Nile"), casting directly from life. Problems arise on several levels, professional and personal disagreements mingling, as one scene after another is interrupted for discussion of the fictional role and the actor's performance. For example, the actress Sheila Harris, who experiments with a religious sect, discovers her worship to be another form of performance, not unlike her devotion to acting. Along with that parallel, comparisons are drawn between the status of the profession in Trinidad and abroad. Whereas there is neglect in Port of Spain, there is injustice in London and New York. In spite of the layered themes and overlapping techniques, one anonymous early reviewer found that the synthesis works well in performance (*Trinidad Guardian*, 10 November 1983).

The publishing of Walcott's *Collected Poems* (1986) is the crowning achievement in a consolidation process that began as far back as the writing of *Remembrance* and his resignation from the Trinidad Theatre Workshop in 1976. Selections from his successive works afford the reader a view of Walcott's developing style through *Midsummer*. As for *Midsummer* itself, its direct candor is the mature extension of an allusive, confessional style dating back to Walcott's earliest verse. From *Three Plays*, *A Branch of the Blue Nile* is equally close to Walcott's own life. It provides exposition, then dramatizes the impact of theater on a group of people struggling to discover themselves and the meaning of their lives. The combined effect of the two collections is to affirm the centrality of West Indian experiences in the New World.

The two-part division of his next poetry collection, *The Arkansas Testament* (1987), into sec-

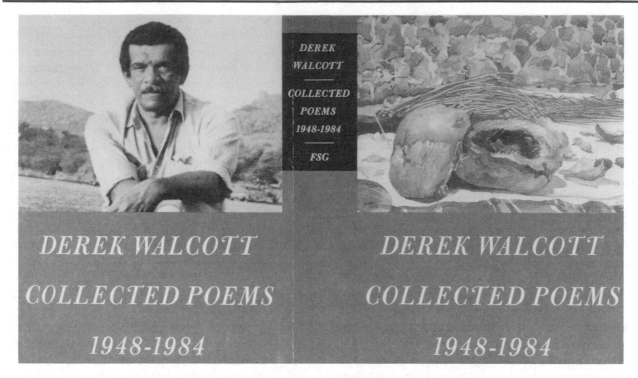

Dust jacket for the volume that includes Walcott's selection of his major poems

tions entitled "Here" and "Elsewhere" reflects the enduring bifurcation of colonialism. Walcott's familiar themes emphasize home, memories, the past, and contrasts among cultures both ancient and modern. Suspended between his native Saint Lucia and his adopted North America, he weaves a poetic synthesis that consoles even as it fails to reconcile his displacement.

Walcott's propensity to turn all of Western culture to his own purposes reached new heights with the publication of *Omeros* in 1990. Combining Homeric and Dantean elements within a New World context, Walcott undertakes nothing less than a New World epic of the dispossessed. On the figurative level a striking, black Helen embodies the island of Saint Lucia. Whether they are descendants of African slaves or representatives of the waning empire, the author and the separate protagonists ultimately discover that, through their efforts to take possession of the metaphorical Helen, the island has laid its inextricable claim on each of them. In the bittersweet harmony of *Omeros*, Walcott reflects the unfulfilled promise and the potential of the Americas.

Walcott presently teaches at Boston University, where he has been since 1981. He continues painting, one of his first loves; he writes at a furious pace and still produces and directs plays. His career as a serious writer has encouraged many younger Caribbean artists, and the success of his Trinidad Theatre Workshop has inspired new companies throughout the West Indies. Beyond that, his poetry and drama stand as artistic proof that the most complex issues in Western civilization culminate in the New World. Thus Walcott enjoys an international reputation that by many estimates places him among the greatest contemporary English writers.

Interviews:

Carl Jacobs, "There's No Bitterness in Our Literature, No Matter How Degrading Our History," *Trinidad Sunday Guardian*, 22 May 1966, p. 9;

Dennis Scott, "Walcott on Walcott," *Caribbean Quarterly*, 14 (March-June 1968): 77-82;

Raoul Pantin, "We Are Still Being Betrayed," *Caribbean Contact*, 1 (July 1973): 14, 16;

Pantin, "Any Revolution Based on Race Is Suicidal," *Caribbean Contact*, 1 (August 1973): 14, 16;

Selden Rodman, "Derek Walcott," in his *Tongues of Fallen Angels* (New York: New Directions, 1974), pp. 233-259;

Robert Hamner, "Conversation with Derek Walcott," *World Literature Written in English*, 16 (November 1977): 409-420;

Edward Hirsch, "An Interview with Derek Walcott," *Contemporary Literature*, 20 (Summer 1979): 279-292;

Jo Thomas, "For a Caribbean Poet, Inner Tension and Foreign Support," *New York Times*, 21 August 1979, p. 2;

Sharon Ciccarelli, "Reflections Before and After Carnival," in *Chant of Saints*, edited by Michael S. Harper and Robert B. Stepto (Urbana: University of Illinois Press, 1979), pp. 296-309;

"An Interview with Ned Thomas," *Kunapipi*, 3, no. 2 (1981): 42-47;

James Atlas, "Derek Walcott: Poet of Two Worlds," *New York Times Magazine*, 23 May 1982, pp. 32-34, 38-42, 50-51;

Carrol B. Flemming, "Singing the True Caribbean: The Plays and Poems of Derek Walcott," *Americas*, 34 (May-June 1982): 8-11;

"Walcott Tells of Local Amateur Actors in Disguise," *Trinidad Sunday Guardian*, 11 July 1982, p. 5;

"Derek Walcott Talks About *The Joker of Seville*," *Carib*, 4 (1986): 1-15;

Edward Hirsch, "The Art of Poetry, XXXVII: An Interview," *Paris Review*, 101 (Winter 1986): 196-230;

Edward Baugh, "Derek Walcott on West Indian Literature and Theatre," *Jamaica Journal*, 21 (May-July 1988): 50-52;

Charles H. Rowell, "An Interview with Derek Walcott," *Callaloo*, 11 (Winter 1988): 80-89.

Bibliographies:

Robert Hamner, "Derek Walcott: His Works and His Critics—An Annotated Bibliography," *Journal of Commonwealth Literature*, 16 (August 1981): 142-184;

Irma E. Goldstraw, *Derek Walcott: An Annotated Bibliography of His Works* (New York: Garland, 1984);

Stewart Brown, "Select Bibliography," in *The Art of Derek Walcott*, edited by Brown (Bridgend, Mid Glamorgan, U.K.: Poetry Wales Press / Chester Springs, Pa.: Dufour, 1991), pp. 215-224.

Biography:

Edward Baugh, *Derek Walcott: Memory as Vision* (London: Longman, 1979).

References:

Funso Aiyejina, "Derek Walcott: The Poet as a Fed-

erated Consciousness," *World Literature Written in English*, 27 (Spring 1987): 67-80;

Albert Olu Ashaolu, "Allegory in *Ti-Jean and His Brothers*," *World Literature Written in English*, 16 (April 1977): 203-211;

Edward Baugh, "Metaphor and Plainness in the Poetry of Derek Walcott," *Literary Half-Yearly*, 11 (July 1970): 47-58;

Stephen P. Breslow, "Trinidadian Heteroglossia: A Bakhtinian View of Derek Walcott's Play *A Branch of the Blue Nile*," *World Literature Today*, 63 (Winter 1989): 36-39;

Lloyd W. Brown, "Caribbean Castaway New World Odyssey: Derek Walcott's Poetry," *Journal of Commonwealth Literature*, 11 (December 1976): 149-159;

Brown, "Dreamers and Slaves—The Ethos of Revolution in Walcott and LeRoi Jones," *Caribbean Quarterly*, 17 (September-December 1971): 36-44;

Brown, "The Personal Odyssey of Derek Walcott," in his *West Indian Poetry* (Boston: Twayne, 1978), pp. 118-138;

Frank A. Collymore, "An Introduction to the Poetry of Derek Walcott," *Bim*, 3 (June 1949): 125-132;

Theodore Colson, "Derek Walcott's Plays: Outrage and Compassion," *World Literature Written in English*, 12 (April 1973): 80-96;

Michel Fabre, " 'Adam's Task of Giving Things Their Name': The Poetry of Derek Walcott," *New Letters*, 41 (Fall 1974): 91-107;

Elaine Savory Fido, "Value Judgements on Art and the Question of Macho Attitudes: The Case of Derek Walcott," *Journal of Commonwealth Literature*, 21 (August 1986): 109-119;

Robert Elliot Fox, "Derek Walcott: History as Dis-Ease," *Callaloo*, 9 (Spring 1986): 331-340;

Robert D. Hamner, *Derek Walcott* (Boston: Twayne, 1981);

Hamner, "Exorcising the Planter-Devil in the Plays of Derek Walcott," *Commonwealth Essays and Studies*, 7 (Spring 1985): 95-102;

Hamner, "Mythological Aspects of Derek Walcott's Drama," *Ariel*, 8 (July 1977): 35-58;

Errol Hill, "The Emergence of a National Drama in the West Indies," *Caribbean Quarterly*, 18 (December 1972): 9-40;

Patricia Ismond, "*Another Life*: Autobiography as Alternative History," *Journal of West Indian Literature*, 4 (January 1990): 41-49;

Ismond, "Walcott Versus Brathwaite," *Caribbean*

Quarterly, 17 (September-December 1971): 54-71;

Ismond, "Walcott's Latest Drama: From *Joker* to *Remembrance*," *Ariel*, 16 (July 1985): 89-101;

Biodun Jeyifo, "On Eurocentric Critical Theory: Some Paradigms from the Texts and Sub-Texts of Post-Colonial Writing," *Kunapipi*, 11, no. 1 (1989): 107-118;

Lloyd King, "Derek Walcott: The Literary Humanist in the Caribbean," *Caribbean Quarterly*, 16 (December 1970): 36-42;

Travis M. Lane, "At Home in Homelessness: The Poetry of Derek Walcott," *Dalhousie Review*, 53 (Summer 1973): 325-338;

James McCorkle, "Re-Mapping the New World: The Recent Poetry of Derek Walcott," *Ariel*, 17 (April 1986): 3-14;

Pamela Mordecai, " 'A Crystal of Ambiguities': Metaphors for Creativity and the Art of Writing in Derek Walcott's *Another Life*," *World Literature Written in English*, 27 (Spring 1987): 93-105;

Mervyn Morris, "Derek Walcott," in *West Indian Literature*, edited by Bruce King (London: Macmillan, 1979), pp. 144-160;

Morris, "Walcott and the Audience for Poetry," *Caribbean Quarterly*, 14 (March-June 1968): 7-24;

Yvonne Ochillo, "Aspects of Alienation in the Poetry of Derek Walcott," *Journal of West Indian Literature*, 3 (September 1989): 39-52;

Erskine Peters, "The Theme of Madness in the Plays of Derek Walcott," *CLA Journal*, 32 (December 1988): 148-169;

Daizal R. Samad, "Cultural Imperatives in Derek Walcott's *Dream on Monkey Mountain*," *Commonwealth Essays and Studies*, 13 (Spring 1991): 8-21;

Denis Solomon, "Ape and Essence: Derek Walcott's *Dream on Monkey Mountain*," *Tapia*, 7 (19 April 1970): 6;

Patrick Taylor, "Myth and Reality in Caribbean Narrative: Derek Walcott's *Pantomime*," *World Literature Written in English*, 26 (Spring 1986): 169-177;

Valerie Trueblood, "On Derek Walcott," *American Poetry Review*, 7 (May-June 1978): 7-10;

Clement H. Wyke, " 'Divided to the Vein': Patterns of Tormented Ambivalence in Walcott's *The Fortunate Traveller*," *Ariel*, 20 (July 1989): 55-71.

Papers:

There is a small depository of Walcott's personal papers at the University of the West Indies in Saint Augustine, Trinidad.

Denis Williams
(1 February 1923 -   )

Louis James
University of Kent at Canterbury

BOOKS: *Other Leopards* (London: New Authors, 1963);

The Third Temptation (London: Calder & Boyars, 1968);

Image and Idea in the Arts of Guyana, Edgar Mittelholzer Memorial Lectures (Georgetown, Guyana: National History and Arts Council, 1969);

Giglioli in Guyana, 1922-1972 (Georgetown, Guyana: National History and Arts Council, 1973);

Icon and Image: A Study of Sacred and Secular Forms of African Classical Art (London: Allen Lane, 1974; New York: New York University Press, 1974);

Contemporary Art in Guyana, by Williams and others (Georgetown, Guyana: Bovell's Printery, 1976);

Ancient Guyana, Edgar Mittelholzer Memorial Lectures (Georgetown, Guyana: Department of Culture, 1985);

The Archaic of North-Western Guyana (Turkeyen, Guyana: History Society, University of Guyana, 1989).

OTHER: "The Sperm of God," in *New Writing in the Caribbean*, edited by A. J. Seymour (Georgetown, Guyana: Caribbean Festival, 1972);

Guyana: Colonial Art to Revolutionary Art, 1966-1976, introduction by Williams (Ruimvelt, Guyana: National Service Publishing Centre, 1976).

Although Denis Williams is best known as a painter, archaeologist, and social anthropologist, his first novel, *Other Leopards* (1963), made a major contribution to the Caribbean literature of the 1960s. In the years of widening political independence for the region, West Indian writers were seeking an identity, trapped, as many saw it, between the intellectual hegemony of Europe and the ancestral culture of Africa. Williams, writing out of his own experience, created in his pro-

tagonist Froad an archetype of this dilemma. Yet, at the same time, Williams's highly individual imagination created a work that undermined the very stereotype it invoked and that remains as immediate today as when it was first written.

Denis Joseph Ivan Williams was born in Georgetown, Guyana, to Joseph (a merchant) and Isobel Adonis Williams, on 1 February 1923 and studied there until he got his Cambridge Senior School Certificate. In 1946 he went to London and attended the Camberwell School of Art until 1948. He then became lecturer at the Central School of Fine Art in Holborn and visiting tutor at the Slade School of Fine Art. He mounted exhibitions of his paintings in both London and Paris. In 1957 he moved to Africa, where he was to deepen his major interests in archaeology and anthropology. While in the Sudan beginning work on *Other Leopards*, he lectured in fine art at the Technical Institute in Khartoum until 1962. He then pursued research with the Institute of African Studies at the University of Ife, Nigeria (1962-1966), and the School of African and Asian Studies at the University of Lagos (1966-1968). He moved back to Guyana in 1968 and lived in the Mazaruni area of the interior, studying Amerindian remains and culture until 1974 and living virtually outside the twentieth century. For the sake of his children's education he moved into Georgetown, where he held various government posts, including that of director of art for the Ministry of Education. Although now based mainly in Georgetown, as director of the Walter Roth Museum of Archaeology and Anthropology, he is still actively involved in research. He is also working on his third novel, part of which was published in 1972 as a short story, "The Sperm of God."

His first novel, *Other Leopards*, focuses on Lobo Lionel Froad, a Guyanese whose divided racial and cultural background is indicated in his two names, the African Lobo and the European Lionel, while his failure to find an identity in either culture parallels his last name, Froad (resem-

Denis Williams (photograph by Vic Krantz, Smithsonian Institution)

bling fraud). A Guyanese massa/slave relationship is intimated in his relationship with Hughie King, the English archaeologist for whom he works as a historical draftsman, and he is in love with two women, the black Eve and the English Catherine. His personal relationships are as disastrous as his intellectual ones, and he is only able to express himself in violence.

The novel is set in the Sudan, a transitional area between equatorial forest and the Sahara, between the cultures of West Africa and of the Nilotic region, and between Arab and African. The country is in a period of political unrest, with two evangelizing groups, Muslim and Christian, attempting for political reasons to recruit Froad for Pan-Africanism and the Negro Christian church respectively. Hughie wishes to prove that African identity lies in the past, and in the Nilotic civilization.

At every point Froad finds himself an alien. Even history fails him. He views the image of Queen Amanishakete on her tomb as the image of both history and humanity. But later in the novel she is shown flogging her slaves, indicating

for Froad a desolate vision of impersonal cruelty. In a desperate attempt to liberate himself from the burden of imposed identities, he murderously attacks Hughie and flees without clothes but covered with mud to protect against blister beetles and hide his human odor. He hides in a tree, uncertain whether the approaching light is a pursuer or just the dawn.

The novel suggests schematic interpretations only to undermine them. Eve, for instance, with her black sensuousness, is the African woman of negritude, linked both with the earth and creative sexuality. But the stereotype here and elsewhere is largely in Froad's mind. Impulsive, needy, trapped between a Black Christian upbringing and repressive Muslim marriage, Eve is driven by the desire to assert her individuality. Froad is at one level the representative of moral and intellectual forces, but he is part tragic, part clown—a confused and violent mixture of intellectual and emotional need. The setting that surrounds him is both an Africa of the mind and a graphic, physical landscape, with heat, dust, insects, and overflowing latrines.

Dust jacket for Williams's first novel (1963), in which the mixed-race protagonist is alienated from black and white cultures

The meaning of the work remains open. Edward Baugh argues, drawing on views Williams expressed in his 1969 Edgar Mittelholzer Lectures, that Froad initially fails to accept the fact of West Indian miscegenation. In responding to outside claims on his identity, Froad misses the creative potential of his cultural emptiness: at the end he has come to a hopeful self-realization. At the other pole, Mark Kinkead-Weekes, equally persuasively, sees Froad as a "mordant exposure of what it means to be uncommitted, without identity." But the novel in fact ends with uncertainty even as to Froad's sanity or survival, and it is an imaginative creation that raises rather than answers questions.

Williams's second novel, *The Third Temptation* (1968), transfers the theme of identity and responsibility to Caedmon, a seaside town in Wales. The deliberately difficult form of the novel is in-

fluenced by French new-wave writing as practiced by Alain Robbe-Grillet. The structure, comprising twelve hours, midnight to noon, holds both an objective account of life on the main street and a narration of some of the accumulated memories of Joss Banks, businessman and newspaper proprietor, his thoughts set in motion by a street accident. His position of power has led him into the seduction of the wife of a designer in his employ, starting a chain of violence and suicide that explores the nature of Christ's "Third Temptation"—to use power selfishly. Joss is left sunk in stoic paralysis. *The Third Temptation* is an original and often powerful short novel that nevertheless fails to find what gives *Other Leopards* its strength—the perfect coherence between private and public worlds.

Williams has spent the later years of his life researching the historical roots of the Guyanese peoples, and working as a cultural archaeologist. In 1979 the Guyanese government awarded him the Golden Arrow of Achievement for this work. He will be remembered more for his practical achievements than for his fiction, but both his life and his slim body of creative writing are marked by the same integrity and originality of vision.

Interview:

Margarita y María Elena Mateo Palmer, "Denis Williams: 'Ahora pertenezco al Caribe,'" *Anales del Caribe*, 4-5 (1984-1985): 409-423.

References:

F. Aiyejina, "The Backward Glance: Lamming's *Season of Adventure* and Williams' *Other Leopards*," *African Literature Today*, 14 (1984): 118-126;

Edward Baugh, Introduction to Williams's *Other Leopards* (London: Heinemann, 1983), pp. v-xvii;

Wilfred Cartey, "The Rhythm of Society and Landscape," *New World: Guyana Independence Issue* (1966): 94-104;

Michael Gilkes, *The West Indian Novel* (Boston: Twayne, 1981), pp. 142-144;

Louis James, ed., *The Islands in Between* (London: Oxford University Press, 1968), pp. 7-10;

Mark Kinkead-Weekes, "Africa—Two Caribbean Fictions," *Twentieth Century Studies*, 10 (1973): 37-59;

Gerald Moore, *The Chosen Tongue* (London: Longman, 1969), pp. 119-125;

Kenneth Ramchand, *The West Indian Novel and Its Background* (London: Faber & Faber, 1970), pp. 159-163;

Adrian Rowe-Evans, "Other Freedoms," *Transition*, 3, no. 10 (1963), 57-58.

APPENDIX

Olaudah Equiano and Unfinished Journeys: The Slave-Narrative Tradition and Twentieth-Century Continuities

APPENDIX

Olaudah Equiano and Unfinished Journeys: The Slave-Narrative Tradition and Twentieth-Century Continuities

Paul Edwards and Pauline T. Wangman
University of Edinburgh

See also the Equiano entries in *DLB 37: American Writers of the Early Republic* and *DLB 50: Afro-American Writers Before the Harlem Renaissance*.

The wide range of eighteenth- and nineteenth-century slave narratives—Anglo-African, French, Caribbean, North and South American, and Cuban—maps a long, diverse journey from slavery to freedom, which roots twentieth-century Caribbean and black African writing, as well as black British and African-American writing, in a creative tradition. Continuities have been noted from Olaudah Equiano (circa 1745 - 31 March 1797) to nineteenth-century West African writers James Africanus Horton and Edward Wilmot Blyden, and to Chinua Achebe, who has described Equiano as his literary ancestor. The slave-narrative tradition contextualizes modern fictional treatments of slavery by rooting them in a specific historical and literary context and by providing a precedent for telling about slavery from the point of view of slaves. Alex Haley's well-known search for his family's African ancestry, *Roots* (1976), and the Caribbean writer Caryl Phillips's novels *Higher Ground* (1989) and *Cambridge* (1991) are indebted to the sense of detail, subject matter, and dominant themes characteristic of *The Interesting Narrative of Olaudah Equiano, or Gustavus Vassa, the African, Written by Himself* (two volumes, 1789).

The recent trend in African-American fiction—from Margaret Walker's *Jubilee* (1966) to Sherley Anne Williams's *Dessa Rose* (1986) and Toni Morrison's *Beloved* (1987)—suggests not only a persistent interest in the experience of slavery but also concern for the marginalized, and thus silenced, slave woman. Both *Dessa Rose* and *Beloved*, in different ways, problematize telling the story of slavery, both as a public political act and as a private process that inevitably involves painful surfacing of memories and recognition of loss. The settings of *Beloved* and *Dessa Rose* in the era of nineteenth-century American slavery and its aftermath; the main focus of these two novels on female characters in sometimes problematic relationships to their families and communities; and a preoccupation with issues of silence and memory in coming to terms with the experience of slavery—all of this draws from and comments on the slave-narrative tradition, in which Equiano's autobiography participates in a powerful way.

Scholars of early black writing are establishing the range and diversity characteristic of the slave-narrative tradition, and such attention encourages comparative studies within the tradition, on the basis of gender as well as historical and regional differences, and between slave narratives and their literary relations in contemporary fiction. Identifying such continuities is facilitated by scholarship that retrieves and contextualizes the works of eighteenth-century writers such as Equiano and his contemporaries Ottobah Cugoano, Ignatius Sancho, and others. This critical activity has developed in parallel with the retrieval and recognition of early black women's writing, one result of which is the thirty-volume Schomburg Library of Nineteenth-Century Black Women Writers (1988), edited by Henry Louis Gates, Jr., which includes slave autobiographies by the African-American Harriet Jacobs and the West Indian Mary Prince, as well as the work of eighteenth-century poet Phillis Wheatley. Commentators who have placed Equiano in the Ameri-

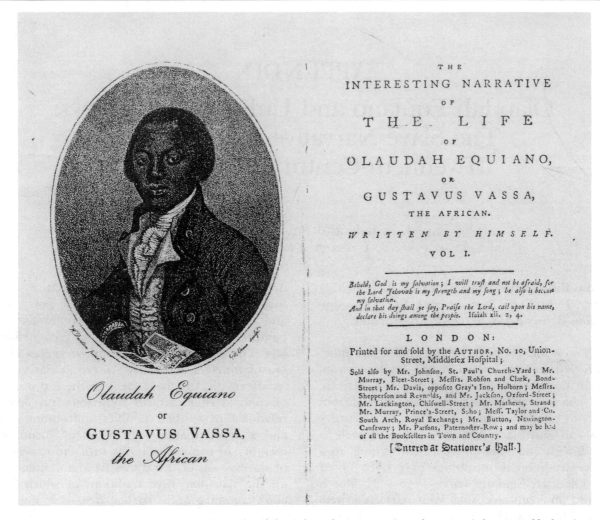

Frontispiece and title page for the autobiography of the eighteenth-century writer whom twentieth-century black writers regard as a literary ancestor

can slave-narrative tradition have initiated steps toward expanding and reevaluating the historical, geographical, and literary features by which readers know and name features of that tradition.

Comparing Equiano's narrative with the first and best-known of Frederick Douglass's autobiographies, *Narrative of the Life of Frederick Douglass, An American Slave, Written By Himself* (1845), and with Harriet Jacobs's *Incidents in the Life of a Slave Girl, Written by Herself* (1861) suggests ways in which different historical and gender realities shaped both the slave narrator's use of literary conventions and the extent to which the narrators felt compelled to mask problematic elements of their tales. Differences and similarities also emerge in the treatment of recurrent themes in Equiano's tale: the search for home and familial connection; relations with surrogate parent figures in the form of masters and mis-

tresses; dilemmas of gratitude and repressed anger, often emerging as crucial silences in the story; and the liminal position of the slave narrator in relation to Christian white society. Phillips's *Higher Ground* tells three different tales—the first set on the West African coast during slavery, the second on death row in a U.S. prison in the 1960s, and finally, in London, as experienced by a Polish Jew separated from her family during World War II. The novel's unifying themes, historical range, and focus on female as well as male characters all pay tribute to the slave-narrative tradition and move beyond it.

The experience of motherhood is central to Jacobs's *Incidents* and to *Dessa Rose* and *Beloved*, but one may also look to male writers to explore maternity and images of women in general. In Equiano's narrative a persistent and varied presence of women, and a significant mother figure, can be identified; Douglass's second autobiography, *My Bondage and My Freedom* (1855), restores the presence of his grandmother and mother to his life story, and it roots Douglass's love of learning in his mother's own literacy; the hero of *Cambridge*, whose words are often taken directly from Equiano, examines the place of both white and black women in slave society. The place of Equiano's autobiography in the slave-narrative tradition and the links between *The Interesting Narrative* and novels by writers such as Achebe, Phillips, Morrison, and Williams demonstrate that slave narratives make up an engaged body of writing, which participates in contexts, for example, of African cultural practices—vital presences in the slaves' lives and in the narratives through which many former slaves were able to account for their experiences in slavery. Slave narratives reflect mythic dimensions that transcend them: realms of family, community, and religion are seen shaping childhood, adolescent struggles, and adult dilemmas. That slave narratives present the reader with unfinished journeys is immediately evident in the black creative tradition that acknowledges the slave's voice—spoken, sung, and written—as its first utterance.

Equiano was the author of the most remarkable, the fullest, and the most authentic of several slave autobiographies published in English in the late eighteenth century, and thus a full understanding of his life and work is vital as a background for the slave-narrative tradition. He was born circa 1745, probably not far from the modern Nigerian city of Onitsha, in an Igbo village he calls Essaka, which has been variously identified, most recently by Catherine Obianuju Acholonu as Isseke. At around the age of eleven he was kidnapped by a band of Africans raiding for slaves, carried to the coast by land and river, and sold to white slave traders "with horrible looks, red faces, and loose hair." He was taken to Barbados, then to Virginia, where he was purchased by a Lt. Michael Henry Pascal of the Royal Navy, who gave him the name Gustavus Vassa. He served Pascal throughout the Seven Years' War, with Gen. James Wolfe in Canada and Adm. Edward Boscawen in the Mediterranean fleet.

Equiano's master arranged for him to attend school when ashore, and Equiano also received education in schools aboard the ships on which he served. He mixed freely with British families whenever Pascal was on leave. Thinking that his master held him in genuine affection,

Equiano suffered another profound shock when Pascal sold him back to American slavery: he passed into the hands of a Philadelphia Quaker, Robert King, on whose merchant ships he worked for several years, earning enough money, at the age of twenty-one by trading on his own account, to buy back his freedom. His subsequent travels included a voyage to the Arctic as assistant to the surgeon on the Phipps expedition (1772-1773); a tour of the Mediterranean as a manservant to an English traveler; and a period of six months among the Miskito Indians of Central America. He was appointed commissary for stores for the expedition that was to return many freed slaves to Africa in 1787 and create the settlement at Freetown in Sierra Leone; but before the ships finally left England, he was dismissed after disagreements with the organizers of the expedition. He had by this time become the leading spokesman for the black population of London, and his dismissal might be seen as a blessing in disguise: it gave him the opportunity to complete his autobiography, which he had been working on for many years.

Equiano's book was well supported and well received. The first edition lists over three hundred subscribers, and it went into eight British editions in Equiano's lifetime, as well as an American edition (1791), and translations into Dutch, Russian, and German; it continued to be read after his death, going into many more editions in the first half of the nineteenth century. Equiano was also a regular contributor of letters and reviews to the *Public Advertiser*, and one of his letters, to Lord Hawkesbury, was presented as evidence to the 1789 government committee investigating the slave trade. In the years following his return to England from slavery, he devoted much of his time to active involvement in the fight for abolition; it was he, for instance, who informed the abolitionist Granville Sharp of the murder of 130 slaves aboard the *Zong*, a case that shocked the public in 1783. Equiano was also involved in securing the freedom of black people who had been captured and threatened with a return to West Indian slavery.

After his book had been published, he traveled widely throughout Great Britain, selling copies and speaking publicly against slavery. In England he traveled to Birmingham, Durham, Stockton, Hull, Bath, Devizes, Liverpool, Manchester, Sheffield, Nottingham, and Shrewsbury; a record of his visit to the last survives in an unpublished diary (in the Cambridgeshire Record Of-

Notation by Equiano in a copy of An Exposition of all the Books of the Old and New Testaments *(eighth edition, 1772) by Matthew Henry (Edinburgh University Library)*

fice), that of Katherine Plymley: "my brother had then purchased of him the memoires of his life written by himself; and I believe his business at that time was to get introduced wherever he could, and to dispose of them—my Brother was rather concerned at his going through the country for this purpose, as he feared it would only tend to increase the difficulty of getting subscriptions when wanted, for carrying on the business of abolition. The luke-warm would be too apt to think, if this be the case, and we are to have Negroes come about in this way, it will be very troublesome; my brother thought there was something not quite right about him, or he would have been at Sierra Leone." But Katherine's sister-in-law, Ann, and the children took to Equiano: "the little people, though they had never been accustomed to blacks, immediately went to him, offered their hands, and behaved in their pretty friendly way," and eventually Equiano was awarded the stamp of approval. Though he appears to have made many white friends, there are indications that even the supporters of abolition could be paternalistic and insulting, as his account of his dismissal from the post of commissary for stores demonstrates (in volume two of his autobiography), and as does a letter from one of his white friends, Mrs. Susannah Akinson, trying to cheer him up after an unhappy visit to some abolitionists at Elland, near Leeds, in 1791:

"I am sorry to hear you are low—suffer yourself not to be hurt by trifles, since you must in this transitory and deceitful world meet with many unpleasant changes. I was sorry we should be so unfortunate as to recommend you to any who should in the least slight you . . . but I sincerely hope you have since experienced that friendship and civility from those you have been with, which has amply made up for the treatment you there received." (This letter is in the Cambridgeshire Record Office.)

On 7 April 1792 Equiano married Susan Cullen of Soham. There were two children of the marriage: Anna Maria Vassa died at age four in 1797 and is commemorated on a memorial tablet in St. Andrew's Parish Church, Chesterton, near Cambridge. Her mother had died two years before, and Equiano himself three months before, on 31 March 1797. One daughter, Johanna, survived. Equiano left enough to provide her with a good education and upbringing, and on her twenty-first birthday in 1816 she received, as a posthumous gift from her father, the sum of £950. In his will Equiano, after making provision for his two daughters, requested that, should they not outlive him, his estate should pass to the Sierra Leone Company, half of it to be used expressly for the establishment of schools. Sharp was at Equiano's side when he died. There appears to have been something of a rift in their friendship at the time of Equiano's dismissal from the company: Sharp wrote to his brother in 1787 that "all the jealousies and animosities between the Whites and Blacks [on the Sierra Leone expedition] had subsided, and that they had been very orderly since Mr. Vassa and two or three other discontented persons had been left on shore in Plymouth." But this rift was later healed: Equiano continued to speak of Sharp and other abolitionist leaders such as Thomas Clarkson and James Ramsay with affection and respect, and Sharp wrote to his niece, Jemima, many years later, when she asked about Equiano, "He was a sober, honest man—and I went to see him upon his death bed, and he had lost his voice so that he could only whisper."

Equiano probably had a hand in a book published two years before his autobiography. There is evidence that he gave some assistance to his friend Cugoano in the writing of the latter's *Thoughts and Sentiments on the Evil and Wicked Traffic of the Slavery and Commerce of the Human Species* (1787). But Cugoano's book, though it contains elements of autobiography, is essentially an abolitionist tract and has little of the range of individual observation and lively storytelling of Equiano's autobiography. The opening section of *The Interesting Narrative* deals in some detail with Igbo village life as Equiano remembers it. There is every indication that his memories are accurate, and in a crucial paragraph he establishes the values of this society as underlying the whole of his life, which he repeatedly suggests was as deeply grounded in his memories of Igbo childhood as in the Christian values he adopted, seriously but sometimes ambiguously, in later times:

> I hope the reader will not think I have trespassed on his patience in introducing myself with some account of the manners and customs of my country. They had been implanted in me with great care, and made an impression on my mind which all the adversity and variety of fortune I have since experienced served only to rivet and record; for, whether the love of one's country be real or imaginary, or a lesson in reason, or an instinct of nature, I still look back with pleasure on the first scenes of my life, though that pleasure has been for the most part mingled with sorrow.

The Interesting Narrative returns to such a theme in several passages, notably in the comparisons between white Christian society and those of the Muslim Turks of Smyrna and of the Miskito Indians of Central America. He also notes his delight at discovering in the Bible "the laws and rules of my country written almost exactly here; circumstances which I believe tended to impress our manners and customs more deeply on my memory." In this respect Equiano is a forerunner of a tradition—including Horton's *West African Countries and Peoples* (1868) and the modern novels of Achebe—of restoring honor to the Igbo ancestors. Equiano's account of his experiences in Smyrna apparently influenced Edward Wilmot Blyden's *Christianity, Islam and the Negro Race* (1887) and the rise of the Black Muslim movement. Were one to seek further lines of continuity, one might turn to recent American commentators: William L. Andrews, for example, has seen Equiano as "the prophet, if not the father, of Afro-American autobiography"; and Angelo Costanzo sees him as "setting the pattern of countless narratives—both non-fictional and fictional—that have influenced American literature to the present."

Another recurrent theme is Equiano's search for human relationships with his sometimes appalling, sometimes disconcertingly benevolent captors; this often manifests itself as a struggle in Equiano's own heart between his need for a "father" and his desire to break away from the paternal and become his own "captain." Of his shipmate Daniel Queen, Equiano writes, "In short, he was like a father to me; and some even used to call me after his name; they also styled me the black Christian. Indeed I almost loved him with the affection of a son." Equiano's own father he describes with pride as "one of those elders or chiefs which I have spoken of . . . styled Embrenche . . . a term, as I remember, importing the highest distinction, and signifying in our language a *mark* of grandeur." His first master, Pascal, appears to adopt him, and Pascal's failure as a "father," when he resells Equiano into slavery, is one of several traumas of relationship in the autobiography. Later, the role of "captain" and "father" is transferred to Capt. Thomas Farmer, who is a principal aid in Equiano's regaining his own freedom. Of Farmer, Equiano writes on this occasion: "Every one I met I told of my happiness, and blazed about the virtue of my amiable master and captain." At the same time, Equiano wishes to return to London in order to confront Pascal: "I determined that the year following, if it pleased God, I would see old England once more, and surprise my old master, Captain Pascal, who was hourly on my mind; for I still loved him, nothwithstanding his usage of

*Cover for the abridged, 1988 edition of
Equiano's autobiography*

me, and I pleased myself with thinking of what he would say when he saw what the Lord had done for me. . . . " Farmer, however, his benefactor, still needed him aboard ship: "Here gratitude bowed me down; and none but the generous mind can judge of my feelings, struggling between inclination and duty." Equiano's relationship with Farmer became strained, but Farmer soon died, resolving Equiano's struggle. Farmer's death was seen by Equiano as yet another sign of God's providence. On one hand, Equiano tells the reader that "Every man on board loved this man, and regretted his death. . . . I was exceedingly affected at it, and I found that I did not know, till he was gone, the strength of my regard for him"; yet, on the other hand, this leaves Equiano in charge of the ship, "and I now attained a new appellation, and was called Captain."

What becomes apparent is Equiano's need to free himself from the paternalistic, almost as much as from enmity and contempt, and this section of the autobiography is a striking demonstration of the psychology of paternalism, as regret for Farmer's death is inextricably entangled with Equiano's resentment toward the benevolence that had been imposed on him, and his delight (which he is prepared to reveal as having its streak of vanity) at the opportunity to display his skills as a navigator, a leader of men, his own captain. His ambivalence toward authority is brought out by persistent ironies, often in the guise of naiveté: "I have often seen slaves, particularly those who were meagre, in different islands, put into scales and weighed; and then sold from three pence to six pence or nine pence a pound. My master, however, whose humanity was shocked by this mode, used to sell such by the lump."

It is important that the reader should bear in mind the demands placed upon Equiano that determine the tone of his narrative. On one hand he was a man who had every reason to detest the slave trade on personal grounds and was one of the few articulate representatives of the African slaves themselves; on the other, he was a committed Christian, a prominent member, however ambivalently, of white society, and a spokesman for a white-led abolitionist movement. The prevalent tone of the narrative shows in this passage from the opening chapter:

> People generally think those memoirs only worthy to be read or remembered which abound in great or striking events, those, in short, which in a high degree excite either admiration or pity; all others they consign to contempt or oblivion. It is therefore, I confess, not a little hazardous in a private and obscure individual, and a stranger too, thus to solicit the indulgent attention of the public; especially when I own I offer here the history of neither a saint, a hero, nor a tyrant. I believe there are few events of my life which have not happened to many: it is true the incidents of it are numerous; and, did I consider myself an European, I might say my sufferings were great: but when I compare my lot with most of my countrymen, I regard myself as a *particular favourite of Heaven*, and acknowledge the mercies of Providence in every occurrence of my life.

The tone is of the European man of reason and sensitivity; but far from simply aligning himself with European values, Equiano sets up conflicts and tensions that are to characterize his narrative. His phrase "the mercies of Providence" suggests a Christian view of the world, but later in the narrative, in the midst of a series of references to fate, fortune, and Providence, he reminds the reader that "as I was from early years a predestinarian, I thought that whatever fate had determined must ever come to pass," and as a result he roots what appear to be Christian beliefs in his pre-Christian Igbo upbringing. The italicized words, *a particular favourite of Heaven*," have similarly to be set against his Ibgo name, Olaudah, which he tells the reader a few pages later, "in our language signifies vicissitude or fortune also, one favoured. . . ." When he refers to himself as "a private and obscure individual, and a stranger, too," then adds "did I consider myself an European," with the subsequent ironic contrast with the "sufferings" of white men and black, he establishes the separation of himself from civilized Christian gentlemen and notes his relationship to "most of my countrymen" in the very process of acknowledging his better "fortune" and consequent status in white society. Finally, in stressing that he is to present himself as "neither a saint, a hero, nor a tyrant," he prepares the ground for an often equivocal self-display: he subsequently presents himself as naive as well as innocent, vain as well as justly proud, self-seeking as well as practical, and in this avoidance of a mere stance of saintliness and heroism establishes himself all the more firmly both as himself, and as part of humankind. But when he adds "tyrant" to the list of what he is not, he reminds readers once again of the brutalities that lie beneath the surface of their benevolence.

References:

Catherine Obianuju Acholonu, "The Home of Olaudah Equiano: A Linguistic and Anthropological Search," *Journal of Commonwealth Literature*, 22, no. 1 (1987): 5-16;

Acholonu, *The Igbo Roots of Olaudah Equiano* (Owerri, Nigeria: AFA, 1989);

William L. Andrews, *To Tell a Free Story: The First Century of Afro-American Autobiography, 1760-1865* (Urbana & Chicago: University of Illinois Press, 1986);

Houston A. Baker, Jr., *Blues, Ideology and Afro-American Literature* (Chicago & London: University of Chicago Press, 1984);

Baker, *The Journey Back: Issues in Black Literature and Criticism* (Chicago & London: University of Chicago Press, 1980), pp. 1-26;

Chinosole, "Tryin' to Get Over: Narrative Posture in Equiano's Autobiography," in *The Art of Slave Narrative: Original Essays in Criticism and Theory*, edited by John Sekora and Darwin T. Turner (Macomb: Western Illinois University, 1982), pp. 45-54;

Angelo Costanzo, *Surprizing Narrative: Olaudah Equiano and the Beginnings of Black Autobiography* (New York: Greenwood, 1987);

Ian Duffield and Paul Edwards, "Equiano's Turks and Christians: An Eighteenth Century African View of Islam," *Journal of African Studies*, 2 (Winter 1975): 433-444;

Paul Edwards, "Black Writers of the Eighteenth and Nineteenth Centuries," in *The Black Presence in English Literature*, edited by David Dabydeen (Manchester: Manchester University Press, 1985), pp. 50-67;

Edwards, "A Descriptive List of the Manuscripts in the John Audley Papers in the Cambridgeshire Record Office, Relating to the Will of Gustavus Vassa (Olaudah Equiano)," *Research in African Literatures*, 20 (Fall 1989): 472-480;

Edwards, "Eighteenth-Century Writing in English," in *European-Language Writing in Sub Saharan Africa*, edited by Albert Gérard (Budapest: Akademiai Kiado, 1986), XI: 57-76;

Edwards, "Equiano and His Captains," in *Common Wealth*, edited by Anna Rutherford (Aarhus, Denmark: Akademisk Boghandel, 1972), pp. 18-25;

Edwards, "Equiano's Round Unvarnished Tale," *African Literature Today*, 5 (1971): 12-20;

Edwards, " 'Master' and 'Father' in Equiano's *Interesting Narrative*," *Slavery and Abolition*, 11 (1990): 216-226;

Edwards, "Three West African Writers of the 1780's," in *The Slave's Narrative*, edited by Charles T. Davis and Henry Louis Gates, Jr. (New York: Oxford University Press, 1985), pp. 175-198;

Edwards, " . . . 'written by Himself . . .': A Manuscript Letter of Olaudah Equiano," *Notes and Queries*, 15 (June 1968): 222-225;

Edwards and Rosalind Shaw, "The Invisible *Chi* in Equiano's *Interesting Narrative*," *Journal of Religion in Africa*, 19, no. 2 (1989): 146-156;

Edwards and James Walvin, *Black Personalities in the Era of the Slave Trade* (London: Macmillan, 1983);

Edwards and Dabydeen, eds., *Black Writers in Britain, 1760-1890* (Edinburgh: Edinburgh University Press, 1991);

Henry Louis Gates, Jr., *The Signifying Monkey: A Theory of Afro-American Literary Criticism* (New York & Oxford: Oxford University Press, 1988);

Sharon M. Harris, "Early American Slave Narratives and the Reconfiguration of Place," *Journal of the American Studies Association of Texas*, 21 (1990): 15-23;

Sidney Kaplan, "Olaudah Equiano: The Image of Africa," in his *The Black Presence in the Era of the American Revolution, 1770-1800* (Washington, D.C.: New York Graphic Society and the Smithsonian Institution Press, 1973), pp. 193-207;

Victor C. D. Mtubani, "The Black Voice in 18th Century Britain: African Writers Against Slavery and the Slave Trade," *Phylon*, 45, no. 2 (1984): 85-97;

S. E. Ogude, "Facts Into Fiction: Equiano's Narrative Revisited," *Research in African Literatures*, 13 (1982): 31-43;

Ogude, *Genius in Bondage: A Study of the Origins of African Literature in English* (Ile-Ife, Nigeria: University of Ife Press, 1983);

Ogude, "Olaudah Equiano and the Tradition of Defoe," *African Literature Today*, 14 (1984): 77-92;

James Olney, ed., *Autobiography: Essays Theoretical and Critical* (Princeton: Princeton University Press, 1980);

Wilfred D. Samuels, "Disguised Voice in *The Interesting Narrative of Olaudah Equiano, or Gustavus Vassa, The African*," *Black American Literature Forum*, 19 (Summer 1985): 64-69;

Keith A. Sandiford, "Early Traditions of Learning in Europe: Renaissance to Enlightenment," in *Images de l'Africain de l'antiquité au XXe siècle / Images of the African from Antiquity to the 20th Century*, edited by Daniel Droixhe and Klaus H. Kiefer (Frankfurt: Lang, 1987), pp. 73-83;

Sandiford, *Measuring the Moment: Strategies of Protest in Eighteenth-Century Afro-English Writing* (Selinsgrove, Pa.: Susquehanna University Press, 1988);

Folarin Shyllon, *Black People in Britain, 1555-1833* (London: Oxford University Press, 1977);

Shyllon, "Olaudah Equiano: Nigerian Abolitionist and First National Leader of Africans in Britain," *Journal of African Studies*, 4 (1971): 433-451.

Papers:

Equiano's papers and first editions of his works are held by the Schomburg Collection, New York Public Library; Library Company, Philadelphia; Ridgeway Brothers, Philadelphia; Boston Public Library; Yale University; Harvard University; Atlanta University; and the Hornby Collection, Liverpool City Library.

Books for Further Reading

Achebe, Chinua. *Morning Yet on Creation Day: Essays*. London: Heinemann, 1975; enlarged edition, Garden City, N.Y.: Anchor/Doubleday, 1975.

Awoonor, Kofi. *The Breast of the Earth: A Survey of the History, Culture and Literature of Africa South of the Sahara*. Garden City, N.Y.: Anchor, 1975.

Barthold, Bonnie J. *Black Time: Fiction of Africa, the Caribbean and the United States*. New Haven: Yale University Press, 1981.

Baugh, Edward. *West Indian Poetry 1900-1970: A Study in Cultural Decolonisation*. Kingston, Jamaica: Savacou, 1971.

Baugh, ed. *Critics on Caribbean Literature*. London: Allen & Unwin / New York: St. Martin's Press, 1978.

Brown, Lloyd W. *West Indian Poetry*. Boston: Twayne, 1978.

Brown. *Women Writers in Black Africa*. Westport, Conn. & London: Greenwood, 1981.

Cartey, Wilfred G. *Whispers from a Continent*. New York: Random House, 1969.

Cartey. *Whispers from the Caribbean*. Los Angeles: Center for Afro-American Studies, University of California, 1991.

Chinweizu, Onwuchekwa Jemie, and Ihechukwu Madubuike. *Toward the Decolonization of African Literature*. Washington, D.C.: Howard University Press, 1983.

Cudjoe, Selwyn R. *Resistance and Caribbean Literature*. Athens: Ohio University Press, 1980.

Cudjoe, ed. *Caribbean Women Writers*. Wellesley, Mass.: Calaloux, 1990.

Dance, Daryl C., ed. *Fifty Caribbean Writers: A Bio-Bibliographical Critical Sourcebook*. New York, Westport, Conn. & London: Greenwood, 1986.

Davies, Carole Boyce, and Anne Adams Graves, eds. *Ngambika: Studies of Women in African Literature*. Trenton, N.J.: Africa World, 1986.

Davies and Elaine Savory Fido, eds. *Out of the Kumbla: Caribbean Women and Literature*. Trenton, N.J.: Africa World, 1990.

Etherton, Michael. *The Development of African Drama*. London: Hutchinson, 1982.

Fraser, Robert. *West African Poetry: A Critical History*. Cambridge: Cambridge University Press, 1986.

Gérard, Albert, ed. *European-Language Writing in Sub-Saharan Africa*. Budapest: Akadémiai Kiadó, 1986.

Gilkes, Michael. *The West Indian Novel*. Boston: Twayne, 1981.

Goodwin, Ken. *Understanding African Poetry: A Study of Ten Poets*. London: Heinemann, 1982.

Griffiths, Gareth. *A Double Exile: African and West Indian Writing Between Two Cultures*. London: Boyars, 1978.

Harris, Wilson. *Tradition, the Writer and Society: Critical Essays*. London & Port of Spain: New Beacon, 1967.

Irele, Abiola. *The African Experience in Literature and Ideology*. London & Exeter, N.H.: Heinemann, 1981.

James, Louis, ed. *The Islands in Between: Essays on West Indian Literature*. London: Oxford University Press, 1968.

JanMohamed, Abdul. *Manichean Aesthetics: The Politics of Literature in Colonial Africa*. Amherst: University of Massachusetts Press, 1983.

King, Bruce, ed. *West Indian Literature*. London: Macmillan, 1979.

Lamming, George. *The Pleasures of Exile*. London: Joseph, 1960.

Larson, Charles R. *The Emergence of African Fiction*, revised edition. Bloomington: Indiana University Press, 1972.

Moore, Gerald. *The Chosen Tongue*. London: Longmans, 1969.

Ngara, Emmanuel. *Stylistic Criticism and the African Novel: A Study of the Influence of Marxism on African Writing*. London & Hanover, N.H.: Heinemann, 1985.

Ngugi wa Thiong'o. *Decolonising the Mind: The Politics of Language in African Literature*. London: Currey / Portsmouth, N.H.: Heinemann, 1986.

Ngugi. *Homecoming: Essays on African and Caribbean Literature, Culture and Politics*. London: Heinemann, 1972.

Ngugi. *Writers in Politics*. London & Exeter, N.H.: Heinemann, 1981.

Obiechina, Emmanuel. *Culture, Tradition and Society in the West African Novel*. Cambridge: Cambridge University Press, 1975.

Omotoso, Kole. *The Theatrical into Theatre: A Study of the Drama and Theatre of the English-Speaking Caribbean*. London: New Beacon, 1982.

Palmer, Eustace. *The Growth of the African Novel*. London & Exeter, N.H.: Heinemann, 1979.

Ramchand, Kenneth. *An Introduction to the Study of West Indian Literature*. Sunbury-on-Thames, U.K. & Kingston, Jamaica: Nelson Caribbean, 1976.

Ramchand. *The West Indian Novel and Its Background*. London: Faber & Faber, 1970.

Soyinka, Wole. *Art, Dialogue and Outrage: Essays on Literature and Culture*. Ibadan: New Horn, 1988.

Soyinka. *Myth, Literature and the African World*. Cambridge: Cambridge University Press, 1976.

Taylor, Patrick. *The Narrative of Liberation: Perspectives on Afro-Caribbean Literature, Popular Culture, and Politics*. Ithaca, N.Y.: Cornell University Press, 1989.

Van Sertima, Ivan. *Caribbean Writers: Critical Essays*. London & Port of Spain: New Beacon, 1968.

Wauthier, Claude. *The Literature and Thought of Modern Africa*. Translated by Shirley Kay. London: Heinemann, 1978.

Webb, Barbara J. *Myth and History in Caribbean Fiction: Alejo Carpentier, Wilson Harris, and Edouard Glissant*. Amherst: University of Massachusetts Press, 1992.

Contributors

Cecil A. Abrahams ....*Brock University*
Kofi Ermeleh Agovi ....*University of Ghana—Legon*
Kofi Anyidoho..*University of Ghana—Legon*
Wolfgang Binder ....*Universität Erlangen-Nürnberg*
Frank M. Birbalsingh ....*York University*
Elaine Campbell............................*Massachusetts Institute of Technology*
Selwyn R. Cudjoe ....*Wellesley College*
Jean-Pierre Durix ....*Université de Dijon*
Paul Edwards ....*University of Edinburgh*
Ernest N. Emenyonu ....*Alvan Ikoku College of Education, Owerri, Nigeria*
Elaine Savory Fido ....*University of the West Indies, Barbados*
Robert D. Hamner ....*Hardin-Simmons University*
Michael E. Hoenisch............................*Freie Universität Berlin*
Naana Banyiwa Horne ....*University of Wisconsin—Madison*
Louis James ....*University of Kent at Canterbury*
Abdul R. JanMohamed ....*University of California, Berkeley*
G. D. Killam ....*University of Guelph*
Thomas R. Knipp ....*Saint Louis University*
Greta D. Little ....*University of South Carolina*
Ernest Mathabela ....*University of Texas at Austin*
Alan L. McLeod...............................*Rider College*
Ian H. Munro...............................*William Jewell College*
Charles E. Nnolim ....*University of Port Harcourt, Nigeria*
Emmanuel Obiechina...........................*University of Nigeria at Nsukka*
Chikwenye Okonjo Ogunyemi...........................*Sarah Lawrence College*
Kirsten Holst Petersen ....*Aarhus, Denmark*
Patrick Scott...............................*University of South Carolina*
Michael Wade...............................*Hebrew University of Jerusalem*
Pauline T. Wangman ....*University of Edinburgh*
Robert M. Wren ....*University of Houston*
Derek Wright...............................*Northern Territory University, Darwin, Australia*

Cumulative Index

Dictionary of Literary Biography, Volumes 1-117
Dictionary of Literary Biography Yearbook, 1980-1990
Dictionary of Literary Biography Documentary Series, Volumes 1-9

ISBN 0-8103-7594-X

90000

9 780819 375940